Alphabetical list of revision symbols

The Holt Guide to English

The Holt Guide to English

Third edition

A comprehensive handbook
of rhetoric, language, and literature

William F. Irmscher
University of Washington

HOLT, RINEHART AND WINSTON
New York   Chicago   San Francisco
Dallas   Montreal   Toronto

9/1981
Eng.

Library of Congress Cataloging in Publication Data

Irmscher, William F
    The Holt guide to English.

    Includes index.
    1. English language—Rhetoric.   2. English language
—Grammar—1950–   I. Title.
PE1408.I67   1981   808'.042   80–25168
ISBN 0–03–044451–9

Acknowledgments

Excerpt from *The American Dream* by Edward Albee. Reprinted by permission of Coward, McCann & Geoghan, Inc., and William Morris Agency, Inc., on behalf of author. Copyright © 1960, 1961 by Edward Albee.

Excerpts from "1924" by Alistair Cooke. Copyright © 1974 by *Saturday Review*. All rights reserved. Reprinted by permission of *Saturday Review* and the author.

"My sweet old etcetera" by E. E. Cummings. Copyright 1926 by Horace Liveright, copyright 1954 by E. E. Cummings. Reprinted from *Complete Poems 1913–1962* by E. E. Cummings by permission of Harcourt Brace Jovanovich, Inc., and MacGibbon & Kee.

Excerpt from *Pilgrim at Tinker Creek* by Annie Dillard. Copyright © 1974 by Annie Dillard. Reprinted by permission of Harper & Row, Publishers, Inc.

Excerpt from "The Population Explosion: Facts and Fiction" by Paul Ehrlich. Copyright *The Sierra Club Bulletin*, October 1968. Reprinted by permission of Dr. Paul R. Ehrlich.

Excerpts from *Murder in the Cathedral* by T. S. Eliot. Copyright 1935 by Harcourt Brace Jovanovich, Inc.; copyright 1963 by T. S. Eliot. Reprinted by permission of Harcourt Brace Jovanovich, Inc., and Faber and Faber, Ltd.

Excerpt from "A Harmonious Gathering" by Paul Froiland, *TWA Ambassador*, October 1979. Reprinted from *TWA Ambassador* magazine with permission of the author and publisher; copyright © 1979 by Trans World Airlines, Inc.

(Continued on page 535)

The purpose of this handbook is to provide a comprehensive and flexible text which will serve both reference and teaching purposes. To this end, it gives full attention to rhetoric, language, literature, criticism, and composition. The ever-expanding nature of English studies makes it increasingly difficult to keep up with both past and current developments. Thus, this book attempts to assemble in one place a variety of background information for the study of English and to explain with a completeness that is adequate for most general purposes.

The basic objectives of the third edition of this text remain essentially the same as those of the first and second:

1. To set positive guidelines for the discussion of writing and to maintain a positive emphasis in the discussion of revision and usage by pointing out what writers should *strive for* rather than what they should *avoid*.
2. To bring new thought and treatment to such topics as the writer's attitudes toward writing, the audience, the drama of thinking, nonlinear logic, the paragraph bloc, variations of prose style, and, in specific terms, the characteristics that mark good writing.
3. To give background about the nature of literature and the genres of fiction, drama, and poetry as a means of understanding them and to supply specific suggestions for writing on literary topics without inviting the stereotype of a student theme about literature instead of a personal, meaningful commentary.
4. To provide adequate information for the preparation of a reference paper without creating a special mystique about its difficulties.
5. To give a coverage of grammar that recognizes the contributions of several grammars without setting forth the complete description of any particular one.
6. To inform the reader about English usage on the assumption that flexible standards of usage do operate, subject to dialectal and individual variations; to leave appropriate choices, then, to the informed reader in terms of style and audience without imposing prescriptions or proscriptions.
7. To supply a full reference guide to manuscript form and to offer a workable approach to spelling problems.

The Holt Guide represents a sound, practical guide to writing that recognizes the importance of a process in writing as well as the importance of qualities of the product that represent good writing.

The new edition is organized in four parts rather than three, giving greater focus to revising and proofreading. Material formerly included in Chapters 10 and 19 is now grouped as four chapters in Part II, Toward Better Writing. An especially practical section on readability has been added.

Chapter 3 on "The Subject: Generating a Topic" adds a second heuristic model to the Pentad, used in the second edition. Chapter 4 on "Order, Logic, and Mode" adds a new section on the syntax of thought that is designed to help students who have difficulty developing the all-important middle section (the Main Body) of an essay. Two chapters on grammar have been combined into one. Other parts have been abbreviated or revised. Many examples have been updated. A general effort has been made to make the text more readable by relaxing the prose style and to make it as sound as possible by strengthening those sections that reviewers said needed reinforcement.

The manual for instructors comments on the purpose of many assignments and suggests additional ones. My book *Teaching Expository Writing*, published by Holt in 1979, is a full treatment of the process of writing and the practice of teaching it.

The appearance of a third edition is gratifying because it means that *The Holt Guide* has found an audience of instructors who recognize its value as both a teaching text and reference book. I continue to be grateful to Phillip Leininger, who initiated the project and saw the first edition to completion, and also to Kenney Withers and to Susan Katz of Holt, Rinehart and Winston for their continuing support. Throughout the working period of all editions, Richard S. Beal has served as an invaluable adviser. Pamela Forcey and H. L. Kirk, editors at Holt, have also contributed immeasurably to this edition.

For comments on the preceding edition, my appreciation to William Babner, R. S. Beal, Bruce Beiderwell, Cheryl Bolin, Santi Buscemi, Patrice Caldwell, Mary Alice Lo Cicero, Leigh Clark, Jeffrey T. Gross, Deborah Kreda, Richard Larson, Jane W. Lucas, Walter E. Meyers, Joan Quarm, David Roberts, Greg Ross, Eric James Schroeder, Steve Ward, Heinz D. Woehlk, and Lee Zimmerman.

I continue to owe a special debt to my secretary, Shirley Hanson, who has now worked with me for twenty years and has been an integral part of seeing each of the editions to completion. I cannot adequately acknowledge the extent of her contribution.

All of these people have given the book strength; its limitations to be sure, are my own.

W. F. I.

Contents

Part II Toward better writing

Part III Special kinds of writing

The English language and its use   Part IV

The Holt Guide to English

Elements of writing *Part I*

We commonly refer to writing as a skill. We are therefore inclined to think of it as we think of other skills like driving a car, sewing on buttons, playing the piano, serving a tennis ball, and thousands of others, some domestic, some recreational, some artistic. We know also that we can sometimes learn skills easily, but then, after practicing them for a long time, we develop them into an art. A carpenter who begins with the most basic skills of sawing, beveling, hammering, and sanding may eventually become a master cabinetmaker. A beginner who first learns how to stroke, kick, and breathe rhythmically may eventually become a champion swimmer. Mastery of basic skills is only the beginning of a process of development.

Further, we commonly describe skills in terms of steps: collect flour, milk, baking powder, and salt, measure them each in turn, combine them in the order the cookbook says, do this, now that, and the result is biscuits for breakfast. The process is describable, and the order of the steps is important.

In view of the way we learn and practice other skills, now think again about writing as a skill. Clearly writing is something you do. But do you need to start with basic terms? Do you have to move step by step? Do you have to proceed in a certain order? The answer to all of these questions is "No." Each person goes about the job of writing differently. There is no set procedure for everyone, although doubtless some ways are more efficient than others.

You will come to a closer understanding of writing and how to write better if you do not oversimplify the process and expect a list of ten easy steps. Writing is a complex form of behavior, much more like acting on the stage than using a power saw. It involves your mind, your senses, and your feelings as well as your hands. The handwriting is a relatively unimportant part of the process. Writing involves the total self. The very first time you compose, whether you are talking or writing, you are concerned with the whole process. You have to have something to say, a point to begin and a point to end, words to express your thoughts and feelings, a tone to indicate your intentions, and—if the words are written down—certain punctuation to mark the sentences and make the meanings clear. Showing improvement after that first performance is a matter of gaining self-confidence, becoming more consciously aware of ways to vary the expression, and, overall, learning to control language so that words in action do what you want them to do.

If you consider writing in these more complex terms, not as a simple skill that someone else can teach you, you will begin to understand why many people have hangups about writing and find all kinds of excuses for not writing. You may very well find your own views or feelings reflected in these statements, written by students like yourself:

- *Blank-paper paralysis:* "When I look at a blank piece of paper, all I can think about is that I can't write what I think in a way that will do me or the reader any good. It's a defense mechanism."
- *Anxiety:* "I spend time fidgeting and twitching nervously before actually struggling with a rough draft. I get anxious because my main desire is to think of a good opening statement that will inspire me and help me go on with the piece."
- *Procrastination:* "I got up this morning thinking that I would write after breakfast. Then I noticed how dirty the kitchen floor looked. I couldn't stand that, so I got out the bucket and mop. Then I decided it was time to clean out my closet. After a whole day of puttering, I'm now sitting at my desk waiting for the pressure to build."
- *Defeatism:* "When I have to write a paper, I receive the first signal of distress, a physical reaction in my neck right under the jawline. First I feel hopeless, then I feel inadequate, and, finally, I get to a stage of catatonic resignation. When I'm in the third of these mental states, I decide that nothing will be lost if I try to begin because I am already defeated."
- *Perfectionism:* "In everything I've undertaken, I've tried to be the best, number 1, not some clod who gets trapped in the average. I've always tried to put forth the effort it takes to be an example for others. I strive for utter perfection in writing."
- *Gamesmanship:* "I use a method of looking at the clock and saying 'I'll start in five minutes' or 'At a quarter after, no more fooling around.' The trick is that when I check the time, if it is past the designated mark, say sixteen minutes after instead of fifteen, I figure that section of time is blown and wait for the half-hour. The game can be played almost endlessly until guilt finally takes over."
- *Ritualism:* "To write, I have to find a quiet room with no distractions such as music. It has to have enough lighting to keep me from squinting at anything in the corners of the room—I have to have at least two or three lights on around me. The chair must be fairly straight-backed but have a soft seat—an armchair puts me to sleep and a hard seat makes me squirm. I clear the table of all

encumbrances except the paper. My best time for writing is between dinner and midnight."

- *Struggling:* "My writing is a long struggling process. It does not come naturally. I know the only way I'm going to improve my writing is to make myself write."

These statements are typical. They tell us about the attitudes of people as they approach the job of writing. Here we have evidence of reluctance, resistance, fear, frustration, insecurity, and even self-delusion. What is less evident from the words themselves is that most of these writers also feel that their egos are at stake. Yet they all try. They all get over the hump of beginning, gain self-confidence by the act of writing itself, and, when the words are down on paper, even take pleasure in seeing the record of their thoughts. Yet it is worth asking why anyone should bother to write anyway, when it is clearly easier not to write. What purpose does writing serve?

Why write, anyway?

First of all, writing is an important means of communication. The age of specialization has not decreased the need for writing; it has actually increased it. More and more people must record on paper their findings, their opinions, and their procedures. Telephones and tapes do not meet all of the demands. Individuals who think they can get by without developing their abilities to write underestimate the role that writing assumes in the lives of educated people and ignore the dependency and inconvenience that result when they lack confidence to do the job adequately. Writing provides us a way to get out of the boxes we represent as separate beings. It is a connector. Besides the bond of communication with others that writing provides, it also demands a kind of internal communication, the "I" addressing its "me," as Margaret Mead has described the inner dialogue. Writing frequently reveals to us what we know and feel or what we may think we know but cannot verbalize. In Philip Roth's novella *Goodbye, Columbus,* Neil Klugman says of his relationship with Brenda Patimkin:

Actually we did not have the feelings we said we had until we spoke them—at least I didn't; to phrase them was to invent them and own them.

Talking, like writing, defines our thoughts, but talking is ordinarily a dialogue between two people who support and reinforce one another. Writing, however, leaves us alone with ourselves. In this state, we cannot very well fool ourselves, because writing proves whether we have produced anything in our thinking.

Writing also organizes what we think. At a certain stage, thinking may be a mixture of experience, ideas, and sensations, but writing cannot be produced in an electronic flash like television. It has to be drawn out word by word and set down in successive sentences. The linear form of words does not mean that ideas and feelings lose their force, but they are put under control for useful purposes.

Writing also helps us to weigh thought. The fact that writing is a slower process than talking gives us an advantage. We make discoveries as we write. We may suddenly see the limitations of our own thinking, or we may see relationships that we have not seen before. One thing suggests another. Setting down a thought helps us to reflect on it. Once down on paper, it is separated from us and we are sometimes able to see our own ideas and hear the tone of our own remarks quite objectively, particularly if a period of time has elapsed. To write clearly is to perceive clearly.

Finally, writing inescapably mirrors the self. It is something unique, something we have said that no one else can say in exactly the same way. As a personal act, therefore, writing is a strong force for individualism against massive pressures to conform. In struggling with complexities, we need to remind ourselves of the etymology of the word *compose*. Its roots mean "to put together." As a form of composing, writing can help us put ourselves together. To this point, Eldridge Cleaver makes an impressive comment in *Soul on Ice:*

I lost my self-respect. My pride as a man dissolved and my whole fragile moral structure seemed to collapse, completely shattered.

That is why I started to write. To save myself.

Writing may not necessarily be easy, but it is a way for individuals to find themselves, to know who they are, where they are, and what their purposes are. These are practical values to the individual that go beyond simple communications with others. They are the reasons individuals continue to find writing a worthwhile activity, no matter how modest their achievements.

The writer and the reader-critic

The reluctance that many people show toward writing can often be traced to an unexpressed view they hold about the reader-critic, particularly in a classroom situation. First, they see the reader as an enemy, not a friend. And, in truth, if an instructor consistently has only negative things to say about a student's writing, it is easy for the student to turn in routine work—writing that plays it safe, ventures nothing, and falls into dullness. Because all writing, no matter how good or bad it is, is a personal creation, the writer is naturally sensitive. The respect of a critic for the integrity of the writer and, in turn, the respect of the writer for the critic's intelligence and judgment are necessary conditions for criticism to function constructively.

Further, writers have to accept the hard fact that the reader is the final judge of the prose. You may think you have been clear, but if the reader does not understand, then you have fallen short. You may be too close to your own thoughts to decide. The outside viewer can sometimes reveal that the pen has leaped over thoughts that only you can supply to fill the gap. The enemy of the writer is not the reader, but the chaos and confusion that both of them seek to overcome.

Finally, a good working relationship between a writer and the reader-critic depends on the two of them seeing eye to eye on certain basic questions: What is the function of criticism? What essentially does improvement in writing mean? Does it mean proofreading? Does it mean eliminating errors in grammar, spelling, and punctuation? Does it mean learning the refinements of usage—what offends some people and what doesn't? Does it mean realizing the full potential of language by learning how to write things in varied and interesting ways? Does it mean being able to analyze more carefully, to support opinions, to organize thoughts, and to put them down persuasively? All of these are improvements of one kind or another, but they cover a wide range. Some relate to matters of correctness, some to appropriateness, some to content and form and style. If writer and reader do not share common expectations, then they may be working at cross-purposes. If you think writing is a mechanical skill and all you need to do to improve is to discover the rights and wrongs, but the teacher-reader thinks it is a dynamic process and that you need to learn to make choices appropriate to the purpose and occasion, then the difference between the two of you is great.

A book like this is intended as a kind of forum about writing. You must feel free to test the ideas, for what will finally be useful is what will work for *you*, what will help you to write more easily and effectively, what will help you become more self-sufficient as a writer.

How people write

Every writer can find consolation in the writing experiences of others. If you have had some doubts about your own attitudes toward writing, you may be interested in these remarks that represent a composite of what numerous students have said about themselves and their practices as writers:

1. Writing is painful and agonizing and joyful and passionate, sometimes all at once.
2. Writing depends on both know-how and intuition; that is, some things can be learned, while others happen quite spontaneously.
3. A genuine part of the process is the mulling, the fermenting, the questioning, the mental fooling around, the planning—however one wants to explain what takes place before the first word ever gets on paper.
4. Procrastinating is so common that it can be considered a way of getting ready. Readiness is all. Getting started is a major problem.
5. Writing usually gets easier as the writer continues. It picks up momentum.
6. Editing or revising varies with the individual. Some people are revise-as-you-write writers; some are revise-after-you-write writers; a few produce finished products with little or no editing.
7. Seeing the final product brings relief. It also gives the kind of satisfaction that comes from having won in any struggle.

In fact, we might think of all writers (writers as creators, writers as reporters, writers as persuaders) as wrestlers, not physical ones, but mental ones, as wrestlers with thoughts and feelings, motivated by purpose, agonized by the struggle to make words mean, spurred by a desire to break the hold of incommunicableness, aided by intuition, finally finding form as a way of meaning, willing to repeat the struggle, even grateful therefor.

Projects

1. List what you consider the responsibilities of the instructor in your writing course. What, then, are your responsibilities as a student where your own progress in writing is concerned? What basically do you think improvement in writing means?

2. As something we do, what is writing like more than anything else? Seek out comparisons and see if they test whether you think writing is primarily a skill, a creative process, a performing art, or some combination. For instance, is writing like driving a car? Building a house? Making a vase? Acting on the stage? Gymnastics?

3. List what seem to be the differences between unfocused thinking, conversational talking, and expository writing; that is, do we produce them differently? For instance, is thinking always verbal? Do these differences explain why many people consider writing difficult.

Suggestions for writing

Various kinds of free-association and forced-thinking methods are useful to loosen up and get the pen or typewriter keys moving. The first thing to do in this kind of writing is to discard the tendency to make a judgment about a thought before you write it down. Simply write as uninhibitedly as possible whatever occurs to you.

1. Write continuously as you listen to a musical selection or watch a nonnarrative film. Associate freely. What are you reminded of? What are your responses? Try to censor as few of your thoughts as possible.

2. For about five minutes, force your mind to come up with thoughts and words by doing "wet-ink" writing; that is, keep the pen moving without stopping to ponder. In the absence of something to say, write repeatedly, "I can't think of anything to say" until you do find something to say. Examine what you have written. How many ideas have you produced? Is putting pen to paper, whether you think you are ready or not, a way of getting over the hump of beginning?

3. Tape about five minutes of your own talking as if you were casually explaining something to someone else. Transcribe on paper what you said. To what extent do you want to edit what you said when you see it written? Is talking a way of getting started?

4. Keep a journal as a way of recording thoughts and finding the most natural way you express them. To be of value, a journal should not be a diary of what you do from day to day but a record of your observations, reactions, and speculations—a reflection of your intellectual activity. Above all, worry as little as possible about form, correctness, and style. Write in a way that you find comfortable. What you write should be your own choice, but a few suggestions may help:

A. Register your support of or objection to something you heard in class.

B. Summarize briefly something you have read, and let your own thoughts go on from there.

C. Simply ask questions that haunt your thinking. Attempt answers if you wish.

D. Catalog sounds and sights and smells as you sit in a particular place.

E. Use the journal for trial writing. Try something you have not tried before. Write a dialogue or a poem, or imitate someone else's style.

F. Tell what you gain by getting in the habit of regularly recording your thoughts and feelings on a daily basis. What do you discover about yourself?

5. We all have fantasies. They may be enormously important (such as Kekulé daydreaming about polygons and then coming up with the benzene ring); colorful, outrageous, full of sound and fury; or farfetched (like piloting a sailplane over the Swiss Alps at sunrise while listening to Beethoven's Ninth Symphony over stereo earphones). In a short piece, realize one of your fantasies.

Chapter 2   *The audience*

Writing is a personal and private act, but all the while you are writing you may be aware of outside influences on the choices you make. These are sometimes determined by your potential readers, if they are known, or by the situation you are addressing, or by the conventions that are largely formed by the society in which you live. The interaction between writer and reader through writing is often expressed in terms of the communications triangle:

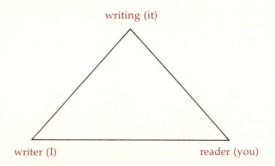

The triangle is a useful way of showing how awareness of an audience can vary considerably with the kind of writing you are doing. While writing in a diary or journal, you may be almost completely immersed in your own thoughts, unaware of any outside audience. While writing up a chemistry experiment, you may be totally concerned with facts—the writing itself—not with yourself as a writer or someone else as a reader. On another occasion, while trying to correct a misimpression you have given of yourself, you may be fully conscious of the readers you are trying to convince. Thus, focus upon audience shifts as the purpose of writing changes.

Writer–audience relationship

Even though when writing we usually assume someone will ultimately read what we write—a reader out there apart from ourselves—the important question is what you think about in terms of audience when you actually write. If you are writing a letter to a friend whom you know well, the matter is relatively simple. If you are writing a paper for a professor, you might ask yourself how much you actually know about that professor as a person. Are you writing for a person you know well or for an image of professors in general? Or for the expectations the professor sets? Writing to an abstraction is far less definite than writing to a person, but it is also far less threatening in some cases.

If, then, you are writing for an altogether unknown audience, what do you do? If you assume an audience is educated or is youthful, that may help in a few decisions about usage and tone, but will probably not help in other ways because groups are highly fragmented by sex, background, social status, and personal preferences of all kinds. Because our knowledge about potential readers is often vague and trying to conjure up a hypothetical audience can actually be distracting, many writers simply write for a kind of fictitious audience that is essentially a projection of themselves—a generalized "I"—a group of readers, for instance, who share their thoughts, enthusiasms, and values and who therefore pose no threat. If you worry too much about pleasing an audience, you may very well create a mental block for yourself. You must first please yourself. In doing that, you may very well please an outside audience.

Audience, therefore, need not be thought of as a specific reader or a group of individuals outside yourself. You can have an inner sense of audience that acts as a guide in making decisions. The more you write, the more intuitive a sense of audience is likely to become. You will finally recognize that "audience" is built into the language itself. Choose certain words, and you have created one kind of audience. Choose other ones, and you have accommodated the language to another audience. It is helpful, however, to think of the relationship between you and readers. Are you and they on a par with one another, and you are therefore writing for your peers? Or, must you accommodate your language to them because they are much younger or less informed than you on a particular subject? Or, must you address an audience that is essentially more informed than you on a particular subject, like writing for your professors? At one time or another, we all find ourselves in one of four basic relationships between writer and audience, writing as a specialist to specialists, as a specialist to generalists, as a generalist to generalists, or as a generalist to specialists.

1 *Specialist to specialists*

Everybody is a specialist in something, whether in ordinary things like cooking and swimming or unusual ones like gyrostatics and Platonism. *Specialist* is a relative term indicating that some people either know more or have greater experience than other people, who by comparison have only a general and somewhat superficial knowledge of that subject. On most topics, the great majority of people fall into the category of generalists; only a few are specialists.

Specialization is by no means limited to scholarship. There are specialists on any subject or activity—jazz, football, drag racing, astrology. Specialists in a particular area usually represent an ingroup. There may be differences of interpretation among them, but not great differences in their commitment to the subject. They speak the same language; they have mastered their own jargon. Their common interest bridges their differences and gives them shortcuts in communication. Specialists are demanding of one another, but a specialist writing for other specialists has a considerably easier job than a specialist writing for generalists.

2 *Specialist to generalists*

A specialist writing for generalists can encounter innumerable pitfalls. In a typical situation, the specialist-as-authority writes for an amateur audience—an audience supposedly interested in learning more, but not yet experienced enough to be members of the ingroup. What can the writer assume this audience knows? Does the writer begin from zero? What terms need to be defined? What language will be completely unfamiliar? Will explaining too much seem condescending? Will explaining too little produce vagueness? The basic problem, therefore, is one of accommodation—simplifying the concepts, at times giving generalizations without extensive support, and popularizing the language. The more specialized the topic, the more difficult the translation. In the preface to *The Miracle of Language*, a popularization of scholarly approaches to the English language, Charlton Laird comments on the dilemma of the specialist writing for a broad audience:

In the belief that promoting the popular understanding of language is a worthy endeavor, I have tried to write so that a dogged person can understand me and a charitable reader can stay awake. Popularization has necessitated simplification; I hope it has not led me into downright error.

Popular magazines are, of course, expert in this kind of accommodation, but very often their writers are not true specialists; they are generalists writing for generalists.

3 *Generalist to generalists*

No writer-reader relationship exists on a completely equal basis, because the writer always has a temporary advantage over the reader—a moment of control, as it were. The free-lance writer is a good example of the generalist who becomes a temporary expert. Professional writers have to be generalists on many subjects, or they run out of magazines to submit to. Typically, a free-lance writer may read seven or eight books on a subject, interview several professionals, attend a number of perform-ances or lectures if they are relevant, and with newly acquired "expertness" write the kind of article that appeals to a wide audience. The extent of that audience, of course, depends on the level of knowledge and language the writer chooses. In one of his so-called nonlectures delivered at Harvard University, E. E. Cummings tells about the editor of the magazine "possessing the largest circulation on earth," whose first rule for writers supposedly was "eight to eighty"—every article had to appeal "to anybody, man, woman, or child, between the ages of eight and eighty years. . . ." The anecdote hits upon the idea of a common denominator, particularly the writer's decision on how low the common denominator should be.

The generalist who writes for generalists can never assume a captive audience. The audience has no obligation to read. Naturally, these readers don't want to be bored. Unless the writer lures them at the outset and sustains their interest, they give up. In this particular category of writing, therefore, rhetoric is a strong factor. Appealing to the audience is a way of holding them.

4 *Generalist to specialists*

At first thought, it might seem that there would never be need for the generalist to write for specialists. Yet almost all student-to-teacher writing falls into this category. It is not surprising, therefore, that students often approach this kind of "test" writing with a lack of confidence. What every generalist needs to realize, however, is that lack of knowledge about a special subject can be offset by fresh perception. If it were possible, many specialists would undoubtedly trade some of their knowledge for the completely unencumbered perspective of the newcomer. A beginning stu-dent in American literature can say something new about *Moby Dick*. In fact, students have to take advantage of the unique position they are in: they are experi-encing for the first time something that to the specialist has become dulled by repetition.

Another familiar generalist-to-specialist kind of writing is the open inquiry, com-mon in the daily newspaper. It often takes the form of a letter. The writer seeks information or advice, writing openly about a situation and then posing a question. Often the circumstances of the individual voluntarily looking to an authority affect the whole content and tone of the writing.

It should be added here that student-to-teacher writing can conceivably fall into any of the four categories, although it seems to be concentrated in this last one. As specialist to specialist, the student would have to know in advance that student and instructor share a common specialty, perhaps jazz recordings, and that the student is as advanced and as experienced as the instructor. As specialist to generalist, a young woman might be, for example, an expert photographer and the instructor only an amateur. Her responsibility of accommodating the subject to the audience would then be the same as that of any other authority writing for an interested reader. Age or sex or professional status would be irrelevant. A student who writes a term paper on a topic outside the instructor's specialty becomes basically the generalist writing for the generalist, and the responsibilities to inform and to create interest are no less than those of the free-lance writer preparing an article for sale. Yet term papers, although they may be sound in their facts, frequently suggest that the writer feels no particular obligation to win the audience. Unfortunately, the student all too often takes the captive teacher for granted.

The extended audience

Besides thinking of an audience as a fairly well-defined group of readers at a particular time or as a kind of inner sense that keeps writers aware of their obligations to someone besides themselves, it is also possible for a writer to address a situation rather than a particular audience. In such cases, the audience is, in an extended sense, everyone. For example, public figures quite often make use of special occasions like after-dinner speeches, graduation addresses, and dedication ceremonies to discuss a national or world situation. They may be speaking to a particular group gathered to listen, but the speech has been written with the extended audience in mind. Because of the extended audience, the arguments are general and the tone impersonal.

Proclamations, manifestoes, demands, and open letters are all forms of public writing. In that they are often declarations, they attempt to influence an audience, not let the audience shape what will be said or how it will be said. Such writing obviously does not deny that an audience exists, but it can be said to ignore the audience and its preferences in order to change it. Essentially, all revolutionary writing—revolutionary in idea or technique—dares to intimidate and antagonize the audience. Experimental writers have reason to complain that an audience can be tyrannical, for an audience in the most general sense is conventional. It likes predictable patterns and temperate expression. It prefers meaning to be explicit, not implied. It is not surprising, therefore, that writers who have influenced prose style in the past have been those who were willing to forgo the favor of one audience in order to create a new one. It is also not surprising that most writers seek common ground with their audience.

The continuing audience

The great unknown is the continuing audience. Any published work has a potential audience beyond its writer's own lifetime. Every surviving work has had a history of its own—where it has been read, when it has been revived, for what purpose it has been used, who has been influenced by it. Sometimes writers who begin to envision their immortality run the risk of losing their present audience. Perhaps the biggest mistake writers can make is to try to write for the future rather than for their own time. It is true that purely topical works will pass away quickly, but it is also true that the universality of a work beyond its time is a judgment of the future, not a quality that the writer can inject. Big thoughts do not necessarily ensure universal truths. It is unlikely that the writer of the ancient biblical tale of Joseph and his brothers thought that he was writing a story for future ages. That writer simply wrote with honest insight, and that quality has made the story durable. Every writer, no matter how modest, can try to do the same.

Audience and style

Finally, the writer-audience relationship gets translated into a particular kind of style that results from the choices a writer makes. As readers, we may encounter as many as six major styles of expository writing; as writers, we seldom write more than two or three of these. The categories are broad, yet each differs in purpose and design. The following examples from each of the six suggest the range of the styles and illustrate the assumptions the writers seem to be making about their readers.

1 Legal and technical writing

Legal and technical writing is a special kind of practical prose designed by the specialist for the specialist. General readers do not encounter it frequently, but when they do, they are likely to find it as obscure as a foreign language.

The first example is taken from the *Canadian Journal of Biochemistry:*

> The occurrence of organophosphonic acids and their derivatives has been reported in a variety of invertebrate biological material. However, a recent report by Alam and Bishop (1) describing the presence of lipid-bound choline-phosphonate in human aortas with athero-sclerotic plaques shows that the occurrence of organophosphonic acid derivatives is not confined to the lower forms of the animal kingdom. Rouser *et al.* (2) were the first to isolate an intact phospholipid deriving from phosphonic acid. While investigating the composition of phospholipids of the sea anemone *Anthopleura elegantissima* by a combination of column and paper chromatographic methods, they obtained a sphingolipid differing from known sphingolipids in that on acid hydrolysis it gave a mixture of fatty acids, long-chain bases, and 2-aminoethyl-phosphonic acid. Examination of the long-chain bases by paper chromatography revealed the presence of *erythro-* and *threo-* sphingosine, *erythro-* and *threo-* phytosphingo-sine, and related compounds of different chain length (2).
>
> Erich Baer and G. Raphupati Sarma, "Phosphonolipids. XX."

Apart from the highly technical vocabulary, the most noticeable feature of the style is its compression. This introductory paragraph refers to two research studies and manages to summarize the relevant findings of each in a few sentences. Even though the words themselves are obscure to the general reader, we may assume that to the biochemist they are precise ones. Others would not substitute. Thus, technical writing of this order is a kind of private language.

When the specialist element is reduced, the prose becomes more generally understandable, as in this example from the magazine *Scientific American:*

Toads respond to small objects, such as a piece of white cardboard moved over a black background, with a series of prey-catching reactions. First there is orientation toward the prey, then binocular fixation, then snapping, gulping and mouth-cleaning. Two basic processes are required to produce the overall orienting reaction: the identification of a stimulus and the location of it in space. The identification process determines the type of behavior. It is dependent on specific features of the stimulus such as its angular size, the orientation of the boundaries between light and dark, its angular velocity, its contrast with the background and so on. A detection process then localizes the stimulus and, together with the result of the identification process, determines the motor response, which can be either to turn toward the stimulus if it is identified as prey or to avoid it if it appears to be an enemy. In what follows I shall attempt to analyze the neurophysiological basis of signal identification, localization and the triggering of the associated instinctive actions.

Jörg-Peter Ewert, "The Neural Basis of Visually Guided Behavior"

The third example is a paragraph from the mortgagee clause of a homeowner's insurance policy:

Whenever this Company shall pay the mortgagee (or trustee) any sum for loss or damage under this policy, and shall claim that, as to the mortgagor or owner, no liability therefor existed, this Company shall, to the extent of such payment, be thereupon legally subrogated to all the rights of the party to whom such payment shall be made, under all securities held as collateral to the mortgage debt, or may at its option pay to the mortgagee (or trustee) the whole principal due or to grow due on the mortgage, with interest, and shall thereupon a full assignment and transfer of the mortgage and of all such other securities; but no subrogation shall impair the right of the mortgagee (or trustee) to recover the full amount of said mortgagee's (or trustee's) claim.

Even though copies of insurance policies are given to purchasers, the prose is not written for them. It is written by lawyers for lawyers in case of any disagreement about the provisions of the policy. The policy is a contractual agreement couched in legal jargon. The language must be exact, therefore, carefully qualified to cover all possible alternatives, and punctuated so that as few ambiguities as possible occur. Like other technical writing, the prose is completely impersonal and formal, limited to bare facts. The need for accuracy in documents, laws, and contracts allows for little flexibility of language. The result is a style that is often rigid and cumbersome and essentially unreadable except as a matter of necessity.

2 *Popular reporting: the plain style*

The style of popular reporting retains both the factual and impersonal emphasis of technical writing, but its chief difference as a style is that it is written to be read and understood by a wide audience. We encounter it in news reporting, program notes, announcements, business letters, and encyclopedia articles. It is also the style of written examinations that call for facts and analysis. It is often unsigned prose, but signed or unsigned it is anonymous in effect because the writer excludes feelings and avoids coloring the prose by any unusual words or strategies. The style therefore includes much writing in an extremely simple and practical form.

The first example is an excerpt from a university bulletin, briefly describing a course of special interest being offered during the summer quarter:

Beginning and advanced mountain climbing have been scheduled for the full quarter in order to provide a complete summer of climbing. Evening lectures and practice sessions are combined with weekend field trips to nearby mountains. An additional fee of $25.00 will be charged for registration in either course. No auditors will be allowed.

The basic course (PE 136) includes evening lectures or practice sessions and weekend field trips. No prior experience is necessary. Two sections are offered; the first begins Tuesday, June 24, the second on Wednesday, June 25.

The advanced course (PE 137) includes instruction and practice in techniques used in high-angle rock, snow, and ice climbing. Evening lectures and weekend field trips are planned. Interested students must have successfully completed any basic mountain climbing course (or have equivalent experience) and must obtain the instructor's permission. The course will meet on Monday evenings beginning June 23.

One of the most noticeable features of the style is the consistent use of the passive voice in order to maintain an impersonal tone. This passage uses no connectives. The facts are set down in sequence in relatively brief, uncluttered sentences. The vocabulary is undemanding.

The second example is a news report:

Typhoon Judy gained strength today and dumped 7 inches of rain on parts of Okinawa, forcing the postponement of a huge American military exercise and virtually halting air, ground and sea transportation.

Up to 7 inches of rain were recorded in Naha, Okinawa's capital, and wide areas of the Pacific coast of Japanese main islands were doused. Airline, bus and ferry services serving Okinawa were canceled.

A United States Marine Corps spokesman in Okinawa said a two-day amphibious exercise, code-named Fortress Gale, originally scheduled to begin tomorrow, was postponed till Saturday because of the typhoon.

Seattle Times, August 23, 1979

This weather report is factual, although the writer colors the information slightly by the choice of words like "dumped" and "doused." Nevertheless, the sentences are clearly phrased. The paragraphs, typical of journalistic prose, are brief. The report efficiently condenses at least eight or nine separate facts into a short space. The writer is unidentified. Essentially, the prose is anonymous in its tone.

3 *Learned discourse*

Although legal and technical writing treats specialized material, not all discourse of this nature needs to read as laboriously as an act of Congress or an insurance policy. Learned discourse may be described as a style also written by specialists for specialists with the broader purpose of analyzing and expanding upon a topic, as opposed to prose that sets down facts in the most abbreviated way possible. Because learned discourse may also need to argue and persuade, it depends on rhetorical strategies. Topics are often of limited interest to a general audience, but it is possible for the prose to be read by educated readers outside the field if they have enough knowledge of the terms and references.

The first example is taken from a paper read by Alfred North Whitehead before a meeting of the Aristotelian Society. He himself considered this writing less complex and technical than material he was writing concurrently for books on the same subject:

I presume that the fundamental position of idealism is that all reality can be construed as an expression of mentality. For example, I suppose that Mr. Alexander is a realist because for him a mind is one among other items occurring in that evolution of complexes which is the very being of space-time. On the other hand, Mr. Wildon Carr is an idealist because he finds ultimate reality in the self-expression of monadic mentality. The test, therefore, of idealism is the refusal to conceive reality apart from explicit reference to some or all of the characteristic processes of mentality; it may be either thought, or experience, or knowledge, or the expression of valuation in the form of historical process, the valuation being both the efficient and the final cause of the process. Now Berkeley's argument in favor of this central position of idealism is that when you examine the objects of sense-perception they are essentially personal to the observer. He enforces by a variety of illustrations the doctrine that there is nothing left when you have torn the observer out of the observation. The planet, which is no bigger than a sixpence, is the observer's planet, and he walks off with his own property.

"The Philosophical Aspects of the Principle of Relativity"

Whatever difficulty there may be in reading this passage perhaps derives more from the concepts than the language. Although Whitehead uses several terms that have special meanings in philosophy, all of them are defined in a standard collegiate dictionary and are therefore accessible to the educated reader who is interested in capsule definitions without doing extensive background reading. But more important about the prose is that Whitehead seems interested in helping the reader follow the line of reasoning. There are markers like "on the other hand," "therefore," and "now." There is an elaboration of the definition in sentence 4 and a moving from the general to the particular in the last three sentences, ending with a comparison. These are all signs of the writer's concern for the reader, even to involving the reader personally by the use of "you." All in all, though the learnedness of this writing is apparent, so also is the writer's willingness to expand on his phrases and seek understanding.

Scholarly journals are filled with writing in the style of learned discourse. In a book entitled *Tough, Sweet, and Stuffy,* a book describing three styles of American writing, Walker Gibson uses scholarly writing as a typical example of the stuffy style. Little wonder that being published in a scholarly journal becomes a way of being entombed in a library.

4 *Popular discourse*

Popular discourse varies as widely as the audience it is written for. What all of it seems to have in common is an interest in communicating feeling as well as fact. At times, the feeling is expressed in a direct personal way. At other times, it is implicit in the choice of words and strategies that play on a reader's emotions. Popular discourse need not be less serious in its subject matter than learned discourse, although characteristically it is written in a more flexible and informal manner which allows the writer's voice to come through. It uses almost any device that will convince, appeal, influence, sell, amuse, or attract a reader. It turns often to description and narration for purposes of illustration. It is prose written from a personal viewpoint for a general audience.

A passage from E. B. White's *One Man's Meat* suggests how radically the style of popular discourse can differ from that of learned discourse:

I keep forgetting that soldiers are so young. I keep thinking of them as my age, or Hitler's age. (Hitler and I are about the same age.) Actually, soldiers are often quite young. They haven't finished school, many of them, and their heads are full of the fragile theme of love, and underneath their bluster and swagger everything in life is coated with that strange beautiful importance that you almost forget about because it dates back so far. The other day some French soldiers on the western front sent a request to a German broadcasting studio asking the orchestra to play *"Parlez moi d'amour."* The station was glad to oblige, and all along the Maginot Line and the Siegfried Line the young men were listening to the propaganda of their own desire instead of attending to the fight. So few people speak to the young men of love any more, except the song writers and scenarists. The leaders speak always of raw materials and *Lebensraum.* But the young men in uniforms do not care much for raw materials (except tobacco) and they are thinking of *Liebestraum*, and are resolving their dream as best they can. I am trying hard to remember what it is like to be as young as a soldier.

"First World War," written October 1939

This prose has all of the marks of easy informality—uncomplicated sentences of varied length (some very short), relatively simple words except for the play upon the two German words *Lebensraum* and *Liebestraum*, parenthetical asides, and a brief narration to illustrate. The writer characterizes himself in this short paragraph as a man who, twenty years after World War I, finds it hard to remember how young a young soldier is. The manner is appealing; the tone inviting.

Even though some prose written in the style of popular discourse is clearly different from the learned style, it is also true that there has been a narrowing of the differences between the two. Writers of learned discourse, particularly in the humanities, often tend toward an informal manner and pursue their subjects with a kind of easy discursiveness that makes the prose popular in its appeal. The result is simply more readable prose without the writer necessarily suggesting that the audience is being talked down to. Most student writing, in fact, seems to fall within this overlap of the two styles—what might be described basically as an informal (but not casual) treatment of a subject, which by its words and ideas still assumes that the reader has reached an advanced level of education. A student theme illustrates this kind of writing; it was written in response to a selection from James Baldwin's *The Fire Next Time:*

James Baldwin's story is not unique. It can be told and retold in various ways by other men in other cities. Their versions may differ slightly from Baldwin's; some more shocking than others; some less involved; others more ruinous. Yet all these stories are alike. Their causes are the same and their themes identical—fear, hate, mistrust, despair, apathy, and hopelessness.

Baldwin mirrors these feelings clearly. Even though he has found his "gimmick" and has apparently escaped from the clutches of the world he discovered when he became fourteen, his essay still reveals the fear and despair that he shares with thousands like him. He attempts to portray himself as a calm, experienced man saying quietly, "Listen to me. I know. I've been there." But whether he wants to or not Baldwin says more than that. He says "hate." He says "despair." He says "mistrust"—mistrust of society, mistrust of his own community, mistrust of his father, even mistrust of his God.

As I said before, these feelings of Baldwin are not unique. In fact, in the black community they are the rule rather than the exception. Nearly all blacks in the ghettoes of this country share this attitude toward life. It is not normal. This is not just "the way the black is" or a trait of the race. Rather it is a pathological condition in which the black finds himself. It is a continuing cycle of despair and apathy. Baldwin says that ". . . the girls were destined to gain as much weight as their mothers, the boys, it was clear, would rise no higher than their fathers." This cycle, of course, is the result of the breakdown in the structure of the black family. The family breakdown is directly attributable to the days of slavery, the years of legal segregation as a result of the infamous Jim Crow laws, and the black migration to the northern cities in the 1940s and 1950s. Slavery removed the black male from the family picture. It took away all his pride as leader of the family and source of authority. Women naturally assumed this role and were able to continue it because they were not a threat to anyone or anything. During the Reconstruction Period, the black faced segregation and Jim Crow laws. The male lost all courage and ambition, for the "sassy nigger" was lynched. With his move to the North, the black was still hemmed in by unemployment and segregation; and the family condition, rather than changing, became more and more matriarchal. Statistics on crime rates, unemployment, divorce rates, and illegitimacy in the black community demonstrate vividly what this family breakdown has created.

Our society has caused this breakdown. Americans have allowed it to continue. And now—today—we must correct it.

This essay begins in the first two paragraphs with the impulse that Baldwin's prose has given the writer; in the third paragraph, it includes historical and sociological material to broaden the implications; and it ends in a short fourth paragraph on a persuasive note—a direct appeal to the reader as a part of society to correct these ills. All of this is set forth in a flexible prose that sometimes piles up words in series; sometimes interprets Baldwin by a kind of simulated direct discourse, that is, attributing words to him as if he were speaking them himself; uses repetition for emphasis; and builds the sentences to a climax. All of this is quite different from an unimpassioned factual account; yet in paragraph 3 the writer shows a capacity to write a basically direct style of learned discourse, which is set down factually without commentary. In other parts of the essay, however, the writer's own emotional responses remove the prose from the category of a sociological profile of the black American.

The strategies that generate feeling in the student essay are even more obvious in any prose that is written to be delivered as a speech. The style of public address, therefore, represents a more generous use of rhetorical devices for purposes of persuasion.

The style of public address is shaped by the fact that the writer is present and speaking to a group of people. The presence of an audience does not necessarily mean that the prose will be more informal; it may mean only that the writer will structure the prose more loosely to take into account the fact that a listener cannot easily absorb succinctly stated ideas. Generalizations need to be elaborated upon in order to give the audience time to reflect; they need to be repeated or paraphrased so that they can be absorbed. Crucial words need to be put in emphatic positions; sentences need to be built to a climax to allow the speaker's voice to be effectively used.

Among the kinds of public address that continue to be prepared as written statements to be read are the sermon, the occasional address, and the political speech. The first example is taken from a book of sermons by the well-known American preacher Harry Emerson Fosdick:

Come at this matter now from another angle, and see that hidden in this truth lies the reason for some of our most unintentional, and yet most deplorable, hypocrisies. It is easy to choose the good in general, and then to fail utterly in paying the price of getting it. For Kreisler to say, in general, I want to be an artist, is one thing; it is something else to be willing, day by day, to pay the cost.

The nations of the world now are presenting a fearful illustration of this truth. Have we not chosen peace? Is not that what we want? If anyone should ask for war, would he not be howled down in indignation? It is peace we want, all are saying. But the price of peace—the necessary surrenders of national sovereignty, the cessation of power politics, the ending of competitive armament, the shift of our economy from self-centered nationalism to co-operative internationalism, the overcoming of racial prejudice, the building of a real world government where such suspicious remnants of the old order as the veto power in the Security Council have been overpassed—these conditions of peace, that must be fulfilled as indispensably as in a laboratory the conditions of achievement must be met, we shrink from. Give us peace! we say; but not the cost of it.

Most evident in this writing is an ordering of words and ideas for dramatic impact. There are contrasts, there are rhetorical questions, there is a building to the climactic statement "Give us peace!" and then an intentional trailing off of the thought in the final six words. The whole piece is written with the human voice and actual presentation in mind.

A readjustment of the word order and a few changes in the strategies of the second paragraph will reveal how the total effect changes:

We have chosen peace as the course we want to pursue. If anyone asked for war, he would be howled down in indignation. But peace has its price. It involves necessary surrenders of national sovereignty, the cessation of power politics, the ending of competitive armament, the shift of our economy from self-centered nationalism to co-operative internationalism, the overcoming of racial prejudice, and the building of a real world government where such suspicious remnants of the old order as the veto power in the Security Council have been overpassed. We shrink from these conditions of peace that must be fulfilled as indispensably as the conditions for achievement must be met in a laboratory. We say we want peace, but we do not want the cost of it.

With these alterations of Fosdick's paragraph, the style of public address has reverted essentially to the style of learned discourse. The rhythms have been changed; the sentences have been given a general uniformity of tone. Everything has been moderated to such an extent that the word *howled*, carried over from the original paragraph, actually seems out of place, even though it is appropriate in the more intense and dramatic version.

The second example is taken from a speech called "The Black Revolution," delivered on April 8, 1964, by Malcolm X in New York City:

This is a real revolution. Revolution is always based on land. Revolution is never based on begging somebody for an integrated cup of coffee. Revolutions are never fought by turning the other cheek. Revolutions are never based upon love-your-enemy and pray-for-those-who-spitefully-use-you. And revolutions are never waged singing "We Shall Overcome." Revolutions are based upon bloodshed. Revolutions are never compromising. Revolutions are never based upon negotiations. Revolutions are never based upon any kind of tokenism whatsoever. Revolutions are never even based upon that which is begging a corrupt society or a corrupt system to accept us into it. Revolutions overturn systems. And there is no system on this earth which has proven itself more corrupt, more criminal, than this system that in 1964 still colonizes 22 million African-Americans, still enslaves 22 million Afro-Americans.

There is no system more corrupt than a system that represents itself as the example of freedom, the example of democracy, and can go all over this earth telling other people how to straighten out their house, when you have citizens of this country who have to use bullets if they want to cast a ballot.

The force of this passage is based almost exclusively on its use of repetition. Each short sentence, parallel in form with the one before it, adds to the cumulative effect. The words and phrases are familiar, known both to whites, who constituted almost three-quarters of the audience, and also to blacks. The inconsistency of the American position is highlighted by the final phrase that ironically points out that some citizens who want to cast ballots are forced to use bullets.

The style of public address is, of course, not consistently declamatory. In long passages, it may be expository or conversational or anecdotal, but qualities that identify it as a special style are found in those passages that are designed to give the human voice free play with words and rhythms. None of the other styles employs rhetorical strategies so generously and flamboyantly.

6 *Private discourse*

The style of private discourse is a highly personal kind of writing. It may be the open, perhaps unstructured manner of personal correspondence, doing freely what the writer wants to do because the audience is possibly an intimate friend or relative, not a public one. It may shortcut detail because the reader and writer share a common understanding of the background.

We are all familiar with the style of personal letters we ourselves write. There are no conventions to follow. We can make the prose what we want it to be. Much of the interest in the published letters of famous people lies in the new insights we get of them when they show themselves unmasked and writing with no sense of doing it for the general public. A letter of the well-known American poet Theodore Roethke to the critic Kenneth Burke, whom he often addressed as "Pa" or "Pop," reveals both the openness of his manner in writing to Burke and the difficulty outsiders have in understanding references the two of them share:

Saginaw, Michigan
September 6, 1949

Dear Pa: Your post-natal letter received: forwarded from Washington.

I'm delighted, of course: and pleased that you've documented my pre-human history so extensively. As to the *Sewanee:* they've announced the piece, don't forget. Palmer has been very decent: why shouldn't he be decenter? Tell him that some of the *zeit-geist*, ear-to-ground boys in England like John Lehmann think I'm the only bard at present operating in the U. S. of A., that everybody is tired of Tiresome Tom, the Cautious Cardinal, and wants to hear about the new jump-boy, the master of diddle-we-care-couldly. They have to be told, the goddamned sheep. Boom-boom, you gotta believe. (I don't mean Palmer but the public.)

Sure, I'd love to see it, but that isn't necessary. Anything you say is Ho-Kay mit mich mir. Just so I ain't drummed out of Christendom, or that part of it called Academia. I had to do a loathsome solo job on me & poems for an anthology. I made it in the form of a letter to make the tone less odious: lifted a page out of that letter I showed you (the one to the lady critic). The whole thing ran to 5½ pages, but when I got done I had the sense of not really having come to grips with the subject. But some cracks seem pertinent and I hope I wasn't puke-making.

Only when the references are annotated can the general reader begin to understand the setting and the comments. In the second sentence, Roethke expresses his delight with an essay that Burke has written about him. Tiresome Tom is T. S. Eliot, and the lady critic is Babette Deutsch. The language encompasses foreign words, playful phrases, slang, and profanity. The tone throughout is unguarded.

The same kind of prose, which often shows little concern for coherence and unity and effects calculated to influence a general audience, may also be found in some diaries, memoirs, and journals. The second example is taken from the diary of Mary Walker, who, with her husband Elkanah, served as a missionary among the Spokane Indians:

Saturday, September 1 [1838], Waiilatpu

It was decided that Mr. Smith remain with Dr. Whitman; that Mr. Gray go with Mr. Spalding to assist in building a mill, that Mr. Walker and Mr. Eells go to explore, assist Mr. Spalding, etc. I find it hard to be reconciled, yet trust it is for the best. We are short-sighted creatures, and know not what a day may bring forth. All will be right in the end, although we cannot foresee how it may be. It is very trying to me to think of having my husband gone. Inclination would make me wish to be where no one else scarcely could see me. Had female prayer meeting, a very good one.

Monday, September 10 [1838], Waiilatpu

Rose early; worked hard as I could till Mr. Walker got ready to start which was at three P.M. After crying a little picked up and found myself somewhat tired. Oh! dear how I would like to be at home about this time, and see brothers, hear from all the good folks! I wish I could have a letter from some of them.

These daily notes, clearly unintended for publication, include routine, trivial details of everyday life, but of special importance are those revelations of inner conflict and nostalgia that the writer confesses to her diary. The topics shift rapidly; the thoughts are at times put down in fragments. The manner is strictly private.

The descriptions of the six major styles given here should suggest that no writer writes only one style. We need to write what is appropriate to our purpose and audience. A scientist who tried to give a compact technical report as a public address would be doomed to disaster, even if the audience consisted only of fellow scientists. A writer who used the style of popular discourse for a job that required only reporting of facts would probably seem to be trying too hard. An informal essay or a personal letter written in learned discourse would be a pompous effort. The expectations that people have are conventional, and they judge on the basis of them.

It is probably true that the style of popular discourse is becoming more and more widespread, not only because it is the most spontaneous and natural of the public modes, but because we encounter it most frequently in newspapers, magazines, and books of nonfiction. To be skillful, however, we all need a range of styles and a capacity to adjust words and strategies to meet the demands of varying audiences. We can make these adjustments only if we fully realize that we as writers are able to control stylistic effects by the choices we make. Our flexibility therefore depends largely on the range of choices available to us.

Projects

1. Choose a particular magazine and study three or four issues. What kinds of articles appear? What do the pictures and advertisements tell about the magazine's appeal? In short, what audience does the magazine address? Support your conclusions with evidence.

2. Analyze the kinds of assumptions on which a particular advertisement is based. In what ways did the designer of this advertisement take into account the audience? Consider not only the written copy but also the advertisement as a whole, including pictures and color.

3. Consult a current edition of *Writer's Market,* a reference book listing markets for free-lance writers. Do the guidelines set down in that book suggest that free-lance writers write for an audience or for editors who say what the audience wants?

4. Take a short article or several paragraphs of an article from a special magazine you are familiar with and summarize it for the benefit of an audience of generalists. What changes were necessary? What did you have to omit? To add?

5. Find four prose passages that illustrate each of the four categories of writer–audience relationships discussed in this chapter. If possible, try to find passages on the same subject written for different audiences. What are the main differences in style?

6. Examine a legal document, a policy, or a contract of some kind. Explain the characteristics of the prose in terms of word choice, sentence structure, punctuation, and typography (use of italics, boldface, and variety of typeface). What would be gained or lost if the style were changed?

Suggestions for writing

1. Write an article that would be suitable for your school newspaper. Use a person or an event as your subject.

2. Write a description of a particular sport for a foreigner who is completely unfamiliar with the objectives, rules, and emotions of the game.

3. Determine something in which you are a specialist. Then within that range, select a topic. Write a paper on the specialty for an audience of generalists.

4. In his essay "Real Women," Robert Graves writes "A real woman, by my definition, neither despises nor worships men, but is proud not to have been born a man, does everything she can to avoid thinking or acting like one, knows the full extent of her powers, and feels free to reject all arbitrary man-made obligations." Write a paper giving your reactions to this definition, but assume that your audience will include a large number of ardent feminists. Consider whether your remarks will appeal to them or offend them. Think about the implications of sexism in language.

5. Collect five short examples of writing that seem to be designed for quite different audiences. As if you were preparing a small anthology, write an introduction to these five selections that describes the characteristics and differences in the writing and comments on the audience appeals. (The selections can be Xeroxed and submitted with the introduction as a short anthology.)

Chapter 3   *The subject: generating a topic*

The mind is constantly recording, responding, remembering, reflecting. Seldom, if ever, is it idle, during waking or sleep. It is no respecter of orderly time sequences; the past, present, and future intermingle. It knows no limits of space; it concerns itself with fact or fantasy. Thinking is a free-ranging process. The mind can explore, create, and at times make the intuitive leaps that produce the wholly unpredictable. What we think about may be a mixture of idea and feeling, with no way to differentiate one from the other. A thought may flash in our minds like a picture, a kind of total experience.

If we think about our own mental functioning—the full range of it—we become more fully aware how much unfocused activity goes on. Our verbal thinking may be focused, but a good bit of it is nonverbal and undirected. Thinking may sometimes even be a kind of reverie instead of deliberate analysis of a problem. In the undirected stages, thoughts skitter from one thing to another. What is relevant to this discussion, however, is that writing demands that we bring unfocused thinking under some kind of control. We cannot develop the wholeness of an image on paper, as a photographer can. We must draw out the thought word by word in a linear sequence. Only after readers have followed through the sequence do they get some intimation what our instant mental image may have been.

Because of the difficulty of communicating exactly what we think by means of words, a writer must frequently try to put an idea into a context so that the reader will understand what the writer is trying to say. It is this development of a topic that often gives beginning writers their greatest problem. Rather typically, we are so product-minded—getting the job completed—that we find it difficult to be process-minded—evolving a more efficient way of going about the job.

Are there ways of helping thoughts grow? Are there devices that will help us generate thoughts without limiting the capacity of the mind to range freely? Undoubtedly, there are many. Aristotle set down twenty-eight ways, but for practical purposes, most individuals find a smaller number more manageable.

The twentieth-century rhetorician Kenneth Burke has provided a simple device that applies to any situation; he calls it the *pentad,* a set of five terms, each leading logically to related questions. These terms are action, actor-agent, scene, means, purpose. Trying to answer the questions that spring from the terms becomes a way of gathering resources for writing. The mind may not want to stick to the categories; it has a way of leaping from one to the other. That is not a disadvantage; the way the mind operates merely indicates that the categories are part of a whole. But making an effort to consider the categories separately overcomes haphazard thinking and becomes a way of seeing clearly. Once we begin the process, we may not complete everything at one sitting. Thoughts occur constantly during the prewriting stage and continue even after we have begun to put words on paper. Basically, however, prewriting is advance preparation for all of the stages that follow. Thinking in a structured way has decided advantages. What follows here, then, is an adaptation and simplification of Burke's approach.

The drama of thinking

Burke says that if we think of anything as if it were a part of a drama, we can use certain dramatic terms to help us see the whole thing. A drama has action, setting, actors, and various devices for projecting these, all usually integrated for a total purpose. We can ask questions to find out about each of these: What was done? Who or what did it? When and where was it done? How was it done? Why was it done? It is immediately apparent that all of these overlap and depend upon one another. Given an action (*what*), the most important part of learning *why* the action takes place may be explaining *who* did it, *when* it happened, *where* it occurred, and *how.* Together, the *what, who, when, where, how,* and *why* represent a complete context. It is the interrelatedness of the questions that makes them generating principles, but only, of course, if they can be applied to any topic. The five terms of the pentad, therefore, need further expansion and explanation.

1 Action

An action is anything that has happened or is happening, but is not necessarily limited to physical acts. Anything that exists may be considered a "happening." A poem or a painting, for example, has "happened," has been an action, and it continues to "happen" as long as people react to it. A boxing match is an action; so also is a personal thought like "I wonder why boxing is a popular sport." A scientific discovery, a space feat, an educational experiment, or a Supreme Court decision is an action. An act is very often the starting point of our thinking. If a writing assignment is free choice, our first thought might be as big and general and vague as an urge to write about the generation gap or moral corruption or the population explosion, all actions in that they are events that are happening now; or, conceivably, that first thought might be as limited and personal and specific as "I don't like the taste of curry in food." Nevertheless, general or specific, these are the thoughts that need development.

Let's explore further the implications of the basic question *What?* The question rephrased can open up a number of possibilities:

A. What happened? The question applies to any past deed. Even though this may seem the simplest question of all to answer, it is often one of the most difficult. Immediately following an event, if ten people were asked "What happened?" they might give ten different answers, at least ten answers reflecting different viewpoints and emphases. The more distant the event, the more obscure the facts. Reporters and historians spend much of their time at first trying to find out what happened. New histories now tell us that things did not happen during the Civil War exactly as old histories told us or that old histories did not tell us all that happened. Knowing what happened may make all the difference in answering other questions.

B. What is happpening? The question applies to any event occurring at the present, but also what is happening in any literary work we read or in any performance we see. It also includes the results—namely, the reaction. If the actions of a literary character are puzzling to the reader, the motives of the character may be also. Television has made us more and more aware of what is going on about us than would ever have been possible in the past. Yet our capacity to see does not always reveal what is happening because we see only parts and are left to construct the whole. In current events, we do not always know what is happening. The assassination of John F. Kennedy, for instance, at the time raised the question whether a conspiracy existed. Was there more happening than we were actually able to observe on film or TV? The question is still an open one. In analyzing literature, on the other hand, we know that writers usually tell us what they want us to know about what is happening. Even though we may have to make inferences about the things they do not tell us, we have the distinct advantage of being limited by their clues.

C. What will happen? What could happen? The questions apply to any speculation about an event or development that has not yet occurred. The answers are almost always based on what has happened or is happening, but they represent the capacity of the thinker to generate ideas beyond the facts at hand. In what direction are things moving? On the basis of what we know now, what can we expect to happen? This kind of thinking is not prophecy, but simple logical projection on the basis of known factors. It is often one of the interesting turns writing can take.

The question applies to any act or thought that requires definition: What is existentialism? What is extrasensory perception? What is the twelve-tone technique? What are the properties, the qualities, or the characteristics that identify them? Often, in order to say what something is, it is also necessary to sort it out from all others like it. In order to talk about love, it would be useful to consider the different ways we use the word: mother love, married love, Platonic love, puppy love, brotherly love. What do these have in common? What is the range of variation? That is, how far can the definition of *love* be extended before it becomes something else? What is not love?

D. What is it?

2 Actor-agent

One part of the drama of thinking logically leads to another. Action is, of course, inseparable from actors or the agents who are responsible for an action. In this sense, an agent does not necessarily need to be a person; it may be a cause or a force or a motivating influence. A storm, for instance, may be used as an agent, as the storm is in Shakespeare's *The Tempest*, which tosses a shipwrecked crew onto a strange island, thus precipitating the action. Or emotions like fear, malice, or greed may be the agent or motivating force which controls the action.

Given any agent, there is the possibility of both co-agents and counteragents—friends and enemies, associates and antagonists, supporting forces and counterforces. Who are the co-agents of Antigone in Sophocles' play? Are the gods on her side? In Thoreau's essay "Civil Disobedience," the government is the antagonist of the individual; the majority is the enemy of the minority of one. The agent within a piece of writing is not the only focus of interest. The author also is the agent of a book, and much interest of a biographical nature often revolves around the writer as a human being. Who is the author? What kind of person? What about this individual throws light on the internal structure of what has been written?

If we are going to generate thoughts that focus upon the agent, we have some basic questions to ask ourselves about the source of action:

The questions apply to any situation in which the agent is unknown. Huge numbers of people read murder mysteries and detective stories, eagerly turning the pages to find out "who did it"—but there the answer is almost always given. In real-life situations, the answer may be speculative. Arson in the cities. Who is responsible? Conflict in the Near East. Who are the co-agents? Racial oppression. Who is involved? Evil in general. Who is responsible for it?

A. Who did it?
Who is doing it?

The question applies to all the impersonal forces that bring about thoughts and actions. At times, these may be only abstract ways of referring to people in a collective sense: society, government, the military, the radical component, religious pressure. These are continuing agents; they persist after the individuals who represent them at a particular time pass from the scene. It is therefore not unusual to explain actions in terms of intangible forces—the conservative mood of the coun-

B. What did it?
What is causing it?

try—particularly when we are attempting to determine causes or trying to philosophize about ongoing history.

C. *What kind of*
agent is it?

This question applies to an agent that is known. It asks for full information concerning the active agents—details about one person or the qualities of individuals who
act as a group. If individuals picket the White House, what do they share in
common? If a new Attorney General is appointed, who is this person? If a woman
produces a bestseller, the public asks who the writer is—not her name but her
identity. The description of an agent quickly overlaps all of the other questions
because we may go on to explain the writer's family background, the influences
upon her, her preoccupations, her techniques, and her purposes. Answers to all of
the basic questions about a person would be capable of generating a complete
biography—a complete context and a complete drama.

3 Scene

Having considered the action and the agents, we may then turn to the scene.
Anything that happens occurs in a setting. There is always a backdrop against which
the action takes place; there is a location for the play of events. Anything that
happens occurs at a particular time; it may be that it could not have happened at
another time.

Time and place are therefore important to the scene. In an extended sense, the
scene might be the environment in which something happens. We can think of
specific areas like an urban ghetto or Miami Beach or the campus of a privately
endowed college. What are the significant details? In a more abstract way, we can
speak of the moral climate of the "roaring twenties" or an age of affluence. These
scenes are less concrete, but they can be meaningful if they are explained and
illustrated.

Besides the immediate scene, events can be considered against the background of
the past. History often attempts to interpret current happenings in terms of the past
or even to set up a theory of history on the basis of recurrences. Literary criticism
evaluates current literary works in terms of tradition and convention. What is
happening in higher education may be better understood by reference to what has
happened in the past. The fact that we think of time as a continuum makes history
relevant. What happens now is at least related to what has already happened, even if
there has been a radical break. Reference to the total scene, past and present, is
therefore a means of generating thoughts.

The questions about the scene of an action are simple and direct:

A. *Where did it*
happen? Where is it
happening? Where
will it happen?

Answering these questions does not mean merely naming the place but describing
the conditions, going beyond surface appearances to determine the true circumstances, giving descriptive details. What was the atmosphere? The morale? The
prevailing situation? What was the scene in Germany when Adolf Hitler came to

power? Where are similar things happening now? Under what conditions is totalitarianism likely to occur in the future?

Literature takes on special interest because writers do not always provide readers with a familiar environment. They may create unusual situations in unusual places in critical times in order to show how men act under extraordinary circumstances. The twentieth-century writers referred to as absurdists depend to a great extent on characters acting in grotesque settings and situations. To ignore the scene in the interpretation of these works is to fail partly to understand the action.

The *where* and the *when* are so closely connected that they are hardly separate considerations. We refer to the timelessness of things, but that is not to say that they are unrelated to a time, only that they persist beyond their time. Beethoven's music may be timeless, but it grew out of the special circumstances that characterized the late eighteenth and early nineteenth centuries.

B. When did it happen?

A particular time is such a crucial factor in shaping actions that we sometimes refer to all of the diversity of a scene simply as "the times"—the times of Michelangelo, the times of Luther, the times of Martin Luther King. What occurs at one particular time may not occur at another because circumstances have changed. The time, therefore, may be the main focus of a writer's attention.

This question applies to the background of an action—the historical scene. It therefore applies to actions that have occurred in the past as well as those that are happening. All actions have references to other actions, either evolving from them or reacting against them. All the action of the present occurs against the backdrop of the past.

C. What is the background?

4 Means

In approaching a general subject, we need to consider further that all actions require means. By what means or methods is the action brought about? The agent needs tools to work, ways of achieving a purpose, methods of development, resources for implementing, instruments for operating. Agents are usually observable, but not always the means. The means, when known, often stir up controversy. Medical research employs vivisection. The war machine uses guns, bombs, gases, tanks, and men. The government depends on laws, taxes, force, authority, and consent for its operation; higher education depends on course requirements, examinations, grades, lectures, research, and experimentation. In the case of higher education, many students want to go to college—an approval of the action—but many object to the way they are asked to learn—a disapproval of the means.

Since the means of any action are constantly subject to change and experimentation, they often create disturbing reactions. Music that employs new harmonies meets with indifference or even hostility. Art that experiments with new materials upsets traditional expectations. Writers who write plotless plays and stories obviously are attempting new means of expression, but readers resist change. In view of the vast implications of means in both concrete and abstract terms, the basic questions will generate an infinite number of other thoughts:

A. *How did the agent do it?*
The question applies mainly to actions in which the agent is a person. In the 1970s women revolutionized the thinking of our society about the status of women. How did they accomplish it? If a man succeeds in finding a cure for cancer, how has he accomplished it? This interest in means can never be ignored because we are always concerned with whether the end justifies the means. In 1945, President Harry Truman made a decision to drop two nuclear bombs on cities in Japan. The vast destruction and loss of life are a matter of record, but a long war ended. Every thinking person weighed the end against the means.

B. *What means were used?*
The question applies mainly to processes and products. Heart transplants became a fact in the 1970s. What means were used to achieve this successful operation? Were human beings used as guinea pigs in the early operations? European films have revolutionized the art of filmmaking. What means do they use? Immediately this question concerning *how* involves *who*—Bergman or Wertmuller or Fellini? We read a newspaper editorial. What arguments does it use to support its position? A Broadway company produces a modern adaptation of Bizet's *Carmen*. What means does it use? In almost any example that might be cited, the means are the substance of the action because through them the action is realized.

5 Purpose

Finally, in the generative process, we can weigh intentions. It cannot be said that everything that happens has a purpose. Some things happen accidentally, some by chain reaction. All happenings may have a cause, but not all have a discernible purpose, because purpose presupposes an actor or agent who has designed an action with intent. Purpose appeals to our intellectual curiosity. We are not satisfied with being only observers. We want to probe motivation. We want explanations. We are endlessly plagued by the recurring thought that there must be a purpose, even when happenings appear purposeless.

The nature of the purpose may or may not justify an action. It is always intimately tied in with the means. In fact, means and ends over a period of time sometimes fuse: the means become an end. At one point in his career, a man may work to make money to do other things that satisfy him. But if he works and works so that he no longer has time for other pleasures, work becomes an end in itself. It may be the purpose and the end of all his efforts.

Many individuals and groups find it necessary to declare their purposes in advance. Without declared objectives, they can win no support; they can gain no resources to bring about an action. At times we may concern ourselves with investigating whether the stated purposes of an organization are its true purposes or whether purposes have changed in the course of action.

Even though a purpose may be apparent, we can always generate thoughts by reasking the basic question: Why?

"Why did the agent do it?" questions personal motives. "Why was it done?" ques- *Why?* tions the objectives and purposes of any movement or institution or phenomenon whose agent is unknown. *Why* is an all-embracing question because it often can be answered only in terms of all of the other questions: *why* in terms of the person, *why* in terms of the time and place, *why* in terms of the means. What is answerable in terms of one question is not always as clearly answerable in terms of the others.

Finally, the question *why* leads us to our most metaphysical speculations about the universe itself. Our knowledge of the universe is limited primarily to the scene—what we observe—and to some of the means—the principles by which it operates. But how it actually came into being—the means—is unknown, and its agent and purpose are likewise unknown. To provide answers, science theorizes about possibilities of origin; religion advances explanations about who and why. Thus, even in our most universal concerns about mankind, *who, what, where, when, how,* and *why* are basic questions on which all other thoughts rest.

The negative question

The negative form of each of the questions we have posed can at times be illuminating and set the mind on a new channel of thinking. Can we answer where in the world a war has *not* occurred in the last fifty years? Or among what groups of people there is little or no incidence of cancer? *Why not* may be a more persuasive question than *why*. What something is *not* may help to identify what it *is* by a process of elimination.

In summary, then, the basic questions of the drama of thinking are listed below. Others can be invented besides the negative ones, but no matter how many new questions arise, they should not obscure the pattern of the basic pentad, for it establishes a way of developing any thought as if it were a total drama.

1 *Action*
What happened?   (the negative form of each question)
What is happening?
What will happen?
What could happen?
What is it?

2 *Actor-Agent*
Who did it?   (the negative form of each question)
Who is doing it?
What did it?
What is causing it?
What kind of agent is it?

3 Scene
Where did it happen?   (the negative form of each question)
Where is it happening?
Where will it happen?
When did it happen?
What is the background?

4 Means
How did the agent do it?   (the negative form of each question)
What means were used?

5 Purpose
Why? Why not?

Scenarios as different ways of seeing

What happens when you attempt to apply the pentad to a specific writing assignment? Suppose you were assigned to choose a painting by an American artist and to write about it. It is the kind of assignment that might invite your objection that you know little or nothing about art. What are you expected to do? Describe it? Say whether you like it or not? What can you do?

Let's use Edward Hopper's *Nighthawks* (p. 35) as a point of departure and see what we can generate, using the pentad as a device. If we consider the painting itself as the action, then Edward Hopper is clearly the agent. But if the action is what is occurring in the transfixed moment of the painting, then the agents are the three men and one woman who are depicted. How, then, do we resolve this confusion and other complexities that arise when we get multiple answers to the same questions? How do we ordinarily resolve the confusion of our own thinking and cope with a problem of this kind?

One way is to establish a series of scenarios in which actions, agents, scenes, means, and purposes vary depending on the perspective we adopt or the context in which we place the painting. Let's see what possibilities Hopper's painting holds. The four scenarios that follow may not all be equally productive as far as writing is concerned, but they open up a number of unexplored avenues. Pay special attention to details.

SCENARIO 1: THE PAINTING AS A WORK OF ART

Action   *Nighthawks* (1942), oil, 30 × 60″, displayed at the Art Institute of Chicago.
What is it?
1. A realistic depiction of an urban scene at night.
2. An example of realism in American painting.
3. A painting with a metaphorical title (not *Nightowls*, but *Nighthawks*).
4. Possibly a psychological study or a sociological commentary or a statement on the human condition.

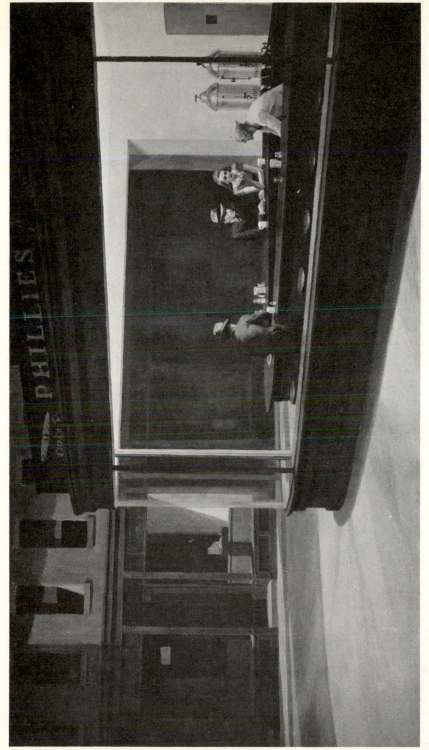

Edward Hopper. *Nighthawks* (1942). Oil on canvas, 30 × 60″. Courtesy of The Art Institute of Chicago.

Actor-agent   Edward Hopper.

What kind of agent is it?
1. Distinguished American painter, 1882–1967.
2. Studied illustration at a commercial art school in New York.
3. Studied under Robert Henri, American realist.
4. Did illustrations, etchings, watercolors, oils.
5. Lived most of his life in New York, spending summers in New England; traveled in Europe and throughout U.S.
6. Married to a painter, Jo Nivison, in 1924; lived together until his death; childless.

Scene   An all-night lunch counter.

Where is it happening?
1. Possibly New York, but could be any urban setting. Only limitation is a sign advertising a 5¢ Phillies cigar.
2. Significant details: (*a*) A clean, well-lighted café, stark in its plainness, occupied by four people. A hawk-nosed man and a heavy-lidded woman sit side by side with coffee cups in front of them on the counter. He is smoking a cigarette; she fingers a matchbook cover. Their hands are close but do not touch. Their faces are masklike. Two coffee urns on the back wall seem to balance the couple. A third customer, a man, sits with his back to the viewer, some distance from the couple. His dark suit and gray hat are identical to those worn by the other man. He is also having coffee. A waiter in white bends over, doing chores and looking outward with an expression of intensity. (*b*) The street, empty, lifeless, dimly illuminated, shadowy. (*c*) Storefronts across the street, unlit, bare windows, and empty display cases, half-pulled blinds on second-floor windows, somber exteriors.
3. Details *not* present: (*a*) Absence of signs, posters, ads, or clutter in the café, buildings, or street. (*b*) No suggestion of sound inside or outside. (*c*) Door of the café to the street not depicted. (*d*) Absence of expression or animation on the faces of the people, except for the waiter. No hurry. No crowd. (*e*) Absence of superfluous detail, decoration, or beauty.

When is it happening?
1. Late 1930s or early 1940s. Time of the 5¢ cigar.

What is the background?
1. Hopper's interest in the visual possibilities of the modern city: forms, surfaces, glass, effect of light on buildings.
2. Hopper's interest in the intimate and ordinary as opposed to the spectacular and dynamic.

Means

What means are used?
1. Contrast of light and dark.
2. Contrast of vivid shades inside and somber ones outside.
3. Emphasis on strong lines and angular structures.
4. Combination of realistic detail and imaginative recollection.
5. Perspective of the viewer looking from outside to inside.
6. Picture almost twice as wide as high to give sense of space.
7. Human figures subordinate to the total scene that goes beyond the dimensions of the canvas.

Purpose
Why?
1. Artistic: "My aim in painting is always, using nature as the medium, to try to project upon canvas my most intimate reaction to the subject as it appears when I like it most; when the facts are given unity by my interest and prejudices."— Edward Hopper, letter to Charles H. Sawyer, October 29, 1939.
2. Personal: to be productive, possibly to sell.

SCENARIO 2: THE PAINTING AS A COMMENTARY ON CITY LIFE

Action Everyday experience of city life. In one sense, nothing is happening—people sitting, thinking. Depersonalization of human beings.

Actor-agent Impersonal agent: urbanization affecting people.

Scene The man-made world of the café. Modern American city, cold, ugly. Silent, impassive buildings, emptiness of street, pervading sense of quiet.

Means Overlaps with Scene. People are submerged in the scene. Everything moves inward, from the darkness outside to the light inside, from the impassive faces of the people to their inner thoughts. Tangible silence.

Purpose Range of interpretation, depending on the viewer:

1. Depiction of life as it is, neither wholly ugly nor glorious.
2. Stoic acceptance of living silent, introverted lives.
3. Statement on the loneliness, sterility, and bleakness of isolation.
4. Depiction of the aesthetic desert of city life.

SCENARIO 3: THE PAINTING AS A COMMENTARY ON THE HUMAN CONDITION

Action Static existence, lingering, passing time, uninvolved, waiting. People escaping the darkness.

Actor-agent
1. God? Chance? The way things are?
2. Modern society? All the factors that collectively intensify the existential dilemma?

Scene
1. People caged in a glass-enclosed, cheerless environment, oblivious of the surroundings, motionless, waiting.
2. All the world where lonely people long for light, warmth, and companionship.

Means Overlaps with Scene. Capacity of people to be together but apart. The artist's techniques (*see* Scenario 1). Darkness outside; light inside. Consuming space.

Purpose Statement on the spiritual and psychological isolation of human beings; alienation; lack of communication. Statement on loss of purpose in living; boredom. Statement on human capacity to ignore time's passing and death's certainty; passive acceptance. There may be none.

SCENARIO 4: THE PAINTING AS NARRATIVE (These details are imaginative conjecture.)

Action   Learning of the death of a mutual friend in World War II. The man with the cigarette has just told the waiter the startling news of the death of a mutual friend. The alarm and concern of the waiter are reflected in his upturned face. The woman's contemplative mood shows careful emotional control. The mood of the trio is one of quiet tension.

Agent   Impersonal: the war. Overlaps with Scene, 1942, when the United States was deeply involved in war.

Scene   The café in 1942.

Means   Expressions, the emptiness, the vacant stools, the absence of cars. No furious war activity or flagwaving at this somber moment.

Purpose   To show human concern. To record a typical scene and reaction. To depict the loneliness of the "home front."

OTHER NARRATIVE POSSIBILITIES:

1. Planning some sinister activity (consistent with the predatory idea of hawks).
2. Contact between a prostitute and a customer.
3. Marital estrangement or a broken affair.

Where do the answers come from?

These particular scenarios, of course, by no means exhaust all of the possibilities; they only begin to suggest what thoughts can be generated by the questions. The answer at times will be simply "I don't know." Every problem has its unknowns. They are often the most challenging part of the investigation, and they will provide the source of the most informative material if you probe. That may require reading and then attempting to see new relationships.

But where do the answers come from? How do you gain the ability to expand kernel thoughts into prose statements?

First, you must depend strongly on *personal observation.* Few people, at least among those who would be looking at American paintings, would find the scene of *Nighthawks* totally unfamiliar. The problem of nonwriters is that they often do not see what is around them, or they see and do not perceive. Hopper's painting can remind you of your own experience and feeling. Writing is also a way for you to alert your senses to what is going on around you.

Second, you can draw on *your own reading,* whether it is the daily newspaper or a current novel. Further, you have the constant bombardment of information from television, movies, and radio. These are all resources that extend your perspectives beyond the limits of where you live. You need to tap these resources and make relationships.

In like manner, you have *your own educational background* to draw on. The significance of a liberal education is its scope. Your knowledge in many disciplines may be superficial, but you at least know what knowledge can be brought to bear on a subject. You can project what a psychiatrist's interest in *Nighthawks* might possibly be or an art historian's or that of a student of literature. An English major might immediately be reminded of Hemingway's story "A Clean, Well-Lighted Place," and that might be the beginning of an illuminating comparison.

Finally, you have *your own reflections*, your own capacity to make inferences, draw comparisons, and form opinions. Final value judgments usually follow the complete drama of thinking: Is what is happening justified? Is an action good in terms of immediate goals? Long-range goals? Has the agent succeeded in terms of stated purposes? Answers to these final questions are often the basis for forming opinions, and they are therefore the starting point for actual writing. Once you have accumulated opinions based on supportable evidence, you can then formulate a thesis and proceed to argue your case or try to persuade others. All that you will say may be entirely worked out before writing the first word of an essay.

Narrowing and selecting

After exploration comes the need to focus. The typical 500-word essay offers a very brief space. It therefore demands a limited topic that can be treated briefly but adequately. Often it helps to ask yourself pertinent questions or to formulate subtopics suggested by the various aspects of the pentad. Topics like those listed in the following pages suggest the kind of selection that would be useful if you were going to write an essay on *Nighthawks*. Some grow directly out of the scenarios given; others are extensions that grow out of an attempt to see the painting in a larger context or in relation to something outside the painting itself.

POSSIBLE TOPICS

Action   (overlaps Actor-Agent)

1. Recognizing that *Nighthawks* presents four individuals in a scene, create a series of events that would lead to these four individuals being together in this place at this time.
2. It is commonplace to say that cities are impersonal places that contribute to the dehumanization of people. Is there any support for that observation in Hopper's painting? Does that necessarily seem to be the way he feels or the way you feel about what he has painted?
3. Using the painting as a point of departure, write an essay on the experience of doing nothing or of waiting.

Actor-agent   (overlaps Action)

1. Consider the metaphorical implications of expressions like "human being in a cage," "in a trap," or "on display under glass." Does *Nighthawks* seem to illustrate any of these metaphors? If not, invent your own and explain.
2. Consider Hopper's painting the scene of a one-act play. Write the dialogue of the characters in the opening scene.
3. Do research on the habits of the nighthawk, and with the information explain how the title is or is not appropriate. Are the people in the painting the hunters or the hunted?

Scene

1. You are a reader for a blind student. Re-create the scene in *Nighthawks* for this unsighted person.
2. In what way is *Nighthawks* typical Americana? Is the significance limited to the place and time of the picture?
3. If *Nighthawks* were a scene from somewhere in your town or city, where would it be? Compare the details of the picture with the details of a setting you know. How would your "painting" be similar to or different from Hopper's?

Means

1. Compare and contrast the interior and exterior in *Nighthawks,* and see in what way you react differently to each. Does this lead you to conclude why Hopper painted the scene as he did?
2. Discuss the dual effect of peacefulness and tension (potential explosiveness) in the painting.
3. In what way would your impression of this painting change if the title were *Early Risers* instead of *Nighthawks*? Suggest other possible titles that would cause the viewer to look at it differently.

Purpose

1. Why would you want or not want a reproduction of *Nighthawks* on a wall in your house?
2. Imagine you saw a friend of yours frowning at *Nighthawks* in the Art Institute of Chicago and asking "Why would anyone want to paint a picture like *that*?" How would you answer? Since the painting would be in front of you, refer to details of the picture to support your ideas.
3. For what company or cause might *Nighthawks* serve as an illustration on a poster? What would be the appropriateness and the comment of the picture?

From focus to thesis

Although the terms of the pentad overlap (agents are almost inseparable from acts), focusing on any two of them may reveal the way you want to interpret a particular experience. Does one cause the other, or does one favor the other? For instance, when tolls were recently removed from a bridge in Seattle and motorists no longer had to stop to pay, one would have expected traffic to move much more quickly. Instead, a tremendous traffic jam occurred. An engineer for the Department of Transportation explained: "There's still a tendency for commuters to slow down and see what the situation is. It's a novelty the first day or two."

In terms of the pentad, this statement may be explained in either of two ways:

Scene–agent   That is, the novelty of the situation prompted motorists to slow down and cause the traffic jam, or

Agent–act   That is, a natural curiosity in people to see what had changed caused people to act as they did.

The two explanations may not be sharply divided, but they are two different readings of the same situation. Consider other examples of relationships:

1. *Scene–act*   In what way does a particular crime (Act) grow out of the conditions in which it occurs (Scene)?

2. *Scene–agent*   In what way are presidents of the United States (Agents) affected by the office they hold or by a situation they must meet (Scene)?

3. *Agency–act*   Does a particular act depend upon the availability of the means to carry it out? Will removing the means eliminate the act?

4. *Agent–act*   Do you characteristically act with consistency in keeping with your fundamental nature as a person? Or is there a split?

5. *Scene–purpose*   Are your personal objectives (Purpose) affected by the situation in which you find yourself—a home situation or a school situation (Scene)?

6. *Agent–purpose*   If you consider your purposes self-determined (Purpose–Agent), how do they differ from those given in Relationship 5 (Purpose–Scene)?

7. *Agency–purpose*   If you had wealth (Agency), how would your purposes change?

Combining the terms in these ways raises questions that might not otherwise occur to you without the nudge of structured combinations.

These combinations also offer suggestions how to get from a general consideration of a subject to a particular thesis. Once you have determined a focus, you need to assume a position. If you decided you wanted to write on the effect of the scene in *Nighthawks* upon the characters, you might choose to see the painting positively as one of tranquility and companionship rather than negatively as one of depression and loneliness. That is a thesis. It becomes the purpose of your writing, and the evidence you present should support that thesis.

Assuming a position on any topic narrows the subject and sharpens the focus. Suppose a student decides to write on the topic "Relationships Between Students and Teachers." The thesis might be "Even though teachers are in the same general age bracket as a student's parents, attitudes toward teachers are, for various reasons, different from those toward parents." This is a Scene–Agent ratio; that is, because the school situation is different from the home situation, a student's attitude toward teachers is different from the same student's attitude toward parents. Or a student might argue that teachers tend to assume autocratic and dictatorial roles. That also is a Scene [school]–Agent [teacher] ratio. The argument might be that teachers become the agents of the school as the official institution of the state to educate children and thus assume authority that they might not otherwise have in an out-of-school setting.

Playing with the combinations, seeing what they imply, and forming an opinion become a way of finding a thesis, the focus that in the final analysis makes a subject manageable and permits you to write about it. More often than not, the thesis comes as an intuitive leap while you are doing the spadework. Without the preparation, however, you are not ready for the jump.

The open topic

The open topic is an assignment that sets almost no limitations on you. You are free to choose your own subject. In such instances, the key dramatic terms help you reduce many possibilities to one or several related ones. In response to an open assignment to write one or more paragraphs on Hopper's *Nighthawks,* the following two brief statements illustrate methods these students used to focus their thoughts.

EXAMPLE 1

Purpose The stark realism of Edward Hopper's *Nighthawks* reveals a harsh, sterile contem-
Means porary society. The observer of the scene remains remote: that viewer can see the customers and waiter only through a glass enclosure. The characters themselves are
Actors not only isolated from the viewer and the bleak external world, but also from each
Scene other. The silent, timeless static world of the café is intensified by the complete absence of life outside—no spontaneous happening will disturb the speechless group or the noiseless city streets. The light of the café does not even brighten the mood or warm the scene: it only emphasizes the pallor of skin tones and the flat sterility of the uncluttered counter tops and shining coffee vats. Ironically, the visual contrast of the internal and external worlds, the bright, gaudy café and the dark, shadowed streets, only reinforces the sameness of the scenes: the psychological isolation within is mirrored in the physical desertion of shopwindows and noiseless streets outside.

EXAMPLE 2

In considering Edward Hopper's 1942 painting entitled *Nighthawks,* our attention
Means is drawn to the contrasts in the picture and to the human scene inside the coffee shop. One of the most striking contrasts is light versus dark: the lighted interior of the shop and the thinner, more anemic light outside contrast with the shadows on the street and the darkness behind the shop. Another contrast lies in the ugly bulk of the boatlike café "cruising" through cement and darkness and the imposing, empty, dark buildings across the street contending with the lighted shop and, in comparison to these structures, the small humans inside the shop. Dark, deep shades dominate the picture and contribute to the prevailing mood of loneliness and foreboding.
Scene Given these contrasts, we look to the shop as a kind of refuge for the four people
and inside. It seems a "clean, well-lighted place" where human beings are together at a
purpose safe distance from the shadows and the darkness. But is it? As we study shop and people "under glass," caught by the artist and held for our inspection, we are struck by how the impersonal loneliness outside the shop is matched by the human loneli-
Actors ness inside it. The clerk looks not at the customers but straight ahead; seen close up,
and his expression is more grimace and preoccupation than a smile. Although the cou-
means ple's hands almost touch, they do not seem really "together." The man's mouth is tight and set, and he looks down and away. Her mouth less set than his, the woman seems abstracted. She studies the match cover she holds, but her attention is else-where. We see the fourth figure only from the back. He slouches slightly and seems even more lonely than they in his distance from the couple and clerk. The two stiff,

metal coffee urns side by side to the woman's left may be a sardonic comment on this human scene. The urns suggest dehumanized automatons rather than human beings. That we do not actually see the *eyes* of the people in Hopper's picture may suggest   *Purpose* their inability to see each other, to reach out and transcend their condition of ennui and isolation.

The limited topic

The limited topic is an assignment that provides a narrower focus, leaving us to restrict it even further by selection of detail. In one sense, this is a more demanding kind of assignment because it cuts out an infinite number of possibilities. In another sense, it helps those of us who find difficulty in narrowing subjects to manageable limits. The following theme topic illustrates that some guidelines have been set by the instructor and other choices left open:

ASSIGNMENT   Compare *Nighthawks* with another Hopper painting entitled *Sunlight in a Cafeteria*. How have the means changed? Is there also a change in mood and effect?

The City by Day or Night   STUDENT PAPER

Does the world change between 3:00 A.M. and 3:00 P.M., or are we led to think so because the light has changed? Venice at night is beautiful and magical; in the sunlight, it is dirty and decaying. But night is not always a cover and light an exposé. Night is also chilly and frightening; day can be warm and inviting. However, in two paintings that contrast night and day—*Nighthawks* and *Sunlight in a Cafeteria*—Edward Hopper does not see such simple opposites. Day may come, but nothing changes too   *Thesis* radically.

    Nighthawks is a cafeteria scene at night. As viewers, we look in from the outside. We   *Scene* stand on a deserted street in the shadowy light of a street lamp. We look through a   *Means* large plate glass window, uncluttered by signs, to see three people sitting at a counter. Most of the stools are empty. A man and woman sit next to one another; a second man   *Agents* sits alone with his back to us; a waiter behind the counter goes about his chores. In the painting, we see no door to the outside. The people seemed trapped in a huge glass cage, illuminated by harsh light. Perhaps they have sought refuge from the bleakness   *Purpose* outside. They sit and think and wait, their expressions impassive.

    Sunlight in a Cafeteria is a scene by day. It is not the same cafeteria as the one in   *Scene* *Nighthawks*, but it is no less stark and unadorned. Only a plant on the window ledge relieves the monotony of bare walls and tables and chairs. But it is not a blooming flower; its stiff green leaves seem to make it as lifeless and formal as everything else. As viewers, we are on the inside looking out of a glass window toward a deserted street   *Means* and bleak, seemingly uninhabited buildings across the way. A man and woman—they   *Agents* could be the same man and woman in *Nighthawks*—sit at separate tables. She sits close to the window in the bright sunlight. He sits on the other side away from the sunlight, not looking at her, but gazing out the window. Their expressions are masklike. The woman is lost in her own thoughts as if she were mesmerized by the sun. A revolving door suggests that these two have an exit if they choose to move. At the moment of the painting, they are immobile.

Means　　In these two paintings, Hopper has changed the arrangment of light and forms and point of view, but he has not changed the basic effect. The human beings are still lost in a scene composed of empty spaces, hard lines, massive structures, and uncheerful colors. In both paintings, there is the same silence, the same spare detail, the same sterility, the same isolation. These are paintings about urban life in America in 1942, *Purpose*　1958, or now. Hopper does not show the excitement, the confusion, and the conflict of the city. He shows the resignation of those who live there. Individuals find strength *Return to* for survival by looking inside themselves. Day or night does not change basically what *the thesis* they are.

In the assignment for which the essay above was written, the writer is limited to particular paintings, with attention directed to the fact that the means have changed, and is asked for a conclusion (whether the change of means has changed the effect). This particular student writes about the scene, including details of the actors and their actions. She describes the painter's means of creating a certain response from the viewer.

Questions of the kind given by this instructor should usually be seen as guidelines for thinking, not as questions to be answered like an examination. In this theme, the writer does not go beyond the painting itself to talk about Hopper as a painter or of loneliness as a fact of life and does not write a narrative about the characters in the painting. She focuses on and sticks to relevant materials in terms of the assignment.

Other aids to thinking

The pentad is called a heuristic device. Etymologically, the word *heuristic* derives from the Greek word *eureka,* meaning "I have found it," usually attributed to Archimedes when he discovered the principle of measuring the volume of an irregular solid by observing the amount of water he displaced in his bathtub. Some people still say "eureka" when they hit upon a discovery. A heuristic device is a systematic way of discovering thoughts. The thoughts may not necessarily be new ones; they may be simply ones that you need to dredge up from the depths of your subconscious. A heuristic device is a formal scanning device. Brainstorming may be faster for some people, but it is less dependable because it can cause you to zoom in too soon on a particular thought without considering other angles that could give you better insights.

Thus, heuristic devices are structured ways of thinking. They are usually phrased as a series of terms or questions, designed to act as guides. The pentad is only one such device. It is useful because the metaphor of drama is familiar, and terms like *act, actor, scene, means,* and *purpose* are self-explanatory.

Another set of terms may be useful for the opposite reason that they are less familiar. A heuristic device designed by the linguist Kenneth Pike, referred to as a tagmemic model, borrows the terms *particle*, *wave*, and *field* from nuclear physics. Whereas the pentad begins with a view of the whole and proceeds to focus on parts, the tagmemic model begins with a part and proceeds to see it in ever-expanding contexts. The difference may make one approach or the other more adaptable to particular subjects. The following version is an adaptation and simplification of Pike's more elaborate scheme.

Particle, wave, and field

First, *think of something as a thing in itself, individual, static, self-contained, describable.*

For instance, think of yourself as a student. What is your identity as a student? What makes you different from other students in your class? In fact, what identifies you as a student rather than a teacher or an assistant?

Second, *think of the same object as it changes, grows, or matures, altering its features in some way.*

Think again about yourself as a student. In what way does formal education change you? How are you different now as a student from what you were five years ago?

Finally, *think of the same object as it is part of a larger context or system.*

Again, in terms of yourself, to what extent is your education affected by your family or the particular school you attend? Or the area in which you live? Or the state system of which your school is a part? There is no limit to the number of expanding contexts you can add as long as you continue to keep your focus on the particle with which you began. The expanding contexts may be seen as a diagram of concentric circles.

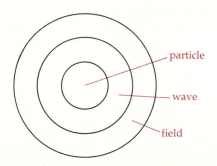

This scheme suggests that anything can be viewed in terms of itself, in terms of change or variation, or in terms of distribution within a larger scene. Many of the questions of the pentad apply to this model. The two are not radically different. They are simply different metaphors. These questions may therefore serve as guides:

1. *Particle*
   What is it?
   What are its features?
   What is its identity as contrasted with others in its class?
   What does it share with others in its class?
2. *Wave*
   How is it changing?
   How much can it change before it loses its identity and becomes something else or is assimilated into a larger context?
3. *Field*
   In what sense is it a self-contained system?
   In what way does it function as part of a larger system than itself?
   How is it affected by the system?

Application of particle-wave-field

A student named Jim Tamble applied the tagmemic model to one of his favorite lakes in Washington. After he followed the model, he began to reflect, and, in a prewriting stage, actually began to write his essay. His reflections are reproduced here because they demonstrate how the generative scheme led him to a thesis and sent him well on his way to writing the essay.

Topic: Spectacle Lake, State of Washington

PARTICLE

1. Spectacle Lake is a high-altitude Alpine lake in the Alpine Lakes area of Washington state (c. 4500 ft.).
2. It is surrounded by steep cliffs on all sides, except the east side, where its waters empty down into the Cooper River canyon in a rampant torrent.
3. It is a cool, clean, clear lake about 75 acres in size. It has many types of Alpine and sub-Alpine trees surrounding it (Western Hemlock, Western Red Cedar, Jack Pine, Ponderosa pine, and Douglas fir).
4. The lake was carved out by glaciers ages ago, and as a result the shoreline and the bottom of the lake itself are extremely smooth rock (a form of granite). The glaciers smoothed down the rock into a smooth, shiny surface. The lake is an open area and gets much sun and wind.
5. Its identity is contrasted to others in its class by the astounding smoothness of the rock base of the lake and the rocks around the lake.
6. It relates extremely well to other things in its geographic area. Since water is the source of life, the lake is the mother of the area.

WAVE

1. Spectacle Lake is changing, as most mountain lakes are changing, by slowly being filled up with silt. Centuries from now it will become a swamp and then a meadow with a stream running through it. Since this particular lake is very deep, it will take many centuries to fill up.

2. It will change from a lake to a swamp to a meadow quite slowly. Thus it will have to change substantially before it totally loses its present identity as a lake and becomes assimilated into the overall area as something else (i.e., a swamp or a meadow).

FIELD

1. From a geographic, ecological, botanical standpoint, the lake and its surrounding area are a totally self-contained area dependent only upon the annual snowfall and the meltoff for its base.
2. The lake itself is part of the total system and still a small part of the total system. In one sense, this Alpine lake is a total universe in itself, while still a part of the universe.
3. It performs a role that consists of being one small part of the balance of nature that operates cyclically. The lake is part of an ever-widening concentric circle of balanced ecosystems that are found in the natural world.
4. If the balance of nature ever became unbalanced or there were any change in the balance of the ecosystem, this lake would be adversely affected. But then all nature would be greatly affected by any drastic change in the balance that exists in nature.

Reflections that followed this objectively written description:

After looking over what I've written thus far, it becomes obvious that I have a very personal feeling for the area. I love Spectacle Lake because it remains an example of nature in a relatively pure state.

Since I used Pike's tagmemic model that flows from specific to general, my thesis statement should also flow from specific to general. Therefore, I hypothesize that the lake area will naturally evolve to its finite stage as long as people do not unduly interfere with the natural process of life and death that surrounds such a high-altitude lake. I also hypothesize that, if people do interfere with the natural evolutionary process, this high-altitude area will not evolve in its proper order and the balance of nature will be upset. If anything symbolizes the fragile yet strong, gentle yet rough dichotomy of what life is for mankind and nature, this lake does. I'm always reminded of antonyms in a language. Antonyms are words that have opposite meanings. Yet I'm struck by the paradox that, in order to be truly opposite, words must be semantically similar in the properties they share. *Death* and *life* are opposites; yet one must be thought of in relation to the other. Death means *not* alive.

The dichotomy of the area around Spectacle Lake stands as the ultimate symbol for mankind as a part of nature. People take natural resources from nature. They also recycle things. Thus, just as mankind has learned to give and take, mankind must sometimes learn to neither give nor take, but let alone. This is, finally, the thesis I want to pursue: mankind, with all of the beauty and pleasure that comes from involvement with nature, must learn at times to leave well enough alone.

The basic questions and the forms of discourse

Traditionally, narration, description, argumentation, and exposition have been spoken of as the basic modes of discourse. Each represents a shifting concern on the part of the writer. We must at times be concerned with setting forth facts (*exposi-*

tion), speaking of them in terms of space, time, and action (*description* and *narration*), and resolving the conflict of facts (*argumentation*). The modes, however, seldom exist as pure forms. We shift naturally from one to the other by turning from one question to another. There is a definite correspondence between the basic questions we ask about a subject and the mode of writing we assume:

What happened? What is happening?	*Narration*
What will happen? What could happen?	*Narration, exposition, argumentation*
What is it?	*Exposition, including definition, illustration, and process*
Who did it? Who is doing it? What did it? What is causing it? What kind of agent is it?	*Description and exposition, including definition, illustration, comparison, and contrast*
Where did it happen? Where is it happening? Where will it happen? When did it happen? What is the background?	*Description, narration, and exposition*
How did the agent do it? What means are being used?	*Description, narration, and process*
Why?	*Exposition and argumentation, including persuasive writing*

In a similar way, note how thinking in terms of particle–wave–field invites particular modes of writing:

- Particle (static): description and analysis
- Wave (dynamic): narrative, contrast, process
- Field (contextual): argument

Once we realize that the modes of writing are not arbitrary inventions but grow naturally out of patterns of thought—or, to put it another way, once we realize that thoughts have a way of shaping themselves—we will also have learned that prewriting is one of the most important parts of writing because it is then that the course of writing is set.

Projects | **1.** In the December 26, 1964, issue of the *Saturday Review*, Henry Seidel Canby presented three questions for reviewing and evaluating:
   A. What was the creator trying to do? [Action and purpose]
   B. How well did he do it? [Evaluation of the means]
   C. Was it worth doing? [Evaluation of the purpose]

Invent variations on the questions of the pentad or the particle–wave–field model that will more adequately satisfy your own approach, but try to preserve the basic metaphors of these approaches.

2. Apply the pentad to topics like distress, frustration, contentment, fulfillment, courage, disaster, depression, euphoria, comfort, extravagance. Observe in what way a topic must be particularized immediately in order to be developed.

3. The use of the pentad is in one sense an application of detective techniques to any problem. Given certain clues, questions follow. Join with a classmate to work jointly on a topic of common interest: the Donner Pass incident, Pearl Harbor, the Chicago fire, Custer's last stand. Where are the unknowns? Eventually, write separate papers; then compare the difference in focus you each assume.

4. Construct as many scenarios as possible based on Winslow Homer's *The Life Line* (p. 50). Compare your results with those of other students during a class session to learn how close observation generates thoughts.

5. As a practice in observing and generating thoughts, list fifty specific observations about something that happened to you this week. Use the pentad as a guide.

1. First, examine how the basic questions of the pentad produce different kinds of writing: a who-paper, possibly a character sketch; a what-paper, a news report; a when-and-where paper, maybe a travelogue; a how-paper, description of a process (how to do it); a why-paper, an analysis of cause and effect. Write a theme, attempting to keep the major focus on one question. For example, topics that begin with: *Suggestions for writing*

Action:	Top TV rating of _____ [popular TV show]
	Proliferation of porno-movie houses
Agents:	Humphrey Bogart as a perennial favorite
	Police in _____ [city]
Scene:	The "climate" on your campus
	The costume period of dress
Means:	A strike as a strategy
	Civil disobedience
Purpose:	Sports cars that go over 100 miles an hour
	Abstract painting

2. Apply the particle–wave–field model to an act or object: a new building on campus, a proposed freeway through the city, a particular strike, a strong opinion you hold. After you have generated your material, see what the possibilities for writing are. What have you discovered? Formulate a thesis, and write an essay, using as much detail as possible.

3. Apply the pentad to one of the Bible stories listed below to determine clearly the pattern of the drama. Then write a modern counterpart of one of them:

A. Solomon's judgment between the two harlots (I Kings 3:16–28)
B. David and Goliath (I Samuel 17:20–58)
C. Samson and Delilah (Judges 16:4–31)
D. Joseph and his brothers (Genesis 37–45)
E. Tower of Babel (Genesis 11:1–9)
F. Ruth and Naomi (Ruth 1:1–22)
G. David and Jonathan (I Samuel 18–20)

4. Cover an event on campus or in town that you can personally observe. Use one of the heuristic models as a guide. Write about the event informatively; that is, explore some of the questions to which there are not ready answers.

5. Apply particular questions of the pentad to any of the broad terms of reference or common phrases we frequently use. Who is a Jew? What are the laws of nature? When is something or somebody old-fashioned? How do we determine right and wrong? Why is "an ounce of prevention worth a pound of cure"? There may be no single answer, but many. Write an explanatory theme answering the question you pose.

Winslow Homer. *The Life Line* (1884). Oil on canvas, 45 x 29″. Philadelphia Museum of Art: The George W. Elkins Collection.

By the time you reach the point of putting words on paper, it is possible that your thoughts have already begun to shape themselves. It is then that you need to give more conscious attention to matters of development.

It is important to recognize that form is not an enemy of writers, any more than it is an enemy of carpenters or sculptors or engineers. Form is a fact of all the arts as well as of nature. It is a means of control over confusion; it is an ordering. Specifically, in terms of writing, it is the writer's way of putting thoughts in sequence so that the reader can see where things are going. The poet William Stafford has said "Form is a way of getting from nowhere to somewhere." In this sense, structuring an essay is different from designing a ten-story building; a detailed blueprint need not be worked out in advance. There are no rigid principles to follow, but of course there are demands. "A work has form," Kenneth Burke writes, "in so far as one part of it leads a reader to anticipate another part, to be gratified by the sequence." In brief, form creates expectation. The purpose of this chapter will be to show in what way you can create form without reference to set models.

Set form and developing form

Set forms of discourse are conventional ones that can be described and imitated. They are almost all limited to imaginative literature. A variety of verse forms, such as the sonnet, the villanelle, and the closed couplet, can be described precisely.

Others, like the epic and the classical tragedy, are longer and more flexible, but they are still bound by an orderly arrangement of parts that can be listed. On the other hand, the contemporary novel gives clear indication of another kind of form, best identified as developing form.

The difference between set form and developing form becomes evident in terms of the reader's approach to each. It is possible for us to have expectations about set form before we ever begin. We simply need to know what a sonnet is, and we know what to expect as far as form is concerned. On the other hand, it is not possible for us to have expectations concerning developing form before we start. Our expectations come only as the writer creates them for us. Form in this sense is not something that exists, like a map you follow; it is discovering a way that will get you and your reader where you want to go.

The essay is clearly a developing form. It has no set patterns. You are free to develop it as you see fit. Yet, even though you have leeway to develop an idea in your own way, you still need to be orderly and to keep in mind that a reader needs cues along the way to follow your thinking.

How to begin and end

There are two ways to think about beginning. One is in terms of effect; the other is in terms of structure. On one basis or the other, we can decide whether a beginning is effective or not. A few examples of student writing will indicate which beginnings work and which do not. Four students, given limited writing topics on Dickens' *Hard Times,* begin in the following ways:

> In *Hard Times,* Dickens compares Fact and Fancy as someone else would compare Good and Evil, Dark and Light, or Heaven and Hell. To him there is only one conclusion: Fact is bad, Fancy is good. Every believer of Fact, every follower of Gradgrindism, is defeated like a villain in a fairy tale. But every believer of Fancy, every member of the proletariat who is able to overcome human suffering, finds the Light of Happiness.
>
> Student 1

This opening is itself a good combination of factual statement and fanciful treatment. The writer very briefly summarizes the themes of the novel and states Dickens' preference, but she does this in the manner of a fairy tale in which the characters are sharp opposites. After this beginning, the writer focuses on two characters who show factual and fanciful attitudes toward religion, but this development is not announced; it grows out of the beginning statement.

> Dickens uses striking contrasts in the characters of *Hard Times* to make his point and get it across to his audience. He does this by taking what he is satirizing, in this case, fact, and placing it beside its opposite, in this case, fancy. An example of such a contrast is the one of Sissy Jupe and Mr. Bounderby.
>
> Student 2

This student has used almost the same approach as Student 1; he is going to compare two characters to illustrate Dickens' commentary on Fact and Fancy and indicates that he will proceed in that way. But this opening is ineffectual, chiefly because it is padded. The facts are lost in a mass of unnecessary words.

The characters of *Hard Times* seem to be divided between the School of Fact and the Circus of Fancy. Bitzer, a colorless, mean, selfish individual, represents the Gradgrindian philosophy of Fact. His opposite is Sissy, the humble, loving, compassionate product of the Circus of Fancy. Dickens uses these two characters to show the dehumanizing influence of Fact and the humanizing power of Fancy.

Student 3

This is yet another version of the same approach, starting with a generalization, quickly narrowed to two characters. The last sentence provides a logical guideline for the discussion to follow. The strength of this opening is its compactness and apt phrases.

How important is fact in our own society? What role does fancy play? When Dickens wrote *Hard Times* in 1854, society was facing the same dilemma we face today. Is fantasy necessary? Dickens says yes. I would like to show how Dickens answers the question by looking at two female characters: Sissy Jupe and Louisa Gradgrind.

Student 4

This opening starts further afield and uses a different strategy. The writer tries to involve the reader by a series of questions and the use of "we" to invite identity. The switch to first person in the last sentence is consistent with the sense of nearness this writer is trying to establish with the audience, but the last sentence is also an outline in miniature. This beginning involves the reader and also anticipates the structure.

The first three openings employ no special device such as the questions in the fourth one. They are simple statements, which depend mainly on generalizations, and they vary in their effectiveness with the writer's choice and arrangement of the words. A survey of the opening sentences and paragraphs by established writers in reputable magazines will indicate that most openings are straightforward statements of fact or opinion, usually wasting no words. Openings of this kind attempt to state the thesis briefly and establish the tone of the article; they provide a clue to both the ideas and the style, and readers sometimes make up their minds after the first paragraph whether they want to continue to read. The importance of a good beginning cannot be overestimated.

How to begin: a dozen suggestions

The dozen examples of opening sentences given below are not beyond the capacities of any beginning writer. What the examples characteristically show is that these writers begin with confidence, even at times with daring. Established writers, however, do not limit themselves to one kind of opening. They begin in a number of different ways:

1. With an anecdote that leads into the main topic:

A student editor, criticizing the draft of a catalogue for a new college, three times deleted the words "liberal education" from the draft. Coming upon it again, she circled the words and wrote in the margin: "What in the world is it?"

Harris Wolfford, "In Search of Liberal Education"

2. With the setting as background for what will follow:

Roman Wortman first decided to turn to organic farming one day in the spring of 1972, when he rode out on his tractor to spray his fields with a new pesticide and found that he was leaving a trail of dead birds behind him. "There was half a dozen of them at the edge of the field," he told me as we stood under a blazing Nebraska sun looking over his cornfields. "I rode back into the yard and there was more dead birds along the driveway where I had sprayed only a half hour before." He fixed his keen brown eyes on me for a moment. "I turned around and I said to myself, 'What the hell am I doing out here?' From that day to this, I've never used another pesticide, herbicide, or fertilizer on this farm." He waved his arm out over his fields of corn and alfalfa, which were shimmering with a bright, deep green. "Look what I have to show for it," he said.

William Tucker, "The Next American Dust Bowl . . . and How to Avert It"

3. With narration, beginning in the middle of things, inviting further reading:

You wake up one morning with a vague sense of unease. Everything seems normal—until you move. And then, brother, you scream. A demon seems to be stabbing at the base of your big toe with a sharp, red-hot poker. Even the light touch of the sheet gouges your nerves. Carefully, delicately, you remove the bedclothes and examine the shiny red swelling at the tender joint. Try to wiggle the toe—and scream again. Cautiously swing your legs to the floor and the whole foot throbs in agony. Wondering how you broke your toe, you limp into your doctor's office and get the news, as I did a few years ago: No broken bones, my friend; it's the gout.

Rafael Steinberg, "If You Are Highly Sexed, Achievement Oriented,
and a Wine Connoisseur, This May Be Your Disease"

4. With a quotation relevant to the thought:

"Yes, we are revolutionaries," acknowledged the fortyish executive, a top salesman for one of America's largest and fastest-growing corporations. "What we are doing will no doubt leave a very lasting impression on America. We are going to turn the world of white-collar work upside down, inside out, and make it do what it's supposed to do—work."

No small boast, that. But this man, who prefers to be an anonymous revolutionary, speaks confidently, for he has seen a vision of the future—and it is electronic.

Jon Stewart, "Computer Shock: The Inhuman Office of the Future"

5. With a firm statement of opinion, arousing the reader's feelings:

The first year of the 1980s may or may not bring a new president to the White House, but it will, for certain, see a new incumbent in a high artistic post that has had a lot less changes over seven decades. After all those years in which the direction of the great Philadelphia

Orchestra has been in the hands of only two men (Leopold Stokowski and Eugene Ormandy), it will pass to Riccardo Muti. This move is somewhat like elevating a parish priest to the papacy.

Irving Kolodin, "Music to My Ears: Provincialism on the Podium"

6. With a prediction:

America is facing a manpower crisis of awesome and dangerous proportions. What is done, or not done, about it in the next few years will affect the quality of life in this country for generations. Nor is it any exaggeration to say that if the correct solutions for the problem are not conceived and carried out, the United States will be confronted with potential disaster.

John Tebbel, "People and Jobs"

7. With unusual or sensational detail:

Physicians may one day treat patients who have shattered limbs, crippled joints, and injured spines in a way that man never before dared to dream of: regrowing the damaged part—whole, perfect, and undiseased.

Susan Schiefelbein, "The Miracle of Regeneration:
Can Human Limbs Grow Back?"

8. With reflective questions:

If, indeed, it is true that taxes are as inevitable as death, what considerations determine whether we must pay more or less? Isn't it simply a matter of how much money "the government" needs to meet its responsibilities to the people? Why can't we take a good, hard look at what we want government to spend money on, set a price tag for these services, and then collect the money deemed necessary according to an ability-to-pay formula, or on some other equitable basis? Wouldn't this be a great deal simpler than our present system of exemptions, deductions, write-offs, and a thousand and one other opportunities for maneuvers that have made a national pastime of searching for "tax angles"? In other words, once we have agreed that, in one way or another, government must collect the tax revenue it needs to stay in business, doesn't it all boil down to finding the fairest means to raise the money?

Haig Babian, "Can Taxes Do More Than Raise Revenue?"

9. With a definition:

Overlive means that we have more than enough for everyone but not everyone gets his share. It's as simple as that.

Charles J. Calitri, "Everybody Wants In"

10. With a figure of speech:

Insomnia is my baby. We have been going steady for a good twenty years now, and there is no hint that the dull baggage is ready to break off the affair.

Roger Angell, "Ainmosni"

11. With a play on words:

A sign over one section of the public library in my town reads "Young Adults Oversize." Although it refers to books too large for normal shelving, it might also stand as a metaphor for the college student who has outgrown the limits of his own collection of textbooks and "favorite" authors, who seeks to pin down the expanding world of ideas into which he is moving to something solid and permanent.

David Dempsey, "Seventh Amy Loveman Award"

12. With humor:

There's good news in the paper. America has its first drive-in funeral parlor. I had almost given up hope that the country could ever reach the goal that it is so obviously striving for—the day when we will be able to do everything without getting out of the car. But now I know that the impossible dream is possible.

William Zinsser, "Time-Saver for Busy Mourners"

Beginnings to avoid   Because the beginning is an important element in establishing a good relation between writer and reader, several kinds of beginning are therefore best avoided:

1. The apology, complaint, or personal dilemma:

I have now read "Love Among the Ruins" for the third and, I hope, the last time. I notice one element which is used sporadically throughout the story. The topic of which I am speaking is the use of the word "State" in the place of God's name.

Student theme

2. The panoramic beginning, typically a survey reaching back to the dim past:

War is a topic which has been handled admirably by poets throughout the course of history and man's conscious destruction of his fellow man. Homer first described "man's inhumanity to man" and the results that war can have in his epic poem *The Iliad.* In the intervening years, the poet has continued to use war as the subject of his poetry, for war begets sorrow, and expressing emotion is the poet's stock in trade. [Written as the opening of a theme asking the student to compare two contemporary war poems.]

3. The mystery opening, making the theme dependent upon material from an outside source known to the instructor but to no other reader:

The main thing that I noticed in the poem was the way the tone changed from stanza to stanza.

Student theme

4. The overworked beginning:

In Book 1 of *Gulliver's Travels,* Swift says . . .

Webster's dictionary defines *love* as . . . [Definitions are fine, but original ones are often more meaningful than dictionary ones.]

5. The perfectly obvious statement:

Brave New World confronts man with a question that has in the past and will in the future most certainly be a human problem.

The utopian society has always been considered the ideal society.

Gulliver's Travels contains a very important thought which everyone should think about.

How to end: a dozen suggestions

Like the beginning of an essay, the ending may be thought of primarily in terms of structure or in terms of effect, but in either case the important thing about ending is to leave the reader with a sense of completeness. Isolated examples of final paragraphs demonstrate very little because as endings they can be judged only in terms of what has gone before. Characteristically, however, writers end in a number of different ways:

1. With a final paragraph or sentence that completes the logical pattern that the essay has been developing.
2. With a restatement of the main thesis.
3. With a concluding opinion supported by the preceding discussion.
4. With a speculative question or statement that leaves the subject open for further thought.
5. With musing on the broader implications of the topic.
6. With a return to a question or image in the opening paragraph so that the essay is rounded out.
7. With an ironic twist or unexpected turn of thought.
8. With a note of high persuasion or challenge, comparable to the peroration of the classical oration.
9. With an appropriate anecdote.
10. With a telling quotation.
11. With a descriptive passage, using the setting as a final commentary.
12. With a laugh.

Essentially, these devices for ending an essay correspond to the kinds of intonations that occur at the end of a sentence, either falling, rising, or level. Those endings that come to a logical conclusion, just as we intuitively know the end of a sentence, are falling. Those that end with a question or move to a persuasive climax are rising. Those that are reflective or leave the subject as an open question tend to be level because we are left to resolve the problem in our own minds.

Endings to avoid

Ending seldom presents the same problem to a writer as the beginning. Once the beginning and middle are complete, the ending usually follows in natural sequence. Several kinds of endings, however, are best avoided:

1. The unnecessary summary

A theme of 500 words seldom requires a formal summary, one that restates in a full paragraph what has just been discussed in two or three previous ones. At times, it may be appropriate to draw together the thought of a short paper, but this can usually be done in one compact sentence. For the most part, summaries are necessary only in long works, where they perform a service to readers by drawing together major points for their final consideration.

2. The postscript

A postscript is simply a thought that the author adds after the ending has already been reached. If the form of the essay has been fully developed, the reader knows where the ending is. A postscript may not necessarily be an irrelevant thought, but it is probably misplaced in the development of the essay proper. An afterthought, therefore, is better dropped altogether or integrated into the essay.

3. The obvious ending

The phrase "In conclusion" is the most obvious of endings. Characteristically, readers don't like to be told the obvious. If the organization of an essay has been thoughtfully developed, the ending is self-evident without a special announcement.

The design of the middle

What is your purpose in writing? To tell what you did? To tell someone else how to do the same thing? To explain what you think about violence on television? Once your purpose is clear, almost immediately certain decisions about arrangement and development have already been made. For instance, telling someone how to do something is called process, and the ways of explaining a process are fairly conventional. Once you determine the purpose, certain steps follow.

In this section, we will discuss six common kinds of writing:

1. Expository narration
2. Expository description
3. Process and analysis
4. Definition
5. Argumentation and refutation
6. Expressive writing

These are all forms of expository writing; that is, they all explain something in some particular way. One explains by setting down facts, another by telling about an incident, another by describing how something works, another by reasoning. Expository writing has the overall purpose of explaining, although the writing itself may vary considerably in content and style. In this sense, exposition is an umbrella term for various kinds of writing.

In a similar way, we will use the term *persuasion* not as a separate mode but to refer to a general quality that we seek in most of our writing of whatever variety it may be—that is, persuasiveness. Surely no one wants to write exposition that is unpersuasive. Ordinarily, we want an audience to accept what we say or write. Persuasiveness is the capacity of writing to appeal. In attempting to persuade, we can appeal in two ways: by pleasing and by seeking approval, either rationally or emotionally. We need not assume that readers are opposed to us. They may be neutral or uninformed. The emphasis of persuasion is therefore to win acceptance, not necessarily to overcome an opponent. A favorable response may at times result from the integrity of the speaker, the authority of the evidence, the fullness of supporting detail, or the ability of the author to bridge the barriers of misunderstanding by the skillful use of language.

In discussing the six modes listed above, we will see how each usually coincides with a particular arrangement you may choose. For instance, a time order leads to narration, or we can say that narration invites a time order. In a similar way, description is practically inseparable from space order. Argument may proceed by induction or deduction. As we discuss the different modes, we will consider seven different ways material can be arranged:

1. Time or serial order
2. Space order
3. Classification and grouping
4. Comparison and contrast
5. Order of logical induction: from the particular to the general
6. Order of logical deduction: from the general to a logical inference, either general or particular
7. Nonlinear order: juxtaposition

1 Expository narration

This book is not concerned with the kind of storytelling included in novels and short stories. That is an art in itself. We are, however, concerned with the kind of narration that is often used in illustrations and examples for purposes of explanation and support. This kind of narration may be brief when the illustration is anecdotal, although it may be more extended in something like autobiographical writing, where the point often emerges only after a complete story has been told.

Narration depends chiefly upon time order. The most obvious time order is serial—that which begins at the beginning and proceeds in chronological sequence to the end. The basic serial pattern is A to B to C, but the skilled narrator will usually arrange the details so that the reader's interest rises to a climax at some point in the narration, as in this passage by Alistair Cooke:

On May 21, late in the afternoon, a 13-year-old schoolboy, the son of a Chicago millionaire real-estate man, stopped on his way home to watch a ball game. A car drove up and carried him away. The following day a special delivery letter assured the parents that the boy was safe but asked for a $10,000 ransom, to be collected in worn bills and put in a cigar box. The father duly obliged and drove off to the specified meeting place. Quite incredibly, he forgot the instructions about where he was to go, and he drove back home. It would have been too late anyway. That morning a laborer found the naked corpse of the boy near a railroad right-of-way. Nearby was a pair of shell-rimmed spectacles. They were the crucial clue that led to the arrest, and subsequent conviction, of two young men, both the sons of millionaires, both brilliant and already, at 19, both postgraduate students at the University of Chicago. In September the two men, Nathan Leopold, Jr., and Richard Loeb, were sentenced to life imprisonment.

"Nineteen Twenty-Four"

In addition to a straight chronological sequence, narration also uses what might be termed artistic time, that is, an arbitrary arrangement of time for a special effect. The narrative may begin at the end of an incident (C), flash back to the beginning (A), and then fill in events until the end is reached again, making the order C to A to B to C. The advantage is that readers are able to reflect on details along the way in terms of what they already know about the ending. Knowing the outcome—something we ordinarily do not know in actual experience—provides the reader with a special ironic perspective on things as they can be told in writing.

In a similar way, a narrative may begin in the middle of a conflict (B), narrate events leading up to that conflict (A to B), and then proceed to carry the story to a conclusion (B to C). Thus, the order is B to A to B to C. The ancients referred to this arrangement as beginning *in medias res,* in the middle of things. It has an obvious dramatic effect that other arrangements do not have. It is frequently used in films.

Thus, by variations of serial order, writers can be makers of their own time, unrestricted by clock, day and night, or seasons.

Writing effective expository narration: suggestions

1. Getting to the point quickly is often the purpose. If the illustration turns out to be a "shaggy dog story," the point may be lost. Expository narration is not a story for the sake of a story; it is support.

2. Expository writers must achieve their effects by compressed action, fragmentary characterization, abbreviated dialogue, and simplified detail. Good joketellers are models; they have mastered these techniques. The more expanded an illustration is, however, the more thoroughly developed any one of these elements may be. Length is determined by the context.

3. Narratives dealing with people, places, and objects are concrete, not abstract. Take advantage of that fact. Writers of expository narration ought to avoid abstractions and strive for vivid detail.

4. Expository narration ought to be well-paced and appropriate. The details should count; they should contribute to the content as a whole; they should keep things moving. In short, a narrative example should make a point.

2   *Expository description*

Description is actually narrative in intent. We usually think of it as a kind of picture-taking, indicating what someone or some place looks like. Thus, spatial orientation is important in description. It may also be thought of as a kind of filmmaking, showing how something happens or how something functions. It therefore has a time dimension as well. Narration and description work hand in hand, but description employs basically different structural principles.

Seeing something for the first time tends to be a total experience. It is only in telling or writing about something that a writer must decide where to start and where to go next. If someone wants to describe a painting, for example, part of the decision about where the writer should start has already been made by the artist. An artist is often able to create a focus in a painting, to make us see one object first, something that calls attention to itself by line, color, or light. A word description of a painting might therefore logically begin with the artist's central focus and proceed to the other things that relate to it. In like manner, any other description might also proceed on that basis. A description of a confused scene—a mass strike, for instance—might focus first on a leader and then proceed to other details to show the effect of the leader on the mass, or the same purpose might be accomplished by focusing on an anonymous person in the crowd to show the effect of the leader.

Any description, of course, depends on the way things are arranged to begin with. If five people are seated in a row, they are likely to be viewed from left to right or from right to left. If we attempt to recall the contents of a room, we may find it helpful to proceed mentally around the walls. These are conventional scanning devices, and they have therefore become the standards for orderly space arrangement. Undoubtedly, the rapid shifting of scene that television and contemporary motion picture techniques have made familiar to all of us will continue to influence patterns of space order in writing because these techniques tend not to move in straight lines and circles but in flashes—back and forth, here and there.

In the following passage, we very clearly have the impression that the author is describing a praying mantis in the same way she would use a movie camera—first a long shot and then, with diminishing distance, various close-ups from different angles:

She was upside-down, clinging by her feet to a horizontal stem of wild rose. Her head was deep in dried grass. Her abdomen was swollen like a smashed finger; it tapered to a fleshy tip out of which bubbled a wet, whipped froth. I couldn't believe my eyes. I lay on the hill this way and that, my knees in thorns and my cheeks in clay, trying to see as well as I could. I poked near the female's head with a blade of grass; she was clearly undisturbed, so I settled my nose an inch from that pulsing abdomen. It puffed like a concertina, it throbbed like a bellows; it roved, pumping, over the glistening, clabbered surface of the egg case testing and patting, thrusting and smoothing. It seemed to act so independently that I forgot the panting brown stick at the other end. The bubble creature seemed to have two eyes, a frantic little brain, and two busy, soft hands. It looked like a hideous, harried mother slicking up a fat daughter for a beauty pageant, touching her up, slobbering over her, patting and hemming and brushing and stroking.

Annie Dillard, *Pilgrim at Tinker Creek*

Since descriptive passages in exposition are frequently brief, patterning may not be as important as creating a single strong impression by a few bold, simplified strokes, something in the manner of a cartoonist. In this kind of description, the choice of words is crucial.

*Writing effective
expository
description:
suggestions*

1. Determine the length of expository description and the development of detail by the purpose it has in the larger context.

2. Observe closely. Select significant suggestive details that will fill out the setting, create a mood, reveal a character trait, or create a special effect: "She seemed more ancient than I had pictured her, more wrinkled and brittle, with sparser hair and duller eyes, as though a translucent yard of shroud had been prematurely wrapped around her for an easier death." (Student sentence)

3. Use all of the senses to vitalize descriptive writing: see colors, hear sounds, savor smells, record tastes, be aware of touch sensations. Consider using one of the senses metaphorically to describe the perception of another sense (synaesthesia): "The faint silvery warblings heard over the partially bare and moist fields from the bluebird, the song sparrow, and the redwing, as if the last flakes of winter tinkled as they fell!" (Thoreau, *Walden*, Chap. XVII)

4. Choose precise words and phrases; a "slashing switchblade" is a more telling phrase than "knife" alone. Use apt metaphors as a way of extending the connotations: "A bevy of bosomy women, of indeterminate ages, emerged as simultaneously and importantly as seals stirred by the promise of fish." (Student sentence)

5. Think of "Happiness is a warm puppy," not as a touchstone of excellence but as a reminder that abstractions ought to be treated in terms of specific examples.

6. Vary the ways of adding detail. Description is more than adding adjectives to nouns; a sentence or passage can move from a general statement to more and more particular details: "Voices mingled in the auditorium—loud, raucous voices, excited voices, authoritative voices, commanding, ordering, reverberating, augmenting each other, then diminishing reluctantly." (Student sentence)

3 *Process and analysis*

Process and analysis are forms of explanatory writing dealing with the basic question *how*. They may vary from simple how-to-do-it recipes to highly complex and technical analyses of how something works, how it is organized, or how it originated. The question we ask ourselves will often suggest the structure.

How-to-do-it papers, for instance, suggest the most basic narrative technique of serial order—from step 1 to step 2 to step 3—although a writer who is interested in persuading others to follow the same process may entice the reader by beginning with a description of the finished product and then going through the sequence of how it is made.

Basic to process and analysis are grouping and classification. Grouping is a pattern of order based on selection. It is not limited by time order or space order because the writer is free to select those materials that relate to one another regardless of their time or place or origin. They must simply be able to fit a particular category. For example, if a woman wanted to write about the New Conservatism of the early 1980s in the United States, she might choose to proceed by listing a number of different categories:

THE NEW CONSERVATISM OF THE EARLY 1980s IN THE UNITED STATES
   I. Attitudes toward law
  II. Attitudes toward morality
 III. Attitudes toward education
 IV. Attitudes toward religion

She might not decide on the order of these four groups until she had begun to write. For instance, she might discover that, if she started with education, she might want to go next to law, then morality, and finish with religion. Someone else might see the order differently.

Any one of these groupings, of course, invites subgroups based on various comparisons with the past:

Attitudes toward morality
  A. Sexual mores in the 1930s
  B. Sexual mores in the 1980s

Or comparisons with other cultures:

Attitudes toward morality
  A. Oriental attitudes toward women
  B. Western attitudes toward women

What is included or excluded would of course be determined by the thesis of the essay and the relevance of the subgroups to the controlling idea.

Classification is a form of analysis, a breaking down of a broad topic into parts. The parts may be thought of as variations on a theme. For instance, sports are sometimes classified as team or individual sports. Or as contact or noncontact sports. Or as sports requiring strength and endurance, requiring speed, or requiring skill and maneuvering. The choice of categories would of course depend on the writer's purpose and emphasis. Their order would also be largely a matter of individual decision. Whether team sports come first and individual sports come second does not so much depend on logic as on the effect a writer might want to create. In this brief passage, John Alan Lee classifies kinds of love:

For thousands of years writers and philosophers have debated the nature of love. Many recognized that there are different kinds of love, but few accepted them all as legitimate. Instead, each writer argues that his own concept of love is the best. C. S. Lewis thought that true love must be unselfish and altruistic, as did sociologist Pitirim Sorokin. Stendhal, by contrast, took the view that love is passionate and ecstatic. Others think that "real" love must be wedded to the Protestant ethic, forging a relationship that is mutually beneficial and productive. Definitions of love range from sexual lust to an excess of friendship.

"The Styles of Loving"

In arranging their material, writers who want to make a special point ordinarily hold their strongest evidence till last. That choice, however, is a rhetorical decision, not a logical one. Admittedly, the line of distinction between the two is very fine.

When a comparison is employed, two basic approaches suggest themselves. One thing might be explained in its entirety, then compared or contrasted with the other: A, then B. On the other hand, if several points of comparison can be drawn, the writer may choose an alternating order: A^1, B^1, A^2, B^2, A^3, B^3. How this formula works can be seen in a carefully structured passage by Bertrand Russell:

Lenin, with whom I had a long conversation in Moscow in 1920, was, superficially, very unlike Gladstone, and yet, allowing for the difference of time and place and creed, the two men had much in common. To begin with the differences: Lenin was cruel, which Gladstone was not; Lenin had no respect for tradition, whereas Gladstone had a great deal; Lenin considered all means legitimate for securing the victory of his party, whereas for Gladstone politics was a game with certain rules that must be observed. All these differences, to my mind, are to the advantage of Gladstone, and accordingly Gladstone on the whole had beneficent effects, while Lenin's effects were disastrous. In spite of all these dissimilarities, however, the points of resemblance were quite as profound. Lenin supposed himself to be an atheist, but in this he was mistaken. He thought that the world was governed by the dialectic, whose instrument he was; just as much as Gladstone, he conceived of himself as the human agent of a superhuman Power. His ruthlessness and unscrupulousness were only as to means, not as to ends; he would not have been willing to purchase personal power at the expense of apostasy. Both men derived their personal force from this unshakable conviction of their own rectitude. Both men, in support of their respective faiths, ventured into realms in which, from ignorance, they could only cover themselves with ridicule—Gladstone in Biblical criticism, Lenin in philosophy.

"Eminent Men I Have Known"

Writing effective process and analysis: suggestions

1. Make certain that you yourself understand clearly the procedure you are describing or the structure you are analyzing. It is difficult to make clear to someone else what is vague to you.

2. Anticipate the kinds of questions readers may pose about your subject. Do terms need to be defined? If so, define them in advance. Do points need illustration? If so, provide graphics or written examples.

3. Provide as much explanation as may be needed to be clear. Remember that overly technical language may be confusing. Being too obvious may be boring.

4. Use precise language. If technical terms are used, determine in your mind whether the audience will understand them.

5. Be certain that all major groupings or categories are included. A serious omission may be reason enough to discredit the believability of the whole classification.

6. Mark the steps of a process. Then adopt a clearly established order and stick to it.

7. Be certain that classifications are parallel. If the general topic is Dance

Steps, then Fred Astaire is not parallel with the foxtrot, rumba, tango, and waltz. He may be used as an example, but he fits into another classification that would include the names of dancers or movie stars.

8. Determine the parts to be included in an analysis, then choose an appropriate order. If a logical order is apparent, follow it. If not, determine an order of importance or an order of effectiveness.

9. If possible, seek new ways to classify familiar topics. A new classification is a fresh perspective. For instance, dogs are conventionally classified by breed. But they might also be classified as (1) those owned by people with incomes over $50,000; (2) those owned by old people; (3) those owned by farmers; (4) strays; (5) mine. This classification would obviously produce a different kind of paper from one that simply listed breeds.

4 Definition

Definition is one of the purest forms of exposition because its main purpose is to explain. It answers the basic question "What is it?" or "What does it mean?" Everyone, of course, is familiar with cryptic dictionary definitions. At times, they may be all that we need to understand the use of a word in a particular sentence. Yet such definitions have limited usefulness where general understanding is concerned. For example, the dictionary definition of *hemidemisemiquaver* is "a sixty-fourth note," but that is not wholly meaningful unless we have additional knowledge about musical timing and notation. An extended definition might discuss the larger context of musical timing, explain the notation system, and finally make clear how *hemidemisemiquaver* relates to other notes. After that explanation, we might then by extension understand why a short section in *The New York Times* consisting of brief items about musical events and personalities was for years entitled "Hemidemisemiquavers."

We need not always think of definition as a bland statement of fact. Definition can often be a delightful source of humor that includes a commentary on human nature. In "Education in a Post-Literate World," John M. Culkin defines an Eskimo family as "a father, a mother, two children, and an anthropologist." James Agee classifies and defines laughs as follows: "In the language of screen comedians four of the main grades of laugh are the titter, the yowl, the bellylaugh, and the boffo. The titter is just a titter. The yowl is a runaway titter. Anyone who has ever had the pleasure knows all about a bellylaugh. The boffo is the laugh that kills."

Extended definition invites almost any of the structural arrangements listed above:

Time order   Defining by giving an illustration (*Anarchy occurs when . . .*) or by tracing the origin and development of something (the etymology of O.K., for instance).

Space order   Defining by describing what something looks like or how it works.

Classification   Defining by placing something in a general category (*Monarchy is a form of government*) and then indicating how it differs from others in the same classification (*Monarchy is a form of government in which authority is invested in one person*).

Comparison and contrast   Defining by saying how two or more things are alike or different (*Monarchy is a form of government in which authority is invested in one person, as opposed to oligarchy, in which authority is invested in a few privileged persons*). Or defining by analogy: *I'd rather be a hammer than a nail.*

Order of logical induction, from the particular to the general   Defining by giving examples or enumerating details and then making a covering statement.

Order of logical deduction, from the general to a logical inference, either general or particular   Defining by making a relationship between two things that have elements in common. The arrangement is similar to comparison, but may also be based upon a conditional statement: *If the government you have described is totalitarian, then our government is also totalitarian because of the elements the two have in common.*

Nonlinear order: juxtaposition   Defining by setting down a series of statements or impressions that add up to something more than the logical sum of the parts—the description of a dream, for instance.

Writers sometimes unabashedly interrupt the development of a thought to define for the reader, as David L. Bazelon does in this passage:

Psychiatrists are not alone, of course, in their failure to comprehend the nature and the importance of the adversary process. A word of explanation about what I mean when I use the term is in order here. The adversary process is the central feature of the system of legal institutions and procedures set up by our society to resolve controversies that arise between contending interests, values and ideologies. The adversity—to use the word in its old dictionary meaning—is supplied not by the process but by the parties to the conflict; the adversary process is merely the decisional mechanism for resolving their conflict. Decisions must be reached even in the absence of any source of perfect information or wisdom. We therefore arrange an orderly contest of the parties in the courtroom, in which adversary roles are assigned to reflect the reality of the underlying dispute. Those of us who are engaged in conducting these proceedings have an awed awareness of the risk of arriving at an imperfect decision often with enormous consequences for the individual and for our society.

"Psychiatrists and the Adversary Process"

Writing effective definition: suggestions	**1.** Be certain that definition is necessary and purposeful. Knowing what to define is being aware of who the audience is. **2.** Make certain that words, images, and comparisons are exact, familiar, and appropriate. **3.** Make certain a definition is adequate. Think of defining as providing a bridge for readers to get where you want them to go. **4.** Be certain that basic formal definitions are not circular; that is, definitions that use a derivative term of the word being defined: "Comparing means drawing comparisons."

Argumentation, by definition, is dispute. It implies that there are opposing positions. Someone might claim that on the basis of such a definition anything in the
world can be argued. Perhaps so, but some things are less arguable than others. It
is hardly worth arguing whether newspapers should or should not have headlines if
no issue is involved, or whether Hemingway should have written *A Farewell to
Arms* before *The Torrents of Spring,* since he didn't. Any viable issue, however,
naturally lines up arguments for and arguments against.

Any structure will have to take into account the pro-and-con nature of argument.
We can argue in three different ways. First, we can take an affirmative position and
set forth our own arguments. Second, we can add further evidence that will counterbalance the arguments of our opponents. If these arguments have not yet been
advanced, we can try to anticipate them. (Aristotle thought that those who argued a
case should know the opposing position as well as their own. Lawyers still seem to
follow this advice.) As a third means of argumentation, we can point to fallacies in
our opponents' arguments as a way of discrediting them. Strong argumentation,
therefore, demands careful study of evidence, and it requires perceptive reasoning to
detect flaws in an argument, whether it is an opponent's or our own.

The nature of the logic helps further to shape the structure of an argument. It
follows, therefore, that different kinds of reasoning will determine different arrangements of material. A discussion of these will suggest various structures.

Inductive reasoning is a way of thinking that enables us to make general statements *Inductive reasoning*
on the basis of particular examples and evidence. It is therefore both a way of
discovering (making an inductive leap) and a way of explaining. The generalization
may take the form of a definite conclusion, an hypothesis, or a recommendation. On
the basis of certain kinds of evidence, a generalization may be 100 percent true. For
example, if a professor says "No one in my 9:30 class received a failing grade," the
generalization can be accepted as universally true, since it is based on all possible
examples. Any generalization based on less than complete evidence is held to be
generally true. In fact, most generalizations that we make are based on high probability rather than absolute certainty, simply because generalizations about human
behavior and attitudes cannot be made on all possible cases, only on representative
samplings. Doctors prescribe on the basis of high probability, following certain
hypotheses drawn from medical research and practice. For example, barbiturates are
useful as sedatives, but they may also be fatal if mixed with alcohol. Neither of these
facts is an absolute certainty, but each is a sufficiently authoritative generalization to
deserve respect, and one fact does not necessarily contradict the other. It cannot be
said that barbiturates are fatal drugs because in most instances, properly used, they
are not.

Judgments, recommendations, and predictions tend to be the most controversial
kinds of conclusions, and their general acceptance depends on the strength of given
evidence. A jury's decision of "guilty" or "not guilty" is made after it weighs the
evidence for and against the accused; but the more circumstantial the evidence, the

less certain the decision. In a series of articles, a local newspaper may list reasons for the city to move as quickly as possible to increase mass transit facilities. If the arguments are convincing, the recommendation may get results. If they are not, it will fail.

Since inductive reasoning ordinarily is based on conclusions drawn from evidence, the test of an argument that uses this approach therefore lies in key questions directed to the nature of the evidence and the nature of the conclusion:

1. Is the evidence reliable? Does it seem to be objective? Is it representative? Where did you get it? Does it reflect a certain bias or prejudice?
2. Is the evidence adequate? Is there enough of it to justify a conclusion? Are there a sufficient number of cases or samples?
3. When several inferences are possible, which is the simplest and least forced? Is a common-sense explanation dismissed in favor of an unlikely or farfetched one?
4. Does the cause adequately explain the effect? Has the obvious obscured any other possible explanations? Has the relationship of cause and effect been affected by pure coincidence or possibly even superstition?
5. Are there obvious exceptions to a generalization? If so, does the generalization still hold as generally true if not universally true? Can the exceptions be explained in other terms?

Structuring inductive reasoning is mainly a matter of deciding whether the arguments will be stated first followed by the conclusion or the conclusion stated first followed by the evidence. Either is acceptable, depending on the effect we may want. In this passage by Naomi Weisstein, the evidence is first narrated, then the conclusion is given:

> In Milgram's experiments a subject is told that he is administering a learning experiment, and that he is to deal out shocks each time the other "subject" (in reality, a confederate of the experimenter) answers incorrectly. The equipment appears to provide graduated shocks ranging upwards from 15 to 450 volts; for each four consecutive voltages there are verbal descriptions such as "mild shock," "danger, severe shock," and finally, for the 435 and 450 volt switches, simply a red XXX marked over the switches. Each time the stooge answers incorrectly the subject is supposed to increase the voltage. As the voltage increases the stooge begins to cry in pain; he demands that the experiment stop; finally, he refuses to answer at all. When he stops responding, the experimenter instructs the subject to continue increasing the voltage; for each shock administered, the stooge shrieks in agony. Under these conditions, about 62.5 percent of the subjects administered shock that they believed to be possibly lethal.
>
> "'Kinder, Küche, Kirche' as Scientific Law: Psychology Constructs the Female"

Deductive reasoning   Deductive reasoning is a way of thinking that draws inferences from general statements or uses generalizations to apply what is true in one instance to what is true in another related instance. Deduction therefore has a certain predictive value in the sense that one statement can be used to imply another if the proper connections between the two can be made. Even though deductive reasoning is commonly explained as a movement from the general to the particular, it is wholly possible that reasoning of this kind will move only from one general statement to another general statement. The important thing, however, is that one of the generalizations must be prior to the conclusion and the two logically connected by certain terms. The structure of a deductive argument is, therefore, bound by the pattern of certain basic syllogisms.

The categorical syllogism may assume several forms, but a few principles are common to all of them:

*The categorical
syllogism*

1. The syllogism is limited to three statements: a major premise, a minor premise and a conclusion.

Major premise: All men are mortal.
Minor premise: Socrates is a man.
Conclusion: Socrates is mortal.

2. The syllogism is also limited to three and only three terms. Every syllogism must include one term that is common to the major and minor premise but does not appear in the conclusion. This link is called the *middle term.* In the model syllogism, "man" is the middle term. The *major term* is the predicate of the conclusion ("mortal"); the *minor term* is the subject of the conclusion ("Socrates").

3. The middle term must be distributed at least once. A distributed term is one that includes all members of its class. An undistributed term is one that is not all-inclusive. In the model syllogism, "men" is distributed in the major premise. The reference to Socrates is also distributed because an individual by name is considered the only member of his class.

4. If a particular term is distributed in the conclusion, it must also be distributed in the premises. If a term is undistributed in a premise, it cannot be distributed in the conclusion.

5. If one premise is negative, the conclusion must be negative.

6. If both premises are negative, no conclusion can be drawn.

7. If both premises are qualified, that is, made particular by a word like *some* or *most,* no conclusion can be drawn.

Syllogisms that violate these rules are invalid and, as arguments, are unsound.
Almost all propositions may assume one of four forms: universal affirmative, universal negative, particular affirmative, and particular negative. A statement that refers to all instances is called *universal;* a statement that is qualified is called *particular.*

Universal affirmative: All mailboxes in this city are green.
Universal negative: No mailboxes in this city are red.
Particular affirmative: Some mailboxes are indoors.
Particular negative: Some mailboxes are not outdoors.

Although other propositions may not be phrased in the exact words of the models, they may still be included in these four categories. For example, "a majority" may be interpreted as the equivalent of "some," since a qualified phrase is less than the universal "all."

Even though the categorical syllogism may be the backbone of a particular argument, most written argument employs a telescoped version of the syllogism called an *enthymeme*, which may omit one of the premises or even the conclusion if the conclusion is obvious. Reconstructing the basic syllogism of a written enthymeme is often a way of testing the validity of an argument. For instance, a woman student argues:

Any interpretation a student writes is bound to be better than the professor's because it will come closer to the student's understanding than to the professor's.

This sentence makes a comparison, but it is first based on some principle of what the student thinks a good interpretation is. In an attempt to penetrate the fuzziness of the thinking, we might try to formulate a syllogism:

Major premise: All interpretations that are close to a student's understanding are good.
Minor premise: An interpretation a student writes is close to her understanding.
Conclusion: An interpretation a student writes is good.

From these statements, we might also establish that a professor's interpretation that goes beyond the student's understanding is bad, forming the basis for the comparative judgment in the original statement. What this kind of demonstration reveals is that we may disregard a person's valid conclusions if we reject any one of the premises. Given certain premises, many ridiculous points can be argued, but if we examine the premises and find them to be true, we are then obligated to accept the conclusion if it has been validly drawn from the true premises.

The conditional syllogism

Conditional syllogisms are those that can be phrased in terms of *if . . . then.* One premise implies the other: If gambling restrictions are lifted, organized crime will take over. If admission standards to the university are raised, the student body will become more select. Of these two examples, the first is more controversial; that is, the connection between the condition and the conclusion would be more difficult to establish.

It should also be noted that the parts of the conditional syllogism—the *if* clause, called the antecedent, and the *then* clause, called the consequent—are not reversible. It does not necessarily follow that if a student body becomes more select, the admissions standards have been raised. The cause may be a substantial increase in fees.

The conditional syllogism is not limited to one antecedent; it may have any number of conditions. When a writer is trying to establish a point, the structure suggests itself: *if . . . if . . . if . . . then.* The effectiveness of such an argument, of course, depends on the relations between the conditions and the conclusions. If too many variables can be shown to intervene between the *if* and the *then*, the argument is weakened.

Alternative syllogisms are those that can be phrased in terms of *either . . . or.* One premise excludes the other, although at times an *either . . . or* relation means "perhaps both."

The alternative syllogism

Premise 1: In order to arrive on time, you have to take either the 6:30 A.M. or 10:30 A.M. flight.
Premise 2: Not 6:30.
Conclusion: Therefore, 10:30.

This happens to be a syllogism in which either of the alternatives is possible. In other instances, however, the alternatives are exclusive:

Premise 1: Either we choose to meet once again this quarter, or we adjourn for the summer.
Premise 2: Decision to adjourn.
Conclusion: Therefore, we choose not to meet once again this quarter.

One alternative may be true and the other false, leading to a faulty conclusion:

Premise 1: Either the judge is a Democrat, or he is against free enterprise.
Premise 2: He is not against free enterprise.
Conclusion: Therefore, he is a Democrat.

When both alternatives are true and possible, an inference cannot be made by simply affirming one; there is always the possibility that both will occur.

Premise 1: Either taxes will have to be raised, or inflation will continue.
Premise 2: Taxes will be raised.
Invalid conclusion: Therefore, inflation will not continue.

In this case, the conclusion is invalid because control of inflation may depend on many complex factors. Raising taxes may not solve the problem. Only when an argument can deny one alternative in order to assert the other does it become valid.

The structure of an argument based upon *either . . . or* reasoning would follow basically the skeleton form of the syllogism. The options, however, must be clearly drawn. If both alternatives can be maintained, no choice may be necessary. In a particular election, the choice finally must be Candidate A or Candidate B. But in arguing how to solve the city's traffic problems, an argument based on alternatives can be refuted if it can be shown that the best choice is not A *or* B, but A *and* B—in short, that they are not exclusive alternatives. An argument based on alternatives can persuade only if the listeners believe that all of the alternatives are real ones in the first place, that they are exclusive of one another in the second, and, finally, that they consist of the genuinely possible alternatives as opposed to others that may not be included. Only then is a clear choice possible.

Reasoning by analogy

Reasoning by analogy is the weakest of all the forms of argument because no conclusion can be logically established by this method. The writer may state a conclusion, but we are not bound to accept it on the basis of the reasoning simply because two contexts are brought into relation with one another, which may involve quite different principles and values. Can the fact that wild male animals roam in packs be used to justify a man's desire to spend one night a week away from home? Can the slaughter of animals for meat to used to justify the slaughter of human beings in warfare? These analogies are farfetched, but they show how comparison can give a distorted and oversimplified view of a situation.

Yet analogy is useful for purposes of illustration; and if the similarity between two things or two situations is close enough, we may choose to ignore the lack of necessary connection and accept the conclusion of the argument. Often it is necessary to examine the language of an analogy carefully to determine whether the argument is misleading. For example, a student justifies his negative feelings toward blacks by drawing parallels between them and other minority groups:

It is very true that we Americans, like many Europeans, brought African people to our country to be our slaves. But today they are on their own, a free people. They had a difficult time in America proving themselves to the rest of the Americans, but so have the Jews, the Japanese, and the Chinese. The fact is that the Jews, Japanese, and Chinese have succeeded in being accepted, and the blacks have not. It seems to me that the answer is simply that these other people have helped themselves; they had initiative.

This paragraph is based on a premise that those minority groups that "prove themselves" are accepted by Americans. This in itself is a shaky premise, but the writer goes on to assert that the Jews, Japanese, and Chinese have met this test and the blacks have not. The analogy breaks down in at least two places. It first ignores the significant difference in the history of these groups. Only the blacks came as slaves; the others did not. But the passage goes on: "But today they are on their own, a free people." In what sense are blacks free? Constitutionally free? Economically free? Socially free? On this point, close parallels exist between all of the minority groups because they have all been subjected to restrictions of freedom, but even then the differences between them are perhaps greater than the similarities. What at first seems like a logical parallel turns out to be a flimsy comparison.

Comparison can be highly illuminating if it is not pushed to prove a point. It is interesting to draw analogies, as Plato did, between the government of the individual soul and the government of the city-state, since, as he reasoned, the state is made up of individuals; but it is another matter to justify aristocracy over democracy as a form of government on the basis of such an analogy. It may be useful to consider what happened in Germany in the early 1930s in terms of what happened in the United States in the 1970s if the comparison is not used to infer that we were moving inevitably toward a dictatorial state. Many historical analogies are instructive, but it is another thing to conclude that the pattern of the future follows precisely the pattern of the past. The more closely related two things are, the more sound an analogy based on them will be, but close similarity then works against the purpose of an analogy to create a fresh perspective by bringing two quite different things in relation to one another.

Writing effective argument: suggestions

1. Accumulate reliable, adequate, and verifiable evidence to support any point that you wish to establish. *Reliability* often depends on the source of the evidence. Is the writer or speaker informed and dependable? *Adequacy* depends on the representativeness of the evidence. Has a generalization been made on the basis of numerous examples, and has contrary evidence been considered? *Verifiable evidence* depends on its basis in fact. Is an opinion mere prejudice, or does it reflect actual experience?

2. Define terms. In order to avoid confrontation and quarreling, one of the first considerations in argument is to eliminate a possible misunderstanding of crucial words. Writers must establish the context of their arguments by definition. For instance, one writer might oppose war on humane grounds; another might support it on economic grounds. Those are different and separable arguments.

3. Group arguments. Related reasons reinforce one another. An outline will help a writer see what might be the most effective order of the categories.

4. Anticipate the arguments of the opposition. Answering objections in advance is a way of filling possible loopholes in your own argument.

5. Argue in a clear, unconfused sequence. Organization and well-defined connections are especially important in advancing a convincing argument.

6. Use precise and appropriate language. Failure to do so makes your own argument vulnerable to the charge of being fallacious.

7. Detect fallacies. Because arguments depend on words, facts, and relations, fallacies arise from the way these are handled. Fallacies may best be described as counterfeit arguments, ones that have market value because they pass as the real thing. Many of these are self-evident. They spring from faulty kinds of reasoning: a hasty generalization unwarranted by the evidence, a forced analogy, a vague appeal to unnamed authorities, a substitution of simple, extreme alternatives for a careful weighing of several choices. These are all false ways of arguing, although, as experience shows, at times very powerful ways.

There are many fallacies, because for every principle of inference or deduction, there is the possibility of a violation. These are considered formal fallacies. Three are particularly common in everyday reasoning.

A. **Begging the question.** The fallacy of "begging the question" occurs when the conclusion is essentially a rephrasing of the beginning assumption. The argument therefore is circular, getting nowhere in proving a point because it assumes to be true what should be proved. Someone might say, "Use of marijuana is bad because it is illegal." But why illegal? "It's illegal because it's immoral." The reply merely rephrases the original premise; it makes "bad," "illegal," and "immoral" synonymous terms. The reply begs the question.

B. The confusion of *all* and *some*. Reasoning that misleads the reader to substitute "all" for "some" is more formally known as the fallacy of the undistributed middle. It is a form of hasty generalization. This kind of thinking often has serious consequences. For instance, during World War II, Japanese-American civilians on the West Coast were transferred to detention camps because it was thought potential enemies of this nation had to be confined. All were evacuated. Some of these people may have been potential enemies, but most of them were responsible citizens who supported the war effort just as other Americans. Substituting *all* for *some* becomes a way of incriminating innocent persons. In this instance, fallacious reasoning caused a loyal group of citizens severe hardship.

C. *Post hoc, ergo propter hoc.* Literally translated, the Latin words mean, "After this, therefore on account of this." It is erroneous cause-and-effect reasoning: one thing happens, another follows; the first is inferred to be cause of the second. Of course, one thing that happens before another need not necessarily be its cause. The *post hoc* fallacy can be easily reduced to absurdity. A grandmother tells a young bride that, as soon as she knows she is pregnant, she can control the sex of her child by sleeping on her left side if she wants a boy and sleeping on her right side if she wants a girl. In the course of years, the young woman, faithful to the practice, has two boys and two girls in exactly the order she wants them. She recommends the method to her friends because the results have been perfect.

Apart from formal fallacies that violate the rules of inference, there are a number of informal fallacies. These seem to function by confusing the argument, evading the issue, or substituting emotion for evidence.

A. Confusing the argument. An argument can be confused mainly by two methods: using ambiguous language or distorting the evidence. Sound argument rests on clear and precise terms. Many arguments bog down because words are used vaguely or the terms shift in their meaning. For example, a student writes "A person who has compassion and understanding for everyone and hatred for none is Christlike. He is a Christian." This conclusion is either based on the untenable assumption that all Christians are Christlike, or there has been an unconscious shift of terms in the last sentence from "Christlike" to "Christian." The two words cannot substitute for one another.

Confusion, whether deliberate or not, also arises from the manipulation of evidence, particularly statistical evidence. Figures can be made to prove almost anything, usually by suppressing some of the evidence. One store may advertise that its prices are lower but suppress the fact that its interest rates are higher. A high school administration may publicize that its current graduating class has received more scholarships than any other class in the history of the school but suppress the fact that the class is larger than any previous one and the percentage of scholarships is 5 percent lower than that of three other classes. The distortion of evidence is actually a device of oversimplification.

B. **Evading the issue.** Ignoring the question and introducing irrelevant issues are also common fallacies of everyday reasoning. Ignoring the question is usually a deliberate attempt to avoid controversial or unpleasant issues. In one sense, a reply that ignores the question is a total irrelevancy; yet it is particularly common in personal interviews involving direct questions. A diplomat asked to comment on our present relations with Israel may begin with a review of our past relations, stopping short of the current situation. If further questions explore new issues, he manages to skirt the original question. The practice also occurs among student writers who, asked to analyze some particular work, merely summarize and fail to come to grips with the question.

Irrelevant arguments are more subtle. They may appear to be related, particularly if they are wrapped in syllogistic phrasing. For example, a graduate student attempts to explain the unpopularity of a particular freshman course in this way:

> There are two possible explanations: something is wrong with the students, or something is wrong with the course. If something is wrong with the freshmen, then I don't see why the same things aren't wrong with graduate students. Therefore, the faculty ought to consider the desires of graduate students to the same extent that graduate students are willing to consider the desires of freshmen.

The argument begins logically by setting up an alternative, but it then turns quickly to graduate students. It is not clear what they have to do with the argument about freshmen, except that the writer wants to add a bit of special pleading that is totally irrelevant to the main point.

C. **Substituting emotion for evidence.** Arguments that substitute emotion for evidence are also irrelevancies, but they represent a special kind of fallacy in that they shove reasoning aside and appeal to feelings. In so doing, they actually cloud the issues. One of the most common is an *ad hominem* argument. In simplest terms, an *ad hominem* argument attacks the "man" instead of the issues. It is a common political practice, particularly when the issues are sticky or when the candidates are not sufficiently different in their views to represent opposing sides of an argument. In such cases, the contest may shift to personal grounds. Attacks can be forthright, but often they are couched in simplified language that condemns by association. One senator or another will be labeled a hawk, an isolationist, a left-winger, or a negativist. All of these words are intended to draw responses, but not rational ones.

Other appeals that play on the emotions and prejudices of people but do not necessarily involve personalities are called *ad populum* arguments (literally, "to the people"). These appeals cover a wide range of feelings, but a few are more commonly exploited than others: blind patriotism (*if minorities don't like what is going on in this country, let them go back where they came from*); self-interest and bigotry (*Approval of the open housing law will ruin property values in the suburbs*); anti-intellectualism (*Immorality among young people has been encouraged by the weirdo professors of our universities*); suspicion and prudishness (*There is a nationwide Communist-supported plot to encourage the moral decay of our youth through sex education in schools and lewd motion pictures featuring perversion and nudity*). Even though any of these positions may be argued on legitimate grounds, the *ad populum* approach shortcuts the process of careful support and takes advantage of the readiness of many people to jump to quick conclusions.

Expressive writing

Expressive writing is highly personalized. It may concern an individual's feelings, preoccupations, moods, or opinions. It may be a writer's unique response to some object, person, or experience. It tries to record the writer's reactions. It is therefore self-expressive. In an extended essay on trying to come to terms with a young man's death, his sister writes:

It was a cold wintry day. There was a brisk wind blowing, the clouds were moving in and out, the sun was shining brightly, as if to warm the numbness of my heart. It was the day of Steve's funeral. He was just twenty-two. His life had just begun. Now it was over.

The opening natural description of this essay creates a poetic effect. We often think of poetry as an essential form of expressive writing, but expressive prose can be no less moving or imaginative.

Words often do not catch either the subtlety or the complexity of our emotions. It is hard to say in a straightforward, linear way what simultaneously involves the eye, the hand, and the ear, as well as the brain. In fact, music, film, abstract art, and multimedia forms seem particularly successful in expressing emotions because they allow several things to occur simultaneously as they actually happen in experience. In order to get closer to the totality of experience, writers also turn to a technique that we have learned to accept in other art forms. It is a nonlinear approach that depends on the juxtaposition of parts rather than a close linking of them. It suggests a variety of meanings rather than a single one. It can best be described as a cinematic technique applied to writing.

For a moment, we need to explore further the differences between a nonlinear approach and the more traditional linear model of logical thinking.

First, we should consider that our ways of thinking about things do not always correspond to our ways of experiencing them. We observe and feel and absorb. What we ordinarily call logical thinking is a special way of interpreting experience. For instance, in our culture we think of time in terms of minutes, hours, days, months, and years; and these are logically laid out in a straight line. We refer to someone's living from age one to age seventy, each year in sequence. A clock measures time. Yet neither time nor growing old is in actuality the kind of experience we talk about. In one way or another, time can be ignored, transcended, speeded up, turned backward or forward, even though measurements continue uniformly, falling bodies accelerate at 32 feet per second, and the alarm clock rings at 6:30 sharp. Time is a continuum, but whether it exists in the manner that we think about it is another matter. Aging is growth and change and has nothing much to do with marking off the passing days on a calendar. Some people of fifty are older than others at sixty. Nevertheless, straight-line thinking is the traditional standard for logical thought. It is a one-directional sequence of sentences, with parts connected link by link to form a chain of reasoning. When it is put down in writing, it represents connected, successive discourse.

On the other hand, nonlinear logic may be described as fluid, mosaic, or kaleidoscopic—whichever word best conveys the notion of a multidimensional effect that does not so much lead the audience as a group in one direction and to one conclusion as allows them to participate individually in their own way. It is a logic that may jump instead of moving step by step. It does not necessarily bridge the gaps. It is suggestive and expressive.

Two paragraphs will illustrate both nonlinear and linear structure:

Firmly planted. Not fallen from on high: sprung up from below. Ocher, the color of burnt honey. The color of a sun buried a thousand years ago and dug up only yesterday. Fresh green and orange stripes running across its still warm body. Circles, Greek frets: scattered traces of a lost alphabet? The belly of a woman heavy with child, the neck of a bird. If you cover and uncover its mouth with the palm of your hand, it answers you with a deep murmur, the sound of bubbling water welling up from its depths; if you tap its side with your knuckles, it gives a tinkling laugh of little silver coins falling on stones. It has many tongues: it speaks the language of clay and minerals, of air currents flowing between canyon walls, of washerwomen as they scrub, of angry skies, of rain. A vessel of baked clay: do not put it in a glass case alongside rare precious objects. It would look quite out of place. Its beauty is related to the liquid that it contains and to the thirst that it quenches. Its beauty is corporal: I see it, I touch it, I smell it, I hear it. If it is empty, it must be filled; if it is full, it must be emptied. I take it by the shaped handle as I would take a woman by the arm, I lift it up, I tip it over a pitcher into which I pour milk or pulque—lunar liquids that open and close the doors of dawn and dark, waking and sleeping. Not an object to contemplate: an object to use to satisfy someone's thirst.

A glass jug, a wicker basket, a coarse muslin huipil, a wooden serving dish: beautiful objects, not despite their usefulness but because of it. Their beauty is simply a gratuitous gift, like the perfume and the color of flowers. It is inseparable from their function: they are beautiful things because they are useful things. Handcrafts belong to a world antedating the separation of the useful and the beautiful. Such a separation is more recent than is generally supposed. Many of the artifacts that find their way into our museums and private collections once belonged to that world in which beauty was not an isolated and autonomous value. Society was divided into two great realms, the profane and the sacred. In both, beauty was a subordinate quality: in the realm of the profane, it was dependent upon an object's usefulness, and in the realm of the sacred it was dependent upon an object's magic power. A utensil, a talisman, a symbol: beauty was the aura surrounding the object, the result—almost invariably an unintentional one—of the secret relation between its form and its meaning. Form: the way in which a thing is made; meaning: the purpose for which it is made. Today all these objects, forcibly uprooted from their historical context, their specific function, and their original meaning, standing there before us in their glass display cases, strike our eyes as enigmatic divinities and command our adoration. Their transfer from the cathedral, the palace, the nomad's tent, the courtesan's boudoir, and the witch's cavern to the museum was a magico-religious transmutation. Objects became icons. This idolatry began in the Renaissance and from the seventeenth century onward has been one of the religions of the West (the other being politics). Long ago, at the height of the Baroque period, Sor Juana Inés de la Cruz coined a witty little phrase poking fun at aesthetics as superstitious awe: "A woman's hand is white and beautiful because it is made of flesh and bone, not of marble or silver; I esteem it not because it is a thing of splendor but because its grasp is firm."

Octavio Paz, "In Praise of Hands"

These two paragraphs make different demands upon us, and the first paragraph is clearly more demanding. It asks us to experience the prose; the second asks us to follow the thought. The second paragraph begins to identify the objects and explain them; it proceeds with logical connections. Paragraph one leaves things out. We have a series of associations. When we cannot make conventional connections between two thoughts, we usually say that one is a *non sequitur,* meaning literally "it does not follow." Yet our thinking is filled with non sequiturs. The first paragraph of Octavio Paz's writing may be difficult to understand in terms of conventional logic. Thoughts that seem at first to have no obvious connection are put side by side, and we are left to make something of the meaning. At that point, we have to help ourselves because the writer has chosen not to help. We therefore become active participants, not just interested spectators.

The effect of nonlinear prose is different from that of linear prose. It is fast-moving. It can create a total impression without explaining all of the details. It is a way of translating sensory experiences into writing. If writers want to explain their ideas carefully or present an argument, they need to write linear prose because only in connected discourse of that kind do a writer's precise intentions come through clearly and unambiguously. If their purpose is expressive, however, then nonlinear prose offers another way.

Effective expressive writing: suggestions

1. Since nonlinear writing makes intense demands on readers, they may not be able to sustain involvement with this kind of prose for a long time. Consider how long a passage of nonlinear prose can be sustained.
2. Let the structure be guided primarily by intuition.
3. Although nonlinear prose may represent a "free-fall" style, free-falling is not totally uncontrolled. Let the purpose guide the choices you make.
4. Use novel language (coinages, images, and metaphors) as a way of individualizing your experiences.

Why does writing usually get easier once you are over the hump of beginning? One of the reasons is that developing a thought depends little upon formal knowledge of logic and strongly upon the ways we characteristically relate objects, experiences, and ideas. One thing suggests another because it is like the first or because the second is different from the first. Or one causes the other. These are familiar principles of association. They are implicit in the structure words of the language— the various words and phrases that act as connectors, chiefly conjunctions and conjunctive adverbs. Lists of these words are included in other parts of this book, but here we are interested in only a few that represent the basic relationships of written discourse. These can be reduced to nine:

and as simple addition, coordination, or juxtaposition
and further as reinforcement, qualification, emphasis, or expansion
and then as narrative sequence
or as alternative
but as discrimination, exception, or negation (*not*)
for instance as illustration or particularization
thus/then/because as linking a cause and the consequences (*because . . . thus*), a condition and the result (*if . . . then*) or the conclusion and the reasons (*because*)

Clearly, there are other words that fit into each of these categories. For instance, *meanwhile* is a word likely to appear in a narrative sequence, or *in spite of* will signal discrimination (*We went in spite of the rain*). Accept the nine words and phrases, however, as representative of all of the others that connect words, sentences, paragraphs, and larger units of thought. Sometimes the connectives are written in; sometimes they are implicit. In the following paragraph, the author includes only one connective, *however.* The other implied ones are inserted in brackets.

Everyone is by now familiar with the fact that newspaper printing technology is in the midst of an historic revolution. [because] The computer has entered the ancient production routines of the newspaper, disturbing the cobwebs, making the floorboards creak in unaccustomed places, sending the workers out on strike. [and] A great convulsion is taking place, the main result of which, in the layman's eyes, is a reduction in the total hours of labor that go into the setting of type and the presswork. [but] To all outward appearances the new printing equipment, which has abolished the use of molten lead, reduced all the hot and heavy labor of heaving heavy stereotype plates around the plant, and turned newspapering largely into a white-coated and white-collared affair, has merely substituted one production process for another. [thus] The newspaper when it reaches us looks exactly as it did before, cleaner in appearance, often containing more mistakes, with better pictures and more of them in color, just a little smarter. *However,* in no sense is it a different *medium.*

Anthony Smith, "All the News that Fits in the Databank"

Both as writers and readers we make connections intuitively. The main purpose in bringing them to the surface is to become aware that as a writer you can fall back on these connectives if you get stuck. They can help you determine where to move next.

The syntax of thought

If you talked to yourself as you wrote, you might say something like this: "Up to this point I have been writing about X; now I am going to write about Y." As you develop thoughts in writing, you periodically experience a sense of closure. You experience it at the end of a sentence. You experience it at the end of a paragraph. You know you have come to the end of something. Your sense of closure is dependent upon the degree to which you are familiar with patterns—the patterns of sentences and the patterns of paragraphs. But are there also patterns that determine the overall development of an essay? If so, how do these affect the way you write?

The basic patterns

You are undoubtedly familiar with a popular bit of advice to beginning writers that an essay ought to have three main parts: an introduction, main body, and conclusion. This model tells you only that a composition ought to have a clear beginning, middle, and end, but it tells little else about developing the parts.

As an alternative, think of an essay as divided into slots, each slot having a function. Here are five basic slots that writers commonly use and four others that serve more special purposes:

T: theme, thesis, or topic

The T-slot has an introductory function, but it is more than that. Unlike an introduction, it may be repeated any number of times throughout an essay. When you have completed one topic of discussion and begin another, T reoccurs.

The T-slot may be a statement of the thesis, theme, or purpose. It may raise a question. It may pose a problem. It may provide a definition. In short, it is the point of departure.

R: restatement or reinforcement

The R-slot commonly follows T. It is an expansion of the theme or purpose. It clarifies and emphasizes. It develops the thought. The implied connective "and further" signals the R-slot.

I: illustration

The I-slot is one of the most important in writing because it provides concrete details for general statements. This slot includes various kinds of support in the form of examples, anecdotes, or practical applications. It logically follows the connective "for instance."

The A-slot is also important as a way of developing a thesis. It includes evidence, facts, reasons, and causes. It may explain a process or provide a classification. In some instances, the slot follows the connective "because."

A: analysis

This slot represents the logical completion of a pattern. It need not be thought of as something tagged on at the end. C-slots may occur at various points in an essay whenever a pattern has been completed. It often follows a connective like "thus" or "therefore."

C: closure, culmination, consequences, or conclusion

These five slots combine into any number of patterns, such as TRIC, TAC, TRAC, ITRC, or ITAC.

At least four additional slots are worth identifying because they represent other characteristic ways of thinking.

The S-Slot can take the form of a setting in a descriptive passage, retrospective narration in a narrative, summary of research in a report, or the context for an argument in a persuasive paper. S may on occasion be the point of departure instead of T. It is the background against which the topic will be discussed. It has variable uses and positions. S may even occur in final position as a summary conclusion.

S: scene, setting, or summary

Even though the E-slot may be thought of primarily as a fictional category, essayists often begin with a brief narration. E thus becomes a point of departure, substituting for the T-slot or S-slot.

E: episode

The L-slot develops a comparison or analogy in order to explain a point.

L: likeness

The D-slot discriminates by contrasting or drawing lines of distinction between two or more things. The D-slot also includes negation, telling what something is not.

D: difference or discrimination

In summary, therefore, we have five basic slots:

- T: theme, topic, thesis
- R: restatement, reinforcement
- I: illustration
- A: analysis
- C: closure, conclusion

and four special-purpose slots:

- S: scene, setting, summary
- E: episode
- L: likeness
- D: difference, discrimination

These nine slots define how we think. In combination, they become the basis of our sense of structure. The development and organization of an essay, therefore, can be thought of as combining these slots to form repeatable patterns throughout an essay. The following analysis indicates the structural patterns in an essay entitled "The Gaming of America" by Karl E. Meyer.

The Gaming of America

S

I was intrigued to learn when Philo T. Farnsworth transmitted the first wireless television images in San Francisco in 1927, the test pattern was a dollar sign. This fact was among the tidbits in a bulky press kit distributed by the makers of *Deal*, a feature film (which premiered at the Public Theatre in September [1978]) about the most lucrative of TV game shows, *Let's Make a Deal.*

Farnsworth, the co-inventor of all-electronic television, lived until 1971, and thus was able to see the full flowering of that epiphany of greed, the daytime game show. Participants gurgle and squeal with almost orgasmic ecstasy as goodies are flashed before them, and the winners gape like zombies at the loot they have acquired. Around 40 million Americans regularly watch these shows and salivate.

[thus]

T

Two independent film directors, John Schott and E. J. Vaughn, had the interesting notion of exploring the surreal world of *Let's Make a Deal.* If a bit overlong (95 minutes), the documentary movie is devastating in what it tells about the great American capacity for self-deception. To hear the makers of this game show tell it, *Let's Make a Deal* is really a high-minded charity almost as worthy as the Community Chest.

[because]

A

After all, they argue, host Monty Hall and his producer-partner Stefan Hatos are giving viewers what they want—an innocent escape from everyday tedium. Moreover, since the program began in 1965, it has dispensed more prizes and cash—$31 million worth—than any game show in history. Someone has calculated that Monty Hall has been kissed 20,000 times in the course of 3,800 shows, which in their peak period have attracted 9 million daytime viewers and 27 million evening viewers. So loyal is *Deal*'s audience that when the program switched in 1968 from NBC to ABC, it transformed the daytime ratings of the latter network.

[but]

> But the creators of *Let's Make a Deal* are more reticent about the program's profit yield to the networks, stations, and its producers—there is not even a rough estimate of the overall total available. In 1976, the income to Hatos and Hall together was $11 million, and it has been conjectured that since 1965 the pair has earned $44.8 million. In the process, thousands of manufacturers have had their giveaway prizes plugged, gratis.

T_1

[but]

> No doubt about it, there is a perverse genius in *Let's Make a Deal.* It is unlike other game shows in that not a scintilla of skill is needed to become a big winner but the ability to catch the emcee's attention. Years ago a would-be contestant put on a bizarre costume, and the practice caught on. Today, ticket-holding Martians and Munchkins, cowboys and Indians, belly dancers and bumpkins turn up at the studio by the busload. All assemble for inspection as Monty Hall selects the 31 "traders" from a lineup that even a Fellini could not have invented.

D

[and]

> In the documentary, a single program is anatomized, and we are taken backstage to writers' conferences, negotiations with sponsors, and the plotting of camera positions. There is hardly any commentary and none is really needed; the creators of *Let's Make a Deal* are permitted to speak for themselves, with revealing results. All are defensive, and obviously stung by critical derision. They want the program to be seen as a symbolic statement about the glories of competition and the rewards of American life. Anything that so many people like must have a redeeming merit, or so they argue. (The same case, of course, can be made for *Hustler.*)

T_2

[and further]

> This self-deception has a certain pathos. The contestants, dressed in their imbecilic costumes, are at least under no delusion about their motives—they want something for nothing. How refreshing if Monty Hall and Steve Hatos would be as honest, and simply remark that no one has ever lost a dime by overestimating the tastelessness of the public.

R

[for example]

> Hatos, it turns out, was once a promising oboist and played under Toscanini, Stokowski, Reiner, and Walter. He quit when he discovered how little money even the greatest oboists could earn. Only at the very end of the documentary does Hatos—a street-smart Hungarian with the pate of a Kojak—confess to any doubts: "And if I could have had the life of a musician and ultimately conducted and so on, that would have been a hell of a lot more gratifying for me. . . . In the next life I'll come back as Leonard Bernstein."

[thus]

> If *Let's Make a Deal* does make a statement about America and television, it is implied in this poignant admission of lost opportunities. Messrs. Schott and Vaughn have come up with a fine documentary, and I only wonder why it is being distributed as a feature film. As soon as possible, *Deal* should be given prime-time exposure, preferably on a network, since game shows now account for 34 percent of all daytime programming on commercial television, and are indeed as American as instant gratification.

Karl E. Meyer

The structure and development of this essay may be described as follows:

Pattern 1	*Pattern 2*	*Pattern 3*
S	T_1	T_2
T	D	R
A		I
		C

It begins with general background material on Farnsworth (S), providing a setting for discussion of a documentary film. At the end of paragraph 3, a thesis about the worthiness of the program is stated (T), followed by reasons for that position (A).

The essay returns to another general statement about claims the creators make for the TV program (T_1). This program is then differentiated from other game shows (D).

The essay returns to the creators, who now claim the program is a "symbolic statement about the glories of competition" (T_2). This self-deception is elaborated upon in the following paragraph (R). The kind of honesty that would be admirable is illustrated by statements from Hatos (I), and the essay moves to completion with a final evaluation of the documentary (C).

In diagrammatic form, we can therefore see the patterning—the ebb and flow of thought from general to particular—and the orderly way in which Karl Meyer leads the reader from the opening S to the final C.

You too can think in terms of these slots as you write. They show you what you can do next. They set the direction for your thinking. They provide clues for paragraphing.

The outline has two functions: it can help you find an overall pattern for your thoughts, or it can help you analyze the structure of an essay after you have written it. A distinction needs to be made between outlines written in advance of writing and outlines written after at least the first draft has been completed.

Inasmuch as we often generate thoughts in the act of writing and even discover new directions, an outline written in advance is most useful if it does not attempt to freeze the organization. Clearly, it should show the overall pattern and major topics, but these should be flexible. The chief advantage of making an outline at all is that it permits you to see if you actually do have a plan and purpose in mind. Like all writing, if you have nothing specific in mind, you can put nothing down.

The outline done after the essay has been written is primarily a self-testing device. If the outline indicates an obviously illogical arrangement or a disproportionate treatment of one topic and neglect of others, you are still free to make adjustments. If an outline is thought of as planning and testing, then it is not merely an exercise. It is order visualized; it is structure diagrammed.

Working outlines, of course, may be merely notes or jottings, but beginning writers will learn that the demands of formal outlining are in part also the demands of controlled writing: order, proportion, and parallelism. Attempting to meet these demands is a means of cultivating an intuitive sense of order.

Formal outlines follow several conventions:

1. They frequently begin with a one-sentence thesis statement, designed to help the writer formulate the essential point.

2. They subdivide topics by a system of numbers and letters followed by a period.

   I.

      A.

      B.

         1.

         2.

            a.

            b.

3. Dividing ordinarily implies a minimum of two parts: if I, then II; if A, then B. If the writer wants to discuss only one subcategory under a main heading, it may be separated from the main topic by a colon:

I. **The Sound of the New Rock: Electronic Amplification**

4. Introduction and conclusion, if listed at all, are not indicated as numbered parts. They are followed by brief statements of purpose and not subdivided:

Introduction: **Circumstances leading up to the launching of Skylab, May 1973.**
Conclusion: **Skylab as the forerunner of future space ventures.**

5. Numbered topics are phrased consistently. If the outline is a sentence outline, topics are phrased as complete sentences. If the outline is a topic outline, parallel topics are phrased in parallel fashion: nouns with other nouns, adjectives with adjectives, phrases with phrases, and clauses with clauses:

I. Effects of fluoridated water on tooth decay	Parallel phrasing with nouns
II. Effects of fluoridated water on other parts of the body	

or

I. How fluoridated water affects tooth decay	Parallel phrasing with clauses
II. How fluoridated water affects other parts of the body	

Outlines, therefore, may assume slightly different forms, but the forms should not be mixed. The exception is that a thesis sentence is almost always phrased as a complete sentence whether the form is a topic outline or a sentence outline.

On the following two pages a planned essay is outlined, first in sentence form and then in topic form. This particular outline shows balance in the subdivisions because each of three parts is divided in turn into four parts. But no such exact balance is necessary. What the outline suggests is that the writer is probably interested in giving proportionate treatment to the three stages of childhood, adolescence, and adulthood. Section IV might conceivably be listed as a conclusion. One would expect it to be briefer than the preceding sections because it is a drawing together of the evidence, a final commentary on the nature of humor. This outline reveals that the writer has planned the essay by proceeding from the particular to the general in terms of an orderly time sequence.

The sentence outline

Thesis: The nature of humor remains basically unchanged throughout life; it only grows more sophisticated.

   I. A child typically finds fun in antics.
     A. Clowns and pets appeal because of their silliness.
     B. Animated cartoons appeal because they are exaggerated and imaginative.
     C. Riddles and rhymes are amusing because of their sounds and suspense.
     D. Unexpected falls are funny.

  II. A teenager adds additional sources of amusement.
     A. Jokes, clean and dirty ones, play upon words and situations.
     B. Mockery provides cruel amusement.
     C. Practical jokes entertain because of one-upmanship.
     D. Unexpected falls are funny.

 III. An adult typically adds other sources of amusement.
     A. Grotesque happenings are absurd.
     B. Slapstick is a form of release from inhibitions.
     C. Subtle jokes and ironic humor are intellectually delightful.
     D. Unexpected falls are funny.

 IV. Humor at all levels depends on incongruities, turns, twists—the unexpected.

Thesis: The nature of humor remains basically unchanged throughout life; it only   *The topic outline*
       grows more sophisticated.

I. The appeal of antics to children
   A. Silly clowns and pets
   B. Exaggerated and imaginative movie cartoons
   C. Tricky riddles and rhymes
   D. Unexpected falls

II. The added appeals to teenagers
   A. Verbal and situation humor in jokes
   B. Cruel mockery
   C. Surprising practical jokes
   D. Unexpected falls

III. The further sources of amusement for adults
   A. Grotesque happenings as absurdities
   B. Slapstick as release of pressure
   C. Intellectually appealing jokes and irony
   D. Unexpected falls

IV. Humor at all levels based upon incongruity and the unexpected

1. Study the format (pattern, structure, matrix) of a current TV program,   *Projects*
possibly a variety hour, game show, comedy program, or serial. Into what
chunks does the program fall? What would be appropriate terms to label the
parts, such as the chase, the complication, the moment of crisis, the disclosure or discovery, the unraveling? Is there movement toward a climax? How
does it end, typically? Is the arrangement ever varied? Does this kind of
structuring of parts have any relation to writing? Is there such a thing as
finding a new structure for writing, or would it be only a variation on an old
one?
2. Examine a painting or photograph, either abstract or representational.
How is it organized? What technique does the artist use to make you perceive the organization? If you were writing about the painting or photograph, where would you begin? Where would you go from that point?
3. Test your responses to the opening sentences given below. Is your initial
reaction favorable or unfavorable? Why? Would you want to read on? Do any
of these fall into the dozen categories described on pp. 53–56? If not, how
would you describe these openings?

> A. I am 29, going on 32 and I have a Ph.D. in English literature. I am also an
> assistant professor at Franklin & Marshall College, a small, liberal-arts institu-
> tion nestled somewhat uncomfortably between the Amish farms and tourist
> traps of southeastern Pennsylvania. This is not to brag, mind you, or to com-
> plain either, but merely to state what are the banal facts.
>
> Sanford Pinsker, "Confessions of a Recent Ph.D."

B. It used to be Know Thyself, but now it's Be Thyself. On that small change of emphasis lies a world of difference, not all of it to the good. The one attitude is inquiring, the other condoning.

Rolf Stromberg, Seattle Post-Intelligencer, Sept. 20, 1969

C. Saints should always be judged guilty until they are proved innocent, but the tests that have to be applied to them are not, of course, the same in all cases. In Gandhi's case the questions one feels inclined to ask are: to what extent was Gandhi moved by vanity—by the consciousness of himself as a humble, naked old man, sitting on a praying mat and shaking empires by sheer spiritual power—and to what extent did he compromise his own principles by entering politics, which of their nature are inseparable from coercion and fraud? To give a definite answer one would have to study Gandhi's acts and writings in immense detail, for his whole life was a sort of pilgrimage in which every act was significant.

George Orwell, "Reflections on Gandhi"

D. What is Truth? said jesting Pilate; and would not stay for an answer.

Francis Bacon, "Of Truth"

E. Real buttonholes. That's it! A man can take his thumb and forefinger and unbutton his sleeve at the wrist because this kind of suit has real buttonholes there. Tom, boy, it's terrible. Once you know about it, you start seeing it. All the time! There are just two classes of men in the world, men with suits whose buttons are just sewn onto the sleeve, just some kind of cheapie decoration, or—yes!—men who can unbutton the sleeve at the wrist because they have real buttonholes and the sleeve really buttons up. Fascinating!

Tom Wolfe, "The Secret Vice"

4. Choose the opening of one of your recent themes. Attempt to rewrite that opening in each of the twelve ways suggested on pp. 53–56. Are some of the approaches inappropriate? Are some of the new openings better than your original version?

5. Formulate subgroups for the following topics. All of these invite certain obvious classifications. Try to avoid the self-evident ones; subdivide them in a way you would consider interesting. Compare your groupings with those of other students.

A. Students in your English class
B. Students in your college
C. Automobiles
D. Occupations
E. Social levels
F. Religious faiths

6. Write several brief humorous definitions like these in Ambrose Bierce's *The Devil's Dictionary:*

immigrant, *n.*   An unenlightened person who thinks one country better than another.

pulpit, *n.*   An elevated box, into which the person gets, for fear
                      that people would not otherwise notice his superiority over his
                      congregation.

7. As a class or small group, select an essay that everyone can first outline individually. Then make comparisons. What overall pattern reveals itself? Do the writer's techniques (transitions, paragraphing, announced purpose) help to determine the pattern? Do some of you see the organization differently from others? Can some of you be said to be wrong, others right?

8. Select an essay. Analyze its development in terms of the slots described on pp. 80–81. What patterns emerge?

NARRATION AND DESCRIPTION

Suggestions for writing

1. For practice in expository description and narration, write the script for a two-minute teleplay advertising a product, promoting a cause, or featuring a candidate for office. Begin with FADE IN; end with FADE OUT. Write camera directions as you visualize them: LONG SHOT, MEDIUM CLOSE SHOT, CLOSE-UP, CUT TO. Include precise descriptions of the setting and people and what action will occur. Insert the dialogue. If you wish, consult a book on television writing for more terms and teleplay techniques.

2. Select a cartoon. Describe it with sufficient completeness so that anyone who has not seen the cartoon will understand it. Then explain the significance or the cartoonist's attitude or the purpose. Do *not* submit the cartoon with the essay.

3. If you were a photographer and were paid to take pictures of this country that would represent it in some way to a foreign audience, what scenes would you include and why? Limit yourself to four or five. Describe them in some detail.

4. Describe and elaborate on two or three qualities of a "survivor personality," a type of person who consistently survives life's crises.

5. The name of the cartoonist Rube Goldberg has become a byword. His particular gimmick was to draw fantastically elaborate machines to do simple tasks. His name is now commonly used as a term to describe any outlandish contraption or scheme. Invent your own "Rube Goldberg." Then describe its appearance, operation, and purpose as clearly and imaginatively as you can.

PROCESS AND ANALYSIS

1. Choose a subject about which you have some knowledge, such as auto mechanics, music, sailing, football, baseball, tennis, photography, or nuclear physics. Write an essay explaining a process, technique, or principle to a reader who is presumably unfamiliar with the subject. You may have to use specialized terms, but try to tell about something you do without letting those terms confuse the reader.

2. Tell how something (an airplane, an organization, or a game) functions. Pay attention to the structural principles.

3. Tell how a natural phenomenon (lightning, earthquake, rainbow, or snow) occurs.

4. Pick a comic strip; read back issues covering several weeks. Write an analysis of the values represented by the major character or characters in this strip.

5. We are fond of thinking in dichotomies, either consciously or subconsciously: liberals and conservatives, the good and the bad, those who work and suffer and those who think life is made for pleasure. Find a dichotomy that you essentially adhere to, and analyze the difference between the two categories as fully as you can.

6. Analyze the logic of statements like the following or any other that you consider equally outrageous: (*a*) Dropping out is simply a way for some students to indulge their own laziness. (*b*) Long hair is the first clue to subversive activity. (*c*) If students are happy, then the college standards must be too lax.

DEFINITION

1. Francis Bacon said that writing makes an "exact man." Fill in the blank in the following statement: "Television makes a [an] _____ person." Then define what you mean, and defend the choice of the word you chose.

2. Much has been written in recent years about the so-called sexual revolution. What does that term mean to you? In your opinion, has such a revolution really taken place? Cite specific evidence from books, articles, or surveys to support your opinion.

3. A favorite modern term is *complexity*: "the complexity of the modern world" or "the complexity of man." Define what *complexity* means by writing an essay about something that at one time seemed simple to you but turned out to be complex. Explain the significance of the more complex view that you eventually reached.

ARGUMENTATION AND PERSUASION

1. For years there has been an almost continuous argument between those who oppose abortion and those who defend it. Determine on what grounds each side bases its argument. Then demonstrate why the two views either can or cannot be compromised. Is there a possibility that the argument will ever be resolved?

2. During the 1970s, there was a good deal of discussion about academic freedom. Suggest what the limits on academic freedom should be, if any. For instance, should a professor be allowed to teach a philosophy that either explicitly or implicitly advocates the subversion of the national government? If you think there should be no restraints, indicate why. Use specific examples.

3. A father thought that his refusal to eat anything he didn't eat in his mother's house was a sign of character and a well-developed point of view. His daughter considered it a narrow and unreasonable prejudice. Yet she held views that the father called prejudices. Write about a view you hold or someone else holds that might be considered reasonable in some ways and unreasonable in others. Attempt to present both sides.

4. Argue for or against the current trend toward childless marriages.

5. A good fantasy often begins with an unlikely hypothesis: that men can read women's minds or that flowers grow and reproduce but never die. Formulate an hypothesis of your own, and then develop its consequences as logically and realistically as you can.

6. Defend the virtues or value of a film you consider worth defending but whose merit has been questioned by many people or by critics. Convince a reader that it is worth money and two hours to see the picture.

7. Politics in the United States has long been dominated by two major parties, even though many people may find neither party congenial to their political and social beliefs. Discuss whether this two-party system still effectively provides choices to the public with regard to laws that influence them as individuals. In brief, how alike are the major parties?

EXPRESSIVE WRITING

1. Convey your feelings about a particular song, poem, person, flower, or color.

2. Convey a mood: melancholy, release, elation, depression, loneliness.

3. Choose a word or phrase (like *American, youth, old people*) and respond to it.

4. Choose a favorite word, one that has special personal significance to you. Try to convey what that "specialness" is.

5. Attempt to convey the sensation of a daydream, a nightmare, a rapturous experience.

Chapter 5 *Paragraphing*

Paragraphing is a way of dividing continuous discourse into convenient segments to make it meaningful and readable. A paragraph cannot be defined as a grammatical unit in the same way a sentence can because it varies in size and shape as its function varies. Emphasis therefore should be placed on what a paragraph *does,* not what a paragraph *is.* Basically a paragraph is what you make it, subject to practices and standards that have become common in writing. This chapter will try to illustrate what those expectations are.

Paragraphing practices vary greatly. Some writers paragraph solely on the basis of content. To them, the paragraph highlights the logical development, each division expanding on one point in some depth. Other writers operate on wholly different premises. Some of their paragraphs are logical units, but others are rhetorical, separated from one another for purposes of emphasis and variety. Rhetorical paragraphing, for the most part, uses the visual effect of short paragraphs to do in writing what a speaker can do by intonation and gesture. A student, asked to write about her notion of a modern-day Utopia, begins in this way:

Temperamentally unsuited for safety and security, restless in stable circumstances—in short, as a human being preferring a roller coaster's careening and lurching to the merry-go-round's even circling—I am perhaps unfit to design a Utopia pleasing to most people.

But what would I wish if what I wish were possible?

I would like men and women to be free.

Free, not from the necessity of working, but from any need to work in any way at any task whose purpose is lost in the doing of it.

I do not mean that every person's work would be a means of feeding mind and body, or that everyone who did not work in this way would hurry home to read *Saturday Review*—there are more important things—but that no work of any man or woman would repudiate their human dignity by leaving their lives in the end cheap as a beast's, and that no one—whether because of extreme poverty or extreme greed—would be so caught up in the grind of getting and spending that he would lay waste his powers of joy and love and openness to beauty.

This particular essay continues with two more paragraphs of approximately a hundred words each, so that the short paragraphs—the question, the answer, and the elaboration in paragraphs 4 and 5—are not typical of a writer who does not know what she is doing. They can be taken as wholly intentional. In fact, they focus on the key ideas and provide a rhythmic contrast to customary even-flowing paragraphs of one or two hundred words each. Perhaps, in the writer's own words, these short paragraphs represent "careening and lurching," which she prefers to the "even circling" of longer ones.

Therefore, one standard of measurement cannot be applied to all paragraphs. They may be visual devices, as newspapers use them; they may be logical divisions, as we most commonly think of them; and they may also be rhetorical units, as individual writers use them for special effects. In all of these uses, however, the paragraph represents a relatively short unit of varying length that divides discourse for purposes of readability and better understanding.

Levels of generality

The shaping of a paragraph may be best understood in terms of an ebb and flow of sentences between the general and the particular. If the relation between a reader and writer were completely intimate, so that they shared the same knowledge and the same background, generalities could be written without support. But even when a writer and reader share the same knowledge and experience, detail is still necessary as a means of making perfectly clear what the writer has in mind.

Buckminster Fuller begins a paragraph with the following sentence, actually two sentences that support one another: "Vision is an unlimited universal language; speech is local and limited." He could have stopped at this point, and there would have been a good bit of implicit understanding, especially if you supplied your own example. But because he is an experienced writer, Buckminster Fuller does not take things for granted. He follows the general statement with a further elaboration and then an example.

Though we have no sound name for an object, we can see and understand much of its behavioral pattern. To a person speaking only French, a horse race in Japan looks just like a horse race in France or in any other country.

The final sentence of this paragraph restates the first sentence in more particular terms: "You don't need to know the language; the horses are numbered."

Thus, the paragraph begins on a general level, moves to particulars, and concludes with a statement reinforcing the generalization at the beginning. Both the generalizations and particulars are necessary for a fully developed statement. Particulars are the writer's way of earning the right to make generalizations. Generalizations, in turn, interpret and show the significance of particulars.

All paragraphs, of course, do not move on a simple two-level alternation of general and particular. Whenever any statement needs further elaboration, a paragraph may move to further particulars. The alternating movement from general to particular and back again may be shown by a kind of rhetorical diagram that records the changes. Indentation to the right indicates a more particular statement than the previous one; movement to the left, a more general statement. Sentences diagrammed on the same level are coordinate, suggesting that a sentence may expand or elaborate on or restrict a preceding sentence at approximately the same level of generality. Sentences at the same level are often signaled by balanced phrasing such as "On the one hand . . . On the contrary" or "For most of history . . . In recent times," or by similarity of phrasing as in these three sentences by James Thurber: "He learned to say funny things. He learned to smoke and blow smoke rings. He learned to earn money."

The following diagram of a paragraph by Bertrand Russell shows the movement of his sentences:

Generalization Of the two [Gladstone and Lenin], I should say that Gladstone was the more unforgettable as a personality.

Extension of sentence 1 I take as the test what one would have thought of each if one had met him on a train without knowing who he was.

Detail about Gladstone In such circumstances Gladstone, I am convinced, would have struck me as one of the most remarkable men I had ever met, and would have soon reduced me to a speechless semblance of agreement.

Detail about Lenin Lenin, on the contrary, might, I think, have seemed to me at once a narrow-minded fanatic and a cheap cynic.

A comment on his own judgment I do not say that this judgment would have been just; it would have been unjust, not positively, but by what it would have omitted.

Return to details about Lenin When I met Lenin, I had much less impression of a great man than I had expected; my most vivid impressions were of bigotry and Mongolian cruelty.

Examples of cruelty When I put a question to him about socialism in agriculture, he explained with glee how he had incited the poorer peasants against the richer ones, "and they soon hanged them from the nearest tree—ha! ha! ha!"

A comment on the laugh His guffaw at the thought of those massacred made my blood run cold.

"Eminent Men I Have Known"

This paragraph begins with a generalization that sets up a comparison. Because it is the point Russell wishes to establish, it can be identified as the *topic sentence* of the paragraph. A topic sentence is usually a brief general statement of the main point being discussed. But equally necessary in a paragraph are support and illustration.

The topic sentence may also be thought of as the top sentence, the thought representing the highest level of generality within a particular paragraph. Every paragraph does not necessarily have a topic sentence because, as we will see, several paragraphs sometimes operate as a single unit and one sentence serves all of them.

Topic sentences characteristically appear in first position as in the Russell paragraph. In the following one, however, Buckminster Fuller begins with details:

In 1961, we have Gagarin, the first human safely orbited in space and returned to earth. *Detail 1*

In 1966 we have the first successfully controlled soft landing on the moon photographi- *Detail 2*
cally radio viewed on earth.

When I was young, the most hopeless category of humans were lunatics. *Detail 3*

People who had gone so far off their heads that they had "touched the moon" *Particular explanation,*
(*luna*–moon; *tic*–touch). *phrased as a fragment*

In 1969 we have the first real lunatics, humans touching the moon. *Contrast to Detail 3*

The meaning of the word, like all other opinions and beliefs, had become completely re- *Topic sentence and top*
versed. *level of generality*

"Cutting the Metabilical Cord"

A topic sentence therefore may come first, last, or possibly in the middle. Placing it is seldom a conscious decision. Its position reflects our thinking and approach. The fact that it often occurs first perhaps indicates that we most characteristically think first of the general and then move to particulars. Other ways are more conscious and deliberate strategies.

Developing paragraphs: a dozen suggestions

What are your resources for developing paragraphs? How do you add support? What form do various details take? In answer, here are twelve ways:

1. You can qualify, elaborate, or restate in different words:

This is the function of the clock. It will not retreat one second in all the millennia to come. *Lead-in sentence*
It will cut you down, replace your future with a past, and put you under the sod. At the age *Elaboration*
of sixty, you will have spent twenty years sleeping, twenty more growing up, and twenty *Topic sentence*
trying to leave your mark on our cave.

Jim Bishop, "Time Is the Only True Enemy"

2. You can define and give examples:

Jewish jokes are not funny. They are not even jokes, but potted observations about *Topic sentence*
Jewishness given anecdotal form and a punch line. The response is laughter, though not the
sort of laughter that greets the regular (usually obscene) male-company story; it is ambiguous, *Definition*
it conceals, or fails to conceal, a ruefulness, a reflectiveness, a sense of resignation. How true

Example that is, we are meant to feel, how wry, how inescapable, how Jewish. Cohen at the travel agency rejects ex-pro-Nazi Italy and Spain, not to speak of Germany and Austria, for his vacation trip; the busy clerk leaves him thoughtfully spinning a globe; when the clerk returns, *Restatement of topic* Cohen says, "Maybe you got another globe?" That is the basic Jewish joke; hardly a joke at *sentence* all.

Kingsley Amis, "Waxing Wroth"

3. You can classify:

Lead-in sentence There are roughly three New Yorks. There is, first, the New York of the man or woman who was born here, who takes the city for granted and accepts its size and its turbulence as *Classifications* natural and inevitable. Second, there is the New York of the commuter—the city that is devoured by locusts each day and spat out each night. Third, there is the New York of the person who was born somewhere else and came to New York in quest of something. Of these *Topic sentences* three trembling cities the greatest is the last—the city of final destination, the city that is a goal. It is this third city that accounts for New York's high-strung disposition, its poetical deportment, its dedication to the arts, and its incomparable achievements. Commuters give the city its tidal restlessness, natives give it solidity and continuity, but the settlers give it *Examples* passion. And whether it is a farmer arriving from Italy to set up a small grocery store in a slum, or a young girl arriving from a small town in Mississippi to escape the indignity of being observed by her neighbors, or a boy arriving from the Corn Belt with a manuscript in his *Restatement of major* suitcase and a pain in his heart, it makes no difference: each embraces New York with the *premise* intense excitement of first love, each absorbs New York with the fresh eyes of an adventurer, each generates heat and light to dwarf the Consolidated Edison Company.

E. B. White, "Here Is New York"

4. You can summarize and analyze:

Summary MacArthur had spent part of his youth after the Spanish-American War in the Philippines where his father, the military governor, was almost a feudal lord. Young Douglas was later to return to Manila as a Philippine field marshal. As U.S. Far East Commander during WW II *Topic sentence* he fought brilliantly. But one felt that he was fighting "his" war as much as that of his country. (He got away with openly defying the Joint Chiefs and retook the central and southern Philippines, his beloved islands.) As the SCAP [Supreme Commander for the Allied *Summary and analysis* Powers] during the occupation of Japan, he ruled benevolently, with incomparable finesse and intelligence. But again, it was almost as if the occupation of Japan were "his" rather than his country's. MacArthur spent 14 consecutive years in the Far East, and every year it seemed as if the gravitational pull of Washington grew weaker and weaker, until the government appeared to be nothing more than a distant annoyance. MacArthur treated Washington as if it were a glorified supply depot from which he might requisition men and material.

Orville Schell, Review of *American Caesar* by William Manchester

5. You can present arguments:

Lead-in sentence One hears a great deal about the coming decline of the hardcover book, particularly from *Topic sentence* the young. The point of a hardcover book is the durability of its paper and binding, and therefore of its contents. The performing arts, even when captured on film or tape, are a part of our culture that cannot effectively be passed from generation to generation. A 1930s movie today is seen out of context. Technological developments make films of just a decade or two ago different in a way that a book of a previous period is not. The performances of Shakespeare's plays can be described for us—interpretations vary greatly from period to period— but only the texts, passed down in book form, can remain the same. Reading about the performing arts of the past is like reading about sex; it is not the same as the experience. Hence the only precise way that culture is transmitted from generation to generation is in the durable book.

Comparative arguments

Conclusion and restatement of topic sentence

Sol Stein, "The Future of the Arts"

6. You can refute arguments:

There is no escape, it seems to me, from the conclusion that the vice presidency is not only a meaningless but a hopeless office. Truman said, and many have repeated, that "there is no officer in our system of government besides the President and Vice President who has been elected by all the voters of the country," as if this somehow sanctified the vice presidency. Truman's proposition, advanced nine weeks after Roosevelt's death, was natural enough to a man interested in legitimating his own recent succession to the presidency. But it is an amiable myth. No one votes for a Vice President. He is a tie-in sale, an inseparable part of a package, "a sort of appendage to the Presidency" (Truman's own phrase), not an independent choice. And, once carried to the vice presidency as second rider on the presidential horse, where is he? If he is a first-rate man, his abilities will be wasted, turn sour, and deteriorate. If he is not first-rate, he should not be in a position to inherit the presidency. Why not therefore abolish the vice presidency and work out a more sensible mode of succession?

Basic premise

Evidence to the contrary

Refutation

Conclusion

Arthur Schlesinger, Jr., "Is the Vice Presidency Necessary?"

7. You can present facts:

The Mexican has made an important place for himself in the railroads of the country. Thousands are employed by the Atchison, Topeka & Santa Fe Railroad on all its lines, and other thousands on the Rock Island. From information available we estimate nearly ten thousand Mexicans on these two systems alone. The Denver & Rio Grande Western Railroad reports three thousand; the Great Northern Railroad from five hundred to one thousand (varying with the season); the Southern Pacific Lines, 4,276 in Texas and Louisiana alone; the Northern Pacific several hundred and the Pennsylvania Lines 1,290 regular Mexican employees and several hundred additional seasonal workers.

Topic sentence

Supporting facts

Jay S. Stowell, "The Danger of Unrestricted Immigration"

8. You can compare and contrast:

The standard of American skiing is amazingly high. I find the average skill of American skiers higher than that of Europeans, even though skiing in the United States has been popular for a relatively short time. It must have something to do with the fact that Americans, when they start something new, want to do it well and therefore work hard at it. Europeans are inclined to take skiing more as a relaxation and fun than as a sport. They are content with being just proficient enough to enjoy it.

Topic sentence

Comparison

Contrast

Henry Brandon, "Nixon Starts Down the Run"

9. You can describe:

DESCRIBING A PLACE

Overview   Before me the creek is seventeen feet wide, splashing over random sandstone outcroppings and scattered rocks. I'm lucky; the creek is loud here, because of the rocks, and wild. In the low water of summer and fall I can cross to the opposite bank by leaping from stone to stone. Upstream is a wall of light split into planks by smooth sandstone ledges that cross the creek *Specific focus* evenly, like steps. Downstream the live water before me stills, dies suddenly as if extinguished, and vanishes around a bend shaded summer and winter by overarching tulips, *Overview* locusts, and Osage orange. Everywhere I look are creekside trees whose ascending boles against water and grass accent the vertical thrust of the land in this spot. The creek rests the eye, a haven, a breast; the two steep banks vault from the creek like wings. Not even the sycamore's crown can peek over the land in any direction.

Annie Dillard, Pilgrim at Tinker Creek

DESCRIBING EVENTS

Lead-in question   How can you explain to someone who was not there what it was like to live during the ghastly months just before Franklin D. Roosevelt took office for the first time? So many millions were *Detailed description* out of work, some of them actually starving, that one American family in two was directly affected. Trade was as close to a complete standstill as trade can get, the United States as near economic collapse as a growing young country can become without actually being in physical revolution. With the economic and social motors groaning toward a breakdown, with banks closing in every state, and money gradually becoming a scarce and fearsome thing, with panic everywhere and hunger stalking the cities as Iowa farmers dumped their milk because there *Conclusion and topic* was no market for it at any price, the early days of 1933 were undeniably among the most *sentence* difficult any American has ever lived through, an unforgettable moment of personal and national agony.

Richard L. Tobin, "A Year to Remember"

DESCRIBING A PERSON: MARIAN McPARTLAND

General observation   I see she is not one of those players who float dreamily over the keyboard with no apparent effort, or sit back and just jolly the piano along. Her hands are not particularly large, but they *Details* are strong, and when she plays it looks like concentrated *thought!* She "thinks" bent slightly forward over the keys, with a small smile, head cocked to facilitate the dialogue between ear and fingers, and the resultant music is, like her, a lovely mix of introspection and style.

Annie Gottlieb, "Marian McPartland—Everything a Jazz Musician Is Not Supposed to Be"

10. You can narrate:

Details,   Half an hour after swallowing the drug I became aware of a slow dance of golden lights. A *chronologically* little later there were sumptuous red surfaces swelling and expanding from bright nodes of *arranged* energy that vibrated with a continuously changing, patterned life. At another time the closing of my eyes revealed a complex of gray structures, within which pale bluish spheres kept emerging into intense solidity and, having emerged, would slide noiselessly upwards, out of *Details not present* sight. But at no time were there faces or forms of men or animals. I saw no landscapes, no enormous spaces, no magical growth and metamorphosis of buildings, nothing remotely like a drama or a parable. The other world to which mescalin admitted me was not the world of *Summary* visions; it existed out there, in what I could see with my eyes open. The great change was in the realm of objective fact. What had happened to my subjective universe was relatively *Topic sentence* unimportant.

Aldous Huxley, "The Doors of Perception"

11. You can use an allusion and quote relevant material:

When Don Quixote interrupts Sancho Panza, complaining that a tale he is telling is too full *Allusion with relevant* of repetitions and diversions, the redoubtable Sancho defends his method simply. "The way *quotation* I'm telling it," he says, "is the way all stories are told in my country. It isn't fair for your *Application of the* worship to ask me to get new habits." With as little fuss Jean Stafford has clung tenaciously *anecdote and topic* for twenty-five years to her established short story strategies. It is as if, having long ago found *sentence* her special country and habits, she too sees no use for newness. *Elaboration*

Robert Maurer, "The Deceptive Facade"

12. You can develop an analogy or figure of speech:

I have an image of my own death which is probably unique. It stems in part from the *Lead-in sentence* phrase "when we have shuffled off this mortal coil," and in part from the fact that I can do a shuffle-off-to-Buffalo, however clumsily. Years ago, I showed a French friend my shuffle-off-to-Buffalo, and, thanks to her misunderstanding of the term "shuffle off to Buffalo" and my own unusual dancing style, she thought I was doing a creditable imitation of a water *Development of the* buffalo. *analogy*

Anyway, "when we have shuffled off this mortal coil" brings to my mind the image of a man—myself—doing a shuffle-off-to-Buffalo exit to the great Unknown. Step, tap-tap hop; step, tap-tap hop. Since I can do the tap-tap hop only with my right foot, I always travel to my left when I shuffle off to Buffalo. So my personal image of my own dying is "Exit, stage *Topic sentence* left, shuffling off to Buffalo."

Thomas H. Middleton, "Shuffle Off to Valhalla"

A few of these techniques, like 11 and 12, are fairly sophisticated ones, but the others are quite spontaneous ways of expanding a topic that you use in both speaking and writing.

Paragraph patterns

The arrangement of sentences within a paragraph normally follows a limited number of patterns:

1. From general to particular
2. From particular to general
3. Alternating order
4. Time order
5. Space order
6. Climactic order

1. From general to particular

Paragraphs of this order characteristically begin with a topic sentence and proceed to give support of some kind:

Lead-in generalization

The drugstore was a horse of a different color (and odor), but it was circumscribed by equally strict rules. Often, in the thirties, it boasted one of the few neon signs seen on Main Street, usually a blazing vermilion vertical down the side of the building, spelling our "Nyal" or "Rexall" and sometimes the pharmacist's name as well. The window displays, as opposed to the workaday pumps and pipe fittings of the hardware store's unchanging (and fly-specked) windows, were quasi works of art. Loose swags and taut diagonals of pleated crêpe paper in jungle hues formed a nest for the product of the month, often a patent medicine or a new tooth powder; over the crêpe and cardboard burned the store's invariable trademark, a pair of glass urns filled with red and blue colored water and lighted from behind. Inside, the store, except in the poorest towns, was rather splendid: after you recovered, reeling slightly, from the rich, mingled fumes of iodoform, chocolate soda syrup, and the essence of a thousand biologicals, you strode across the marble floor to the marble soda fountain (for a malt or phosphate) or to the pharmacist's counter at the back, behind which were ranged multiple rows of functional apothecary jars. Here you would ask the white-coated (and often rimless-spectacled) druggist for aspirin or Four-Way Cold Tablets or Bromo-Seltzer, or perhaps for paramedical advice, which he was glad to give. (When "a lady" fainted "right on the street" in those days, she was carried directly to the drugstore and ministered to by the druggist, who was often known as "Doc.")

Details about outside appearance

Details about inside appearance

L. E. Sissman, "Int'l Jet Set Hits Watkins Glen"

2. From particular to general

Paragraphs of this order characteristically begin with details of some kind—possibly narrative, descriptive, or expository—and proceed to offer some general statement at the end.

Three particular theories

Galileo said that the earth moves and that the sun is fixed; the Inquisition said that the earth is fixed and the sun moves; and Newtonian astronomers, adopting an absolute theory of space, said that both the sun and the earth move. But now we say that any one of these three statements is equally true, provided that you have fixed your sense of "rest" and "motion" in the way required by the statement adopted. At the date of Galileo's controversy with the Inquisition, Galileo's way of stating the facts was, beyond question, the fruitful procedure for the sake of scientific research. But in itself it was not more true than the formulation of the Inquisition. But at that time the modern concepts of relative motion were in nobody's mind, so that the statements were made in ignorance of the qualifications required for their more perfect truth. Yet this question of the motions of the earth and the sun expresses a real fact in the universe, and all sides had got hold of important truths concerning it. But, with the knowledge of those times the truths appeared to be inconsistent.

Elaboration

General observation

Alfred North Whitehead, "Religion and Science"

Since paragraphs of this kind often begin with the familiar and proceed to the unfamiliar, they reflect our natural way of learning. We explore known facts in order to arrive at new hypotheses; we proceed from particular details to theoretical principles; we put pieces together to reconstruct a whole. We also narrate and describe in these terms, first giving details which suggest some observation to be made later:

Springtime, about to ripen into sultry summer in Charleston, was breathing its first in the North Carolina mountains. White dogwood blossoms blanketed the slopes, and azaleas were blushing into bloom. Maple, hickory, birch, and oak trees, not yet come to full leaf, spread a filmy green shadow across the land. On the drive from the airport to Asheville, I opened the window of the Austin-Healy and pushed my face into the cool gush of air, breathing it in like a transfusion. I ask: Is there a sweeter affirmation of life than a cruise through the highlands in a sports car on a shining spring day? *Descriptive details* *Observation*

David Butwin, "A Climate Fit for Weathermen"

3. Alternating order

Alternating order is the natural movement of comparison and contrast or of pro and con discussion. The shifts may be frequent—back and forth from A to B, A to B, A to B—or the details may be presented in simple complementary order—A, then B. The following paragraph follows the simple A and B pattern:

The protagonists in the stories are generally poor, but well educated, having seen better days. They are patient and deserving, people of family, who have nice but run-down old houses with a few good antiques. They are ladies and gentlemen in every sense. Crooks are easily identifiable, because they are vulgar, bad-tempered, and have an unfortunate tendency to raise their voices to people. They have red or coarse, bushy black hair, and nicknames like "Spike," "Red," "Snorky," or "Flip," They further identify themselves by their regrettable preference for checkered suits, yellow overcoats, elevator shoes, and (for the oilier, better-educated crook) striped pants, spats, and goatees. Criminals always have a physical oddity: a long nose, or a missing middle finger. *Part A* *Part B*

Arthur Prager, "The Secret of Nancy Drew—Pushing Forty and Going Strong"

The paragraph falls into two parts: details about the protagonists; then, by contrast, details about crooks.

In a more involved comparison, an anonymous writer in *Time* compares two football players, alternating from one to the other in terms of various topics:

It was perhaps inevitable in the Age of Aquarius that two young men born in the first week of February would ultimately battle for the same prize. But when Quarterbacks Roger Staubach of the Dallas Cowboys and Bob Griese of the Miami Dolphins meet in the Super Bowl for the National Football League championship this week, they will have more in common than their Aquarian fixity of purpose. *Lead-in statement*

Staubach was raised in the Midwest. So was Griese. Staubach was a class president and star baseball, basketball and football player in high school. So was Griese. Staubach was turned down by Notre Dame, the college he passionately wanted to attend. So was Griese. Staubach was named a college All-American in his junior year. So was Griese. Staubach is a Roman Catholic, is married to a former nurse, sells real estate, has blue eyes, short-trimmed hair and is modest and reserved. Ditto for Griese on all counts. Staubach is the leading passer in the National Football Conference. Now, on the eve of the sixth annual Super Bowl, the two best young quarterbacks in professional football are preparing to establish a crucial difference in their parallel careers: the difference between winner and loser. *Alternating details about each* *Topic sentence*

"Bullet Bob v. Roger the Dodger"

4. *Time order*   Time order is most closely associated with narrative, but any collection of material—for example, a body of information about submarine plant life—may be presented in the order that the findings were made. Any material, of course, can be simply enumerated as if the details were being given in a list from first to last:

Topic sentence

Support arranged in time order   Our life in the sanatorium was like that of hogs, nothing but eating and sleeping. At seven a bell rang for breakfast. We had to bathe at eight and at nine we had to go back to sleep until eleven, which was lunchtime. From twelve to three we had to sleep again. From three to four, which was dinner time, we were allowed to be awake, and after eating we had to sleep once more. They didn't allow us to walk around much, and an asthmatic like me needs to walk.

Oscar Lewis, "One Can Suffer Anywhere"

This paragraph is actually a description of sanatorium life ordered in terms of the events of a typical day.

The second example is not a description of actual events like the first one but a hypothetical reconstruction of the career of a developing novelist from his twenties to his forties. The writer divides the time sequence into two paragraphs. The first paragraph states the thesis and treats the early career:

Topic sentence

The writer in his twenties   Over the last fifty years in America, we've developed a bad habit of trying our young writers by fire and ice. In the beginning is the fire. A first novelist in his early twenties, filled with a delicate balance between confidence and insecurity—a balance that should be labeled DO NOT DISTURB—is suddenly thrust into the limelight, lionized, publicized, enriched, and adulated to gratify the machinery of publishing. If his head isn't turned, if the humble doggedness that took him successfully through his first novel isn't dissipated, if he isn't marginally corrupted by his first taste of love and money, then he must be an unusually strong

Second stage of early career   and wise young man. And after the fire, comes, in too many cases, the beginning of the ice: the sophomore jinx of a second novel, with mild reviews or bad reviews or no reviews at all.

L. E. Sissman, "John Updike: Midpoint and After"

In a long second paragraph, Sissman continues to trace the career of the novelist into his thirties and forties. At the end of these two introductory paragraphs, chronologically arranged, he then turns to John Updike as a particular case in point.

5. *Space order*   Space order is most closely associated with description:

It is a "round" village, with the houses lining the edges of the perimeter lanes, but with shops, church, pub, school, chapel, spread along a central road following the bank of a creek officially known as the Potsford River but called locally the "Black Ditch." The center of the village remains self-contained and quiet in spite of farm machines, motor-bikes, and the dull murmur of summer holiday traffic. Jets from the American base at Bentwaters occasionally ordain an immense sound and the place seems riven, splintered—yet it resumes its wholeness the second the plane vanishes. Nobody looks up . . .

Ronald Blythe, "England's Cruel Earth"

This particular description is conceived in terms of a circle and its center. At first, the perspective looks downward, then shifts upward to the jets in the sky.

A second example makes us particularly aware of a road as the point from which a couple walking along look about them to see one thing, then another. The writer seems keenly aware of other linear forms: the "streaks of yellow wild flowers in the fields" and the rows of growing cabbages. The writer covers space much in the same manner that a movie camera would view it:

Shoshone and I walked back to the main road that cuts across the 320-acre ranch. The sun had burned through the fog, highlighting streaks of yellow wild flowers in the fields. Black Angus cows were grazing by the road. People in hillbilly clothes, with funny hats and sashes, were coming out of the bushes carrying musical instruments and sacks of rice and beans. About a mile from the front gate we came to the community garden, with a scarecrow made of rusty metal in the shape of a nude girl. Two children were chasing each other from row to row, shrieking with laughter, as their mother picked cabbage. A sign read, "Permit not required to settle here."

Sara Davidson, "Open Land"

In addition to scenic description, space order may also be used as the basis for arranging expository details. An essay on archeology, for example, might discuss findings in terms of their place of origin: discoveries at Corinth, discoveries at Athens, discoveries at Delos.

Climactic order implies both a rising to a climax and a falling away from it. It depends on an order of sentences from least important to most important, from the known to the unknown with a sense of suspense, from the lowest to the highest, or in any number of other ways that produce a cumulative effect. It therefore applies to any mode of writing, whether it is argument, narrative, description, or persuasion.

6. Climactic order

[Description of James Brudenell, later Lord Cardigan, commander of the famous Light Brigade, which made its charge at the Battle of Balaclava in 1854]

It was to be expected that his parents and sisters should be passionately attached to him, and natural affection and pride were immensely heightened by the circumstances of his extaordinary good looks. In him the Brudenell beauty had come to flower. He was tall, with wide shoulders tapering to a narrow waist, his hair was golden, his eyes flashing sapphire blue, his nose aristocratic, his bearing proud. If there was a fault it was that the lower part of his face was oddly long and narrow so that sometimes one was surprised to catch an obstinate, almost a foxy, look. But the boy had a dash and gallantry that were irresistible. He did not know what fear was. A superb and reckless horseman, he risked his neck on the most dangerous brutes. No tree was too tall for him to climb, no tower too high to scale. He excelled in swordsmanship and promised to be a first-class shot. He had in addition to courage another characteristic which impressed itself on all who met him. He was, alas, unusually stupid; in fact, as Greville pronounced later, an ass. The melancholy truth was that his glorious golden head had nothing in it.

Cumulative details

Climax

Anticlimax

Cecil Woodham-Smith, *The Reason Why*

The rising and falling motion of this paragraph is so sharply defined that the reader cannot fail to respond to its effect.

In the following example, Martin Luther King achieves a cumulative effect by piling one fact upon another, repeating the same words at the beginning of each of six sentences. The final sentence ends with a sense of drama:

All of this represents disappointment lifted to astronomical proportions. It is disappointment with timid white moderates who feel that they can set the time-table for the Negro's freedom. It is disappointment with a federal administration that seems to be more concerned about winning an ill-considered war in Vietnam than about winning the war against poverty here at home. It is disappointment with white legislators who pass laws in behalf of Negro rights that they never intended to implement. It is disappointment with the Christian church that appears to be more white than Christian, and with many white clergymen who prefer to remain silent behind the security of stained-glass windows. It is disappointment with some Negro clergymen who are more concerned about the size of the wheel base on their automobiles than about the quality of their service to the Negro community. It is disappointment with the Negro middle class that has sailed or struggled out of the muddy ponds into the relatively fresh-flowing waters of the mainstream, and in the process has forgotten the stench of the backwaters where their brothers are still drowning.

Martin Luther King, *Where Do We Go from Here: Chaos or Community?*

The test of a successful paragraph

Even though paragraphing is a highly flexible system, almost wholly controlled by the writer, the results are nevertheless more successful in some instances than in others. Because the paragraph is a conventional unit of discourse, certain expectations persist in the minds of readers. A successful paragraph, therefore, must ultimately meet these tests:

1. Is it functional? This question assumes that paragraphing aids the reader in various ways by making meaningful divisions in the development of the thought, by marking shifts of focus to new topics, by intentionally separating material for emphasis, by slowing or accelerating the pace of reading. An indifferent writer can defeat these purposes and actually confuse the reader by failing to paragraph when the sense of the content demands it. Most writers know that they discover paragraphs as they go along; they end them and indent just as naturally as they supply periods and capital letters to sentences. These writers treat paragraphing as if it were punctuation. They recognize it as a means of clarifying and interpreting subject matter in order to make their intentions precise.

2. Is it adequately developed? The development of a paragraph, of course, depends on its purpose. If a paragraph is transitional, it may be brief. In Chapter I of *The Decline and Fall of the Romantic Ideal*, F. L. Lucas pauses momentarily after eight pages of discussion to write:

What in fact is "Romanticism"? What, historically, has it been? What can or should it be?

In terms of its purpose, this paragraph is adequately developed because it poses three questions he intends to answer in the first three chapters of the book. His plan is laid out fully but briefly. The answers come later.

Adequate development means that a satisfactory paragraph is as long as it needs to be. If it provides a transition, it may be one sentence. If a writer wants to make a point and support it, however, the paragraph may be 200 words or more.

Yet it is possible to make judgments about inadequate paragraph development. Unless short paragraphing is used for rhetorical purposes, we tend to think that a paragraph is inadequately developed if the writer supplies too little evidence and leaves the reader unfulfilled; if it poses a question and gives no answer; or if it supplies a group of details without a conclusion. A sense of paragraph patterns helps you to know when you have reached an ending, at what point you can most effectively make a paragraph break.

3. Is it sufficiently varied in relation to other paragraphs?

Paragraphs set up a rhythmic effect in a composition just as variation of sentence length produces a stylistic effect within a paragraph. Many nineteenth-century prose writers are now difficult to read because we have become accustomed to more rapidly paced prose produced by shorter sentences and relatively shorter paragraphs. Prose reads rapidly or slowly in proportion to paragraph length. Narrative with frequent divisions for dialogue and separate actions reads quickly. Analysis with an intricate interweaving of sentences within lengthy paragraphs reads more slowly. Undoubtedly, the newspaper, with its typically brief paragraphs designed for rapid reading, has been a major influence on the faster pace of twentieth-century prose. The short snatches of journalistic prose, however, are as unsatisfactory for most expository writing as long, ponderous segments. A variation of paragraph lengths serves to keep the pace moving while still allowing the writer occasion to expand fully on the topics.

4. Is it unified?

The unity of a paragraph should not be thought to mean that it has only one idea. A paragraph contains many ideas, but taken together those ideas ought to have a singleness of purpose. They ought to hang together on one thread. That common thread is frequently expressed in the topic sentence, although the unifying theme may extend beyond a single paragraph. Unity, therefore, is a test of relevance. Do all of the sentences in a paragraph belong there? Has the writer allowed the thoughts to drift? Occasionally, a writer digresses, that is, wanders aimlessly from the topic. This can be done purposefully, however, to provide what the writer considers necessary background, but if done, it should be declared with a phrase like, "To digress momentarily to explain why. . . ." In this way, the writer shows that the digression is purposeful.

The unity of the parts in a paragraph can be judged only in terms of the purpose of the whole. In reading the following sentences, we are pushed to find a unifying theme:

Cooking is more prefabricated. Few clothes are sewn. Fire and heat are not made. Among poor people there used to be more sweated domestic industry, which didn't do the adults any good but taught something to small children.

Even though these particular sentences do not seem to relate to one another, each of them relates to the common thesis of a paragraph written by Paul Goodman in *Growing Up Absurd*:

Lead-in example   People use machines that they do not understand and cannot repair. For instance, the electric motors: one cannot imagine anything more beautiful and educative than such motors, yet there may be three or four in a house, cased and out of sight; and when they blow they are
Generalization and taken away to be repaired. Their influence is then retarding, for what the child sees is that
topic sentence competence does not exist in ordinary people, but in the system of interlocking specialties. This is unavailable to the child, it is too abstract. Children go shopping with Mama; but
Supporting details supermarket shopping for cellophane packages is less knowledgeable and bargainable than the older shopping, as well as providing tasteless Texas fruit and vegetables bred for nonperishability and appearance rather than for eating. Cooking is more prefabricated. Few clothes are sewn. Fire and heat are not made. Among poor people there used to be more sweated domestic industry, which didn't do the adults any good but taught something to small children. Now, on the contrary, the man and perhaps the woman of the house work in distant offices and factories, increasingly on parts and processes that don't mean anything to a child.
Restatement of topic A child might not even know what work his daddy does. Shop talk will be, almost invariably,
sentence in more griping about interpersonal relations. If the kid has less confidence that he can make or fix
specific terms anything, his parents can't either; and what they do work at is beyond his grasp.

With the total context available, we can see how the pieces fit together to form a whole. Submitting the paragraph to a rigid testing, we might question the relevance of the phrase "as well as providing tasteless Texas fruit and vegetables bred for nonperishability and appearance rather than for eating." It is not totally necessary, although it is clearly suggested by Goodman's total theme of the relations between youth and organized society.

Unity, therefore, depends on the writer's capacity to keep sentences under control. If they are allowed to take their own course, there is no telling where free association will lead them.

5. Is it coherent?   Unity and coherence are closely related. Whereas the first is a test of relevance, the second is a test of connectedness. Coherence is the way both the sentences in a paragraph and the paragraphs in an entire composition are interlocked. Anything within paragraphs or between paragraphs that links, draws together, or associates is a means of coherence. Some of these devices are more obvious than others.

The most obvious device of coherence is the use of transitional words and phrases, which indicate relationships and signal the direction in which the prose is moving. In the following paragraph, the connecting links are italicized:

I believe that the disestablishment of the school has become inevitable and that this end of an illusion should fill us with hope. *But* I also believe that the end of the "age of schooling" could usher in the epoch of the global schoolhouse that would be distinguishable only in name from a global madhouse or global prison in which education, correction, and adjustment become synonymous. I *therefore* believe that the breakdown of the school forces us to look beyond its imminent demise and to face fundamental alternatives in education. *Either* we can work for fearsome and potent new educational devices that teach about a world which progressively becomes more opaque and forbidding for man, *or* we can set the conditions for a new era in which technology would be used to make society more simple and transparent, so that all men can once again know the facts and use the tools that shape their lives. *In short*, we can disestablish schools or we can deschool culture.

Ivan Illich, "The Alternative to Schooling"

Even though Illich depends heavily on the formal device of transitional words, another factor is also working strongly to hold this paragraph together. In a tightly unified paragraph, we would normally expect a recurrence of certain words or equivalent terms. In this particular paragraph, there are two chains that can be linked together. One begins with "disestablishment," which is followed by words such as "end," "breakdown," "demise," and "deschool." The second is the one that includes all of the references to "school" and "education."

Some paragraphs may depend wholly on chains of words rather than conventional function words to hold them together. The following paragraph by Marshall McLuhan has only one formal phrase: "In a word" at the end introduces a brief summary. Otherwise, the paragraph hangs together on its thematic associations and chains of equivalent words. Two of these interlinking chains are indicated by the circled words:

A century ago the British craze for the monocle gave to the wearer the power of the camera to fix people in a superior stare, as if they were objects. Erich von Stroheim did a great job with the monocle in creating the haughty Prussian officer. Both monocle and camera tend to turn people into things, and the photograph extends and multiplies the human image to the proprtions of mass-produced merchandise. The movie stars and matinee idols are put in the public domain by photography. They become dreams that money can buy. They can be bought and hugged and thumbed more easily than public prostitutes. Mass-produced merchandise has always made some people uneasy in its prostitute aspect. Jean Genêt's *The Balcony* is a play on this theme of society as a brothel environed by violence and horror. The avid desire of mankind to prostitute itself stands up against the chaos of revolution. The brothel remains firm and permanent amidst the most furious changes. In a word, photography has inspired Genêt with the theme of the world since photography as a Brothel-without-Walls.

Understanding Media

Another analysis of the same paragraph indicates that other word connections are also operating. Of particular importance are pronouns that have their antecedents in previous sentences, words that refer to one another, and the repetition of particular words:

A century ago the British craze for the monocle gave to the (wearer) the power of the camera to fix people in a superior stare, as if they were objects. (Erich von Stroheim) did a great job with the monocle in creating the (haughty Prussian officer.) Both monocle and camera tend to turn people into things, and the photograph extends and multiplies the human image to the proportions of mass-produced merchandise. The (movie stars and matinee idols) are put in the public domain by photography. (They) become dreams that money can buy. (They) can be bought and hugged and thumbed more easily than public prostitutes. Mass-produced merchandise has always made some people uneasy in its prositute aspect. (Jean Genêt's) *The Balcony* is a play on this theme of society as a brothel environed by violence and horror. The avid desire of mankind to prostitute itself stands up against the chaos of revolution. The brothel remains firm and permanent amidst the most furious changes. In a word, photography has inspired (Genêt) with the theme of the world since photography as a Brothel-without-Walls.

Besides formal transitions and word associations, sentences and paragraphs are also linked to one another by rhetorical strategies: repetition, series, parallel structure, question and answer, and contrast. A variety of these is illustrated in a paragraph by Archibald MacLeish:

Two questions repeated for emphasis

Two sentences with parallel beginnings

Repetition for emphasis

Four sentences with common subject and parallel structure

Repetition for emphasis

But nevertheless the uneasiness remained and became more and more evident in our books, our painting, our music—even the new directions of our medical sciences. Who were *we* in this strange new world? What part did *we* play in it? Someone had written a new equation somewhere, pushed the doors of ignorance back a little, entered the darkened room of knowledge by one more step. Someone else had found a way to make use of that new knowledge, put it to work. Our lives had changed but without *our* changing them, without our intending them to change. Improvements had appeared and we had accepted them. We had bought Mr. Ford's machines by the hundreds of thousands. We had ordered radios by the millions and then installed TVs. And now we took to the air, flew from city to city, from continent to continent, from climate to climate, following summer up and down the earth like birds. We were new men in a new life in a new world . . . but a world *we* had not made—had not, at least, intended to make.

Archibald MacLeish, "The Great American Frustration"

The marginal notations identify the strategies that connect these sentences, but the same kinds of repetition and parallelism are also operating within sentences. The entire paragraph demonstrates an intensive use of repetition and parallelism as ways of tying thoughts together.

Coherence, therefore, cannot be reduced to the simple mechanical matter of inserting a few *therefores* and *yets* in the prose. These may help, but in the final analysis, the essential ties are those that grow out of the thought and structure of the composition.

Do you ordinarily know the number of paragraphs you will write in an essay before you begin? If you plan the topic well, you may have several major points in mind, but each could take two or three or even more paragraphs to develop fully. What you are likely to know in advance is that the essay will have several parts, each developing a major topic. A unit consisting of several related paragraphs traditionally has had no name. You can think of it as a *paragraph bloc.*

The paragraph bloc is a unit of discourse that has not been given adequate recognition or study until recently. Its meaning is closely related to the political use of the word *bloc.* In politics, a bloc is a group of people who work together for some common cause. In writing, a bloc is a group of paragraphs that work together to develop a major segment of thought. It is an important unit in terms of the logic of the essay as a whole. It closely resembles the major headings of an outline, for those sections do not necessarily correspond to the paragraphing of a paper but to the main points being discussed. The extent to which each is developed determines the number of paragraphs.

The paragraph bloc, therefore, cannot be defined arbitrarily in terms of length. In a short theme, it may consist of two paragraphs, or possibly the entire theme will be a single bloc of four or five paragraphs. In a book, a bloc may be eight or ten paragraphs or the equivalent of a numbered section within a chapter. It cannot be defined as a set pattern, but it can be clearly recognized. In Chapter II of *Patterns of Culture,* Ruth Benedict discusses the diversity of cultures. She begins with a narrative bloc of four paragraphs about a California Indian named Ramon, whose cultural values are quite different from those of most Californians. It is a story in itself. She then follows this with a bloc of three paragraphs developing the idea of selection as a prime factor in cultural life: each culture chooses to emphasize certain aspects of life and regard others lightly. Then extended illustrations follow. Fourteen paragraphs are given to a discussion of adolescence and adulthood. These represent one bloc. She signals a change to another topic by the opening sentence of a new bloc:

Warfare is another social theme that may or may not be used in any culture.

This new bloc on warfare consists of four additional paragraphs, each beginning in the following way:

There are even quainter notions, from our standpoint, associated with warfare in different parts of the world.

On the other hand, it may be just as impossible for a people to conceive of the possibility of a state of war.

I myself tried to talk of warfare to the Mission Indians of California, but it was impossible.

War is, we have been forced to admit even in the face of its huge place in our civilization, an asocial trait.

When the next paragraph begins with the words "Warfare is not an isolated case" and moves to the subject of mating and marriage, we know that the warfare bloc has been completed. Thus, each of the blocs throughout the chapter becomes an illustration of the cultural diversity indicated by the title of the chapter.

In an article in the *TWA Ambassador* entitled "A Harmonious Gathering," Paul Froiland writes about the annual International Convention of the Society for the Preservation and Encouragement of Barbership Quartet Singing in America. The article falls into three paragraph blocs. The first bloc describes the gathering of conventioneers in the lobby of the Leamington Hotel in Minneapolis. This is the setting or scene. It includes ten paragraphs. The next bloc, reproduced below, sets forth the criteria for selecting a winner of the competition. It includes six paragraphs. The final bloc, including eighteen paragraphs, tells about the winning quartet, four young men who call themselves Grandma's Boys.

The middle bloc treats a single theme: the way in which a winner is chosen. These six paragraphs are interwoven so that they represent a single unit. The whole bloc follows a TDA pattern. Four paragraphs are given to details of analysis. This paragraphing permits each point to be developed in considerable detail.

The quarterfinals begin on Thursday and run to completion and the selection of an international champion by Friday evening. Forty-eight quartets are in competition, winners, runners-up and, in some cases, third-place finishers in each of the society's sixteen districts. All of the groups are from the United States, with the exception of three from Canada. Each group sings a set of two songs, judged in four categories: sound, interpretation, stage presence and arrangement.

From the beginning it becomes instantly apparent that the woodshedders in the lobby are no accurate advertisement of the quality of current championship barbershop singing in this country. Within the limits of the form, the groups in the quarterfinals are schooled in nuance and finesse. The variation in quality between groups that had finished high in recent years and groups entering their first competition is so slight that an inferior placement might hinge on the slight mistiming of a hand clap or the improper shaping of a single vowel.

Dress varies from comical to nostalgic to baroque. One group shuffles onstage dressed as hobos, with a stereotyped belongings-wrapped-in-a-bandana-on-a-stick, battered shoes and hats with burst crowns. Other groups haul out the inevitable and retrograde spats and straw boaters. The majority of groups, however, wear dazzling tuxedos, or suits in lime, melon or cream, looking like groomsmen lately escaped from summer weddings.

A group's "act" is judged within the category of stage presence. Three types of acts predominate. The theme act combines dress, song choice and choreographed movements into a unified presentation—the hobos, for example. They at first appear to be mere farce, but perform with remarkable restraint, never breaking character, singing sad, desperate songs and finally plodding offstage at the end, too hopeless even to acknowledge the crowd's hearty applause.

A second type of act is the traditional barbershop presentation, feet rooted to the floor, gestures minimal and stylized, with the focus purely on the music and vocal interpretation. A majority of the groups opt for this old standard.

Finally, the comedians, distinguished from the first type in that the comedy isn't implied in dress or props, but in comedic interaction between quartet members. Typically, the burden of humor is carried by a barrel-chested bass, whose role in many cases lapses into buffoonery.

Another member of the group acts as the scold, wagging his finger at the bass's periodic irreverence.

The sentence following the bloc reads: "The winning quartet, as it turns out, is the master of all three types of act." This is a transitional sentence; it signals the beginning of a new bloc that discusses the winning group in extended detail.

Here we see that a paragraph functions as part of a larger segment, the paragraph bloc, just as blocs in turn combine to shape the entire essay. The individual paragraphs mark off the divisions of thought. They contribute to readability, and they give special emphasis to individual parts. In this way, they function logically, visually, and rhetorically. In the final analysis, paragraphing is the writer's way of orchestrating the prose, for the writer can divide and arrange the parts to achieve different effects. It is therefore not as important to determine what a paragraph *is* as it is to realize what a paragraph *does*.

Projects

1. Examine the paragraphing of an article on the front page of the newspaper. Then examine paragraphing in a short story or novel. Then, further, examine the paragraphing in an essay or book of nonfiction. What observations can you make? Do the operating principles seem to be different? If so, try to define them.

2. Examine the following paragraph by Peter Blake. Try to define the function of each sentence. What does each sentence do in relation to the one preceding it? Use your own terms, but ones like the following will work in many instances: introduces, restates, expands, defines, qualifies, supports, illustrates, refutes, contrasts, parallels, evaluates, summarizes.

> What the ground floors of cities need is not wide-open spaces, but tightly structured spaces full of shops, restaurants, theaters, markets, and all the rest. The one sure way to kill cities is to turn their ground floors into great, spacious expanses of nothing. Jane Jacobs was one of the first people to point this out, almost fifteen years ago, but cities are still being built of glassy towers on pilotis, with nothing at ground-floor level except windswept plazas and terrible sculpture and sometimes a fountain or a bank that closes at 3 P.M. Such diagrams for modern cities are sure death for their inhabitants—and that is not a rhetorical statement: Sixth Avenue, in New York, whose upper reaches consist almost entirely of glass towers on pilotis, with lots of empty space at ground level, is one of the most dangerous *modern* avenues in Manhattan. I know—I live around the corner from it. And before those pristine diagrams were constructed, the avenue was full of little shops and restaurants and bars and movie houses that stayed open most of the night—and nobody was stabbed. Now the place is an architectural gem, more or less—and a human disaster area.
>
> "The Folly of Modern Architecture"

3. Consider the following paragraph bloc written by Leonard Koppett. First, try to justify his paragraphing. Then consider other ways the sentences might be grouped.

It is the best of games, it is the worst of games, it is a game of cleverness, it is a game of foolishness, it makes one a believer, it arouses incredulity, it swirls in one second from the Spring of Hope to the Winter of Despair, it inspires the Spirit of Light, it stirs the Forces of Darkness, it has everything before it, it has nothing before it, it takes us directly to Heaven, it takes us directly to the other place—in short, its world is so much like the present world that it is peculiarly at home in the America of the second half of the twentieth century.

"It," of course, is basketball.

The essence of the game is deception. Deception is an important feature of all games, of course. Any tactic works better if it takes the opponent by surprise, and the surest way to create surprise is to make the opponent expect something other than what you actually do.

But in basketball, deception is more than the natural accompaniment of seeking competitive advantage. It is more than one of the means used to accomplish your goal. It is, in a very real sense, the goal itself.

The Essence of the Game Is Deception

4. The nature of a particular thought will usually determine the manner of development. Explain what possible modes of development each of the following thoughts invites:

A. She is a different person since she lost weight. [e.g., contrast]

B. He always reminded me of a penguin.

C. The essay sets forth four main ideas.

D. This is the way I usually go about the job.

E. No one could completely understand how I felt.

5. Rhetorical diagramming, illustrated on pp. 94 and 95, is a visual picture of what is going on in a paragraph. Select a paragraph from one of your previous themes and diagram it by this scheme. Does the diagram reveal that the paragraph is fully developed, or do you see in what way more particulars would fill out and support the general statements? Is there an orderly movement in the paragraph?

6. Examine one of your previous themes. Justify the paragraphing by writing in the margin a reason for each indention. In view of your study of this chapter, would you realign any of the paragraphing? If so, why?

7. Pick out the transitional words and phrases in the following paragraph by Kenneth Keniston. What other factors are operating to hold the paragraph together as a unit?

Drug use is no different from any other form of human behavior, in that a great variety of distinct motives can cooperate to produce it. The particular weight of each of these motives and the way they are combined differs in each individual. Furthermore, drug use is affected not only by motives and forces *within* the individual, but by what is happening *outside* of him in his interpersonal environment, and in the wider social and political world. Thus, any effort to delineate "types" of motivations that enter into drug use is bound to be an oversimplification. For example, there are many individuals who share common characteristics with drug users but who do not use drugs because drugs are not available on their particular campus. Similarly, there are individuals who have little in common with other drug users, but who nonetheless use drugs.

"Heads and Seekers"

Suggestions for writing

1. Describe two of the following in interesting detail. Adopt an attitude toward your subject; that is, treat it sympathetically or mockingly or humorously.

A. A man or woman in a supermarket.

B. A student taking an important examination.

C. A person in a restaurant confronted for the first time with eating an artichoke.

D. People at a religious ceremony.

E. A group of young people at a common meeting place (drive-in, beach, tavern).

2. Choose one of the following topic sentences to develop a paragraph of approximately 150–200 words:

A. All students cannot be lumped into one big category.

B. The movie and live theater are two quite different experiences.

C. People often wander around in a kind of daze; they don't see small but significant things happening around them.

D. A gym is a mass of bodies and noises and smells.

E. The purpose of a university [your own school] should be clarified.

3. Write three short anecdotes (possibly 75–100 words) that support or refute familiar proverbs and sayings like these:

A. A stitch in time saves nine.

B. An ounce of prevention is worth a pound of cure.

C. A bird in the hand is worth two in the bush.

D. Don't put all your eggs in one basket.

E. Every cloud has its silver lining.

F. All that glitters is not gold.

G. Pride goeth before a fall.

H. Love conquers all.

4. Choose an object you can see from where you are sitting. Write a paragraph describing that object as favorably as you can, concentrating perhaps on its beauty or its usefulness. Then present the same object negatively, detailing its defects or uselessness. In each instance, try to be convincing.

5. Narrate an event in an irritated tone. Then narrate the same event in a more positive tone (objective, sympathetic, enthusiastic).

6. Write a unified paragraph that uses the following pattern: I used to think . . . , but now . . .

7. Write a unified paragraph on one of the choices: I am like the color [number, animal, object] because . . . Invent your own beginning; avoid writing "I am like . . . because. . . ."

Chapter 6   *The Rhetoric of the Sentence*

The sentence is a means of dividing discourse into finite and separable parts. In speech, any group of words signaled by some kind of final juncture is a sentence. In writing, words beginning with capitals and ending with a terminal mark of punctuation are called sentences. But all units spoken or written as sentences are not grammatical sentences. *A grammatical sentence is a unit with a subject and a predicate that contains a finite verb.* Although a sentence with a subject and predicate is grammatically complete, the completeness of its thought may depend on sentences preceding or following it.

In grammatical terms, sentences are classified as simple, compound, and complex. The three, of course, may be combined in various ways:

1. Simple sentence A simple sentence is a complete grammatical unit that has one subject and one predicate, either or both of which may be compound. A simple sentence is an independent clause.

> The Emperor of Japan visited the United States.
>
> The President and the Secretary of State received the visitors.
>
> The Emperor and his wife attended ceremonial functions and created general good will.

A compound sentence is a combination of two or more independent clauses:

I could arrange to come late, or I could send a substitute.

The drive takes twenty minutes with no traffic, but we should allow at least forty minutes at the rush hour.

In typical fashion, a few members were strongly in favor of the motion, a few were violently opposed, but the majority seemed to be indifferent.

A complex sentence combines one independent clause and at least one dependent clause:

Even though the government took action, the measures were too few and too late.

The audience applauded enthusiastically when the new choral group sang a Bach cantata.

The terms that you stated are agreeable.

In rhetorical terms, sentences have been traditionally classified as *declarative*, stating facts; *interrogative*, asking questions; *imperative*, giving commands; and *exclamatory*, expressing feeling. The terms merely explain the effect of the sentences:

My notes are lost. [declarative]

Did you misplace my notes? [interrogative]

Look for the notes as soon as possible. [imperative]

What luck that we found the notes quickly! [exclamatory]

Sentence length 6A

The single most important principle of variety in prose style is writing long and short sentences—not long, short, long, short, but long and short as the purpose dictates and as your ear hears them rhythmically. There is no particular stylistic virtue in a long sentence per se, or a short sentence, or one of moderate length. There is virtue, however, in enough variety to avoid the ponderousness of too many long sentences, the choppiness of too many short ones, and the monotony of too many medium-length ones. Sentences need to be considered in context because they set up their own rhythms, sometimes accelerating the movement, sometimes slowing it. Many writers operate on an intuitive basis; others read their sentences aloud to themselves. Whatever you do, it is valuable to be aware how other writers vary sentence length.

The sharp contrast of long and short is one of the most effective ways of making a point. The short sentence is climactic; it is forceful.

The first and most evident of the conflicts is that between choosing, on the one hand, to publish whatever most easily interests the largest number of readers most quickly—that is to say, yellow journalism—and, on the other hand, to provide, even at a commercial loss, an adequate supply of what the public will in the longer run need to know. This is responsible journalism.

Walter Lippmann, "On the Importance of Being Free"

To do battle man must give only his life, but to love he must give his soul. Battle is easier.

Student sentence

The strength of these short sentences following longer ones grows out of the rhythmic contrast. The period following them speaks with strong finality. The point has been made.

In the following paragraph, John Updike describes a home run hit by Ted Williams on the day of his announced retirement at age forty-two. The number of words in each sentence is indicated by the superscripts:

Like a feather caught in a vortex, Williams ran around the square of bases at the center of our beseeching screaming.[21] He ran as he always ran out home runs—hurriedly, unsmiling, head down, as if our praise were a storm of rain to get out of.[26] He didn't tip his cap.[5] Though we thumped, wept, and chanted "We want Ted" for minutes after he hid in the dugout, he did not come back.[22] Our noise for some seconds passed beyond excitement into a kind of immense open anguish, a wailing, a cry to be saved.[22] But immortality is nontransferable.[4] The papers said that the other players, and even the umpires on the field, begged him to come out and acknowledge us in some way, but he declined.[28] Gods do not answer letters.[5]

"Hub Fans Bid Kid Adieu"

If we record the figures—21–26–5–22–22–4–28–5—we get some notion of the rhythmic contrast of long and short. The number of words in a sentence does not tell the whole story, however. It should be apparent that a sentence of monosyllables like "He didn't tip his cap" moves more rapidly than one like "But immortality is nontransferable." Or that a sentence with subordination or with parenthetical elements reads differently from one with none. Attention to such matters of rhythm, however, is one of the things that can improve your prose style.

6B   *Cumulative sentences*

A cumulative sentence is grammatically constructed so that the main thought is first stated and then added to by various phrases and clauses. It differs from the periodic sentence in that it might be terminated at any of several points beyond the basic pattern without altering the meaning. Detail is not worked into the basic sentence itself; it is usually added at the end.

The cumulative sentence is typically informal in its effect because the additions often suggest the kind of thoughts that develop when we speak but cannot go back to add. Or to express the matter another way: a painter has said that writing a cumulative sentence is the closest she has come to feeling with words the way she feels when she handles her brush, highlighting detail, shading, touching up. The cumulative sentence is typically a loosely structured sentence, but not a disorderly one. It demands no regularity of structure, although it often invites parallel phrasing. The following sentences show a variety of ways in which detail can be added—by means of participial phrases, prepositional phrases, absolute phrases, noun phrases, and clauses; and these do not exhaust the possibilities:

I used to park my car on a hill and sit silently observant, listening to the talk ringing out from neighbor to neighbor, seeing the inhabitants drowsing in their doorways, taking it all in with nostalgia—the sage smell on the wind, the sunlight without time, the village without destiny.

Loren Eiseley, The Immense Journey

We would sit round the long shiny table, made of some very pale-coloured, hard wood, with Sim goading, threatening, exhorting, sometimes joking, very occasionally praising, but always prodding, prodding away at one's mind to keep it up to the right pitch of concentration, as one might keep a sleepy person awake by sticking pins into him.

George Orwell, "Such, Such Were the Joys . . ."

All marriage is a sort of gambling, like blackjack or poker, with a slight finality to it, a decision about eternity and forevers, with irrevocable implications, and losing naturally a part of it.

Student sentence

He arrived on horseback, the reins loose, the stirrups tossing free.

Student sentence

Periodic sentences 6C

A periodic sentence is grammatically constructed so that the main thought is suspended until the end of the sentence. It therefore has a forward thrust. The reader must wait until the end for the meaning to emerge. It is a sentence that reserves its climax for the final position. It ends with a note of emphasis. The meaning of each of the following sentences would be completely altered by changing several words at the very end:

It comes as a great shock to discover that the country which is your birthplace and to which you owe your life and identity has not, in its whole system of reality, evolved any place for you.

James Baldwin, "The American Dream and the American Negro"

For, in all this passionate protest, there is virtually no intimation, even in the loud negatives, of what these young people are *for*.

Philip Wylie, "Generation of Zeroes"

Perhaps the greatest value of having roommates is that it provides what a professor of mine used to call a Cross Cultural Experience.

Joan Paulson, "Why Roommates Make the Best Wives"

When you considered liquor harmless and fashionable, the fact that it was illegal seemed laughable.

Richard Goldstein, "1 in 7: Drugs on Campus"

Examination of the structure of these sentences indicates that three of them depend on the anticipation created by using "it" or "there"; the fourth uses the construction "the fact that . . . ," which has the same effect of postponing the completed thought until the final word has been added. The periodic sentence characteristically depends on some structure that delays the completion of a sentence pattern until the last moment.

6D *Questions*

Strictly speaking, a rhetorical question is one to which no direct reply is expected. It is a device that makes readers feel they are weighing the issues. Sometimes you may not even have an answer to your own question, or you may not care to offer one; but by posing a question, you focus on a problem. In an essay on the poet Dylan Thomas, Richard Whittington-Egan stops at one point to question whether or not "Dylan-the-actor was playing the role which he had created for Dylan-the-poet":

Was it really, then, all make-believe? Or was he a fringe alcoholic, stalwartly refusing to admit the fact even to himself?

"The Tosspoet"

These particular questions are not answered directly in the essay, but they do suggest possible interpretations.

The rhetorical question can also function as an argumentative device if its answer appears completely self-evident:

Who can argue on the side of poverty, or against justice, or against the idea of a Great Society?

Norman Mailer, "Lyndon Johnson"

Here Mailer uses the question to make a concession, only to follow it in succeeding sentences by reservations about the Johnson administration.

In a different way, a question may actually contain its answer and only invite assent. When Thoreau asks "This American government,—what is it but a tradition, though a recent one, endeavoring to transmit itself unimpaired to posterity, but each instant losing some of its integrity?" the form of the question is only a means of making a statement. In another passage, he uses questions to pose alternatives. His subject is military men:

They have no doubt that it is a damnable business in which they are concerned; they are all peaceably inclined. Now, what are they? Men at all? or small movable forts and magazines, at the service of some unscrupulous man in power?

"Civil Disobedience"

Other writers, however, use the question as if they were carrying on a dialogue with themselves. They pose a question, then answer it. The question becomes a structural device; it is a convenient way of introducing a new topic, particularly at the beginning of a paragraph. "How is the humanization of sex impeded?" asks a writer; then he offers two reasons.

Other questions are mere springboards: "What are the facts?" "How typical is all this?" "What consequences can we expect?" These are followed by answers, but the questions themselves, empty as they are of content, merely add variety to the majority of declarative sentences.

A fragment is a word or any group of words, short of a complete grammatical sentence, set down as a thought and punctuated as a sentence. Often, in student writing, fragments are unintentional; they betray the writer's inability either to write a complete sentence or to punctuate one correctly. For instance, in response to an examination question, one student wrote these fragments:

Since Gordon is a man. One with a family to support. I think he should take the job with his brother-in-law.

The obvious point here is that all of the words together represent a complete sentence; the student simply does not punctuate the introductory clause and the appositive phrase properly:

Since Gordon is a man, one with a family to support, I think he should take the job with his brother-in-law.

In fairness, we should ask whether the student's punctuation represents a deliberate strategy for emphasis. Or, even if it has a purpose, does the punctuation interfere with the meaning? In this instance, the student's punctuation does seem to interfere with expressing a clear, direct thought, since the appositive phrase, which closely modifies the subject, belongs closely connected to it. The same kind of observation may be made about the following fragments:

I would take the job with my brother-in-law. *Because of the money involved.* [prepositional phrase as sentence]

Having a job you like is important to your well-being as a person. *While having one you don't like could cause frustration and lack of motivation.* [dependent clause as sentence]

I think it would be to the family's best interest for Gordon to take the job that pays less. *The first job giving him a chance for advancement.* [absolute phrase as sentence]

If I were Gordon, my choice would be determined by today's living standards. *Giving myself a chance for a few luxuries.* [participial phrase as sentence]

Gordon has two responsibilities. *To accumulate as much money as he can for his family and also to satisfy himself.* [infinitive phrases as a sentence]

In every instance, these phrases and clauses, which seem to be contributing little to the effectiveness of the writing as fragments, could be attached to the main clause by punctuation, at times with slight rephrasing, as demonstrated below:

I would take the job with my brother-in-law because of the money involved. [no punctuation required]

Having a job you like is important to your well-being as a person, while having one you don't like could cause frustration and lack of motivation.

I think it would be to the family's best interest for Gordon to take the job that pays less, as it is the first job giving him a chance for advancement.

If I were Gordon, my choice would be determined by today's living standards, in order to give myself a chance for a few luxuries.

Gordon has two responsibilities: to accumulate as much money as he can for his family and also to satisfy himself.

At times, fragments may be used conveniently and effectively as transitions: *To move then to a second argument. And now for the implications. A final point.* In the appropriate context, a fragment can also create an emphasis that the writer clearly intends and the reader perceives:

The community was liberal, but that does not imply that it was permissive, disorderly, or immoral. Quite the contrary.

Student sentence

Minorities have always wielded the cutting edge of history; that is, change. Not always well or wisely, to be sure. But that is the process and we are bound to report it, and by a higher law than the law of habit or the law of the box office.

Eric Sevareid, "The Quest for Objectivity"

Since a fragment is an attention-calling device, it should be used only for instances when emphasis is clearly needed.

6F Coordination and subordination

Coordination links sentences and shorter units with conjunctions; subordination transforms sentences into dependent structures. The two processes produce different stylistic effects. Coordination tends to loosen the prose style; subordination, to tighten it. Coordination is expansive; subordination is economical. Coordination is common in speech because one thing merely follows another in sequence. Subordination predominates in writing because it requires forethought. We commonly speak sentences like this one:

The baseball game has been postponed, so we have to find something else to do.

But in writing we would probably subordinate one of the sentences to get rid of an overused *so:*

Since the baseball game has been postponed, we have to find something else to do.

Coordination may be said to have a horizontal, forward-moving effect; subordination, a vertical, in-depth one. Studies of children's writing at various grade levels indicate rather consistently that the use of various kinds of subordinate structures increases with age. Subordinating, then, can be taken as one of the marks of a mature style, permitting compactness and variety in expression.

Coordinating conjunctions 6 FA

Coordinating conjunctions connect words, phrases, dependent clauses, and complete sentences. The four main connectives express different relationships between the parts: *and* is the only conjunction that joins in the sense of "adding to"; *but* excludes or contrasts; *or* and *nor* provide alternatives. A few other words like *for*, *yet*, and *so* are also used at times as coordinating conjunctions.

Principles of coordination 6 FB

Coordination implies a balancing of equal parts. Sentences that are not clearly coordinate are therefore better separated, rephrased, or joined by words other than coordinating conjunctions. A number of illustrations will show how coordination can be faulty and can be easily remedied:

coord

James Bond has a helper and guide named Quarrel. Quarrel has a wife and two children, who are never shown in the movie but mentioned, and he has qualms about murdering his fellow man.

Faulty coordination; parts seemingly unrelated

James Bond has a helper and guide named Quarrel, a man with a wife and two children, who are never shown in the movie but are mentioned. Unlike Bond, Quarrel has qualms about murdering his fellow man.

Rephrased with parts regrouped and relation between them shown by a transitional phrase

There are some people who seem to have their world so well organized that they need no extra support beyond themselves, and these atheists are frequently scientists who have been trained to think in terms of absolute facts and proofs.

Faulty coordination; parts related but disconnected because writer makes a leap in his thinking

There are some people who seem to have their world so well organized that they need no extra support beyond themselves. This kind of self-sufficiency sometimes leads to atheism. Scientists who have been trained to think in terms of absolute facts and believe only what they can prove are frequently atheists.

Rephrased with the parts separated and the gap bridged

I was standing there minding my own business, and a man came up and insulted me.

Faulty coordination

I was standing there minding my own business when a man came up and insulted me.

Rephrased with one sentence subordinated

I was standing there minding my own business. Without warning, a man came up and insulted me.

Separated with a transitional phrase

By his explanation, this writer strikes me as a person who wouldn't listen to reason, and I don't like that kind of person.

Faulty coordination; loosely connected

By his explanation, this writer strikes me as a person who wouldn't listen to reason. That's the kind of person I don't like.

Rephrased with greater emphasis

Faulty coordination; superfluous use of coordinating conjunction	My ideals are not his ideals, and therefore I don't believe we would get along together.
Rephrased with coordinating conjunction eliminated	My ideals are not his ideals; therefore, I don't believe we would get along together.
Rephrased with one sentence subordinated	Because my ideals are not his ideals, I don't believe we would get along together.
Faulty coordination; related but not parallel	The poem expresses a great struggle, but he talks about life in the ghetto as if he were just passing through.
Rephrased with parallel subjects	The poem expresses a great struggle, but the poet talks about life in the ghetto as if he were just passing through.
Faulty coordination; excessive use with loss of effect	I think that this person had a rough time getting through life and then trying to get through the pressures of college. I think when this girl was writing this poem she was a little depressed but I also think that she had the desire and will to make it to the top and nothing was going to stop her.
Rephrased with the thoughts compressed, subordinated, and separated	I think that this girl had a rough time getting through life and surviving college. Although she seems depressed when she writes this poem, I think she shows the desire and will to make it to the top. Nothing is going to stop her.
Faulty coordination; phrasing weakened by unnecessary linking	The student's statement is completely true and I believe life will be hard for him, but if he tries he'll succeed.
Rephrased with unrelated parts separated	The student's statement is completely true. Life will be hard for him, but I believe if he tries he'll succeed.

Excessive coordination in writing tends to be amateurish, unless it can be used with a special stylistic effect, as Tom Wolfe does in this sentence:

> Out in the club the Epics, with four electric instruments going, are playing "Doing the Dog," and Misty is doing the Dog, and Janet is doing the Mashed Potatoes, and Jerrie Miller is doing the Monkey, with a few baroque emendations, but Marlene reflects a moment, as if upon her busy round of work with the churches, the benefit balls, the women's groups and the youth.
>
> "The Peppermint Lounge Revisited"

The tendency merely to string thoughts together can be offset by a greater awareness of subordination.

6FC *Subordinating conjunctions*

Subordinating conjunctions that introduce dependent clauses also define a relationship between the clause and the remainder of the sentence. Several categories suggest the range of these relationships:

Cause: *because, in that, since*

We will postpone the vote since we no longer have a quorum.

Condition: *if, although, unless, whereas*

Unless you keep the flame low, you run the risk of burning yourself.

Manner: *as, as though, as if,*

The apples, as though they knew ripeness had come, fell to the ground.

Result: *in order that, so that*

I deliberately called so that you wouldn't make an unnecessary trip.

Time: *after, before, since, until, when, whenever, while*

Since the book was published, she has been living in Paris.

These examples indicate that a dependent clause may assume any number of positions in a sentence. Even when the clause stands in first position, the subordinating conjunction still acts as the connecting link between the clause and the remainder of the sentence.

Relative pronouns *6FD*

Relative pronouns are a special category of subordinating words that introduce noun clauses and adjective clauses. *Who, whom, whose, which, that,* and sometimes *what* are the simple relatives. All of these words except *that* combine with *ever* to form additional relatives: *whoever, whomever, whosever, whichever, whatever.* The forms *whosoever, whichsoever,* and *whatsoever* are archaic.

We were willing to do *whatever we could to help.* [noun clause]

I wonder *which of these is better.* [noun clause]

Individuals *who think they cannot help* are often making excuses. [adjective clause]

I made the motion *that the delegates are now discussing.* [adjective clause]

Principles of subordination *6FE*

sub

It should be noted that some phrases and clauses that are subordinate in structure are not necessarily subordinate in meaning. In fact, the subject of a sentence may be expressed in a noun clause, and sentences beginning with expressions like "It is true . . ." or "It is questionable whether . . ." put the important thought into the dependent clause that follows. In most instances, however, subordination is a way of giving secondary emphasis to a thought, even though it may be the more important fact. The following sentence, for example, is clearly designed to emphasize a personal detail rather than the world event:

I was stationed in Marseilles, France, in 1945 when the first atom bomb was dropped.

Ordinarily, most writers place the principal idea in the main clause, although the writer often determines which is the principal idea. The following sentences illustrate how a reversal of subordination shifts the emphasis from the deed in the first example to the time of the deed in the second example:

When John Kennedy was in the third year of his administration, he was assassinated.

When John Kennedy was assassinated, he was in the third year of his administration.

In the matter of subordination, the writer must also consider what a reader's normal expectations will be. Adverbial clauses, for example, are sometimes subject to upside-down subordination; that is, the main focus of the sentence seems to be misplaced in a dependent clause. Reading the following sentences aloud will indicate that their intonation patterns are quite different:

Upside-down subordination   The wrecking ball swung forward again, when the last wall collapsed.

Rephrased with emphasis more appropriate to the meaning   As the wrecking ball swung forward again, the last wall collapsed.

Excessive subordination consists in piling up clauses to the detrimental effect of the sentence as a whole:

I was reading about Pieter Brueghel, a Flemish artist, who painted in the seventeenth century when it was common to treat biblical subjects in terms of contemporary thought, which consistently sought out moral parallels between the Bible and the times and which did not hesitate to satirize what was immoral.

Improved phrasing:

I was reading about Pieter Brueghel, a seventeenth-century Flemish artist, who followed the then current fashion of treating biblical subjects in terms of contemporary thought. Artists of his day consistently sought out moral parallels between the Bible and the times and did not hesitate to satirize what they considered immoral.

6G *Passive voice constructions*

pass   Phrasing a sentence in passive voice is a means of transposing the doer of an action and the receiver of an action for a different stylistic effect. Subject and object are reversed by a change of the verb form:

A tornado hit Biloxi, Mississippi.

Biloxi, Mississippi, was hit by a tornado.

The difference between these two sentences is essentially one of emphasis, and the preference of one over the other would depend on the writer's intentions. Newspaper reports commonly focus on the object of a crime, particularly if the agent is yet unknown or unidentified:

The First National Bank was robbed by an unidentified group of teenagers at 2:30 this afternoon.

In other instances, however, passive voice tends to be a feeble way of expressing what can be said much more forcefully in active voice:

Passive construction: "Down with Nukes" was chanted by thousands of marchers in the street.
Active construction: Thousands of marchers in the street chanted "Down with Nukes."
Passive construction: It was known to me long before the teacher found out.
Active construction: I knew about it long before the teacher found out.

The passive voice is often used in technical, scientific, and other kinds of scholarly writing both as a means of establishing an impersonal tone and as an economical way of setting down thoughts when the actions and facts are of primary importance, not those who performed them or discovered them. Passive voice is particularly common in historical writing. In the following passage, it is used conveniently and unobtrusively:

How deep the hatred against the new Christians had become was demonstrated in 1449 when Toledo was called upon to contribute a million maravedis for the defence of the frontier. The community refused and tax-gatherers—most of them *marranos*—were sent into the city to enforce the collection. Not only were they assaulted, but the houses of all the new Christians were destroyed and those who attempted to defend them or their property were brutally beaten or killed. All of the king's attempts to restore order failed, and he was compelled to watch feebly as the council passed an edict forbidding new Christians to hold any public office. The envenomed wording of the edict, the *Sentencia Estatuto,* demonstrated clearly that the animosity sprang from more than a religious difference. It had become a genuine race-hatred.

Abram Leon Sachar, *A History of the Jews*

Inversion **6H**

Inversion is a device of reversing the customary word order of a basic sentence. As a strategy, it works because most sentences follow a regular pattern. Therefore, moving a word or phrase or clause from its usual position to a less regular one gives it a special emphasis:

Regular word order: I may be hungry, but I'm not desperate yet.
Inversion: Hungry I may be, but I'm not desperate yet.
Regular word order: He was ready to sacrifice his money if necessary.
Inversion: His money he was ready to sacrifice if necessary.

In these examples, words like "yet" and "if necessary" can also be transposed; e.g., "If necessary, he was ready to sacrifice his money." Of course, any movable part of a sentence can be rearranged for a slightly different effect:

Basic sentence: We find these facts to be unalterable: that war is inevitable; that pride, greed, and lust for power are weapons of destruction within man.

Other arrangements: These facts we find to be unalterable: that war is inevitable; that pride, greed, and lust for power are weapons of destruction within man.

That war is inevitable; that pride, greed, and lust for power are weapons of destruction within man—these facts we find to be unalterable.

Inversion is a strategy that must be handled cautiously because it can result in awkwardness:

Regular word order: Alexander the Great was not only a great general but also a disseminator of Greek culture.

Awkward inversion: Not only a great general but also a disseminator of Greek culture was Alexander the Great.

Like most other strategies, inverted structures have to be tested in context, since they clearly tamper with rhythmic patterns that we normally expect. When aptly used, however, they can do exactly what they are intended to do.

My point is that a very large proportion of the progress during those years must be attributed to the influence of Bentham. There can be no doubt that nine-tenths of the people living in England in the latter part of the last century were happier than they would have been if he had never lived. So shallow was his philosophy that he would have regarded this as a vindication of his activities. We, in our more enlightened age, can see that such a view is preposterous; but it may fortify us to review the grounds for rejecting a grovelling utilitarianism such as that of Bentham.

Bertrand Russell, "The Harm That Good Men Do"

The inversion "So shallow was his philosophy" in the third sentence manages to be both unobtrusive and at the same time emphatic; it shores up the meaning but does not call attention to itself as a device. Effective inversion operates that way.

6I *Interrupted movement*

The interruption of a sentence to insert comment may be a deliberate strategy to call attention to an aside, a means of moving a word, phrase, or clause to a more emphatic position, or simply an effort to make the writing a little more informal. In tightly controlled prose, the incidental thoughts that pop into our minds are ordinarily censored out. In a freer style, these are included by means of some punctuation device—sometimes commas, sometimes dashes, sometimes parentheses or brackets. Some writers are obviously more disposed to this kind of rearrangement and side discourse than others, but almost everyone comes upon some occasion that invites an interpolation. The chief caution is to avoid chopping up the prose to such an extent that the reader is left without a clear line of thought.

The following sentences represent a variety of uses (italics added):

The evidence, *if reliable*, is highly incriminating. [*compare* If the evidence is reliable, it is highly incriminating.]

The party was, *as they say*, a bash.

Governments—*ours as well as theirs*—are responsible for the conditions that will permit open access to the major canals of the world.

Beauty devoid of responsibility might be a way of describing a familiar kind of female punk: the Hollywood star who makes marriage a game of musical chairs (*or beds*) and love a five-star final.

Marya Mannes, "Let's Stop Exalting Punks"

My still inchoate but nevertheless clearly heretical sentiments about literature and my incipient rebellion against the academic life had been causing me a good deal of anxiety—*was I turning into a "sellout"?*—and I had feared that they might shock Trilling, who had, after all, followed the very course I was half-consciously proposing to desert on the ground—*was it a rationalization?*—that there was something false in such a life for someone like me.

Norman Podhoretz, *Making It*

The last example illustrates the use of the interrupter as a stylistic device for suggesting hesitation and uncertainty—something comparable to a stream-of-consciousness technique that tries to catch vacillations of the mind. The interruption, however, is not eccentric; it is common in most conventional kinds of prose, representing only a break in rhythm that keeps the reader alert to the meaning.

A writer has to guard against one major pitfall, that is, separating related structures that we ordinarily expect to follow one another. The following examples illustrate the kind of confusion that can result:

It was a not-to-be-forgotten and not-too-pleasantly remembered incident. [wide separation of determiner and noun]

Rephrased: It was an incident not to be forgotten and not too pleasantly remembered.

A ballpoint pen, formerly bright blue but now faded by the weather and at the moment I saw it covered with raindrops, was lying under a bush. [wide separation of subject and verb]

Rephrased: Lying under a bush was a ballpoint pen, formerly bright blue but now faded by the weather, covered with raindrops at the moment I saw it.

I requested, even though I knew the deadline was past, permission to submit my application. [wide separation of verb and object]

Rephrased: Even though I knew the deadline was past, I requested permission to submit my application.

The use of dashes or parentheses invites two other common pitfalls. One is a tendency to attach extra material as an afterthought instead of rewriting the sentence to integrate the added information smoothly. Sometimes the revision may require a major reorganization of the sentence, but at other times it can be done quite easily and simply:

Taking the high-risk drivers (*teenage*) off the road until they are eighteen or twenty-one doesn't eliminate the problem.

Rephrased: Taking high-risk teenage drivers off the road until they are eighteen or twenty-one doesn't eliminate the problem.

The other pitfall is inserting interruptive material that does not fit grammatically or consistently into the sentence:

During your first year in college—*it is perhaps the first time it has ever happened*—you experience the freedom that gives you confidence to think for yourself.

Rephrased: During your first year in college—perhaps for the first time in your life—you experience the freedom that gives you confidence to think for yourself.

6J   *Balance and parallelism*

bal
par

Whereas interruption operates by breaking regular rhythmic patterns, balance operates on the principle of recurring pattern. Balance within a sentence weighs one part evenly with another. Parallelism, which refers simply to similarity of structure, frequently works hand in hand with balance. Two parts alike in structure are possibly alike in rhythm as well. But balance and parallelism do not necessarily imply completely symmetrical phrasing:

But individuals like students are by virtue of their stage in life changeable and changing, malleable yet often intransigent.

Kenneth Keniston, "The Faces in the Lecture Room"

In this sentence, "malleable yet often intransigent" has the same one-two effect of balance as "changeable and changing," but when the two are put together the result is something slightly asymmetrical because the rhythms are different and the patterns are not exactly parallel.

Thus, balance and parallelism are closely tied with matters of symmetry and asymmetry. There is a tendency sometimes to think of symmetry as a righting of something that is wrong, an arranging of something that is crooked—therefore, a special artistic virtue. Yet we need to observe that the unbalanced and asymmetrical are as common in our experience as the balanced and symmetrical. Nature itself is filled with asymmetrical forms: trees, cloud formations, streams, and mountains. We may be less aware of asymmetrical forms, but they are wholly natural—all of which is to say that some writers reject balance and parallelism as contrived and artificial. Ultimately, the use of balanced and parallel structures is a private choice, a mark of individual style. Some writers cannot avoid them because these strategies satisfy a feeling. We can see this affinity operating in each of the following sentences:

We are an active, ingenious, pragmatic race, concerned with production rather than enjoy- *Balance and* ment, with practicality rather than contemplation, with efficiency rather than understanding, *parallelism* and with information rather than wisdom.

Dwight Macdonald, "Howtoism"

The moon was always measured in terms of hope and reassurance and the heart pangs of *Balance and* youth on such a night as this; it is now measured in terms of mileage and foot-pounds of *parallelism* rocket thrust. Children sent sharp, sweet wishes to the moon; now they dream of blunt-nosed *Balance without* missiles. *parallelism*

Eric Sevareid, "The Dark of the Moon"

For in sports, as in gambling, and as in most of the activities that we think of as peculiarly *Parallelism and* masculine, the greater the risk, the more serious the play, the keener the fun. *imbalance*

George Stade, "Game Theory"

The love of liberty is the love of others; the love of power is the love of ourselves. *Exact balance and*

William Hazlitt, "Political Essays" *parallelism*

The Hazlitt quotation illustrates a sentence that can be easily memorized, and dictionaries of famous quotations are filled with similar examples. It is one of the fringe benefits of balance and parallelism. But quotability sometimes raises the question whether an easy phrase does not also kill "analytical invigoration," a phrase once used by William F. Buckley, Jr., in deploring the resounding but empty phrases of a political figure. Of course, balance and parallelism need not be either false or superficial. Their effectiveness is a matter of appropriateness; John Kennedy's words remain both memorable and meaningful:

Ask not what your country can do for you—ask what you can do for your country.

The way parallel phrasing obligates a writer to remain consistent can be illustrated by a diagram that puts balanced and parallel structures under one another:

There must be understanding in any home situation:
  <u>understanding</u>
    <u>that lets</u> each member of the family accept the others
      <u>for what</u> they are,
  not <u>for what</u> someone thinks they should be;

  <u>understanding</u>
    <u>that makes</u> each one <u>notice</u> the good and positive things in others and
                <u>not dwell</u> on the faults and shortcomings that each of us has;

<u>understanding</u>
<u>that makes</u> each one realize <u>that</u> it is terrible to reject others,
<u>that</u> to put someone down is
<u>to create</u> tension and
<u>provide</u> barriers to happiness.

Student sentence

In its usual form, the sentence would read:

There must be understanding in any home situation: understanding that lets each member of the family accept the others for what they are, not for what someone thinks they should be; understanding that makes each one notice the good and positive things in others and not dwell on the faults and shortcomings that each of us has; understanding that makes each one realize that it is terrible to reject others, that to put someone down is to create tension and provide barriers to happiness.

This long sentence of 84 words works because the balance and parallelism divide it into readable segments and keep it orderly.

6JA *Correlative conjunctions*

Correlatives are connectives that are typically used in pairs and therefore invite balanced and parallel phrasing. The common ones are *either . . . or, neither . . . nor, both . . . and, not only . . . but also, so . . . as,* and *whether . . . or. Neither . . . nor* is the negative equivalent of *either . . . or. Or* is not an acceptable substitute for *nor* after *neither,* although it may follow other negatives:

I got *neither* money *nor* glory.
I got *no* money *or* glory.

A basic principle of correlative conjunctions is to place to correlatives as close to the words they join as possible—words that are the same part of speech or the same grammatical construction:

Misplaced: Either I must *send* a telegram or *make* a long distance call.
Rephrased: I must either *send* a telegram or *make* a long distance call.
Misplaced: Not only is she *bright,* but *pretty* too.
Rephrased: She is not only *bright* but *pretty* too.

Again, we can demonstrate by a diagram:

This poem gives me a vivid mental picture
  not only *of an empty lot*
      but *of an empty life.*

This reading is considerably better than "This poem not only gives me a vivid mental picture of an empty lot but of an empty life," because the correlatives should be placed to highlight the contrasting phrases.

Repetition can work subtly as a way of insinuating a thought, or it can work much more obviously as a device of emphasis. In prose, whole sentences are never repeated consecutively as speakers do occasionally for emphasis. But a sentence can be repeated intermittently to make a point. Undoubtedly, one of the best-known examples is Iago's speech to Roderigo in Shakespeare's *Othello*—a speech that has a remarkable insinuating effect:

Come, be a man. Drown thyself? Drown cats, and blind puppies. I have professed me thy friend, and I confess me knit to thy deserving with cables of perdurable toughness. I could never better stead thee than now. Put money in thy purse; follow thou the wars; defeat thy favour with an usurped beard. I say, put money in thy purse. It cannot be that Desdemona should long continue her love to the Moor—put money in thy purse—nor he his to her. It was a violent commencement in her, and thou shalt see an answerable sequestration; put but money in thy purse. These Moors are changeable in their wills—fill thy purse with money. The food that to him now is as luscious as locusts shall be to him shortly as bitter as coloquintida. She must change for youth; when she is sated with his body she will find the error of her choice. Therefore put money in thy purse. If thou wilt needs damn thyself, do it a more delicate way than drowning. Make all the money thou canst. If sanctimony and a frail vow, betwixt an erring barbarian and a super-subtle Venetian be not too hard for my wits, and all the tribe of hell, thou shalt enjoy her—therefore make money. A pox of drowning thyself, it is clean out of the way. Seek thou rather to be hanged in compassing thy joy, than to be drowned, and go without her.

Othello, I, iii

The effect of any repetition varies with the number of occurrences; that is, anything beyond two or three repetitions assumes emotional overtones rather than a calculated effect of stress. The first example below illustrates repetition used with restraint and emphasis:

The Father in *Six Characters* expounds almost continually upon a philosophy of denial—denial that a man has a consistent identity, denial that one man has always been viewed the same by himself and those around him, even denial that philosophizing about anything will get anyone anywhere.

Student sentence

The second example, by its repetition of five words and use of italics, shows greater intensity:

There *must* be a language in which all but the most highly technical matters can be discussed without distortion or falsification or watering-down; there *must* be a language impartially free of all the various jargons through which the "disciplines" maintain their proud and debilitating isolation; there *must* be a language in which the kinship of these disciplines is expressed and revealed and reaffirmed.

Norman Podhoretz, "In Defense of Editing"

The final example shows how completely devastating repetition can be. The passage is taken from Mary Campbell's newspaper review of Brian Bedford's performance as Hamlet:

Bedford's Hamlet has no personality, no depth and no motivation. He shows no melancholy, no fears or turmoil, no antic humors, no dissembling, no "almost blunted purpose."

Repetition can hardly be considered apart from parallelism and cataloging, because frequently they all work together to reinforce one another. Overused, they all become uneventful. As strategies, their effectiveness springs from contrast—departures from the usual and expected.

6L Series

Like repetition, a series has a cumulative effect. A series of two we often take for granted. Sentences with compound subjects, compound verbs, or compound objects are extremely common:

The fancy is a kaleidoscope; it shifts and lights a path into the world of everyday.

Student sentence

He loved the cutthroat and the steelhead with their brilliance and spirit.

Student sentence

At times, the meanings of the words do not vary greatly from one to another, but the preference for two rather than one seems to satisfy the writer's sense of balance. The tendency to write doublets constantly instead of a single word needs to be guarded against, because a habit of twoness can accumulate a good number of unnecessary words.

Series beyond two items are capable of a whole range of effects, and those effects are also conditioned by the use or absence of connectives. Whether or not to use conjunctions depends on the way readers will respond to the rhythms that the writer sets up. The patterns of the following sentences seem to have a rightness about the way they read, but they vary in their use of conjunctions:

It is worth noting that when individual nations can no longer trust their leaders they also cease to trust or believe or understand each other.

Student sentence

The makings of an All-American amateur athlete are agility, courage, two strong legs, and a private patron.

Student sentence

The dingy hall sighs and moans and cries and thunders, as clusters of bodies tumble out of classrooms, and the classrooms grow gradually quieter and quieter until they are silent.

Student sentence

The ultimate in writing a series is the catalog, a device of overwhelming the reader with a list of representative examples that seem to be all-inclusive. The catalog is panoramic; it expresses scope, sweep, fullness. Tom Wolfe uses it often in his writing:

Good old boys from all over the South roared together after the Stanchion—Speed! Guts!—pouring into Birmingham, Daytona Beach, Randleman, North Carolina; Atlanta, Hickory,

Bristol, Tennessee; Augusta, Georgia; Richmond, Virginia; Asheville, North Carolina; Charlotte, Myrtle Beach—tens of thousands of them.

"The Last American Hero"

A Truman Capote catalog pushes even further:

Father is a world traveler. Cards arrive: he is in Seville, now Copenhagen, now Milan, next week Manchester, everywhere and all the while on a gaudy spending spree. Buying: blue crockery from a Danish castle. Pink apothecary jars from an old London pharmacy. English brass, Barcelona lamps, Battersea boxes, French paperweights, Italian witch balls, Greek icons, Venetian blackamoors, Spanish saints, Korean cabinets, and junk, glorious junk, a jumble of ragged dolls, broken buttons, a stuffed kangaroo, an aviary of owls under a great glass bell, the playing pieces of obsolete games, the paper moneys of defunct governments, an ivory umbrella cane *sans* umbrella, crested chamber pots and mustache mugs and irreparable clocks, cracked violins, a sundial that weighs seven hundred pounds, skulls, snake vertebrae, elephants' hoofs, sleigh bells and Eskimo carvings and mounted swordfish, medieval milkmaid stools, rusted firearms and flaking waltz-age mirrors.

"Brooklyn Heights: A Personal Memoir"

In such an example, the eccentricity of the extended catalog matches the eccentricity of the subject matter, but, no doubt fully aware of the length, the writer skillfully groups the items and varies the connectives. The final test of a catalog is its capacity to be exhaustive without being exhausting.

Strategies of sound 6M

Just as words on a page cannot be separated from the rhythms they produce, so words cannot be separated from their sounds, whether they are spoken or not. The inner sense of sound is not necessarily dependent on the ear, but the things that we hear and like no doubt affect the "sounds" that we see and like.

Phrasing that repeats words or plays upon words that sound alike tends to attract attention. For that reason we see them frequently in advertisements and on bumper stickers and signs; they serve as repeatable slogans:

When guns are outlawed, only outlaws will have guns.

It's hard to keep your body in good physical shape; it may be even harder to keep your money in good fiscal shape.

In general, when sober communication is in order, this kind of playfulness, particularly punning, has no place because it often smacks of triviality and forced cleverness.

On the other hand, alliteration is both tasteful and pleasing when it acts as an unobtrusive link between the words of a sentence. It is necessary to separate subtle examples from forced ones. In general, any use of alliteration becomes excessive when sound predominates over sense.

Subtle alliteration:

A vast and inventive organization of living matter survives by seeming to have lost.

John Steinbeck

We are more and more conversant with the chemistry of that clod of clay on a speck of star-dust, that we call human life.

Irwin Edman

Too deliberate alliteration:

Traffic cannot untangle in Boise and Bozeman, as well as Boston and Bobo, Texas. All movement has ended in Seattle, Seaside, Secaucus, and Sand Flea, Fla. There is a national dragon, stretching everywhere. All, commerce, all continuity, all congress has ceased.

Lorenzo Milam

It could be that this explosion of special levy nay-sayers results from the belated suspicion that, in the past, some legislators, proud and powerful legislators, "dressed in a little brief authority," have played such fantastic partisan pranks for possible personal political profit so persistently as to preclude passage of any program of tax reform.

Letter to the Editor, *Seattle Post-Intelligencer*

Clearly, some cases of alliteration are more obvious than others, but it is not too difficult to determine when the bounds of discreet use have been passed. Some writers have a more natural tendency to alliterate than others; they therefore need to be more cautious of the way sounds intrude on meaning.

Sentence choice

The kinds of sentences you choose depend upon the effect you want to create. Some choices tighten the prose; some loosen it. Some speed the pace; some slow it down. Some choices personalize the writing; some depersonalize it. Some make it formal; some, familiar. Here are a few guidelines:

1. A short sentence lends forceful contrast or emphasis to a long sentence in both thought and rhythm.
2. A series of short sentences gives a well-paced, staccato-like effect to the prose.
3. A long sentence allows for deliberation, qualification, and explanation, usually slowing the forward movement.
4. A sentence punctuated with interruptions or asides creates a casual, colloquial effect.
5. A cumulative sentence serves descriptive and narrative writing especially well because it invites concrete detail.
6. A periodic sentence lends a climactic, somewhat formal note to prose because it suspends the main thought until the end.
7. A question creates interest by opening up a new thought or anticipating an answer yet to come.
8. A fragment, by its elliptical nature, creates a clipped, emphatic effect.
9. A balanced sentence highlights a balanced thought by its structure; it is consciously formal.

10. A sentence phrased with the verb in passive voice weakens the active force of the verb and depersonalizes the prose.

Strategy and emphasis

The rhetoric of the sentence, of course, finds extension in the paragraph and paragraph bloc. Sentence strategies such as climactic arrangement, variation of length, inversion, interruption, balance, parallelism, repetition, and sound devices operate on a larger scale as well as within the sentence. Actually, they are the writer's substitutes for stress, intonation, and pause, the speaker's stock-in-trade for emphasis. You can also resort to mechanical devices like underlining, italics, capitals, boldface type, and large print, but strategies like the ones discussed in this chapter are more natural because they grow out of your own thought and inventiveness. They must be used unaffectedly, however, to reinforce thought, not ornament it. A deliberate display of rhetorical strategies may indicate a kind of virtuosity, like that of some pianists who are anxious to show off their technique. But showing off risks superficiality—in music and in writing. The timeless principle that art disguises artfulness applies to writing as well as to other modes of expression.

Learning what other writers do is one way to learn further what you may possibly try. As you become more confident of your own abilities and more sure of the craft of writing, you can concentrate more and more on effectiveness. It helps to be able to choose among a number of ways of expressing a thought in order to find the most suitable one. In fact, an awareness of sentence strategies may give you the major resources you need to develop an appealing prose style.

A close examination of a passage of nonfiction by Richard Wright will show how many things are happening in a piece of prose to influence us as readers. Further, it should be apparent that these techniques are not additions or contrivances but integral parts of the prose. They reflect Wright's manner and feeling. He uses strategies naturally, without self-consciousness. In similar ways, you can learn to combine words effectively, but learning to do so will require the kind of hard work and practice that are always basic to the achievements of a skilled craftsman or artist.

Buttressed by their belief that their God had entrusted the earth into their keeping, drunk with power and possibility, waxing rich through trade in commodities, human and non-human, with awesome naval and merchant marines at their disposal, their countries filled with human debris anxious for any adventures, psychologically armed with new facts, white Western Christian civilization during the fourteenth, fifteenth, sixteenth, and seventeenth centuries, with a long, slow, and bloody explosion, hurled itself upon the sprawling masses of colored humanity in Asia and Africa.	*Series of six introductory phrases, varied in structure*

gth of ntences

84

Transposition and interrupted movement

I say to you white men of the West: Don't be too proud of how easily you conquered and
24 plundered those Asians and Africans. You had unwitting allies in your campaigns; you had
Fifth Columns in the form of indigenous cultures to facilitate your military, missionary, and
25 mercenary efforts. Your collaborators in those regions consisted of the mental habits of the
people, habits for which they were in no way responsible, no more than you were responsible
30 for yours. Those habits constituted corps of saboteurs, of spies, if you will, that worked in the
19 interests of European aggression. You must realize that it was not your courage or racial

Balance and parallelism

Alliteration

Repetition of "habits"

Balance and parallelism with inversion

Question with interrupted movement

Cataloging

Single-word question

Inversion

superiority that made you win, nor was it the racial inferiority or cowardice of the Asians and Africans that made them lose. This is an important point that you must grasp, or your concern **33** with this problem will be forever wide of the facts. How, then, did the West, numerically the **22** minority, achieve, during the last four centuries, so many dazzling victories over the body of colored mankind? Frankly, it took you centuries to do a job that could have been done in fifty **24** years! You had the motive, the fire power, the will, the religious spur, the superior organiza- **17** tion, but you dallied. Why? You were not aware exactly of what you were doing. You didn't **18–1–** suspect your impersonal strength, or the impersonal weakness on the other side. You were as **14** unconscious, at bottom, as were your victims about what was really taking place. **16**

Average: **24**

White Man, Listen!

Projects

1. Count the number of words in each sentence of your last essay. Record the figures to see what the variations in length are. Then average the numbers. If you arbitrarily accept 20 or 21 words as the length of an average sentence written by a professional writer, you may get some idea whether you need to expand sentences or shorten them. Sentence averages are revealing if they hit the extremes. A consistently low average of 12 or 15 may suggest that you are writing only the simplest sentence forms. A preponderantly high average of 35 or 38 may imply a lack of variety of long and short that explains, in turn, a lack of pace or emphasis in your prose.

2. Repeat the count using several paragraphs of at least two professional writers. What is their average? What is the pattern of variation? The longest sentence? The shortest sentence? How do their counts compare with your own?

3. Choose one of your own sentences. Then write 15 variations of it, changing the word order, varying the subordination, altering the voice of the verb, introducing new words if necessary, but not changing the basic meaning as you perceive it. When you have completed the exercise, mark with a B the sentence that you consider best; mark with an A the sentences that might be acceptable in some context; and finally mark with an M sentences that seem to be monstrosities under any circumstances.

4. Examine carefully all of the strategies that are operating in the following sentences. Identify the strategies by name. Then decide whether the total effect is pleasing or not.

A. Poetry is not a turning loose of emotion, but an escape from emotion; it is not the expression of personality, but an escape from personality.

T. S. Eliot

B. If experience teaches anything, it is that economic policies aimed exclusively at short-term relief too often bring long-term grief.

Richard M. Nixon

C. If I had to choose pictures of the American people that would represent them to a foreign audience, I would choose scenes that emphasize the likenesses shared by all of the world's peoples. Corny, cliché pictures—children playing, people crying, people dying, people spending their lives in hard work—seem more important to me than any pictures of football games or hot dogs or American apple pie.

Student sentence

D. Approaching Concord, doing forty, doing forty-five, doing fifty, the steering wheel held snug in my palms, the highway held grimly in my vision, the crown of the road now serving me (on the righthand curves), now defeating me (on the lefthand curves), I began to rouse myself from the stupefaction which a day's motor journey induces.

E. B. White

E. Knowing things is not being them, nor being them knowing them.

José Ortega y Gasset, trans. by Toby Talbot

5. Choose a passage of 100–150 words from a writer of your choice. Using the analysis of the Richard Wright selection on pp. 135–136 as a model, identify the techniques the writer uses. The idea is not just to "name the parts," but to see what effects are gained by particular strategies.

6. Imitation is a special way of gaining insights into the ways writers work; it can create an awareness of structures and strategies that you yourself can develop. This exercise is not intended to discourage originality, but to open up potentialities for inventiveness that you may have but may not be using.

The procedure is to take a sentence that you find effective, analyze its structure and devices, and then write another one like it, using new subject matter and current idiomatic English. Retain the structure words, like prepositions and conjunctions, so that the relationships stay the same.

Example: Reputation is an idle and most false imposition, oft got without merit and lost without deserving.

William Shakespeare, *Othello*

Student imitation: Love is a fragile and most fickle condition, often won without intent and lost without knowing.

Write similar adaptations of four of the following sentences, and add one of your own choice:

A. New York is the concentrate of art and commerce and sport and religion and entertainment and finance, bringing to a single compact arena the gladiator, the evangelist, the promoter, the actor, the trader, and the merchant.

E. B. White

B. The other day I was shoving some of my originals around on the floor (I do not draw on the floor; I was just shoving the originals around) and they fell, or perhaps í pushed them, into five separate and indistinct categories.

James Thurber

C. I think; but who, as yet, knows?

Daniel Lerner

D. I had never before been so aware of policemen, on foot, on horseback, on corners, everywhere, always two by two.

James Baldwin

E. To speak critically, I never received more than one or two letters—I wrote this some years ago—that were worth the postage.

Henry David Thoreau

When you have completed each imitation, write what you have discovered, either about the way the sentence works or about the success or failure of your own imitation.

7. The cumulative sentence is based on the principle of addition, moving to more and more particulars. Attempt to add at least three particulars to each of the following base sentences, using any kind of phrase or clause:
A. I walked slowly down the street to the drug store at the corner . . .
B. I heard all of the sounds of early morning . . .
C. We were completely confused . . .
D. Memories surged into my mind . . .
E. Cars were jammed bumper to bumper for miles on the freeway . . .

8. Use a rhetorical diagram as a way of composing parallel structures. Invent your own beginning. For instance

He made the assumption
  that we were basically naïve,
  that we would follow if ordered,
  that we were incapable of seeing what the consequences would be.

Suggestions for writing

1. Fill in the blank: Who is _____? It may be a guru or your roommate or a person who smiled or didn't smile at you today. Answer the question in an essay.
2. Write a description of a movie you have seen recently. Consider especially the selection of important detail.
3. Write a restaurant review. Be precise about details.
4. Tell why a particular musician (singer, group, composer) strikes you as being unusual or great. Choose details that are specific and meaningful.
5. It is often said that clothes reflect the personality or mood of the wearer. Discuss this idea, perhaps in terms of how true you think it is or how it needs to be qualified. Consider the tendency of many people today to dress in "costumes." What is the reason? Use people you know as illustrations.
6. Some people perform better if they are awake for longer or shorter periods of time; some are "morning people," some "night people." Describe your own time-style. Do the things you have to do (your job or your schedule at school) conflict with your preferences?

Speech and writing are codes of communication dependent mainly on words. Writing is even more dependent on words than is speech because a speaker has many nonverbal means of influencing an audience. Further, we have other nonverbal codes for communicating thoughts and feelings—mathematical symbols, musical notations, and ideograms. Each of these codes or languages has its own basic principles which permit the system to operate. We characteristically refer to the principles that make words operate efficiently as the grammar of the language.

From time to time, codes are displaced almost entirely because they have lost their efficiency or their magic. Smoke signals, drum beats, and flag signaling—all once significant systems of communication—exist today only in rare circumstances and situations. The fading of old codes and the emergence of new ones have prompted some thinkers of our day to question whether writing has the capacity to survive when computers and electronic devices offer vastly more efficient means of communication. By learning to master words and structure them, do we continue to learn an already outmoded code?

Even though many of us would answer that bold question with a "No," the threat of more efficient languages and modes of communication must prompt us at least to ask ourselves what magic we still find in words, even though as a total system they may now have lost some of their efficiency. A short quotation by Leo Rosten will suggest one man's answer:

I fell in love with words at a very early age—perhaps because I was an immigrant child, brought to Chicago (from Poland) when I was three. It was an indescribable, invaluable experience to be transported from one world of words to another, entirely alien, with elders who cannot help you, since their knowledge of the new tongue is no greater than yours.

"The Hypnotism of Words"

To Rosten, language was a lure. To him and to all of us, it is a natural and personal means of expression. We do not need complicated technology to produce words. They are still the most characteristic stamp of our human identity.

In the preceding chapters on the paragraph and the sentence, we considered the structuring and organizing of words. In Chapter 18 on usage, we will consider words in sociocultural contexts. In this chapter, we are concerned primarily with words as words and the choices that make a difference to any writer.

The lexicon of the language

The total stock of words in the English language is its lexicon, not just those that appear in standard dictionaries but all words that are used in speech or writing. In fact, the bound dictionary with its label "unabridged" creates an illusion that the verbal resources of the language are contained within its covers. The truth is that only the more stable words are recorded there—words that have been established by use and words that for the most part fall within the category of standard English, essentially the words that are appropriate for writing. The nonstandard, dialectal, obscene, and archaic words are numerous enough to supply material for many other dictionaries. Even though supplementary dictionaries of this kind do exist, dictionary makers cannot possibly keep up with a living language that permits its users to invent new words constantly and to reinterpret old words in new contexts. New words in the language originate in four main ways: by borrowing, combining, shifting, and inventing.

Borrowing

The vocabulary of Old English was relatively stable, forming new words by joining native words. *Wīs*, meaning "wise," was combined with *dōm*, meaning "judgment," to make *wīsdōm*, the word for "wisdom" and "learning." English, however, was not always able to supply equivalent words for new ideas and situations. For example, when Christianity was adopted in A.D. 597, English borrowed words like *mass* and *alms* from Latin.

From the twelfth century on, English resorted more and more to borrowing from foreign languages to supply its needs, at first mainly from Latin, French, and the Scandinavian languages, but eventually from the languages of many nations, particularly as transportation and communication brought the far-flung people of the world in touch with one another. A selected list of borrowed words in English reads like an inventory of languages, both ancient and modern:

African dialects	gumbo, banjo, voodoo
Algonquin	moccasin, toboggan, wigwam
Arabic	coffee, harem, zero
Assyrian	ziggurat
Australian	boomerang, kangaroo
Celtic	down [hill], vassal, Avon
Chinese	silk, tea, yen
Czech	polka, robot
Dutch	buoy, easel, sleigh
Eskimo	igloo, kayak
Finnish	sauna
French	bourgeois, cabaret, resume
Gaelic	bard, bog, whiskey
German	delicatessen, nickel, wanderlust
Greek	academy, catastrophe, stoic
Hawaiian	hula, luau, ukulele
Hebrew	amen, cherub, jubilee
Hindu	punch, shampoo, thug
Irish	colleen, leprechaun, shamrock
Italian	bankrupt, confetti, soprano
Japanese	haiku, jujitsu, tycoon
Latin	appendix, interim, prospectus
Malay	bamboo, gingham, orangutan
Mexican Spanish	enchilada, mesquite, taco
Norwegian	fiord, ski, slalom
Persian	lilac, shawl, turban
Polish	mazurka, polonaise
Polynesian	taboo, tapa, tattoo
Portuguese	cuspidor, flamingo, tank
Russian	boyar, tundra, vampire
Sanskrit	ginger, jute, swastika
Scottish	kale, plaid, skulduggery
Spanish	adobe, canyon, sombrero
Swedish	ombudsman, troll, smorgasbord
Tibetan	polo, yak
Turkish	odalisque, seraglio, tulip
Yiddish	schnozzle, schlemiel, bagel

Even though it is obvious that many of these words are native terms for products or activities associated with a foreign country or cultural, commercial, and political words for which English has no equivalent, it is also true that all of these words are fully Anglicized; that is, we think of them as English words, not as foreign words. In print, they are not italicized as unadopted words characteristically are. They have full status in our own language.

In the history of borrowing, foreign words have on many occasions displaced words of Old English origin. Thus, today we use the Latin importation *library* instead of a modern version of the Old English words for a library of manuscripts and documents, either *bōchūs* (book-house) or *bōchord* (a book hoard). The oft-repeated generalization that all of the short, vivid words of the English language are of Old English origin does not hold consistently. *Mount, firm,* and *flame* were borrowed from Latin through French (compare *ascend, secure,* and *conflagration* borrowed directly from Latin). *They, die, egg,* and *sky* were borrowed from the early Scandinavian dialects. At times, words have entered the language by different routes at different periods, so that two English words that have the same meaning may have different forms, like *cipher* and *zero.* Both are derived from Arabic. The first entered the language about the sixteenth century through Old French. The second entered about one hundred years later through Italian. The two forms are called doublets. *Regal* and *royal* and *compute* and *count* illustrate the same phenomenon. Whether a writer chooses one or the other does make a difference in the tone. Other doublets, deriving from a common source, sometimes take on completely different meanings. Thus, pairs like *cruise* and *cross* and *dainty* and *dignity* are related to one another by a common parentage, although they are quite unlike in their implications.

The examples of borrowing already cited indicate that some foreign words are adopted ready-made into the language with no change in form or spelling, whereas others are adapted to English. Among French borrowings in the first category that have become common English words are *apropos, cliché, devotee, etiquette, prestige,* and *souvenir.* Among other words less obviously French in form are *government, attorney, jury, estate, soldier,* and *vestment.*

Needless to say, the English language makes use of a number of purely foreign words and phrases for which it has no equivalent. These keep their foreign spellings, and we usually think of them as foreign. Many of them are professional and technical terms like *doppelgänger, pas de chat,* and *medulla oblongata.* Others are highly useful phrases, like *sine qua non* and *raison d'être,* that we cannot very well get along without. Despite the indispensable nature of some foreign words, however, we have to recognize that using them is frequently looked upon as either affectation or exhibitionism. Their use always requires discretion on the part of a speaker or writer.

Combining: derivation, compounding, blending

Combining as a source of new English words occurs by means of derivation, compounding, and blending. The forming of words by adding prefixes and suffixes to word stems is called derivation. Foreign influence is particularly strong in this kind of word-making. The word *translation,* for example, combines the Latin prefix *trans-* ("across") with the Latin participle *latus* ("carried") and adds a typical noun suffix, *-ion.* At other times, Latin or Greek prefixes and suffixes are attached to familiar words, thus *atypical.* The Greek prefix *a-* means *not,* similar to the Latin prefix *in-* (insane) and the English *un-* (unjust). Knowledge of word elements, therefore, often provides a quick clue to the meaning of words derived by this process.

LATIN PREFIXES USED IN ENGLISH

ab-, abs-	from away	*abstain*
ad-	to, toward	*address*
ante-	before	*antebellum*
bene-	well	*benefactor*
bi-	two	*bimanual*
circum-	around	*circumnavigate*
con-	with	*concurrent*
contra-	against	*contradistinction*
de-	down	*depress*
dis-	apart, opposite of	*distrust*
ex-	out, from	*excavate*
extra-	beyond	*extracurricular*
in-, il-, im-, ir-	not	*inapt, illicit, immature, irrational*
in-, im-	in	*infringe, impress*
inter-	between	*intercede*
intra-	within	*intramural*
intro-	within, inside	*introspection*
juxta-	near	*juxtapose*
non-	not	*nonconformist*
per-	through	*perforate*
post-	after	*postdoctorate*
pre-	before	*premature*
re-	again, back	*reclaim, recoil*
retro-	backward	*retroflex*
sub-	under	*subside*
super-	over, beyond	*superscript, superman*
trans-	across	*transplant*
ultra-	beyond, extremely	*ultraconservative*

GREEK PREFIXES USED IN ENGLISH

a-, an-	not	*amorphous, anhydrous*
ambi, amphi-	around, on both sides	*ambidextrous amphibious*
ana-	back, opposite	*anaphase*
anti-	against	*antibody*
cata-	down	*cataclysm*
dia-	through	*diatribe*
dys-	bad	*dysfunction*
epi-	upon	*epigraph*
eu-	good	*euphony*
hyper-	beyond, excess	*hyperthyroid*
hypo-	under	*hypotension*
meta-	beyond, denoting change	*metalinguistics, metamorphosis*
para-	side by side, near	*paraphrase*
peri-	around	*perimeter*
proto-	first	*prototype*
syn-, sym-	together	*synchronize, symphony*

PREFIXES OF NATIVE ORIGIN

a-	in, on, of	*ashore, akin*
be-	near, about	*bemoan*
for-	off, extremely	*forswear, forbear*
mis-	wrong, bad	*misconduct*
out-	beyond	*outlaw*
over-	too much	*overeat*
un-	not	*unbeaten*
with-	against	*withstand*

In addition to the lists above, English adverbs and prepositions have the force of prefixes when they combine with other words, like *backhand* and *uphill.*

English words are also derived by adding suffixes. The suffixes are of special importance because they permit the words of the language to shift from one part of speech to another. Thus, *emotion* can be changed to *emotional* and, in turn, to *emotionalize, emotionally, emotionalist,* and *emotionality.* The suffix in each case marks the change and varies the meaning. Thus, suffixes are best grouped in terms of the parts of speech they ordinarily identify.

Suffixes marking nouns: -acy, -age, -an, -ance, -ancy, -ant, -ar, -ard, -ary, -ate, -cy, -dom, -ee, -eer, -ence, -ency, -ent, -er, -ery, -ess, -ette, -hood, -ice, -ie, -ier, -ite, -ism, -ist, -ity, -ive, -kin, -let, -ment, -mony, -ness, -or, -ory, -ship, -ster, -teen, -tion, -tude, -ty, -ure, -y, -yer

Suffixes marking verbs: -ate, -en, -fy, -ify, -ise, -ize

Suffixes marking adjectives: -able, -ac, -aceous, -al, -am, -ar, -ary, -ate, -ble, -ent, -er, -ern, -escent, -ful, -ible, -ic, -ical, -id, -ile, -ine, -ish, -less, -like, -ly, -ory, -ose, -ous, -some, -ty, -ulent, -wise, -y

Suffixes marking adverbs: -ally, -fold, -like, -ly, -ward, -ways, -wise

In recent years, new words ending in *-ize* and *-wise* have flourished. We now encounter *functionalize, finalize, optimize,* and *winterize* as well as *learning-wise, weather-wise, time-wise,* and *money-wise.* Undoubtedly, a number of useful words will survive out of this language fad, but coinages of this kind have become so much associated with bad jargon that careful writers will at least use them with caution.

Even though derivation is one of the common means of forming words, English also uses compounding, that is, joining together stems of words to form new ones. The process is by no means limited to native words. Relatively recent additions to the language like *television, telethon, astronaut, neutrosphere, bathysphere,* and *helicopter* show the tendency to combine Latin and Greek roots to supply our contemporary needs, particularly in science and technology.

The meanings of native compounds are sometimes self-explanatory when two elements are combined, like *newsworthy, teenage, lackluster,* and *flowerpot.* In other instances, however, they assume meanings beyond the literal addition of the two parts, like *henpeck, ladykiller, browbeat,* and *handbook.*

Compounding is particularly common in popular speech. One form will often spawn numerous others. By analogy with established words like *manpower* and *horsepower,* the late 1960s coined *black-power, white-power, flower-power, green-power,* and *boy-power.* Other popular compounds were *sit-in, stand-in, camp-in, love-in,* and *be-in,* possibly by analogy with *drive-in.* Many compounds of this kind are colorful and expressive, but often short-lived, as we can already see by viewing these words from the perspective of the 1980s.

Blending is a third means of combining words; the resulting forms are called portmanteau words. Some of these are long-established words, like *flare* (a combination of *flame* and *glare*), *glimmer* (*gleam* and *shimmer*), and *smash* (*smack* and *mash*). More recent ones like *motel* (*motor* and *hotel*) and *smog* (*smoke* and *fog*) are relatively self-explanatory. *Napalm* makes a short pronounceable blend of its two main ingredients, naphthenic and palmitic acids. Some blends are informal, like *josh* (*joke* and *bosh*) and *chortle* (*chuckle* and *snort*). Others are puns or deliberately humorous combinations, like *dognap* (cp. *kidnap*) or *drismal* (*dreary* and *dismal*).

Shifting

The discussion of derivational suffixes above has shown how words of one part of speech can be made to serve as another part of speech by actually changing the form of the word. The English language, however, also permits a functional shift of a word without an actual change of form. A word need only be moved from its accustomed position to a position usually occupied by another part of speech. Thus, the space-age phrase "All systems are go" changes *go* from a verb to an adjective. In the sentence "She won't believe in you hereafter," *hereafter* functions as an adverbial modifier. In "She believes in the hereafter," the placement of *hereafter* in an object position after the preposition *in* indicates that it is used as a noun in this sentence. Thus, by a constant process of shifting, words of the language assume new functions and meanings. The basic reason, of course, is economy. No new word needs to be created if an old one will serve.

Economy operates also in two other forms of shifting: clipping and back formations. Clipped words are essentially only shortened forms of other words, like *quote* for *quotation, gym* for *gymnasium, exam* for *examination.* In these instances, both forms are retained, the shortened form usually associated with informal speech and the longer one with more formal occasions of speaking or writing. In other instances, however, the shortened form has become as firmly established as the standard form, and both are used interchangeably. We do not ordinarily think of *fan* as short for *fanatic* or of *pants* as short for *pantaloons.* Clipped forms like *gas* (for *gasoline*), *flu, phone,* and *plane* (for *airplane*) have a similar independence from their sources and are used freely in writing as well as speech. The most extreme form of clipping, of course, occurs when a word or phrase is reduced to its initials, like *TV, U.S., DDT,* and *P.M.*

Back formations are another kind of shifting and shortening to make current words do additional work. Some back formations have been accepted for so long that the only way to determine whether they were created by back formation or by derivation is to consult a historical dictionary. For example, the *Oxford English*

Dictionary indicates that *commune* is a back formation from *communion*, *educate* from *education*, and *edit* from *editor*. At the time back formations are introduced, they are almost always condemned as gaucheries and continue to have that reputation until such time as usage has established the back formation and no one knows any longer which word preceded the other. Back formations of relatively recent origin, like *enthuse* from *enthusiasm* and *destruct* from *destruction*, are still in that period of transition when favor and disfavor counterbalance one another.

Inventing

Combining words and shifting them are actually forms of inventing, in that new words are created as a result. But invention often takes a more ingenious twist. Existing elements are sometimes combined in highly unusual ways, or new words are created without reference to existing forms. Trade names, echoic words, nonce words, acronyms, and folk etymologies are the clearest signs of inventiveness at work.

Trade names would be no more important than any other proper names that are invented except that they often change their status as patented trademarks to become a class name for all other products of the same kind. *Zipper, nylon, kleenex, xerox,* and *escalator* have become utility words of the language.

Echoic words are combinations of letters that are invented to approximate sounds. Some like *whew, whoa,* and *boom* are conventional sound words recorded in the dictionary, but others like *ssh, psst,* and *hmm* continue to be used only as symbols of sounds rather than words. Closely related to the imitative words are reduplicating words that seem to play with sound for the sake of sound. Some of these words are slangy, like *super-duper, helter-skelter,* and *wishy-washy,* but others like *knicknack, humdrum,* and *zigzag* have lost most of their colloquial flavor.

Nonce words, or neologisms, are words and phrases invented for a particular context or occasion. In one sense, all new words might be considered nonce words when they first appear, but the fate of some words seems clearer than that of others. The limited usefulness of a nonce word frequently dooms it to a short life. A few like *boondoggle* and *gobbledygook* have become established; Winston Churchill's phrase "iron curtain" also survives. But blends like *psychedelicatessen* (a store to buy psychedelic posters), *archeolatry* (reverence of the past), *magnicide* (murder of an important man), and *numbskulduggerous* are not likely to find many users. They are left to perish in their newborn state. The stillbirth of many words, however, should not discourage you from trying your hand at coining new words that seem to meet a need in a particular context, particularly if the established lexicon does not meet that need.

Acronyms are words whose individual letters are telescoped from a series of several words. *Snafu* (situation normal, all fouled up), a popular word of World War II, has been cleaned up and finds general acceptance in the language. Organizations with long titles provide one of the most common sources of acronyms; UNESCO (United Nations Educational, Scientific, and Cultural Organization), NASA (National Aeronautics and Space Administration), and PAWS (Progressive

Animal Welfare Society) are only three among thousands of examples. Acronyms are either pronounced as words or, when unpronounceable, are sounded as individual letters, like TVA.

Folk etymologies are inventions in that they are usually popular translations of difficult words or phrases that people do not understand. *Varicose veins* is first heard and then written as *very close veins; cole slaw* becomes *cold slaw*. Foreign terms are given the same treatment; *cucaracha* is simplified to *cockroach*, and *coquetier* to *cocktail*. The unfamiliar in general is made familiar. Thus, *crayfish* becomes *crawfish* and *groseberry, gooseberry*. Comparable to these are simplified spellings of difficult words, like *pigeon English* for *pidgin English* and *shammy* for *chamois*. The interesting thing about many folk etymologies and simplified spellings is that their use sometimes prevails, so that in time we wonder why they are called what they are. A primrose, for example, looks nothing like a rose. The word is actually a folk version of the Middle English and Old French word *primerole*, which was the early word for the flower that we recognize as a primrose.

Changing meanings and values of words

Etymology, the study of the history of words, satisfies our perennial fascination with detection and our delight in narrative. It seeks out the origins of words and traces the changes that have occurred during the period of their use. New words constantly emerge; others, like *olden* and *bestow*, grow obsolescent; innumerable others are obsolete. Apart from being born and dying, however, words represent other kinds of changes. They move in and out of fashion or up and down the social ladder. Seldom do they retain absolute meanings, because meaning is a property that exists in the minds of individuals, not in the words themselves. Words are being constantly reinterpreted by their use. Their meanings may be extended or narrowed, improved in their connotations or debased. These four changes are customarily referred to as generalization, specialization, amelioration, and pejoration or by an alternate set of terms—extension, limitation, regeneration, and degeneration.

Generalization

Extensions of meaning are almost always gradual and may be either logical or figurative extensions. The change a word undergoes is not always limited to a single language. If the word has been borrowed, its meaning in another language is a part of its history. The word *governor*, borrowed from French, comes from a Latin word that originally meant "the steersman of a boat." Rather interestingly, we still retain the association between government and sailing in the cliché "ship of state." A governor, however, is not literally a "steersman," only a figurative one.

Words as unlike in meaning as *assassin* and *hashish* are related by their history. *Assassins* were originally members of a Mohammedan sect who ate hashish to fire up their zeal to kill Christians during the time of the Crusades. *Assassin*, of course, is now a general term for murderer, not specifically one who has taken hashish to inspire the act.

Extensions of meaning frequently result from a change whereby some common usage displaces the particular meaning of a word. For example, in the sixteenth century, a madhouse in London named the Hospital of St. Mary of Bethlehem was commonly known as *Bedlam* (an old form of Bethlehem). *Bedlam* now means "confusion," only an association with the original place and clearly an extended meaning.

Almost all words derived from proper names necessarily show an extension of meaning. *Sadism, silhouette,* and *dunce* are derived from the names of men; *maudlin, georgette,* and *marijuana* from the names of women; *utopia, serendipity,* and *quixotic* from the titles of books; and *wiener, paisley,* and *bourbon* from place names. To these might be added countless others drawn from mythology. The qualities associated with the original person, book, or place are universalized and made generally useful.

Synecdoche and metonymy are figures of speech that ordinarily represent extensions of meaning. *Synecdoche* involves the substitution of a part for the whole—*boards* for "the stage," *hands* for "workers," *mouths* for "persons to feed." In each instance, the part stands for the meaning of the whole. *Metonymy* describes a similar kind of association by which one term loosely substitutes for another related one; thus, *sweat* for "energy," the *press* for "newspapers" or "newspaper reporters," *tongues* for "languages," *Milton* for "Milton's works." The close relation between metonymy and synecdoche has blurred a hard and fast distinction between them.

Words are also capable of taking on metaphorical extensions at the same time that they retain their basic meanings. This transfer of association is no more obvious than in the use of the names of animals, fish, and birds to describe people, either in complimentary or insulting ways. Most of the terms are highly colloquial. *Chicken, sparrow,* and *pigeon,* are sexist but complimentary terms for females; *crow, cat,* and *vixen* are of another order. Men seem to inspire consistently negative terms like *wolf, goat, rat,* and *worm.* Anyone, male or female, can be a *shark, louse, pig,* or *dodo.* All kinds of popular usages seem to tend toward generalization. *Guy,* originally a term used only for males, now includes both sexes. *Great* and *fantastic* take on more and more burdens of meaning, and the list of words could be extended to great length. Words subjected to endless extension, however, finally signify almost nothing at all. For example, *cute, nice, great, cool,* and *tough* have accumulated so many meanings that they are now mainly general expressions of approval and disapproval. Such words with a wide variety of meanings are called *counter words.* Slang and nonstandard dialects are responsible for a great number of counter words. It has been estimated that *mess* as one part of speech or another has more than fifty meanings. Because counter words are "umbrella" terms, imprecise in their meanings, careful writers usually avoid them.

Specialization

Specialization denotes a narrowing of meaning rather than an extension. Usage alone is responsible for the change. Outside the United States, *corn* refers to grain in general rather than to the one we identify with the word. *Vest* originally meant any garment; now it is one particular article of clothing. *Undertaker* was a general term for anyone undertaking a job; now it is used only for a mortician. *Computer*, once a term for a person who computes, now refers almost exclusively to an electronic device. The monopoly of the medical profession on the word *doctor* has tended to obscure its more general meaning as one who holds any doctoral degree. Professors now have to identify themselves as "teaching doctors," not "doctor doctors." *Doctor* has been specialized.

The continued narrowing of a word's meaning over a period of time ultimately places its lifespan in jeopardy. A word may possibly become a purely technical term used in very limited contexts; in rapidly changing times, it may disappear when the specialty has faded. Innumerable terms associated with early sciences and heraldry died out when those pursuits were no longer viable, although a few like *quintessence, chevron, humor,* and *tincture* took on extended meanings and have survived.

Amelioration

Amelioration, a word derived from the Latin word *melior,* meaning "better," identifies the kind of change that occurs when the meaning of a particular word improves. A word itself does not become better or worse because of changes, but its associations do. The word *nice* has made a complete shift. Its original negative connotations of "foolish," "stupid," and "wanton" have changed to current meanings that are consistently agreeable. A *brave* in the sense of a warrior was used in the sixteenth century as a term for a bully or hired assassin. *Enthrall* originally meant "to enslave." By a transfer of meaning from literal enslavement to a captivation of the senses, it has come to have its present meaning of "to charm." The fine print of historical dictionaries reveals the questionable origins of many reputable words in use today. *Jazz* is only one example.

Pejoration

Pejoration is a process that attaches negative connotations to a word. Often it occurs simultaneously with changes in specialization or generalization. *Spit* once referred to anything spewed from the mouth. We retain that sense of the word when we say something like "He spits out bitter reproaches." When *spit* became more specialized to refer mainly to ejecting saliva, it underwent pejoration. It usually carries unpleasant associations. *Idiot* originally referred to a private citizen who preferred not to hold public office. The transition from "an uneducated private citizen who prefers not to hold office" to "one totally incapable of holding office" accounts for the negative associations that the word now has.

The reputation of words is sometimes relative. Among people of liberal, nonauthoritarian thought, words like *reactionary, fundamentalist,* and *purist* are used pejoratively. Among ultraconservative thinkers, *liberal, left,* and *intellectual* are used with scorn. Over a long period of time, negative connotations that spring up may at times stick. *Pontificate* is almost exclusively used today in a negative, uncomplimentary sense. Ingroups frequently borrow words of the standard vocabulary and give them private associations for their own purposes. These secondary meanings, compared with their usual ones, are often pejorative. One might list *acid, lid, gay,* and *powder* as words looked upon differently depending on the context and the user. If as a writer you are unaware of the pejorative meaning of many words, you can fall into unintentional blunders.

The appropriate use of words

Accuracy of meaning: denotation

Mrs. Malaprop in Sheridan's play *The Rivals* (1775) is the matron-saint of all blunderers with language. She easily confuses two words that sound alike regardless of their meaning; "supercilious knowledge" is her version of "superficial knowledge." All such confusions and near-misses are now referred to as *malapropisms.* Mrs. Malaprop's humor is of course a reminder of the need to know the exact meanings of words. In fact, you could not even respond to her humor if you did not know the difference between the words she uses.

Any writer needs an adequate stock of words to draw from and an accurate knowledge of what they mean. We do not have much difficulty with the words of the language that have specific referents, that is, with words that refer to something concrete in time and space. *Fire* in its basic sense has reference to our common perception of burning and flame. It can be seen and felt and smelled, and heat is as inseparably connected with it as light. Whether fire refers to the flame of a match, burning logs in a grate, or a conflagration, the word has a hard core of meaning that we understand. We know that *fire* is not *rain,* and *wood* is not *fur.* It is true that we each choose a particular referent from own experience; we have not all seen the same fire, but your capacity to communicate a concept like *fire* lies in your ability to link the right word with the right referent. The basic meaning of a word—its hard core of meaning—is commonly referred to as its *denotation.*

Further, a concept like *fire* represents a family of words, but kinship ends at some point; that is, every word has a limited range of meaning. We have no difficulty including *flame, blaze,* and *conflagration* in the *fire* family (in the sense of a chemical reaction), but *spark* seems to have only a borderline relationship (fire reduced to an ember or a small piece of fire spewed from a burning substance). When *spark* is used to mean an electrical discharge, it loses the essential denotation of *fire* altogether. A holocaust of fire falls within the burning family, but a holocaust in the generalized sense of any widespread destruction clearly moves beyond the range. Thesauruses do not sufficiently make clear these variations and limits of meaning. For instance, *inferno* is at times listed as a synonym of *fire.* Even though *inferno* may in the minds of some people be associated with flames, the denotation of the word as a "place of torment" puts it in quite a different family. To describe a fire in newspaper style as a "raging inferno" simply adds metaphorical implications to the fact of intense burning.

A word is capable of operating in different contexts without confusion. For example, we set aside the literal meaning of *head* as a biological term when it is used figuratively in new contexts such as "the head of a pin," "the head of a boil," "the head of a department," "the head on beer," "a river's head," "the head word of a phrase," or "bringing matters to a head." With varying degrees of generality, each of these uses has a carryover meaning of "something at the top," but the context in each case determines a more specific meaning that does not permit us to mistake one for the other.

Not all words are as simple to differentiate from one another as *fire* and *head.* A somewhat different problem arises with words like *practical* and *practicable, sensuous* and *sensual, incredulous* and *incredible.* In these instances, we are dependent on literal meanings as defined by the dictionary; there are no specific referents. Their denotations are matters of written record. The fact that you recognize what some words mean in one context does not guarantee that you will be able to use them accurately in another unless you are sure of their precise denotations. For that reason, a dictionary is indispensable. You should use one to check words you use, particularly if there is any doubt in your mind about their exact meanings.

Synonyms

Both dictionaries and thesauruses list synonyms. These are helpful guides as long as you remind yourself that words often have subtle differences of meaning. *Ethical* has reference to moral principles, but *ethical* and *moral* are not necessarily interchangeable. *Opponent, antagonist,* and *adversary* seem to share a common denotation, but they would not all fit the same context because they suggest different kinds of opposition. A tackle playing opposite another tackle in football has an *opponent,* not necessarily an *antagonist* or *adversary.* In the classroom, they might be antagonists. In the courtroom, they might be adversaries.

Further, we should note that alternate patterns of the same word are not always synonymous. "He fights" and "He is a fighter" do not any more mean the same than "He types" and "He is a typist." The second statements differ from the first because *fighter* and *typist* are noun forms that are more specialized in meaning than *fights* and *types.*

Shifts in meaning of this variety are important in the revision process, particularly if someone else edits your writing and tries to cut out unnecessary words. It is true that "Dead leaves covered the ground" is shorter, more direct, and possibly more emphatic than "There were a great number of dead leaves lying on the ground," but one critic has made the interesting observation that the second sentence does not mean exactly what the first sentence means. There are more leaves on the ground in the first sentence; there could be a bit of ground showing through in the second sentence.

Meaning, therefore, depends on the preciseness with which words are used, the arrangement of them, and, finally, the total context in which we find them. In larger contexts, words begin to acquire extended meanings.

Puns

Puns actually trade on the multiple meanings of words. They invite a double take; they play on more than one context at one and the same time. For example, shortly following the first orbital trip around the moon, a scientist, wanting to emphasize that exploring the depths of the sea was as important as probing the far reaches of space, chose to make his point by means of a *double entendre:* "The ocean's bottom," he said, "is infinitely more attractive than the moon's behind." Before a national audience, former President Gerald Ford did not hesitate to say "I am a Ford, not a Lincoln." Garry Wills, writing for *Esquire,* described the successes of opera star Beverly Sills as "singing in the reign." As we all know, to a tennis player love is nothing.

Even though punning is one of the humorous things you can do with language, you should realize that its effectiveness depends on contrast—that is, not doing it too often.

Associations and extended meanings: connotation

What a dictionary cannot indicate is what happens to particular words when they become a part of your own experience. If you once severed a finger with a garden sickle, just the mention of a sickle or a knife may cause you to respond emotionally. Words conjure up past experiences; they act as a stimulus to subconscious feelings.

If you consider the denotation of a word its nucleus of meaning, then consider all your private associations with a word as satellite meanings. The associations words have for you are its connotations. Some of these we all share; some are purely personal. For instance, if we list names of insects like cockroach, fly, butterfly, mosquito, and centipede, some of these will prompt more emotional reactions than others, depending on your familiarity with them. Many people think of cockroaches as noisome, flies pesky, butterflies beautiful, mosquitoes irritating, and centipedes possibly amusing, at least at a distance. Many connotations are similar because we share common human experiences. We often say impetuous and temperamental people are "full of fire." Common associations of this kind ultimately result in extended meanings of words. In fact, *fire,* used to refer to human temperament, means "ardor," "enthusiasm," or "inspiration."

Other associations with *fire* may be completely private. In *The Shape of Content,* Ben Shahn narrates what personal associations *fire* has for him and how in a painting entitled *Allegory* he transformed those experiences into a highly formalized wreath of flames, which one critic interpreted as a Communist symbol. Shahn denies that the wreath has any political significance and states that it expresses abstractly his private feelings about fire. These associations can be understood, however, only when Shahn explains his private feelings. In writing, you too have to realize that readers will not understand your most personal associations with a word unless you supply a context by which they can begin to understand how you feel.

Connotations are a fact of language use. They cannot be prevented, and they cannot be ignored by a writer. A writer cannot use the word *slob* and expect a pleasant response, unless the context is humorous. And we don't know to what extent a different word like *slobber* overlaps and affects our reaction to *slob*. These are complex responses to language. Words are like Rorschach tests; they are indexes to our personality and experiences.

Metaphor

Metaphor is one of the major sources of expressiveness in language, not reserved for poets but used constantly by ordinary people in everyday talk. Consider these sentences:

I dived into the food.

The audience sat glued to their seats.

That job was tough sledding.

She was swept into office.

The darkness swallowed them.

That decision was a shot in the dark.

Money talks.

These are fairly commonplace expressions, but they are all metaphoric. Each involves using words in a context they do not literally belong to. "Diving into food" suggests a full commitment, something like plunging into water, not literally, but figuratively.

Metaphor is a process of comparison. Its use is clearly more conscious in some instances than in others. When particular metaphors are used constantly, they lose their power of analogy. For example, clouds seem to have their own way of drifting. We don't have to think about water when we say clouds drift. Nor does "He jumped at the suggestion" cause us to think of a sudden physical action. And we may be little aware of the mixture of sense impressions in phrases like "loud colors" and "piercing sounds." The language is filled with faded metaphors, comparisons that no longer cause us to think of two separate contexts.

All fresh metaphors, however, act by giving us two perspectives at once. They bring two frames of reference to bear upon one another. Attempting to explain that every step and movement in ice dancing has equal value, Walter Terry writes:

We all love to jump, but jumps are important only when skillfully placed in a sentence of movement.

We are left to spell out the correspondence between two contexts. Just as words become meaningful when they are combined into sentences, so jumps take on importance when they are made a part of the total movement of a dance. The metaphor contained in the word *sentence* suggests the idea of wholeness.

In expository writing, metaphor is frequently used to explain the abstract in terms of the concrete. For example, Suzanne Langer introduces a simile (a special form of metaphor) to explain an abstract concept of language:

As it is, however, all language has a form which requires us to string out our ideas even though their objects rest one within the other; as pieces of clothing that are actually worn one over the other have to be strung side by side on the clothesline.

Philosophy in a New Key

The homely image permits us to understand more clearly.

In a book entitled *Timewarps*, John Gribbin refers to the "Holy Grail of time travel," a reference to the possibility of crossing into other time frames through space travel. The "Holy Grail" is both a metaphor and an allusion. Understanding the reference depends upon knowing that much medieval literature was devoted to stories about knights seeking the Holy Grail, the chalice from which Jesus drank at the Last Supper. The Holy Grail signifies an ultimate quest, the sense in which Gribbin uses it. Clearly, this is a learned metaphor, yet one that the author assumes most of his readers will know.

If a metaphor is not sufficiently familiar, however, a reader may simply be left with puzzlement. For instance, Daniel Bell writes, "New York is a palimpsest." Realizing that this comparison is not self-evident, he goes on to explain:

Successive layers, never wholly erasing the earlier ones, have provided different outlines for the profiles of New York.

"The Forces Shaping the City: The Four Faces of New York"

Yet even this sentence is unilluminating unless one knows that a palimpsest is a parchment or tablet "that has been written upon or inscribed two or three times, the previous text or texts having been imperfectly erased and remaining, therefore, still visible" (*Webster's New World Dictionary*). Readers who know that fact will understand the metaphor; others will be mystified.

Familiarity is therefore an important element in choosing a metaphor. "Black holes" is a scientific metaphor for a phenomemon of space. Even though you may not grasp the technicalities known to physicists, you at least, through metaphor, have an image of what they are talking about. If you think of metaphor as a way of explaining and clarifying, then metaphor is truly functional, not just ornamental.

Abstract and concrete

Do words divorce thought from feelings? Only in the sense that some words fail to touch nerve responses at all. We can think first of structure words like *that, for, whereas*, and *however;* we can then think of abstract words like *result, tendency*, and *distribution*. These are essentially unfeeling words. As a generalization, words that have concrete associations tend to be more capable of emotional expression than abstract words. In one sense, anything written is more abstract than the experience itself, because writing is a symbolic transcription of the experience. The word *fire* is more abstract than the actual burning, but among words themselves *fire* is less abstract than other words. Both *passion* and *zeal*, as synonyms of *fieriness*, are more abstract than the word *fire* itself because they are further removed from the referent and more generalized. Further, words like *feeling* and *endeavor* seem even more abstract and generalized than *passion* and *zeal*. An abstract word, therefore, functions as a kind of summary term; a concrete word, as a specific example. Only when abstract words are tied to experiences—like *resistance* to the French underground during World War II or a small boy's refusal to be bullied by a bigger one—can their meaning be made specific and forceful. All the dictionary can say by way of definition is that *resistance* means "the opposition offered by one thing, force, etc., to another." This is an abstract definition devoid of specific meaning or feeling, although it is a covering definition. In writing, abstract words act similarly as ways of grouping and generalizing individual experiences.

It is apparent that some subjects invite the use of more abstract words than others; or, to put the matter differently, some subjects invite more words with precise denotative value to the exclusion of words with expressive qualities. It is one thing to discuss death as man's inevitable fate; it is another to describe a fatal accident that takes the lives of three young men. One topic is by nature theoretical and generalized; the other, actual and specific. The first would probably be more abstract than the second, but it does not necessarily follow that the total effect of writing on an abstract subject has to be vague and unfeeling. Its effect is influenced by the balance of abstract and concrete words working together in a total context. An excess of abstract words invariably produces an impenetrable and dull style:

> The reason people exclude strange or "wrong" ideas is out of fear. But the same fear prompts them to use the same methods everyone else uses to obtain the same goals, spiritual or mental. The point is not that it is undesirable to want certain middle-class material things or to have a certain set of values. The most important part of life is to be free enough within one's own spirit so that other values and wants and methods of obtaining them can be seen and tolerated.
>
> Student paragraph

A paragraph of this kind causes the reader to wonder what the writer has in mind. Each of the following phrases lacks a sense of the specific: "strange or 'wrong' ideas," "the same fear," "the same methods," "the same goals," "certain middle-class material things," "certain set of values," and "other values and wants and methods." These indefinite references make the prose diffuse. Although each one cannot be spelled out, some of them can be illustrated to clarify the meaning and liven the prose.

Clichés

The cliché is prefabricated language; it is packaged and ready for immediate delivery. Because of its accessibility, it also tends to be overused language: "He told it like it was without beating around the bush." The cliché is the mark of the tried and tired style. Yet it is misleading to assume that novelty will necessarily produce vigorous language. You do not need to be inventing new words constantly to give your writing a sense of freshness. It is mainly a matter of avoiding tired combinations.

Various free-association tests indicate that people respond to stimuli with a high degree of uniformity. When given a stimulus word like *color,* they will most commonly say "red," or in response to *flower* they will say "rose." Most respondents will also say "dark" in response to *light* instead of "lamp," "bright," "sun," or "bulb." Because informal talk allows little time for careful choice of words, it depends very heavily on the cliché, which is actually a kind of conditioned response. The stereotyped expression occurs to us first.

What is true of speaking, of course, need not be true of writing. When the ready phrase presents itself, the writer without too much deliberation can decide whether it has been overworked. All of the following sentences fall into highly familiar, almost set expressions:

His comments are applicable to all walks of life.

They think they should have their lives given to them on a silver platter.

Within the past few years, a new ray of hope has shone on allergy sufferers.

If we turn back the pages of our history books, we will find the account of Seward's Folly.

We had ham, beef, crab, shrimp—you name it.

One might continue to list inevitable combinations like "thick and thin," "sum and substance," "rank and file," and "good clean fun." To illustrate further would be to quote the slogans and pet phrases that are current, better left unquoted because they are "here today, gone tomorrow." Hackneyed expressions do not fail to communicate anything at all, but they fail to do it with much vigor, particularly if the expressions are figurative, like "smart as a whip," "deep as the ocean," or "a square peg in a round hole." If the function of figurative language in expository prose is to make the ideas and feelings more concrete, then tired expressions tend to lose effectiveness simply because their meanings are ignored. They arouse no reaction; they set up no stimulus that alerts the reader to new associations and implications. In order to keep language vigorous, therefore, you first have to be able to recognize what is trite; then you have to decide that you will avoid ready-made language.

Avoiding a cliché is not always easy, but you can at times get mileage from one by twisting it, echoing it, or substituting words:

Nothing succeeds like excess.

Better done than said.

A nickel a day keeps the crooks away. [ad for light bulbs]

A shirt for all reasons. [advertisement]

Describing the flight of the Egyptians before their Roman conquerors, Bernard Shaw writes "The battle was not to the strong, but the race was to the swift," recalling Ecclesiastes 9:11, which reads: "I returned and saw under the sun, that the race is not to the swift, nor the battle to the strong. . . ."

Monosyllables and polysyllables

In "Politics and the English Language" George Orwell sets forth several rules that "one can rely on when instinct fails." His second one reads: "Never use a long word where a short one will do." His advice stems from the tendency among many people, particularly the politicians he is writing about, to do just the opposite.

We need not take George Orwell's rule too literally. The polysyllables of the language are both necessary and often appropriate. What Orwell is saying in effect is "Don't use too many big words all at once" or "Don't use too many unfamiliar words together." To do so may be to inundate and obfuscate readers and even exacerbate their annoyance. The polysyllabic style is very easy to make fun of.

What many writers seem not to realize is that big words do not accomplish what they think big words do. College freshmen writing their first themes frequently haul out all the polysyllables they know because they seem to think the "educated style" is the style of big words. In their honest effort, they create an impression of being pompous.

Big words are sometimes used as an evasion of hard facts. During the government scandals of 1973–1974, the Attorney General of the United States asked that the former Vice President "not be incarcerated in a penal institution." His choice of words seemed to suggest that it would have been inappropriate to ask that a wrongdoer in high government circles "not be put in jail" or possibly "not be imprisoned." On another occasion, a TV commentator explained that a senator of the United States was guilty of "grave improprieties in his fiscal management." What he meant simply was that the senator had some irregularities in spending to explain. Unfortunately, when we are personally involved in difficult situations, we too are capable of inventing elaborate phrases when the force of few words is too great.

Jargon

Jargon is special talk. Jargon is inside talk understood mainly by those who are insiders. "Insiders" are members of a profession; they are special practitioners (plumbers, truckers, waiters); they are devotees of an art or sport. All specialists have their own lingo. Thus singers talk about the "tessitura" of a song when they refer to the level of tone; doctors are more likely to refer to "cardiac arrest" than to a heart attack.

Even though jargon is often condemned because it tends to narrow the circle of communication, we must also recognize another argument. Mastering a jargon is essentially the way individuals prove they are members of a group. They can talk the lingo. Jargon is therefore a badge. It certifies entry. No matter how horrid the lingo may sound to unattuned ears, the sound is familiar and comfortable to those who use it. The use of jargon has to be gauged in terms of audience. If specialists speak to specialists, jargon is in order. If specialists speak to generalists, then some translation and accommodation have to be made.

Verbal taboos: euphemisms

Modern taboos against words result from an attitude of purism about language or from moral bias. Modern taboos are scarely more rational than primitive taboos, but they do make sense in terms of the sensibilities of people who are offended by specific words. Needless to say, there are far fewer taboos in the 1980s than there were in the 1880s or even in the 1920s, but taboos are not necessarily limited to matters of sex and obscenity. It is equally important what words we use to address Italians, Jews, or the person who collects the garbage or the one who cleans our office building. All inappropriate terms become taboo. Glossaries of usage are filled with taboos that threaten the offender with social disapproval if they are used. They supply soft and inoffensive substitutes. Modern English has a plentiful supply of euphemisms to ease the sting of harsh words. All supposedly is good that sounds good.

Thus, euphemisms protect the status and feelings of individuals and, in that way, provide a service. At other times, however, euphemisms represent doublespeak, a deliberate cover-up, an evasion of the truth, particularly in military language, sometimes referred to as Pentagonese. "Protective reaction" and "air strike" are euphemisms for bombing. The CIA used "termination without prejudice" as a mask for political assassination. One writer has advanced the idea that six months of reading materials issued by the United States government would teach students more about the uses and abuses of language than years of college courses.

Letters of recommendation represent another form of doublespeak. In their zeal to put nothing outrightly bad in black and white, recommenders fall into a code language. In certain contexts, they say someone is "quiet" when they mean "ineffectual"; "solid," when they mean "mediocre"; "unflamboyant," when they mean "dull"; and "versatile," when they mean "not particularly good in anything." In such examples, we find a reversal of the basic premise that words are used to communicate. Unfortunately, words can also be used to obstruct communication.

A matter of fundamental importance in writing is whether you control words or whether they run away with you. If you hold a tight rein on words, you seldom risk the danger of saying what you never intended.

Projects **1.** The language is constantly gaining new words to meet advances in science, technology, and communication, deriving them in traditional ways: borrowing (Apollo, Antares), combining (supersonic, feedback), shifting (solid state, jet), and inventing (laser, radar). Choose twenty-five words of recent vintage and categorize them by origin.
2. Invent a new word by any of the means that new words are ordinarily formed. Following the exact form of a dictionary, write an entry for your

word, including an example or two of its use in a context. Add a brief justification for the addition of this word to the language.

3. Determine the meanings of the following foreign phrases:

ad hoc	*non sequitur*
ad nauseam	*per capita*
alter ego	*per diem*
de facto	*per se*
ex cathedra	*persona non grata*
ex officio	*pro tem*
modus operandi	*sine qua non*

Make a list of other foreign phrases you commonly use or see. If you are in doubt about the foreign words you use, think of certain subjects like ballet, music, or medicine.

4. Write a list of technical terms associated with one specialty you are familiar with. Then write a corresponding list of their colloquial equivalents; for instance, *herpes zoster* is the technical term for what is commonly called shingles.

5. Explain the etymology of the following words: advent, antedeluvian, belligerent, dunce, epicurean, holocaust, maudlin, ostracism, pandemonium, postlapsarian, satellite, simony, venereal.

6. Check the *Oxford English Dictionary* for the different sources of the following pairs:

abbreviate, abridge	mint, money
blame, blaspheme	regal, royal
compute, count	sever, separate
frail, fragile	travel, fare
help, assistance	truth, veracity

7. Make a list of current slang terms that in meaning are extensions of words in standard use—*pot*, for instance.

8. Some words we use are complimentary, some disapproving. Set up a chart with the terms below down the left side. Add two column headings to the right: "Complimentary terms" and "Disapproving terms." Then try to fill in at least five complimentary nouns or adjectives, standard or slang, for each of the terms, and then five disapproving adjectives or nouns for each:

an old soldier
baby in arms
child in diapers
a teenager, between 11 and 15, male
a teenager, between 11 and 15, female
a teenager, between 16 and 20, male
a teenager, between 16 and 20, female
a woman in distress
a young cripple

a senator
a hit record (music)
a $100,000 house

9. Determine what current terms are being used to refer euphemistically to the following: gardener, janitor, street cleaner, death, war, disease, sickness, students with low IQs, the blind, the crippled, a toilet.

10. List pejorative terms—slang or otherwise—for doctors, dentists, lawyers, professors, preachers, politicians, salesmen.

11. The following list represents a ladder from general to particular, from abstract to concrete: communicated, spoke, spoke loudly, shouted, megaphoned his words (metaphorical extension). Move the following words and phrases to greater precision by constructing similar ladders: color, late in the year, drove fast, passed the time, crowded street.

12. *Sweet* is a general word that applies to many contexts. Determine five or six more particular adjectives that convey the idea of "sweetness" in terms of each of the following:

a flower   a person
a food product   a sound

13. Determine in what ways the following pairs share a hard cord of meaning and then in what ways they differ. Do you consider the words synonymous?

happy—euphoric
sad—morose
quarrelsome—litigious
impatient—petulant
firm—adamant
proud—pompous

Suggestions for writing

1. Choose several terms you and your friends commonly use to describe experiences or states of mind (for example, "spaced out" or "blow my mind"). Use them as a point of departure to write an essay about people of your age. What images do the words create? You may want to include an analysis of the metaphors involved in some of the terms.

2. Think of a group to which you belong, possibly your family, that has its own system of communication or evasion. Write an essay about the ritual of language in this group. What are the members trying to say? What are they trying to avoid saying? Do you get along better as a result of this mode of communication?

3. Write an essay on the language of the newspaper, particularly the euphemisms. What language does the newspaper you read characteristically use for references to sex, handsome diplomats, high society, the aged? Do the terms applied to women as opposed to those applied to men indicate a sexist view?

4. Read an article or speech by a political figure. Write an essay on the diction used, considering such things as circumlocutions, euphemisms, and clichés. Is the thought clear or foggy?

5. Watch television for two or three hours, taking notes on the words and expressions you hear. Can you classify them or make generalizations? Is the language of the advertisements different from that of entertainment shows or talk shows? Does the audience being appealed to have something to do with the usage? Does the seriousness of purpose? Write an essay about your findings.

6. Write an essay on a subject of your own choice in which you consciously experiment with language.

7. Examine the words of one of your favorite songs. Do you find that you can accept the meanings literally? Are there meanings and implications beyond the literal ones? Write an essay about the meaning of a song.

Chapter 8 Style

To the perennial question of the beginning writer, "What can I do to improve my style?," there is no simple answer, because style is the total effect of all the things you do when you write. The previous chapters of this book have each discussed elements that enter into the making of an identifiable style. It is not something that you put on like a costume; it is something that grows out of the qualities you have as an individual and the things you do as a writer. The important thing to note is that you do not write just one style; you write various styles that reflect different selves on different occasions. The style of the one true self is a fallacy. You change, adjust, and express yourself in various ways. The style that identifies you results from a merging of inward motives and outward strategies. You are in control of that style only if you are aware of what you are doing.

Beyond technique

Jonathan Swift defined style as "proper words in proper places." The definition implies that context determines what is suitable. Undoubtedly, this is true. Yet Swift's definition may lead too easily to the conclusion that the choice of words is mechanical: all seems to depend on knowing what is proper and the rest will follow, like putting together a jigsaw puzzle. Much more is involved, of course. Yurek Lazowski seems to get at the heart of the matter in commenting on style in dance:

It is not enough in ballet just for the people to move in the right places at the right time. That is only the skeleton, but the heart doesn't beat yet. You have to give life to it.

In short, says Lazowski, style in dance is not technique alone. Style is beyond technique. The same applies to writing. You have to be involved with words to give life to them. Precisely how to do that no one will be able to tell you, but the degree of your involvement with your subject and your audience will serve as a starter. If you care about something or someone, you are likely to care about the words you use to tell about them.

The writer's point of view

The term *point of view* can be taken quite literally. It is the way you view your material; it is the stance you take. You can be on the inside or the outside, close or far away, beneath or above. These are figurative ways of saying that you can be a participant or an observer, close to your subject or removed from it, or looking at it from different angles. These perspectives will also determine the degree of subjectivity or objectivity in a piece of writing.

Subjectivity and objectivity

Subjectivity and objectivity are relative terms that attempt to define the degree to which the treatment of the subject is colored by the writer. Every writer has to recognize the distinction between fact and opinion. "The house across the street from mine is fifty years old" is a fact. "The fifty-year old house across the street is a blight on the neighborhood" is an opinion. The difference is not that one is measurable and verifiable and the other is not. A survey of the neighborhood might very well confirm that all the neighbors think the same thing. The difference between the two is that the first statement is objective, impersonal, and unbiased; the second statement is subjective, individual, and judgmental. An opinion does not become less subjective because many people share it; it is simply more widespread.

Subjectivity results when you are close to the subject you are writing about or when you make no effort to censor feelings and opinions. Objectivity results from the attempt to assume other perspectives than your own, to get outside yourself to see the matter as others may see it. Objectivity therefore represents a detached point of view. It requires some capacity for distancing.

Inasmuch as anything you think or write filters through your own mind, we might question whether any statement you make can be objective in an absolute sense. We may be forced to admit that all statements reflect only varying degrees of subjectivity, but objectivity still remains a useful and relative term that permits us to speak of opposites, just as heat is defined as the absence of cold, but we speak of heat and cold as opposites. The more you deliberately strive for fact instead of opinion, the more objective writing becomes.

It should not be assumed that subjectivity is bad and objectivity good or even that subjective writing is full of feeling and objective writing passionless. If you adopt an objective point of view, you can certainly come to conclusions and express them with emphasis. That is the nature of effective argumentation. Objective consideration of an issue means that your views are supported by facts and balanced against other viewpoints. The degree of subjectivity or objectivity, therefore, does produce a difference in style. The appropriateness of one stance or the other depends upon your own purposes and your reader's expectations.

The writer's voice: tone

Voice is another dimension of point of view; it is the tone that results from the writer's involvement and energy and manner. Almost any passage of prose can be characterized in terms of its voice. Voice is simply an analogy, a way of saying that the voice of the writer can be perceived on paper as readily as if the words had been spoken. Voice is something partly under your control by the choices you make about point of view and words and strategies; it is also something beyond your control because the personal voice, as Robert Frost has phrased it, gets "somehow entangled in the words and fastened to the page for the ear of the imagination." Frost thinks that voice is the only thing "that can save prose from itself."

A particular tone—humorous, solemn, satiric—may reflect your attitude toward the subject. Formality or informality may reflect your attitude toward the audience. A tone of superficiality or offensiveness may be wholly unintentional yet grow out of your own choice of words. In fact, tone can vary with all of your possible moods and attitudes.

If someone is called on to write anonymously—a committee report, for instance—the prose can be voiceless. The directions on a box of frozen vegetables are not intended to reveal anything about the writer. The he/she of such prose is an undifferentiated voice that is supposed to sound factual, precise, bland, controlled. Completely impersonal prose of this variety is actually difficult to write for an extended space because essentially it requires the writer to blot out personality and individuality. Voiceless prose is often referred to as the *plain style*, a kind of writing whose main purpose is to provide facts without commentary or editorializing, prose that informs rather than persuades.

Note the essentially bland tone of the following account of living conditions of a family in Alabama:

PASSAGE 1

George Gudger, 31-year-old Alabama tenant farmer, and his wife Annie Mae, 27, are no strangers to hard living. As a sharecropper with no land, no home, no mule, and no tools, Gudger is financially dependent on the landlord, who each Spring loans him equipment to work the land and rations money to support himself while the crop is growing. This debt is paid back, with interest, through the labor of Gudger and his family. The best the Gudgers have ever cleared after these annual transactions is $125. From this remaining sum they pay doctors' bills, repay any other debts plus interest, and make an attempt to clothe and feed four children under the age of ten until the following Spring.

This is an almost completely undramatized statement. There is no noticeable sign that the writer has personally observed the situation; these are all facts that might have been read in a book. In fact, their source is actually James Agee's *Now Let Us Praise Famous Men.* The account is sympathetic, but there is no special pleading. About the only sign of an attempt to influence the reader's feelings comes in the second sentence: " . . . with no land, no home, no mule, and no tools. . . ." This brief piling up of phrases which repeat the word *no* builds to a momentary climax and reveals a show of feeling. Otherwise, the facts are left to speak for themselves.

The relative objectivity of this passage may be compared with another view of the same scene:

PASSAGE 2

In the midst of the hurried world of white collar workers, factory men, and the others who fill up spaces in the melange of today's metropolitan society, it is reassuring to stop for a moment to remember that to the south of our industrial cities lies a countryside of quaint sharecroppers, earning a living off nature's soil. A visit to this area will leave one with an understanding of the words "If I did not work, these worlds would perish," and of the important vision which inspired Markham's "Man with a Hoe." For here, a man's work is his life: from the moment he is old enough to pronounce the word until the last time he methodically returns his hatchet to its appropriate place among the other crude but highly valued tools, his life is spent in honest toil, the backbone of a great nation.

If we were not told that this is an account of the same situation in Passage 1, we would never know it from the prose. The viewpoint has changed completely; there are no hard facts. The writer looks upon the scene as if it were a nineteenth-century landscape in an art museum. In fact, it would seem that the spirit of Millet's *The Angelus* has served as a model for interpreting the facts. This Alabama is a serene countryside dotted with "quaint sharecroppers," but we cannot get a close look at them because the wide-sweeping perspective diminishes them. The vast canvas also includes "white collar workers, factory men, and others who fill up spaces in the melange of today's metropolitan society. . . ." At such a distance, the writer can romanticize, make pronouncements about the nobility of honest labor, and moralize with pious phrases. The passage expresses feeling, but it is feeling without involvement. The attitude is superficial, the tone sentimental, the style glossy. Writing of this kind tells us more about the writer than about the subject.

In a technical sense, these two passages use the same approach; that is, both are third-person accounts, the writer is apart from the material, and the reader is an observer limited by what the writer tells. The treatment is quite different from that of still another writer who involves the reader by telling about herself and the kind of life she lives:

PASSAGE 3

In two rooms of bare boards and a kitchen slapped up against the side of the house, six human beings sleep, eat, work, grow, and die in the midst of dirt, filth, and insects that they can't get away from. I can go running back to Spic and Span floors, Windex windows, Glade-filled rooms, and Blue Cheer clothes; but these people are stuck here, trapped by the life they lead, forced to stay on the land and forced to stay together.

This passage describes a personal reaction and intensifies the emotion by contrasting the living conditions of the sharecropper family with the writer's own style of living. It is written as if the author had seen with her own eyes. Each of these three passages, therefore, demonstrates how the writer's relation to the subject creates a different effect.

Another description of the sharecropper and his family will indicate what a difference point of view makes. This passage takes the form of a personal letter from a young woman to her parents:

PASSAGE 4

Well, I'm finally here. It seemed as if the train would never arrive, but I'm now situated in the backroom of a schoolhouse. I've even begun to meet the people I will work with during the coming months. All the knowledge of an expert could not have prepared me for the sickening conditions I find here! And in America too! One family, the Gudgers, lives in such a pathetic situation that I practically cried when I visited them. The six of them have a tiny shack, half of which is unusable. It is filthy and stinks from a combination of many, many odors. Their food is all but inedible, and the beds are overrun with a variety of bugs. I saw the baby scratch at some!

This is a highly subjective paragraph because the writer cannot escape her own personal observations and feelings. The purpose of writing is, of course, different from that in either Passages 1, 2, or 3. This is a personal letter. The writer is actually the subject of the letter—how she feels and why she feels as she does. There is no attempt to get beyond the self, as the writer of Passage 3 does, for example.

The way we react to a writer's voice is almost completely based on the things a writer does with language. Knowing the writer personally does not change what the prose says of its own accord. But we are also conditioned by a number of conventional associations. Exaggeration ordinarily conveys emotion. Moderate words and balanced sentences imply rational control. Punning and playing with sounds suggest informality and lightness of tone; ornateness is associated with the grandiose and formal. Relationships of this kind prevail in our thinking because they are true of the responses we make not only to writing but to other art forms as well. Agitated lines and sharp contrasts of color are the painter's way of expressing strong feeling. A musician uses dynamics for emotional effects. Order and symmetry in a fugue are intellectually appealing. We might add similar examples from architecture, dance, or landscape gardening. It is questionable how far anyone can go to upset these normal expectations. They are cultural factors that influence our taste and judgment.

The personal pronouns and style

Comparison of Passage 2, written in third person, and Passage 4, written in first person, indicates that subjectivity does not depend wholly on the choice of pronouns. Ordinarily, anything written in first person singular tends to be more personal and intimate than anything written in third person. Yet you should be aware, both in your reading and in your writing, that pronouns shift in their uses. They may have a variety of implications, and you may use them to represent yourself in different ways.

I—the writer by name, as an individual, bringing personal experience to bear upon the writing:

At the moment I am writing these words, I am distinctly depressed.

J. Middleton Murry

I—the writer as a representative of a group or spokesman for it:

What to the American slave is your Fourth of July? I answer: a day that reveals to him, more than all other days in the year, the gross injustice and cruelty of which he is the constant victim.

Frederick Douglass (1852)

I—the writer in some capacity as an official or as an authority upon a special subject:

From the moment I examined the preliminary drawings I was disturbed and puzzled by its design, and I am still disturbed, though further reflection and observation have revealed a little of Wright's intentions and decisions.

Lewis Mumford, an authority on urban architecture,
commenting on Frank Lloyd Wright's drawings
for the Guggenheim Museum in New York

I—the writer as a neutral, hypothetical subject:

When I refuse to obey an unjust law, I do not contest the right of the majority to command, but I simply appeal from the sovereignty of the people to the sovereignty of mankind.

Alexis de Tocqueville

I—the writer as an impersonal editorial guide:

I have already suggested that our sexual uncertainties reflect a deep conflict we feel in areas other than those of our sexual emotions.

Diana Trilling

We—a plural that embraces the writer and reader:

Now comparing these instances together, we shall have no difficulty in determining the principle of this apparent variation in the application of the term which I am examining.

John Henry Newman

We—representatives of a group; editorial *we:*

What we propose to do here, then, is to examine the word *antonym,* to determine the concept it involves, and to state its definition in as clear terms as possible.

Introduction to Webster's New Dictionary of Synonyms

We—a disguised *I* (closely related to the editorial *we*):

We have already suggested a doubt whether indecent books or performances in fact either alter people's natures for the worse or even stimulate them to immoral behavior. . . .

Unsigned article,
The [London] Times Literary Supplement, August 4, 1961

We—representatives of an identifiable group, possibly excluding the reader:

Revolutions and civil wars are brutal and messy things, and the results are rarely satisfactory. At least, that was so with the Irish Revolution. We had forced the English to come to terms and then had a civil war as to whether the terms were good enough.

Frank O'Connor, an Irishman speaking for Irishmen

We—all humanity, including the writer and the reader:

The realist at last loses patience with ideals altogether, and sees in them only something to blind us, something to numb us, something to murder self in us, something whereby, instead of resisting death, we can disarm it by committing suicide.

George Bernard Shaw

Uses of one

One—representing the writer and reader:

Remembering that, one sees what function these post cards, in their humble way, are performing.

George Orwell

One—indefinite reference to all persons, including the writer:

Can we invent rituals? Can one artificially create collective art?

Erich Fromm

One—an extended *I;* one of the speaker's kind:

I learned in New Jersey that to be a Negro meant, precisely, that one was never looked at but was simply at the mercy of the reflexes the color of one's skin caused in other people.

James Baldwin

One—a disguised *I:*

One is finally driven to conclude that all Huxley's intellectual paraphernalia conceals an intelligence at war with itself, or struggling vainly for a clear position from which to attack. And while in this essay I am interested directly only in the early novels, it would be unrealistic not to bear in mind also the constant gropings and changes of position in his later work.

Sean O'Faolain

Adams had looked at most of the accumulations of art in the storehouses called Art Museums; yet he did not know how to look at the art exhibits of 1900.

Henry Adams, writing about himself

Mailer always supposed he had felt important and unimportant in about as many ways as a man could feel; now he felt important in a new way.

Norman Mailer, writing about himself in *The Armies of the Night*

Other indirect references to the speaker or writer

The chair wishes to thank . . .
This writer was present when . . .
The editors have attempted to . . .

It should be apparent from the examples above that the ways in which you can represent yourself vary greatly in their formality and directness. The more indirect the form, the more it tends to be contrived. The simple use of *I* remains your most natural and inconspicuous way of referring to yourself. The use of *I* does not necessarily make prose egocentric. The element of subjectivity is much more affected by your view of the world than by your choice of pronouns. If you have only one perspective—your own—you will find it difficult to escape the limitations of your view. If you have a world of perspectives, you will be capable of broader vision and more perceptive analysis.

Uses of you

The point of view and the corresponding pronouns you choose reflect how you want to involve your audience. Of course, in a third-person account, the audience is not addressed; its presence is implicit. The audience is actively involved only when you use first person plural (*we, us, our*) or second person singular or plural (*you*). All of these pronouns invite an identity of the audience with the writer. When you write a third-person account, however, you do not necessarily ignore your audience. You simply involve it in a different way by selection of detail, choice of words and images, and the tone of your remarks.

The use of *you* is a definite decision to address the audience directly, but it can be a formal or an informal *you*, a specific or a general one. The implications will vary:

You—the immediate reader, addressed as an individual:

Recall, then, some event that has left a distinct impression on you—how at the corner of the street, perhaps, you passed two people talking.

Virginia Woolf

You—the reader, but also in an extended sense all people:

169

If you look into your own mind, which are you, Don Quixote or Sancho Panza? Almost certainly you are both.

George Orwell

You—an indefinite reference, essentially informal in tone:

It is a professional warning, not at all unlike what a golf professional means when he tells us to keep our eye on the ball. Once lift your eye from the actuality of the moment, he seems to say, and you are distracted, deceived, deflected, lose focus, strike without accuracy, and the next thing you know you are in the rough of the sentimental, or the bogus.

Sean O'Faolain

You—reference to a particular group, not necessarily including the reader:

That my first novel should win this most coveted prize [National Book Award] must certainly indicate that there is a crisis in the American novel. You as critics have told us so.

Ralph Ellison

Thus, the decision to use second person *you* may not always add a personal note to the prose. And if *you* is overused, the pronoun can lose its effect as personal address; it becomes simply a generalized *other*. In many instances, a sentence can be made more precise by eliminating an indefinite *you* and substituting the exact reference:

Indefinite: In school, you weren't permitted to wear slacks.
More precise: In school, girls weren't permitted to wear slacks.

A discriminating use of *you* can be a factor in keeping your own prose style clear and personally appealing.

Variations in tone

If you were listening to a horn player, you would be acutely aware of the control of tone or the lack of control. And, without doubt, a good horn player could tell you specifically how to maintain control of that instrument. Control of tone in writing is equally important, although it may be less clear exactly how that is accomplished. Perhaps more than anything else it has to do with your intuitive sense of what is excessive and what is restrained and how practiced you are in maintaining a particular manner or tone. Some discussion of variations in style may indicate in what ways you can exercise control over the effects that words create.

Variations of plain and fancy

Plainness of style is a quality of restraint—an absence of excess and complication. One kind of plain style is purely utilitarian. Its chief purpose is clear communication. It therefore avoids irony, figurative language, and strategies that from the standpoint of pure practicality seem to divert interest from *what* is said to *how* it is said. Prose of this kind is factual and impersonal. It is efficient. It is the typical language of reporting and informing:

Zachary Taylor National Cemetery—4701 Brownsboro Road—A monument marking the grave of the 12th President dominates the reservation. Taylor was less than a year old when he moved with his parents to Kentucky and settled in the home which is within sight of the cemetery.

At the cemetery entrance, turn right and drive past one road to Blankenbaker Lane and turn right. A marker a quarter of a mile down Blankenbaker locates Springfield, the home of Taylor, now privately owned and not open to the public. Continue north to Locust Grove, the mansion where George Rogers Clark spent his last years.

Tourist guidebook

The plain style of the guidebook, textbook, manual, and communiqué is indispensable for factual communication—we encounter it constantly—but, as a style of writing, it also tends to be commonplace. Nevertheless, *plain* and *prosaic* do not have to be accepted as counterparts of one another. A plain style is also capable of simple elegance:

In the beginning, there was the land, stretching in majesty from ocean to ocean. The land was rich in its diversity—of mountains and valley, of deserts and grassy plains, of singing brooks and rushing, mighty rivers, of plant and animal life.

Beneath the surface of the land, greater riches were hidden—life-giving water, fuel to fire man's industries, ore to build his cities of steel in a far distant time.

And there were no people. The land was virgin; prostitution of the land was in the unknown future.

Muriel Crosby, "English: New Dimensions and New Demands"

The plainness here is the simplicity of words and structure. Yet, at the same time, there is a subtle intricacy of series, balanced constructions, and parallelism. The style recalls both the restraint and techniques of narrative passages of the Book of Genesis. In fact, the best description of the tone is biblical. Yet the strategy that produces this stylistic effect does not degenerate into fanciness, if fanciness is understood to mean a purely ornamental device that actually disguises meaning because it calls too much attention to itself. A too conscious striving for effect can defeat the writer's purpose:

Forgive! For forgiveness is the fragrance of a violet on the heel of the one who crushed it.

Abigail van Buren

This brief sentence is both elaborate in language and profuse in feeling to the point of sentimentality. It is a fancy style, not because the words are extraordinary but because the total effect is excessive and the metaphor more decorative than functional.

Another kind of fanciness results from overwriting—trying too hard, pulling out all the stops, striving for the grandiose:

The educator should approach his class not as the chemist appraises his retorts nor the astronomer his nebulae but rather as the conductor confronts his symphony orchestra. From the breathless whisperings of the strings, from the clarion peals of the brass, from the muted thunder of the percussion, the conductor will weave the very fabric of great music, threaded throughout with the polychromatic strands of his own genius. Even so will the teacher evoke from the myriad experiences and abilities of his pupils the chords which, laced and interwoven with something of himself, will ring gladly in the harmony of life.

Max Rafferty, Suffer, Little Children

Between stark simplicity and extravagance lies a whole range of effects. One extreme is not categorically good and the other bad. In the hands of one writer, plainness can be barren or extravagance capable of grandeur. In the hands of another, plainness can be imaginative and extravagance gaudy. One effect or the other depends on your own capacity to perceive differences in tone. You may then be able to exercise some control of tone by the choices you make.

Variations of exaggeration and understatement

Exaggeration and understatement are opposite techniques, but they are not necessarily different in their purpose. Both are ways of trying to get an emphasis beyond simple factual statement. Exaggeration, or hyperbole, is the easier and more obvious of the two. It depends simply on adding words, enlarging the scope, magnifying the idea, heightening the effect, or overstating the problem. As a writing technique, it deliberately distorts, but the distortion is not intended to falsify, only to intensify. For example, a writer may try to arouse strong feelings by exaggeration. When it is applied to personal attack, the result is invective—a particular kind of abuse Westbrook Pegler was capable of when he wrote about Franklin D. Roosevelt:

> That Mr. Roosevelt has his faults I would be among the first to admit under very little pressure, but as a social and political liver-shaker he has had no equal in our time in this country. Ornery, tricky, stubborn, wayward and strong as a bull, he has bucked, wheeled, kicked, walked on his hind legs, tried to mash us against the barn and scrape our heads off under the door in more than five years of continuous plunging, and he apparently isn't even breathing hard yet.
>
> Pull him out of one willful, pesky trick and he will stand there a minute with his head down, showing the whites of his eyes and then go tearing off across the yard hell-bent, rattling our teeth and every bone and joint in our body.
>
> "Rough Riding"

Paradoxically, the same technique can be employed to produce humor. The extent of exaggeration can produce anything from mild amusement to verbal slapstick. Broad comedy is the stock-in-trade of a columnist like Erma Bombeck:

> I have never taken household hints too seriously.
>
> Once I sent a suggestion to *Good Housekeeping* pointing out that dust balls stored under the bed throughout the year make wonderful, safe toys for the baby and were unique stocking stuffers.
>
> They cancelled my subscription.

Another writer exaggerates less and creates a wry kind of humor:

1968 was a rotten year—a succession of jolts, shocks, fingers in the eye, and knees in the groin for all of us. You could sit for the next five hours trying to think of something cheerful that happened during 1968, and every time you came up with something someone would point out that the good thing you recalled actually took place during 1967 or 1945 or 1066.

Patrick Butler, "1968—And the Hell with It"

The alternative to adding and magnifying for a special effect is minimizing. It is a device of withholding rather than overwhelming, and its element of restraint seems to carry over emotionally to the reader. The reader knows when a controlled or casual statement is disproportionate to the writer's far more intense feelings. The disproportion between the writer's intention and the phrasing that produces understatement can also create an ironic tone, often with overtones of humor. There is no mistaking this quality in Swift's writing:

Last week I saw a woman flayed, and you will hardly believe how much it altered her person for the worse.

In a more subtle, seemingly casual way, Carl Rowan writes:

It has been said that, by nature, the American people love the underdog. It must be true, for we create so many of them.

Knowing that Carl Rowan is a black writer adds even further to the intensity of his statement.

Because understatement is a form of calm expression, it is probably a tone that some writers are incapable of. It would be difficult to imagine that the writer of the following sentence would be much disposed to understatement under any circumstances:

I have had it with the continual effrontery of the bleeding-heart do-gooders, and their latest whine, urging investigation of a police officer for doing his duty.

In matters of feeling, the person and the style are likely to be one.

Hyperbole and understatement, of course, can be sustained at much greater length than these examples. One of the great challenges to writers all over the world occurred in July 1969 when they were faced with the task of trying to write about the drama of the space voyage that would put man on the moon for the first time. Many writers attempted to match the magnitude of the event by inflated prose; adjectives like *great, wonderful, fantastic,* and *fabulous* quickly became feeble resources. The descriptions began with the blast-off at Cape Kennedy on July 16; the departure of Apollo 11 invited flamboyant kinds of prose like the following:

Just before the emissaries left the cape, the morning star, Venus, fading in the early sunlight, seemed to wink down at Pad 39-A. It reminded some that men were just inching into space by going to the moon. But no step would be tougher than this one, the first step.

The launching to the moon came in a litany of thunder and light on Cape Kennedy's Pad 39-A.

The sun-orange flame from the Saturn V rocket's mighty booster snaked out to sear the pad and blacken the palmetto scrub that struggles to exist on this sandy cape.

The sound—a chest-thumping staccato—poured across the barren flats and pounded into the nearest observers more than three miles away.

A few cruising pelicans dived for safety. Some men cried.

The mighty Boeing-built booster agonizingly lifted its 6½ million-pound burden away from the pad. The booster was devouring fuel at a rate of 30,000 pounds a second, but the rocket seemed to only inch up and away from the launching tower.

There was a moment of silence before the sound reached the observers, then a whispered "Go, baby, go" and finally a wild cheer as the rocket cleared the tower and the thunder reached the viewing stands.

William W. Prochnau, Seattle Times, July 16, 1969

Much more rare among various reports was an attempt to get the same effect by a relative kind of simplicity and understatement. By comparison with the previous example, the following one shows restraint:

It is in many ways the most stunning of all the spectacles man has created, the sight not so much of a lifetime as of a millennium. You have to see this rising star in person. No one is going to tell you about it and make you understand.

If the American republic should live for a thousand years, 9:32 A.M. EDT July 16, 1969, may not be kept as its finest hour. But, in the last thousand years, man's world cannot have held a more exciting minute.

A tongue of incandescent flame—so bright that it pained, so mystic in flow that it held one's eye on the symmetry of its slow arc—rode the Florida sky in the name of Apollo 11. At least one viewer among the thousands who stood watch this hazy day thought of the word apocalypse.

The view of an Apollo ascent—given the portent of this one—can be a revelation, a striking visual disclosure, of what man has done at the tail end of his first million years as a definable entity.

H. D. Quigg, Seattle Post-Intelligencer, July 17, 1969

Significantly, however, the impact of the entire event was perhaps most remarkably expressed in the simple, understated phrases of Neil Armstrong in his first words from the moon:

That's one small step for a man, one giant leap for mankind.

Variations of informal and formal

Informal and formal are measures of distance between the writer and the audience. Informality narrows that distance; formality widens it. Either effect may or may not be appropriate to a particular situation. An old-fashioned word used to describe appropriateness of manner is *decorum*. And usually *decorum* was preceded by the word *proper*—"proper decorum," a standard for polite speech and behavior. Our more informal age is less concerned with strict propriety; yet we are constantly reminded of inappropriate language. For example, a student being admitted to the graduate program of a large university failed to indicate on her application which degree she wanted to work for. When asked, the student replied by mail:

If this letter may be appended to my application, I hereby proclaim my intention to proceed to the Ph.D. degree after earning the M.A.

In this case, the relation between the writer and the chairman of graduate studies was not a close one, but it hardly justified the tone of a public proclamation in the letter. The candidate might have responded in a simple, direct manner:

After I finish the M.A., I intend to study for the Ph.D.

This rewriting eliminates the verbiage of the unnecessary clause and the passive voice construction; it drops the pompous language of "hereby proclaim" and substitutes "finish" for "earning" and "study" for "proceed" to make the tone throughout less guarded.

Formal tone does not need to be either pompous or stiff, although it is characteristically temperate in its language and uses strategies that preserve an impression of full control:

I am a man of the law. I have dedicated myself to uphold the law and to enforce its commands. I fully accept the principle that each of us is subject to law; that each of us is bound to obey the law enacted by his government.

But if I had lived in Germany in Hitler's days, I hope I would have refused to wear an armband, to *Heil Hitler*, to submit to genocide. This I hope, although Hitler's edicts were law until allied weapons buried the Third Reich.

Abe Fortas, Concerning Dissent and Civil Disobedience

These two paragraphs show some slight variation in formality. In the first, Mr. Fortas speaks as a judge, and the choice of words and the arrangement sound familiarly like a formal oath of office. In the second paragraph, Mr. Fortas speaks as a private citizen. The series of three infinitives—"to wear," "to *Heil Hitler*," and "to submit"—and the repetition of "I hope" give a somewhat more relaxed tone to the writing, but it is in no sense as open and free as the following prose:

When I saw *Planet of the Apes* a couple of months ago, I liked it. I just plain liked it—an ingenious, adventurous, humorous, deliciously spooky example of one of my favorite popular genres, science fiction, that was smartly made and contained a useful moral or two. I should have trusted my instincts, stood up and proclaimed my affectionate regard for the thing right off.

Richard Schickel, "Second Thoughts on Ape-Men"

We can observe first that the subject matter of this writing is less weighty than that of Mr. Fortas, and Richard Schickel, as the movie reviewer of a popular magazine, occupies a position considerably less dignified than that of the former Associate Justice of the Supreme Court. Therefore an easy manner is appropriate both to this writer and his audience. His phrasing is conversational—"I liked it. I just plain liked it"; he does not hesitate to throw in a bit of current jargon like "spooky." When he uses a word like "proclaimed," he follows it with an unstilted object: "my affectionate regard for the thing right off." Yet the writing is not overly familiar; its variety of words is unforced. Even though Schickel mixes a few learned words and ordinary ones, there is no marked change in tone, as in the following sentence:

In my growth from mushroomhood to "scholar" it was necessary for me to find a personal language which would give intelligible form to my own instincts and judgments in situations where intelligent critical reaction was called for.

This passage is taken from a statement of personal objectives written by a student applying for a graduate assistantship. Its playful phrasing at the beginning is hardly consistent with the density of the words that follow. It is an odd mixture of coyness and pomposity, and the writer seems clearly uneasy. Only when the writer and the reader are at ease with one another does informality result. A reader, however, can be put off either by chumminess (an abuse of informality) or aloofness (an abuse of formality).

Most student writing is informal and appropriately should be, because informality comes naturally to young people. Further, informality does not have to be taught. In many instances, however, it has to be encouraged, chiefly because many students have a mistaken notion that informality is inappropriate to serious writing. Informality in writing is seldom inappropriate if informality helps to make the prose spontaneous, flexible, and sincere.

Variations of clear and obscure

Everyone is capable of occasionally writing an unclear sentence. But a single vague sentence does not produce an obscure style. Obscurity grows out of repeated habits in a writer's prose that leave the reader doubtful about precise meanings. The following illustrations are brief, but they should be looked on only as typical of many other passages that are considered unclear. Obscurity results from:

1. The tendency to use more words than necessary:

This acquired privilege to regulate the activities of the family invites the possibility and probability of censorship of conflicting opinions without further investigation into which side could be right.

Student sentence

2. The tendency to write unduly long sentences:

And even after it was done, the victim had no recourse whatever since, unlike sacrilege and obscenity, we have no laws against bad taste, perhaps because in our democracy the majority of the people who make the laws don't recognize bad taste when they see it, or perhaps because in our democracy bad taste has been converted into a marketable and therefore taxable and therefore lobbyable commodity by the merchandising federations which at the same simultaneous time create the market (not the appetite: that did not need creating: only pandering to) and the product to serve it, and bad taste by simple solvency was purified of bad taste and absolved.

William Faulkner,
"On Privacy: The American Dream, What Happened to It?"

3. The tendency to use too many abstract polysyllables and circumlocutions:

The problem of modality leads directly and immediately to the problem of historicity. The talk-write pedagogy is essentially ahistorical on two different levels. Like all behavioral techniques, it is ahistorical with regard to the origin of scribal non-fluencies: it attacks the nonfluency-as-dysfunction, with no attention to originating cause. Much more to the point here, talk-write is philosophically ahistorical regarding the relationship between vocal and scribal activity: it handles both as equivalent modalities of verbal behavior. This places it in sharp contrast with the current think-write pedagogies, which exhibit an historicity which has been largely confirmed by linguistic research. Indeed, one of the great anomalies of the current compositional situation may be that the conceptual framework we have borrowed in part from linguistics is actually inhibitive of genuine progress in scribal pedagogy. The linguistic viewpoint is largely historico-descriptive. It is also, and as a consequence, pervasively hierarchic.

Robert Zoellner, "A Behavioral Pedagogy for Composition"

4. The tendency to be abstruse:

What is reality, and what is pretense in Pirandello's *Six Characters?* Through the Father, one may feel that Pirandello is saying that the character is more real than the actor, since the character's personality does not change. On the contrary, while the character's personality may be more stable, the actor is real, and his personality is, at any instant, real. Like the characters in the play, reality knows no past or future, except what may be implied by the present. Pretense includes any influences of the past or thoughts of the future.

Student paragraph

5. The tendency to garble words and constructions:

Swift so cleverly approaches and attacks human deficiencies that even after the readers realize it is them that Gulliver is talking about they submit not only to Swift's veracity, but begin to, I feel, exhibit the same incensement Swift has in hope of finding a Utopian society.

Student sentence

6. The tendency to leave gaps in the development of a thought:

Some of the excesses in the current excursions into aural, oral, tactile, and kinetic experience may in fact be directly responsive to the sensory deprivation of the print culture. Nature abhors a vacuum. No one glories in the sight of kids totally out of control in reaction to the Beatles. Some say, "What are the Beatles doing to these kids?" All the data isn't in on what it means to be a balanced human being.

Student paragraph

The ways of obscurity are many, but chief among them is *redundancy*. First of all, you must recognize that thoughts need to be expanded to be made clear. If you reduce a complete message to a telegram or a headline, you increase the amount of work the reader has to do to understand what you mean, and you also increase the probability that the message will pick up ambiguities. However, you need to make a distinction between the necessary elaboration of a thought to make it clear and the piling up of unnecessary words that can obscure it. That kind of excess is redundancy. For the most part, profuseness in writing tends to obscure thought; spareness and directness are assets to clear expression.

Fuzziness of meaning also results from too many private and obscure allusions, from the use of words known only to extremely restricted groups (*fugleman, hyparistic, ontogentically*), from ambiguous phrasing, and from general disorganization. All of these tendencies can be called the noise factors of writing, the things that interfere with clear reception. A completely lucid style is so unusual that critics often mention clarity as a special mark of praise, like the following comment by Caskie Stinnett in *Holiday:*

> Lillian Hellman has written her memoirs, *An Unfinished Woman* (Little, Brown), and it's surprising how clear, intelligent writing can seize a reader and thrill him in a way no other medium can.

Similarly, critics almost always condemn persistent fogginess. The smog of writing is often referred to as *gobbledygook,* a word coined in the 1940s to describe the impenetrable jargon and style of government documents but that has stuck in the language because the style is by no means limited to bureaucratic prose.

Punctuation and style

On a sheet of music, dynamic markings would be meaningless without the notes, but the rhythm and style of the music would be less apparent without these notations added to the notes. In a similar way, punctuation has no value except as it reveals the writer's intentions about the meaning and effect of the words set down on paper. Punctuation is a way of doing in writing what the speaker can do by variations of pitch, stress, and pause. But the writer does not do what the speaker does to the same degree. If you merely transcribe all the pauses of your speech, you will end up with superfluous punctuation marks. It should be emphasized that punctuation is designed for *readers.* There is not an exact equivalent among these marks for everything that you do with the voice for listeners.

Nevertheless, all punctuation has a phonological dimension. A period, for example, is the equivalent in writing of a falling pitch that we use to indicate the end of a sentence, and commas and other internal marks of punctuation mark pauses of varying degrees. They do not mark all the pauses that occur in speech. Spaces between words, sentences, and paragraphs may also be considered punctuation devices in the sense that they also clarify the author's meanings and intentions.

Punctuation is always closely related to the syntactic structure of the language, and its importance increases as sentences become more complex and sophisticated. A basic sentence pattern requires no internal punctuation. There is no need for it, because the simple sentence is a single unit. But as soon as the kernel sentence is added to, transformed, reordered, or interrupted—any change that alters the simple structure or invites misreading—then punctuation becomes necessary. Some marks are indispensable to prevent misreading; others are optional and therefore dependent on the writer's own style.

As soon as the element of choice enters, punctuation takes on a stylistic dimension. Some writers make spare use of marks of punctuation; others try scrupulously to avoid all ambiguity by punctuating as precisely as possible. These tendencies produce two general styles of punctuation: open and close. The choice between them is not always the writer's own. Legal and technical writings clearly cannot risk possible misreading and therefore demand close punctuation. Some newspapers and publishing houses establish their own practices. Yet in most informal, personal prose, you are free to deviate from conventional practices if you find punctuation a way to gain emphasis or add variation to the rhythms.

Conventions of punctuation are not inviolable rules, but they are in most instances sound guidelines because they reflect the typical uses of most writers. They follow several principles: (1) some marks of punctuation signal end breaks; (2) some separate various words and structures within a sentence; (3) some enclose others; (4) some serve a variety of conventional purposes that simplify the transcription of thoughts on paper, as the apostrophe indicates possession, for instance. For each of the first three functions, several marks of punctuation are commonly used and are at times interchangeable:

1. End breaks: period, question mark, exclamation point
2. Separating within the sentence: comma, semicolon, colon, dash
3. Enclosing: commas, dashes, parentheses, brackets, quotation marks
4. Conventional uses: ellipsis points, quotation marks, hyphen, apostrophe

Often, you can be quite versatile in your use of punctuation as long as you understand what is possible. The limitations and open possibilities of marks of punctuation become fully known only after you become familiar with established practices. Then you can begin to see that the interchangeability of marks and the frequency with which you use particular ones produce shifts in style. The dash, for instance, can in many sentences freely substitute for commas, colons, parentheses, and even semicolons and periods. To depend on it almost exclusively, however, produces a highly fluid, loosely connected prose style that is appropriate to certain kinds of expressive writing but not to more formal kinds of expression. How a change of punctuation alters the effect of a sentence can be demonstrated by a few examples:

1. When Picasso decides to disregard the laws of perspective, that means he has passed through and beyond a certain technique—unlike the Egyptian painter, who has never acquired it.

Arthur Koestler

Repunctuated: When Picasso decides to disregard the laws of perspective, that means he has passed through and beyond a certain technique, unlike the Egyptian painter, who has never aquired it.

The repunctuated sentence indicates immediately that Koestler's use of the dash provides a sharper break than the comma and takes us back to Picasso at the beginning of the sentence. The main contrast is "Picasso—unlike the Egyptian painter. . . ."

2. I Ate, I Vomited, I Died   Title of an oil painting by Menahem Lewin

    Repunctuated: I Ate; I Vomited; I Died
                I Ate. I Vomited. I Died.

The original punctuation of the title clearly emphasizes the sequence. We read quickly one short sentence after another and perhaps recall Caesar's famous statement "I came, I saw, I conquered," which is also traditionally punctuated with commas. The semicolons seem to introduce an unnecessary formality. The periods add a dramatic effect to each part of the series, if a writer wants emphasis.

3. In South Africa, the English, it is said, are against the Afrikaner; both are against the Jews; all three are opposed to the Indians; while all four conspire against the native black.

                                  Gordon W. Allport

    Repunctuated: In South Africa, the English (it is said) are against the Afrikaner; both are against the Jews; all three are opposed to the Indians, while all four conspire against the native black.

The substitution of parentheses for commas to enclose "it is said" unnecessarily emphasizes a mildly qualifying statement and even seems to add a coy note. The second change of the semicolon to a comma is a wholly conventional change; commas, not semicolons, are ordinarily used to separate dependent clauses from main clauses. Yet if we examine the structure of the sentence as a whole, we see what Allport is doing with the punctuation. He does not want to lose the cumulative effect of "the English," "both," "all three," and then "all four." These thoughts are coordinate; the consistent punctuation with semicolons helps to keep them that way.

4. I had not been mistaken as to the size of the men's yard: it was certainly not more than twenty yards deep and fifteen wide.

                                  E. E. Cummings

    Repunctuated: I had not been mistaken as to the size of the men's yard; it was certainly not more than twenty yards deep and fifteen wide.

The two main clauses could also be separated with a period. What the colon adds that the semicolon or period does not is a special quality of anticipation: what is not explained in the first part of the sentence is completed in the part following the colon.

Examples such as these indicate that the guidelines for the use of particular marks of punctuation are flexible. If you have mastered the basics so that you understand what the marks can do, you are then free to use them effectively. Even though changes of punctuation may at times seem slight, they are capable of conveying subtle differences in meaning, emphasis, and attitude. They are one additional factor in gaining control of style.

Projects | **1.** **Professor Wayne Booth has defined the rhetorical stance as "a stance which depends on discovering and maintaining in any writing situation a proper balance among three elements that are at work in a communicative** effort: the available arguments about the subject itself, the interests and peculiarities of the audience, and the voice, the implied character of the speaker." He speaks of three corruptions that represent unbalancing: the pedant's stance, depending on the subject to do the job and forgetting the audience; the advertiser's stance, depending on pure effect to influence people and undervaluing what is said; and the entertainer's stance, projecting more personality than substance.

In what ways do the following situations often invite a corruption of a balanced rhetorical stance?

A. A freshman writing a paper assigned by an English instructor

B. A comedian going through his act in a nightclub or place of entertainment

C. A television announcer doing a detergent commercial

D. A politician campaigning for a seat in the legislature

E. An ecologist lecturing on pollution

2. Compare your responses to something you have experienced (speech, theater production, movie) with the way it was reported or reviewed in the newspaper. How much of the newspaper account was fact, speculation, opinion, misrepresentation? How did the point of view differ from your own?

3. Examine an essay written in first person. Are the implications of *I*, *me*, and *my* consistent throughout? Does the use of *I* do more than identify the writer as an individual? Examine the possible shifts of meaning in the use of other personal pronouns.

4. Without seeking biographical information, make as many inferences as you legitimately can about a writer (or the voice of the writing) from a prose selection: background, sex, age, education, the writer's attitude toward the reader, tone. Where do doubts begin to arise about the inferences you can make?

5. Write metaphors suggested by one or more words in each of the lists given below:

I	*II*
cars	birds
freeways	desert
speed	flower garden
crowding	garbage
commuters	wind

Example: A line of cars on the freeway moving occasionally as if they were a stem imperceptibly nudged by a breeze.

6. Examine the phrases, particularly the metaphors, used by sportswriters in newspapers and magazines. What are some of the characteristic phrases associated with particular sports?

7. In an effort to determine the statistical dimensions of a writer's style, analyze several paragraphs of an assigned essay in terms of the following:

A. Proportion of short words to long words (use one- and two-syllable words as an arbitrary definition of "short")

B. Variety of sentence length

C. Variety of sentence patterns

D. Degree of subordination

E. Degree of coordination

F. Nature of the paragraphing

G. Dependence on transitional words and phrases or relative absence of them

H. Proportion of verbs in passive voice

I. Proportion of verbs that are a form of *be* (standing alone, not used as auxiliaries)

J. Proportion of contractions

K. Special or unusual uses of punctuation

L. Dependence on particular strategies: balance, parallelism, repetition, alliteration, puns, metaphors

M. Point of view and corresponding use of pronouns: first person, second person, third person

8. What evidence can you give that the following article from the *University of Washington Daily*, March 12, 1974, is a put-on?

> Editor:
>
> The other night, while on my way to an American Legion meeting, I was shocked to see three totally unclad perverts (I shouldn't say totally as they were wearing skin diving fins) prancing across my lawn.
>
> While chasing these degenerates with my trusty axe-handle, one of them had the audacity to suggest that I remove my new $22 Hart Shaffner & Marx suit, and join them in this degrading act of immorality.
>
> Ever since this country and its permissive society has allowed men to wear topless swim wear, I have seen the moral fiber disintegrate before my eyes.
>
> Of course, we all know that this outbreak of nudity was perpetrated by the communists, liberals, Ted Kennedy and other such weird types.
>
> As the good book says, "the road to paradise is very narrow, and those who are fully clothed shall make it."
>
> Block Streaking

9. Write three versions of each pair of sentences, combining them in various ways:

A. It was a pleasure to me. I found the house.

B. I said this. The greatest discoveries are accidents.

C. I chided myself. I failed.

D. I live in New York. I am happy.

E. The policeman arrested the criminal. The criminal was fleeing.

10. Without changing any of the words or the order of the words, choose alternate punctuation for the following sentences. Then determine what difference, however slight, the changes make in the implication or effect of the sentences:

A. It was just like Ootney—whenever something had to be done, Ootney was there to do it.

Joe Eszterhas, "Charlie Simpson's Apocalypse"

B. Sometimes—though not often enough—official science admits that its field, though large, is limited; that its methods are not applicable to every subject of investigation; that it is not, in a word, omnicompetent.

Joseph Wood Krutch,
"Are the Humanities Worth Saving?"

C. And no doubt the children, in their disturbed and guilty state, were almost ready to believe this: he had been remote enough to be anything.

James Baldwin, "Me and My House"

D. With languages which have not been used in writing and thus subjected to a special kind of grammatical analysis—it is worth recalling that grammar takes its name from writing—there is often very great uncertainty as to where one word ends and another begins.

I. A. Richards, *The Philosophy of Rhetoric*

E. The Lysenko crisis is quiet at present (though not necessarily settled; see for example "The Third Stage in Genetics," by Donald Michie, in *A Century of Darwin*, ed. S. A. Barnett, London, 1958), but not the least of its effects while it lasted was the widely disputed question whether there could be not one but two biologies, a Soviet one identified with Stalin and Lysenko fundamentally opposed to a bourgeois or capitalist one identified with Mendel and Weismann (at least not with the head of a state, to be thankful for small mercies).

Howard Nemerov, "The Dream of Reason"

F. Sport, then, in this mechanized society is no longer a mere game empty of any reward other than the playing: it is a profitable business: millions are invested in arenas, equipment, and players, and the maintenance of sport becomes as important as the maintenance of any other form of profit-making mechanism.

Lewis Mumford, *Technics and Civilization*

Suggestions for writing

1. Choose an incident that you have witnessed, such as an accident, an arrest, or a fire. Write several versions of the same incident from different points of view: (*a*) as a news story, (*b*) as a dialogue between you and someone at home, (*c*) as a letter to a friend who did not witness the incident, (*d*) as a discussion with a friend who saw the same incident, (*e*) as a reflection on how the people who were actually involved seemed to feel.

2. Choose a cartoon that interests you. Write a descriptive sketch about it, employing the same technique of exaggeration or distortion used in the cartoon. Determine, first of all, the difference between writing *about* the cartoon and trying to create the dominant effect *of* the cartoon as if it were your own. Then reproduce the effect in writing.

3. As an experiment, write a short descriptive passage in which you deliberately try to minimize the use of descriptive adjectives without loss of the detail you want to include. (Frequently, the detail can be incorporated into the verb or the adverb modifying it.) Repeat the experiment attempting to eliminate all verbs of being. Write another paragraph forcing yourself to use passive voice as often as you can. Then rewrite the paragraph converting the passive voice constructions to active voice. Assess the differences in style.

4. Find an example of what you consider bad writing. Without changing the meaning, rewrite one paragraph. After you have finished, analyze essentially what kinds of changes you made.

5. Climb a tree or go to the top floor of a building; look down, up, and around. Write a paper describing what you see from the height and that perspective.

6. G. K. Chesterton once said that at some time since the age of Chaucer human society had been converted from a dance to a race. In what ways is your life a dance? (Think about the element of pattern in a dance and the number of people involved.) In what ways a race? Would you prefer to substitute another metaphor? If so, develop a different analogy.

7. Write a short satire on circumlocutions, newspaperese, or another fashion in language, using slang, clichés, colloquialisms, or jargon for your purpose.

Toward better writing *Part II*

Often, books talk about drafting and writing as one stage of composing and then about revising and proofreading as another. In actual writing, things are not quite as neatly divided. Revision goes on constantly in the writing process. You no doubt write several sentences, then read them over to pick up cues where you are, and proceed to write several more sentences. Writing is much more a series of starts and stops than it is a steady, deliberate process from beginning to end. Each of those stops is a kind of revising—quite literally, in the original sense of the word, "seeing again"—a pausing, reflecting, evaluating, perhaps changing something, and then moving on again.

Revising as you write is therefore one step. Some people are more disposed to do this than others. In fact, some writers can actually tie themselves up if they try to get everything exactly right as they complete the first draft. It is advisable to curb the tendency to revise too much as you write because you need the perspective the final composition gives you, particularly if you reread after a cooling-off period. It is then that you can ask yourself bigger questions: Are the things I've said worthwhile? Have I said them in sufficient detail to be convincing? Does the whole thing hold together? Is the tone right for the intended audience? The answers to questions like these may lead to substantial changes in the organization, to the deletion or addition of certain details, or to the reformulation of some of the thinking.

It is therefore important to make a clear distinction between revising as a reseeing and reviewing process for general effectiveness and, more specifically, revising as a testing of the readability of sentences. Are the meanings clear? Are the sentences ambiguous? Do parts need to be cut, added, or transposed to eliminate problems that might confuse a reader?

Finally, revision consists of one other step: proofreading. In this instance you ask yourself a different kind of question: Have I observed the conventions of grammar, punctuation, capitalization, and spelling? Is the writing correct?

Actually, many students think of revising only in terms of proofreading. If, however, you check only grammatical and mechanical details and neglect a broader assessment of your work in terms of readability and effectiveness, you have neglected the most essential part of the review process—reseeing it to make it better.

As a general rule, most writers find that revising can improve their prose as long as they know when to stop reworking it. Too much revision can erase the spontaneity of the first version and leave you dissatisfied with everything. It is best, therefore, to think of rereading and revising not as a testing of every word and sentence but as an attempt to get some sense of the strengths and weaknesses of your prose. That depends on being able to recognize good and bad qualities of writing. The following chapters are designed to help you become a better critic of your own writing as well as that of others.

Revising: readability and effectiveness   Chapter 9

Progress toward better writing depends on some awareness of the qualities that you should be seeking, even though good writing cannot be defined as just one thing. It may vary with the purpose. Nevertheless, a few guidelines are helpful in learning how to revise.

Readability

All of us are capable of writing complicated or totally unreadable sentences. The crux is to understand how we fall into that trap. What contributes to unreadability? Or, more important, what promotes readability?

The term *readability* is used here objectively: how easily can a reader process the words that you write? This is not a question of effectiveness; it is one of efficiency.

Readability is closely related to the limits of short-term memory. Psychologists have tried to define these limits by determining the number of discrete items we can hold in memory at any one time. The title of George A. Miller's study, "The Magical Number Seven, Plus or Minus Two," suggests these limits. We need only remind ourselves that our license plates usually have six units, telephone numbers, seven, and Social Security numbers (much more difficult to remember), nine. More recent studies indicate that the "magical number" may be more accurately set at five, plus or minus two.

These facts suggest that we need short stretches of words to understand readily—phrases and clauses that convey their meaning within five or seven words. We need frequent closure in order to grasp meaning. As soon as we write longer units, we begin to tax the limits of the reader's short-term memory, especially if we separate words that regularly should follow one another, like subject and verb or preposition and object. Note this sentence:

Specific agents that cause maldevelopment of the embryo or fetus resulting in a miscarriage, a still birth, or the presence of congenital defects are called teratogenic agents or teratogens.

Student sentence

Compare that sentence with this one:

Teratogenic agents or teratogens are specific agents that cause maldevelopment of an embryo, miscarriage of a fetus, a still birth, or congenital defects.

The second sentence is clearly more readable simply because it puts less burden on the memory. We are able to read subject and verb without interruption. In the first sentence, twenty-two words separate the subject and verb. In addition, the parallelism of the series within these twenty-two words is broken.

Consider another example:

The waking up early in the morning, to see the sun rise, and the companionship of meeting other neighbors to participate in an activity were all part of the thrill of running.

Student sentence

In this sentence, we have to read twenty-four words before we ever get to the verb, and we do not learn what the sentence is about until the last three words. Compare the readability of a revision that follows the more familiar grammatical pattern of subject/verb/object and makes the series parallel:

The thrill of running includes waking up early in the morning, seeing the sun rise, and meeting neighbors who are also running.

Some arrangements therefore are more readable than others if they observe certain rules.

9A *Rules of readability*

1. *Keep words and phrases that refer to one another as close together as possible.* These include verbs and subjects, words and their objects, and modifiers and the words they modify. Shifts are distracting.

Student sentence

The most frequently type of person seen in the library is a fellow slouched in a chair with a book resting on his chest.

Revision

The type of person most frequently seen in the library is a fellow slouched in a chair with a book resting on his chest.

Student sentence

The conclusion is that by making these actors and actresses look the way the ad producers think Americans want to or do look, this creates motivation to buy the product.

Revision

Ad producers hope to motivate viewers to buy a product by making actors look the way producers think Americans want to look.

2. *Meet the expectations you set for the reader.* If you set up a series, make the phrasing parallel. Let the parts of the series follow one another with as little interruption as possible.

Student sentence

There are five different health aids, be it vitamins or cold repressives, one shampoo, panty hose, and two color TV commercials in a two-hour time period.

Revision

In a two-hour time period on TV, I saw nine commercials: five for health aids, one for shampoo, one for panty hose, and two for color TVs.

Student sentence

The herds consisted of sheep for wool and meat and oxen to provide working power.

Revision

The sheep herds provided wool and meat; the oxen, working power.

3. *Eliminate circumlocutions.*

Student sentence

I would be very supportive of any legislation that would ban selling beer at sporting events.

Revision

I would support any legislation that would ban selling beer at sporting events.

Student sentence

My opinion of people in this country who take everything for granted is not a good one.

Revision

I have a low opinion of people in this country who take everything for granted.

Student sentence

Intelligence was one of his prominent traits.

Revision

He was a highly intelligent man.

Other circumlocutions:
   is dependent upon
   is indicative of
   was responsive to

Verb equivalents:
   depends on
   indicates
   responded

4. *Eliminate deadwood that adds nothing to the meaning.*

Student sentence	**Revision**
For me, music has become a major part of my life through the playing of a woodwind instrument called the clarinet.	Playing the clarinet has made music a major part of my life.

Student sentence	**Revisions**
There is a theoretical point where the voter's pamphlet will have so much material in it that it will discourage readers from spending the time to read it.	In time, the voter's pamphlet will have so much material that voters will not take the time to read it. If the voter's pamphlet gets too long, people will not read it.

Student sentence	**Revisions**
I have always considered the sport of running a field in which I have a high level of expertise.	I have always considered myself an expert runner. I am an expert runner.

5. *Eliminate self-reflective and self-protective phrases that dilute the essential message of a sentence.*

Self-reflective phrases	**Self-protective phrases**
I can't think of a better example than . . .	in all probability
In every case I know . . .	in most instances, usually, often
Without a doubt, obviously	perhaps, to a certain extent, sort of
It is my hope that . . .	if I may say
One reassuring note is . . .	in my opinion

These expressions represent a running commentary by the writer on the act of writing. They frequently reassure the writer more than the reader.

Student sentence	**Revision**
Small children sometimes seem to be bored. I have concluded that this is because they don't know how to entertain themselves.	Sometimes small children seem to be bored because they don't know how to entertain themselves.

6. *Eliminate redundancies and unnecessary repetitions.*

Student sentences	**Revisions**
The gleam in my eye is very effective in nagging. It is effective be-	I can nag best when I get a threatening gleam in my eye.

cause it helps me gain a threatening image. Thus, the gleam in my eye is effective because it enhances the power of my nagging.

My nagging is most effective when I have a threatening gleam in my eye.

7. *Eliminate ambiguities.*

Student sentence

My attitude toward violence and abuse used by coaches in college football is one of anger.

Possible revisions with different meanings

I am angry about violent and abusive tactics used by college football coaches.

I am angered by violent and abusive college football coaches.

I get angry when I hear about abusive college football coaches.

8. *Prefer familiar words to unfamiliar ones, short words to long ones, English expressions to foreign ones.*

Student sentence

The procurement of a quality bicycle warrants some forethought.

Revision

Buying a good bicycle requires forethought.

Student sentence

Organized labor has engendered a better life to many Americans.

Revision

Organized labor has given many Americans a better life.

9. *Prefer the verb to the noun form of the same words.*

Nominalizations

I came to the realization
held a discussion about
had no intention of insulting
is in expectation of
to offer an explanation of
to get relaxation
was in competition with

Verb equivalents

I realized
discussed
did not intend to insult
expects
to explain
to relax
competed with

Eliminating a noun form frequently eliminates a prepositional phrase or *that*-clause following it.

10. *Prefer active forms of the verb to passive forms.*

Student sentence

The Pacific Ocean is cold when you first swim in it. When you get used to it, the cold is forgotten.

Revision

The Pacific Ocean is cold when you first swim in it. When you get used to it, you forget the cold.

Student sentence	*Revision*
There is one test to be taken by all students.	All students have to take one test.

Acceptable use of passive voice

Smoking in public places should be restricted.

11. *Prefer verbs of action to verbs of being.*

Student sentence	*Revision*
The weather was a sort of symbol of her defeat.	The weather symbolized her defeat.
Student sentence	*Revision*
The sport that gives me most enjoyment is tennis.	Among various sports, I enjoy tennis.
Student sentence	*Revision*
My attitude toward rowdy behavior in public places is negative.	I dislike rowdy behavior in public places.

12. *Prefer positive statements to negative ones.*

Student sentence	*Revision*
This nation's unions have not been free of controversy.	This nation's unions have been controversial.
Student sentence	*Revision*
The general public does not perceive a strike in an unambiguous way.	The general public looks upon a strike ambiguously.

Clearly, you cannot apply all of these guidelines consistently, but they help to test sentences that are wordy and unreadable. They are things to look for. Yet any list of rules about writing ought to have one important disclaimer. Here it is:

Break any of these rules rather than write anything downright dull.

Effectiveness

As you have noted, readability can be defined in terms of specific guidelines that are the equivalent of rules. They are not inviolable rules, but paying attention to them can keep you out of a good bit of trouble as a writer.

Effectiveness is another matter altogether. It is far less specific. Some writing problems cannot be met by changing a word or phrase because they derive from the thinking and attitude of the writer. Qualities of the individual constantly get written into the prose. To change a word here and there cannot get to the heart of the matter at all. Such passages have to be reconceived. Difficult as it is to talk about qualities that are intangible and intuitive, to ignore them would be to ignore an important element of style. If you want to improve your prose style, you have to become fully aware of things you do that interact to create the total effect of your writing. It needs to be emphasized that revising is not just catching errors. It is trying to get qualities into the writing that will make it attractive as well as meaningful. The issue therefore in learning how to revise is not always trying to find out what to avoid, but also in a positive sense what to do to become better. Think of effectiveness as strengths to be developed. Those strengths are identified here and arranged in categories to give you a clearer idea of the focus. Even though many of the qualities overlap, they are separated to give due attention to each one.

Focusing on the writer **9B**

Are the statements made with confidence, or are they weakly phrased or unduly qualified so that your voice is ineffectual?

1.   Effectiveness of voice

voice

Samples	*Revisions*
1. I think what is considered funny now is to a certain extent the same as what was considered funny twenty or maybe even fifty years ago.	1. What is funny now is basically what was funny twenty or even fifty years ago.
2. One of the major characteristics of a black in a big city is that he lives in one certain area. This area is generally not the best part of the city.	2. One of the marked features of black life in the big city is that it is usually confined to one inferior ghetto area.
3. Throughout the book Burgett expresses the violence in the world. He shows it with very good description, giving the reader a feeling of being part of it.	3. Throughout the book, Burgett reveals violence in the world by vivid descriptions that make the reader a part of the scene.

ANALYSIS   In sample 1, weakness derives from a hesitancy on the part of the writer seen in such phrases as "I think what is considered . . . ," "to a certain extent," and "maybe even." Such phrases are often useful as qualifiers, but an accumulation of them expresses doubt. In sample 2, the weakness derives from the uncertainty of such roundabout phrases as "one certain area" and "generally not the best part of the city." In the final example, the weakness is chiefly a matter of vagueness. In order to strengthen the statement, the revision substitutes more specific phrases for "very good" and "a feeling of being part of it."

COMMENT   Keep the writing direct and specific as a way of creating a clear voice and confident tone.

2. Insight

Do the sentences make worthwhile assertions or merely echo the trite and obvious?

ins
trite

Samples

1. Each and every college girl is different; therefore, each one is amused in a different way.

2. We can now kill a great number of people at one time, whereas in the beginning we could kill only one at a time.

3. If people were more honest, the world would be a better place to live in.

ANALYSIS   The obviousness and generality of these statements need not be labored. They indicate either a lack of perception on the part of the writers or a failure to think hard about the things they are writing.

COMMENT   Slice out obvious statements that are self-evident to most people.

3. Honesty

Will the reader be persuaded that your personal voice is sincere? Are you conveying what you actually feel?

hon

Samples

1. I was struck by Jarrett Boone's "Poem." It's difficult for me to verbalize what this poem means to me, but it is especially descriptive of what I do at night. Sitting in bed in the dark, I think. There's a peacefulness and quietness at midnight that one rarely has access to during the day. Some of the thoughts I have then "filter through" or some float around—the others, settled or gone, return at various intervals into my consciousness. It's rather amazing how precise and clear everything becomes at these times. Maybe I've been worried about something for days, and then one night, very suddenly, the solution sort of slides into my mind, whole and so timely it is refreshing. Like a mint, its sweetness can be tasted.

2. Since I am from the ghetto and dropped out of school, I can agree that sometimes it seems like an impossible task to get a good education. At the high school I attended, I got with the in-crowd. That's what I wanted, but this was a wrong move because these were the most affluent students and the best dressed, who had plenty of spending money and nice cars. The other students just settled for the fancy dress, which after a period of time I couldn't keep up with. This annoyed me very much, and I kept a chip on my shoulder and got expelled for assaulting an instructor. You see, because I wasn't able to keep up with the fellows, I caused a lot of trouble and almost ended my education altogether.

3. The return to the rough and tough ways of the pioneers is good for all concerned. Father may fish for delightfully-tasting Rainbow or Eastern Brook trout; the children may wander through well-traveled trails and pick blueberries, huckleberries and blackberries; Mother may cook over an open fire and watch chipmunks, squirrels, deer and occasionally the black or brown bear wandering through the campground.

So, for a delightfully worthwhile and relaxing experience, try camping sometime. Can't you just smell the aroma of fresh, hot coffee being perked over a crackling campfire?

4. The most essential part of being "cool" is being an individual with a compatible personality—a person who could get along with most people, even people who have nothing in common with him. This person would have the ability to compromise and gain friendship with an intrinsic motivation. This person should have a sparkling personality that gives others a refreshing feeling. This requires a good sense of humor and skillful gregarious techniques. It would make other people wanting to be with him. Therefore, being "cool" is having an almost impeccable image that shines upon others and being a compatible individual who has the ability to cope with different types of people.

ANALYSIS   Honesty in writing should not be identified with unpolished writing. On the other hand, polished writing need not be thought of as dishonest. Sample 1 is not less honest because it ends with a polished figure of speech. In fact, that comparison makes the previous thoughts wholly convincing. The writing reveals thoughtfulness and sensitivity. In sample 2, the facts speak for themselves, but what is important about the writing is its openness, its frankness, its lack of self-pity, and the clear sense that education is now of foremost importance to the writer. What is important about samples 3 and 4 is that the writers seem more interested in impressing a reader with the choice of words than concentrating on the subject matter. These samples illustrate that words on paper, no matter how sincere the writers may protest they are, stand separated from the writer. Both passages seem as glossy and idealized as the advertisements in the latest issue of *Sunset* or *Family Circle* or *Woman's Day*. If the writer of sample 3 thinks she describes the "rough and tough ways of the pioneers," then she deludes herself. If the writer of sample 4 thinks being "cool" is displaying a shining image, then she has succeeded in being cool at the expense of being forthright. Writing can be a mask, as it is in 3 and 4, but it can also be a mirror of the writer, as it is in 1 and 2.

COMMENT   Use personal experiences and firsthand observations whenever possible; don't invent hypothetical characters and situations. Above all, be natural in the expression of feeling.

Have you controlled your tone so that it is appropriate to the subject matter and the audience? Have you channeled and supported your feeling so it works for you instead of producing doubts about your sincerity?

4. Control of tone and feeling

cont

Samples

1. In evaluating a professor, I place the highest importance on the three following qualities: (1) mastery of the subject, (2) enthusiasm of the instructor for his subject, (3) the warmth with which he regards and responds to his subject. (1) Mr. H. is very able not only in understanding and explaining the material, but also in relating subject matter to other things, idealism, beliefs, etc. (2) He is apparently eager to think about further implications of literature and readily accepts different ideas with a necessary amount of disciplined thought. (3) He shows warmth by his responses to students and his interest in literature.

2. Get every person in class to talk—not just a few. Don't give your own opinions (although they're good) because so many individuals depend on them. Even if the student is off base a mile, don't raise your voice: you'll never get another response. Suggestion: Have a minor fraction of the final grade depend on participation. I believe this would stimulate some of the "bumps on a log" and make those who participate talk more frequently.

3. He always came to class prepared with good questions and ideas to stimulate our thinking. He respected our opinions and never embarrassed or hurt anyone. If he disagreed with a comment, he would state why. I feel that his method of teaching was very effective. Until this course I had never enjoyed English. Now it's my favorite subject. He was very easy to get along with and was much more helpful than I expected. He was reasonable in his assignments, although he was not an easy instructor. The questions or topics we were given to write about in our themes were easy for the students to relate to.

4. I feel Mrs. S. has done an excellent job as a teacher. Her classes were intellectually stimulating to the extent that once you got out of the classroom you remembered what was discussed and made it part of your life. Through this class I have become much more socially aware of the problems we are confronted with in the world today and am able to deal with them better. The course has opened up a whole new world for me—one in which creativity is presented as something fun as well as beneficial. Reading became meaningful and the writing became exciting. I felt like I could express myself without having to worry about what anyone else thought. Mrs. S's class was a beautiful, growing experience for me. Our confrontations with poetry were enlightening as well as delightful. Her attempts at drawing the class out as individuals worked fantastically to the point where as a class we became one. This has never happened before in a class, and I think this closeness between a teacher and students is essential and very important to the relationship of learning and growing. The idea of the journal of our thoughts was a new experience for me and one which helped me understand myself as I never thought possible. Another thing which impressed me was Mrs. S's interest in us outside of teaching as well as in class. Many times after class or during her free moments, we talked and discussed things which I was upset about. Her time was always our time and made readily available. I appreciated the interest she showed in us as human beings and not just as students. Very rarely is a teacher sincerely concerned with his students. When a teacher is concerned, I think that says an awful lot about the teacher as a person. This class was really a joy and a fantastic experience. I only hope I can take another course from Mrs. S. or that my other encounters will be as happy.

5. He has a thorough knowledge of the material, and he seemed interested in actually teaching the class something. He was also willing to discuss problems with students. In general, he seems to be a thoroughly devoted instructor with a good deal of knowledge to transmit to the students. His main weakness lies in the way he presents it. Instead of lecturing, he should encourage more participation. I realize this is often difficult to do when the students will not cooperate, but he seemed to jump at the chance to lecture when the students failed to show an immediate understanding of the material. When the students fail to respond at first, it would be better if he would ask more leading questions so the students can dig out the answers bit by bit. This would help the student to analyze literature himself, instead of taking notes on the instructor's ideas.

6. For some reason undefined, it annoyed me to have Mr. K. announce one day near the middle of the quarter that we need not bother ourselves very much with satire or *Gulliver's Travels* anymore. Our future themes need not be concerned with previous material, but with opinions on overworked subjects like race problems and education. Ecch! It shook my confidence. We should have pursued a straight line through the material intended. Once when I chose not to correct a certain commonplace paper, Mr. K. assigned me another paper, after I had already received a satisfactory grade on the stupid paper. (It was a boring paper, I admit.) But the second paper was on an obscure subject, which I thought wholly unfair. If I had known the alternative, I would have gladly, even joyously rewritten the first horrendous paper.

ANALYSIS   All of the samples are taken from survey forms of student opinion and therefore record the responses of these students to their instructors in Freshman English. Among many varied responses, which ones does an instructor take seriously? Which ones say more about the writer than about the instructor? Samples 1 and 2 contrast two students who are both orderly in their responses. The essential difference is not that one tends to be positive and the other negative but that the writer of sample 1 seems both sensitive and reasonable, while the writer of sample 2 makes himself appear both dogmatic and uncompromising.

   Samples 3 and 4 illustrate two highly favorable responses. Sample 3 is enthusiastic but controlled; sample 4 is exuberant. Probably no one would question the honesty of the writer of sample 4, but we might question her judgment because everything seems so indiscriminately "fantastic," almost miraculous. In fact, the instructor of this student reported that this young woman had come from such a restricted home and school environment that everything at the university seemed great and marvelous. The prose catches that glow.

   Samples 5 and 6 record negative comments. The differences are obvious. The writer of sample 5 attempts to balance good and bad, although the remarks hint more at dissatisfaction than satisfaction. Nevertheless, the student tries to be fair. The writer of sample 6, above all, records his own peevishness and self-indulgence. The entire blame is placed on the instructor. Even though the comment may raise questions in the reader's mind about the instructor's actions, it fails to carry weight because of the writer's uncontrolled tone and unchanneled expression.

COMMENT   Control the tone of writing so that a worthwhile idea has its full effect.

Focusing on the subject 9C

Is the prose vague because the concept and words are abstract rather than concrete?   *1. Concreteness*

conc

Sample	**Alternate Version**
Americans have always considered the problems of education. They want a good education for their children.	I have attended more than a dozen schools in California, Nevada, and Washington. Some of them were little

Sometimes though, they weren't having a major say, or sometimes they didn't want it bad enough. For a lot of areas in American education have been hurt, better teachers for one, buildings to house our students, the best of books, all have suffered. Why blame one area, why try to correct it in just one area? Because that one area in which action is implied won't solve the problem. It would be just the first step in deciding which areas will suffer for the benefit of others. The reason it won't work is because you are not improving the total picture, just going back to what you generally had to start with. We shouldn't discriminate within but rather go outside of the system and get help. This way the total picture will be improved, not just part for the expense of another. My value judgment would be that not enough value on education as a whole is being seen, not that a minority of our school buildings are getting too much value placed upon them.

more than a collection of quonset huts and portables, some a sprawling maze of well-lighted classrooms and landscaped play areas. Stadium High School, which I now attend, is a huge brick edifice nicknamed "The Old Brown Castle" by generations of students admiring its castle-like architecture and decrying its falling plaster and exposed overhead pipes. I have found these schools similar in almost every respect except architecture. The administrators and financial directors have been caught up by the rising maintenance and budget expenditures of existing schools and the need for yet more school buildings and more teachers. Teachers find themselves in larger and larger classrooms, some even teaching double sessions. There is a real need for more classrooms and more teachers: we hear it over and over again from journalists and educators. The answer always seems to be the same: criticism of the extravagance and waste in American education. Nothing is really being done to ease the situation.

ANALYSIS Both samples are the opening paragraphs of responses written in answer to the question, "In the light of your own observation and experience, to what extent do you think the United States places more value on elaborate school buildings than on expert teaching?" The specific nature of the question throws some light on the meaning of the first sample, but much of its vagueness grows out of the writer's failure to focus on the topic, falling into a general discussion of problems of education. Undefined abstractions occur in almost every sentence: "problems of education," "good education," "major say," "areas," and "the total picture." To be revised, a paragraph of this kind has to be reconceived in new terms, with an attempt to approch the question concretely. The alternate version, written by another student, does that. It illustrates how she starts by thinking in terms of actual places and buildings in relation to education. As a result, she writes a more satisfactory response.

COMMENT Try to think in terms of the specific and concrete. In revision, consider whether some abstract words can be replaced by more concrete ones. If simple changes cannot be made, rethink and rewrite the passage in different terms.

2. Credibility

cred

Are the statements believable in terms of facts and experience that we know or that you supply?

Sample

The one institution today which most openly practices the discouragement of ideas is the church. Essentially it tells its members not to think. From birth to death it controls its members' intellectual environment.

Revision

[The writing itself needs no revision, but this particular man might possibly revise his opinion or qualify it if he knew more about the great differences among churches.]

ANALYSIS If this statement were made in terms of one particular religious sect, it might be credible, although it would still be difficult to conceive of the total control of an individual's "intellectual environment." The writer generalizes about all churches in terms of some churches and, as a consequence, falls into the *all–some* fallacy (see p. 74). The third sentence of the statement is also difficult to accept as an unsupported statement, but in the next paragraph the writer explains more precisely what that sentence means.

COMMENT The bald statement is impressive but not often persuasive. In writing, consider the credibility of broad generalizations, particularly those that are unsupported.

Is sufficient detail given to support statements that are made? Does the evidence given actually support the generalizations?

3. Support

sup

Samples

1. We tend to laugh at others because of their shortcomings. For instance, if we see someone hit in the face with a cream pie we see it as absurd and very unreal.

2. Paul Goodman labels subject matter, especially on the college level, as abstract and barren. He says that "the lessons are only exercises, with no relation to the real world. They are never for keeps." I agree with him to some extent. I'm sure that memorizing all the presidents of the United States is something that will stick with me forever.

Revisions

1. We sometimes laugh at others because we see some incongruity between what is happening to them and what ordinarily happens. Thus when we see someone get hit in the face with a cream pie we laugh because the action is unexpected and absurd.

2. . . . I'm sure that being able to identify thirty-five passages of English literature on the basis of style and content will have little or no relevance to anything I will ever do again.

ANALYSIS In samples 1 and 2, the illustrations do not support the statements that the writers make. In the revision of sample 1, the lead statement has been changed so that the evidence is appropriate. In the revision of sample 2, a more appropriate example has been substituted.

COMMENT Provide as much relevant detail as necessary to support statements that cannot stand upon their own assertion.

9D *Focusing on the audience*

1. Appropriateness   Is the language appropriate to the subject and the audience, and is the usage appropriate to the overall style?

appr
colloq

Samples	*Revisions*
1. I think meeting and knowing Gordon would be a good experience. If a person can come right out and say that criminals should be treated real nice because they create jobs for other people, he's got to be nuts.	1. I think meeting Gordon would be a good experience. If a person can say outright that criminals should be treated tolerantly because they create jobs for other people, I think he's eccentric enough to be worth knowing.
2. As for adults who wish to crack down on this younger generation and teach them some respect and manners, I would like to clobber them all. They seem to forget that most of the vandalism is caused by a few. They wish to punish us all for being young. They advocate more police and stricter laws. They assure us that they know how we should be handled. The most saddening part of this is that they have no understanding of us at all.	2. Adults, although they are more sophisticated and experienced, tend to come to solutions which they think are best without fully understanding that young people's reactions are different from theirs. Teenagers, although they are often immature, have their own ideas about solving a problem like vandalism. Neither side, however, gives in sufficiently, and in the end harsh feelings result.

ANALYSIS   The first sample illustrates the mixture of an informal writing style with a much freer conversational style. Phrases like "right out," "real nice," and "got to be nuts" are unobjectionable as everyday expressions, but, in writing, more precise and appropriate choices can be made, as the revision shows.

The second sample is part of a student's response to a topic on a college entrance test that described a public meeting of citizens who were undecided how to solve the problem of teenage vandalism in their city. One group wanted a curfew and a larger police force; the other wanted expanded programs and facilities for the amusement of teenagers. Students were asked to discuss which group they would support and why. The directions added the statement, "You are expected to express your best thought in your best natural manner." The writer of sample 2, like the writer of sample 1, shows some tendency to fall into speech patterns, but the writing is basically inappropriate in a different way. The student overreacts and is carried away by sweeping and thoughtless accusations. What we read seems natural enough, but it is doubtful whether it was the best manner for the occasion or the audience who would read the test. Sample 2 cannot be revised; it needs to be rewritten. The revision is actually an alternate version written by another student, who gives a more balanced and appropriate statement of the differences between adults and teenagers.

COMMENT Choose expressions and a tone of writing appropriate both to the audience and the purpose of the writing.

Does the prose have the necessary links to hold it together closely? Are the statements rationally consistent with one another so that the development is orderly?

1. Coherence

coh

Sample

Is higher education suited for all students? Paul Goodman feels that "lessons are only exercises, with no relation to the real world." Philip Wylie finds that to the founding fathers of higher learning universal education consisted of "teaching everyone the language, simple arithmetic, and the structure of eighteenth century society. Science was elementary. Industry was nil, as we know it. There is no such society today." Yet their higher education has practically remained the same. They both feel that there should not be just one type of college institution, but a variety of schools where advanced instruction is taught so that all knowledge is represented and each student can pick where his interest and ability lie, whether it is computer processing, ancient Greek, or dancing. No more single college degree.

Revision

Is higher education suited for all students? No, it isn't, because higher education still tries to make a general program apply to all students. Classes designed for all students are irrelevant. Paul Goodman thinks that the typical lessons of higher education are only "exercises, with no relation to the real world." Philip Wylie touches on a similar kind of irrelevance in discussing the original concept of universal education envisioned by the founding fathers. "Universal education consisted, then," Wylie writes, "in teaching everyone the language, simple arithmetic, and the structure of eighteenth century society. Science was elementary. Industry was nil, as we know it. There is no such society today." In similar terms, higher education seems to hold to principles of the past. It does not address today's society. Both writers see the need for innovations in the total structure of education that will bring about relevance. If varieties of schools were created at the lower levels, then advanced instruction could not be as much one thing as it now is. There would be no such thing as a single college degree.

ANALYSIS The opening question of the sample is precise. A previous paragraph of the theme has asked, "Are all students suited for higher education?" The second basic question, then, reverses the emphasis: "Is higher education suited for all students?" That is, is higher education suited for those students who presumably have the potential to do college work? What follows the question, however, lacks coherence for several reasons. First, this young man gives only a vague answer. Second, he forces his illustrations to say things that the essays themselves do not say. It is not surprising, therefore, that his examples do not seem to fit together. The phrasing of the quotation from Philip Wylie indicates clearly that he is talking about education in the lower schools. The writer attempts to make the statement relevant by referring to "the founding fathers of higher learning." Wylie says simply, "The idea of universal education sounded sensible to the founding fathers," and then moves into the sentence which the student quotes.

Coherence is closely linked with clearness, logic, relevance, and unity. The revision attempts to use the same illustrations as the original, but to use them honestly and to relate them to one another by appropriate explanations. The new paragraph has both an answer to the question and a thesis of its own to develop. The revision is longer than the original because it fills in the missing links.

COMMENT   Consider the gaps in thoughts that keep a reader from following the line of development easily. Provide bridges and links in the prose.

2. Consistency of person

person shift

Do the personal pronouns shift needlessly?

Samples	**Revisions**
1. I think if I try to succeed I can. If one has the will to try and has people who want to help, you should be able to do something with your life.	1. I think if I try to succeed I can. If we have the will to try and have people who want to help, we should be able to do something with our lives.
2. If a person buys something from Woolworth's or Kress's and one of your friends finds out, you will be laughed at and considered "uncool."	2. If you buy something from Woolworth's or Kress's and one of your friends finds out, you will be laughed at and considered "uncool."

ANALYSIS   In sample 1, the writer begins from a personal point of view; the second sentence generalizes but does not follow through consistently with the pronoun. The revision does. The second sample shifts from third person to second person; the revision uses a consistent second person.

COMMENT   Revise personal pronouns that alter the point of view already established in a sentence or in the essay as a whole.

3. Proportion

prop

Are the topics given space and development in proportion to their importance? Is the reader left with a sense of completeness?

Samples

1. Movies are one of the worthwhile national pastimes in America. They not only can be entertainment to the people but they also can be educational as well.

People react to the movies in one way or another, especially young people in today's society. They take the movies as their guide. Rather than thinking of this particular movie as good or bad, they will try to follow the same procedures or patterns they saw in the movie.

Strangely enough, many people do think that movies are parallel to education today. Movies can affect the younger generation in the way they behave. Producers try to simplify the meaning of the purpose of the movies for the people as best they can. But some people do take them for granted. Why is this so? The answer will depend upon each individual's family background and his environment.

2. Of the national pastimes available, I feel bicycling is the most worthwhile. From the standpoint of exercise, it develops many muscles not used in our relatively sedentary daily life. Stimulation to the circulatory system can be invaluable to persons of all ages. The entire family can become involved together, including the grandparents who would otherwise rarely participate or exercise.

The most important aspect of bicycling, however, is the beneficial effect on the emotional system. In the pressured world of the executive or the busy but frequently nonstimulating world of the housewife, there are few moments to relax and simply watch things as they exist. The schoolchild can be so wrapped up in schoolwork and extracurricular activities that he becomes nearly unaware of the world about him. The suburban family typically whirls in a self-absorbed circle. Bicycling offers an escape from routine and a chance to stand apart and see oneself and things about him.

ANALYSIS Sample 1 begins with two sentences which state that movies are worthwhile because they are both educational and entertaining. We might expect that each of the paragraphs following would develop one of these points. Instead, the writer writes first about the manner in which young people indiscriminately accept movies as a guide. The second paragraph then turns to the general populace, but its point is not wholly clear. Neither paragraph is adequately developed, and nothing is said about movies as entertainment. The reader is left with a sense of disproportion and incompleteness. It is apparent that this young woman has major difficulties with writing, but she needs help first in the prewriting stage; she needs to focus on a limited topic, estimate how much or how little she has to say about it, generate more ideas, and learn to develop them as fully as she can.

The writer of the second sample treats the same topic in a modest way, but the aims are clear. Bicycling, the writer points out, benefits both young and old physically and emotionally. Since the effect on the emotional system is a less obvious point, it receives the greater emphasis. Despite the briefness of the treatment, the reader nevertheless perceives that the topic has been developed with a sense of proportion.

COMMENT Consider the size of the topic in relation to the space available, make appropriate limitations, and develop individual points to the extent of their relative importance.

4. *Unity*

Do the sentences have a oneness of purpose? Do the ideas have a point?

U   **Samples**

1. The lust for power and material values corrupts the mind. The power of oil as an implement of war is a terrible wrong to humanity. Only for peace can we find true happiness. Today we seek peace for the preservation of humanity, but progress is making this a difficult task. Modern devices are slowly taking over man's mind. No longer do they conform to us but we to them. We are slowly losing our identity and individualism, becoming just a number. With the push of a button the destruction of the earth and its life can come about. Maybe it would be better to be dead than to live in a huge machine.

2. In rock music there is a distinct and almost overpowering beat. There is not a single beat characteristic of the music today, but each song has an easily audible rhythm. As you listen to a song, your foot usually starts to pick up the beat. Before long, your entire body seems to be moving with it. Your head pounds with the beat, and there is no room for thought. Only the music is important.

ANALYSIS   It is impossible to know precisely what the point of sample 1 is. It touches on the evils of materialism, the need for peace, the dehumanization of man, and the possible destruction of the earth, but these statements do not seem to support the topic the first sentence sets forth. By contrast, sample 2 states a precise topic in the first sentence and in four succeeding sentences sticks closely to it.

COMMENT   Establish a main theme for a paragraph or an essay and keep the ideas related to it.

9F *Focusing on style*

1. *Balance and parallelism*

Do the sentence constructions satisfy the reader's sense of uniformity, balance, and parallelism?

bal
par

Samples

1. James, a young teenage black, experienced an exhilarating, soul-searching encounter with God which he thought was something to cling to, protecting him from the immoral clutches of the Avenue and that would relieve his feelings of despair. It didn't.

Revisions

1. James, a young teenage black, experienced an exhilarating, soul-searching encounter with God which he thought was something to cling to, protecting him from the immoral clutches of the Avenue and relieving him of feelings of despair. It didn't.

or

. . . something to cling to, something to protect him from the immoral clutches of the Avenue and relieve him of feelings of despair.

2. The black motorist claimed that the officer was discriminating against him in terms of racial prejudice and not only because a law had been broken.

2. The black motorist claimed that the officer was discriminating against him because of racial prejudice, not because of a traffic violation.

or

The black motorist claimed that the officer's motive in charging him was racial prejudice, not the traffic violation.

3. Not only was he seeking self-respect, which he could not have hoped to achieve in his base condition, but also for respect from the white man, who had built the cage he was trapped in.

3. He was seeking not only self-respect, which he could not have hoped to achieve in his base condition, but also respect from the white man, who had built the cage he was trapped in.

4. The cartoonist brings out the satire vividly by comparing the tragedy with the trivial.

4. The cartoonist brings out the satire vividly by comparing the tragic and the trivial.

ANALYSIS Each of these sentences becomes more readable and clear by a few simple changes: shifting the position of words or using parallel phrasing in balanced constructions.

COMMENT Take advantage of the effects that can be gained by balanced and parallel phrasing.

Is the figurative language consistent with the overall style and consistent in itself?

2. Consistency of figurative language

fig

Sample

Putting on the breastplate of rhetorical technique and taking up the sword of Dante and the Bible, Buckley pulls out all the stops in this paragraph.

Revision

Using a full range of rhetorical techniques and literary allusion, Buckley pulls out all the stops.

ANALYSIS This sentence is taken from a student's analysis of William F. Buckley's prose style. In context, it seemed unduly elaborate; it is the kind of metaphor that calls attention to itself, not to the thought of the sentence. The revision reduces the mixed metaphor to one clear, consistent analogy which is appropriate to the meaning—an organ. In the original, the image of Buckley dressed as a warrior playing an organ at full volume is an unintentional bit of humor.

COMMENT Strive for the expressive metaphor, not the ornamental one. Be on the alert for mixed metaphors that turn out to be more amusing than meaningful.

Are the words and sentences arranged to gain emphasis? Have the most appropriate words been chosen to make an emphatic statement?

3. Emphasis

emph

Samples	**Revisions**
1. The statement that was written was a good one.	1. The statement was perceptive.
2. There are educated people who engage in crime on an organized scale, and I would say that their purpose would be money.	2. There are educated people who engage in crime on an organized scale to make money.
3. A history shows, with the decreased control of the aristocracy over the working class, freedom of the press developed, which is an interesting point.	3. History reveals the interesting fact that with the decreased control of the aristocracy over the working class, freedom of the press increased.
4. That man is naïve in that he thinks that criminals are an asset to the economy and he doesn't realize that they are a liability to the community.	4. That man is naïve if he doesn't realize that criminals are not primarily an asset to the economy, but basically a liability to the community.

ANALYSIS   Emphasis is an effect related both to the choice of words and their arrangement. In some instances, like sample 1, the sentence might be quite satisfactory in a particular context. If the writer wanted to create a more emphatic statement, however, he might eliminate "that was written" (unless those words were necessary to contrast the statement with one "that was spoken"). He might also substitute a more explicit adjective for "good." The revision uses "perceptive," but other adjectives like "original" or "purposeful" would be more precise and emphatic than "good." The revision of sample 2 tightens the prose for emphasis. The nine words of the second sentence are easily compressed into the phrase of three words used in the revision. The final clause in sample 3 is the writer's own judgment, but from the reader's point of view, it is an afterthought tagged on ineffectually. The revision incorporates the thought into the main sentence. The balancing of "decreased" with "increased," a substitute for "developed," adds further emphasis. Sample 4 demonstrates how a perceptive idea can be weakly phrased. The revision emphasizes the contrast of the two views by using the "not primarily . . . but" construction.

COMMENT   Look at various words and constructions that can be altered to produce more emphatic effects.

4. Euphony

eu

How would the written words sound if they were read aloud? Do the words read rhythmically?

Samples	**Revisions**
1. In the first three books of *Gulliver's Travels*, Swift jests objects of his displeasure in witty and imaginative ways.	1. In the first three books of *Gulliver's Travels*, Swift attacks objects of his displeasure in witty and imaginative ways.

2. Her world is based on values that mean something—something not shallow but which you can draw a sense of fulfillment from.

2. Her world is based on values that mean something—something not shallow but fulfilling.

3. I would like to know G. P. because he seems sensible, cynical, and sincere.

3. I would like to know G. P. because he seems cynical and sincere.

ANALYSIS   All of the samples illustrate combinations of words that make the alliteration of sounds too obvious. The revision of sample 1 substitutes a more pleasant and idiomatic word for "jests." The revision of sample 2 not only eliminates an awkward alliteration at the end of the sentence but improves the rhythm and emphasis as well. The revision of sample 3, although it cuts out only one word, seems to eliminate the objectionable hissing of the original and to create a rather appealing alliteration. It also sharpens the antithesis of "cynical and sincere," which seems to be the point of the statement.

COMMENT   Consider the potential sounds of words when they are combined on the page, even though they may never be read aloud.

Is the language stale and meaningless because it falls too easily into the familiar phrase?

5. Freshness

fr
cliché
trite

Samples

1. Persons who stubbornly remain unaware or ignorant of the other side of a picture are usually so emotionally involved with their opinions that they refuse to envision the other side of the story.

Revisions

1. Persons unaware of other viewpoints are usually so emotionally involved with themselves that they stubbornly refuse to listen to other opinions.

2. Living in the ideal commonwealth is not all roses.

2. Living in the ideal commonwealth is actually less than ideal.

3. Everywhere one sees nature dressed in her best attire.

3. Everywhere nature is luxuriant and beautiful.

ANALYSIS   "The other side of the story" and "the other side of the coin" are clichés. In sample 1, the writer uses only one of these, but thinking in terms of these clichés produces a relatively meaningless phrase, "the other side of a picture." Here the writer falls into an easy expression without thinking that it does not actually say anything in this context. The revisions of 2 and 3 avoid the tired phrases of the originals.

COMMENT   Sidestep hackneyed words and expressions.

6. Naturalness

awk
id

Does the prose sound like the English language? Are the expressions grammatical and idiomatic and the arrangements unforced? Are the words and phrases idiomatic?

Samples

1. When people cease to tolerate themselves is the time hypocrisy comes about.

2. With physical death does not, nor cannot die the existence of the achievements of a man.

3. These people are kept at a minimum as to being able to outwardly express their opinions, which is wrong.

Revisions

1. Hypocrisy comes about when people cease to tolerate themselves.

2. With physical death, the achievements of a man do not and cannot die. [The credibility of this statement can be questioned.]

3. It is wrong that these people are discouraged from openly expressing their opinions.

ANALYSIS   In sample 1, the awkwardness results from trying to make a *when* clause the subject of the sentence. In sample 2, the inverted structure serves no purpose except to make the sentence difficult to read. Sample 3 simply does not sound like English. The revisions eliminate these difficulties.

COMMENT   Rewrite involved and obviously unidiomatic expressions. Consider whether departures from normal word order add to or detract from the effect of the sentence.

7. Pace

pace

Does the prose move? Are the sentences varied so that the pace slows or quickens to suit the meaning?

Samples

1. One criterion is obvious and of special importance for the present discussion; namely, that sets of such primitives should be comprised of *observational*, or as we shall sometimes say, *experimental*, terms (i.e., that such predicates should refer to observable features of the universe). The import of positivist, pragmatist, and operationalist philosophies of science on the thinking of methodologically self-conscious scientists has no doubt been so pervasive as to require no extended comment here on this point. But from the foregoing discussion, it should be clear that one way of meeting the demand of experimental testability on any candidate concept that we are considering introducing into a theory is to introduce it through definition by primitives which, themselves, *are known to have experimentally testable reference*. Thus, an important by-product of the experimental-testability criterion for a set of primitives lies in the fact that any set that meets this condition in a theory guarantees that all new concepts introduced through definition will, in turn, be experimentally testable concepts.

Richard S. Rudner, *Philosophy of Social Sciences*

2. It must be admitted that when people speak of using experimental methods in social enquiry, they are frequently using the word 'experiment' in a narrower sense.

They would not, that is to say, regard mere learning by trial and error in the normal course of life as satisfying the conditions of a properly conducted experiment. For this they would require that we also have control over the conditions in which we act, and arrange these conditions so as to eliminate the influence of factors other than our action. It is this control which we have in its most developed form in a laboratory, and action under 'real life conditions' rarely attains it, even when there is a merely theoretical end in view. In any discussion of experiment, therefore, the distinction between the narrower and the wider sense should be kept in mind.

Quentin Gibson, *The Logic of Social Enquiry*

ANALYSIS Pace involves more than a variety of sentences to produce the right rhythms. It also means eliminating obstacles that keep the reader from moving easily, with understanding, through the prose. The illustrations above by two social scientists are compared with each other, not with a different kind of writing altogether, like narrative, that moves with a different pace because its purpose is different. In neither sample is there a striking variety of sentence length. However, the length of the sentences in sample 1 ranges from 33 words to 48 words; in sample 2 from 22 to 34. The sentences of sample 1 therefore begin at the upper reaches of those in sample 2. An accumulation of long sentences naturally slows the pace of prose.

More significant, however, is the difference in the diction of the two samples. The prose of sample 1 becomes bogged down in an impenetrable jargon and a mass of polysyllables. The sentences are overloaded, making it difficult for the reader to carry the burden of the thought. The writer of sample 2 chooses a different vocabulary altogether, even though his book is addressed to a comparable audience. The prose of sample 2 also shows careful attention to the linking of sentences, enabling the reader to follow the thought easily. The result is well-paced, more readable prose, even though the subject is specialized.

COMMENT Note that almost all elements of writing—the diction, the structure, and the style—make the difference between well-paced and ponderous prose. Read prose aloud to test its sound and movement.

Are words used accurately and precisely so that the meaning is unconfused?

8. Precision

prec
D
ex
WW

Samples	*Revisions*
1. The main theme of *Hamlet* can generally be summed up in the Greek word *nemesis*, meaning the weakness in a character causing disaster to that person.	1. The plot of *Hamlet* turns upon the Greek idea of *nemesis*, that is, a concept that the gods demand the punishment of those who disrupt the harmony of the moral order.
2. To use violence as a means of obtaining a goal is a far too poignant dosage of barbarism for most people to sympathize with.	2. The use of violence to obtain a goal is a stronger dose of barbarism than most people can take.

3. Bitzer would probably be a great success in business, but a man so deficit of emotion cannot be considered a whole man.

3. Bitzer would probably be a great success in business, but a man so deficient in feeling cannot be considered a whole man.

ANALYSIS   In sample 1, the writer does not understand what *nemesis* means because the definition is inaccurate. The second example seems to be saying that violence is a dose of medicine that is too strong for most people to tolerate. But "poignant" and "sympathize" are inaccurately used. The third example confuses "deficit" and "deficient."

COMMENT   Consult the dictionary for various meanings; then consider whether the words mean precisely what they should mean in a particular context.

9. Variety

var

Are the sentences sufficiently varied, particularly in length, to avoid a monotonous effect?

Sample

Bob Dylan's message is clear to anyone who reads or listens to the songs. He finds fault with many facets of our society. The one I have chosen to discuss is war. These three songs were written prior to 1963 before there was a great deal of outspoken opposition to the war. So I imagine one could say that these songs apply to past, present, and future wars. The first two are about his feelings toward war and injustice. The last is, I think, an explanation of why he feels the way he does.

Revision

Bob Dylan's message is clear to anyone who reads or listens to his songs. Many of them, particularly those written about war, find fault with society. I have chosen three songs on war that were written prior to 1963. Because they were written before there was a great deal of outspoken opposition to the Vietnam war, one could say that these songs pertain to past and future wars as well as the present one. The first two songs tell about Bob Dylan's feelings toward war and injustice; the third tells why he feels the way he does.

ANALYSIS   The original seven short sentences, which vary from 9 to 20 words in length, have a choppy effect. Not only are they relatively short, averaging less than 14 words, but they are for the most part similar in construction: simple sentences beginning with a subject which is followed by the predicate. In four of the seven sentences, moreover, the principal verb is a form of "to be." In the revision the number of sentences is reduced to five, with an average length close to 18 and a range between 12 and 36. Sentence variety has been achieved further by skillful use of subordination, which also helps show relationships among the various statements made. Only one sentence, the first, now uses a form of "to be" as the predicate for a main clause.

COMMENT   Test the variety of sentences by their readability. Consider both length and structure.

Proofreading: punctuation and mechanics   *Chapter 10*

Correctness is a part of effectiveness. Error gets in the way in the same sense that static gets in the way of radio reception. It doesn't actually keep you from understanding. It is just an annoying interference.

Correctness also helps to create the writer's voice. It indicates an attitude—an intention to observe the familiar norms of English expression. Error therefore becomes noticeable, not just because it is a blunder but because it represents an inconsistency in voice. Tone changes when error occurs. It becomes discordant.

Some people consider correctness a neutral factor. They want a manuscript or book to be accurate so that they can concentrate on the thought and the subtleties of the way it is written. Because correctness allows readers to pay attention to what they want, it becomes an indirect way of pleasing them.

The graphics of writing are largely conventional. The uses do not necessarily have logical explanations; they are just the way people have used them, and these conventions are perpetuated by the schools and all of the publishing media. Thus, getting familiar with the conventions can make writing much simpler for you. If you have mastered mechanics, you too can pay attention to both the matter and the manner of what you are writing.

1. To mark a full end-stop, whether the break comes at the end of a sentence or at the end of a fragment written as a sentence.

From time to time, he would glance at his notes to regain his confidence.

I think we must set up priorities among values. Human beings first. Yes. No doubt about the first priority.

Note: When the period substitutes for a question mark, the question may be interpreted as a polite directive:

Would you please make the changes and return the manuscript to us by June 15.

2. To indicate abbreviations:

Mr.—Mister	M.A.—Master of Arts
Mme.—Madame	S.J.—Society of Jesus
Esq.—Esquire	A.D.—Anno Domini

Abbreviations that tend to be pronounced as words or sounded as letters are often written without periods:

AAUP—American Association of University Professors
USSR—Union of Soviet Socialist Republics
YMCA—Young Men's Christian Association
VIP (informal)—very important person
BMOC (informal)—big man on campus
CORE—Congress of Racial Equality

As a general principle, the use of abbreviations varies with the formality of the writing: the more formal, the fewer abbreviations. Yet, even in the most formal contexts, abbreviations may be required to avoid the unnecessary repetition of long names and involved titles. They are, of course, standard in footnote forms, lists, tables, and so on. A few are commonly required in prose of almost any variety:

Titles:	Mr., Mrs., Ms., Dr., Sr., St. (saint)
Degrees:	B.A., Ph.D., D.D.
Time:	P.M., A.M., B.C., A.D.
Foreign terms:	i.e., e.g., viz., cf.
Names:	AP (Associated Press), IPA (International Phonetic Alphabet), IRBM (intermediate-range ballistic missile).

Two guidelines will serve almost all situations:
A. Follow with consistency throughout a work whatever practice is initially adopted.
B. If in serious doubt about the appropriateness of any abbreviation, spell it out.

3. To indicate dollars and cents ($7.10), percentages (5.3%), divisions by act, scene, and line (*Hamlet* I.i. 5–6), and other divided numbers in itemized lists (14.17, 14.18).

Notes:

A. Periods are placed inside quotation marks:

The title was an allusion to a phrase in Goethe's "Erl-King."

He said, "One example can be found Whitman's 'Song of Myself.'"

B. When a quotation comes at the end of a question, the period is dropped:

Who said "I think, therefore I am"?

C. If a sentence ends with an abbreviation, no second period is necessary:

I attended a professional meeting in Washington, D.C.

D. Periods and commas are commonly used together:

Whenever he encountered John, Jr., he was sure to have an argument.

E. When parentheses or brackets are used, the period may be placed inside or outside the parentheses depending upon the context or dropped altogether:

His ten years in Rome were unhappy ones (the decade discussed in Chapter 3).

His ten years in Rome were unhappy ones. (See the discussion in Chapter 3.)

His ten years in Rome (see the discussion in Chapter 3) were unhappy ones.

Use of the question mark **10B**

1. To terminate a question:

Regular questions: Do you know about the new policies? Is it not possible that you may be wrong and she right?

Intonation questions: She failed?
I am the one to blame for this mess?

Note: In an intonation question, the question mark indicates the change of *pitch* when speaking the sentence. It is the only way to identify a question whose word order is the same as that of a statement. See "Segmentals and Suprasegmentals," pp. 463–464.

2. To indicate questions inserted parenthetically for rhetorical effect:

He was cocksure—is it so bad to be cocksure?—that he was going to win.

3. To indicate the uncertainty of facts:

The comedies of Aristophanes (445?–385? B.C.) provide glimpses of what Athenian life was actually like.

Notes:

A. The question mark is placed inside quotation marks if the question is part of the quoted material, outside if the question is being asked by the writer.

I am certain I heard him ask "What do you want me to do?"

Have you read Francis Thompson's "The Hound of Heaven"?

B. The indirect question requires no question mark:

I asked what was required of me.

Cf. the equivalent direct question:

I asked, "What is required of me?"

C. The use of the question mark to make an ironic commentary is generally considered obvious and amateurish:

The newspaper reported that unarmed (?) policemen were present at the gathering.

10C *Use of the exclamation point*

1. To add force or agitation to almost any kind of emotional expression or interjection:

Please! Give the man air!

O Lord our Lord, how excellent is thy name in all the earth!

Psalm 8:1

Notes:

A. The exclamation point is placed inside quotation marks if the statement is a part of the quoted material, outside if the emphasis is being added by the writer:

He ended his remarks with a cynical mumble, "What's the use!"

Every English major should certainly know Chidiock Tichborne's "Elegy"!

B. The exclamation point is actually an intensifier. The solution to adding greater intensity to a remark, however, does not lie in multiplying the number of exclamation points (!!!) but in choosing words that will convey the writer's sense of stress and tension.

Use of the comma **10D**

The comma is a utility mark of punctuation. It is used to join, separate, and enclose elements of a sentence. The principle of restrictive and nonrestrictive provides such an important guideline for the use of the comma to separate or enclose that an understanding of that principle should come first. The principle applies to all modifiers, including single words, phrases, and clauses.

A *nonrestrictive element* is basically a free modifier; that is, such an element is not bound to the antecedent it modifies: if it were omitted, the meaning of the antecedent would not change:

Old Nick, *which is a common term for the devil,* **continues to be used as a way of saying that someone is mischievous.**

The relative clause, set off by commas and thus marked by the writer as nonrestrictive, undoubtedly adds a fact that the reader may not know; but if the information in this clause is dropped from the sentence, the meaning of the subject is not affected. Thus, the nonrestrictive clause is not binding grammatically. The same applies to a clause that is added:

I support your program, *although I do not agree with all its details.*

In this example, the meaning of the main clause does not depend on the added details of the nonrestrictive dependent clause, as opposed to this sentence:

I will support a program *that reduces costs.*

The restrictive clause binds the meaning of *program*—not *any* program, only one *that reduces costs.*

A *restrictive element,* therefore, is a bound modifier; that is, such an element is essential to the meaning of the antecedent and cannot be dropped without radically altering the meaning of a sentence. Compare *Men who hate football should stay home* with *Men should stay home.* The meaning has changed radically. Either sentence might represent someone's viewpoint, but they are two entirely different statements. The relative clause *who hate football* places a necessary restriction on the subject. A restrictive clause is a means of limiting the general classification of *men* to a narrower classification of *men who hate football.* If the clause in this particular sentence were punctuated as if it were nonrestrictive—*Men, who hate football, should stay home*—it becomes apparent that the incidental comment would be false, because all men obviously do not hate football.

Restriction or nonrestriction, therefore, is an interpretation placed on the material. *Nonrestrictive elements are punctuated; restrictive elements are not.*

Commas are used:

1. To join compound sentences linked by *and, but, or, for, nor, yet,* and sometimes *so:*

> The whole matter is beyond our control, and it is now so confused that we have little hope of saving any lives.
>
> The more we earn, the less we seem to care, for money does not bring the satisfaction we thought it would.
>
> He was persuaded that he wanted to visit Mexico, so he went.

Note: If internal punctuation blurs the break between the main clauses, the comma can be raised to a semicolon:

Mass media include printed materials, radio, and television; and they, after all, must bear some responsibility for the consequences of their productions.

2. To join short sentences in series, usually with parallel or balanced phrasing:

> I know, I was there, I saw him.
>
> Cats shrieked, dogs barked, horses neighed.
>
> We can, we will, we must.

3. To separate words in series:

> He acted the role of a lost, searching, anguished youth.
>
> The needs, interests, and dignity of these people must be respected.
>
> We had to consider time, place, occasion.

Notes:
A. In series arranged as A, B, and C, the comma before the final *and* is optional unless misreading results from its omission. The choice of one way or the other ought to be followed consistently.
B. If the items of a series are separated by conjunctions (A or B or C), the commas may be omitted completely: *Give him a tie or a shirt or a belt.*
C. Being able to distinguish between *coordinate adjectives* and those that are not relates directly to the use of the comma. Adjectives that show an equal relation to the noun they modify are considered coordinate and are separated from one another by commas: *a perceptive, concise, interestingly presented speech.* In a phrase like *the warped kitchen cabinet,* the words *warped* and *kitchen* are not coordinate. *Kitchen cabinet* is the equivalent of a single word modified by *warped.* The common test is to see whether *and* can be used between coordinate adjectives and still sound natural: *a perceptive and concise and interestingly*

presented speech, but not *the warped and kitchen cabinet*. Punctuation can be omitted from the following phrases because the adjectives are not coordinate: *an elegant walking stick, a fast running jump, an irritating old man.*

4. To separate phrases and dependent clauses in series:

Phrases: The movie continued boringly without change of pace, without variation of tone, and without particularly interesting technique.

He was received enthusiastically wherever he went: in Milan, in Bayreuth, in Munich, and in London.

Clauses: If there are no good hotels, if there are no outstanding restaurants, if there are no sports activities, what is the attraction of the place?

We should stress that one out of four marriages ends in divorce, that a large majority of divorced couples marry again within four years after their split, and that being remarried will soon be a more common phenomenon than being married only once.

5. To separate introductory words, phrases, and clauses from the remainder of the sentence:

Words: Yes, I agree with you.
Nevertheless, we have to proceed with caution.

Phrases: Convinced that we had followed the wrong sign, we turned around.
To get recognized, we had to shout.
His fist clenched in defiance, he cursed.

Clauses: When people have been saying for years that vaudeville is dead, it is surprising how its ghost continues to appear in many places.

If the circus disappeared, we would lose one of the "greatest shows on earth."

Because the nation is slow in grappling with accumulated problems, a new era of peace escapes our grasp.

Notes:
A. When an introductory phrase is followed by inverted word order, no comma is used:

From the wings of the stage emerged a slow-moving procession.

B. If an introductory clause is short and allows no misreading, the comma is sometimes omitted:

As soon as he arrived he began to cause trouble.

6. To separate words, phrases, and clauses added to the end of a sentence:

Direct address:	I compliment you, fellow citizens.
Tag question:	I would like to go, wouldn't you?
Direct quotation:	"I can't, I can't," he shouted.
Nonrestrictive element:	We should agree on the basic costs, such as travel, meals, and lodging.
Absolute phrase:	There was nothing else to do, the celebration having ended.
Transitional words:	We ought to listen, nevertheless.
Suspended elements:	My reading speed is as slow as yours, if not slower.

7. To enclose parenthetical, explanatory, or interruptive words, phrases, and clauses:

Nonrestrictive appositives:
The captain of the ship, Joe Delano, was only thirty-five years old.

Some of Shakespeare's plays, such as *Hamlet, Othello, Macbeth,* and *The Merry Wives of Windsor,* have been made into operas.

The prestige schools, namely, Harvard, Princeton, and Yale, are beginning to have strong competitors.

Cf. the restrictive appositive with no punctuation:
The director Antonioni was mainly responsible for the failure of the movie. William the Conqueror became William I of England.

Inserted phrases and clauses:
Cheryl, being one of those naturally impulsive people, dived in with her clothes on.

We had to consider him, so to speak, a newcomer.

In ordinary circumstances, when they are not playing a game, the players still stick together.

Transitional words and phrases:
I would, however, like to try.

One of the more interesting varieties, for example, is the Golden Retriever.

Direct address:
One of the purposes of this meeting, my friends, is to enlist volunteers for the campaign.

You know, George, that you can't take on another job.

Split quotation:
"The manpower programs," he began his address, "are classic examples of waste."

"I am going," she said with determination, "even if you don't think I should."

8. To emphasize a contrast or to give added emphasis to a particular word, phrase, or clause:

This was our first attempt, though by no means our last.

Critics in the United States, not European critics, have tended to intellectualize literature.

The more limited the supply, the higher the price.

9. To prevent misreading or to accommodate the reader when rephrasing does not seem to be the best solution:

As soon as he got in, the car pulled away.
(Cf. As soon as he got in the car pulled away.)

To Mary, Anne was very special.

What will be, will be.

10. To indicate an ellipsis in sentences where the parallel structure makes clear what the omission is:

We were leaving for Europe; they, for Mexico.

I began to remind myself that the race was almost over; he, that it had to be won.

11. To increase the readability of addresses, place names, dates, statistics, and measurements and to serve other conventional purposes:

Addresses and place names:
His new address is 117 Shiga Lane, San Francisco, California.

Mail to: University of Washington, Seattle, Washington 98195.

Note: Zip codes are not separated by commas.

Dates:
Pikes Peak was discovered by Zebulon Pike, born January 5, 1779.
In December, 1941, the United States made a formal declaration of war.

Notes: Open style omits the comma when only the month and year are used:

In December 1941, the United States made a formal declaration of war.

Or when the date is reversed:

On 7 December 1941, Pearl Harbor was attacked.

Statistics:
By 1900, Pennsylvania's population had already reached 6,000,000.
He was six feet, five inches tall.

Note: The comma is sometimes omitted in numbers of four digits (2000 people), but it is always used in numbers ranging from 10,000 up.

Titles and degrees:
Henry Webster, Vice-Provost, was coordinator.
He always signed his name George Miller, M.D.

Names reversed:
Shakespeare, William
Patton, George S., Jr.

Salutation and complimentary close in informal letters:
Dear Esther,
Sincerely,
Regards as always,

References: (See footnote and bibliographical forms, pp. 390–398.)

Notes:

A. The comma is always placed inside quotation marks.

He was an exponent of "art for art's sake," a true aesthete.

When direct quotation invites the combination of the comma with the exclamation point or question mark, the comma is usually dropped in favor of the more expressive mark:

"Quiet!" he shouted with a sense of desperation.

"Do you know why?" Ethel inquired.

When the direct quotation ends with a dash, the comma is retained to separate the quoted material from the words that follow:

"This is one of those—," but he was unable to continue.

B. The comma is not used before parenthetical material; it is held until the parenthesis is closed:

I was idling along at 30 miles per hour, looking at the scenery (the mountains were snow-capped), listening to the radio (B. J. Thomas was singing "Raindrops Keep Falling on My Head"), not paying attention to the old hay wagon in front (going slower than I was).

Thomas Campbell's *The Pleasures of Hope* (1799), a long poem, is now virtually forgotten.

C. The comma is not added to dashes that set off parenthetical material:

He had fallen in love again—one of his weaknesses—but this time the affair was to last.

1. To separate two closely related sentences joined *without* a connective:

Practice to him came easy; he did it routinely and ungrudgingly like all of the other things in his life.

This is the major portion of the manuscript; the rest will be finished in another month.

Daniel Webster spoke of government "made for the people, made by the people, and answerable to the people"; Lincoln, of course, spoke the more familiar phrases "of the people, by the people, and for the people."

2. To separate more than two sentences or elliptical sentences arranged as a series:

She considered the policies of her company objective and fair; she never questioned the reasons they were adopted; she never concerned herself with their consequences.

At least ten people were killed in the tornado; property damage amounted to more than $10,000,000; the entire tourist season was jeopardized.

In Florida, the membership was strong; in Tennessee, less strong; and in Kentucky, negligible.

3. To separate sentences joined by conjunctive adverbs (e.g., *however, moreover, therefore*) or other transitional expressions (e.g., *in brief, by the way*):

Winter lasted on into May; therefore, no one could begin early spring planting.

There are a number of things she could do to improve her writing; for example, she could try to learn how to work several ideas into one sentence rather than stringing them out in primer sentences.

The total cost is high; thus we cannot make the planned changes.

Notes:
A. The comma following the connecting adverb is frequently optional.
B. Conjunctive adverbs and other connectives may be grouped in terms of their functions:

Addition: also, too, furthermore, likewise, moreover, besides, in fact

Emphasis: indeed, that is to say, to be sure

Discrimination: however, nevertheless, anyway, on the contrary, on the other hand

Illustration: namely, that is, for example, for instance, by way of illustration

Conclusion and result: accordingly, consequently, hence, so, therefore, thus, as a result, in conclusion

Time and space: first, second, then, later, finally, at the top, further on.

4. To substitute for a comma when sentences joined by coordinating conjunctions contain enough internal punctuation to obscure the main break:

Some of the streets ran north and south, others east and west, and yet others diagonally; but the whole city was so well plotted that it was practically impossible to get lost.

The professor encouraged students to collect samples of water from dormitory water taps, coffee urns, and the stream that runs through the campus, which is heavily polluted; and he then had them do water analysis as a laboratory exercise.

5. To substitute for the comma when internal punctuation obscures the main division of any series:

The sights in Venice continue to attract tourists: the Rialto Bridge, always a place of great activity; the Cathedral of Saint Mark, which is perhaps second only to Santa Sophia in Istanbul; and, of course, the Grand Canal, with its array of interesting buildings.

He quoted a number of Biblical passages: Job 1:21; Psalm 61:1–3; Proverbs 8:13–14.

Notes:

A. The semicolon is ordinarily placed outside quotation marks, unless in rare instances it is used as a substitute for a comma:

He was very fond of using "and what not"; it was a part of every other sentence.

Thoreau wrote, "I heartily accept the motto, 'That government is best which governs least'; and I should like to see it acted up to more rapidly and systematically."

Rare: A rave review is the kind that talks about a "funny furious narrative;" the kind that says the story is "tearfully humorous, triumphantly sad;" and the kind that closes with the remark that the book "has added something fine and important to the literature of our age."

B. When a direct quotation ends in a semicolon, the semicolon is dropped.

C. The semicolon is placed after parentheses, not before:

She was a strong young woman (the second child in a family of five); she was unbeatable.

D. The semicolon does not combine with the comma or the end marks of punctuation unless the period marks an abbreviation:

The package came C.O.D.; it was clearly something Mandy had bought.

Use of the colon *10F*

1. To introduce a list or an enumeration of items or examples:

The axial skeleton is made up of the bones of the head, neck, and trunk: the skull, the spinal column or backbone, vertebrae, the sacrum, and coccyx.

Here is a checklist for the camping trip: food, utensils, canteen, bedroll, personal necessities.

2. To indicate that an explanation, example, elaboration, or correlation will follow:

The redwood tree is matchless: it has antiquity, great size, and hardihood.

He lusted for one thing above all: an original Cézanne.

This is the dilemma: can an honest person be found anywhere anymore?

Note: When a complete sentence follows a colon, the capital letter at the beginning of the sentence is optional.

3. To introduce quotations or formal statements, with or without a verb of saying:

With an old-style prophet's indignation, he burst out: "Evil has come upon the nation."

Pascal's observation on atheism is thought-provoking: "Atheism is a sign of mental strength, but only up to a certain point."

4. To mark conventional separations:

Formal salutation:
Dear Senator Cummings:
To whom it may concern:

Hours from minutes:
9:45 P.M.
6:30 A.M.

Rhymes and related terms:
room:doom, black:white

Chapter from verse:
Micah 6:8

Volume from page:
English Journal 58:1307–1315

Title from subtitle:
Phantoms: A Collection of Stories

Introductory tags:
From left to right: Sadat, Carter, Begin
SPEAKER NO. 1: What's your name?
SPEAKER NO. 2: Norman.

Numerals in ratio:
3:6::4:8

Place from publisher:
New York: Holt, Rinehart and Winston

Notes:
A. The colon is placed outside quotation marks and parentheses. If a quotation ends
   in a colon, the colon is dropped.
B. The practice of combining the colon and the dash (''the line goes as follows:—''),
   common in earlier typography, is now considered outmoded.

10G *Use of the dash*

1. To introduce a summary statement following a series of words or phrases:

   Literature, philosophy, religion—these are disciplines that overlap.

   1918 and 1945—the dates mark the ends of two world conflicts.

2. To indicate a break, shift, or interruption in the writer's thought:

   No, not again—surely we cannot repeat the same mistakes over and over.

   He was born six hundred years too late—a truly chivalrous knight if there ever was
   one.

   I liked it—but then *chacun à son goût*, wouldn't you say?

3. To indicate an unfinished remark or to simulate faltering, broken, or confused
   speech:

   ''And it's just—'' but the voice was stifled.

   I—I—no, I can't tell you—but I must!

4. To add a sharpened emphasis to parenthetical material which might otherwise be
   separated by commas or parentheses:

The scholastic record—at first good and then deplorably bad—could not be ignored.

She was a woman of firm conviction—I suppose she would be typical of the Silent Majority—but she was not inclined to sign petitions.

5. To expand on an idea, often going back to pick up a word or phrase already used:

    This was an ailment that had bothered the horse for years—an ailment that was not going to be easily cured now.

    Her book is clearly distinguished—distinguished in the sense that it represents not only a fair reflection of accumulated knowledge but a significant addition to it.

6. To serve as a less formal substitute for the colon in introducing an explanatory statement, list, or quotation:

    There were only two things to do—run or jump.

    Three patients are ready for release—the one in the first bed, the one in the second, and the one in the fifth.

7. To serve conventional purposes:

    Omission of a word or letters:
    When I look at ———, I think of ———.
    The story identifies her only as Madame G—d.

    Inclusive dates, times, references:
    April 11–13, 1981
    5:30–7:30 P.M.
    pp. 38–45

    Before citations of author or source:
    "The vanquished have no friends."
    —Mussolini

Notes:

A. In printing, inclusiveness, such as 12–14, is shown by en dashes, longer than hyphens and shorter than em dashes. Em dashes are used to show omission of letters.
B. On the typewriter, a hyphen is used for an en dash, two hyphens for an em dash, and occasionally four hyphens for a long dash.
C. The dash is used inside or outside quotation marks, depending on the context. Ordinarily, the period, comma, semicolon, and colon are dropped when the sentence seems to invite double punctuation. The question mark and exclamation point may be retained.

    The whole scene—what an outrage!—was shown on television.

    The question—what do we do now?—simply can't be answered at the moment.

10H Use of the hyphen

1. To form familiar compounds:

brother-in-law   ill-concerned
cross-examine   Johnny-on-the-spot
double-jeopardy   single-breasted
heavy-handed   storm-swept

Note: Over a period of time, the hyphen may be dropped and the hyphenated compound may become one word. You should therefore check a recent dictionary for changing usage.

2. To form one-time-only compounds and special coinages:

an I-don't-care-what-you-think-of-me type
the beep-beep-beep of the horns
a motorcycle's pb-pb-b-b-b!

3. To form coined words with a prefix or suffix:

pro-Communist   president-elect
trans-Asia   stand-in
ex-husband   bell-like

4. To form numbers, fractions, ratios, and compounds with numbers:

twenty-two   three-day pass
seven-eighths   twentieth-century concept
20-20-20 soluble fertilizer   thirty-story building

Note: When fractions are used as nouns, the hyphen is sometimes omitted:

We completed one fourth of the assignment.

5. To divide a word into syllables:

re-tort   tem-po-ral
sep-tu-ple   tran-spire
spon-ta-ne-ous   vac-ci-nate

6. To transcribe the kind of suspended expression that might be spoken:

This was a three- to five-thousand-year-old vase.

He was informed in both socio- and psycho-linguistics.

1. To indicate the possessive case of nouns and indefinite pronouns:

Singular possessive:

a father's devotion	anybody's privilege
The New Yorker's wit	another's interests
my brother-in-law's car	everyone else's ideas
a master's degree	each one's turn

Note: Singular possessive is formed by adding an *'s*. The use of the apostrophe with words ending in sounds of *s* or *z* ordinarily depends upon the pronounceability of the syllable. If the syllable is pronounced, the *'s* is kept (*class's*); if the syllable is not pronounced, the apostrophe is kept and the *s* dropped (*Dickens'*). Usage will therefore vary with the individual, who may or may not want to indicate the extra sound.

PRONOUNCED ADDITION	UNPRONOUNCED ADDITION
Marx's doctrine	for righteousness' sake
Mr. Gomez's store	Aristophanes' plays
Brutus's betrayal	Ulysses' journey
Mars's strength *or* Mars' strength	Archimedes' screw

Plural possessive:

his sisters' devotion	ten years' time
two cents' worth	the Browns' cooperation

Note: Plural possessive is formed by adding an apostrophe to the plurals of words that end in *s*. If the plural is irregular, an *'s* is added to the plural form:

women's courage	a children's book
the geese's pond	mothers-in-law's luncheon

Joint or collective possessive:

Beaumont and Fletcher's dramas	University of London's location
Simon and Garfunkel's songs	fathers and sons' banquet
Lerner and Lowe's musicals	

Note: When the writer does not wish to indicate joint effort, a distinction can be made:

Donne's and Marvell's poetry is Metaphysical in style.

Or rephrase: The poetry of Donne and Marvell is Metaphysical in style.

2. To indicate contractions or the omission of numbers:

isn't	would've	we'd	xerox'd
haven't	the class of '36	OK'd	ma'am

3. To form plurals of numbers, letters, signs, abbreviations, dates, and words used as words:

6's and 7's	78 rpm's
p's and q's	GI's
+'s and −'s	the 1930's (or 1930s)

He had difficulty pronouncing his *this*'s.

10J *Use of parentheses*

1. To enclose explanations, digressions, and interruptions to the main thought of the sentence.

The selling price is twenty-four thousand, five hundred dollars ($24,500).

The trend indicates (see Table 2) that unemployment is increasing.

Many composers (for example, Mozart, Verdi, and Saint-Saëns) have used the fugue for dramatic purposes.

The idea of consubstantiation (Burke discusses it in *A Rhetoric of Motives*) makes possible a different concept of rhetoric.

2. To enclose numbers and letters marking divisions included in the main text:

The two writers might be compared in terms of (1) their similar background, (2) their preoccupation with psychology, and (3) their tendencies toward the macabre.

The geological changes can be observed in (a) Siberia, (b) China, and (c) Northern India.

Note: Commas, semicolons, and colons follow a closed parenthesis. Terminal marks may be included within the parenthesis depending on the context.

We observed one main rule (with appropriate flexibility, of course): everybody had to get at least seven hours of sleep.

The speaker cited innumerable examples of oxymoron (most of them from Elizabethan sonneteers).

A global language seems more and more a necessity. (There are at least three thousand spoken languages in the world today.)

10K *Use of brackets*

1. To insert editorial comment or explanations within a direct quotation:

"Persons of genius are, *ex vi termini* [by definition], more individual than any other people. . . ."

John Stuart Mill

"They [the Athenians] were the most religious of the Greeks."

Lord Acton

"Arnold demonstrated his classical spirit in his long narrative poem *Sohrab and Rustrum* [*sic*]."

Student sentence

Note: *Sic* means "thus," indicating that the misspelling of *Rustum* appeared thus in the original.

2. To serve as parentheses within parentheses:

In the edition of 1890, Thomas Wentworth Higginson had made changes in Emily Dickinson's poems. (For the original and unreconstructed texts, see *The Complete Poems of Emily Dickinson*, ed. Thomas H. Johnson [Boston: Little, Brown, 1960].)

3. To enclose phonetic transcriptions:

He had visited Jaffa [jaf′ ə].

Note: Angle brackets ⟨ ⟩ are sometimes used for this same purpose.

Use of quotation marks   *10L*

quot

1. To identify direct quotations:

G. K. Chesterton wrote: "To say that a man is an idealist is merely to say that he is a man."

Coleridge wrote: "Love is flower-like; / Friendship is a sheltering tree."

One definition of *moral* is "sanctioned by or operative on one's conscience or ethical judgment."

2. To identify spoken dialogue:

We were standing around. "You know what?" one fellow blurted out as if he had the world's greatest idea.
"Naw, we don't know what," Snoopy sneered.

Note: Conventionally, a new paragraph marks the words of a new speaker. Narrative and descriptive detail may be included in the same paragraph.

3. To enclose titles of newspapers and magazine articles, essays, stories, poems, and parts of books as differentiated from the title of the book as a whole:

"Out of Place in America: Confessions of a Chauvinist" by Peter Schrag in *Saturday Review*

"Pulvis et Umbra" by Robert Louis Stevenson

"My Oedipus Complex" by Frank O'Connor from *The Stories of Frank O'Connor*

"As I Grew Older" by Langston Hughes from *Collected Poems* (1954)

Chapter II, "Humanistic Ethics: The Applied Science of the Art of Living" from Erich Fromm's *Man for Himself*

Note: Quotation marks are not used to set off the title of a student theme at the beginning of the paper.

4. To set off the names of songs, short musical compositions (not symphonies or operas), radio and TV programs.

Grieg's *"Ich liebe dich"*
"Sympathy for the Devil" performed by The Rolling Stones
Ravel's "Bolero"
NBC's "Tonight Show"

5. To set off a particular word under discussion:

The popular music of the 1940s was called "Swing."

If we consider what Plato meant by "realism," we will have some insight into the basis of his philosophy.

"Disinterested" and "uninterested" can mean quite different things.

6. To indicate awareness of an obvious shift in usage or to suggest irony:

It's one thing to use "people's talk"; it's another to be obscene.

Marlowe might have been the "hip kid" of the sixteenth century.

7. To indicate italics within italics:

The title of his book was *A Modern Guide to James Joyce's "Ulysses."*

Notes:
A. As a general principle, periods and commas are always placed inside quotation marks; semicolons and colons, almost always outside; and other marks, inside or outside, depending upon the context. If the quotation comes at the end of a sentence, only one terminal mark is necessary, not double punctuation.
B. Single quotation marks are most commonly used for quotations within quotations:

She had very clearly said, "I am going to sing 'Jesu Joy of Man's Desiring.'"

(British usage frequently follows the reverse pattern of American usage: single marks first, then double.)
C. The distinction between indirect and direct discourse should be kept clear; no quotation marks are necessary in indirect discourse.

Direct discourse: I said, "I will help if I can."

Indirect discourse   I said I would help if I could.

Direct discourse: He said, "Reason must prevail."

Indirect discourse: He said that reason must prevail.

D. Quotations of approximately fifty or more words of prose or two or more lines of poetry are most conveniently set off by special indentation and single-spacing in typewritten papers and by special typography in printing. When the indented block style is used, opening and closing quotations marks are not used, and any quotation marks within the text are left as double quotation marks, not converted to single quotation marks.

Samuel Johnson was notorious for his blunt and bristling comments. One passage from *The Life of Samuel Johnson* by James Boswell will illustrate:

> When invited to dine, even with an intimate friend, he was not pleased if something better than a plain dinner was not prepared for him. I have heard him say on such an occasion, "This was a good dinner enough, to be sure: but it was not a dinner to *ask* a man to."

Use of ellipsis points **10M**

1. To mark an omission from a direct quotation. Three points indicate that one or more words have been deleted; four points indicate that the deletion occurs at the beginning or end of a sentence (the actual deletion may include one or more complete sentences). When four points appear, one of the points is the period marking the end of a sentence.

Original	*With omissions*
You can vitiate the air by your manner of life and of death, to any extent. You might easily vitiate it so as to bring such a pestilence on the globe as would end all of you. You, or your fellows, German and French, are at present vitiating it to the best of your power in every direction; chiefly at this moment with corpses, and animal and vegetable ruin in war, changing men, horses, and garden stuff into noxious gas. But everywhere, and all day long, you are vitiating it with foul chemical exhalations; and the horrible nests, which you call towns, are little more than laboratories for the distillation into heaven of venomous smokes and smells, mixed with effluvia from decaying animal matter, and infectious miasmata from purulent disease.	You can vitiate the air by your manner of life and of death, to any extent. You might easily vitiate it so as to bring such a pestilence . . . as would end all of you. . . . you are vitiating it with foul chemical exhalations; and the horrible nests, which you call towns, are little more than laboratories for the distillation into heaven of venomous smokes and smells. . . .
John Ruskin, *Fors Clavigera*	

Note: The overuse of ellipsis points is likely to create suspicion because too much omission may well distort the exact intention of the original.

2. To indicate an interruption or an unfinished sentence, particularly in spoken dialogue:

   "There is one thing I want to . . . ," but the mumbled words were lost in a final effort to take one last deep breath.

3. To indicate the omission of one or more lines of poetry or one or more paragraphs of prose by the use of a full line of spaced ellipsis points:

These beauteous forms,
Through a long absence, have not been to me
As is a landscape to a blind man's eye:
But oft, in lonely rooms, and mid the din
Of towns and cities, I have owed to them,
In hours of weariness, sensations sweet,
Felt in the blood, and felt along the heart;

. . . .

For I have learned
To look on nature, not as in the hour
Of thoughtless youth; but hearing oftentimes
The still, sad music of humanity,
Nor harsh nor grating, though of ample power
To chasten and subdue.

William Wordsworth,
"Lines Composed a Few Miles above Tintern Abbey . . ."

Note: This ellipsis represents the omission of sixty lines.

10N *Use of the slant or virgule or slash*

1. To indicate alternatives:

   The tour included England/France and Germany/Austria.

   Traditional Africa was—and can/must/will become again—a continent of Life and Art.

2. To act as a dividing line between a period of time extending over successive years (academic year 1976/1977), shillings and pence (8s/3d), fractions set into a line of type ($y/b = 1$), and run-in lines of poetry ("Oh, lift me from the grass! / I die, I faint, I fail!").

3. To stand for *per* in abbreviations like 6 ft./sec. (feet per second) or km/hr (kilometers per hour).

4. To set off phonemes and phonemic transcriptions:

/p/ as in *pat*

5. To suggest a kind of jazz rhythm or syncopation, as used in some current poetry:

the Jess B. Semple hip sneer
the bassist/drummer/pianist/guitarist/rhythm on top of Caldonia

Ted Joans, from "Passed on Blues: Homage to a Poet,"
in *Black Pow-wow: Jazz Poems*

Use of capital letters 10O

1. To begin the first word of a sentence, a line of poetry, or a fragment written as a sentence:

cap
lc

Books surrounded me to the point of suffocation.

How do I love thee? Let me count the ways.
I love thee to the depth and breadth and height
My soul can reach, when feeling out of sight
For the end of Being and ideal Grace.

Elizabeth Barrett Browning

The state decided to close the express lane of the freeway. A completely arbitrary decision.

2. To identify proper nouns, words derived from proper nouns, and the initials and abbreviations of those words:

Don Phillips has expressed the Afro-American point of view more forcefully than anyone else in Washington, D.C.

Note: Usage is often divided on the capitalization of nouns. Although proper nouns are capitalized and common nouns are not, the distinction between the two is not always clear-cut. A few principles seem to operate, however:

A. When a word is used in a restricted sense, it is capitalized: *China, the country*; when its meaning is extended, it is not capitalized: *china, the pottery*.

B. The descriptive references of geographical names and organizations are usually capitalized: *Black Canyon, Howard Street, Democratic Party*. Informal usage, however, may drop the capital: *Black canyon, Howard street, Democratic party*.

C. Points of the compass when used as nouns are capitalized: *he grew up in the West*. When used as adverbs, they are not: *we drove west*.

D. University ranks are capitalized: *Freshman year, Senior standing*. The member of a class is not: *a sophomore* or *a junior*.

E. The names of specific courses are capitalized: *History 214, Introduction to Biology*; the names of the subjects are not: *history, biology*. The names of languages are capitalized, however, because they are proper nouns.

F. Second references to titles and names are capitalized only if the context makes the reference specific and clear:

> The Governor spoke.   [Previous reference would make clear which
> We go to the University.   governor and which university are meant.]

G. References to the President and Constitution of the United States are customarily capitalized.

H. Capitalization of a noun to attach special meaning or effect to it is an optional matter of style, not one of established usage:

> He believed in the idea of Universal Grammar.

3. To set off references to a deity, titles, the pronoun *I* and the interjection *O:*

> Let my cry come near before thee, O Lord: give me understanding according to thy word.
>
> Psalm 119:169
>
> Professor Lichter recited the verse.

4. To mark the first word and all the principal words of a title:

> Have you read "Who Has Poisoned the Sea?"
>
> Helmut Nickel's *Warriors and Worthies: Arms and Armor Through the Ages* is a fine book for both information and browsing.
>
> Roger van der Weyden's *Descent from the Cross* is a remarkably moving painting.

Note: All words of a title are capitalized except the articles *a, an,* and *the,* conjunctions, and prepositions of five or fewer letters.

5. To indicate that a word is personified:

> As our Religion, our Education, our Art look abroad, so does our spirit of society.
>
> Ralph Waldo Emerson
>
> Return, return, O eager Hope,
>   And face man's latter fall.
>
> Herman Melville

6. To set off words typographically for unusual emphasis:

> There was the sign in all of its blatant defiance: NO DOGS ALLOWED, OR EVEN WANTED.

10P *Use of italics*

ital   *Italic* is actually a type style, used in contrast to the kind of roman type most commonly used for ordinary reading matter. There are numerous other type styles, but their uses are more specialized—for titles and for special printing like announcements, stationery, and advertisements. Italic, however, is designed to match all roman typefaces and is considered an indispensable part of routine printing. Because of the common use of italics, single underlining has been adopted as the way to show on a typewriter and in handwriting what would appear in print as italic. Italics and underlining are therefore one and the same.

1. To indicate foreign words and phrases not yet fully assimilated into the English language:

After disagreeing for an hour about the merits of the performance, we could only fall back upon the inevitable saying: *de gustibus non est disputandum.*

The latest Wertmuller film is her best, *nicht wahr?*

Note: Doubt may exist whether a word or phrase has become fully anglicized. Usage may therefore vary with writers, depending on their education and cosmopolitanism. The foreign words in the following sentences might well be italicized by some individuals:

Slum housing usually leads to de facto segregation.

We had a good old-fashioned kaffeeklatsch.

2. To designate titles of books, periodicals, newspapers, dramas, operas, symphonic works, works of art, movies, ships, and aircraft:

Dickens' *Great Expectations*	Leonardo's *The Last Supper*
Newsweek	Michelangelo's *David*
Seattle *Times*	Ghiberti's *Gates of Paradise*
Hansberry's *A Raisin in the Sun*	*Midnight Cowboy*
Verdi's *Aïda*	*Titanic*
R. Strauss' *Tod und Verklärung*	*Apollo 13*

3. To add emphasis to a word or phrase:

It is not *what* you said; it's *how* you said it.

I am interested in *people*, not their clothes.

Note: A device of this kind remains effective only if it is used sparingly and then with good cause.

4. To refer to letters as letters, numbers as numbers, and words as words:

My name has a *c* in it.

The sign had a large *5* on it.

The word *affect* as a noun is seldom used except by psychologists.

The quatrain rhymed *abab.*

10Q *Use of figures*

The representation of numbers by figures or by written words varies widely with the nature of a work. Business, scientific, technical, and legal writings tend to prefer figures to written forms. In less specialized prose, however, numbers are frequently written out. A few specific guidelines will reflect the most common practices for prose in standard English:

1. To represent numbers that require more than one or two words when written out:

   875 people, but ten men
   $1,365,748, but a million dollars
   1983, but the twentieth century or the 20th century
   1940s or 1940's, but the forties

Note: If various statistics are included in one sentence, all are given in figures for the sake of consistency:

   The attendance at the workshops varied from 125 at Language and Composition to 75 at Rhetoric and Composition, to 35 at Literature and Composition.

2. To represent:

Dates:	May 11, 1980 or 11 May 1980
Addresses:	1823 West Kentucky Street, Apt. 4
Time:	4:30 P.M., but half-past four
	8:00 A.M., but eight o'clock in the morning
	2315 hours (11:15 P.M. in military time)
Dollars and cents:	$3.55, but $5 per person and 15 cents each
Decimals:	3.1416
Measurements:	4-by-6-inch cards
	5'11" tall, but six feet tall
Code numbers	Army serial number: 35481990
	Telephone number: 206-543-2190
	Social Security number: 410-17-8404
	Zip code number: 98105
Percentages:	6% or 6½ percent (*also* per cent)
	one-fourth of 1 percent
Set forms of reference:	4-H Club, 35 mm lens, 50 mph, 7-Up, pp. 104–105, Flight 107. Gate 3, Channel 7

3. To prevent misreading or to serve as a greater convenience in reading:

$8.5 billion deficit   ten 6-foot stakes or 10 six-foot stakes

Note: Numbers at the beginning of a sentence are ordinarily written out. If such a number requires several words, the dilemma can be avoided by a simple rephrasing:

Generally avoided:	4300 students participated in the drive.
Rephrased:	A total of 4300 students participated in the drive.
	Approximately 4300 students participated in the drive.
Acceptable:	1976 was the bicentennial year.

Word division at end of line: syllabication **10R**

Dividing of words at the end of a line should be done by syllables and then with certain limitations. Not all breaks are appropriate or clear:

1. Words should not be divided if only one letter (*man-y*) or two letters (*mon-ey*) carry over to the next line.
2. Words should not be divided if the syllable leaves only one letter remaining at the end of a line (*e-ject*).
3. Hyphenated words should be divided only at the hyphen, not at other syllables (*self-deceit,* not *self-de-/ceit*).
4. Monosyllables cannot be divided.
5. Contractions should not be divided (*they're, weren't*).
6. Numbers stated in figures should not be divided (5,000,000).
7. Words that would have a misleading appearance when hyphenated should not be divided (*wa-ter, of-ten*).

Note: The dictionary is an indispensable source of information concerning syllabication, although all dictionaries do not share common principles of word division. (*Webster's Eighth,* for example, divides *English* as *En-glish; Webster's New World* gives *Eng-lish*). Hundreds of examples might be cited, indicating, of course, that English syllabication has not been completely standardized. These variations suggest two useful guidelines for writers:

1. If possible, avoid word divisions at the end of a line.
2. If a word division is necessary, use one dictionary consistently as a reference.

Typing conventions **10S**

1. On 8½″ × 11″ paper, use a 15-space margin on the left side and leave approximately 1″ on the right side and at the bottom; approximately 1½″ at the top.
2. Indent paragraphs 5 spaces.
3. Leave 2 spaces between sentences.
4. Leave 2 spaces after a colon; one space after all other marks of punctuation.
5. Use the period for ellipsis points. Put a space between each one. When an ellipsis occurs at the end of a sentence, the fourth point is a period.

6. Use underlining for italics.
7. Distinguish between a single hyphen and a dash (2 hyphens) or a long dash (4 hyphens).
8. If your typewriter does not have square brackets, write them in by hand or use a combination of slashes and underlining (⟦ ⟧)
9. If your typewriter does not have an exclamation point, use a combination of the apostrophe and the period.
10. Never begin a line with a mark of punctuation that belongs at the end of the previous line.

Proofreading: common grammatical faults   **Chapter 11**

Every language has its pitfalls. English is no exception. And every speaker and writer is vulnerable. The best protection is one of prevention—becoming aware of your own shortcomings and learning how to control constructions that give you trouble. If you characteristically have trouble with dangling constructions, make sure you get in the habit of asking "Who is the agent? Who is doing this?" If an answer is not actually written in the sentence, then you have a construction that needs revision. Keeping yourself alert to your own particular problems is a key to writing correctly.

This section discusses those problems that commonly cause difficulty.

Agreement of verb and subject   *11A*

Verbs agree with the grammatical subject of the sentence in number and person. At times, the grammatical subject may be singular in form, even though the thought is logically plural. A few constructions cause most of the problems in agreement:

agr

1. Compound subjects take plural verbs whether or not the subject is inverted:

   Music, theater, and art *are* grouped as the fine arts.

   Both men and women *are* included.

   On top of the buildings *were* TV antennas.

2. Compound subjects or plural subjects that express a unit idea take singular verbs:

   Sears, Roebuck and Company *is* an established store.

   My friend and neighbor *comes* over often.

   Ten dollars *is* a good price.

   The New York Times maintains its reputation.

3. Compound subjects expressing mathematical relations may be singular or plural:

   One and one *makes* [*make*] two.

   Six from twenty-one *leaves* [*leave*] fifteen.

4. Singular subjects joined by *or* or *nor* take singular verbs; plural subjects joined by the same words take plural verbs:

   A graduate student or an undergraduate *is* eligible.

   Either graduate students or undergraduates *are* eligible.

   If one subject is singular and the other plural, the verb agrees with the nearer form:

   Either the seniors or John *has* to do it.

   Neither she nor other women *want* the job.

5. Singular subjects joined by *and* but introduced by *many a, such a, no, every,* or *each* take a singular verb.

   Many an actor and actress *has* triumphed here.

   No student and no faculty member *is* expected.

   Every chair, table, and lamp *has* to be moved.

6. The agreement of the verb with a singular subject is not affected by any intervening phrase, even though the phrase seems to make the meaning plural:

   One of my reasons *is* purely personal.

   The scout leader, as well as the whole troop, *is* being honored.

   The coach, not any of the assistants, *has* to be present.

   The representative from the Soviet Union, together with the delegates from the satellite countries, usually *votes* negative on this issue.

7. Collective nouns are an exception to the general principle that a verb agrees with its grammatical subject (the form of a particular word), not its logical subject (the general idea). Deciding whether to use a singular or plural verb with nouns like *means, Cherokee,* and *sheep* is a logical decision. The choice will vary with the interpretation of the sentence:

The Cherokee were a people originally from the mountains of Tennessee and North Carolina.
The Cherokee was a tribe originally from the mountains of Tennessee and North Carolina.

The brood of chickens *were* scattered in the yard.
A brood of pigeons *tends* to be small.

8. Indefinite pronouns cause considerable difficulty in agreement because their number may be doubtful, or usage may be changing. The following guidelines reflect common practices in making pronouns agree with antecedents and verbs with their subjects:

   A. Clearly singular: *another, anything, each one, either, everything, many a, much, neither, nobody, no one, one, other, someone, something.*
   B. Clearly plural: *both, few, many, several.*
   C. Singular or plural depending on the implication and on whether they are used with mass nouns or count nouns: *all, any, each, none, some.*

      None *is* **correct.** [singular implication]
      None *are* **more successful than she.** [plural implication]

      All of the land *is* . . . [mass noun]
      All of the boxes *are* . . . [count noun]

   D. Changing usage: *anybody, anyone, everybody, everyone,* and *somebody* are singular in form and take singular verbs. Because of their plural implication, however, usage has established the use of plural pronoun references to them: *Everybody took their seats.* The traditional usage, however, is no less natural: *Everybody took his seat,* with *his* used in a generic sense to refer to mankind in general. *Everyone clapped their hands* makes sense. *Everyone clapped his hands* does not.
   E. The number of pronoun phrases like *each of you, none of us, either of them, some one of you* depends on the number of the head word:

      Either of them *is* **an acceptable choice.**
      None of us *are* **going.**

9. Words ending in *s* but singular in meaning usually take singular verbs. A few are singular or plural depending on the interpretation of them as mass nouns or count nouns.

   Mass nouns treated as singular: *aesthetics, economics, linguistics, mathematics, measles, news, semantics*
   Words treated as singular or plural: *athletics, acoustics, statistics*

   Athletics *has* **always had a place in society.** [mass noun in the sense of a "general activity"]

   Athletics *are* **supposed to build character.** [count noun in the sense of "various games"]

10. A verb of being agrees with its subject, not the complement following it, unless the subject is a *what* clause followed by a plural subject:

His mania *was* cameras.

Diplomatic relations between the United States and Japan *are* an interesting topic for discussion.

What concerns me most *are* the conditions they have to endure.

11. A verb of being that is introduced by *there* agrees with the subject following it:

There *are* many problems to be met.

There *is* no reason to be upset.

12. When the antecedent of a relative pronoun is either of two words, one singular and one plural, it is difficult to determine which of two words should govern the number of the verb:

He is one of those who *are* [*is*] constantly complaining.

The plural usage may be interpreted as follows: The antecedent of *who* is *those;* the entire adjective clause (*who . . . complaining*) modifies and tells about all the people in the group, not just a single member. *Are* agrees with *those.* The sentence might be paraphrased: *There are those who are constantly complaining. He is one of those.*

The use of the singular verb *is* would be more a matter of emphasis than of logic, making *one* the antecedent of the relative pronoun rather than *those.*

Since all relative pronouns can be singular or plural, depending on the antecedent, some reputable writers prefer to use the singular. The weight of evidence, however, favors the conservative use of a plural verb in instances of this kind.

11B *Agreement of pronoun and antecedent*

agr   1. Personal pronouns agree with their antecedents in number, gender, and person:

Sue had an office to *herself.*

The mail clerks seldom have offices to *themselves.*

Each one is doing *his* share.

Note: Because the English language lacks a generic pronoun to express the singular idea of this sentence, established magazines continue to use *his* as a general reference to mankind or persons of both sexes. The use of *he/she* and *his/her* recognizes sexual differences but introduces stylistic awkwardness. An alternative is to rephrase so that the subject invites a plural reference:

All of us are doing our share.

All are doing their share.

See Glossary under *he/she, his/her,* and *man, person.*

2. A relative pronoun does not itself show number, gender, or person, but, by

connecting a relative clause to its antecedent, it determines the number, gender, and person of elements that follow it:

  Pl.   *Pl.* *Pl.*

Those who are willing to donate *their services* should sign now.

    S.   *S.*   *S.*   *S.*

The *girl* who *has* confidence in *her* own ability now *has* a chance.

3. If a pronoun refers to two or more antecedents joined by *and,* the number is plural; if it refers to two or more joined by *or* or *nor,* the number is singular.

   Jim and Carol moved into *their* new home.

   Neither Mike nor Phil met *his* quota.

Agreement of demonstrative and noun   11C

Demonstratives agree in number with the nouns to which they refer. Words like *kind, sort,* and *type* invite errors in agreement, particularly if the noun is followed by a prepositional phrase.

Correct: that kind   this type
               those kinds   those types

          That kind of jade is rare.

          Those sorts of games are now unknown.

Case of nouns and pronouns   11D

1. The case of a pronoun is determined by its function in a sentence:

   Someone must act quickly. [subject]

   Did the fire cause *that?* [direct object of verb]

   Most of *them* responded. [object of preposition]

   He owes *me* money. [indirect object]

   Thanks were given *us.* [retained object]

   I know *who* you are. [subjective complement]

   We made him *one.* [objective complement]

   Otello, the *one* by Rossini, is less well known. [appositive]

   Hey, *you!* Come here. [direct address]

2. Self-consciousness about correctness often leads to the mistaken notion that *I* is categorically more proper than *me,* whereas the object form may be both correct and natural, particularly when the object of a verb or preposition is compound:

   Misuse: She told my secretary and *I* to take the day off.
   Rephrased: She told my secretary and *me* to take the day off.

Misuse: Between you and *I*, I think he's wrong.
Rephrased: Between you and *me*, I think he's wrong.

Misuse: Let's you and *I* cooperate on this job.
Rephrased: Let's you and *me* cooperate on this job.

Note: Here *me* is used in apposition: *Let us—you and me —cooperate on this job.*

3. The use of the subject form after the verb of being continues to be standard in written prose and is applied particularly when writing is edited. Thus, *it is I, it is he, it is we,* and *it is they* may be used quite unpretentiously when the context tends to be formal. However, the position of the subjective complement in the object position causes the object forms like *it's me* and *it's them* to predominate in speaking. These also now commonly appear in informal prose. Most people who are aware of the differences adjust their usage to suit the purpose and occasion of speaking or writing.

4. Constructions with *than* and *as* are sometimes shortened so that the case of the pronoun depends on elements that are understood:

He got a bigger raise than *I* [did].

We like him better than [we like] *her.*

She is as old as *I* [am].

5. *Who* and *whom* hold more pitfalls for misuse than any of the other relative forms. Standard written English observes the distinction between subjective and objective cases when the pronouns are used as relatives or as interrogatives:

Who is he?

Who does he think he is?

He is one person *who* should be invited.

He is one person *who* I think should be invited.

List the ones *who* you think should come.

To *whom* did he refer?

Whom did he refer to?

He is a man *whom* everyone should know.

However, the subject position that the relative pronoun occupies has the force in speech of dulling case distinctions. In speaking, usage favors the general substitution of *who* for all uses of *whom* except in highly conventional phrases like *to whom it may concern.* This common practice now affects writing, even by respected authors, so that it is possible to say that *who* is rapidly becoming an invariable form like *how, what, where, when,* and *why.*

6. The use of the possessive with *-ing* forms in the subject position causes no problem: *The President's coming is a special event.* The use of the possessive with *-ing* forms in the object position, however, may be easily confused with a

construction consisting of a noun and a participle. The two constructions are capable of different meanings:

Possessive with gerund: We saw the boy's whipping. [being whipped]
Noun plus participle: We saw the boy whipping. [doing the whipping]

The distinction is clearer when pronouns are substituted:

We saw *his* whipping.
We saw *him* whipping.

Possessive with gerund: We expected the President's coming. [the event]
Noun plus participle: We saw the President coming. [the action]

Other uses, however, cannot be decided on the basis of meaning, but only in terms of emphasis or rhythm:

The hope of man ending war is dim.
or
The hope of man's ending war is dim.

Comma splice or comma fault   *11E*

The comma splice or comma fault represents the writer's failure to see that a comma used to join certain sentences will not suffice, because a semicolon or period is clearly demanded. The seriousness of the comma splice, therefore, is that it invites misreading, not that it is a mortal sin of punctuation.

cs
cf

Samples

1. One group was pushing Congress to enact a law that would permit federal authorities to fingerprint, photograph, and run identification checks on people who had no criminal charge placed against them, that would be unprecedented and probably unconstitutional.

2. The commune had no written rules, however the members were morally obligated to share all of their earned income.

Comma splice eliminated

1. One group was pushing Congress to enact a law that would permit federal authorities to fingerprint, photograph, and run identification checks on people who had no criminal charge placed against them. That would be unprecedented and probably unconstitutional.

2. The commune had no written rules; however, the members were morally obligated to share all of their earned income.

Alternate reading

2. The commune had no written rules, however; the members were morally obligated to share all of their earned income.

The comma splice can be corrected by:

1. Repunctuating with a semicolon or period.
2. Subordinating one of the clauses:

   Since the commune had no written rules, the members were morally obligated to share all of their earned income.

3. Eliminating the conjunctive adverb and adding a coordinating conjunction that permits the use of a comma:

   The commune had no written rules, *but* the members were obligated to share all of their earned income.

11F *Comparison*

1. The comparative degree is ordinarily used to refer to one of two objects; the superlative to one of three or more, either expressed or implied.

   Comparative: She is the *taller* of the two.
   Superlative: She is the *tallest* girl in her class.

   Comparative: This article is *more informative* than that one.
   Superlative: This is the *most informative* article I have ever read on the subject.

2. Double comparisons (*more better, most ugliest*) are now considered strictly nonstandard. It is also nonstandard to inflect adjectives that are usually compared with *more* and *most* (*wonderfullest* time, *dancingest* kid, *lovinger* child) or to use regular comparisons for forms compared irregularly (*worser*).

   Nonstandard: A mental institution is more worse than a penal institution.
   Standard: A mental institution is worse than a penal institution.

3. An absolute adjective is one that does not lend itself to comparison. Adjectives like *prior, daily*, and *principal* present no problem, but words like *equal, essential, unique, round, perfect*, and *black* are subject to divided usage. Phrases like *more nearly perfect* or *almost round* are precise ways of preserving the absolute meaning of these terms, but usage among reputable writers has established *more perfect, more round*, and *blackest black* as acceptable ways of expressing relative degrees that are less than absolute. Nevertheless, the comparison of absolutes remains a taboo among many persons. You therefore have to consider your audience and the formality of the writing in deciding on usage.

4. The use of *any other* indicates that things of the same class are being compared; the use of *any*, that things of a different class are being compared:

   My aunt thinks she can cook better than any other woman.

   My nephew thinks he can cook better than any woman.

   The doubling of a comparison may be expressed in either of two ways:

   He is as old as, if not older than, I am.

   He is as old as I am, if not older.

A third version occurs in standard English, but shows less regard for exactness:

He is as old if not older than I am.

5. Some comparisons are left incomplete because the context makes clear what the implication is and completing them would only add unnecessary words. An advertisement that reads "Oldsmobiles cost less at Richie Center" means that they cost less there than at any other Oldsmobile dealer in town. The full statement would sound pedantic. Phrases like *better stores* and *higher prices* are commonly used without completing the comparisons.

6. *Different from* has traditionally been the preferred form in America; however, *different than*, the British usage, has become more and more common and acceptable in this country because it avoids the piling up of words that the use of *different from* sometimes requires. Two groups of sentences will illustrate:

The spirit of Franz Hals's painting is considerably different from that of Rembrandt's.
The spirit of Franz Hals's painting is considerably different than Rembrandt's.

It's different from what you think.
It's different than you think.

Dangling constructions *11 G*

Dangling constructions violate the fundamental grammatical principle that adjectives or words that function like adjectives should modify specific nominals. Danglers either modify nothing or modify the wrong word. More important than the grammatical lapse, however, are the uncertainty of meaning and the unintended humor that usually arise from the implied agent-action relation. The misuses can be corrected by simple rephrasing.

DM

1. Dangling participles:

Dangling:	Coming up the steps, the statue stood at the top.
Rephrased:	Coming up the steps, we saw the statue standing at the top.
or:	As we came up the steps, we saw the statue standing at the top.
Dangling:	Caught in the act, her excuses meant nothing.
Rephrased:	Inasmuch as she was caught in the act, her excuses meant nothing.
or:	Caught in the act, she could not make her excuses convincing.
Dangling:	Having been told that he was out of order, the judge held the attorney in contempt of court.
Rephrased:	Having told the attorney that he was out of order, the judge held him in contempt of court.
or:	Having been told that he was out of order, the attorney was held in contempt of court by the judge.

Note: Although dangling constructions ordinarily occur in a position preceding the main clause, they may occur in other positions as well:

> *Dangling:*   A bow showed her appreciation, knowing the audience loved her.
> *Rephrased:*   She showed her appreciation with a bow, knowing the audience loved her.

2. Dangling gerunds: When a gerund is the object of a preposition, the agent must be apparent in the subject of the main clause or in the possessive modifier of the gerund, especially when the phrase precedes the main clause:

> *Dangling:*   By comparing Wordsworth and Coleridge, Romanticism can be better understood.
> *Rephrased:*   By comparing Wordsworth and Coleridge, students can better understand Romanticism.

> *Dangling:*   By explaining clearly what to do, we got the problem right.
> *Rephrased:*   By Bill's explaining clearly what to do, we got the problem right.

Note: In post-position, a statement is often clearly understood to be a generalization referring to everyone so that specific mention of an agent is unnecessary:

> *Acceptable*   Arguments are rarely won by name-calling and shouting.

3. Dangling elliptical clauses: When words have been deleted from a clause, the reference must still be clear.

> *Dangling:*   If adopted, I hope the new law solves the problem.
> *Rephrased:*   If adopted, the new law will, I hope, solve the problem.

> *Dangling:*   At the age of three, my father taught me to swim.
> *Rephrased:*   When I was three years old, my father taught me to swim.

4. Dangling infinitives

> *Dangling:*   To apply for the job, four recommendations are needed.
> *Rephrased:*   To apply for the job, you need four recommendations.

> *Dangling:*   To read *War and Peace*, plenty of time is needed.
> *Rephrased:*   To read *War and Peace*, a person needs plenty of time.

Note: Words like *considering, according, providing, assuming,* and *speaking* take on the function of prepositions rather than participles when they introduce phrases of a general or impersonal nature. These might be termed "acceptable danglers":

Considering the implications, the decision was the only one that could be made.
Speaking of fashion, a show is going to be held soon.

These particular phrases are used independently. They have no grammatical link with the main clause. Since mentioning the specific agent is not crucial to the meaning, they are not considered dangling modifiers. Infinitive phrases also function in a similar way in highly idiomatic constructions that state generalizations:

To tell the truth, the boat should never have sailed.

To illustrate the point, Büchner was ahead of the times.

The double negative is a construction with a respectable history, though it is no longer accepted in standard English as a device of emphasis. The tendency to attach the negative to the verb is strong. However, the usage is clearly nonstandard in a sentence like *Nobody won't do nothin'.* Expressions like *can't hardly, couldn't scarcely,* and *won't barely,* although commonly heard in speech, are inappropriate in writing. A combination of a negative with an adjective or adverb as a device of understatement is, however, an acceptable usage: *not infrequently, not wholly unsuccessful, not impoverished.*

1. Using *they, you,* and *it* as indefinite pronouns rather than personal pronouns *ref* with well-defined antecedents leads to vagueness and redundancy in writing, although the use is common in speech.

Vague	*More precise phrasing*
When I was in Paris, *they* said that hemlines were going to change again.	When I was in Paris, dress designers said that hemlines were going to change again.
At the Vatican, *you* have to wear a hair covering.	At the Vatican, women have to wear a hair covering.

Redundant

On the form *it* says that the bill is due now.	The form says that the bill is due now.

2. Demonstratives are commonly used to refer to the entire idea of a previous sentence rather than to a specific word in that sentence. The use is acceptable when the meaning is unambiguous:

Ambiguous: Everyone has to work hard if we are not going to fail in this venture. This is what we really want.

Rephrased: Everyone has to work hard if we are not going to fail in this venture. We really want everyone to cooperate.

Unambiguous: Germany lost World War I. That explains much of the history of the next fifty years.

This and *that* are sometimes used as synonyms for *the former* and *the latter. So* and *such* at times serve as demonstratives in the sense of *that:*

I will be glad to do *so.*

Such are the circumstances.

3. Tagging on a *which* clause to refer to the complete idea of a sentence is a questionable usage. This kind of tagged-on thought is better rephrased:

Tagged-on: The union is going to strike, which I thought was the only solution.

Rephrased: The decision of the union to strike seemed to me the only solution.

11J *Omissions and substitutions*

1. It is common to omit some portion of a clause if the understood element is perfectly clear from the context:

   I remember the first time [that] we met.

   When [he is] on the job, he's usually sober.

   This flour is a better quality than that [flour is].

   Some of the revelers had on masks, others [had on] massive heads, and a few [had on] almost nothing at all.

2. The relative pronoun may be omitted:

   The car [that] I bought recently was stolen.

3. The omission of the preposition in speech is particularly common in certain expressions like *What size shoe do you wear? A couple minutes ago* is wholly as acceptable as *a couple of minutes ago. He came Monday* is also standard for *He came on Monday.* Clearly, many of the common prepositional structures are undergoing change. Omitting the preposition in writing except for the clearly idiomatic expressions is always a questionable usage. Certainly, using the preposition would be playing safe.

4. Although *to* is the mark of the infinitive, it is omitted in some constructions:

   He helped [to] lift the piano. [optional omission]

   He need not [to] come. [obligatory omission]

5. The use or omission of conjunctions in a series is a stylistic difference, not a matter of grammar:

   Omission of connectives: The garden was an array of spring flowers—crocuses, daisies, peonies, carnations, iris, lilies-of-the-valley, lilac.

   Varied use of connectives: The garden was an array of spring flowers—crocuses and daisies and peonies, carnations, iris, lilies-of-the-valley, and lilac.

6. Since *which* has no possessive form, *whose* has been established as an acceptable substitute for awkward constructions beginning *of which*:

   Awkward: The mountain, the top peak *of which* you can see now, is Mt. Rainier.

   Preferred: The mountain *whose* top peak you can see now is Mt. Rainier.

7. *What* is frequently a simple substitute for more involved constructions like *that which, that of which,* or *the thing which*:

   Stilted: He was held at fault for *that of which* he knew nothing.

   Rephrased: He was held at fault for *what* he didn't know.

8. In compound expressions with a suspended object, one of the prepositions is often dropped, particularly in speaking:

Omitted preposition: We were interested and anxious for a change. [*for* is not an idiomatic preposition with *interested*]

Rephrased: We were interested in and anxious for a change.

or: We were interested in a change, and anxious for it.

If two words combine with the same preposition, the preposition does not have to be repeated.

Acceptable: We were anxious and agitating for a change.

Placement of adverbs 11K

The placement of the adverb is often a device for giving emphasis to a particular word or thought in a sentence. You therefore have to be aware of interpretations differing from your own and varying degrees of emphasis that are possible. Compare the differences among the following sentences:

He *just* nodded to me as I was about to get up. [emphasis on the manner, possibly suggesting that the nod was given in a grudging way]
He nodded to me *just* as I was about to get up. [emphasis on the timing and simultaneous action]

He stopped *only* to say hello. [emphasis on the shortness of the greeting]
He *only* stopped to say hello. [emphasis of above sentence lost, no new emphasis gained]

As a general principle, adverbs should be put as close as possible to the words they modify. In certain contexts, however, adverbs may seem to modify either of two constructions. Because they look in two directions, they are called *squinting modifiers:*

Squinting: The new play that we hoped to support *completely* disappointed us.

Moving the adverb clarifies either of two meanings:

The new play that we hoped to *completely* support disappointed us.
The new play that we hoped to support disappointed us *completely*.

In speech, adverbs tend to move forward in sentences. Thus, we commonly hear:

She *just* plays golf on Tuesday.
The boss *only* fired two men.

These sentences would be more emphatic, particularly in writing, if they read:

She plays golf *just* on Tuesday.
The boss fired *only* two men.

The same tendency to move the negative *not* forward in the sentence is acceptable in both speaking and writing. *I don't believe he is honest* is the equivalent of *I believe he isn't honest.* Compare also the greater naturalness of *He is not interested in painting but in sketching* as opposed to *He is interested not in painting but in sketching.*

11L *Preposition at end of sentence*

One of the most carefully preserved bits of folklore in usage is the old taboo about not putting a preposition at the end of a sentence. Normally, because prepositions introduce phrases, they don't come at the end of a sentence anyway. But what does come at the end of a sentence very naturally is a preposition used with a verb (or it may be an adverb form identical with it), particularly if the sentence is a question:

What are you waiting for?

To say or even write "For what are you waiting?" is an affectation. And this kind of cultivated usage often leads to worse blundering—saying the same thing twice:

Here is the place *to* which he was going *to.*
This is a matter *of* which I was speaking *of.*

Of course, thinking that the preposition at the end is always a virtue is as wrongheaded as believing that it is a sin. At times, a preposition is left dangling ineffectually at the end:

It is one of the things which he was willing to give his faithful and undying attention *to.*

This particular sentence can be strengthened by moving the particle forward:

It is one of the things to which he was willing to give his faithful and undying attention.

In most instances, you will do best to follow your natural sense of word order and then revise only if there is a change you really care about.

11M *Run-on sentence or fused sentence*

fs   The run-on sentence represents a failure to mark the ends of sentences, even though they may be well formed:

Run-on: You are probably wondering why I am writing you I am angry.
Corrected: You are probably wondering why I am writing you. I am angry.

Run-on: I have had four years of college (without a degree) maybe I am foolish not to go back.

Corrected: I have had four years of college (without a degree). Maybe I am foolish
not to go back.

Sequence and consistency of tenses   *11N*

The sequence of verb tenses within a sentence of some complexity is largely a matter
of your natural sense of time. If the main verb is present tense, for example, any
tense may logically follow:

I realize that you are going.
          that you were going.
          that you will be going.
          that you have been going.
          that you had been going.
          that you will have been going.
          that you can be going.
          that you may be going.

If the main verb is past tense, past time imposes limits on the sequence that follows:

I realized that you were going.
          that you had been going.
          that you would be going.
          that you could be going.
          that you might be going.

If the main verb is future tense, the past forms are logically excluded:

I will see you because I am going.
              because I will be going.
              because I have been going.
              because I will have been going.

The tense of participles is also governed by the verb of the main clause:

Present Now realizing what the problem is, we offer this solution.
Past: Having realized what the problem was, we offered a solution.

In units of discourse beyond the sentence, you should ordinarily maintain an
order of tenses consistent with natural time; that is, use present tense forms for
matters of the present and past tense forms for matters of the past. Your point of
view will establish a time base for a series of sentences. If this base is present tense,
maintain a sequence of tenses consistent with the present unless the thought recalls
an event from the past. Then, logically, turn to the past tense to narrate the past,
only to return to the original present tense when the narration has ended.

Two exceptions are conventional. First, it is customary to write about any published document, particularly literary works, in the present tense, for example: *The*

Consitution says . . . or *In "Walden," Thoreau writes*. . . . Second, you may narrate past events in the present tense in order to add immediacy and color to your prose. This adjustment of point of view is referred to as the *historical present*.

11O   *Split infinitive*

A firm denunciation of the split infinitive is a carryover of the grammatical tradition that consistently looked to Latin for models. The infinitive in Latin (*amāre,* "to love") cannot be split. The infinitive in English, however, must at times be split to express the writer's exact intentions:

The agency was determined to deliberately spread subtle propaganda.

This sentence with a split infinitive is different in meaning and emphasis from any of the following:

The agency was deliberately determined to spread subtle propaganda.

The agency was determined deliberately to spread subtle propaganda. [squinting modifier in this sentence]

The agency was determined to spread deliberately subtle propaganda.

The agency was determined to spread subtle propaganda deliberately.

Widely split infinitives, with several words inserted in between, appear to be forcing the issue of the split infinitive:

He was inclined *to* sometimes but not always *tell* the truth.

The writer who splits all infinitives as a sign of rebellion shows as little good sense as the writer who avoids all split infinitives as a mark of virtue.

11P   *Unnecessary commas*

Of the various marks of punctuation, the comma is most subject to overuse. In the following cases, the circled commas can be omitted altogether:

1. Commas are not used to separate subject and verb:
   Unnecessary: The most important thing today, is to save.

2. Commas are not used after the last item of a series of adjectives before the noun:
   Unnecessary: She was a particularly honest, forthright, stimulating, speaker.

3. Commas are not used *after* the coordinating conjunction separating the clauses of a compound sentence:
   Unnecessary: We ought to know the solution but, we obviously do not.
   Corrected: We ought to know the solution, but we obviously do not.

4. Commas are not automatically used before quotation marks, only those that introduce direct quotations:

Unnecessary: We read, "The Fall of the House of Usher."
                 A representative of **HEW** asked the president of a college for a, "list of faculty broken down by sex."

Correct: The president replied, "That's not our problem. It's alcohol."

5. Commas are not automatically used after verbs of saying, only those that introduce direct discourse:

Unnecessary: One of the things the union leader said, was that the workers would have to sacrifice.
                 She said, that paintings for the home should be pleasant. [indirect discourse]

Correct: She said, "Paintings for the home should be pleasant." [direct discourse]

Use of the subjunctive   11Q

It is common to say that the subjunctive is disappearing from English and that it remains only in set expressions like *Long live the king* and *Peace be with you.* This is true as far as it goes because the subjunctive has only a few forms that distinguish it from the indicative, and some of these like *if I be* and *though he were* sound archaic. It might be more accurate to say that the use of the subjunctive to express wish, condition, and doubt has been largely assumed by the auxiliaries *may, might, shall, should, can, could, will,* and *would* and by adverbial modifiers of the verb like *hopefully* or *perhaps.* In modern prose, *though he live* becomes *though he may live* and *if he go* becomes *if he should go.*

Despite this shift of function, the subjunctive still crops up naturally in a few sentences, particularly with verbs of saying, asking, and wishing and those that express condition contrary to fact:

I asked that he *be excused* from gym.

It is important that this statement *be given* special consideration.

I wish I *were* you.

Even if she *were* to come now, she couldn't participate.

Chapter 12 *Spelling*

Anyone who has written the English language knows why misspellings occur. Some difficulties are rooted in the spelling system itself, others in the people who try to use the system. These are two separate issues.

First, English spelling is not strictly phonetic. To make this observation is not to say that phonics do not help in learning to spell. Phonics will help as long as you realize that particular sounds are not always spelled consistently and that only twenty-six letters are available to transcribe almost twice that number of sounds in the language. People who are interested in establishing that the English spelling system is chaotic point out that the *sh*-sound can be represented by at least fourteen different spellings. What they do not add is that at least nine of these transcriptions tend to be rare, used in such words as *schist, fuchsia,* and *pshaw.* Most *sh*-sounds are spelled in five fairly common ways, like the spellings of *shoe, mansion, nation, suspicion,* and *conscious.*

It is true that the English spelling system in a very conservative way retains the remnants of older spellings, for example, in the silent letters of *governor* and *descend.* It is also true that orthography changes much more slowly than the sound system. For that laggardness, you need to be grateful. What you learn today is likely to hold true tomorrow. If the system changed as rapidly as sounds, spelling would be chaos. If the campaigns for spelling reform and simplification consistently succeeded, every book in our libraries would soon be archaic.

Spelling reformers from Benjamin Franklin to Bernard Shaw have given most of the reasons why English words are difficult to spell. Yet, despite whatever difficulties exist, the system we have is in general use, masses of people accept the ability to spell correctly as one of the marks of an educated person, and most people, accordingly, learn to spell—not perfectly but adequately. Everyone misspells occasionally, usually because of carelessness or simple failure to observe closely. Good spelling requires an eye for detail.

Your attitude toward spelling often correlates directly with your performance. If you think good spelling is important for whatever reason—social, economic, or academic—you usually go to some trouble to see that your words are right. If you dismiss spelling as a trivial matter and rationalize your own inadequacies by dumping the blame on the spelling system, you are likely to be indifferent to correctness. Good spelling requires concern. If you believe it makes a difference whether a word is spelled correctly or incorrectly, you have acquired a basic attitude that will permit you to go further in analyzing and understanding your own spelling problems.

How do people misspell?

Familiar lists of spelling demons include words that are most commonly misspelled. They sometimes divide the words into syllables; they sometimes identify spelling traps. But they never show exactly *how* words are misspelled. Of course, two individuals are capable of misspelling a word in different ways. One may fail to double a consonant, and the other may use a wrong vowel in an unaccented syllable. Yet for all of these potential differences, misspelling is not as erratic as it sometimes appears. Particular words are misspelled in characteristic ways, but very seldom do the misspellings of one individual fit all patterns. In many instances, you may repeatedly do only one thing wrong. The only sensible approach to spelling, therefore, is for you to list the words you personally misspell and then over a period of time see if your misspellings group themselves. In most cases, one predominant pattern will emerge. That pattern, then, can be studied and worked on.

In order to determine typical patterns of misspelling among college students, 225 misspelled words from themes of approximately 100 students were listed and then grouped. The study produced eleven categories, although most of the misspellings fell into three of these. These categories, therefore, provide comparisons for an analysis of your own misspellings if you want to find out what you need to do to become a better speller.

Misspellings categorized

1. In the total number of 225 misspellings, almost no one, even the worst spellers, missed the first letter. There were six misspellings involving the first letter, and they fell into two categories:

UNACCENTED FIRST SYLLABLE

incourage (encourage)
indeavor (endeavor)
enevitably (inevitably)
enialate (annihilate)

SUBSTITUTION OF S FOR C

sensuring (censuring)
synical (cynical)

What this observation suggests is that even the poor speller is not completely handicapped in looking a word in the dictionary. If you become aware that syllables like *in-* and *en-* are easily confused in unaccented positions or that *s* and *c* spellings may actually sound alike, you should not have undue difficulty in finding a word.

2. By far the greatest number of spelling errors were made by missing only one vowel in an unaccented syllable. There were only three errors in the vowels of accented syllables: *complecency* for *complacency*, *combersome* for *cumbersome*, and *curtesy* for *courtesy*. Some of the words misspelled were fairly difficult ones, but all of the letters were exact except for the one representing a neutral sound (the schwa). The following lists show that the error occurred most commonly in a middle or final syllable:

ERROR IN UNACCENTED FIRST SYLLABLE

discribe (describe)
dispise (despise)
distroy (destroy)
granade (grenade)
rediculously (ridiculously)

ERROR IN UNACCENTED MEDIAL SYLLABLE

catagories (categories)
emphisis (emphasis)
emphisize (emphasize)
exhilerating (exhilarating)
exhileration (exhilaration)
gallary (gallery)
hypicritical (hypocritical)
imaginitive (imaginative)
incapibility (incapability)
instramental (instrumental)
jealosy (jealousy)
manditory (mandatory)
oppertunity (opportunity)
oppurtunity (opportunity)
prevelent (prevalent)
princepals (principals)
seperate (separate)
simularly (similarly)

ERROR IN UNACCENTED FINAL SYLLABLE

e–a

allience (alliance)
challange (challenge)
competant (competent)
existance (existence)
guidence (guidance)
importence (importance)
panal (panel)
personel (personal)
privilage (privilege)
relevence (relevance)
speciman (specimen)
vengence (vengeance)

e–i

tangeble (tangible)

e–o

ancester (ancestor)
poisen (poison)
prospor (prosper)
rotton (rotten)

3. The next greatest number of errors were made by adding an unnecessary letter, either by doubling a consonant, inserting a syllable which the writers used in their own speech, or spelling the word like another one.

UNNECESSARY DOUBLING OF CONSONANT

aggreement (agreement)
arrises (arises)
arroussing (arousing)
assett (asset)
ballance (balance)
beautifull (beautiful)
begginning (beginning)
controll (control)
derrogatory (derogatory)
dissadvantage (disadvantage)
donnate (donate)
exposses (exposes)
illussions (illusions)
impartiallity (impartiality)
impersonnally (impersonally)
laggs (lags)
neccessary (necessary)
oppinion (opinion)
parrallel (parallel)
proffesional (professional)
reffer (refer)
stiffles (stifles)
symbollic (symbolic)
truthfull (truthful)
untill (until)

ADDED LETTER, PROBABLY PRONOUNCED

athelete (athlete)
barbarious (barbarous)
monsterous (monstrous)

ADDED LETTER, PROBABLY INFLUENCED BY ANOTHER WORD OR THE SAME WORD IN ANOTHER FORM

amoung (among)
arguement (argument)
beyound (beyond)
confrounts (confronts)
eleveating (elevating)
loyiality (loyalty)
predjudices (prejudices)
proceedures (procedures)
scence (scene)
truely (truly)

4. An almost equal number of errors were made by dropping a letter, a syllable, or parts of two syllables from a word. Many of these misspellings involve unaccented or silent consonants and vowels; others reflect the writer's own pronunciation of these words; still others reflect the tendency to look at the beginning and end of a word, not its middle.

OMISSION OF ONE LETTER, OFTEN SILENT OR ELIDED IN PRONUNCIATION

adultry (adultery)
aquired (acquired)
backwars (backwards)
choclate (chocolate)
cleary (clearly)
convenieces (conveniences)
curisity (curiosity)
delt (dealt)
diagoses (diagnoses)
envirnment (environment)
futher (further)
impetous (impetuous)
mathmatics (mathematics)
minature (miniature)
obviosly (obviously)
pobable (probable)
realty (reality)
temperture (temperature)

OMISSION OF A SILENT E

completly (completely)
creats (creates)
definitly (definitely)
involvment (involvement)
severly (severely)

OMISSION OF ONE CONSONANT THAT SHOULD BE DOUBLED

accomodate (accommodate)
aparent (apparent)
begining (beginning)
dilema (dilemma)
disatisfied (dissatisfied)
embarass (embarrass)
exagerated (exaggerated)
folies (follies)

occured (occurred)
sadest (saddest)
supressed (suppressed)
totaly (totally)
unoticed (unnoticed)
writen (written)

OMISSION OF ONE VOWEL THAT SHOULD BE DOUBLED

smothest (smoothest)

5. The next greatest number of misspellings involved the confusion of two words. At times, the word used was correctly spelled, but it was the wrong word. At other times, the misspelling represented an integration of two words:

TWO CORRECT SPELLINGS INTERCHANGED

cloths for clothes
course for coarse
deep-seeded for deep-seated
isle for aisle
local for locale
loose for lose
loosing for losing
site for sight
their for they're
they're for their

charature for character (*compare* caricature)
choosen for chosen
desserted for deserted
idealogies for ideologies
incidences for incidents
layed for laid
numberous for numerous
planely for plainly
realitively for relatively
sqwiggles for squiggles (*compare* wiggles)
wheather for weather
wheren't for weren't

TWO WORDS CONFUSED IN ONE SPELLING

boarder for border
cann't for can't (*compare* cannot)

6. A number of words were misspelled by transposing two letters, immediately following one another or in two key syllables.

TRANSPOSITION OF I AND E

beleifs (beliefs)
nieghborhood (neighborhood)
peice (piece)
percieve (perceive)
recieve (receive)
sieze (seize)
soceity (society)
wierd (weird)

TRANSPOSITION OF OTHER LETTERS

chruch (church)
gagued (gauged)
enviornment (environment)
irrevelant (irrelevant)
niave (naive)
perscribe (prescribe)
plauge (plague)
prespiration (perspiration)

7. Another group of words was misspelled by interchanging two letters that have the same sound value:

SUBSTITUTION OF S FOR Z

characterisation* (characterization)
realised* (realized)
recognise* (recognize)
satirising* (satirizing)

SUBSTITUTION OF S FOR C

consentrate (concentrate)
consise (concise)
devises (devices)
sensuring (censuring)
synical (cynical)
vises (vices)

SUBSTITUTION OF Z FOR S

raized (raised; *compare* razed)
suprize (surprise)
surprized (surprised)

SUBSTITUTION OF C FOR S

fantacy (fantasy)
inconciderate (inconsiderate)

SUBSTITUTION OF CIOUS FOR TIOUS

ficticious (fictitious)

8. Several words were misspelled by failing to substitute *i* for *y* when the basic word was changed:

Plural: berrys (berries)

Third person singular: exemplifys (exemplifies)

Suffix: livelyhood (livelihood)
                        uglyness (ugliness)

9. Several words ending in *o* were misspelled in either the singular or the plural.

heroe (hero)   proes (pros)
heros (heroes)   torpedos (torpedoes)
Idahoe (Idaho)   zeroe (zero)

10. Spelling difficulties increase, of course, when the writer makes two or more mistakes: transposing letters and using the wrong letter in an unaccented syllable, omitting a syllable and adding an unnecessary one, failing to double a consonant and using the wrong vowel, and so on. These words when misspelled often appear highly distorted:

ciriculum (curriculum)   occurances (occurrences)
distory (destroy)   remencsent (reminiscent)
groes (grows)   tradgety (tragedy)
inconvieniant (inconvenient)

11. The final group of misspellings are those that might be identified as phonetic spellings. A few patterns emerge, like the use of *ee* for any *e* sound, but for the most part these are inventions writers substitute to approximate what they say:

---

*These four spellings, however, are acceptable British ones. See 12 D.

connisuer (connoisseur)	rightchusness (righteousness)
definetly (definitely)	sargeant (sergeant)
enialate (annihilate)	squeemish (squeamish)
extreemly (extremely)	sumething (something)
journees (journeys)	venir (veneer)
metemorphius (metamorphosis)	

How to remedy misspellings

One obvious but important conclusion to be drawn from the spelling study just described is that most spelling errors occur inside a word (medially), not at the beginning or the end. This observation reflects our tendency to recognize words quickly as we read without ever stopping to examine exactly how the letters are arranged. If you are a poor speller, the first and main job you have, therefore, is to look at words and see what you are looking at. If dividing a word into syllables helps you to look at each letter, then you should divide words in that way. If closing your eyes helps you to obtain a clear mental picture of the word, then you should try that device. If enunciating precisely and exaggerating some sounds helps you get a sound image, then you should try the oral approach. If writing certain letters large (temper-Ament) helps you visualize a trap in a word, then you should dramatize it in that way. If typing forces you to think about the order of letters, you should practice on the typewriter. There are many useful aids for the poor speller, but whatever you do should be designed to get at the proper arrangement of letters, either by sight or by sound.

The analysis of your own spelling errors represents a kind of amateur psychotherapy. If you become aware of a particular spelling problem, and especially if you learn that it may not be as severe a problem as you think it is, then you can direct your attention to certain helpful principles of spelling. Of course, there are exceptions to all of these principles, but you can always cope with the exceptions if you first learn the mass of words that follow the pattern.

Some kinds of spellings must simply be memorized. For example, there is no useful guideline for differentiating between words that add *-able* and those that add *-ible* or those that end in *-ance* and those that end in *-ence.* Yet, where guidelines do exist, these are useful. The following twelve sections illustrate how common spelling difficulties can be eliminated by keeping in mind certain model words that illustrate fundamental spelling guidelines. You may have to concentrate on only one or two of these. The others you have already mastered, whether you are aware of that fact or not.

12A Model words

As a remedy for particular spelling problems, model words can serve as reminders of basic spelling principles.

Ordinarily, *i* comes before *e* except after *c* when the pronunciation sounds like the *e* in *be*.

1. *The* achieve–deceive *model*

WORDS LIKE ACHIEVE

believe	relieve
chief	reprieve
field	siege
fierce	thief
niece	wield
piece	yield

WORDS LIKE DECEIVE

ceiling	perceive
conceit	receive

Exceptions

either	leisure
neither	seize
financier	weird

Exceptions: words pronounced like neighbor

eighty	vein
freight	weight
sleigh	

When a word ends in *y*, preceded by a vowel, the *y* is kept and *s* added to form the plural (*alley, alleys*).

2. *The* alley–ally *model*

When a word ends in *y*, preceded by a consonant, the *y* is dropped and *ies* added to form the plural (*ally, allies*).

WORDS LIKE ALLEY

attorney	attorneys
boy	boys
day	days
chimney	chimneys
donkey	donkeys
key	keys
monkey	monkeys
turkey	turkeys
valley	valleys

WORDS LIKE ALLY

army	armies
baby	babies
body	bodies
city	cities
copy	copies
fly	flies
library	libraries
sky	skies
study	studies

Exceptions: proper names

Marys
Overburys
Emorys

Application of the *y* to *i* principle can be made to other formations: the third person singular of verbs, comparatives, and changes from nouns to adjectives, adjectives to nouns, adjectives to adverbs, and verbs to nouns.

THIRD PERSON SINGULAR

bury	buries
marry	marries

COMPARATIVES

easy	easier
empty	emptier

ADJECTIVES TO NOUNS

fiery	fieriness
lovely	loveliness

ADJECTIVES TO ADVERBS

crafty	craftily
mighty	mightily

NOUNS TO ADJECTIVES		VERBS TO NOUNS	
beauty	beautiful	carry	carrier
mercy	merciless	fly	flier

3. The drop–
dropped–dropping
model

Monosyllables ending in a single consonant, preceded by a vowel, double the consonant when a suffix begins with a vowel.

WORDS LIKE
DROP–DROPPED–DROPPING

WORDS LIKE
DROP–DROPPING

brag	bragged	bragging		bet	betting
can	canned	canning		cut	cutting
plan	planned	planning		bid	bidding
ship	shipped	shipping		get	getting
rob	robbed	robbing		put	putting
sin	sinned	sinning		run	running
snap	snapped	snapping		sit	sitting
stab	stabbed	stabbing		spin	spinning
stop	stopped	stopping		swim	swimming
whip	whipped	whipping		win	winning

SAME PRINCIPLE APPLIED TO
OTHER FORMATIONS

big	bigger
clan	clannish
gun	gunner
mad	madder
man	mannish
pig	piggish
red	reddish

4. The refer–
referred–reference
model

Words of more than one syllable ending in a single consonant, preceded by a vowel, with the accent on the final syllable (*refer*), double the consonant when a suffix begins with a vowel (*referred*) and the accent stays on the same syllable. If these conditions do not hold, the consonant is not doubled (*reference*).

WORDS LIKE REFERRED

WORDS LIKE REFERENCE

admit	admitted	admittance		confer	conference
allot	allotted			defer	deference
compel	compelled			prefer	preference
control	controlled				
concur	concurred	concurrence			
occur	occurred	occurrence			
omit	omitted				
permit	permitted				

SAME PRINCIPLE APPLIED TO OTHER FORMATIONS

bevel	beveled	(*alternate:* bevelled)
benefit	benefited	(*alternate:* benefitted)
counsel	counseled	(*alternate:* counselled)
kidnap	kidnaped	(*alternate:* kidnapped)

Words ending in a silent *e* (*amuse*) drop the *e* when a suffix beginning with a vowel is added (*amusing*). They retain the *e* when a suffix beginning with a consonant is added (*amusement*).

5. *The* amuse–amusing–amusement *model*

WORDS LIKE AMUSE–AMUSING

argue	arguing
arrange	arranging
come	coming
dine	dining
have	having
hope	hoping
judge	judging
sacrifice	sacrificing
shine	shining
write	writing

APPLICATION EXTENDED

arrive	arrival
assure	assurance
bride	bridal
force	forcible
guide	guidance
imagine	imaginary
live	livable
move	movable
use	usage
value	valuable

Exceptions

dye	dyeing	(*compare:* die, dying)
hoe	hoeing	
singe	singeing	(*compare:* sing, singing)

WORDS LIKE AMUSE–AMUSEMENT

achieve	achievement
arrange	arrangement
encourage	encouragement
require	requirement

APPLICATION EXTENDED

entire	entirely
sincere	sincerely
hate	hateful
use	useful
care	careless
hope	hopeless

Exceptions

acknowledge	acknowledgment
argue	argument
awe	awful
judge	judgment
nine	ninth
true	truly

Words ending in silent *e* preceded by *ce* or *ge* retain the *e* before a suffix beginning with *a* or *o*, if the sound of the consonant is soft.

6. *The* outrageous *model*

advantageous	manageable	pronounceable
changeable	noticeable	serviceable
courageous	peaceable	

Words ending in *c* add a *k* when a suffix beginning with *e*, *i*, or *y* is added.

7. *The* frolic–frolicking *model*

WORDS LIKE FROLIC, FROLICKED, FROLICKING (compare *frolicsome*)

mimic	mimicked	mimicking	(*compare* mimicry)
panic	panicked	panicking	panicky

picnic   picknicked   picknicking   picknicker
traffic   trafficked   trafficking   trafficky

8. *The* illiterate–soulless–roommate *model*

When a prefix ends in the same letter that begins the main stem, both letters are retained. When a word ends with the same letter as a suffix or a combined word, both letters are retained.

WORDS LIKE ILLITERATE	*WORDS LIKE* SOULLESS	*WORDS LIKE* ROOMMATE
dissatisfied	accidentally	barroom
dissimilar	critically	bathhouse
dissuade	commonness	beachhead
illogical	drunkenness	bookkeeping
irrational	finally	cannot
irresponsible	formally	cattail
misshapen	meanness	cutthroat
misspelled	morally	glowworm
override	occasionally	penname
overrule	physically	rattrap
unnamed	stubbornness	yellowwood
unneeded	suddenness	
unnoticed	totally	

Exceptions

wherever   whosever

9. *The* maintenance *model*

Certain words show a significant change of spelling when the part of speech changes, like the difference between *maintain* and *maintenance*.

WORDS CHANGING LIKE MAINTAIN-MAINTENANCE

concede	concession	pertain	pertinence
curious	curiosity	proceed	procedure
describe	description	pronounce	pronunciation
explain	explanation	recede	recession
omit	omission	repeat	repetition

10. *The* sede–ceed–cede *words*

Only one word ends with *sede,* three with *ceed;* all of the others are spelled with *cede.*

-sede	*-ceed*	*-cede*	
supersede	exceed	accede	precede
	proceed	cede	recede
	succeed	concede	secede
		intercede	

11. *The* raspberry *model*

The *raspberry* model involves silent letters that reflect the origin of the word and its early spelling in English: *raspis* (wine) + *berry.* These are consistently tricky words to spell:

WORDS LIKE RASPBERRY

silent b
climb
debt
doubt
dumb
lamb
subtle
thumb

silent c, ch
indict
muscle
scene
schism
yacht

silent d
handsome
Wednesday

silent e
eagle
manure

silent g
gnat
gneiss
gnome
sign

silent h
ghoul
ghetto
ghost

silent k
knife
knight
knot
know

silent l
calm
could
palm
salmon

silent m
mnemonic

silent n
condemn
hymn
solemn

silent o
courtesy

silent p
comptroller
pneumonia
psychology

silent r
February

silent s
aisle
island

silent t
listen
mortgage
often

silent u
guess

silent w
answer
grow
snow
write

Some words ending in *o* form their plurals by adding *es* (*echoes*); others, including a large number of musical terms, add only *s*. A few have optional spellings.

12. The echo–solo
model

WORDS LIKE ECHO

hero	heroes
mosquito	mosquitoes
mulatto	mulattoes
potato	potatoes
tomato	tomatoes
tornado	tornadoes
veto	vetoes

WORDS LIKE SOLO

alto	altos
canto	cantos
Eskimo	Eskimos
folio	folios
piano	pianos
ratio	ratios
soprano	sopranos
studio	studios

WORDS WITH OPTIONAL PLURALS

buffalo	buffaloes (buffalos)
ghetto	ghettos (ghettoes)
halo	halos (haloes)
motto	mottoes (mottos)
no	noes (nos)
volcano	volcanoes (volcanos)
zero	zeros (zeroes)

12B Homophones

Words that sound alike but have different spellings and meanings are a common source of spelling errors.

air, heir
aisle, isle
allowed, aloud
altar, alter
ascent, assent

bail, bale
ball, bawl
bare, bear
base, bass
beach, beech
beat, beet
beau, bow
bell, belle
berry, bury
berth, birth
blew, blue
boar, bore
board, bored
bough, bow
brake, break
bread, bred
bridal, bridle
but, butt
buy, by

cannon, canon
capital, capitol
cast, caste
cell, sell
cent. scent, sent
cereal, serial
chord, cord
cite, sight, site
climb, clime
colonel, kernel
complement, compliment
council, counsel
creak, creek
currant, current
cymbal, symbol

days, daze
dear, deer

dew, do, due
die, dye
discreet, discrete
done, dun
dual, duel
dyeing, dying

earn, urn
earnest, Ernest

faint, feint
fair, fare
fate, fete
flea, flee
flew, flue
flour flower
fore, four
forth, fourth
foul, fowl

gait, gate
gamble, gambol
gild, guild
gorilla, guerilla
grate, great
gray, grey
grisly, grizzly
groan, grown

hail, hale
hair, hare
hall, haul
hart, heart
heal, heel
hear, here
heard, herd
him, hymn
hole, whole

idle, idol
in, inn
it's, its

knead, need
knew, new

knight, night
knot, not
know, no

lain, lane
lead, led
lessen, lesson
lie, lye
load, lode
loan, lone

made, maid
mail, male
main, mane
manner, manor
meat, meet
medal, meddle
mussel, muscle

naval, navel
nay, neigh

pain, pane
pair, pare, pear
pale, pail
patience, patients
peace, piece
peak, pique
peal, peel
pearl, purl
pedal, peddle
peer, pier
plain, plane
pray, prey
pride, pried
principal, principle

rain, reign, rein
raise, rays, raze
rap, wrap
read, red
real, reel
right, write, rite, wright
road, rode, rowed
role, roll

root, route	son, sun	vain, vane, vein
rote, wrote	staid, stayed.	vale, veil
rye, wry	stair, stare	vial, vile
	stake, steak	
sail, sale	stationary, stationery	wail, whale
scene, seen	steal, steel	waist, waste
sea, see	step, steppe	wait, weight
seam, seem	stile, style	waive, wave
serf, surf	straight, strait	ware, wear, where
serge, surge		way, weigh
sew, so, sow	tail, tale	weak, week
shear, sheer	taught, taut	weather, whether
shone, shown	team, teem	wet, whet
sign, sine	tear, tier	which, witch
slay, sleigh	there, they're, their	while, wile
sleight, slight	threw, through	whine, wine
soar, sore	throne, thrown	
soared, sword	tied, tide	yoke, yolk
sole, soul	to, two, too	
some, sum	toe, tow	

Similar words **12C**

Words that look alike or sound somewhat alike are a common source of spelling confusion.

advice, advise	loose, lose
angel, angle	medal, metal
biding, bidding	moral, morale
breath, breathe	personal, personnel
choose, chose	quiet, quite, quit
cloths, clothes	statue, statute, stature
counsel, council, consul	thorough, though, through, thought
dairy, diary	were, where
decent, descent	
desert, dessert	
elicit, illicit	
ever, every	
formally, formerly	
hoping, hopping	
human, humane	
later, latter	
local, locale	

British and American spellings **12D**

Variations between British and American spellings cause some confusion. If you are aware of these differences, you can avoid writing perfectly acceptable British spellings only to have them read as incorrect American ones. A comparison of some common words that vary also shows how easily a written language can be made to appear foreign by very minor changes:

BRITISH	AMERICAN
annexe	annex
centre	center
cheque	check
colour	color
connexion	connection
defence	defense
draught	draft
gaol	jail
kerb	curb
labour	labor
pretence	pretense
programme	program
pyjamas	pajamas
tyre	tire
utilise	utilize
waggon	wagon

The dictionary as an aid

Knowing how to spell is, of course, an economy measure. It saves time; it saves embarrassment. But to answer the questions that crop up in everyone's mind, the dictionary is the best source of information concerning common spellings and possible variants. Among the variants, most dictionaries will suggest which is preferred or at least which is more common. If you care about the way you spell, you cannot afford to be without a good dictionary.

Projects

1. Choose a subject you are currently studying in another class. Assemble a special word list of twenty-five terms and proper names that commonly occur. Check the text or dictionary carefully to make sure you have each word spelled correctly.

2. Assemble a special word list of twenty-five terms and names drawn from a topic or hobby or job that is of immediate concern to you. Again, check carefully to see that the words are spelled correctly.

3. Think of at least two words from each of the following categories that would cause you some doubt about spelling if you had to write them. Check the dictionary for the correct spelling.

A. automobile parts
B. banking terms
C. government terms
D. grocery items
E. hardware products
F. legal terms
G. medicines or drugs
H. musical terms

4. Complete the following words with the suffix indicated by copying them on a separate sheet of paper. First, determine which ones you are sure of; then check the dictionary for the ones you are doubtful about.

-able/-ible

access( )	innumer( )
admiss( )	laud( )
contempt( )	leg( )
excus( )	lov( )
indispens( )	vis( )

-ance/-ence

abstin( )	influ( )
admitt( )	penit( )
counten( )	remembr( )
eloqu( )	subsist( )
guid( )	turbul( )

-ant/-ent

adolesc( )	insist( )
appar( )	irrit( )
consult( )	persist( )
descend( )	reluct( )
incumb( )	respond( )

-ary/-ery

bound( )	moment( )
cemet( )	refin( )
compliment( )	sanit( )
confection( )	second( )
mercen( )	treach( )

-or/-er

act( )	direct( )
collect( )	don( )
comput( )	employ( )
conquer( )	instruct( )
counsel( )	profess( )

5. Keep a notebook listing your own misspelled words—listing them first *as you misspelled them* and then as they should be correctly spelled. Periodically, check the lists to see if patterns emerge; that is, do your spellings fall into a limited number of the categories suggested in this chapter? If so, review the principles involved.

Special kinds of writing   Part III

What literary criticism is and is not

We all tend by nature to be critics. This does not mean that we want to find fault with things. What it does mean is that we want to ask questions, try to understand, and come to conclusions about things we like or do not like. In other words, we respond. We respond, either consciously or subconsciously, every time we hear a speech, see a film, or listen to a concert. We respond in the same way when we read. Criticism is simply a type of response to reading. Yet when we suddenly introduce the rather formidable term *literary criticism,* we seem to remove reading from common experience and turn it into a specialized process. Actually, the opposite is true: literary criticism enables us to bring what we read into our own personal experience and thus to respond to it fully and completely. This complete response can sometimes awaken strong feelings within us and lead us to insights about experience that are totally revealing.

What further is literary criticism? In simplest terms, it is an orderly way of looking at a literary work—asking questions about it—what has been called "discovery of design." It might also be called "discovery *by* design." For criticism is discovery. It is not a deathblow to the literary work. It is not necessarily a negative judgment. Criticism can be both positive and negative. It is not necessarily a tearing apart, a way of spoiling enjoyment. It is actually a way of enhancing enjoyment. It is most meaningful when it provides a fresh way of seeing—a new view and a new kind of understanding.

Criticism, then, can be thought of as a kind of exploring, probing, playing with possibilities, gambling and usually winning, if only a little. It always demands thought and involvement. It does not always have to be strictly writing *about* literature; it can also be personal expression. It can be writing *through* literature, *with* literature, *by means of* literature, and always, one hopes, *for* literature.

The nature of literature

The meaning of literature

Literature is an art expressed in words. Thus, it is not dance; it is not music; it is not cinematography. It may have elements in common with each of these other arts, but each art has its own identity and special means of expression. Each must be understood in terms of its own forms, conventions, and effects. Literature as a verbal art must also be understood in its own terms.

Today, we have come to think of literature almost exclusively as written expression, forgetting that much of what we now preserve in written form was once perpetuated by an oral tradition. Literature, of course, may be either written or spoken. As the term has been narrowed in one sense, it has been extended in another. That is, the word *literature* also is frequently used in a very general sense to refer to the whole body of writing in a culture, regardless of its purpose. In this sense, both informative writing and imaginative writing clearly belong to our literature. In a restricted sense, however, literature has come to be identified particularly with artistic forms of verbal expression, especially fiction, drama, poetry, and kinds of prose that reveal an imaginative mind at work—some familiar essays, biographies, autobiographies, and letters. All of these may be differentiated from prose that is designed primarily for explanation and persuasion—what we commonly call expository prose. Thus, not much journalistic prose, for example, has gained literary status, and seldom does technical, scholarly, and, alas, textbook writing achieve such status. Nevertheless, the distinction between imaginative and expository writing is not necessarily based on quality, but on purpose and method.

How do these purposes and methods vary? Let us take one topic as an example—the kind of injustice that can occur in the exercise of the law, particularly in the courts. Is there such a thing as an appeal to a higher justice beyond the laws that men make and judges enforce? Suppose a writer—one like Herman Melville, for instance—takes the position that civil law as he observes it is not in harmony with what he thinks is a higher order of justice, what we rather abstractly call natural law or moral law. How can this distinction be made clear?

Presumably, one way a writer can make the distinction clear is to write an essay that tries to define terms. He can attempt to define *moral law* and state what its source is and how it operates. Then, if moral law and civil law conflict with one another, he can weigh the claims of each. He can try to explain and illustrate, proceeding by fairly standard kinds of reasoning, expanding the thought and trying to make the abstractions as concrete as possible. But the problems of this approach are apparent even in this somewhat brief description of it. Abstractions are difficult to grasp.

A writer has an alternative, however. Instead of dealing directly with ideas, he can attempt to represent them indirectly by creating a fictional world. Typically, this is the way of the storyteller, dramatist, and poet. This is the way Melville treats the conflict between civil law and moral law in his story *Billy Budd.* He makes the conflict clear through narrative and actually causes us to take the side of one law against the other.

The main character of Melville's story *Billy Budd* is a youthful seaman, an almost unnaturally naïve and innocent young man. We seldom meet people like Billy, but we would like to believe they exist. Or perhaps we would like to believe we have an element of Billy's innocence in our own nature. At any rate, we like him. We do not want to see him unnecessarily harmed. Yet, in the course of this story, we see him falsely and helplessly accused of plotting mutiny by a strangely diabolical figure named Claggart, whom we instinctively dislike. In a climactic confrontation between Billy and Claggart, Billy in anger strikes Claggart with his fist and kills him. All of the circumstances outlined in the story are against Billy. The military court is obligated to call the act murder under the dictates of military law governing a ship in time of war. Yet, as much as we know that the law has been impartially applied, we also know that even as Billy hangs upon the gibbet the sentence against him has been cruel and unjust, that a higher law exonerates him.

Do we know precisely what this higher moral law is after having read *Billy Budd?* Perhaps not. Melville's story certainly gives us little rational justification for belief in a higher justice, but, without doubt, it gives us a strong moral conviction that such a force operates in our thinking and influences our decisions. Melville makes us first feel a position, then reflect upon it. He presents a paradox of innocence and guilt strangely reversed. Billy is sentenced to die by the decision of the military court, and we are left to accede to the practical and pitiless claims of human law if we also believe that individuals cannot be their own law. But Melville also lets us know that Billy is innocent. For the short span of time that we read the story, Melville creates a world for us that we cannot change. It is a world in which the central issue of justice is dramatized by characters who involve us not only in their own dilemma but in the total continuing human dilemma of which we are all a part.

Who will say that literature of this kind is incapable of explaining or promoting belief or of moving people to action?

The fictional universe

Characteristically, literature acts through a world of its own; it creates its own fictional universe. It may be as completely fanciful as the setting of *Alice's Adventures in Wonderland* or as graphic as scenes in *Crime and Punishment.* Perhaps one of the greatest obstacles to understanding literature is to assume that the literary work, even when it seems most factual, is an actual transcription of real life. No matter how faithfully writers hold to experience, what they write is only an approximation of actuality. We read only a digest, a selection of details from the multitude of words and gestures and actions that are a part of everyday living. In the universe of fiction, we encounter only segments and scenes of the lives of characters. Almost all of the repetitious details of everyday living are taken for granted—bathing, taking out the garbage, washing the car, going to the supermarket, writing the monthly checks. These may be included only if they provide the writer an occasion to reveal something of significance about a character; otherwise, they are simply omitted in the abbreviated world of fiction. The world of fiction has an existence independent of anything else. It does not need to correspond to what we see about us. It is not justified by saying that it is very much like the world we know. In fact, though fiction may at times be grotesque, it is more often less strange than truth. It has to be. If writers included in stories the kinds of incredible accidents and deaths we read about in the daily newspaper, they would be accused of cheap sensationalism. In creating an illusion of reality, a writer is first bound to what is probable, not what is possible.

Even though the fictional universe respects natural law and circumstance, it is not necessarily held to it as the real world is. When the ancient storyteller chooses to have the goddess Artemis seize Iphigenia from the sacrificial altar and carry her off in a cloud to a distant land, he has introduced a miraculous event that dramatizes his concern for the innocence of Iphigenia. He would have us believe that there is a force which preserves good in the world. It is his viewpoint—not universally accepted, to be sure, but one that many people believe. The narration of the ancient myth, therefore, may not correspond to the external system of logic and law in nature we subscribe to, but it does correspond to an inner psychic system within those who choose to believe in a moral and purposive universe. The rescue of Iphigenia is an objectification of a way of feeling and believing which is not less true because it is improbable; it may be less true literally, to be sure, but not less true metaphorically. We need only remind ourselves that Superman is a modern mythological figure who serves the same purpose. He arrives always in the nick of time to save the innocent and foil the forces of evil. He also is a fictional objectification of basic beliefs that are common in our society.

Misconceptions about the fictional universe may account for the fact that some readers are actually alienated by what they find in literature. They do not see what they hope to see; they do not find out what they want to find out. The world of a literary work is incomplete. We do not know how Hamlet spent his days at Heidelberg University, if that concerns anyone. A literary work operates on its own assumptions; Humpty Dumpty's famous statement to Alice "When *I* use a word, it means just what I choose it to mean—neither more nor less" is sometimes more true of literature than we would like it to be. A literary work functions by its own internal laws; it observes its own conventions; it promotes its own values. All of these may be different from what we are familiar with. They require us to suspend our own beliefs in order to accept others' beliefs. The world we experience in a novel or play may be a world that an author thinks ought to be, not what is. It may be a world imaginatively created to move readers beyond the narrow limits of their own thinking and experience. Yet, for all of the unfamiliarities we may encounter in the world of a literary work, we know from the vast literature that has been written that most works touch on human experience, even when they are helping us escape the harshness of everyday living. We know also that literature is capable of transcending time and place. *Gulliver's Travels* is not irrelevant to modern times because it was written in the eighteenth century. It is still readable and meaningful because it embodies a host of universal truths.

In a play by Oscar Wilde, one of the characters says, "Life imitates Art far more than Art imitates Life." The statement reverses what many people may think about literature. But if that statement is essentially true, then we do not need to use experience as a measuring stick for literature. We may learn from it. In fact, it may well set the measures for us.

The influence of literature

What is literature capable of doing? What means does it use to affect the reader? An attempt to answer these questions directly forces us to see that literature shares many elements in common with other art forms, even though the total effect of each may be different; but that, finally, literature is distinct from dance or painting or music in the particular effects it can create.

How, then, does literature function and with what effects?

1. Through *character*, literature reveals human motives; it invites identification and reaction.
2. Through *actions* and *situations*, literature brings characters into relationships with one another or into relationships with institutions and forces beyond their control; it reveals human beings in conflict.
3. Through its own *compressed world*, it focuses on its central concern without being distracted by other details of life; it sorts out and orders the experiences of its characters; it objectifies experience so that it can be viewed as a whole and reflected on; it shields the reader from the intensity of actual experiences.
4. Through *form*, it orders the action, shapes the thought, and channels the feeling.
5. Through *language, symbol,* and *imagery*, it creates effects of beauty and ugliness; it stimulates the imagination; it moves the audience to respond.
6. Through *style*, it embodies the uniqueness of one writer's way of looking at things and provides pleasure in reading.
7. Through *thought*, it mirrors experience, embodies wisdom, anatomizes the world, raises issues, and searches for solutions.

It should be emphasized here that these are the basic concerns of anyone writing about literature. Everything in the following sections is expansion and illustration of these seven major points.

Characters

Literary characters are those creations that permit artists to play deity—to populate a fictional universe with people and creatures of their own making. This power of creativity exceeds the human being's capacity to reproduce, for in physical reproduction the offspring is determined by natural law and heredity. The imagination can exceed those bounds; it can permit individuals to create what their bodies cannot. Early mythology is filled with hybrid beings—part woman and part serpent, part man and part goat, part woman, lion, and bird. Of course, the imaginative power of writers is not measured by their capacity to create the grotesque, but by their ability to shape with words an artistic world so that readers will view it with credibility. In writing about literature, you need to take into account different kinds of characters and the roles they assume in any particular story, poem, or play.

Kinds of characters

Stereotypes

Stereotypes are conventional characters representing a particular group or class or occupation. Because the characters are conventional, they act according to set patterns. Their appearance is familiar; their speech is predictable; their actions are standardized. Thus, anyone who has read a story or seen an old movie knows how to impersonate a Southern gentleman, a Jewish mamma, or a British lord with the aid of only a few gestures, props, and speech intonations. Imitations of this kind border on caricature; that is, they take identifiable characteristics of people and exaggerate them. People get classified by this means.

All stereotyping, of course, is not caricature; it can be a simplified way of looking at people as representatives of a group rather than as individuals. In Giraudoux's *The Madwoman of Chaillot*, the cast includes characters such as The President, The Ragpicker, The Prospector, The Doorman, and The Sewer Man, all unnamed, identified only by their rank or occupation. Yet these are not wholly wooden characters. Stereotypes often seem true to experience, not because they are exact replicas of people who walk the streets, but because people whom we meet show some of the same traits of talking, dressing, and acting associated with types: hard sell with salesmen, flashy clothes with dudes, and shuffling with cowboys. Unquestionably, stereotypes in literature and other art forms have had their effect on social attitudes, often with serious and unjust consequences. Stereotyping conditions the way we look at one another, so that we tend to see a type that may not be at all accurate. Such typing is, obviously, a superficial way of looking at people.

Despite the serious social and personal implications of stereotyping, it persists in literature as a quick means of characterization. The typical senator, the typical Texan, the typical evangelist—these are all characterizations that may be used by writers for a purpose, perhaps for comedy or satire. Because background characters of a story or drama make only brief appearances, they may have to be made recognizable quickly by typing.

To label a literary figure as a type does not provide you much material for writing, but it does help as a starter if you can estimate how far beyond the typical a particular characterization moves. The Nurse in *Romeo and Juliet*, for example, could have been only a functional type, performing routine duties and making brief, innocuous responses. As it is, she does far more, but this limited conception of a servant role in other plays makes clear how far Shakespeare went to create an individual and colorful character who defies the conventions of her role.

Closely related to stereotypes are stock characters. Even though the word *stock* has close associations with drama, stock figures appear in other kinds of literature also. They are figures who because of their customary association with a dramatic situation have become conventions. Thus in Ovid's elegies, a young wife and a secret lover are haunted by the jealous eyes of an old, repulsive husband. These are stock figures who have been recast with variations over and over again throughout literature. The triangle situation is, of course, perennial. The philandering husband is as common as the erring young wife within the triangle.

Stock characters

Today we identify the snarling, moustachioed character of nineteenth-century melodrama as one of the stock villains, but that figure is only an exaggerated portrayal of a long tradition of dark villains, including giants, misers, and magicians who pervade even the early mythology and literature. Among other stock characters, we could talk of traditional fools, scapegoats, sworn brothers, and fallen women. To see how Falstaff is a variation of a stock comic figure of the braggart soldier in Roman comedy or how Hamlet fits into the tradition of the revenge hero helps you to come to a deeper understanding of Shakespeare's powers of characterization, but this knowledge is not necessary to respond to these characters as they are revealed in the play.

Stock figures need not be stereotypes. Willy Loman in Arthur Miller's *Death of a Salesman* might be considered the stock figure of the traveling salesman, but Miller does not treat Willy Loman in stock situations. Even though the world of salesmanship has been his whole life, the play itself focuses on Willy's private life as a husband and father. As a consequence, *Death of a Salesman* seldom permits us to cater to stock responses. Willy Loman is one of the most pathetic of modern characters—a far departure from the prototype of the salesman in the common joke.

In a letter to Sir Walter Ralegh, the English poet Edmund Spenser explained that he intended the long poem he was going to write to be read as an allegory. It would tell stories about knights who would represent the moral virtues set down by Aristotle, and Arthur himself would represent Magnificence, the perfection of all the other virtues. The poem he was planning became *The Faerie Queene*, written over a period of many years and never completed. The poem was not done exactly as Spenser described it to Ralegh, but his basic intention of writing an allegory did not change. Thus, the incidents of the poem tell a story not only of knightly adventures but also of moral and political struggles. Many of the characters in the poem have

Allegorical characters

obvious counterparts in the political world of the 1500s, and they can be aligned on the side of good or evil, as Spenser sees them. His allegory was a protective cloak in an age when criticism could seldom be spoken forthrightly. John Bunyan, a prose writer of the seventeenth century, also allegorizes throughout his long work *The Pilgrim's Progress.* It is the story of a Christian man's search for salvation. Its central character is called Christian, and his travels lead him finally to the Celestial City. On his journey, he encounters figures like Giant Despair, Mrs. Diffidence, Neighbor Pliable, and Neighbor Obstinate, all of whom personify the obstacles to virtuous living.

In works as obviously allegorical as Spenser's and Bunyan's, our response to the characters is shaped by the nature of the work. But it does not follow that all allegorical figures are two-dimensional, cardboard personifications. In depicting the temptations of life, for instance, Bunyan is often as incisive in his brief characterizations as early painters like Brueghel were successful in depicting the sins of mankind on vast canvases populated by hundreds of allegorical figures. The characters of allegory can be as cartoonlike as George Orwell's menagerie in *Animal Farm* or as lively and intense as the children in William Golding's *Lord of the Flies* or as dramatic and memorable as the seamen of Melville's *Moby Dick.*

Full-dimensional characters

Just as individuals interest us more than masses of people representing movements, so also the full-dimensional characters of literature have attracted most of the attention to themselves. They are described at greater length and revealed in more detail; they are capable of greater individuation. No doubt, many people whom we encounter casually and see only as stereotypes—the waitress, the cab driver, the elevator operator—would be interesting subjects for study, but, just as in life, literature does not permit us to know every character equally well. Leading characters of a literary work are drawn in full; other figures are sketched in to fill out the scene. Although poetry ordinarily does not permit the same space for character development that fiction and drama do, it still manages by implication to suggest the full dimensionality of its characters. T. S. Eliot creates the memorable figure of Prufrock in only 131 lines; Chaucer uses 32 for the Wife of Bath.

Nevertheless, the very length of fiction and drama permits the possibility of presenting characters who grow and change over a period of time. A novelist like Dickens very often accounted for the full lifespan of his characters, from birth to death, even though his story might focus mainly on one period. The final chapter of *Oliver Twist* gives an accounting of "the fortunes of those who have figured in this tale. . . ." A long novel following characters through many years, through many experiences at different ages, allows us to know them as intimately as we know only those who are closest to us. And the probing of a twentieth-century author like James Joyce into the inner minds and motivations of characters permits us to know them even more intimately than we know our friends. Literature gives us an opportunity to stop the life of a character, to turn back pages, to reread, to reflect, to examine motivations, to be involved and detached at one and the same time; and, after the story has been completed, to reconsider those thoughts and feelings we have accumulated in the course of the novel. Seldom do we think of any living person's actions in such detail, even our own. Literature is a public view of private matters; it is both open and intimate.

The permanence and universality of characters

The permanence of literary characters in their written form raises a question about their true nature. They are persistent and stable because they cannot change; only readers can change their attitudes about them. They continue to live on for centuries, whereas living creatures die. Yet we constantly differentiate fictional characters from real people, implying that their reality is of a different nature. Indeed it is, but not necessarily of an inferior nature. Literary characters are limited by the qualities and situations and scenes given to them by the author to live over and over again, but they enjoy an earthly immortality that living beings achieve only by also becoming, like them, characters in history books, novels, and biographies.

Nevertheless, the permanence of fictional characters is tenuous. It is dependent on more than the durability of the manuscript on which the character is recorded. Granted that manuscripts and their contents can always be reproduced (what likelihood is there that *Huckleberry Finn* will be lost to subsequent generations?), volumes of books continue to exist either as inert museum pieces or as vital creations. Literary figures must constantly experience an imaginative revival in the minds of readers to gain their immortality. In this respect, they are subject to the whims of people. Only those characters who continue to meet the test of future generations become the truly universal figures.

Characters are not universal in the sense that they are everybody. A character who is Everyman is probably no person at all, only a symbol. A universal character is first an individual whose qualities can be generalized. Not many men, like Oedipus, kill their fathers and marry their mothers. His particular dilemma is not the bond between him and us, but his reactions are. Given equally catastrophic circumstances, how would we respond? Would we feel within ourselves Oedipus' stubborn resistance to fate and show our persistence to dig out the truth? Oedipus is a man of pride and guilt and grief who comes to realize the consequences of his acts and his role as a man of fate. These are dilemmas that many of us have not solved for ourselves. The tragedy of Oedipus teaches us and involves us in an experience that warns us to fear for ourselves.

Paradoxically, writers cannot guarantee the universality of their creations. They can only attempt to create individuals who they hope will continue to appeal to subsequent generations. Once separated from their authors, literary characters begin an independent existence. Like a Falstaff, they may assume an importance that the author probably never intended. Like a Shylock, a stereotype may undergo a complete metamorphosis. Therefore, any reader of a new day holds the capacity to see a literary figure in a new perspective. In writing about literature, you need to realize that the final word can never be said about its truly great figures.

Functions of characters

What also cannot change about literary characters is their relationships to each other within their own fictional universe. A new generation's attitude may change toward matters like adultery, rebellion, and pride, but it cannot alter how the author has structured the characters to reveal their qualities.

In almost any literary work, several characters receive the main focus. Accordingly, they are considered the leading characters or protagonists. When no character receives such an emphasis, as in Gerhart Hauptmann's *The Weavers* or Maxim Gorky's *The Lower Depths*, it is customary to state that the people as a whole—as a force or movement—are the author's central interest.

But given a protagonist, the conflict of a story may depend on the existence of an antagonist. Hamlet's rivalry with King Claudius makes that drama a struggle for survival between "mighty equals." In other instances, like Stephen Crane's *The Open Boat*, the antagonist is a natural element—the unconquerable sea. With varying degrees of emphasis, the sea or the desert or the mountains or the elements can assume such a role.

A foil is a character who serves as a contrast to another, usually in such a way as to work to the advantage of the leading character. At times, the foil may also be the antagonist, as Hotspur is to Henry IV in Shakespeare's history play or even as Laertes, a foil to Hamlet, eventually becomes his antagonist. One of the most memorable of all foils is Sancho Panza, the earthy companion of the lofty-minded Don Quixote in Cervantes' novel.

A confidant, often used in drama, is a character to whom the protagonist reveals inner thoughts; a confidant becomes a convenient device for the protagonist to speak thoughts to without addressing them to the audience in the form of a soliloquy. Thus, Hamlet, who at times does soliloquize, takes Horatio into his confidence. The confidant may play an active role in the drama but in many instances is only a passive character, perhaps a servant or close friend, whose main purpose is to listen, not to advise or influence the main character.

A narrator is consistently a special kind of character because, in fiction, this person either shapes the entire story by his or her point of view or, in drama, acts as a kind of one-person chorus commenting on the action. The narrator may play a double role; that is, that person may be involved in a particular set of circumstances, and may also be the one who at some future time chooses to tell the story. Thus, Melville's *Moby Dick* begins with the words "Call me Ishmael." Ishmael is the narrator. He is also a seaman who accompanies Ahab in the pursuit of the white whale and survives. Ishmael is therefore a character in the novel who is as subject to analysis as any other character. On the other hand, the narrator in Thornton Wilder's *Our Town*, even though he is one of the townspeople, views the dramatic scene as if it were framed. He is identified as a stage manager and plays that role. At various times, he narrates the history of the characters; he interrupts the action to shift the scene; he communicates with the living and the dead; he philosophizes. He is a wise, interested observer, but one whose special role as stage manager and narrator and chorus makes him a unique character.

Finally, in almost all stories and plays, there are background characters who populate the scene. Ordinarily, these are of no special interest unless, as a mass, they assume an active role. In Ibsen's *An Enemy of the People*, the people as a group are the antagonists of Dr. Stockmann. He is the individual who has to stand up against the many. They are the composite economic society; they are the ones who want to maintain their investments even at the expense of human life. As individuals, they are not greatly differentiated. But as people in a community they can be discussed as if they were one.

Methods of characterization

Because of the fixed nature of literary characters, writing about them depends to a great extent on being able to seek out meaningful clues and determine what techniques the writer has used to reveal the characters. In character analysis, it is helpful to begin with the assumption that a character is coherently developed. Characters may change within the course of a story or play and still be coherent. But the idea of a coherent character does assume that certain values and motives and beliefs—a kind of functional philosophy—cause a character to act and speak in a particular way; and, if the character deviates, he or she is performing inconsistently. Interpretations about motivation and action will vary, of course. Much discussion about a complex character like Hamlet hinges to a great extent on differences of opinion about his madness or his feigned madness and the extent to which he fully controls his words and actions, to what extent he is deliberate and purposeful, to what extent he is frenzied and impulsive.

Even though we can assume that artistic creations are coherent, careful readers will nevertheless approach characterization inductively, beginning first with details of characterization and then coming to some conclusions about the elements of coherence: Are a character's actions adequately explained? Are they justified by the causes for them? Do a character's responses seem consistent with all of the other things we learn? Literature provides a map of character. We can trace the starting points, the directions, and the destination. The whole terrain is laid out to be viewed and examined. Analysis depends on a presentation of detailed evidence about a character with the intention of seeing that character as a whole being.

The actions of characters

Clearly, the reader has to be alert to the actions of a character because actions are the author's way of showing, not telling, what the characters are like. Yet surface appearances must be questioned. In one scene of Melville's *Benito Cereno*, Babo appears to be a faithful servant shaving Don Benito in the presence of Captain Delano, the visiting captain aboard ship. At that moment, however, Babo, with razor in hand, is actually terrorizing Don Benito in order to keep him silent. The suspense of a story like Melville's *Benito Cereno* depends on the unsuspecting nature of the American Captain Delano, who is deceived by what he sees and through whom we as readers view the scene. Only when, at the end of the story, Babo jumps into a boat in an effort to kill the escaping captain is Delano's deception illuminated. In an instant, his mind moves to review all of the previous events in the light of a newly discovered truth that the slaves have mutinied and have already massacred most of the Spanish crew.

The appearance of characters

In some stories and plays, appearance may be taken as a clue to the nature of a character if the author leads the reader to attach significance to it. Most people today tend to look on ugliness and distortion without suspicion, but in times past, outer flaws were taken as a sign of inner corruption. From early childhood, fairy tales and mythological stories have conditioned us to accept the literary fact that dwarfs and witches and monstrous creatures are servants of evil, and heroes and heroines are handsome, beautiful, and good. The world of the fairy tale is one of simple contrasts.

Yet, even when the fictional universe is not quite so simplified and stories are not told to enforce moral platitudes, writers continue to attach significance to physical appearance. The brief sketches in the Prologue to Chaucer's *Canterbury Tales* consistently include descriptions of physical details and dress that give significant indexes to character and social station. Chaucer's description of the squire includes the line "Short was his gowne, with sleves longe and wyde"—usually understood to be details that indicate the Squire was dressed in the very latest fashion. Chaucer describes him as a young and lusty fellow, gaily dressed, and full of spirit—a sharp contrast to the divinity student, the Clerk, whose coat is threadbare and whose horse is as lean as a rake.

Shakespeare uses appearance in a play like *Richard III* as a psychological motivation. In the opening soliloquy of the play, Richard reveals the thoughts about his deformity that prey on his mind, finally declaring:

> And therefore, since I cannot prove a lover,
> To entertain these fair well-spoken days,
> I am determined to prove a villain
> And hate the idle pleasures of these days.

Thus, from the outset, Richard's physical ugliness is announced as a motive for his monstrous actions.

In *Hedda Gabler,* Ibsen provides clues to the interpretation of characters in the brief description he includes in the stage directions at their first entrance. When Hedda enters, Ibsen assumes the part of a narrator: "Her steel-gray eyes express a cold, unruffled response. Her hair is of an agreeable medium brown, but not particularly abundant." When Mrs. Tesman, Hedda's foil and rival, enters, Ibsen writes, "Her eyes are light blue, large, round, and somewhat prominent, with a startled, inquiring expression. Her hair is remarkably light, almost flaxen, and unusually abundant and wavy." If we ignore these contrasting characteristics, we ignore how Ibsen defines the relationship between the two women from the very beginning and how, in particular, the references to hair and stroking hair and pulling hair at scattered points throughout the play are intended as significant clues to Hedda's character.

It is axiomatic that what characters speak ought to be important in learning about them. There is a tendency, however, in reading (as opposed to listening) to concentrate on the what and the why—the substance and purpose—and to pay less attention to the when and the how—the occasion and the manner. In writing about a character's speeches, you have to attempt to project yourself into the character: How would you say the words in the same situation? What is the tone? Does the occasion color the tone? Answering these questions can provide possible insights into meaning, especially extrasensory meaning, which always represents another level of non-verbal communication. When people are speaking, they are also gesturing, grimacing, inflecting the voice, stressing, and in numerous subtle ways influencing the meaning, adding to it, and, when they are being ironic, even reversing the meaning. All of these extrasensory implications have to be inferred from the reading. A fictional narrator may add a few introductory details to a speech, telling how it was spoken, but you are still left to interpret. In a dramatic production, the whole matter is taken over by the actors and the director. It is therefore not at all unusual that different readings of identical roles by different individuals can produce a totally different conception of a character. The rhythms can be slowed or quickened. The lines can be consistently twisted for humor or satire. All of the speeches can be heightened or understated. Nevertheless, the original author by choice of words, usages, structures, and rhetorical devices builds into the speeches a core of meaning and effect that in itself cannot be altered but can be developed as various interpreters see fit, consistent with their total interpretation of the character.

Two strikingly different examples out of context will illustrate what kinds of elements are built into speeches. The first is a speech from a play; the second is a line of dialogue from a novel:

CHARACTER 1, in a play:

> Mount, mount, my soul! Thy seat is up on high,
> Whilst my gross flesh sinks downward, here to die.

CHARACTER 2, in a novel:

> "Don't worry, darling. . . . I'm not a bit afraid. It's just a dirty trick."

What is first obvious is that there is a different rhetoric operating in each speech. It is unlikely that Character 1 could speak Character 2's line. The thoughts are different as well as the ways they speak. The first speech seems to be a dramatic, oratorical apostrophe of the character to his soul at the moment of death. The second is calm and intimate, addressed to another person—a completely different approach to death, since these are also words spoken at the moment before dying. Having to die is the "dirty trick."

Thus, knowing the occasion throws considerable light on the implications of the second speech, but the intimate elements are built in. It cannot be delivered in the manner of the first, because the structures and words do not lend themselves to that treatment. Yet each speech, within the limits of its language, can be interpreted to show different qualities about the characters at the moment of their death. Character 1 could be seen as noble and high-minded or as pompous and shallow. Character 2 could be seen as casual and superficial or as brave and bitter. Or perhaps these are not the exact descriptive adjectives at all in terms of the total characterization and the occasion; they explain only possible effects. Yet we do know that the speeches identify two characters of quite different temperament, and the speeches contain clues to the characterization.

Character 1 is actually King Richard II in Shakespeare's play of that name. Richard has been forced to abdicate and has been replaced on the throne by Bolingbroke (Henry IV). He is imprisoned in Pomfret Castle, reflecting at length on the discontent of his life, daily fearing that his food will be poisoned to end his life. Death, ironically, comes as a rude assault. Men break in, slay the guards, and strike Richard down. In his dying words, Richard damns his slayer and, in a final gesture of kingliness, cries out:

> Mount, mount, my soul! Thy seat is up on high,
> Whilst my gross flesh sinks downward here to die.

His slayer is moved to speak:

> As full of valor as of royal blood.

Character 2 is Catherine Barkley in Hemingway's *A Farewell to Arms*. She is an English nurse serving in World War I. Her lover is Frederic Henry, an American lieutenant attached to an Italian ambulance unit. In the final scene of the novel, Frederic takes Catherine to a hospital where she gives birth to his child. The baby is dead; she knows she is dying and says she hates it. She tries to reassure Frederic, kidding him a bit, vacillating between thoughts of loving and dying. When a doctor directs Frederic to go out of the room, the novel records the scene with simplicity:

"Don't worry, darling," Catherine said. "I'm not a bit afraid. It's just a dirty trick."

They are her last words. They too are "full of valor as of royal blood," but her bravery and nobility are of a different variety.

These two brief speeches do reveal character. Because they are dying speeches, they are particularly important ones. But what each reveals, it reveals not so much by what it says literally as by the way the words are spoken, to whom they are addressed, when, and under what circumstances.

The persona of the poet

Poems, like plays and stories, are sometimes written about people, and we feel essentially the same interest in these characters as we do in other ones in fiction and drama, except that we are seldom provided with the same kind of detail that permits us to understand them as fully developed characters. These, however, are the visible and identifiable characters of a poem. But like the narrator of a story or the director of a play who remains behind the scenes, a similar kind of character frequently appears in a poem. This is a character whose voice we hear but do not see in person. This is a role the author chooses to assume rather than speak in his or her own voice. This voice is ordinarily referred to as the persona of the poet or the persona of the poem.

In Edwin Arlington Robinson's poem "Luke Havergal," the speaker, the "I" of the poem, is clearly not the author:

> Go to the western gate, Luke Havergal,
> There where the vines cling crimson on the wall,
> And in the twilight wait for what will come.
> The leaves will whisper there for her, and some,
> Like flying words, will strike you as they fall;
> But go, and if you listen she will call.
> Go to the western gate, Luke Havergal—
> Luke Havergal.
>
> No, there is not a dawn in eastern skies
> To rift the fiery night that's in your eyes;
> But there, where western glooms are gathering,
> The dark will end the dark, if anything:
> God slays Himself with every leaf that flies,
> And hell is more than half of paradise.
> No, there is not a dawn in eastern skies—
> In eastern skies.
>
> Out of a grave I come to tell you this,
> Out of a grave I come to quench the kiss
> That flames upon your forehead with a glow
> That blinds you to the way that you must go.
> Yes, there is yet one way to where she is,
> Bitter, but one that faith may never miss.
> Out of a grave I come to tell you this—
> To tell you this.
>
> There is the western gate, Luke Havergal,
> There are the crimson leaves upon the wall.
> Go, for the winds are tearing them away,—
> Nor think to riddle the dead words they say,
> Nor any more to feel them as they fall;
> But go, and if you trust her she will call.
> There is the western gate, Luke Havergal—
> Luke Havergal.

The outlines of the dramatic situation seem fairly clear: a girl whom Luke has loved has died; he is left in bewilderment, not knowing what to do. It is then that a voice both commands and lures him to "go to the western gate." Who is the figure who comes "out of a grave" to tell him this? Is it Death? Or Death's agent? Or is it merely an inner voice within Luke that tells him to follow her by killing himself? There are no definite answers as to who the voice is, but any interpretation of the poem must attempt to account for it in some way.

The importance of the persona will, of course, vary from poem to poem, but, after a first reading, you should always attempt to resolve in your own mind who the speaker is. If it is not the author, then the persona is functioning as a dramatic character, assuming a role that is integral to an understanding of the dramatic conflict and meaning of the poem.

Suggestions for writing about characters

Characters are the focus of almost any literary work of a dramatic nature. No one needs to direct attention to them as subjects for writing, but it is not always equally as clear what you can write *about* in analyzing characters. Literary analysis is not pure description or a summary of the action, although it may include elements of these. It is not gossip—the nature of much of our talk about living people. It is more in the nature of amateur psychoanalysis which concerns itself with the way characters act and talk, with the reasons they act as they do, or with the way parts of their lives fit together to create a total impression. Your job as writer-critic, above all, is to convey to the reader your understanding of the character and the character's role in the literary work. You may want to approach the analysis diagnostically, looking at the symptoms and signs that lead to a particular conclusion. A character analysis of this sort may set out to prove a kind of thesis, such as: Nora in Ibsen's *A Doll's House* is a nineteenth-century forerunner of the twentieth-century feminist and career woman, or Henry Fleming in *The Red Badge of Courage* is a central figure in a story about Christian redemption. The first thesis would look at Nora from the perspective of a different age, but it would still be an analysis limited to what actually happens in the play. The second thesis would emphasize how the novel works out a general theme through its characters—Henry's relation to Jim Conklin, for instance. Topics of this variety indicate that it is rarely possible to write about characters without referring to many other elements that go to make up the literary work.

Another approach to writing about character comes close to a completely personal view, because essentially it will be your attempt to get at the nature of a character by an impressionistic sketch. This kind of character analysis is clearly more speculative and intuitive than the first, but it can at times be successful in describing the emotional temperament of a character.

However varied written papers about characters may be, they ought to be true to the details that the author gives about a character in the special fictional world that has been created. Questions like the following will help you come to some understanding of literary characterization as opposed to our usual casual assessment of people in daily life:

1. Into what categories do the characters of a story or drama fall? Are they types? Are some clearly individualized and fully developed?

2. In what ways do characters comment on one another either by their words or their actions? Are they grouped so that they form contrasting views or attitudes or values?

3. What is the author trying to do with particular characters? What is the author's chief intention? To reveal the variety of human nature? To use characters as mouthpieces? To show a certain style of living? To illustrate a theme through them?

4. Is the characterization of the protagonist coherent? Are his or her actions motivated? Are some actions unexplainable in terms of the character or of the continuing story?

5. Does the time span of the action allow for a developing character? What changes take place in the thinking of a character? Why?

6. How do we learn to know the characters? How well? What typical techniques does the author use to reveal character? In what special ways do actions and appearances add to our knowledge of a character?

7. What details about a character seem to give him or her universal appeal? What particular elements are dated?

8. Do you look sympathetically or critically on the characters? What in the literary characterization and action affects you to respond one way or the other? Do you identify or sympathize with a character who in the construction of the plot is not supposed to invite sympathy?

9. In what way do minor characters fit into the total scheme of the story? Why couldn't they be omitted?

10. How do the characters speak?

Action

Things that happen—actions—continue to be a major factor in literature. We might echo one of the great literary passages of Ecclesiastes in the Bible to say that in literature there is a season for everything: "A time to be born and a time to die . . . a time to kill and a time to heal . . . a time to weep and a time to laugh, a time to mourn and a time to lament . . . a time to get and a time to lose . . . a time to love and a time to hate, a time of war and a time of peace."

When Aristotle discussed tragedy in the *Poetics*, one of the earliest and most influential critical works written, he placed prime importance on plot. To him, plot was not the story or the actions alone; it was also the arrangement of the incidents. The same story might be told by a number of different plots.

If we reflect on Aristotle's preference and then think of contemporary writing in terms of the seven elements of literature we are discussing—character, action, setting, form, language, style, and meaning—we would distort considerably if we said that writers today seem primarily concerned with plot and action. Some writers like Bernard Shaw and Katherine Anne Porter seem little concerned with plot. In contrast to earlier stories, plays, and poems, a remarkably static quality seems to pervade much current literature. Characters no longer do things; rather, they talk, not always to others but often to themselves, or they reflect on the things they have done or they contemplate the actions they might have taken but did not. If the description seems also to fit a character like Hamlet, we need to remind ourselves that Shakespeare in that play was basically writing his version of a revenge drama. At the end, the stage is strewn with dead bodies. There is plenty of action.

Action is no longer even the heart of narrative. The clear exceptions, of course, are the murder mysteries, spy stories, science fiction tales, westerns, gothic tales, and historical novels that are constantly produced in huge numbers; these still feature adventures, searches, accidents, and chases. Aside from these works, however, a modern Aristotle observing today's tragedies and other forms would be hard pressed to consider plot of primary importance.

The events

As simple as it is to ask the question What is happening? it is by no means easy to answer it. Your first obligation is to be as clear as you can about the sequence of events. In long narrative poems and novels and plays, the events may be fairly well defined and expanded. The more compressed the form or the more oblique the point of view, however, the more difficult it is to establish the narrative sequence. Readers accustomed to rapid narration will no doubt encounter considerable trouble with Faulkner's "Barn Burning," merely trying to establish what is happening. Or with Pirandello's *Six Characters in Search of an Author*, in which the events are fragmented as if the author tossed the pieces of a puzzle in the air to leave them where they fell. One clue to understanding the drama fully is to arrange the events in the order in which they happened, not the order in which they are revealed. In Marvell's "To His Coy Mistress," some readers miss completely what is happening, because the poem itself is a lover's speech, but it is a speech made to move his coy mistress to act with him like "amorous birds of prey." To miss the seduction that is going on is to miss a good bit of the irony.

Nevertheless, merely to summarize what is happening in any work is not advisable unless you suspect that you have discovered something that no one else has perceived. Determining the events is usually the spadework that needs to be done before you turn to anything else. Yet student themes too often reveal that their writers have failed to start at this most basic level. If they have mastered the sequence of events, they can legitimately write about the kinds of changes in actions that take place. These observations are usually closely related to character analysis because in works of adequate length characters grow and change, not always in terms of time, but in terms of realization and understanding. You can think of the relationship between actions and thoughts in two ways. First, actions sometimes influence characters. These are essentially forces beyond their control, like work, taxes, health, interpersonal relations, whatever affects them externally. On the other hand, characters often determine the action. Motivated by their own needs, desires, or ambitions, they shape the things that occur. They cause actions; they are not acted upon. Inasmuch as the things that happen in a work of literature are the author's invention, even though they may be based on actual fact, we are obliged to draw significance from actions, either as they happen to characters or as they are made to happen. They are clues to change and indications of the forces that are operating to cause them. What is happening or perhaps not happening is therefore one of the sources of learning what a story or play or poem is about.

The length of a work to a great extent determines what is included or omitted. Short stories ordinarily embrace a short span of time and limited situations. Poems may focus on the detail of a single event, sometimes on something of seemingly little importance, like the widening concentric circles caused by a pebble tossed into a pond. If a writer wants to write a short story, that choice of form may influence the scope of the action, or a writer may have the action in mind and choose a form appropriate to it. The epic and the novel (consider Milton's *Paradise Lost* and Tolstoy's *War and Peace*) hold the greatest potential for the panoramic. The drama is less adaptable to densely populated shifting scenes. Ibsen's *Peer Gynt,* for example, suffers from diffuseness. Goethe's *Faust* is essentially a reading drama, not easily presented in the theater. Shakespeare's *Antony and Cleopatra* is without doubt more successful in its revelation of the intimate love scenes between Antony and Cleopatra than it is in its depiction of the political and military events involving Antony, Octavius, and Lepidus.

During two main periods in literary history—the fifth century B.C. in Athens and the Renaissance on the Continent and in England—most dramatists restricted their plays to an observance of what are familiarly called the unities of place, time, and action, that is, limiting the action to one setting, covering a twenty-four-hour span, and using a single plot line, omitting contrasting or supporting subplots and other episodes not immediately necessary to the exposition of the drama proper. What dramas of this kind lost in their illusion of reality they often gained in the intensity of their effects through compression. In a similar way, short stories and poems that represent only a modicum of action may comment more deeply and meaningfully on experience than novels and dramas of far broader scope.

Given the customary limits of the various forms, writers are still left to include and omit what they wish. The reader is left to infer that what writers include they include for a purpose and what they omit they also omit by choice. Analysis of literature, therefore, involves the weighing of all details in relation to the total purpose. Why does Shakespeare have King Lear at the moment of the old man's supreme grief and tragedy concern himself with asking Albany to undo a button? Why does Browning have the Duke in "My Last Duchess" lead the envoy down the staircase and point out a particular statue done by Claus of Innsbruck? These are seemingly unimportant details of action, but the writers have included them at climactic points as touches of humanity or means of commentary. Such details of action cannot be ignored.

Focusing on events

Both distortion and understatement are means of drawing attention to special events. Each is possible because each is a deviation in an opposite direction from what a reader customarily expects. From everyday experience, readers know in a very general way how things usually happen and how people react. This knowledge determines what we might call ordinary expectations. A distortion of action or an understatement of effect, therefore, gets a special response from readers because they consider these changes improbable or unexpected.

Shakespeare's *Richard III* records the desperate measures of that monarch to secure his throne by conniving, imprisonment of enemies, and murder. But his efforts cannot offset the growing rebellion of the powerful lords of the realm. These are matters of historical record. But Shakespeare, although he was writing a play based on history, was not writing history. In scene iv of Act IV, he has a messenger arrive from Devonshire to report to Richard that Sir Edward Courtney and the Bishop of Exeter are in arms. Almost immediately, a second messenger arrives from Kent to report that the Guildfords are in arms. A third messenger enters to report the destruction of Buckingham's army. Though this is a message favorable to Richard's cause, it is quickly offset by the arrival of a fourth messenger from Yorkshire, who reports the disastrous news that Lovel and Dorset are also in rebellion. The distortion of the time element—the coincidence of these arrivals—becomes a dramatic means of conveying the impact of these events on Richard, and the compression of the time permits Shakespeare to have Richard stirred to immediate action against the rebels, saying

> While we reason here
> A royal battle might be won and lost.

Here the depiction of the action is not historically accurate, but it is dramatically valid. A similar device of messengers arriving one after the other to report disasters is used also in the biblical story of Job and retained by Archibald MacLeish in *J.B.*, his modern adaptation of the tale. In all three examples, the overwhelming effect of disaster becomes the test of a man.

Understatement of action also has its own shattering effect. We would be hard pressed to find a more skillful use than the ending of Katherine Anne Porter's *Pale Horse, Pale Rider,* a subtle story of young love during wartime. Miranda, snatched from death after a prolonged illness from influenza during the epidemic of 1918, turns finally to a collection of letters that she has willingly left unopened on her table. Encouraged to read them, she takes them in order—"What a victory, what triumph, what happiness to be alive, sang the letters in a chorus." But one of them is a thin letter notifying her that Adam her lover has died of influenza in a camp hospital. Miranda does not collapse. There is no emotional outburst, no hysteria, no cursing of fate. Porter's closing description of Miranda going about the business of telling a friend what few items she will again need—lipstick, gauntlets, stockings, and a walking stick—and then her awful sense of aloneness—these understated details of action are as overwhelming and dramatically moving as any piling up of effects. Katherine Anne Porter leaves the reader with a paralyzing sense of the irony of the story she has told:

No more war, no more plague, only the dazed silence that follows the ceasing of the heavy guns; noiseless houses with the shades drawn, empty streets, the dead cold light of tomorrow. Now there would be time for everything.

Observations of this kind concerning action in a story or play reveal in what way writers influence our thoughts and feelings. Since a literary work is not bound to fact or nature, writers are free to alter people and circumstances to the extent that they dare. Their skill in doing so may be their major claim to greatness.

Like many other critical principles, the concept of what completeness is derives from Aristotle. Aristotle defined a whole as that which has a beginning, a middle, and an end; and he continued by specifying that a beginning is that which does not follow something else as a necessary result; an ending is that which naturally does follow other consequences; and a middle is something that naturally follows something else as something else in turn follows it. You may think that his definitions are now too obvious to be stated. Nevertheless, though his concept is a strong, inescapable part of our thinking about wholeness, its obviousness can no longer be taken for granted. For more than a hundred years at least, developments in art, music, and literature have been undermining the notion that a whole is that which has a beginning, a middle, and an end. We have come to recognize fragments as wholes, incompleteness as completeness, disorder as a kind of order, and endings as a convenience, not a necessity. The first of these new concepts is already firmly established in literature, and the others continue to make themselves evident in various writings that deviate sharply from conventional norms.

One of the clearest illustrations of the adjustment in our thinking about a fragment as a whole may be observed in our acceptance of what we now familiarly call slice-of-life dramas and stories. The phrase originated in the nineteenth century and now serves as a common descriptive term for plays and stories that do not attempt to account for beginnings and endings in the Aristotelian sense, that give us only a view of the middle—a passing scene through a window, an opening of a door upon a room, only to have it closed again without explanation; figuratively, a slice from the total lives of the characters involved. Thus, middles stand as wholes.

Obviously, every work of literature has some point of starting and stopping, and, in the same line of reasoning, every work of literature may be said to be only a segment of life. Yet these concepts of beginning and ending and the idea of slicing out a middle are quite different from the logical completeness that Aristotle speaks of. What we now read may be only a beginning or a middle or an ending, not necessarily all three. If your aesthetic satisfaction depends on having actions come to completion or complications fully resolved, if your aesthetic satisfaction depends on perceiving the shape of a beginning and a middle and an end, then you will be constantly frustrated by much of the fragmented work that you will encounter in modern literature, and in art and music as well.

Point of view

One of the fascinating things about literature is to consider the action from the point of view of the narrator. Point of view is a less significant factor in drama than in fiction or poetry because in drama many points of view may be operating at the same time. Even though the author may be speaking through one of the characters, this is ordinarily not the only viewpoint represented.

In fiction and poetry, however, the voice of the narrator is of prime importance. That voice may not be the author's own. John Donne wrote a verse epistle entitled "Sappho to Philaenis." In the poem, he adopts the thoughts and point of view of

Sappho. Sappho is a persona; a mask for the writer. Donne assumes the mask as readily as Shaw writes speeches for Eliza Doolittle in his play *Pygmalion*. Always basic to reading a poem, therefore, is considering who the speaker is, whether the speaker and author are identified with one another, and, if not, who the speaker really is and what the speaker represents.

In far more intricate ways, the point of view in fiction determines what action can be narrated. If the point of view is omniscient, that is, if the author assumes the role of all-knowingness, anything can be included. But space does not usually allow the writer to penetrate and make clear the motives of all of the characters. The author may therefore focus on several of the main ones. In the following passage from Thomas Hardy's *The Mayor of Casterbridge*, the author's omniscient point of view permits him to see the entire scene, to describe sounds both outdoors and indoors, to give close details of a woman's appearance, and to know the thoughts of another woman and her daughter:

Other clocks struck eight from time to time—one gloomily from the gaol, another from the gable of an almshouse, with a preparative creak of machinery, more audible than the note of the bell; a row of tall, varnished case-clocks from the interior of a clockmaker's shop joined in one after another just as the shutters were enclosing them, like a row of actors delivering their final speeches before the fall of the curtain; then chimes were heard stammering out the Sicilian Mariners' Hymn; so that chronologists of the advanced school were appreciably on their way to the next hour before the whole business of the old one was satisfactorily wound up.

In an open space before the church walked a woman with her gown-sleeves rolled up so high that the edge of her under-linen was visible, and her skirt tucked up through her pocket hole. She carried a loaf under her arm from which she was pulling pieces of bread, and handing them to some other women who walked with her; which pieces they nibbled critically. The sight reminded Mrs. Henchard-Newson and her daughter that they had an appetite; and they inquired of the woman for the nearest baker's.

In a somewhat different approach to narration, authors can voluntarily place limits on their point of view and let one of the characters within the scene narrate, limiting themselves only to what the character can see and hear. In the following passage from *The Sound and the Fury*, Faulkner narrates from the point of view of the thirty-three-year-old idiot Benjy:

Through the fence, between the curling flower spaces, I could see them hitting. They were coming toward where the flag was and I went along the fence. Luster was hunting in the grass by the flower tree. They took the flag out, and they were hitting. Then they put the flag back and they went to the table, and he hit and the other hit. Then they went on, and I went along the fence. Luster came away from the flower tree and we went along the fence and they stopped and we stopped and I looked through the fence while Luster was hunting in the grass.

"Here, caddie." He hit. They went away across the pasture. I held to the fence and watched them going away.

Once authors choose a limited point of view, any number of other options present themselves. They can turn over the narration to the main character of the story and let that person relate the story, or they can choose any other character involved in the story. Each change of focus, of course, holds the possibility of an entirely different kind of story because, obviously, no two people view the same situation in the same way. One of the fascinating demonstrations of a story told from a variety of points of view is Robert Browning's long narrative poem "The Ring and the Book." In ten of the twelve books composing this long poem, we read the contrasting views of different characters and groups concerning the story of Guido, Pompilia, and Caponsacchi. The reader is not finally given the author's definitive version; the truth is left to be interpreted as the reader wishes to view it through the eyes of one of the characters.

Suggestions for writing about action

Writing about action or plot depends on being able to answer questions like the following as they may apply to a particular story, play, or poem:

1. Why has the author selected certain details of action and not others which we may possibly know from another source, for example, from a different version of the same story by another author (various works based on the Trojan war) or from actual experience (Truman Capote's *In Cold Blood*)? What actions does the writer fail to narrate that would affect the way we respond to the story? Where are the gaps? Why do particular actions seem to be omitted?

2. What is gained by the particular point of view the author chooses for the narration?

3. What particular effects of suspense, irony, or discovery are gained by the arrangement of the incidents, particularly if they depart from a straight chronological scheme? Why does the story begin or end as it does? What actions seem to be basically cinematic? In what way?

4. What significant changes occur in the course of the action that lend themselves to interpretation? In what way do changes in action act as clues to changes that occur in characters?

5. What is the actual sequence of events? Is one situation the cause of another? What elements of foreshadowing permit the reader to foresee the eventual outcome of the action?

6. Is more than one story operating at one and the same time in the same work (subplots)? Do various lines of action comment on one another? Do they reinforce one another, or do they contrast?

7. What characters or forces determine the action?

8. What are the key events in the narration? Why are these more important than others? What seemingly unimportant details of action take on special significance in terms of the writer's overall purpose?

9. Why are some events that may seem strange or improbable included in the action? How are events narrated that seem to deviate from the way we would normally expect them to happen?

10. In what way do actions shape and change characters?

Setting

Setting, of course, is closely associated with the staging of drama and with descriptive passages in fiction and poetry. In drama, the scene may be served by a simple backdrop and a few props. Even if these are dispensed with, as they frequently are in modern productions, it can be supplied by the imagination of the audience. But in either case, the physical properties creating a setting are not as important as the function of the scene in the mind of the writer and reader.

The setting in fiction

In Conrad's *Heart of Darkness*, the setting of the story is literal and vivid, but it is also a means for revealing the significance of the action. Each move that Marlow makes into the interior of the Belgian Congo of the nineteenth century seeking out Mr. Kurtz—a journey Conrad himself had taken in 1890—retraces the adventures of Kurtz's soul on this earth to its final state of deepest horror and savagery. A journey to another place would not have told the same story. Only the setting in Africa provides Conrad with the symbolic implications that he needs for this commentary on humanity. In this story, as in many others, he describes a special world, a setting removed from the familiar scene and the usual trappings of civilization—a moral island, as it were—that tests people's essential values and capacities when they are released from the ordinary pressures of everyday life. The setting of a typical Conrad story is almost as restricted as a theatrical stage, and it must almost always be taken into account in speaking of the characters and the action.

In other fiction, of course, the setting may be a less integral part of the story than it is in *Heart of Darkness;* it may be only a landscape in the background. Modern writers, however, tend less often to treat the setting perfunctorily. The development of the social sciences in the twentieth century has placed strong emphasis on the total environment, including the actual place one lives; a corresponding school of realistic writers in the early twentieth century and thereafter devoted new attention to the influence of environment on their characters. Thus works like Sherwood Anderson's *Winesburg, Ohio,* Sinclair Lewis' *Main Street,* and James Farrell's *Studs Lonigan* are almost as much stories about places as they are about people.

In reading and writing about fiction, it is important first to dismiss the idea that description is only pictorial filler, that you can skip over it quickly to get on with what will happen next. Ironically, the same reader who would skip description might be aghast at the idea of buying a recording that included only the "great moments" of a symphony, only the melodies without any of the preparation, transitions, or development. Even though description may seem to be a delay in the action, it may very well be the part that helps you understand more fully what happens next and why it happens. When and where are inseparably tied in with who, what, and why.

The setting in drama

A setting in drama can be scenery against which the characters in a play move, or it can represent a more intangible, symbolic force, acting on the characters and reinforcing the thought of the play. The setting of Ibsen's *The Wild Duck,* for example, is conceived in symbolical terms, even though in an actual stage production the setting would demand nothing more than the usual accumulation of household furniture to suggest rooms in a house. Four of the five acts of the play take place in a combination studio-sitting room in the home of Hialmar Ekdal. Constantly referred to throughout the play, however, is an adjoining garret. A producer would have the option of making part of this garret visible to the audience, but that would not be necessary because Ibsen supplies all the necessary details about it in the dialogue.

Inside the garret are boxes to serve as nests for poultry, pigeons, rabbits, and a wounded wild duck that can no longer fly; four or five withered Christmas trees; a cupboard full of picture books; and a large clock that no longer runs. One of the characters says that the books belonged to an old sea captain called "The Flying Dutchman," who used to live in the house.

All of the details and implications of the garret cannot be explored here, but the relationship of each of the main characters to the garret is a means of characterization in the play. Old Man Ekdal has come to think of the garret as a real world where he can hunt and putter about; the young girl Hedvig loves the wondrousness of the books and the otherworldliness of the room; Hialmar Ekdal, the girl's father, is constantly tempted to spend more time in the garret than at his photography in the studio. It is alternately a timeless world of illusion, romance, and escape. Some of the characters in the play prefer the garret to the studio; some never enter it; some stay outside but look in. All in all, Ibsen has translated the theme of reality and illusion that pervades the play into the very setting in which his characters move. The play cannot be fully understood without considering their actions in terms of the scene.

The setting in poetry

At a particularly breathtaking sight, people are often heard to say "Words cannot describe such a scene." Yet poetry among the forms of literary expression often catches the quality of the indescribable; it often succeeds in conveying what the writer has seen and thought and felt. Reading the British poets from Chaucer to Thomas is to gain a knowledge of and familiarity with the English countryside that are second only to seeing it, and some of what they have seen in times past can no longer be seen. Descriptive poetry, however, is not merely scenic. It is often the point of departure for reflection, a typical pattern in Wordsworth's poems. The description cannot be dismissed as ornamentation. It is the source of the thought; it permits the reader to have some sense of the poet's experience. In "Lines Composed a Few Miles above Tintern Abbey," Wordsworth first describes the scene, then comments:

> These beauteous forms,
> Through a long absence, have not been to me
> As is a landscape to a blind man's eye:
> But oft, in lonely rooms, and 'mid the din
> Of towns and cities, I have owed to them,
> In hours of weariness, sensations sweet,
> Felt in the blood, and felt along the heart;

And passing even into my purer mind,
With tranquil restoration:—feelings too
Of unremembered pleasure: such, perhaps,
As have no slight or trivial influence
On that best portion of a good man's life,
His little, nameless, unremembered acts
Of kindness and of love. Nor less, I trust,
To them I may have owed another gift,
Of aspect more sublime; the blessed mood,
In which the burthen of mystery,
In which the heavy and the weary weight
Of all this unintelligible world,
Is lightened: . . .

The setting is the inspiration of the poem.

In other kinds of poems, more dramatic in quality, the description serves as a substitute for a stage. Often, however, the scene needs to be inferred, as in Archibald MacLeish's short poem "The End of the World":

Quite unexpectedly as Vasserot
The armless ambidextrian was lighting
A match between his great and second toe
And Ralph the lion was engaging in biting
The neck of Madame Sossman while the drum
Pointed, and Teeny was about to cough
In waltz-time swinging Jocko by the thumb—
Quite unexpectedly the top blew off:

And there, there overhead, there, there, hung over
Those thousands of white faces, those dazed eyes,
There in the starless dark the poise, the hover,
There with vast wings across the canceled skies,
There in the sudden blackness the black pall
Of nothing, nothing, nothing—nothing at all.

In this poem, the setting itself is a metaphor: the world is a circus, a variation upon those more familiar lines from Shakespeare:

All the world's a stage
And all the men and women merely players.

MacLeish again used the particular implications of the circus metaphor years later when he wrote his drama *J.B.*, based on the story of Job. In that play, all of the action takes place inside a circus tent—a kind of total universe that includes man and God.

In a poem entitled "Come Up from the Fields Father," Whitman describes the reactions of a family to a letter carrying word that the only son has been gravely wounded in the war. The poem begins with the lines:

Come up from the fields father, here's a letter from our Pete,
And come to the front door mother, here's a letter from thy dear son.

After this brief stanza with its sense of foreboding, the narrative shifts to describe the setting, but the reader learns almost immediately that Whitman is providing more than a physical setting—he is describing an emotional setting for the news that will arrive:

> Lo, 'tis autumn,
> Lo, where the trees, deeper green, yellower and redder,
> Cool and sweeten Ohio's villages with leaves fluttering in the moderate wind,
> Where apples ripe in the orchards hang and grapes on the trellis'd vines,
> (Smell you the smell of the grapes on the vines?
> Smell you the buckwheat where the bees were lately buzzing?)
> Above all, lo, the sky so calm, so transparent after the rain, and with wondrous clouds,
> Below too, all calm, all vital and beautiful, and the farm prospers well.

Into this world of calm and sensuous delicacy the harsh news of the outside world comes as a stroke of lightning. Thereafter, we read of trembling and grief and, finally, death. The contrast the poet provides serves to intensify the feeling.

The time of the setting

A setting does not need to be current to seem familiar, nor do we necessarily need special historical knowledge about the past to appreciate a particular scene. Past and present have a remarkable way of fusing in the imagination, and anachronisms do not disturb us much. Writers have characteristically looked to the past to seek out parallels to the modern scene. Getting readers to involve themselves in the past is a device to detach them from immediate concerns, even though they know that the author is commenting on current problems. We are often willingly led by literature to consider what we would otherwise reject if it were treated directly. Giraudoux's *Tiger at the Gates*, for instance, is set in ancient Troy. The war between the Greeks and Trojans serves as a background for the dialogue. The play continues to enjoy revivals, some in modern dress, not because it retells an old story, but because it has become a perennial commentary on the theme of warfare. Yet the play was written by a man who was a member of the French government and, at the time of its production, it had special relevance to the situation in France in 1935. The scene of Giraudoux's play is a strategy that actually helps you gain a perspective on current turmoil. Of course, writers of stories, novels, and poems utilize the same technique. The revival of the past is a constant reminder not only that there is nothing new in human affairs, but also that the past holds infinite wisdom for the future.

Suggestions for writing about setting

To give a few examples of the uses of setting in literary works is only to suggest in this short discussion the kind of thought and emotional impact setting can convey, not to explore the full range of possibilities. You need first to be aware of setting, then to look at details. These offer you an opportunity to interpret. For instance, there is Melville's use of a high brick wall in "Bartleby the Scrivener" to objectify the barrier within Bartleby's mind. And there is Chekhov's use of the barren cherry trees in his play *The Cherry Orchard* to comment, not without irony, on the changing social and political scene in Russia of the early twentieth century. These are all imaginative means of involving you in a concrete experience, tied to a place and time, and valuable clues to the thought of the literature.

Writing about setting should include enough description to make the reader familiar with details of the scene. These need not be quoted; they can be paraphrased and abbreviated. The next and more important step is to say in what way the setting functions in the literary work. Questions of the following kind will provide guides for the reader:

1. In a play, how much detail do the stage directions give in describing the setting? Is the playwright explicit, or can the scene be interpreted in various ways? Can you supply an interpretation? In what way could the play be staged meaningfully?

2. If stage directions are sparse, to what extent can the setting be reconstructed from the dialogue? What are the essential props?

3. In a story or play, to what extent is the setting literally realistic or symbolical? If it is symbolical, in what way does the setting function? What clues does the writer give?

4. In a literary work, in what way does the setting relate significantly to the action? Are the two working together? Do they clash?

5. In what way does a character's response to the setting reveal things about that character?

6. In what way is the setting a reinforcement of the theme of the work?

7. Particularly in poems, is the setting the point of departure for the thought or emotion expressed? Does it serve as contrast? Does the description supply commentary on the author or the speaker in the poem?

8. How is description narrated? Who is telling what is seen and what is happening? What difference does the point of view make in the nature of the description? What methods of description are used? Does the writer depend on precise details, lyrical suggestion, comparisons, and allusions? What is the effect on you?

9. If the scene is remote in time or place, what correspondences can be found in the details of setting and situation that will permit you to draw parallels between the past and the present? How contemporaneous is the setting?

10. To what extent do elements of nature or of the environment become active forces in the literary work, changing the action and determining the fate of characters?

Form and structure

There is no question of the need for structure in the useful arts as opposed to the fine arts. An engineer who builds a bridge has to work with a design first and then with actual structural plans. In like manner, an architect works both with external shape and interior arrangement. Though the function of form and structure in literature is not as readily apparent as it is in construction, it is not less basic to the art. The principles may be less mechanical, but they are no less functional in making a literary work what it is.

Because the external appearance of a literary work is one of the first ways to classify it as fiction, drama, or poetry, form must be discussed in terms of each of the genres, not as a general principle common to all. Further, of the various elements that concern the reader of literature, form is perhaps the most technical. The more knowledge you have of structural matters, the more aware you will be of the way form is operating to shape the literary work and increase its readability. But a brief discussion cannot make professionals out of general readers. So we will consider here those matters of form and structure that are readily observable to the nonprofessional and can aid your understanding and appreciation of literature if you are more conscious of them. Sean O'Faolain, himself an accomplished short story writer, speaks of the short story as showing the "most highly perfected technique in prose-fiction" and emphasizes that we read these stories not alone for what they say but "for the joy we get out of seeing a craftsman doing a delicate job of work." Every reader should have some awareness of how writers do their job.

Form and structure in fiction

Tradition and experiment in fiction

The novel and the short story are perhaps the least formally structured of the various kinds of literary works that are produced; that is, fiction seems to be less bound by set conventional forms than drama or poetry. Drama is linked to the theater and poetry to recitation—at least in times past—but fiction continues to be a form designed mainly to be read silently from the printed page. Characteristically, it is written in prose, and its appearance on the page is fairly uniform. Long works are divided into chapters or sections. In such relatively superficial matters, most novels are alike; but, as far as the form of the novel is concerned, there is no designated length, no set number of parts or divisions. You might note that some experiments in fiction often hinge on trying to make the external appearance of the printed page look different, thus trying for new effects. An early experimental novel like Dos Passos' *The 42nd Parallel* includes newspaper headlines and biographical sketches, so that the novel takes on an effect similar to what we now call multimedia. An experimental work by Willard Bain entitled *Informed Sources* is called a novel, but its typography sometimes resembles verse, sometimes cartoonlike designs, often with symbols and single letters splashed on the page instead of words. Attempts such as these are designed to break down the deadening effects of habit in readers so that their customary assumptions about fiction are challenged. Readers have the option of trying to come to grips with a new approach, figuring out what serious purpose it may have, or dismissing it as mere foolishness. Experiments always meet with detractors because the familiar is pleasant and comforting. Works that alter patterns are disturbing.

Internal structure of fiction

Basic to understanding structure in fiction is coming to a realization that it can be thought about in several ways. The concept of structure does not have to be limited to the most apparent one of putting parts together in an orderly way. That is one concept, but it is essentially a static notion to think of a literary work as if it were a construction. Literary structure needs to be thought of in active terms, not so much as the assemblage of parts according to a blueprint, but as an ongoing process in which characters interact and ideas, images, and themes recur and connect. A novel can be thought of as a developing form, assuming a shape as the writer writes.

Novels do not have set forms that can be labeled and followed exactly. The terms that are used refer to specific techniques or general approaches. Thus, an epistolary novel is one like Samuel Richardson's *Pamela* that uses the letter as its chief device of revealing the characters and their story. A picaresque novel is one like Fielding's *Tom Jones* that uses a series of rambling episodes as a means of taking its rogue hero through adventures that comment on everyday life. But these are essentially structural patterns in very broad terms; they can assume many different forms in the hands of different writers. For purposes of writing about form in fiction, four structural features are worthy of attention: time structure, space structure, character patterns, and motifs.

TIME STRUCTURE Every novelist and short story writer has to come to terms with chronology. Given a set of circumstances that represent the story, where do writers begin? If they begin at the culmination of events, then they transfer the attention of the reader from a concern with what will happen to a concern with how it happened and why it happened. Time structure obviously affects the dramatic impact of the narration. If you know the outcome in advance, your attention is drawn to the ironies of circumstance, because at any point in the story it is possible for you to know through the narrator what characters themselves cannot know about their future. Rearrangement of time by the author, therefore, can cause you to be emotionally concerned about the characters in a way that would not otherwise be possible in a straight chronological sequence.

In addition to the actual chronology of events, there is also the matter of timing in a story, which is in part structural and in part stylistic. It concerns the time at which the narrator chooses to reveal details about the characters, particularly about their past. It is one technique to begin a story at the beginning and move to the end. It is another to start at a given point and then with calculation reveal only what needs to be known at any particular time. In F. Scott Fitzgerald's "Babylon Revisited," we are first told that Charles Wales has returned to Paris, where he once spent a wild two years with his wife Helen. Then we learn that he is returning to visit his daughter Honoria, who is living under the legal guardianship of his sister-in-law Marion. These are all current circumstances in the story. Details of the past begin to unfold. We learn that Helen, his wife, is dead and only later in the story that she died of a heart attack and still later that Charles had locked Helen out of the house during a snowstorm. Each of these details moves the story back in time and helps to explain the conflict between him and Marion and the reason she will probably not release Honoria again to her father. This structuring of the action clearly becomes a matter of interest in itself and affects the entire pace and emphasis of the story.

SPACE STRUCTURE　Space structure refers simply to the geographic bounds writers limit themselves to. The choice of location is usually closely tied to the time element, and the two affect the scope of the story. If a story has only one location and a brief time span, then the writer usually treats only a fairly limited set of circumstances. Narrative devices like the flashback, the interior monologue, the dream, or the vision allow writers to go beyond the immediate geographic dimensions of the story they are telling.

One of the remarkable things about James Joyce's *Ulysses* is that it manages to compress the epic dimensions of Homer's *Odyssey*, the model for the characters and their relationships, into a twenty-four-hour period in Dublin. In linear sequence, from the time of Odysseus' departure from home to his return, Homer's epic ranges to distant places over a period of twenty years. Joyce's reduced space and time structure has altered the effect of the original completely and placed demands on the author to achieve the scope and complexity that he does by a variety of narrative techniques. What is most obvious is that Joyce's novel is no longer a tale of adventure as Homer's epic is; *Ulysses* is a psychological exploration.

Writing about time and space structure mainly involves two things: (1) deciphering and describing it and (2) discussing the effects gained by the choices the author has made. Fitzgerald's "Babylon Revisited," already discussed briefly above, treats two Parises: Paris, the Babylonlike city of young Charles Wales's two-year binge, and the Paris of the immediate present of the story, seemingly tame, empty, and provincial. This contrast simply reflects the way the new Charles sees things and thus becomes a means also of revealing changes that have taken place in him. We see that the elements of literature are never independent of one another, but that the *who, what, where, when, how,* and *why* combine to create the organic structure of the literary work.

CHARACTER PATTERNS　Thinking of characters in terms of structure will often reveal that they fall into groupings that reinforce the theme of the story. The division may be as simple as that between characters who are good and those who are evil, particularly in stories like Hawthorne's, which are strongly allegorical. In other instances, the interrelationships may be more involved. To illustrate again from "Babylon Revisited," there are six main characters in Fitzgerald's story. The protagonist is Charles Wales, eager to gain possession of his daughter Honoria, who in turn is anxious to live with her father. They represent one group. Charles's attempt to establish this relationship permanently is the object of the action. Marion, the sister-in-law, is Charles's antagonist; she resists his effort to regain Honoria. Although her husband Lincoln is not wholly unsympathetic toward Charles, he stands by his wife and therefore represents with her a second group of characters who will determine the future of the first group. The remaining two characters are "sudden ghosts out of the past"—Duncan Schaeffer and Lorraine Quarrles. They are carryovers from Charles's earlier experience in Paris. When they intrude into the household of Marion and Lincoln, all six characters for the first time are brought face to face with one another. It is a decisive scene in the story, and the result is that

Charles's hopes to have Honoria are frustrated. The characters are forced into two groups of three. Charles is associated with Duncan and Lorraine, whether he chooses to be or not; under the circumstances, Honoria is forced to remain with her aunt and uncle. Father and daughter are together only for the duration of the story.

In a similar kind of analysis, examination of character patterns in other works can sometimes provide a means for writing about the story that might not otherwise be possible if the characters were viewed only one at a time.

MOTIFS   Motifs are an expressive means of repeating the same idea a number of times throughout the story, creating a kind of repetitive form. Motifs are structural in the sense that they connect parts of the story by taking us back to an earlier scene or reminding us of a constant feature about a character that remains unchanged. "Babylon Revisited" again serves as an apt illustration, indicating, of course, that a single short story depends on any number of structural features.

The story opens in the Ritz bar in Paris. Charles Wales has a drink. When the barman asks him if he wants another, he refuses, saying that he is "going slow these days"—a reminder of the days when he was "going pretty strong." Charles later explains that he has vowed to have only one drink every afternoon. In the story, his daily whiskey becomes a motif, indicating Charles's determination not to fall back into old excesses. At the end of the story, when Charles is again in the Ritz bar after he has learned that he will not be able to regain the custody of his daughter, the narrator might have indicated a change in Charles by having him take a second drink. But the motif is not broken. As the story closes, Charles once more shakes his head as the barman looks questioningly at his empty glass. It is a final touch in the story that confirms our sympathies for Charles.

There is nothing particularly subtle about Fitzgerald's use of this motif. Each time it occurs, we are fully aware that it is a test of character that Charles has set for himself and must pass. Yet the motif also adds suspense and connective purpose to the story as a whole. Recurring themes, actions, and symbols are therefore important clues both to the meaning of the story and to its organic unity.

Form and structure in drama

Freedom and convention in dramatic structure   The matter of dramatic structure is so closely linked to the history of the stage and the playhouse that the one can hardly be explained except in terms of the other. Further, the active presence of the audience viewing live performances has an additional effect on the structure of the play. Act divisions which provide a rest for the performers, an intermission for the audience, and an opportunity to reset the stage are the formal solutions to the time and space problems of drama. Even long movies now provide an intermission for the audience, although the break seems to have affected the structure of movies very little as yet; it is merely an interruption of the running of the film at an appropriate half-way point—a matter of stopping the projector rather than a formal division of the action into two parts.

In plays, however, act and scene divisions have very specific effects on the structure of a play because playwrights characteristically seem concerned with drawing the audience back into the theater after each break. Thus, two-, three-, four-, and five-act plays tend to break down into discrete and self-contained parts. The effect is different from that of a one-act play with multiple scenes which have the continuousness of a movie. The kind of theater for which an author writes also frequently determines the structure of a play.

Dramatic structure and the theater

Greek tragedies, which were produced in open-air amphitheaters with little scenery, belong to the tradition of continuous-action plays. The setting did not change. The scene divisions used in printed versions of the plays today marked the coming or going of one of the two or three actors who were available to play a larger number of roles. And scene divisions were also influenced by the role of the chorus, a conventional feature of the theater of that day. Even though Greek plays are not divided into acts, many of them fall into five formal divisions: prologos, parados, epeisodion, stasimon, and exodos. These are determined to a large extent by the entrance, function, and exit of the chorus. Playwrights therefore observed fairly rigid dramatic conventions in a theater that might have been used far more flexibly, as indeed it was on the Elizabethan stage.

The open-air Elizabethan theater, epitomized by the Globe Playhouse, provided at least three main acting areas. The projected platform, the rear stage with a curtain, and the upper stage, which was also provided with a curtain, were all adaptable to different purposes. The characters of the play could act as if they moved from outside to inside, or from place to place, by shifting their location on the stage or by describing the scene in the poetry of their lines. Properties and machinery were used to suggest localities, but the theater was not primarily devoted, as later theaters were, to creating an illusion of reality. The scenes could shift rapidly, and an entire play might be produced in two and one-half or three hours, broken only by convenient musical intermissions for the benefit of the actors and the audience.

Thus, to produce Shakespeare's plays today with the same effectiveness as they were in the Elizabethan theaters demands an equally adaptable stage or a vehicle as flexible as film. Actually, the act and scene divisions in texts of Shakespeare's plays are additions of early editors. The structure of these plays was influenced by the stage itself, not by arbitrary conventions, as in Greek times.

Neoclassical drama of the seventeenth century in France, however, was bound strictly by rules. Playwrights like Corneille and Racine wrote plays in an effort to observe what critics of that time had established as the dramatic unities. The unities limited a play to a single line of action in one place within a twenty-four-hour period. These principles were inferred from Aristotle's *Poetics*, based on observations of plays being produced in Athens in the fifth century B.C., but presumably no Greek dramatist ever considered himself as formally bound to the unwritten unities as the dramatists of the distant future were in their attempts to imitate them. Greek dramatists observed conventions that the theater demanded; they did not have Aristotle as their mentor. Ironically, one of the purest examples of Greek tragedy in the neoclassical sense is John Milton's *Samson Agonistes* (1671), declared by Milton not to have been written for the stage at all.

Despite their differences, Greek and Roman plays, Elizabethan plays, and neo-classical plays are all strongly theatrical; that is, they do not deny the fact of the theater itself, that action takes place on a stage. They do not pretend to present an illusion of life itself. The proscenium-arch theater from 1660 on popularized the concept of illusionism. Elaborate scenery and fixed properties were designed to disguise the stage and transform it into the world of the play. Thus, no longer would it have been possible for a Shakespeare of that day to write the forty-two scenes that make up *Antony and Cleopatra;* Shakespeare's plays themselves were actually cut and adapted to be performed on a far less flexible stage. Drama settled into a conventional act structure, which was to dominate dramatic production until new concepts of staging in the twentieth century once again gave to dramatists a com-plete freedom of form.

What this brief survey of the influence of the stage and convention on dramatic structure suggests is that uniform standards of evaluation about form cannot be applied to all plays. One reader may prefer the economical structure of a Greek play; another, the range of an Elizabethan drama; another, the disciplined unity of a neoclassical drama; and still another, the loose, fragmentary quality of many con-temporary plays. But without reference to stage history, the final test of the form of a play, at least from the viewpoint of a reader, is its suitability to the dramatist's theme and purpose. Dramatists in this century who have attempted to say new things in new ways, and, in particular, have attempted to depict inner actions as well as outer actions have had to seek new structures. Thus, Arthur Miller explains that certain scenes in *Death of a Salesman* are not flashbacks in time but are the past flowing into the present through the mind of Willy Loman. The structure of the play accommodates scenes of this kind because, as Miller describes it, the stage can be adapted either to the world of the moment or to the world of reverie. The fact remains, however, that a drama is not as flexible a form as the novel for purposes of psychological probing. Even though drama has found ways of escaping the immedi-ate stage scene, the form still demands that a character's inner experiences be objectified. Thus in *Death of a Salesman*, Ben, who occupies Willy's thoughts, actually appears on the stage. This is memory objectified. It works as a device in this particular play, but having to show thought places far greater demands on the playwright than telling about it does on the writer of fiction.

Internal structure of drama

Basically, the setting of a play and its time divisions determine the external form of a play. Its internal structure, like fiction, depends on motifs of action, characters, themes, and symbols which run throughout the play as a whole and bridge what may be its leaps in time and place.

Chekhov's plays, for example, depend heavily on internal structure. Externally, his longer plays, all written in four acts, show the strong influence of Greek drama. They have a compactness that is reinforced by a limited setting, a limited span of time, and limited action. Typically, the main action occurs offstage; the onstage action concerns the indirect effects of those offstage occurrences on the characters. Thus, in *The Cherry Orchard*, the important action is the sale of the orchard. It is the major concern of the characters throughout the play, but the auction itself finally takes place between Acts II and III. At the end of Act III, when Lopahin announces that he has purchased the orchard, the play reaches its climax. The final act reflects not only the changes that will take place in the estate but those that will occur in the lives of these people.

Throughout Chekhov's play, the cherry orchard itself is the pervading symbol, and the characters may be classified by their attitudes toward it. They belong either to the old order of Russian society which would seek to preserve the beauty of the trees or to the new order which would chop them down to make the land useful for subdividing and building. Thus, the characters fall into loose patterns in relation to the main symbol of the play.

The recurring motifs—the ominous sound of a breaking harp string, Madame Ranevsky's carelessness with money, the weeping, and mournful music—are important structural features of a play of this nature, because the dialogue is often marked by incoherence. Characters seem primarily dedicated to themselves, thinking their own thoughts, and speaking little monologues. Not much communication takes place in a Chekhov play in the sense of one character talking and responding to another; the dialogue does not build on an idea, as a Shaw play does, for example. Chekhov's dialogue shapes an impression, not an argument, and the motifs are in part responsible for creating that illusive, mysterious quality that often pervades his plays.

Form and structure in poetry

The range of poetic structure

Just as the novel seems better suited than the drama for subjects of broad scope and those of psychological depth, so the poem among the three genres seems best suited for subjects of small dimension and intimate feeling. Even though long poems on epic themes have been written, these tend to be versified dramas and narratives and vary considerably in effect from the lyric poem. Long poems are developed freely, in most instances limited only by a particular metric line but not by the kinds of stanza forms lyric poets follow or impose upon themselves. The obvious exceptions to this statement are Dante's *Divine Comedy*, written in an interlocking rhyme pattern (*aba, bcb, cdc*) called terza rima, and Spenser's *The Faerie Queene*, written entirely in nine-line stanzas with a set rhyme scheme.

Set forms of poetry

As soon as a poet chooses to write in a set form, the form itself exercises a control over the content, not only limiting its range but shaping it as well. The best example is the sonnet, a fourteen-line form with a set line length and rhyme scheme. The fourteen lines of a sonnet limit the expression to a narrow range. "Narrow" in this instance does not mean that sonnets are less profound or less complex or that they have fewer implications than other poems, but merely that they are less expansive. Whatever thought and feeling the poet has must be compressed into that space. Sonnet writing is a severe discipline.

Within the bounds of the sonnet, two rhyme patterns have become traditional: Shakespearean and Petrarchan. The first divides the fourteen lines into three groups of four lines and one of two lines: *abab cdcd efef gg*. The Italian form divides the fourteen lines into one group of eight lines and one group of six lines: *abbaabba cdcdcd*, although the rhyme schemes of both the octave and sestet vary greatly. The effect of these divisions is that the logic of the poem is affected by the form itself. In the Shakespearean sonnet, the final couplet is always a break from the previous twelve lines, and the twelve lines may break down into three very precise logical units, as they do in Shakespeare's Sonnet 30:

> When to the sessions of sweet silent thought
> I summon up remembrance of things past,
> I sigh the lack of many a thing I sought
> And with old woes new wail my dear time's waste.
> Then can I drown an eye (unus'd to flow)
> For precious friends hid in death's dateless night,
> And weep afresh love's long since cancell'd woe,
> And moan th' expense of many a vanish'd sight.
> Then can I grieve at grievances foregone,
> And heavily from woe to woe tell o'er
> The sad account of fore-bemoaned moan,
> Which I new pay as if not paid before.
>   But if the while I think on thee, dear friend,
>   All losses are restor'd and sorrows end.

In this poem, the parts are introduced by the key connective words "When . . . Then . . . Then . . . But." These four words also shape the logic. The poem consists of three variations on a single theme with a final conclusion.

The Italian form achieves a different effect, illustrated by Wordsworth's sonnet to John Milton, given the title "London, 1802":

> Milton! thou shouldst be living at this hour:
> England hath need of thee: she is a fen
> Of stagnant waters: altar, sword, and pen,
> Fireside, the heroic wealth of hall and bower,
> Have forfeited their ancient English dower
> Of inward happiness. We are selfish men;
> Oh! raise us up, return to us again;
> And give us manners, virtue, freedom, power.
> Thy soul was like a Star, and dwelt apart;
> Thou hadst a voice whose sound was like the sea:
> Pure as the naked heavens, majestic, free,
> So didst thou travel on life's common way,
> In cheerful godliness; and yet thy heart
> The lowliest duties on herself did lay.

After a brief opening invocation, the poem describes conditions in England that Wordsworth deplores. A break comes after line 8. The final six lines, then, give reasons why a man of Milton's character and spirit might again be able to help. The thought is conveniently accommodated to the form.

Perhaps in none of the other genres does the form influence the reader as forcefully as it does in the poem. The medium has its own effect quite apart from the content—or if not "quite apart" from the content, then in conjunction with it. But the form has its own message. The sonnet speaks preciseness, logicality, and compactness. The closed couplet of two rhyming lines speaks pithiness and certainty. The limerick speaks bounciness and lightheartedness. The poet's feeling for form undoubtedly influences a choice in the first place, with the result that content and form fuse in such a way that the "message" of the form reinforces the thought of the poem.

The effect of the medium

Form has the capacity to free expression, not inhibit it. The imagination must find ways to circumvent the restraints of form. Form encourages invention. Poetic creation is the act of making concrete the images and sensations of the imagination. It is an act of ordering and channeling thoughts and feelings.

The paradox of form

In an interview, Edward Villella, a distinguished ballet dancer, once referred to this paradoxical effect of form and discipline. He spoke of the highly structured nature of ballet, the way in which each step is prescribed, and the disciplined technique necessary to perform the movements. Yet he added that when he was most in control of his technique, he had the greatest experience of absolute freedom, as if he were floating on air. You might observe that an audience also has the same liberating reaction when artists are in full control. If artists have to struggle or force themselves, then the audience becomes conscious of the form and technique itself, not the total experience and expression. In a similar way, form aids the poet. A parachute in the open sky is not a burden. It is the only safe way down.

Free verse forms do not imply an absence of form, only a greater flexibility and a greater dependence on internal structural features. One of these forms, blank verse, which is unrhymed lines of iambic pentameter, must be considered one of the more flexible forms a poet can use. It is adaptable to almost any subject of any scope. Milton wrote his vast epics *Paradise Lost* and *Paradise Regained* in blank verse; Robert Frost wrote an intimate poem, "Mending Wall," in the same meter.

Free forms: rhetorical structure

Free verse as a form abandons rhyme schemes, stanzaic patterns, and the regular line lengths of set forms, but it cannot escape rhythmic design, controlling images, repetitions, and a variety of rhetorical strategies that bind the parts together. Walt Whitman, who sought freedom from traditional forms and expressed themes of freedom in his poetry, was yet highly susceptible to structural patterns. His short poem "I Hear America Singing" illustrates his strong tendencies toward repetition, parallel structure, rhythmic balance, contrast, and the sustained image:

> I hear America singing, the varied carols I hear,
> Those of mechanics, each one singing his as it should be blithe and strong,
> The carpenter singing his as he measures his plank or beam,
> The mason singing his as he makes ready for work, or leaves off work,
> The boatman singing what belongs to him in his boat, the deckhand singing
>   on the steamboat deck,
> The shoemaker singing as he sits on his bench, the hatter singing as he stands,
> The wood-cutter's song, the ploughboy's on his way in the morning, or at
>   noon intermission or at sundown,
> The delicious singing of the mother, or of the young wife at work, or of the
>   girl sewing or washing,
> Each singing what belongs to him or her and to none else,
> The day what belongs to the day—at night the party of young fellows, robust,
>   friendly,
> Singing with open mouths their strong melodious songs.

In its irregularities, Whitman's poem seeks its own structures. Free verse represents only a different concept of what form can be.

Free verse often sets up its own rhythmic patterns based on a principle of cadences rather than regular accents. Lines of free verse might be thought to fall into arcs rather than feet, suggesting the effect of a musical phrase. Two lines of Whitman's "Out of the Cradle Endlessly Rocking" show the wavelike surging and ebbing of his verse:

> From your memories sad brother,
>
> from the fitful risings and fallings I heard;
>
> From under that yellow half-moon late-risen and swollen as if with tears.

Each of the arcs has from two to four major stresses; these key words are pulses, but they do not come at regular intervals. They are determined by the sense of the line and the rhetorical devices such as repetition and parallelism that the poet chooses to use. The lines may vary in length; stanzas are flexible in form like those of the ode. Free verse accommodates itself to natural speech patterns, to the logic of the writer's thoughts, and to his desire to evolve the shape of his own poem. It need not be expansive, as it often is in poems by Whitman and D. H. Lawrence. It can also convey concise, tight thoughts, as it does in poems by Wallace Stevens, William Carlos Williams, and E. E. Cummings.

A strong precedent for free verse in English comes from Hebrew poetry, particularly as it is translated in the King James version of the Bible. Passages from Job, Isaiah, Song of Solomon, and particularly the Psalms illustrate the dependence of this verse on principles of symmetry:

I am come into my garden, my sister, my spouse:
I have gathered my myrrh with my spice;
I have eaten my honeycomb with my honey;
I have drunk my wine with my milk:
Eat, O friends; drink, yea drink abundantly, O beloved.

Song of Solomon, 5:1

The principles of free verse are also inherent in Old English poetry. The lines are irregular in length, with stresses falling on the words demanded by the sense. Each line consists of two halves divided by a well-defined caesura, with two stresses in each half and an unspecified number of unstressed syllables. The two parts are joined by the alliteration of two or three of the stressed syllables:

Oft Scýld Scéfing   scéaþena þréatum,
mónegum mǽgþum   méodo-sètla oftéah

Beowulf

Despite these requirements, the lines are flexible and clearly rhythmical in the spirit of free verse.

One other variety of the free metrical line is called sprung rhythm, invented by Gerard Manley Hopkins. Its most marked feature is the juxtaposition of stressed syllables without intervening unstressed ones. It is therefore sometimes called an accent meter. A line of sprung rhythm is measured by the number of strong accents, not the number of feet or syllables. Like Old English verse, with which it shares common principles, sprung rhythm also depends heavily on alliteration and other sound effects:

I caught this morning morning's minion, kingdom of daylight's dauphin,
dapple-dawn-drawn Falcon, in his riding

Gerard Manley Hopkins, "The Windhover"

Unlike other free verse poets, Hopkins frequently wrote in traditional stanza forms and used rhyme.

Since the nineteenth century, of course, free verse forms have become more and more common, but the popularity of free verse does not deny the importance of structure. Contemporary poetry simply confirms that poets, with their typical inventiveness, constantly find new ways to shape poems. After all, the imaginative fusion of words into form is the quality that continues to give poetry its uniqueness among the various modes of literary expression.

Suggestions for writing about form

Writing about form depends, first, on a perception of what form is doing in a particular literary work. It further requires a special way of looking in order to see what the structural basis of a composition is. One significant contribution of the cubist painters to our way of looking at things was their idea that everything is a composite of shapes and designs. Their technique demonstrated this concept; their paintings emerged as combinations of triangles, rectangles, and circles. This technique helped others to see what the cubists themselves perceived with a keener eye.

Writing about structure must attempt also to demonstrate what you intuit about form. But vague generalizations are of no help. The demonstration must finally be reduced to hard facts—counting the parts, determining why the divisions are made as they are, seeking out the less obvious connectives, recognizing patterns, determining the way themes and motifs shape the whole, and finally verbalizing what the total effects are.

Questions like the following suggest possible leads for discussion of matters of form:

1. What is the total effect of the work's structure? Does it seem to be a continuum? Is it a combination of fragments? Does the whole fall into an orderly sequence of parts?

2. What is the significance of the parts? At what point is a division made? Why? What effect would be altered if the division had not occurred?

3. Besides identifying the main parts of a work, what patterns emerge either through characters, symbols, motifs, or ideas? Can characters be grouped? Do the groupings shed light on the relationships between characters? Is there any character who does not seem to fit any group. If so, what does that signify?

4. What are the time arrangement and space dimensions of the work? If the author severely limits these, do they work to advantage? What effect is gained?

5. In what way is time treated? Is there a straight chronological scheme? A reversal? What is the purpose of any alteration of the time scheme? What effects would be lost if the time and space plan were changed?

6. What is the particular suitability of the form to the themes and ideas of the work itself? How does the form support the content?

7. Does the choice of form in any way run contrary to the content of the work, so that the form is ironic or satiric? Are all subjects appropriate to every form? Do jingles express profundities? Can an inappropriate form for a particular subject be a way to mock it?

8. In what way can the form of the work as a whole be characterized? What is the "message of the medium"?

9. In what way can the form be the most important part of the work? Why are words arranged as they are (as in a Cummings poem)?

10. In what way is the language itself acting as a structural feature, particularly in a poem? What are the grammatical patterns? The rhetorical patterns? The metric patterns? The rhyme scheme? How are they working together?

Language, symbol, and imagery

A writer's passion for language is often a prime incentive for writing. Words crystallize thoughts, realize emotions, and bring images of the mind to the life of literature. The vitality, the imaginativeness, the beauty of this creation depend on words.

In one sense, the concerns of imaginative writers are not far different from those of any other writers, whether amateur or professional. They need to have adequate stocks of words to begin with. They have to be concerned with their meanings, both the accuracy of their literal use and their extended implications. They have to be concerned with the fact that language grows out of a variety of contexts that relate to age, occupation, education, ethnic background, social status, and a host of other factors, and that words derive associations from all of these sources. They have to be concerned with the interaction of words in any particular verbal context—what I. A. Richards calls the "interinanimation of words"—because in context the words gain a tone and meaning all their own. Words are the writer's paints, and every writer must show some capacity to use their coloration, texture, intensity, and harmony to produce an identifiable style.

Ultimately, however, there is always the distinction between the dabbler and the artist. The concerns of the literary artist characteristically do go beyond those of the ordinary writer because of the artist's desire to tap the powers of language to communicate an imaginative vision and to search for ways to push the limits of language outward in order to express the inexpressible. Because imaginative literature often accomplishes these ends, we look to it as the highest expression of man's capacity with language.

Metaphorical language

Metaphorical or figurative language is perhaps the writer's most important single source of imaginative power. It almost always represents the writer's invasion of an alien verbal context to bring back a word or phrase or image to serve in a different setting. Metaphorical language defies ordinary associations; it makes fresh ones by seeking out likenesses in dissimilar areas of experience.

Metaphor is possible only because our common experiences lead us to use words in familiar patterns. Words cluster around topics; certain words fit together. Thus, phrases like these are totally familiar and factual:

- He was born.
- He served in the air force during the war.
- He was a turret gunner on a plane.
- He was killed during an attack on the enemy.

Randall Jarrell's short poem "The Death of the Ball Turret Gunner," however, shows what a complete transformation can take place when these prosaic phrases are translated into metaphorical language:

> From my mother's sleep I fell into the State,
> And I hunched in its belly till my wet fur froze.
> Six miles from earth, loosed from its dream of life,
> I woke to black flak and the nightmare fighters.
> When I died they washed me out of the turret with a hose.

What Jarrell has added is a whole new set of associations that go beyond the simple facts of being born, fighting, and dying; these additions can be suggested by phrases such as these:

> Being in the womb is like sleeping.
> The rapid time between birth and army service is like a fall.
> The plane is the State.
> The ball turret is the plane's belly.
> Being in the turret is like being in the womb.
> In his furry suit, he is like an animal.
> Life on earth is living in a dream.
> Flying high is like being released from something.
> The attack is a nightmare.
> Dying is an awakening.
> His bodily remains are like debris.

These paraphrases of the metaphors are not an interpretation of the poem, but they do reveal what areas of experience the poet has explored to bring imaginativeness and feeling to the basic experience and to make a shocking commentary on the life and death of a young man. Further, only metaphorical language makes possible the compression that the poem achieves and the intensity that grows out of that telescoping of language. The metaphors add the feeling; the metaphors invite the extensions of meaning. They are the source of the poetry.

The one sustained metaphor of Randall Jarrell's short poem is that of sleeping and waking. Living is sleeping; dying is waking. In fact, the *I* of the poem is awake, telling his experience; only he is dead. The poem therefore turns upon a paradox. We ordinarily think of living as waking; death is like sleep, a comparison invited by the appearance of the body in sleep and in death. The effective metaphor, however, does not always depend on the obvious likeness but frequently on the unexpected similarity, even though the poet might find only one possible link between two verbal contexts. In "A Valediction: Forbidding Mourning," John Donne compares separated lovers to the legs of a compass hinged together at the top. In a sustained metaphor, he relates the movements of the compass to the movements and emotions of the lovers. It is the kind of ingenious conceit that prompted Dr. Johnson to condemn the Metaphysical poets of the seventeenth century when he said that they yoked "the most heterogeneous ideas . . . by violence together."

The effect of a metaphor, of course, does not depend on its ingeniousness but mainly on its concreteness and meaningfulness. As a comparison, the purpose of metaphor is to clarify, not to cloud the thought. If it draws on a subject or experience that is totally unfamiliar to most readers, it cannot succeed in illuminating the thought. If it draws on that which is too familiar, it also fails because we do not respond to the overused metaphor. Nor do we ordinarily recognize the dead metaphors that are the common stock of our daily speech—"the hand of a clock," "the foot of a mountain," "to be keyed up," or "a tubby man." A reexamination of any page of our own writing will reveal the extent to which metaphor is a natural way of thinking. The artist goes further to depend on it as a major means of conveying perceptions.

Symbolic language

Like metaphor, symbol-making is a natural process. It is a way of simplifying the complexities of thought and experience by hitting on one thing as representative of many. The symbol may be used as a reminder, a signal, a call to action. It is a means by which people seek to express the unity of their perceptions and experiences. It is a hook to hang on to.

In 1969, the "closed fist" became the symbol of a whole movement of defiance and protest among militant blacks. It was a symbol that could be dramatized, pictured, and spoken. Even though the symbol had special implications for that particular movement, it was basically a borrowing of a universal symbol. We have always recognized the clenched fist as a symbol of threat and resistance, just as we tend to recognize doves as symbols of peace, the crown as a symbol of authority, and water as a symbol of purification. Symbols such as these which have become traditional are called universal symbols. Literature draws heavily on them, but it also creates occasional symbols, like the duck in Ibsen's *The Wild Duck*, whose significance is apparent only from the context of the work itself.

Language that employs symbols is clearly symbolical, but language that is spoken by a symbolic figure, whether or not it includes specific symbols, also becomes symbolical, by implication; that is, we seek general significance beyond the particular context of the words. The thought is raised to a symbolic level. Jesus' phrase "Turn the other cheek," although it might be interpreted literally, represents, more importantly, a symbolic act expressive of passive resistance. Thus, the use of the phrase is ordinarily symbolical in implication.

In a similar way, literary characters who are drawn larger than life or who are clearly set forth as symbolic figures may often speak lines that hold significance beyond their simplest level of meaning. We sense this quality in lines like the Ancient Mariner's cry of despair when his boat is becalmed on the sea:

> Water, water, everywhere
> Nor any drop to drink.

The context does not demand a symbolical reading, but invites it.

A symbol is also capable of compressing the emotional impact of an overwhelming experience into a brief descriptive passage. In Book IX of *Paradise Lost*, after Eve tells Adam that she has eaten of the forbidden fruit—the act that first marks man's fall from divine grace—Milton expresses Adam's stunned sensation by two simple lines:

> From his slack hand the Garland wreath'd for Eve
> Down dropp'd, and all the faded Roses shed.

Symbolic language of this kind has a vividness and force far beyond any kind of ordinary description.

Imagery

Images are the mental impressions created by words in such a way that we can perceive sensations without actually experiencing them. Metaphor and symbol are, of course, common sources of imagery, but other uses of words can evoke the same kind of image-making. Imagery adds sensuousness to language. The opening quatrain of an Emily Dickinson poem is tense with sensations:

> I heard a Fly buzz—when I died—
> The Stillness in the Room
> Was like the Stillness in the Air—
> Between the Heaves of Storm—

This is not a simple contrast of sound and stillness, because worked within the images of the sound of the fly and the stillness of the room are also images of the stillness of air and the sounds of the storm like the troubled breathing of a person.

A passage from James Joyce's "Araby" also represents a complex interweaving of sense images of all varieties to create a vivid description of a winter's evening:

> When the short days of winter came dusk fell before we had well eaten our dinners. When we met in the street the houses had grown sombre. The space of sky above us was the colour of ever-changing violet and towards it the lamps of the street lifted their feeble lanterns. The cold air stung us and we played till our bodies glowed. Our shouts echoed in the silent street. The career of our play brought us through the dark muddy lanes behind the houses where we ran the gauntlet of the rough tribes from the cottages, to the back doors of the dark dripping gardens where odours arose from the ashpits, to the dark odorous stables where a coachman smoothed and combed the horse or shook music from the buckled harness.

We need only reflect on those details that appeal to sight, touch, hearing, and smell to perceive the rich, sensuous quality of this prose.

Besides the animated effect that imagery gives to poetry and prose, it also provides a basis for analysis. Imagery serves as an index to the author's conception of his work. In fact, if it is used with consistency, it may even mirror the writer's interests, experiences, and temperament. Some writers draw constantly on images of nature or love or domestic images or religious images; in a particular work, images may be prevailingly violent or beautiful or gloomy; images may express sadness or buoyancy or sterility. It is often possible to trace threads of imagery running throughout a work—a color scheme, a concern for sounds, an interest in animals, a sexual motif—patterns of images emerging from the writing as a means of setting the tone, of commenting on a character's action, or indicating the author's attitude toward the material. The choice of imagery may be a clue to where the author's sympathies lie.

Not all references to color, sound, animal life, and sex are, of course, necessarily image-making. These can be discussed in quite abstract, unemotional, encyclopedic terms. But the simplest alteration can change the effect. Even a simple proverb can be expressed by fact or fancy. One proverb explains:

> A wise man will hear, and will increase learning; and a man of understanding shall attain unto wise counsels.

Another proverb expresses its meaning by images:

A whip for the horse, a bridle for the ass, and a rod for the fool's back.

The difference between the two is that the words in the second proverb move the imagination to perceive first, then to interpret; in the first, you need only interpret. Imagery is the link between the imagination of the writer and the imagination of the reader.

Stylized language

In analyzing language in literature, you should keep in mind that even the most realistic work does not record speech as we ordinarily use it. The tone may seem colloquial and natural, but the dialogue we read is a conventionalized speech for literary purposes. It is highly compressed; many of the filler words are omitted. Missing also are the bland phrases that have meaning only because we speak them with a particular intonation, and absent too are the repetition and stammering that are characteristic of speech. Stylization is a way of altering conventional speech to suit the author's purpose. For example, the language of poetry is usually a form of stylization. On the other hand, the dialogue of some plays departs so little from customary patterns of speech that we take no notice of it. It creates an illusion of conversation.

Stylization is relative and dependent to a great extent on conventions that prevail at any one particular time. Elements of an Elizabethan play that may seem highly stylized to us in the twentieth century may have seemed far less so to a sixteenth-century audience accustomed to the diction of the plays and the prevalence of verse drama at that time. In a similar way, the diction and arrangement of words of pre-twentieth-century poetry often seem highly stylized to modern ears accustomed to the words and rhythms of standard colloquial speech in the drama and poetry of today. Reading experience helps to distinguish what is customary for any particular age and what is a departure from the ordinary for special effects.

When T. S. Eliot wrote *Murder in the Cathedral* for the Canterbury Festival of 1935, he chose verse as an appropriate vehicle for the twelfth-century story of Thomas Becket. The chorus, itself a stylized device of drama, speaks in this manner:

> Here is no continuing city, here is no abiding stay.
> Ill the wind, ill the time, uncertain the profit, certain the danger.
> O late late late, late is the time, late too late, and rotten the year;
> Evil the wind, and bitter the sea, and grey the sky, grey, grey, grey.

And the Archbishop achieves high drama even in ordering the door of the cathedral to be opened:

> Unbar the doors! throw open the doors!
> I will not have the house of prayer, the church of Christ,
> The sanctuary, turned into a fortress.
> The Church shall protect her own, in her own way, not
> As oak and stone; stone and oak decay,

Give no stay, but the Church shall endure.
The church shall be open, even to our enemies. Open the door!

In an essay entitled "Poetry and Drama," T. S. Eliot explains that he intended this style to be "neutral" in terms of time. It is neither twelfth-century nor modern; neither Shakespearean nor nineteenth-century. In brief, we can now look on it as highly stylized speech that is appropriate to the tense dramatic action, the elevated nature of the characters, and a subject drawn from the past.

Stylization may, of course, take other forms. In a German play dating from 1919, Ernst Toller's *Man and the Masses,* the characters speak in a telegraphic style. The lines are frequently short, elliptical phrases like the messages of a telegram:

THE WOMAN   You! Who sent you?

THE NAMELESS ONE   The masses.

THE WOMAN   They've not forgotten me?
           The message . . . the message . . .

THE NAMELESS ONE   My mission here is to set you free.

THE WOMAN   Freedom!
           Life!
           We escape? Is everything prepared?

THE NAMELESS ONE   Two keepers have been bribed.
               There's one more at the gate. I'll strike him down.

THE WOMAN   You'd murder him . . . for me?

THE NAMELESS ONE   For the cause.

THE WOMAN   I have no right.
           To win life through a keeper's death.

THE NAMELESS ONE   The masses have a right to you.

THE WOMAN   And the rights of the keeper?
           Keepers are men.

THE NAMELESS ONE   We have no "men" as yet.
               On one side, the group belonging to the mass.
               On the other, the class belonging to the State.

THE WOMAN   Man is naked.

THE NAMELESS ONE   Mass is godlike.

THE WOMAN   Mass is not godlike.
           Force made the mass.
           Evils of property made the mass.
           Mass is the movement of distress,
           Is meek devotion . . .
           Is terrible vengeance . . .
           Is blinded slavery . . .
           Is holy purpose . . .
           Mass is a fertile field that has been trampled;
           Mass is the choked-up, inarticulate people.

(trans. by Louis Untermeyer)

The stylization is Toller's way of trying to write a completely abstract and colorless dialogue that will communicate the intellectual substance and nothing else. The emotion arises out of the circumstances.

In a contemporary play like Ionesco's *The Bald Soprano*, stylization takes yet another form. In this play, the characters speak with deliberate absurdity to express the lack of communication between people and the triviality of their concerns when they do speak. The following lines are only a brief excerpt from a scene between a husband and his wife as they sit facing each other:

MR. MARTIN (*musing*)   How curious it is, how curious it is, how curious it is, and what a coincidence! You know, in my bedroom there is a bed, and it is covered with a green eiderdown. This room, with the bed and green eiderdown, is at the end of the corridor between the w.c. and the bookcase, dear lady!

MRS. MARTIN   What a coincidence, good Lord, what a coincidence! My bedroom, too, has a green eiderdown and is at the end of the corridor, between the w.c., dear sir, and the bookcase!

MR. MARTIN   How bizarre, curious, strange! Then, madam, we live in the same room and we sleep in the same bed, dear lady. It is perhaps there that we have met!

MRS. MARTIN   How curious it is and what a coincidence! It is indeed possible that we have met there, and perhaps even last night. But I do not recall it, dear sir!

MR. MARTIN   I have a little girl, my little daughter, she lives with me, dear lady. She is two years old, she's blonde, she has a white eye and a red eye, she is very pretty, her name is Alice, dear lady.

MRS. MARTIN   What a bizarre coincidence! I, too, have a little girl. She is two years old, has a white eye and a red eye, she is very pretty, and her name is Alice, too, dear sir!

MR. MARTIN (*in the same drawling, monotonous voice*)   How curious it is and what a coincidence! And bizarre! Perhaps they are the same, dear lady!

MRS. MARTIN   How curious it is! It is indeed possible, dear sir. (*A rather long moment of silence. The clock strikes 29 times.*)

Stylization, therefore, represents a deliberate distortion of language for a particular effect.

Paradox, dramatic irony, and verbal irony

Paradox and verbal irony work on a common principle of apparent contradiction. Paradox treats opposites in such a way that both elements of the contradiction are true, but true in different contexts. "Teiresias, who is blind, can see" sounds like a contradiction. It is a paradox stating that Teiresias' physical blindness does not prevent him from understanding. Because a statement of this kind works contrary to what we ordinarily expect, the effect is also ironic. Irony is based on a sense that things are not as they seem, or they do not turn out as they should, or there is a discrepancy between intention and effect. The irony of drama and fiction frequently depends on a situation, hence the term *dramatic irony*. But irony may also be a figure of speech; hence the term *verbal irony*, in which the meaning of the words is simply reversed by the ironic tone. Popular phrases like "the home of the brave," "the land of the free," or "America the beautiful" can easily be twisted to mean just their opposite.

Dramatic irony and verbal irony are not completely separable. Complex circumstances that are themselves paradoxical and ironic often produce language of a similar variety. Sophocles' *Oedipus the King* has become almost the standard example of the way dramatic irony works. The play itself is based on a series of paradoxical situations:

> Oedipus the king, the savior of Thebes, is also its destroyer.
> The curse he places on the killer of Laios he places on himself.
> The tracker of the criminal is the criminal himself.
> Teiresias, who is blind, can see; Oedipus, who can see, is blind.

Each element of these paradoxes holds true because Oedipus, the savior and king of Thebes, is also without his own knowledge the slayer of his father Laios. Separated from his father as a child, he later unknowingly kills him. Thus, the lines of the play are constant sources of irony and paradox. When Oedipus prays that the guilty man waste his life away, he concludes his speech with highly ironic words:

> In my house, I knowing it, he dwells,
> May every curse I spake on my head fall.

Without knowing it, he is the one in his own house on whom the curse has fallen.

A later speech turns on the paradox of seeing and not seeing. After the blind Teiresias has told Oedipus that he is the murderer of his father and the scourge of the land, Oedipus speaks:

> In one long night thou liv'st, and can'st not hurt
> Or me, or any man who sees the light.

Oedipus' mocking of Teiresias as one who cannot hurt him because he cannot see produces irony because all that Teiresias speaks is true and will bring about Oedipus' grief and tragedy.

Irony, however, does not always strike a serious note. The unexpected turn of events that Marvell describes in a short couplet from "To His Coy Mistress" produces a touch of ironic humor:

> The Grave's a fine and private place,
> But none I think do there embrace.

Likewise, the paradox may be comic as well as serious. A short poem by John Donne gives this effect:

Antiquary

> If in his study he hath so much care
> To hang all old, strange things, let his wife beware.

Irony and paradox can be sought out in almost any literary work, because their concern with self-contradiction is implicit in almost all experience, if you will choose to see it. They can easily be missed unless you read with an eye and ear for them.

Ambiguity and punning

Ambiguity and punning, like irony and paradox, turn on double meanings. Words are used so that they have more than one implication. Punning is basically a twist of a familiar expression ("There's method in his gladness"); a play on words that are spelled differently but sound alike (Max Beerbohm, asked to hike to the top of a Swiss mountain, declined by saying "I am an anti-climb Max"); a play on a single word that may have several possible meanings (*Hamlet:* 'T is for the dead, not for the quick, therefore thou liest. *First Clown:* 'T is a quick lie, sir; 't will away again, from me to you).

Punning is most commonly written for a comic effect, but when the situation is serious, the effect is gently ironic. The literature of the past indicates that writers did not consider it amiss to pun in serious situations. Dylan Thomas seems to follow that tradition in these lines from "Do Not Go Gentle into That Good Night":

> Grave men, near death, who see with blinding sight
> Blind eyes could blaze like meteors and be gay,
> Rage, rage against the dying of the light.

The opening line is reminiscent of the speech of the dying Mercutio in *Romeo and Juliet:*

> . . . ask for me tomorrow, and you shall find me a grave man.

Ambiguity, however, has broader possibilities than punning alone. Generally to be avoided in expository prose because of the uncertainty of meaning that arises, it is intentionally used in literature as a way of revealing the paradoxes and ironies of life that plague thoughtful men. In this sense, ambiguity adds richness of suggestion to the language.

In particular scenes of *Hamlet,* the ambiguity of Hamlet's remarks is appropriate to the character, for we can never be wholly certain when the frenzy of his emotions has carried his feigned madness into true madness. One such scene is his conversation with Ophelia, which follows immediately his thoughts of suicide in the soliloquy "To be or not to be." He taunts Ophelia with questions that are deliberately ambiguous, that seem to doubt her chastity but on the surface seem to question other virtues.

HAMLET   Ha, ha! Are you honest? [chaste?]
OPHELIA   My lord?
HAMLET   Are you fair? [unstained?]
OPHELIA   What means your lordship?

The ambiguity carries over into his phrase "Get thee to a nunnery. Why would'st thou be a breeder of sinners?" A nunnery is a place of refuge from the world, but

Elizabethan audiences would also have known the word as a cant term for a bawdy house. The ambiguity in these lines suggests Hamlet's divided thinking and complicated state of mind, both his concern for Ophelia in this scene and his bitterness toward her.

Ambiguity frequently results when feelings are mixed. At times, the writer may not convey feelings or thoughts with certainty and clarity. In a short poem, "Dust of Snow," Robert Frost leaves his "change of mood" unexplained:

> The way a crow
> Shook down on me
> The dust of snow
> From a hemlock tree
>
> Has given my heart
> A change of mood
> And saved some part
> Of a day I had rued.

It is clear that the falling snow has changed his spirits for the good, but the precise nature of his new mood remains ambiguous. What realization has the experience brought about? Should we place emphasis on *the way* the crow shook down the dust of snow? In this instance, the vagueness of situation and feeling makes the miniature poem a source of wonder and suggestiveness. Ambiguity, like many other effects of language, demands of us the kind of imaginative participation that ultimately draws us into the experience so that we must weigh what we, as well as the writer, understand by the language we read.

Verbal humor

Verbal humor is itself an ambiguous effect because it depends on a reader's responding to an incongruity between the statement and the writer's intention. If the incongruity is lost on the reader, the effect is lost. Some people do not see humor where others do.

Incongruity can exist only in terms of some norm. If incongruity means that something is out of keeping, it is logical to ask in terms of what. Verbal humor has direct reference to ordinary communicable speech, which maintains a semblance of reasonable tone, uniform usage, and orderliness. Any departures from these general norms are capable of producing something comical. Verbal humor has three main sources: disproportion, surprise, and confusion.

Disproportion is the incongruity that arises between the way something is said and what has actually happened. It is therefore the stock and trade of the braggart, the bluffer, and the teller of tall tales. Falstaff's speeches are funny because he is all three of these. In *Henry IV, Part 1*, in the scene at the Boar's Head Tavern in Eastcheap, Falstaff makes a fool of himself by boasting how he overcame a dozen rogues on the road near Gadshill:

I am a rogue if I were not at half-sword with a dozen of them two hours together. I have 'scaped by miracle. I am eight times thrust through the doublet, four through the hose; my buckler cut through and through; my sword hacked like a handsaw—*ecce signum!* I never dealt better since I was a man. All would not do. A plague of all cowards! Let them speak. If they speak more or less than truth, they are villains and the sons of darkness.

Falstaff speaks more than truth, because from an earlier scene the audience knows that Falstaff and his three companions were set upon as a prank by Poins and Prince Hal and that, when attacked, all of them ran, leaving behind them the money they themselves had robbed from pilgrims on the road. As Falstaff is later prodded into telling the incident, the numbers grow from twelve to sixteen to twenty-two or twenty-three and finally to the climactic figure:

If there were not two or three and fifty upon old Jack, then am I no two-legged creature.

Falstaff's story is amusing, not only in the exaggeration with which he tells it but in the way he draws it out. It is disproportionate in its hyperbole and its length.

The second source of verbal humor, surprise, is the incongruity that arises between what is said and what is expected to be said. This kind of humor almost always shifts the tone the author has established, so that a sudden contrast produces a comic effect. One amusing scene in Bernard Shaw's *Pygmalion* occurs when Eliza Doolittle, who has been taught to speak the King's English with propriety, shocks a small group of socialites by letting a vulgarism slip into her speech. Asked by Freddy if she is going to walk across the park, she responds: "Walk! Not bloody likely. I am going in a taxi." The humor is often lost on American audiences because they fail to respond in the same way that proper Englishmen do to the word "bloody." In the musical *My Fair Lady*, based on this play, the device is repeated, but the scene is shifted to a race track. Eliza appears dressed in most elegant fashion and acts with aristocratic grace, but, suddenly excited by seeing her horse fall behind in a race, she yells boldly, "Move your arse." Saying the unexpected is a common source of humor and one that Shaw often used in his writing.

A third source of verbal humor is confusion. It is the incongruity between the disorderliness of what is said and the coherence of what is expected. It is the humor of nonsense. Since the device is more common in spoken than written humor, it is more likely to be found in drama. The fools in Shakespeare's plays are often given confusing wordplay and absurd non sequiturs. In *Twelfth Night* (III, i), a short dialogue occurs between Viola, disguised as a young man, and a clown, carrying his tabor, a small drum:

VIOLA   Save thee, friend, and thy music! Dost thou live by thy tabor?

CLOWN   No, sir, I live by the church.

VIOLA   Art thou a churchman?

CLOWN   No such matter, sir. I do live by the church; for I do live at my house, and my house doth stand by the church.

VIOLA   So thou mayst say, the king lies by a beggar, if a beggar dwell near him; or, the church stands by thy tabor, if thy tabor stand by the church.

This is a way, as the Clown himself says, of showing "how quickly the wrong side may be turned outward."

In Eugène Ionesco's farce *The Lesson,* the Professor tutoring his young pupil walks up and down the room as he delivers a nonsensical lecture on the neo-Spanish languages:

That which distinguishes the neo-Spanish languages from each other and their idioms from the other linguistic groups, such as the group of languages called Austrian and neo-Austrian or Hapsburgian, as well as the Esperanto, Helvetian, Monacan, Swiss, Andorran, Basque, and jai alai groups, and also the groups of diplomatic and technical languages—that which distinguishes them, I repeat, is their striking resemblance which makes it so hard to distinguish them from each other—I'm speaking of the neo-Spanish languages which one is able to distinguish from each other, however, only thanks to their distinctive characteristics, absolutely indisputable proofs of their extraordinary resemblance, which renders indisputable their common origin, and which, at the same time, differentiates them profoundly—through the continuation of the distinctive traits which I've just cited.

Variations of this kind of humor occur in any repartee in which wordplay predominates.

Satire

When humor is given a target, it becomes satire. Satire mixes humor with criticism. Yet not all satire balances the elements of humor and criticism equally. Two traditions have continued since Roman times: one of satire written with geniality and urbanity in the manner of Horace; one of anger and violent lashing out against evil in the manner of Juvenal. The proportion of humor or criticism produces literary works of a quite different nature. If the element of criticism is lost altogether, the work becomes empty farce. If the humor is lost altogether, the work degenerates into invective. Ideally, satire may be said to lie somewhere between verbal abuse at one extreme and buffoonery at the other. Yet since satirists are not of one temperament, the English language offers a generous supply of words to suggest various tones and forms of satire: derision, invective, vituperation, jeremiad, raillery, ridicule, mockery, *reductio ad absurdum,* sarcasm, irony, caricature, parody, burlesque, comedy of manners, mock-epic, *commedia dell'arte,* clownishness, farce. In each of these, satire exists to a greater or lesser degree; the scale ranges from bitter scorn to gentle irony to sidesplitting laughter.

Since satire is actually a mode of perception—a predisposition—which shapes the writer's thought and language, it needs to be discussed in terms of a work as a whole. Unless the reader catches the writer's intention at an early stage, the effect can be lost or misinterpreted. Even the grotesquerie of Swift's "A Modest Proposal" was read straight by members of the eighteenth-century audience, and in our own time some readers fail to perceive the satire of some of their favorite nursery rhymes.

The twist of the satiric manner may be illustrated by the first stanzas of a series of poems that use Marlowe's "The Passionate Shepherd to His Love" as a point of departure. Marlowe's poem is an effervescent expression of love in an idyllic scene:

> Come live with me and be my love,
> And we will all the pleasures prove,
> That valleys, groves, hills and fields
> And all the craggy mountains yields.

In response, Sir Walter Ralegh wrote "The Nymph's Reply to the Shepherd":

> If all the world and love were young
> And truth in every shepherd's tongue,
> These pretty pleasures might me move,
> To live with thee, and be thy love.

Here the note of skepticism in the opening lines gives the poem a gentle satiric edge.

Some thirty or more years later, John Donne wrote another version entitled "The Bait":

> Come live with me and be my love,
> And we will some new pleasures prove,
> Of golden sands, and crystal brooks,
> With silken lines, and silver hooks.

Donne's switch of the scene throughout his poem from valleys and mountains to sands and streams to pursue a metaphor of his love swimming in the river as bait for "enamoured fish" adds a touch of absurdity that makes the poem virtually a parody of the delicate sentiments of Marlowe's poem.

Yet another poem, this one of the twentieth century, C. Day Lewis' "Come Live With Me and Be My Love," adds the strongest hint of satire by again imitating the poem that extols pastoral delights that are no more:

> Come, live with me and be my love,
> And we will all the pleasures prove
> Of peace and plenty, bed and board,
> That chance employment may afford.

These are examples of genial satire, a mockery of Marlowe's starry-eyed but charming view of young love.

In hard-hitting satire, the laugh fades quickly or the pleasantry takes the shape of a sardonic grin. E. E. Cummings, however, is one of the modern writers who maintained a firm grip on humor even when he was being most devastating in his comment. His poem "my sweet old etcetera" represents the art of satire at its best; the criticism and the humor come through equally clear:

> my sweet old etcetera
> aunt lucy during the recent
>
> war could and what
> is more did tell you just
> what everybody was fighting
>
> for,
> my sister

isabel created hundreds
(and
hundreds)of socks not to
mention shirts fleaproof earwarmers

etcetera wristers etcetera,my
mother hoped that

i would die etcetera
bravely of course my father used
to become hoarse talking about how it was
a privilege and if only he
could meanwhile my

self etcetera lay quietly
in the deep mud et

cetera
(dreaming,
et
    cetera, of
Your smile
eyes knees and of your Etcetera)

Suggestions for writing about language

Since literature is a verbal art, it is the word that makes possible all of its effects—not the isolated word, but the word set down appropriately with other words; the words shaped in forms that reveal the author's plan; the words arranged with timing so that the pace and tone are varied; the words chosen imaginatively so that the writer's intentions and feelings are implicit in the style as well as the thought and characters and actions. The language of a literary work can be examined as an end in itself, but ordinarily the language is studied as a source of tone, atmosphere, pacing, characterization, and the implied thoughts of the writer.

Questions like the following therefore suggest possible leads for the discussion of language in literature:

1. Is the language appropriate to the narrator? Does the dialect and style differentiate the narrator from the author?

2. Is the speech of characters in the work differentiated? Does a major part of the characterization spring from the way characters speak, as opposed to the way they act? To what extent does the dialogue create an illusion of reality? To what extent is it conventionalized? Does the author depend on certain techniques for recording speech?

3. Is the language stylized? To what degree? For what purpose? Does stylization seem to draw attention away from the matter of the work to the manner?

4. Are images and symbols natural or contrived? Universal or occasional? To what extent do they seem forcibly imposed on the material? What is gained by images that hit on extremely unlikely comparisons? In what way is the imagery an index to the writer's personality and mind? In what way can the metaphors be paraphrased so that the full meaning emerges?

5. What are the consistent mental and emotional impressions that emerge from reading the work? What areas of experience are drawn from? Do these follow a pattern? Do the sources and patterns comment on the characters? On the author? Do they create a special tone or atmosphere?

6. What explanations can be given that will resolve a paradox? What relation does paradoxical language have to the action and the characters? What relation does paradox have to the author's state of mind?

7. What different meanings grow out of a particular example of verbal ambiguity? What are the implications of any one of them? From what source does ambiguity arise? From the words? From the syntax? From general vagueness? From the tone? Does the thought and structure of the work as a whole help to settle on one interpretation in preference to another?

8. In what terms can the author's language be characterized? Highly figurative or symbolical? Abstract? Colloquial? Mixed? What is the general appropriateness of the language to the theme of the work?

9. What is the source of verbal humor? What is its purpose? Is it used for contrast, diversion, satire? If it is satiric, what is being mocked?

10. What manner does the writer assume to satirize? Is anger evident? Moral indignation? Geniality? Fun? How do these qualities promote criticism?

Stylistic effects

Literary style can refer to a number of different things: the style of a writer, the style of a particular work, the style of a period. These obviously are not independent of one another: writers produce the works that establish the characteristic manner of a movement. Yet the gap between the writer and the period is great enough to cause confusion about what style actually is. Where does it exist? In the writer? In the product? In the mind of the reader?

In this discussion, *style* will be used to describe the effect that grows out of a writer's ways of working with elements that combine to make up a literary work. Style can be discussed in terms of any one of the components: the arrangement of the plot, the details of the setting, the manner of characterization, the effects of form, the choice and arrangement of words, the modes of thought and feeling. In these terms, almost all writing about literature is in some way a discussion of style. Yet beyond particular focuses of this kind, style can also be discussed as a cumulative effect of the various strategies used, as a total impression gained by readers as they read and react. Style is therefore not infrequently discussed in highly impressionistic and metaphorical terms. While he was studying the style of Jonathan Swift, Professor Louis Milic collected a group of adjectives used by critics to describe the writing of Swift. His partial list includes words like *charming, clear, common, concise, correct, direct, elaborate, elegant, energetic, graceful, hard-round-crystalline, homely, lucid, manly, masculine, muscular, nervous, ornamented, perfect, plain, poor, proper, pure, salty, simple, sinewy, sonorous,* and *vigorous*. Some of these are so different that we might wonder if the critics had read the same writer. Of course, writers do not always maintain a consistent and invariable style, so that generalizations may legitimately vary. Writers experiment; they come under new influences; they change with age. Even though we think of their minds and personalities as relatively constant, they may change in philosophy and temperament.

Meaningful discussions of style, therefore, are those that are most specific while at the same time attempting to explain what effects grow out of the writing. The effect of style cannot be dismissed as an illusion, because even after all of the strategies have been explained, the structures analyzed, and the words diagnosed, the dimensions of style extend further into areas of sensory and extrasensory perception. These effects are often contextual; they can be explained only in terms of the whole, as the effect of the parts interacting together. In these terms, a number of stylistic features contribute to the readability of literature.

Climax and suspense

Climax is a part of the dynamics of a literary work. It is a point of culmination, a moment of high tension and involvement. Thus a work might possibly have a number of climactic incidents, but the main one is usually apparent—the confrontation, the discovery, the revelation, the realization, the final struggle—whatever may be the high interest on which the story turns. Tracing the action to a point of climax is a way of recognizing how the writer has built the story and involved us in the process.

Suspense is a tension caused by looking forward. It is the anticipation that accumulates before the climax is reached and is generally limited to works that withhold crucial information. If we know the entire story in advance, suspense is minimized. Both Greek and modern works based on familiar myths have little suspense because the outcome of the events is known from the beginning. The primary interest lies in the writer's way of working out the narrative and his interpretation of the characters and actions. The interest in such works is, therefore, focused on different aspects of style.

Works in which the outcome of the action is unknown generate a strong element of suspense. Thus, the courtroom and trial by jury are a natural setting and situation for suspense. Detective fiction and adventure stories depend heavily on suspense as a main source of interest.

Pace

All writing is based on motion. It is not a static art, as the words on the printed page might lead us to believe. We not uncommonly speak of the pace of a work. Pace is a matter of timing, both writer's own sense of movement in developing ideas and our sense of how the writing moves. A slow pace encourages reflection; it also risks boredom. A rapid pace magnetizes us; it also risks superficiality. Long works, therefore, are paced so that the movement is sometimes slowed, sometimes quickened. The novelist's sense of timing may be not unlike the strategy of a long-distance runner who cannot go the whole way at the same speed.

Pace is often a matter of the relation between action, description, and dialogue, but it is also a matter of specific technique. In poetry, for example, the metrical line has the effect of moving the verse more quickly or slowly. A regular line that runs smoothly and uninterruptedly tends to move quickly. A metrical variation usually tends to slow the rhythm. In a long work like *Paradise Lost,* consisting of more than 10,000 lines of blank verse, Milton depends on deviations from the regular line to vary the effects. In two succeeding lines (108–109) from Book IV, the pace changes noticeably:

> So farewell hope, and, with hope, farewell fear,
> Farewell remorse! All good to me is lost;

The first irregular line is slow and deliberate. The second regular line quickens.

Frequently, the pace of a line suits the thought. The description of Satan's journey through the realms of Chaos and Night (II, 947–950) reflects his changing progress, sometimes fast, sometimes slow:

> So eagerly the Fiend
> O'er bog or steep, through strait, rough, dense, or rare,
> With head, hands, wings, or feet, pursues his way,
> And swims, or sinks, or wades, or creeps, or flies.

In another description of motion (II, 618–621), the final line of eight stressed syllables reflects the arduous progress against obstacles:

> Through many a dark and dreary vale
> They passed, and many a region dolorous,
> O'er many a frozen, many a fiery alp,
> Rocks, caves, lakes, fens, bogs, dens, and shades of death.

These, of course, are variations only within the pattern of blank verse. They do not take into account the variety of pace that can be achieved by different metrical patterns, short and long lines, and the variations within those patterns. Versification is the poet's special way of controlling the pace of words.

The prose style of fiction can also strongly affect the pace of a work. There is little doubt that the characteristic sentence patterns of Melville, James, or Faulkner cause their prose to move at a slower pace than that of Lawrence, Hemingway, or Sherwood Anderson. But, in general, the pace of fiction is much more a matter of the rate at which the narrative moves forward. The action can move ahead rapidly in a linear sense or hesitate and move in a vertical direction, so that the writer or the characters in a sense stop the action to probe, reflect, or philosophize. In long works, there are alternate horizontal and vertical movements. A story of little action in which most of the movement is vertical may well be highly static, not dull as a consequence, but interesting in terms of other than straight storytelling.

The narrative technique of a story may also affect its pace. A cinematic technique, basically one in which fragments are projected before us without obvious transitions between them, is designed as a kind of economical narration. It is less concerned with the linear quality of narration and more with the total effect. It operates like a montage. On the other hand, a story in which the transitions are carefully drawn so that all of the parts are linked and interfused to make a continuous whole may move with less obvious sense of speed, but the logic of its narration may make it read more easily so that it seems to move at an equally rapid pace. Pace is a matter of intuitive perception in fiction, not unrelated to the technique the writer is using.

In drama, pace is largely a matter of the relation between action and dialogue. The drama is not a form that invites large-scale action. If the background is war, the action ordinarily takes place offstage or between acts. The clashes of rival forces onstage in some of Shakespeare's history plays inevitably fail to convey a sense of intense conflict because stage drama is primarily a form for talking about action, not showing it. When a story or play is converted to film, however, more action is always included simply because cinema, with its greater flexibility and pace, is capable of showing far more. To go to the other extreme, when there is almost no action at all in a stage play and only talk remains, then the movement must depend entirely on the pace of the talk—the dialogue.

One notable development in twentieth-century drama has been writers' interest in discursive plays—plays in which the characters drawn together in a common crisis simply talk. Nothing of significance happens; our interest must be in the characters as speakers, or there is no interest. Many of Shaw's plays, particularly one like *Saint Joan,* fall into this category. Plays by Albee, Beckett, Ionesco, and Pinter are similarly discursive. Plays of this kind differ from others in that they lack a strong narrative base. All drama is composed of speaking, and in none is language more important than in Greek tragedies, which traditionally relegated violent action to offstage. Yet these plays were not without violent action. The tragedies were tragedies of dying, not the modern tragedies of living and talking about it. The pace of drama, therefore, seems to relate primarily to the kinds of things characters talk about and the length at which they expound. Drama that utilizes the natural pace of conversation with a strong sense of a developing action is likely to move at a far brisker pace than one in which characters make speeches and only wait for their fate.

Tone and atmosphere

The tone of a literary work derives primarily from the choices and combinations of words that writers use, and we identify these stylistic effects as irony, satire, humor, understatement, hyperbole, or ambiguity. These verbal qualities have already been discussed in "Language, Symbol, and Imagery." Tone, however, may also result from our response to form and rhetorical design, like orderliness or balance. What impresses us as a tone of eloquence in a work may be largely a result of emphasis or repetition or parallelism. Or what impresses us as unpleasant may be a writer's deliberate attempt to avoid the euphony of liquid sounds, appealing alliterations, or rhymes.

One of the chief delights of language is its sound, sometimes its melodiousness, sometimes its suggestion of actual sounds, sometimes the appropriateness of sound to meaning. Word choice is, of course, the most important factor in the creation of sound, but the choices themselves are often determined by devices that writers use. Seven of these are a part of every writer's repertory of techniques, particularly the poet's.

Alliteration, sometimes referred to as beginning rhyme, is limited as a principle to the repetition of beginning consonant sounds, although hidden alliteration often occurs in internal and end syllables of words. In lines like the following from Shakespeare's Sonnet 30, both the alliteration of *s*'s and *w*'s and the repetition of the *s* in medial and final positions are working together to produce the total sound effect:

> When to the sessions of sweet silent thought
> I summon up remembrance of things past,
> I sigh the lack of many a thing I sought,
> And with old woes new wail my dear time's waste.

Alliteration has operated as a major poetic technique in English poetry from Anglo-Saxon times to the present.

Assonance is the repetition of vowel sounds throughout in prose or poetry, either exact duplications or resemblances. The device is frequently used to establish a tone appropriate to the thought. Compare the opening lines of Milton's companion pieces on joy and melancholy:

> Hence loathéd melancholy
>   Of Cerberus and blackest midnight born
> In Stygian cave forlorn
>   'Mongst horrid shapes, and shrieks, and sights unholy!
>   "L'Allegro"

> Hence vain deluding joys,
>   The brood of folly with father bred!
> How little you bestead,
>   Or fill the fixéd mind with all your toys!
>   "Il Penseroso"

Melancholy is described in rounded, back vowels, low-pitched in sound; joy is described in open, front vowels, high-pitched in sound.

Assonance can also be used as a variation on exact rhyme when a word falls in a final stressed position, as in lines from Dylan Thomas' "And Death Shall Have No Dominion":

> And death shall have no dominion.
> Dead men naked they shall be one

> With the man in the wind and the west moon;
> When their bones are picked clean and the clean bones gone,

Consonance is a kind of half-rhyme or consonantal rhyme in which the consonants are parallel but the vowels are different. Wilfred Owen uses consonance instead of exact rhyme in "Arms and the Boy":

> Let the boy try along this bayonet-blade
> How cold steel is, and keen with hunger of blood;
> Blue with all malice, like a madman's flash;
> And thinly drawn with famishing for flesh.

Consonance is sometimes used synonymously with alliteration or as a term to describe the recurrence of consonant sounds at the end of words.

Onomatopoeia is an attempt to reinforce the meaning by using words that suggest the sounds they describe. The device can be used imitatively, as in Kipling's "The Song of the Banjo":

> With my *"Tumpa-tumpa-tum-pa tump!"*

Or it can be used suggestively with varying degrees of subtlety:

> Over the cobbles he clattered and clashed in the dark inn-yard,
> And he tapped with his whip on the shutters, but all was locked and barred.
> > Alfred Noyes, "The Highwayman"

> The ice was all around:
> It cracked and growled, and reared and howled.
> > Coleridge, *The Rime of the Ancient Mariner*

> The curfew tolls the knell of parting day,
> The lowing herd winds slowly o'er the lea,
> > Thomas Gray,
> > "Elegy Written in a Country Churchyard"

> The lark, that tirra-lirra chants,
> > With hey! with hey! the thrush and the jay,
> > Shakespeare, *The Winter's Tale*

Repetition of single words is a technique equally common in prose and poetry; done almost always with a dramatic effect,

> Blow, bugle, blow, set the wild echoes flying,
> And answer, echoes, answer dying, dying, dying.
> > Tennyson, *The Princess*

> We're foot–slog–slog–slog–sloggin' over Africa—
> Foot–foot–foot–foot–sloggin' over Africa—
> (Boots–boots–boots–boots–moving' up an' down again!)
> > There's no discharge in the war!
> > Kipling, "Boots"

> Lisp'd to me the low and delicious word death,
> And again death, death, death, death,
>> Whitman. "Out of the Cradle Endlessly Rocking"

A *refrain* is the repetition of a complete line at the end of a stanza, often with a musical effect or an intensification of the meaning of the words. It is commonly used in French stanza forms like the ballade and villanelle. Henley's "Ballade of Dead Actors" repeats the line "Into the night go one and all" at the end of each of three stanzas and the envoy.

Rhyme is the similarity of two words to one another because of the resemblance of their sounds. If the repetition of sounds is close, like *eyes* and *sighs,* the rhyme is said to be exact or perfect. But many rhymes are suggestive rather than exact, like John Crowe Ransom's rhyme of *drunkard* and *conquered* or C. Day Lewis' *womb* and *home* or Emily Dickinson's rhyme of *shown* and *cocoon.* These are sometimes referred to as half-rhymes, slant rhymes, off-rhymes, or various other terms that suggest their approximate nature.

The most familiar rhyme, of course, is that which occurs at the end of a line of poetry in a stressed syllable, called end-rhyme. Other rhyme, however, may occur internally, tending to divide a long line into two definite parts if it occurs at the caesura, as in Poe's well-known line from "The Raven":

> Once upon a midnight dreary, while I pondered, weak and weary.

Rhymes like *dreary* and *weary,* with the stressed syllable followed by an unstressed one, are called feminine rhymes. Rhymes of single stressed syllables are masculine. Rhymes are designated as double (*bolder, shoulder*) or triple (*intuition, erudition*) in terms of the number of rhyming syllables. Some rhymes appear to be only eye-rhymes, like Marvell's

> And yonder all before us lie
> Deserts of vast eternity.

Although some modern writers use eye-rhymes intentionally, their presence in earlier poems often testifies to changes in pronunciation that have taken place. In fact, rhymes are one of the important sources of knowledge concerning the pronunciation of sounds in the past.

Rhyme can be used as a source of humor by matching unexpected words, as in Gilbert's lyrics for *The Mikado.* The rhyme for *exist* turns out to be *philanthropist.* One of Ogden Nash's favorite devices for humor was to force words into a pattern of rhyme:

> One kind of sin is called a sin of commission, and that is very important
> And it is what you are doing when you are doing something you ortant.
>> "Portrait of the Artist as a Prematurely Old Man"

Functionally, the use of rhyme goes beyond its sound qualities. Its occurrence interlocks the parts of a poem, it gives emphasis, it reinforces the meaning, it establishes the tone of a poem. In these ways, it operates as one of the poet's most effective resources.

In literature, tone is more than the tone of the language. It also depends on other effects, some of which may be essentially nonverbal in nature. These can be grouped as typographical and theatrical.

Typographical effects

Typographical effects include both the use of various kinds of type styles for dramatic effect and the arrangement of words on a page for a rhetorical effect. Both devices are deliberate attempts to escape the most routine form of presentation on the printed page. They force a reader to respond because they deviate from customary practices. The now familiar appearance of the name of e e cummings without capital letters and punctuation reminds us of the kind of awareness we have of changes from conventional practice. Cummings' own poems are familiar examples of rearrangements of words that will not permit the reader to view them thoughtlessly. Such rearrangements are a visual attempt to get away from the routine, just as a fresh image is an attempt to escape the cliché. Or they may be an attempt to get beyond the medium of words—to suggest motion or to appeal to the visual image. Any alteration of type, mechanics, line length, form, or spacing needs to be considered in view of the author's intentions.

Many typographical variations, particularly in fiction, may be best characterized as nonbook effects. They imitate the more spectacular appeals of newspaper and magazine techniques, or they seem to borrow from the movie script or television commercial. Even though some readers may dismiss these as cheap and superficial effects, the conclusion cannot be avoided that they are operating in their own nonverbal way to contribute to the tone of a work.

Theatrical effects

Aristotle, one of the earliest writers on dramatic theory, recognized both music and spectacle as parts of dramatic effect, even though he spoke of them as accessories rather than as essential components. Any overemphasis on them he would have considered a distraction from a tragedy's purpose. The history of dramatic production indicates that the elaborateness of staging has varied with fashion and the availability of resources. Yet before the modern period, the resources of the stage seem to have been looked on as supplemental to the writer's script—something added to give the play dramatic life on the stage. The play could be seen with the additions, but it could also with equal force be read without them. Its meaning was in the language, not in the acting, the lights, and the sounds.

Many modern dramatists, however, have experimented with theatrical resources in an effort to establish tone and atmosphere as a new dimension of meaning. Thus, a language of pantomime, light, and sound at times substitutes for the language of words. The result is that meaning becomes more and more implicit rather than explicit, expressive rather than reasoned, sensuous rather than discursive. These are plays written to be experienced; reading them requires a special kind of imaginative interpretation.

The final stage direction of Ionesco's *Exit the King* is a good example:

Sudden disappearance of QUEEN MARGUERITE *on the left. The* KING *is seated on his throne. During this final scene, the doors, windows and walls of the throne room will have slowly disappeared. This part of the action is very important.*

Now there is nothing on the stage except the KING *on his throne in a grayish light. Then the* KING *and his throne also disappear.*

Finally, there is nothing but the gray light.

This disappearance of the windows, the doors and the walls, the KING *and the throne must be very marked, but happen slowly and gradually. The* KING *sitting on his throne should remain visible for a short time before fading into a kind of mist.*

This particular ending is a tableau in which the most important commentary is made by the language of silence and light. The fadeout is more than a representation of lights going off or night coming on; it is a vehicle that depicts emotionally and symbolically the experience of death and man's disappearance into the unknown darkness.

Many effects of lighting and sound and mime that the dramatist writes into stage directions are not intended to create an illusion. In fact, they may work directly to the contrary. They make the audience aware that the theater is a theater; that characters are actors playing roles; that real life is not being enacted on the stage. At the end of Edward Albee's *The American Dream*, Grandma interrupts the dialogue to speak directly to the audience:

GRANDMA (*interrupting . . . to audience*) Well, I guess that just about wraps it up. I mean, for better or worse, this is a comedy, and I don't think we'd better go any further. No, definitely not. So, let's leave things are they are right now . . . while everybody's happy . . . while everybody's got what he wants . . . or everybody's got what he thinks he wants. Good night, dears.

In its effect, the speech functions somewhat like the ancient Greek chorus, which remained on stage as an observer and commented on the action.

The stage has definite limitations, but the nonverbal effects are deliberate attempts to transcend the limitations and to use them to advantage. At the beginning of Tennessee Williams' *The Glass Menagerie*, Tom, the narrator and also a character in the play, addresses the audience. After speaking of the social background of the play, he says:

The play is memory. Being a memory play, it is dimly lighted, it is sentimental, it is not realistic. In memory everything seems to happen to music. That explains the fiddle in the wings.

These few remarks indicate the extent to which the music and the lighting are an integral part of this play. They must be taken into account not only for production purposes but for reading purposes as well.

In this same play, Williams planned to use a slide projector that would cast titles and images on one of the walls of the stage. The device was not actually used in the original Broadway production but is written into the published manuscript. Williams explains the use of the slides as a structural device—as a means of giving a narrative line to an episodic play and as a way of accenting values in particular scenes. Some of the legends read "After the fiasco," "You think I'm in love with continental shoemakers?" "Things have a way of turning out so badly." The images include "Amanda as a girl on a porch, greeting callers," "Sailing vessel with jolly roger," "Blue Roses," and a "Glamor magazine cover." The screen images, therefore, serve additional purposes: they act as a memory device, they comment on the action, and they create atmosphere.

Theatrical effects of this kind cannot be ignored in reading a play. In fact, stage directions from the time of Ibsen on become increasingly important as explanations of the writer's intentions. They are not exit-and-entrance instructions; they are interpretations. As a reader and interpreter of drama, particularly of modern drama, you must therefore assume the mental role of director, scenic designer, and choreographer in an effort to determine fully the implications of the dramatist's directions. In this way, you must try to interpret the way nonverbal effects have been made an essential part of the style of the work.

Suggestions for writing about stylistic effects

In order to avoid the pitfall of writing only vague generalizations about style, you need to focus your attention on specific strategies that the writer is using to create effects. Your impressions and emotional responses are by no means to be ignored, although they should be only the starting point. You should ask yourself why you respond as you do. Why are you interested? Why must you read to the end without stopping? Why are you moved to pause and reflect? What makes the style compelling?

To get at particular strategies that often make a writer's style what it is, questions like the following provide leads for the discussion of style in understandable and concrete terms:

1. What words best characterize the style of a particular work? Does this manner of style seem to predominate in other works by the same writer? Is there one style of the writer that seems to include many different manners?

2. What identifiable strategies is the writer using? What are they accomplishing stylistically?

3. What are the climactic points in a novel or play? Do these seem to build to one main climax? Do these seem to set up a rhythmic pattern of stress and lack of stress, like the meter of a poem?

4. Where does the main climax occur in relation to the end? Is there an abrupt dénouement after the climax or a continuation of the story? What is the effect of either strategy?

5. What are the main elements that sustain your interest in the literary work? What anticipations are set up? Are there other kinds of suspense than the one that depends on withheld information or wondering what will happen? Can the emotional effects of the literary work be explained in terms of suspense?

6. What elements can be identified that affect the pace of a long work? In fiction, what is the balance of action, description, and dialogue? What makes a drama static or fast moving? Is pace also related to climax and suspense?

7. In what way are the metrics of a poem suitable to its thought? What are the effects that derive almost completely from the versification? What is the degree of irregularity in the meter? Are the lines long or short or alternating?

8. What is the predominant tone of a work? Do the words that best describe the tone tend to be highly metaphorical? Can the impressions be supported by direct reference to particular incidents, scenes, and speeches?

9. What sound effects and nonverbal resources does the writer utilize? What human senses are responding to these strategies? How many are being used simultaneously? To what effect?

10. Does the use of music, symbolic action, or light tend to support the general tone of the work and act in conjunction with the thought? Or do they tend to be accessories? Or do they serve as an ironic commentary on the characters and actions? What are the nonverbal effects doing? What would change if they were omitted? In what different ways could a play be produced to get different effects?

Thought and meaning

The previous elements of literature we have discussed—the characters, the action, the setting, the structure, the language, and the style—all go to make up the literary vehicle. They are the elements that in special ways make a poem a poem or a story a story. The remaining element hinges on the writer's purpose. Why did this writer write what she did in the first place? What is that writer saying?

John Ciardi wrote a book entitled *How Does a Poem Mean?* He explains that an alternate title might have been "How to talk about a poem without paraphrasing." The title of his book can readily be extended to the other forms: How does a novel mean? How does a short story mean? How does a play mean? The answers may begin to shape themselves if we ask, by contrast: How does an essay mean? How does a telegram mean? In every instance, the form itself is a part of the meaning because the author has deliberately chosen it as a way of expressing meaning in preference to some other way.

From literal to metaphorical

Readers who are intent on finding "messages" in literature are applying the principles of the telegram to works that are not operating on those same principles. This is not to say that many poems, stories, and plays do not have explicit statements to make; but it is to say that they do not usually make them with the directness and literalness of the expository statement. In "Song of Myself," Walt Whitman writes:

> I find letters from God dropt in the street, and every one is sign'd
>   by God's name.

Paradoxically, this line uses the letter, a literal form of communication, as a metaphor. In the three preceding lines, Whitman says much more literally what he means:

> Why should I wish to see God better than this day?
> I see something of God each hour of the twenty-four, and each
>   moment then,
> In the faces of men and women I see God, and in my own
>   face in the glass.

To be quite explicit: the letters Whitman refers to are not written ones; they are implied in everything around us; they are metaphors of God. In a similar way, authors do not write letters to us in stories, poems, and plays. They communicate by everything they create, sometimes by simply holding up a glass for us to see ourselves.

The availability of meaning

In writing about the thought of a literary work, you may find it impossible to reduce everything to one generalization that accounts for the work as a whole. Occasionally, a summary can be made in terms of a thesis statement; for example, Turgenev's *Fathers and Sons* reveals the clash that occurs between the old and the young when the values of the older generation can no longer be accepted as the values of the younger. At other times, the meaning may be stated in terms of the commanding image. The thought and tone of Sartre's *No Exit* are expressed by the metaphor of its own title: life is a room with no escape; hell is other people. When authors have come to an understanding about life, when they have formed attitudes, when they have opinions and possibly even solutions to problems, their own convictions come through clearly, so that it may be possible to reduce the thought to a simple statement. This is not to imply that the thought is simple or superficial, only that it is clear and inferable.

All works, however, are not reducible in these terms. Some authors may claim to have no understanding of what they see and know, but by revealing their thoughts, they may bring about awareness and understanding in others. Some literary works, particularly poems, are only observations; others are explorations with no discoveries; others are conjectures, grasping for balance and hope. To say precisely what an author's thought is in works of this kind may be impossible. Those who want answers in literature may not find them in writers who see their role primarily as recorders of experience, not as seers and teachers.

The important thing in writing about the thought of a literary work is not to begin with a single expectation: that the thought is there to be read as it is in an essay, open and available. You must expect to reach for the thought, not to have it handed to you. In works in which the meaning must be inferred, the thoughts are not hidden in the sense that they are removed from view or that they are deliberately secluded to make understanding difficult. Most authors write to be read and understood, but the most thoughtful ones are seldom reductionists. They do not find platitudes and clichés adequate expressions for their insights. They may find it necessary to work out the meaning of a story or a poem in complex ways. It is certainly legitimate to ask what a writer is driving at as long as you do not always expect to be able to come up with a quick and easy answer.

How literature means

To consider how a story or a poem or a play means is to go beyond what the words say. Meaning is not limited strictly to ideas, to its intellectual substance and sense. Meaning cannot always be summarized in a sentence because works of literature have other varieties of meaning. They mean by the feelings they convey; they mean by the attitudes they create; they mean by the style they assume; they mean in terms of the author's intentions and the time and occasion of the writing. Accordingly, new meanings emerge constantly with the passage of time and with the investigations of new readers. Thus, writing about the meaning of a work is always justified because it can never be set down definitely at one particular time. An old work in a new time may be a revelation to its readers. A new reader is capable of seeing new meanings.

Intrinsic sources of thought

Particular ideas can be derived from a number of different sources within the work itself. These are intrinsic sources of thought as opposed to those that are imposed on the work from without. These intrinsic sources are built into the structure itself and, like all meaning, vary from the literal to the metaphorical. Clues to thought and meaning come from four kinds of sources:

Titles

The title ought always to be taken into account; it may hold a key to the author's emphasis and tone. Ibsen's play *Hedda Gabler* is named after the protagonist. It could be a quite literal title, like Flaubert's *Madame Bovary* or Tolstoy's *Anna Karenina*. *Hedda Gabler* is different, however, because in the play Hedda Gabler is married; her name has been changed to Hedda Tesman. In the title, therefore, Ibsen hints at an idea about the main character that is developed throughout the play.

Shaw's title *Arms and the Man* provides a humorous ambiguity; the play concerns both war and romance. In addition, the title is an echo of the opening lines of Vergil's *Aeneid,* another tale of war and romance, but Shaw's play is a satire. Its title therefore suggests its mock-heroic tone. On the other hand, Hemingway's title *A Farewell to Arms,* also a story of war and romance, contains the same ambiguity, but in its combination with *farewell* suggests a tone of serious irony rather than light mockery.

A standard trick question is to ask who the Merchant of Venice is in Shakespeare's play of that name. Why does the title place the emphasis on Antonio when many people think the play is about Shylock? The title invites another way of looking at this play. Joyce's *Ulysses* and Shaw's *Pygmalion* direct our attention to sources outside the works as keys to their understanding. Dickens' *Bleak House*, a novel about people's entanglements with the law, and Whitman's *Drum-Taps*, his collection of poems about the Civil War, establish a tone. Jane Austen's titles *Pride and Prejudice* and *Sense and Sensibility* give the key themes for interpreting these works. Titles like Thomas Wolfe's *Look Homeward, Angel* and Faulkner's *The Sound and the Fury* are literary allusions and therefore metaphorical in their implications. O'Neill's *The Hairy Ape* and Ibsen's *Ghosts* are also metaphorical titles which provide a commanding image for the play's meaning as a whole. Titles need to be carefully examined.

Names

The names of characters and places may have special appropriateness or irony. At times, they may actually mean something significant in terms of the play, as the name Oedipus means "swollen feet." As a baby, Oedipus had been exposed to the elements with his feet pierced and bound, left to die because the oracle of Apollo had told Laios, his father, that he would die by the hands of his own son. Or the names may invite an extended interpretation of the work, as George and Martha in Albee's *Who's Afraid of Virginia Woolf?* may be seen as the primal husband and wife of the United States. The main characters in Shaw's *Man and Superman* parallel characters in Mozart's opera *Don Giovanni*, so that a comparison between the two works is necessary for a full insight into Shaw's intentions. Other names, like Blanche Du Bois and Stanley Kowalski in *A Streetcar Named Desire*, are associative. Others are suggestive, like the array of humorous names in Dickens' novels, which include Mr. Gradgrind, Mr. Bounderby, Mr. Murdstone, Mr. Pumblechook, Mr. Skimpole, and the Hon. Samuel Slumkey. Place names may take on the same qualities—*Streetcar* is set in a slum area of New Orleans called Elysian Fields—but names of this kind are usually not plentiful unless the work is clearly an allegory.

Equally important as the names chosen is the omission of names. Most of the soldiers in Stephen Crane's *The Red Badge of Courage* are nameless. It makes them as anonymous as soldiers become in a war; it also makes them universal. In a similar way, characters in Strindberg's *The Dream Play* are identified simply by their sex or occupation: He, She, The Daughter, The Officer, The Lawyer, The Poet. These are dreamlike figures; they are also universal types.

Allusions

Allusions represent the intricate interweaving of the author's reading and experience into the writng. They are therefore a source of interest about the writer, but they may prove to be essential to a complete understanding of the work. An allusion like "Jonah's Moby" in a sonnet by Dylan Thomas is a kind of puzzle, but an entire poem based on an allusion, like Yeat's "Leda and the Swan," cannot be understood without knowing the mythological story. Frequently, a poet may give almost all of the facts one needs to know about an allusion, as Wallace Stevens in his poem "Peter Quince at the Clavier" tells the story of Susanna, taken from the Apochrypha; yet knowledge of the original story provides a base for knowing how Stevens uses the allusion for his own purposes. Literary references of this kind are clear-cut; they can even be footnoted. But they do not cover all of the subtle echoes of phrase and line in a poem that may give clues to the author's thinking and meaning. In Eliot's *Murder in the Cathedral*, when the Second Priest expresses joy at the impending return of Archbishop Becket, the Third Priest says:

> For good or ill, let the wheel turn.
> The wheel has been still, these seven years, and no good.
> For ill or good, let the wheel turn.
> For who knows the end of good or evil?
> Until the grinders cease
> And the door shall be shut in the street,
> And all the daughters of music shall be brought low.

The last three lines are almost the exact words of Ecclesiastes 12:3–4, and the first four lines suggest the spirit of Chapter 3 of the same book of the Bible. In this instance, the allusion is the meaning.

Allusions are obviously not limited to literary references. A major portion of Auden's "Musée des Beaux Arts" is based on a reference to Brueghel's painting of the fall of Icarus. His poem "September 1, 1939" is a topical allusion to the invasion of Poland by Hitler's troops. The allusion becomes the point of departure for the thoughts of the poem. It cannot be fully understood without that historical background. Allusions in writing are so very numerous that we can only conclude that the more we read and know, the more likely we will be able to come to grips with subtleties of meaning in an author's work.

Dialogue

One obvious source of ideas occurs in the dialogue of the characters. At times, when authors are interested in particular issues, they introduce a discussion among their characters. There seem to be no bounds—from general topics about morality, politics, and women's rights to more specific theories and ideas. Samuel Butler concerns himself with Darwinism in *The Way of All Flesh*, Dickens with Utilitarianism in *Hard Times*, and Shaw with the Bergsonian Life Force in *Man and Superman*. These sometimes take the form of actual intellectual discussion; sometimes they influence the conception of the characters.

What one needs to guard against is to identify the views of a character in a novel or play with the author's unless there is reason to do so. In a time when authors as self-advertisers are given to writing about their own ideas and their own works, identifications are often possible to make. Inevitably, a character who is a free-thinker or reformer becomes the author's mouthpiece. Some playwrights see themselves primarily as teachers or preachers. In the Epistle Dedicatory to *Man and Superman*, Shaw writes:

. . . it annoys me to see people comfortable when they ought to be uncomfortable: and I insist on making them think in order to bring them to conviction of sin. If you don't like my preaching you must lump it. I really cannot help it.

The ideas of a play, therefore, may be its main reason for existence, and it becomes your job to sort out opinions among the characters to see precisely how the ideas develop and how the action comments on them.

Extrinsic sources of thought

Thus far, we have discussed the analysis of a literary work in terms of itself, in terms of the elements that combine to express meanings. This emphasis is sometimes referred to as formalistic; it has been more popularly labeled the New Criticism. What was new about New Criticism in the 1930s and 1940s has in one sense grown old, but it has now become established as an indispensable approach, particularly for the nonprofessional. What it does is assert the primacy of the text—it asks you to look at the text as material contained between the covers of the book and to consider it without reference to all of the other knowledge in the world that can be brought to bear on it.

However, the growing sterility of New Criticism, the social rebellion of the second part of this century, and a new spirit of Romanticism have brought about a shift in critical emphasis—from a consideration of the work as an isolated text, severed from its author and the times, to a consideration of the work in a variety of contexts. Thus, outside knowledge can be brought to bear on a literary work in such a way as to clarify its meaning. These are extrinsic considerations. They are critical frames of reference that require specialized knowledge and are therefore less available to the amateur reader. Yet the perspectives that these approaches represent should be briefly considered.

Biographical considerations

The biographical approach to literature is a standard one of long duration. Its value lies in the extent to which facts about an author's life help to clarify the content of the works. Its value also is relative. Some works contain more of their writers' immediate thoughts and experiences than others. If we had no outside sources of information about John Milton, for example, we would know most of the things we need to know about him from his own works. He constantly reflects on his own experiences in his prose and poetry and sometimes records them quite literally in personal digressions. On the other hand, the person of Shakespeare, about whom we know surprisingly little despite the fact that he is a major figure, cannot be inferred from the plays and poems. The biographies of him are based on a few facts and a mass of inference; they are largely speculative.

Biographical facts should not be absolutely necessary for reading a poem or story or play, but certainly all of the possible meanings have not been explored until they have been investigated. Once a work has been written, it is severed from its author. Yet the author has been the source of the thought and experiences, and some acquaintance with the author's life may account for many things. The writer of biographical criticism needs to bear in mind one major caution: to keep the biographical facts and the critical interpretation in balance. When the life and works are discussed together, all too often works are forgotten and the study becomes a biographical sketch. Biography is valuable as a study in its own right; it is not the same, however, as the critical application of biography to a work of literature.

Every literary work also springs from the context of its times. Yet, like the personal experiences of an author's life, these must be weighed more heavily in some works than in others for the obvious reason that some writers are more socially and politically conscious than others. The slavery issue and the Civil War are hardly reflected at all in the poetry of Longfellow; they are everywhere apparent in the poetry of Whitman. The French dramatist Giraudoux served in the Ministry of Foreign Affairs of France for a major portion of his life, eventually becoming the Minister of Propaganda, a post he held until the German occupation of France. His plays clearly show his interest in political matters.

Most writers at one point or another do make allusions to the times in which they live. What the writer does and what the critic does are two different things, however. What criticism of this variety tends to do is to read a particular work with a bias—to consider it as a political or social document and to consider it from the one view of history which the critic has adopted. Steinbeck's *The Grapes of Wrath* is a moving novel of human interest which can be read in terms of its own intrinsic values as a literary work; it is also an important social commentary on the plight of dispossessed farmers during the depression of the 1930s. In its sympathy with the farmer and its denunciation of the businessman, the work invites the attention of Marxist critics. For them, the analysis of the novel and also its value therefore hinge on the extent to which it is good or bad Marxist doctrine, on the extent to which the author seems to show attitudes of acceptance or rejection. The author's own intentions are in this case irrelevant. It is possible to read any author's work as Marxist if it is critical of capitalism, religion, and traditional social values, although the author's own interests may not be at all political. Criticism of this nature often begins with presuppositions and then measures the literary work in terms of them. It imposes a framework on it. The critic becomes the primary spokesman, not the literary work itself.

The difference between intrinsic and extrinsic considerations needs to be stressed constantly. It is one thing to examine the motivations of the characters in a novel; it is another to begin with a theory and to view all characters in terms of it. Or to take all of the outward signs of a character as symptoms of inner psychic drives so that a psychologist-critic can offer explanations not apparent to the nonspecialist. Criticism of this variety in a sense subjects literary characters or the author to psychoanalysis in terms of a particular school of thought. Freudian criticism is particularly common.

As fascinating as psychological criticism can be at times, its shortcomings should be apparent. The critic is limited to only what the literary work reveals—a selection of outward signs that cannot be expanded. The critic is unable to elicit more information from the subject. It is not surprising, therefore, that criticism of this kind tends to speculate, to fill in the gaps, to extend the meanings beyond those the work invites. The more complex a character is, the more likely the character is to attract the attention of psychological critics. One of the standard works of this kind of criticism is Ernest Jones's study of Hamlet in terms of the Oedipus complex. Any writer whose works tend to dwell on introspection, sex, the macabre, the occult, the visionary, and the dreamlike—Poe, Kafka, Coleridge, and D. H. Lawrence come quickly to mind—is an especially fruitful source for this kind of critical analysis. Above all, however, criticism of this variety requires knowledge.

Archetypal and mythic considerations

Closely related to psychological criticism is an approach that views literature in terms of archetypal patterns and myths. This kind of criticism draws heavily on anthropology, religion, and mythology. It is an exploration of the communal response of all people to certain patterns of experience and phenomena of nature. These are inescapably a part of basic human behavior. For example, one of the archetypal experiences of all people is growth from childhood to adulthood, from immaturity to maturity, from innocence to knowledge. The pattern applies not only to individual experience but to collective experience as well. Thus, one of the best known of all myths, which like all myths may or may not have basis in fact, is the story of Adam and Eve in the Garden of Eden. Adam and Eve become primal father and mother. They are individuals; they are also all humankind. They pass from their state of innocence to a state of knowledge. As a result, they are expelled from Eden. Thus arises another deep subconscious drive in all human beings: the desire to return to the Edenic experience and the quest for a means, often a savior, to achieve it. In turn, other kinds of experience follow: suffering, sacrifice, and death, with the idea that these will bring about redemption, purification, and immortality. All of these human manifestations are reflected in the cycles of nature: all things spring to life, grow, die, and revive. These patterns of nature and experience all people seem to know and understand and believe.

In ancient times, the archetypal patterns were embodied in simple but powerful stories that today we call myths. They are present in almost all cultures. Common motifs run through them, and they share symbols that are only variations on one another. We are still fascinated with the simple mythic stories of the sun, moon, water, and the garden; or of a hero's search against obstacles for the answer to a riddle or a sword or a chalice that will make him a savior; or of a hero's willingness to die to deliver his people or remove the blight of sterility from the land.

These archetypal and mythic patterns continue to emerge in both the structure and imagery of contemporary writers. Critics interested in this approach are sometimes able to demonstrate convincingly that an author, whether intentionally or not, has once again recast one of the ancient myths in a new garb. These strains seem to demonstrate that beneath all of their knowledge and sophistication, modern people still cannot escape the most elemental concerns of their nature.

Like most of the extrinsic approaches, archetypal and mythic criticism requires an acquaintance with a vast body of knowledge on the subject. We may all know instinctively more than we think we know, but anthropology and cultural history provide a rich source of organized knowledge with which to begin.

It is not uncommon for authors to turn to philosophical works for clarification of their own thinking about the universe and to reflect this reading in their own works, sometimes superficially, sometimes profoundly. Therefore, an investigation of an author's own reading has been a fairly standard kind of project among scholars and critics interested in the influence of outside thought on a writer. We can understand Dante better by knowing Aquinas; Alexander Pope by knowing Deistic thought, which he got from his friend Bolingbroke; Wordsworth by knowing John Locke and David Hartley; John Stuart Mill by knowing Auguste Comte; and Shaw by knowing Henri Bergson. In more general terms, certain concepts occur over and over again in literature. Platonic ideas are pervasive in the writings of the Renaissance. The concept of the Great Chain of Being, which had its genesis in Greek philosophy, occurs again and again in philosophy and literature, as Arthur Lovejoy has shown in his book of the same name.

Knowing the philosophical backgrounds of a literary work can add immeasurably to our understanding of it. We should be aware, however, that the lack of this kind of outside knowledge does not necessarily present an insurmountable barrier to understanding a writer. Authors also take on the role of informants. They often explain what they are talking about through one character or another. The purpose of criticism of this variety is finally to verify the accuracy of the writer's ideas and to see what adaptations have been made. This type of analysis is a specialized approach that requires more than the capacity to name sources. If it is of value, it should add to the completeness of the work's meaning.

Criticism that involves literary history amounts to placing writers or a particular work into any number of literary contexts. Authors can be considered in relation to a literary movement, or they can be considered as influencing other writers or being influenced by them. A work can be considered as employing literary conventions or rebelling against them. A particular writer may be more important historically than the quality of his works justifies. Emile Zola is significant for his leadership of the Naturalistic movement in the late nineteenth century. His novels are still read, but they do not equal in reputation those of Stephen Crane, who followed later in the movement. John Lyly's *Euphues*, written in a highly inflated and affected style popular in the sixteenth century, gave the English language a new word, but the work ordinarily is known only through brief excerpts that appear in anthologies to illustrate "euphuism." Sarah Orne Jewett is an important writer of regionalist literature in America, but she has not achieved major stature as a literary figure. Gertrude Stein exercised a powerful influence on a whole group of writers and artists emerging in the 1920s, but many people find her own works largely unreadable. Thus, we can multiply the examples of literary figures and particular literary works that loom large in literary history, although they are not of major interest from other critical viewpoints. It is obvious that this form of criticism depends on knowledge of literary history.

Another kind of critical response as an extrinsic source of thought may best be described as a bringing of the self to the literary work. It is creative rather than analytical; it is often an emotional response rather than an intellectual one. It requires only that you react in some way to the work you have read. You may want to imitate it; you may want to write a poem; you may be moved to give a personal testimonial to how you have responded to the work; you may want to speak to one of the characters. After reading Arna Bontemps' "A Summer Tragedy," one student wrote:

> I became so involved in the story that Bontemps could take me anywhere, have me see the story through any eyes. I could see where the people's outlook stopped and where the living situation began. Bontemps could inject any sensation into the story and I could feel it immediately.
>
> I am—no, it doesn't matter what I am except that I am a reader. Arna Bontemps is a writer. He reached me. He said his thing to me, I listened to him through my own patterns, and I saw things his way all of a sudden. He made my world larger.

These are only the concluding remarks of a critical response that gives specific examples of why this student was moved as she was. This is affective criticism, that is, criticism concerned with feeling. All highly personal criticism may say more about you than about the work itself, but it does testify to the vital effect literature can have on the individual. Criticism does not need to be considered a purely diagnostic art; it can itself be a creative activity that seeks out its own forms and modes.

Since thought and meaning emerge from almost all things that authors do in composing, a few questions like the following help to bring into focus a large and involved topic:

1. To what extent is the author's meaning literal or metaphorical? Can the author's meaning be reduced to a sentence, or can it only be hinted at?

2. Is the author firmly committed to a point of view, or does the work seem only to raise questions? Does the work seem to express a particular philosophy or set of ideas that are peculiarly the author's own? Are the ideas derivative? Does the uncertainty about the author's meaning comment on the complexity of the work or on its purpose only to observe, not to give answers?

3. Does the title give a clue to the work's major emphasis? Does the work seem to be about other things than the title suggests? Is the title ambiguous? Is it derived from another source that will comment on the meaning of this work?

4. Do the names of characters and places seem to have special significance? Are they metaphorical? Associative? Allegorical? Are characters nameless for a particular purpose? Is any character an embodiment of an idea?

5. Are allusions a key to the author's meaning? Of what nature are they? Topical? Literary? Mythological? Natural? Is the allusion a passing reference or an integral part of the structure? What does a comparison with the source reveal about the author's use of it?

6. Do particular ideas dominate the dialogue? Are particular ideas countered by opposite views? What characters speak particular ideas? Are they sympathetic characters? Do they seem to speak for the author?

7. Are the ideas of a particular work dated? Have they been discredited by later findings and developments? Is the work therefore dated because its ideas are outmoded? Do some ideas seem to be perennial, unchanging?

8. What outside sources of knowledge does a particular work seem to invite? Is the work highly autobiographical so that the facts of the author's life are particularly relevant? Is it a work that concerns itself with a special body of knowledge so that full understanding depends on turning to outside sources? Is a special knowledge of psychology, philosophy, myth, or literary history particularly valuable?

9. What are the social and historical issues that will clarify the meaning? Are they still vital considerations? Has the work transcended its own times?

10. How do you respond personally to the work? Does it anger you or sadden you? Are you in some way inspired? Why? What is the vital force of the work?

General approaches to writing about literature

The discussion up to this point has concentrated mainly on the nature of literature and the way it functions as an art form, indicating the kinds of things you can focus on. With this as background, then, what can you do in actually writing about literature?

You can summarize

Summary statements are close to exercises that merely test your capacity to paraphrase the content accurately. If you write a lengthy synopsis as a substitute for an essay, you should realize that you have done little more than given evidence that you have read closely enough to reproduce the details.

Summary may be considered the most elementary and least demanding approach to writing about literature. It does become important, however, when the presentation demands any kind of illustration. Even though you can often assume that your readers know the work under discussion, it is necessary to give brief summaries from time to time to refresh their memories and to establish a common base for understanding. When summary predominates over all other approaches, however, the readers know that you have failed to take the additional step of lending your own thought to the material.

You can interpret

Interpreting is seeing the implications of what is going on or what is being said in a literary work. It goes beyond retelling the story; it says what it is about. It may consist of any number of different approaches. It may involve deciphering the difficult syntax of a poem; it may mean recognizing that the reading of a poem is intentionally ambiguous and that it therefore has several implications. It may mean filling in the details of a story or play which are left implicit. By leaving some things unexplained, imaginative literature differs quite consistently from discursive prose. The essayist characteristically wants to supply as much detail as possible so that meanings are direct and clear. But the writer of literature leaves much for readers to conjecture and imagine. This is part of the appeal of literature.

Interpretation may also be described as translation as opposed to transcription. Nietzsche once wrote, "There are no facts, only interpretations." Once a work of literature is written, all kinds of private, representative, and universal implications may emerge. If a work by its obviousness or superficiality stimulates little thought, then there is little need for interpreting it. Interpretation may consist of working within the framework of the work itself—intrinsic considerations—in order to dig down into the core of meaning. Interpretation may also consist of extending outward—extrinsic considerations—in order to build on suggestions the literary work contains. In either case, interpretation amounts to bringing thought and feeling—your thought and feeling—to the act of reading and then verbalizing those thoughts.

Interpretation is seldom objective, but its subjectivity does not mean that it can be deliberately wrongheaded. When interpretation seems no longer to have any connection with the facts of the literary work, then surely it can be dismissed as farfetched. Interpretation consists of saying what you think, but saying what you think is one thing; saying what you think the writer is saying is another. As a writer and interpreter, you can think of yourself as an orchestral conductor who takes up the score of a musical work. You can make it your own composition by ignoring completely the author's intentions, or you can put the composer first and try to bring out the fullest intentions of the work.

The best criticism makes the work primary; it begins with the work and keeps it always in focus. It is a critic's purpose to provide a number of access routes to understanding. If an interpretation leads readers *to* the work, it provides a service. If it leads readers completely *away* from the work, it has surely lost sight of its purpose as criticism.

You can analyze

Analysis is a kind of internal dissection that permits a reader to come to an understanding of the work as a whole. John Ruskin once defined artistic composition as "the help of everything in the picture by everything else." Analysis does assume that a literary work is organic, its parts working together to produce a total effect. It does not imply that the examination of the parts, like an exploratory operation of the human body, is done to discover the flaws. Analysis reveals weaknesses at times, but it may also increase your understanding of how intricately the parts join together to cause you to respond as you do. Analysis is simply a way of seeking understanding.

Very often the secret of understanding is being able to ask good questions. The suggestions for writing about each of the components of literature given in the sections above furnish an array of questions for purposes of analysis and interpretation. One question—an obvious one—may provide only an obvious answer. Some students know only obvious questions. If they ask a different question, a less obvious one, the answer may provide new insights. Above all, you must learn to ask your own questions—good ones.

The best criticism asks many different questions, although some critics who associate themselves with a particular school of thought may ask only a limited few. Thus, they tend to see every literary work in the same terms. Their remarks become monotonous, pat, and often forced. Certainly as a student-critic you need all of the resources you can find, not only to be able to write about literature, but to form your own standards of critical judgment.

You can evaluate

To say of a literary work only "I like it" or "I don't like it" is not actually an evaluation; it is a dismissal. Personal response is an important beginning, but in some way it must be pushed further to say what the worth of a literary work is or what is lacking that would make it valuable. Evaluations, therefore, extend over a range of possibilities from formal considerations to private ones.

First, a work may be considered in terms of itself, as this book has emphasized. Evaluation of this kind assumes something about what a work of art should do, namely, that all of its parts should be working toward the total effect. Therefore, evaluation of this kind asks how each part relates to the whole—and, equally important, how the parts relate to each other. Why do they follow one another? What are the principles of arrangement? To say that a literary work is "all of a piece" is to commend it.

Although some literary works are not structurally flawless, they are nevertheless impressive. Their worth may rest on other grounds, perhaps on their plausibility: the plausibility of the action, of the characters, of the thought, If the actions are contrived and improbable under the pretense of being lifelike, then the illusion fails. If the characters are appealing but superficial, then they may be wholly forgettable. Yet if the thought, though fragmentary, is penetrating, the work may still have merit. The elements of literature, however, are not ordinarily isolated from one another. Evaluation is simply a way of considering the merits and limitations of a work in separate terms.

A literary work may have worth in still other ways. Its value may be judged in terms of its stylistic effectiveness—its use of specific language and strategies. Criticism of this kind depends to a great extent on reading experience, and comparison may be the way of arriving at a decision about effectiveness. In one of his critical essays on poetry, Matthew Arnold proposed that the best way to determine excellence was "to have always in one's mind lines and expressions of the great masters, and to apply them as a touchstone to other poetry." He goes on to explain that other poetry will not have to resemble these touchstones closely, but they will serve as the means of determining the presence or absence of quality. They are in a sense, then, reminders of what quality is.

Arnold's touchstone method can be easily discredited as too intuitive, too limited, or too backward looking. Yet it does cause us to ask ourselves what criteria we are using when we are moved to praise. Some critics have no outside criteria; their decision about worth depends on themselves alone.

Evaluation that depends wholly on your personal engagement with a work is, of course, a private kind of criticism. You cannot expect others to share your response unless you explain why you feel as you do. That explanation may involve narrating a personal experience which reveals why you have identified with a literary work. You may show your involvement by recording your reactions in a journal. The form of the creative critical response may be as varied as the individual who responds. Susan Sontag has written, "What a few people know now is that there are ways of thinking we don't yet know about. Nothing could be more important or precious than that knowledge, however unborn." Expressive criticism may be a source of thoughts yet unknown. You need not shy away from it.

Formal considerations are essentially irrelevant to the final judgments that expressive criticism makes, although individuals who permit themselves honestly to respond to literature may in time become interested enough to ask themselves what sources of value are in the work itself when many other individuals find it equally meaningful. Writing about literature is one way of discovering what your own and other people's values are.

Specific approaches to writing about literature

The practical problems of writing about literature involve deciding what to write, how to focus and develop the topic, and, then, always a hurdle to get over, how to get started. Here are a few suggestions.

The topic as an aid to writing

Writing about literature in the classroom often depends on the topics assigned. In most instances, these are designed to help you rather than hinder you and to focus your attention on matters that may not have occurred to you on your own. If the topic is completely free choice, the demand is even greater because on your own you must then know how to avoid the completely obvious.

In order to demonstrate the expectations and range of topics—either those assigned or self-designed—eight topics are included in this section. They are all based on a single literary work, a modern one-act play by Dennis Jasudowicz entitled *Blood Money*, described by the author as a play "on the value of money stretching." The play is skeletal in form. It has only three characters: D.H., a black man (the initials are those of D. H. Lawrence), Lady C., a black woman (the name suggests Lady Chatterley, the main character of D. H. Lawrence's most famous novel), and the Oil Magnate, unnamed, but described as an overfat white man. The scene takes place in the mountains in a highly grotesque cabin painted black with black window shutters. Recently, the Oil Magnate has sent a man to the slums to buy a beautiful woman to bring to his mountain retreat, but when Lady C. arrives he pays no attention to her. He has also brought a man, D.H., to paint his cabin. D.H. and Lady C. are physically attracted to one another. When the Oil Magnate appears on the scene, he speaks only the words "Gosh! Gosh!" and obscenely stuffs dollar bills into his nostrils. D.H. and Lady C. defy Oil Magnate by making love together outside the cabin as he listens inside. When he will not readmit them to the warm cabin from the freezing outside, they taunt him. In the cold, they then grow desperate. D.H. first abuses Lady C. and then kills her in order to take for himself her warm clothes against the freezing weather. D.H. perishes in an avalanche of snow when he tries to sit on the roof of the cabin warming himself by the chimney. Oil Magnate remains inside, pinning two signs to the wall. One reads HOMECOMING, I HAVE ARRIVED; the other says MESSIAH.

The comments after each of the following topics suggest what the instructor is trying to get you to see and do.

1. **Which character in this play triumphs?** You may take the position that in such a drama no one "triumphs," that "triumph" is a contradictory term. Whatever position you take, support it with evidence from the play. Keep in mind that the last figure on stage is not necessarily victorious, that the most interesting characters are not necessarily going to come out on top, that death is occasionally a triumph of sorts, and that your own sympathies, attitudes, and preferences have nothing to do with the outcome of the play.

This topic deals with the conflict in the play and its resolution. It asks who wins, if anyone does at all. In the assignment, the instructor tries to help you avoid obvious thinking on the subject and, finally, encourages you in this instance not to let your preconceptions get in the way of letting the play speak for itself.

2. **The Oil Magnate has no lines in the play. What other means does Jasudowicz use to characterize him?**

The topic focuses on one character who is not revealed, as characters usually are, through spoken lines. The Oil Magnate says the words "Gosh! Gosh!" but he does not engage in dialogue. The topic therefore asks you to consider other nonverbal ways in which the nature of this character is made known.

3. **Does the play seem to present only a problem, or does it offer a solution; that is, does the play go anywhere?**

This topic calls for an interpretation of the play as a whole, not in terms of the characters and actions but in terms of the general problem it treats. You must first decide what you consider to be the central thesis of the play and then consider whether the play merely makes observations or offers solutions and criticism.

4. **Color—not only of skin—is used by the playwright, sometimes expressly, other times by implication, in developing his ideas. Focus on one major idea in the play and discuss how the colors help develop that idea.**

This topic focuses on one kind of strategy—the use of colors in the play as symbolical. You are asked to relate the color symbolism to the development of a particular idea. The theme, therefore, should not become merely a catalog or description; it must also be an interpretation.

5. There is an abundance of blood in this little drama. There is also a rich oil magnate who stuffs money in his nose. Comment on the possible significance of this action and try to develop an argument that relates the ideas of blood and money in the play. In other words, why is *Blood Money* a good title, if it is?

This topic assumes that the two key words of the title are especially important; it asks you to consider the action and ideas in terms of them and then to decide whether they are an adequate index to the action and thought in the play.

6. Can you find a parallel between the ill-fated affair of D.H. and Lady C. and the Biblical story of Adam and Eve in the Garden of Eden? How does the recognition of such a similarity add to your understanding of the play?

This topic explores the possible mythic significance of the play. The whole issue would be whether this parallel adds significantly to your insight. If it did not, you obviously could not write at length on a topic like this one.

7. One former student in this course complained that some of the anthology selections exhibited a "hang-up on sex a little outdated for today's young college student." He asked for selections which would express instead youth's "search for relationship and friendship with each other." Do you think this student would object to *Blood Money* on these grounds, or do you think the play expresses his concern for human relationship and friendship? Defend your opinion.

This is a topic that asks for a reaction to someone else's opinion about the play's relevance to current thinking. It involves an evaluation of the play not in terms of itself but in terms of personal standards.

8. Is this a moral play? If so, what moral lesson are we to learn and why? If it is not, why not?

This is a topic that asks for an evaluation, but not in literary terms. The discussion would depend on your concept of what is moral and what isn't and your own response to this particular drama.

Each of these topics hints, leads, or directs in some way. None forbids you from exploring new possibilities, but each urges, shoves, lures you to think about what you may not have thought about before.

The following theme was written in response to number 6 of the topics given above.

Blood Money

Often in modern plays the author creates characters that are concerned with a major problem, but, unlike plays from past centuries that conclude with a moral being learned or a lesson taught, these modern plays generally leave the reader in a state of wonder, not knowing answers, forced to decide for himself. One such play is *Blood Money* by Dennis Jasudowicz. The author presents a problem, but has left the decision-making to the reader: which character is the hero, which is right in his actions, which to believe, what to think.

The love between D.H. and Lady C. resembles the Biblical story of Adam and Eve—lovers in the ideal state who have sinned and are forced to face the consequences of their sin. D.H. and Lady C. willingly sin and realize too late that it means the loss of their re-entry to the paradise of safety, warmth, and shelter. The god they have spurned, the power above them (represented by the Oil Magnate), now spurns them and is deaf to their cries and pleadings. Their faith in each other is destroyed as they realize their situation—that they have caused their own downfall in mistakenly believing and having faith that they will be forgiven.

Faith, here, is an extremely important issue. Do I trust and have faith in those I love, in those who have power over me, or only in myself? In *Blood Money* all these possibilities seem to be ridiculous, since we must watch as Lady C. is murdered by her trusted lover, as the powerful Oil Magnate shows no mercy toward the lesser beings, and as D.H.'s faith in himself is destroyed.

The author has touched on the timeless search of every age. Is it enough to have myself, have faith that I can survive and succeed? Or is it necessary to find another to love, to rely on someone else besides myself for security, happiness, and success? Or are these relationships too concrete and too earthly? By this I mean, does man have to go out of his own personal realm toward faith in and love for a superior being with power over him? Man in himself is so small, but added to another is twice again in size. D.H. and Lady C. could have had so much strength and beauty in their love and unity, but the weak basic nature of man allowed fear and desperation to take the upper hand. Man can add nothing to himself with false relationships; only through honesty and truth can strength and success in friendship and love grow. Perhaps man's belief in a superior being is his only hope, perhaps it is his major downfall. I have yet to come to a decision. . . .

COMMENT　This essay begins by stating that *Blood Money* is the kind of play that leaves moral decisions to the reader. This particular student does not have moral preconceptions that will simplify looking at the play. The essay is an attempt to consider possibilities, to ask questions.

The interpretation begins by rather remarkably condensing into one paragraph a parallel between the Garden of Eden and the situation in *Blood Money*. This comparison then invites the possible solutions to man's plight: faith and love. A kind of self-examination follows, but the answers are prompted by details from the play. At this point, the student has not abandoned the drama to write a personal narrative. The essay reveals the student's mind at work in interaction with the play. The essay concerns itself primarily with the plot and the ideas that grow out of it. It is a mythic interpretation of the play and a personal assessment.

One of the main problems every writer has to solve is how to talk about a literary work as a whole without falling into vacuous generalizations. The problem increases as the length of the work increases, for the accumulation of detail seems always to invite a statement that will include the whole work.

How to focus and develop: suggestions

What happens can be illustrated by a sentence one student wrote in an attempt to cover three stories by D. H. Lawrence.

> In his three short stories, Lawrence deals with love relationships. He reveals the participants' feelings, needs, and desires—both conscious and unconscious—and their resulting behavior—emotional and often irrational—when these needs and desires are not fulfilled.

The weight of the generalization is almost more than one sentence can bear. But, more to the point, it is a high-level generalization that might apply to three stories by three other writers. It is not specifically a meaningful statement about the stories of D. H. Lawrence. How then can you avoid generalizing about all literature and all life so that an essay seems clearly related to the work it is discussing? How do you organize your thoughts so that in a relatively brief space you can indicate your grasp of the whole?

1. You can carefully select a speech or passage or detail that brings many elements of the work into focus. The discussion can then move outward to illustrate the central importance of this passage and its representativeness. The important emphasis here is to begin with the small significant detail and then develop more general thoughts.

2. Instead of the all too familiar summary theme that begins with the beginning, you can start with the end of the work and explain the outcome in terms of the earlier development. This approach invites selection of detail for purposes of illustration. In explaining why the work ends as it does, you often are led to explain the meaning of the whole thing.

3. You can attempt to see the major characters from the point of view of one of the secondary characters. This provides a means of selective analysis and demands an interpretation from a point of view other than the author's own. This approach provides fresh insight because we usually tend to focus on major characters. (Tom Stoppard's play *Rosencrantz and Guildenstern Are Dead* does this very thing. In this play, Hamlet is only a background character.)

4. You can collect small clues and signs that set the tone and create an atmosphere for the whole work. Here you can often be original because you may be sensitive to details that others do not see.

5. You can select one theme for discussion rather than the full breadth of the literary work. This suggestion may also permit you to pursue a personal interest. For instance, you may see chauvinism in the speeches of the men characters, even though the main theme of the play does not concern women's rights.

6. You can attempt to relate selected details of the story to a single emotional effect: one work as a study in horror, another as a study in the grotesque, another as dreamlike.

7. You can examine particular literary devices as a way of discovering how the author creates effects. You, of course, need to know what a literary device is. This book has attempted to explain how literature works through form, language, character, plot, style, and setting.

8. You can begin with what interests you most about the work and then try to account for this reaction in terms of other things that have receded in your attention. How finally does everything fit together?

9. You can begin with an interpretation or critical evaluation written by someone else and then agree or disagree, support or refute, expand or offer an alternate interpretation. This approach requires some outside reading. It has its advantages and disadvantages. You can always learn from others, to be sure, but you want to make certain that you do not use outside criticism as a crutch or, even worse, as a substitute for your own thinking.

10. Instead of writing directly about the work, you can attempt to do a creative piece of your own that either expresses your response to the work you have read (see essay on p. 369) or gives the work a modern or personal setting so that your understanding of the original is fully revealed.

Each of the student themes that begin on p. 360 illustrates a way of beginning. In order, the seven themes begin with:

How to get started: suggestions

1. an evaluation and then an attempt to support that judgment
2. a condensed sketch of the character to be discussed
3. a statement of personal feelings that relate to the work
4. a quotation
5. two questions that attempt to get at the central meaning of the poem
6. a comparison that will be more fully developed
7. a personal narrative

These particular beginnings are in each instance appropriate to the approaches used in those essays.

Even when students are assigned the same topic, they choose different focuses and organization and thus come up with different beginnings. A group of students, after having read Philip Roth's *Goodbye, Columbus*, were asked to describe the world of that novella—the fictional universe Roth creates. They could focus on any character or on any group of characters. Here are five examples of the beginnings these students actually wrote:

> The world of *Goodbye, Columbus* is one of hot summer days, the smell of fresh-cut grass, and two people discovering the meaning of love. Neil Klugman and Brenda Patimkin come from different worlds, but as their relationship evolves, they form their own separate world in which their lives and love coexist. Their "special" world overlaps with the personal worlds that their families and friends are part of.

> *Goodbye, Columbus* deals with Neil Klugman, a middle-class Jew, college graduate, and library employee, who falls for Brenda Patimkin, college student, Jewish, from a wealthy family. They have an affair one summer which comes to a bad end in the fall. So much for the introduction.

> The world created in *Goodbye, Columbus* was formed by a fusion of the two different worlds of Neil and Brenda. The world which existed between these two people did not last, for it was not a real world at all. It was closer to never-never land.

Brenda's world in *Goodbye, Columbus* consisted of her classes, a jealous mother, an adoring father, a typical, spoiled little sister, a collegiate athlete, a black maid, Radcliffe, an empty temple, three hundred dollars that used to be in an old sofa, an old refrigerator full of fruit, a sports tree, a Chrysler and a Volkswagen, and an ego-builder called Neil Klugman.

Her world is a storybook ideal that every little girl dreams of acquiring. . . .

The little black boy in *Goodbye, Columbus* lives in a world of fantasy. It is so much more appealing to him than the environment that surrounds him. His fantasy world is present only at the library.

The worlds of the individual characters in *Goodbye, Columbus* are so different in terms of values and priorities that it is impossible for them to blend into one, and therein lies the conflict of the story.

The world of Neil Klugman is shaped by a middle-class upbringing in Newark, New Jersey. [details follow]

Things have always come easy for Brenda. [details follow]

So we have Brenda and Neil escaping from their own worlds. They find it impossible, however, to make one world acceptable to them both. . . .

The final example indicates in skeletal form the beginning, the development, and the ending of an entire theme. Once a beginning has been determined—a thesis—and some sense of direction has been given, then almost all of the remainder of such an essay is expansion by way of illustration. How this development is worked out completely can be seen in the student essays that follow.

Student examples

1 *Writing about fiction: a critical evaluation*

"Go Down, Moses"—The Old Versus The New

The most successful story in Faulkner's *Go Down, Moses* is the final episode entitled "Go Down, Moses." This story is successful because it achieves, in a simple way, the presentation of the attitudes and misunderstandings which are part of the southern heritage. The story revolves around Mollie Beauchamp, a post-Civil War black, and Gavin Stevens, the county attorney. Mollie represents the old order of black society which is incapable of handling its own affairs after two centuries of slavery, and Gavin Stevens represents a segment of the modern white society that knows it must live with the blacks and senses an obligation toward them. This obligation is unusual, or perhaps it may be said to be traditional in the same sense that the pre-Civil War plantation owner had an obligation to his slaves. Yet, Gavin Stevens does feel a respect and compassion for the downtrodden blacks. This story attempts to determine the extent of the obligation of one race to the other, at least as it is resolved in one man's mind.

The story also probes the questions, How much is a "dead nigger" worth to the white race and ultimately how much is the entire black race worth to the white race? The story is successful because of the way Faulkner arrives at his answers. He sets up a situation in which Mollie's boy has disappeared. She believes that he is in trouble and goes to the county attorney for help. The bulk of the story is concerned with the county attorney's efforts to ease Mollie's burden. In the course of the action, the reader draws several conclusions relevant to southern life and thinking:

1. Mollie and a majority of the southern blacks do not and probably will not understand completely the system of white domination in which they must function.
2. The white race still does not understand the black's thinking and emotional patterns.
3. The black is still treated as a child by the white race as a result of the two races' misunderstandings.
4. There is no immediate solution to the problems between the races.

Yet, why is this story unique? True, Faulkner has explored these same conflicts in other stories, but he has nowhere else crystallized them as he does in the final story of *Go Down, Moses.* He has gotten away from the plantation, where white domination is traditionally expected; he has gotten away from the hunt, where all men tend to be equal in the chase; and in this story he has situated himself in the city, the new center of southern life in the years after the Civil War as blacks drifted from the plantations. He has shown how the same attitudes, prejudices, and misunderstandings that he has so carefully explored in the earlier stories now function in the city, in the new restructured social system.

This story, with the possible exception of the "The Bear," is the most vital in the entire collection, as Faulkner is pitting the old social order against modern society and new situations. He is not simply explaining life on the plantation with its predictable patterns of behavior, but life in the modern world where action does not allow a predictable pattern. It is this unpredictable pattern—that Stevens goes so far out of his way to please the mother of a dead black, who to him is only a criminal— that makes this story unique.

Stevens realizes that the whites have an obligation to the blacks, not as the McCaslins did because they owned them as slaves but because the blacks are people with desires and feelings the same as any member of the white race. Faulkner's characters do not reach this point of understanding in any of the other stories. "Go Down, Moses" is successful because it explores the old relationships in contrast with the new and thus gives us a new perspective on southern life that none of the other stories can provide.

COMMENT The essay begins with an evaluation: the writer's judgment that one particular story in a collection is the most successful of the group because it accomplishes effectively what it sets out to do. The writer immediately begins summary details as a way of justifying the conclusions that follow. The summary naturally involves the characters, action, and setting; the four conclusions are the emerging ideas. In an effort to establish the uniqueness and success of this particular story, the writer then turns to comparison. He says that the setting of this story makes it unique. He refers also to its special vitality and to the depth of its understanding and penetration. He attempts to support each of these points.

In the course of the analysis, the writer has touched on most of the elements of fiction except possibly the style. Even so, there is some concern with tone. The essay indicates clearly how summary, analysis, interpretation, and evaluation depend on one another and how the various components of this story cannot be rigidly separated from one another for purposes of writing.

2 Writing about fiction: a character analysis

The Man and the Bird

When the boat was first visible on the horizon, it must have appeared as only a small dot to the bird that was flying toward it. Somewhere along in its flight, when it got close enough to see that the boat did indeed afford some sort of haven to perch upon, the bird must have changed course toward it. It is not known what the bird's ultimate goal was, but it seems unlikely that it left it point of origin with that particular boat in mind.

In Hemingway's *The Old Man and the Sea,* the boat belongs to the old man, Santiago. Out fishing on his own, the old man has hooked an enormous marlin, whose strength and sheer will to survive draw the old man and his boat far out beyond the sight of land, and deep into the greatest struggle the old man will ever face. When the struggling bird—it is a warbler, and too small for such a flight—comes toward the boat, it is "flying very low over the water"; it sees the struggling man. For a full day and night, he has kept his line and his muscles taut. Morning finds him in much the same position as nightfall had found him the evening before.

The bird flies because he knows nothing but flying. It is his survival, and without it he would die. In a similar way, fishing is all that the old man knows. Each morning he arises and goes out to his boat. He spends his day fishing. It is his life. Each day the bird takes flight. He does his "fishing" from the sky. It is his life. Each has known no other life than the one each is living now. No matter what their location, their basic actions remain the same.

The old man knows of other lifestyles only remotely. The other people of his village are mostly fishermen, and his only other outside contact is with the world the newspapers describe. Even though he follows baseball and "the great DiMaggio," totally comprehending such a lifestyle is as foreign to him as his own life probably is to the bird. Both the bird and the man follow a way of life that seem predestined for them—the bird because he was born a bird; the man because he was born into a fisherman's world. The great difference lies in the fact that the man has the potential to change his lifestyle. But Santiago is so conditioned to this one world that the thought of changing it would never occur to him.

To both the bird and man, the sea plays a major role. It becomes their immediate world, and their actions revolve around it. The man rides on the water; the bird flies above it. The old man's skiff is his sanctuary from the sea. The man gets his food and income from the sea, but he is not in control. He is bound by the narrow confines of his boat. The bird too is confined, for even though it may fly, unless it can reach a perch, it cannot survive for long over the water. The bird can no more control the events of his flight than the old man can control the force that guides a fish to his bait. Both are limited to the favors the sea is willing to toss their way.

When the old man first sees the bird, he welcomes it. The bird represents another living thing involved in a personal struggle. The bird's struggle is to make it to shore safely; the old man's struggle is that more. To him there is much more at stake than just a safe port. The marlin tests the old man's fishing skills. Catching the biggest marlin anyone has ever seen is not only a means of gaining self-esteem in the eyes of the villagers and the small boy who idolizes him, but it is also a means of maintaining respect in his own eyes. It lends proof that he is not ancient, that he is still capable. Further, it is his duty. He is a fisherman; this is his life. He would no more cut the line and give up without a fight than the bird would stay on shore and never venture out to sea. They do what others expect of them and what they expect of themselves.

The old man thinks of the hawks that will come out to meet the small bird. Against such odds and after such a strenuous flight, the small bird does not appear to have much chance. The bird, or so the old man thinks, knows nothing of this. Neither does the old man know anything of the sharks that await him when he finally catches his prize. Or maybe, unconsciously, he is aware that the lasting struggle lies not in the capture of his marlin, but in retaining this trophy. He tells the bird, perhaps with greater insight than he is aware: "Take a good rest, small bird. . . . Then go in and take your chance like any man or bird or fish." The bird leaves the old man's company with as little thought as he entered it. The old man feels remorse, for the bird has provided some small company, if only briefly. But Santiago is soon caught up again in the process of his own life.

In the end, the old man, after winning so hard a fight and having his victory slip so easily from him, is oddly resigned to his luck, perhaps bcause he recognizes the need to learn from each experience, learning to take what is offered and gaining what he can while he can. He does not lose the marlin entirely. It still exists within him, and he is conscious of its strength and his own strength, a strength that he need not justify simply because he himself is confident of it, as confident as the warbler who unknowingly undertakes an enormous flight.

COMMENT The incident of the old man and the bird is a short one in *The Old Man and the Sea.* The bird rests for a few brief moments on the boat; Santiago talks to it and identifies with it. The extended comparison, however, is the writer's own. It is a way of revealing Santiago's character and motivation by shifting the focus away from him, yet always keeping him in view. By seeking parallels, the writer creates better understanding of the character.

The opening description of the boat from the height of the bird at a distance—a kind of zooming in on the scene—is original with the writer. The essay begins with the bird; it ends with the bird. The rounding out of this theme gives the essay a satisfying sense of completion.

3 Writing about fiction: an impressionistic comparison

On Seeing a Blind Bird

There is something about seeing the blind that wrenches horror out of the viewer. Perhaps it is an innate fear in us that we, too, may be blind one day. Or maybe it is an instinctive aversion to weakness. Certainly our immediate reaction to blindness is not sympathy. Every fiber in us resists the humane attitude.

This horrified fascination hits a viewer of "Blind Bird," a black-and-white ink painting by Morris Graves. Grave's bird, black and huddled, clings flightless to a rock, its feet bound down by a tangle of white cobwebs. The bird's eyes are either dark voids or nonexistent. It crouches alone; it touches nothing but its rock, the tangle holding it there, gray mists around it, and whatever its mind contains. The bird looks totally vulnerable, yet somehow utterly impenetrable.

The main character in Dostoevsky's "Notes from Underground" draws from the reader that same "Blind Bird" horror. We may ultimately wring a drop of pity from our hearts over the underground man's plight if we feel no identity with him, yet immediately we feel a revulsion over his condition. The underground man seems to huddle bitterly in his shell as the bird does on its rock, bound to his spot with a web of uncontrollable thought patterns. He broods like the bird; what else can a vulnerable flightless hulk do?

Something about blindness urges us to ask, "How did this happen?" The question is usually not derived from kind concern but rather from a certain morbid curiosity. There is more than a hint of lingering Puritanism in our unvoiced suspicion that somehow the blindness is a result of the afflicted creature's actions: perhaps the bird might still see if it had been a good bird; perhaps the underground man would be a social success if he did not cling so obstinately to his bizarre reflections.

The lingering quality of the "Blind Bird" is a certainty of unalterable isolation. The bird will not enjoy voluntary solitude; the webby tangles imprisoning its feet will keep it on its rock in a most involuntary manner. Yet if the bird had a chance to fly, we can suspect it would react just as the underground man says:

> Come, try, give any one of us . . . a little more independence, untie our hands, . . . relax the control and we . . . yes, I assure you . . . we should be begging to be under control again at once.

COMMENT This essay is an attempt to solve the very difficult matter of expressing one's feelings about a work of literature in such a way that another reader will understand what the effect has been on the writer. With an opening paragraph about human reactions to blindness in general, the writer turns immediately to a painting by Morris Graves. Not until the third paragraph do we come to the literary work under discussion, but the previous remarks have prepared the reader for a meaningful comparison. From that point on, the thought vacillates back and forth from bird to man and from man to bird. The writer has made the two one.

The Hope of Man

"Think of living up there in the top flat, with a beautiful young wife, two pretty little children and an income of twenty thousand crowns a year," yearns The Student in the first scene of Strindberg's *The Ghost Sonata*. To live in a house like that would be the answer to his hopes for happiness. His hope is for a life of sweet, innocent love, of sunshine-filled rooms with pink draperies, of his own children's bubbling laughter, and of money enough to insulate himself from the common worries of existence. This is his personal interpretation of the basic hope of man—that somewhere there is something beautiful and true to make the suffering of life worthwhile. The question asked by The Girl—so often asked but so seldom answered—is therefore central: "Is life worth so much hardship?"

Strindberg's *The Ghost Sonata* is not a play written to fill one's heart with hope for human triumph over the "labor of keeping the dirt of life at a distance," as The Girl aptly phrases the problem. Instead, Strindberg destroys the false dreams of the romantic and through a horror-filled nightmare shows the blackness of reality that is hidden so securely behind a well-scrubbed facade of deceit. This is shown symbolically by the house—modern, pleasant-appearing, so seemingly filled with "beauty and elegance." It is a mansion. To the passerby it is the home of virtuous and high-minded aristocrats: the wealthy colonel, the benevolent consul, the aged spinster, the baron, the beautiful daughter, and the well-mannered servants. But what are these people after Mr. Hummel, the most flagrant deceiver of them all, disrupts their stagnating existence, and "the deepest secret is divulged—the mask torn from the imposter, the villain exposed . . ."? All of these people are tortured by the sins of their past; all live on in the horrid loneliness of a hell full of "crime and deceit and falseness of every kind," in which payment is painfully wrung from their condemned souls.

In this symbolic house of lies, what is more a paradox of appearance and reality than the Hyacinth Room, full of the splendor of nature? The Student extols hyacinths of many colors: "the snow-white, pure as innocence, the yellow honey-sweet, the youthful pink, the ripe red, but best of all the blue—the dewy blue, deep-eyed and full of faith." But The Girl shows the other side of the picture: "This room is called the room of ordeals. It looks beautiful, but it is full of defects." The chimney smokes, the desk wobbles, the pen leaks, the maid makes more work for The Girl, the cook gives her no nutrition. "Living is hard work, and sometimes I grow tired," laments The Girl. Finally, she grows tired from her labors and dies. Her whole life is a hopeless situation; for, as The Student explains, "The very life-spring within you is sick."

There is no hope here for The Girl, or for man in general. But is there hope in the patient Buddha, waiting endlessly for the time when "this poor earth will become a heaven"? I think not. The Student explains, "Buddha sits holding the earthbulb, his eyes brooding as he watches it grow, outward and upward, transforming itself into a heaven." This symbol of man's hopes seems to be contradicted by the meaningless death of The Girl, killed by the world's cruel

365

deceit. Buddha's shallot, blooming beautifully out of the ugly earth, is the hope of man. Yet it may be contrasted with another flower, The Girl, the flower of reality, who withers and dies in this vale of tears we call life.

To end the play, The Student soliloquizes on the hopelessness of finding anything in life worth living for. He hopes that death will liberate, that The Girl will eventually find the hopes of man fulfilled "by a sun that does not burn, in a home without dust, by friends without stain, by a love without flaw."

COMMENT   The clarity and orderliness of this analysis belie what a remarkable accomplishment this short essay is. The student takes a highly complex, symbolical drama and by focusing on selected details of the setting and dialogue by two of the main characters manages to get at the substance of Strindberg's thought. At no point does he summarize the action, although he does suggest in paragraph 2 what the general situation is. He is primarily concerned with the strategies that Strindberg uses: the house, the Hyacinth Room in particular, the Buddha. All of these he interprets so that their significance is made known. But the essay is not all formalistic analysis. When the major topic of the paper—the hope of man—is introduced in the fourth paragraph, the writer expresses his personal opinion. He shares the doubts of the student in the play. He makes clear which character he identifies with.

5 *Writing about a poem: analysis and interpretation*

Organization: A Definition
Anecdote of the Jar
I placed a jar in Tennessee,
And round it was, upon a hill.
It made the slovenly wilderness
Surround that hill.

The wilderness rose up to it,
And sprawled around, no longer wild.
The jar was round upon the ground
And tall and of a port in air.

It took dominion everywhere.
The jar was gray and bare.
It did not give of bird or bush,
Like nothing else in Tennessee.

Wallace Stevens

If there were no black, would white have meaning? If there were no night, what would day mean? It is this basic premise—that a concept has no meaning, or substance, until it is contrasted with an opposite concept—that seems to prompt Wallace Stevens to write "Anecdote of the Jar." The poem is a contrast between jar and wilderness, exemplifying a dependency of jar and wilderness on each other for definition. The jar lends substance to the wilderness, just as the wilderness defines the jar.

Consider the man who, traveling through a presumably unexplored region, comes upon a beer bottle in the midst of it. Not only does he feel a sense of depression at discovering that the region is not unknown but he also is struck by the contrast between bottle and wilderness, or in a broader sense, between that which is man-made and that which is not. In "Anecdote of the Jar" the jar is placed deliberately upon nature by man, perhaps as an experiment, to judge the effect of art on nature. The poem itself is an account, an observation of the contrast it creates.

The jar is "round," suggesting a sense of structured order, but the wilderness is "slovenly" and "sprawled around," portraying a lack of neatness and organization. The jar assumes superiority over the wilderness. It "made" the wilderness surround the hill. It causes the wilderness to "rise" up to it, an image which also supports the idea that the jar is above the wilderness, not only physically but hierarchically. It tames the wilderness until it is "no longer wild"; it is "sprawled around," implying a sense of subservience. The jar is "tall and of a port in air," a note of the jar's height and an observation of its noticeability.

The jar stands out in an unnoticed wilderness, and in this way, the jar grants dimension to the wilderness. Without the jar there is no criterion for judging any aspect of the wilderness. By providing contrast, it is also defining the area, as black defines white.

The idea of the jar's superiority is repeated in the third stanza: "It took dominion everywhere." Man claims no dominion over nature, because he himself is created as wilderness is. But, by means of the jar, man is able to organize wilderness, and in this way, wilderness falls into the order of man. This organized, ordered structure causes wilderness to appear "slovenly" and unstructured, through force of contrast, creating a similar effect to that which one obtains from pondering the question of life's meaning in the absence of death.

The jar is an artifact—a man-made product. It is a functional thing, but it is also unproductive. It is "gray and bare" and does not "give of bird or bush." And so, though the jar can organize and grant definition to wilderness, it cannot produce life. To me, in brief, the poem contrasts man's creativity and nature's. The jar, being man-made, follows a human organization. The wilderness does not; yet it can produce "bird and bush"—life, the most organized structure of all. The jar cannot.

COMMENT Since the Stevens poem is short, the paper attempts to deal with the complete meaning and purpose; it does not touch on other elements of the poem at all. The first paragraph states the basic premise that the essay will develop. It is the student's interpretation of the meaning; it is the conclusion she has come to after her careful reading, which the remainder of the essay suggests. Paragraph 2 offers an analogy. If the experience of the poem seems somewhat abstract and remote, this example makes it familiar. Paragraphs 3 and 4 of the essay proceed line by line through the first two stanzas of the poem, selecting details and relating them to the main idea of the poem. Paragraphs 5 and 6 develop the thought further in terms of the third stanza, constantly phrasing and rephrasing the basic premise. Interpretation throughout is the product of analysis. It is the kind of poem that can be defined in this way.

The Journey of the Magi

"Journey of the Magi" by T. S. Eliot tells about the three Wise Men and their visit to the newborn child Jesus. Although the poem is based on the familiar Biblical story written by Matthew, Eliot's version presents a decidedly different view. In the Bible, Matthew tells these things about the Magi:

Now, when Jesus was born in Bethlehem of Judaea in the days of Herod the king, behold, there came wise men from the east to Jerusalem, saying "Where is he that is born King of the Jews? for we have seen his star in the east, and are come to worship him." . . . When they had heard the king, they departed; and, lo, the star, which they saw in the east, went before them, till it came and stood over where the young child was. When they saw the star, they rejoiced with exceeding great joy. And when they were come into the house, they saw the young child with Mary his mother, and fell down, and worshipped him: and when they had opened their treasures, they presented unto him gifts; gold, and frankincense, and myrrh. And being warned of God in a dream that they should not return to Herod, they departed into their own country another way.

Matthew 2:1, 9–12

Matthew's recounting of the story deals with the journey in a very few words. His is less of a story than a direct narration of facts. He skips over the actual details of the journey, simply saying that the Wise Men "went their way." The main emphasis of his view of the journey is on the moment when the Magi see Jesus. Matthew stresses their worship and rejoicing, and their offerings of precious gifts. Of utmost importance in the Biblical version are the joy and humility of the great Wise Men before Jesus; their worship of him shows the importance of Jesus. The return of the Magi and the outcome of their visit, much like their original journey, is ignored by Matthew. Once the Magi leave Bethlehem and Jesus, Matthew's interest in them fades, and he states simply: "they departed into their own country. . . ."

In telling the same story as Matthew, T. S. Eliot depicts the events quite differently. In great contrast to the Biblical version, Eliot's poem skips over the actual moment when the Magi reach Jesus and his mother. In a monumental understatement, Eliot's Magi state: "it was (you may say) satisfactory." Clearly what is important in the poem is not the circumstances of the meeting itself, but how the Birth affects the Magi before and after they are confronted with it.

Eliot places great emphasis on the details of the journey. He aptly portrays what an ordeal the journey must have been, a journey undertaken at the very "worst time of year," in the "very dead of winter." He stresses the cold, sharp weather, the length of the journey, and the soreness of the camels. He tells of people hostile and unfriendly, going about their careless ways in spite of the great event taking place in Bethlehem. Underneath it all is the great doubt of the Magi, wondering if the destination is worth the ordeal of the journey: "With the voices singing in our ears, saying that this was all folly."

The poem, differing from the Bible, also contains details about the arrival of the Magi in the "temperate valley." They see "a running stream and a water-mill beating darkness," suggesting that growth and thriving life are here conquering darkness. With Jesus' birth, hope is born. Contrasted with these signs of birth and hope are images that the Magi see about the countryside, images recalling death. The "three trees on the low sky" recall the three crosses on Golgotha, and the men in the tavern are at an open door "dicing for pieces of silver," just as men drew lots for Jesus' clothes before he died.

The outcome of the journey, totally ignored by Matthew, is seriously dealt with by Eliot in his poem. He describes how the Magi return to their kingdoms but are not at ease. In losing their ignorance of what is truly right, they have lost their "old dispensation" to lead lives of corruption. They realize that their old life cannot suffice for them any longer. Thus, the Birth is their "death" in that it makes them reject the lives that they had once led. In saying this, Eliot is talking about another "journey," that of the struggle they will have to change their lives completely. His description of the new journey parallels the old. The Magi are confronted with severe hardships; their people are alien to them, clutching "gods" instead of the one true God that the Magi have witnessed. Their new realizations, in the form of the Birth, are "hard and bitter agony" for them. In their first journey they "at times regretted" going; likewise, in the second they "should be glad of another death." What is important is that in both journeys, on the way to Bethlehem and on the way to making a new life for themselves, they overcome their doubts and follow the road that they, despite their misgivings, know to be right.

Because the poem fully explores the journey of the Magi, Eliot's version of the story is infinitely more meaningful than Matthew's simple narration of the events. "Journey of the Magi" carries a special impact because it dramatizes the force and the outcome of the events that Matthew merely describes.

COMMENT The productiveness of this essay springs from the fact that the student has returned to the source from which the story of the Magi is taken and has indicated how the two accounts differ in their interests. By comparing, she is able to see what Eliot has added in his poem and how the additions say something new, not inconsistent with Christian doctrine but a further illustration of it. Eliot has focused his story-poem on the minor characters in the Jesus story, those who came to witness his birth. The writer succeeds in explaining the paradoxes of birth and death as they are developed in the poem. Her approach is simple but effective.

7 *Writing about a popular song lyric: personal response as evaluation*

Silence

Often—and it is becoming a pretty regular thing these days—when I become depressed and tired of the silence of people I step out into the darkness of night to relax and think. I can take people only for so long, and then I want to scream. I find myself asking: "What in the hell is going on here?" I get tired of the usual escapes: drugs, drinking, or talking to my parents or a priest. After a while these human escapes from humanity put me right back where I started. I sometimes find consolation in just being aware of the situation Man is in, but after trying to get action and finding only the silence—it brings me down pretty fast. I'm not sure whether it is better to live with questions unanswered or with answers to questions that no one cares to ask. So I take a walk in the darkness of the night, trying to understand how some people can feel satisfied.

There are several forms of silence: the silence of people who are unaware; the silence of people who are aware; and the silence of those who won't allow themselves the self-education that is required to become aware of the faults that are in need of correction. From "The Sound of Silence" by Paul Simon, I receive the impression that he was trying to break through the silence of aware people—people who talk day after day without saying or hearing a thing; fools who are creating a guiding system of life which is not to be questioned, just accepted as it is now until the end of time. But time is running out for such silence. Today more than ever the silence is being shattered—but time may still run out.

I feel very strongly about the plight of the American Indian and black. It makes me very sad to see so many satisfied people walking around, when there is so little to be satisfied with today. I know life cannot really be described in words, but I feel that whatever it is it is an individual thing. By living every day of our lives honestly, trying to seek out the corruption that must be corrected and to find love instead of quick, unjust hate, perhaps we can manage to create a satisfactory environment for ourselves and each other.

COMMENT   The student's essay reveals a thorough understanding of the song lyrics, even though it does not deal directly with the verses. What is written in the first paragraph parallels the experience narrated in the poem, but it is the student's own. The second paragraph paraphrases several of the ideas in the third stanza of the song. The details of the third paragraph grow out of the previous one and take the reader back to the sense of discontent expressed at the beginning of the essay. The ending reflects the spirit of the original lyrics, although the student expresses a stronger sense of hope and idealism than the composer.

The student's response to the song—being able to express a parallel experience and similar thoughts—comments on the validity of the poem. This is a private, nonformal kind of evaluation, but it is meaningful because one knows that the student has been involved with the verses.

Individuals as their own models

These seven examples of writing—all done by college freshmen—indicate different degrees of excellence, of literary sophistication, of detachment and involvement, and reveal varying interests in the effects of literature. They indicate that writing about literature is within the capability of any thoughtful person. What they by all means should suggest is that there is no stereotype for the theme about literature. In fact, prescribing any kind of model would defeat the main theme of this chapter: the idea that you yourself have to come to some realization about the world of literature and its effects on you. Given some understanding of the elements that go to make up literature, you have to find the best way you possibly can to make clear your own understandings and feelings. In fact, in the process of writing about literature, you may find that you have come to know yourself in a more meaningful way.

The term *reference paper* includes what is familiarly called a library paper or a research paper. It also includes any paper that makes repeated references to primary sources or to an anthology that includes collected materials on a specific topic. Whether you collect your own materials or have them made available to you in a text, your task as a researcher and writer does not change essentially.

In recent times, the word *research* has been closely associated with scientific research and laboratory experimentation, and the emphasis has been placed on finding new knowledge. What this emphasis overlooks, of course, is much routine research that does not result in dramatic discoveries and inventions. Occasionally, the etymology of a word lends insight into the lost meaning of a word or one that has faded because a more popular one has prevailed. The word *research* comes from the French word *rechercher*. There is first the prefix *re-*, which occurs frequently in words borrowed from Latin; it means "again" or "again and again." The *chercher*, meaning "to seek or to search," is derived from the Latin word *circāre*, meaning "to go round or about" or "to explore."

In these original terms of the words, much undergraduate research has meaning and value. It is going the rounds again; it is seeking again and again to see what more may be found; it is taking another look. And often in this kind of review you are able to see what someone else has not seen or to see things in new relationships. To the extent that a reinvestigation of a topic brings new insight, it is original, although it may discover no new facts. The main purpose of most undergraduate research, therefore, would seem to be to learn how to find materials, how to evaluate them, and finally how to integrate them into a new set of relationships. These are the basic research skills; taking notes and documenting are only incidental to them. The basic skills are fundamental to what education is all about—first, looking at what *was* and *is* as a means of looking ahead.

Finding materials

The most resourceful people are not necessarily the ones who carry around the greatest amount of information in their heads but the ones who know where to go to find the answers to their questions. Unfortunately, libraries are either museums or labyrinths to many people. They walk through awed by what they see on display, afraid to touch; or they get lost because they do not know the intricacies of the way through. Libraries are not museums; all materials are there to be used. And they do not have to be labyrinths; there are guides that solve the complexities. Every researcher needs some basic knowledge about getting around a major library.

The card catalog as an aid to research

The card catalog is the "open sesame" to the library. Without it, the books would be almost completely inaccessible to the average user. The card catalog also permits you to learn a great number of facts about a book without ever actually seeing it. In fact, the card catalog may be a great time-saver, revealing to you that a particular book is not what you thought it was; but, more importantly, the card catalog may open up leads to books you would not otherwise have encountered on your own. By its system of cross-referencing, the card catalog sometimes sends you from drawer to drawer. Following through on these leads can turn up the sources you are seeking.

The representative cards in the illustration opposite indicate the kinds of information available in the card catalog. Each book usually has three cards—an author card, a title card, and a subject card; often there is also a series card, as shown. (Some books have additional subject cards and/or one or more additional author cards if there are two or more authors.) The author card is always the basic card; all other cards are duplicates of this card, with the title or specific subject heading typed at the top. Each card, of course, is filed in its alphabetical place in the card catalog.

Standard bibliographical sources

Even though the card catalog is an index to the books in a particular library, it is limited as a subject guide for two reasons: first, sometimes it is easier to know exactly what subject headings to look for after you have done some preliminary reading and researching in general sources, such as encyclopedias and other refer-

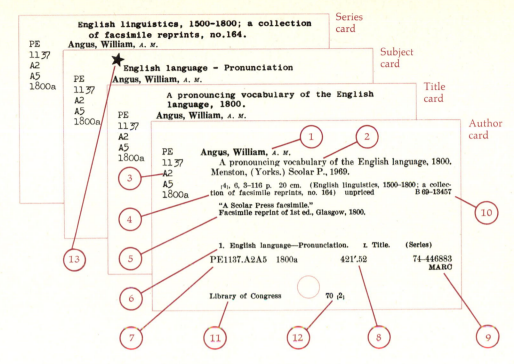

1   Author's name and title or degree.
2   Title of the book, place of publication (Menston, Yorkshire, England), publisher (The Scolar Press, Ltd.), and date.
3   Call number in the library being used.
4   Collation, including preliminary pages (10, of which 4 are used and 6 are blank) and pages in the book proper; height of the book in centimeters; title of the series.
5   Description of special features of the book; other explanatory notes.
6   Other entries in the card catalog. These other cards are shown.
7   Call number under the Library of Congress System.
8   Call number under the Dewey Decimal System.
9   Order number of the card from the Library of Congress and MARC tape availability.
10 Number in *The British National Bibliography.*
11 Indication that the book was cataloged by the Library of Congress.
12 Librarian's information: date of the card and the number of hundreds printed.
13 Identification of a subject entry card.

ence works; second, the card catalog contains virtually no information about material within periodicals. Also, encyclopedias and other reference books usually lead you to specific books that you would not otherwise know about; the card catalog tells you whether or not your own library has them. The library also includes a number of standard guides available as aids in research, at whatever level you are working. These are often located in the reference section.

General encyclopedias

General encyclopedias are a good starting point for the beginning researcher. Since they provide concise summaries of information and scholarly viewpoints, they are useful as an overview that will open up possible topics for detailed investigation. One of the main points to note about an encyclopedia is its date, particularly if current information is vital to the subject being studied. No dates are given here because revisions of some encyclopedias occur frequently.

CHAMBERS'S ENCYCLOPAEDIA

Produced in England, and reflects European viewpoints. Gives standard references on a topic.

COLLIER'S ENCYCLOPEDIA

Bibliography is included in Volume 24.

COLUMBIA ENCYCLOPEDIA

Available in one volume or five. More useful for quick information than for survey of a topic. Brief bibliographies.

ENCYCLOPEDIA AMERICANA

Contains references to source materials.

ENCYCLOPAEDIA BRITANNICA

Provides brief, selected bibliographies. The current edition is now organized in three parts: Propaedia (Outline of Knowledge), Micropaedia (Ready Reference and Index), and Macropaedia (Knowledge in Depth). In addition to the current edition, most libraries keep the 11th ed. (1910–1911) available; some of its fine long articles are books in brief.

NEW INTERNATIONAL ENCYCLOPEDIA

No longer revised under this title, but yearbook continues. Not to be confused with *Encyclopedia International* (1963–1964).

Note: Some encyclopedias attempt to keep current between major revisions by means of yearbooks. These are more useful as collections of information than as comprehensive statements on certain subjects. For yearbooks in specialized fields, see the references listed under Other Standard Reference Works.

AMERICANA ANNUAL, 1923–

BRITANNICA BOOK OF THE YEAR, 1938–

COLLIER'S YEAR BOOK, 1938–

NEW INTERNATIONAL YEARBOOK, 1907–

Formerly *International Yearbook* from 1898.

The main limitation of special encyclopedias and reference works of this kind is that they are not consistently kept current by revisions or yearbooks. But they can be of value to the beginning researcher who may see how bringing one of the topics up to date can be a subject for special study and who will find the selective bibliographies in most of these works an appropriate starting point. The list here is not intended to be comprehensive, only to suggest the wide variety of these aids.

ART AND ARCHITECTURE

Encyclopedia of Painting (1955).
Encyclopedia of World Art (1959–1968).
Larousse Encyclopedia of Prehistoric and Ancient Art (1962), *Byzantine and Medieval Art* (1963), *Modern Art* (1965).

ECONOMICS AND BUSINESS

Encyclopaedia of Banking and Finance (6th ed., 1962).
The McGraw-Hill Dictionary of Modern Economics (2nd ed., 1973).

FOLKLORE AND MYTHOLOGY

Frazer, Sir James G. *The Golden Bough: A Study in Magic and Religion* (12 vols., 1907–1915; Supplement, 1936, 1955).
Funk and Wagnalls Standard Dictionary of Folklore, Mythology, and Legend (2 vols., 1949–1950).
New Larousse Encyclopedia of Mythology (rev. ed., 1969).
Larousse World Mythology (1965).
The Mythology of All Races (13 vols., 1916–1932).

HISTORY

The Cambridge Ancient History, ed. John B. Bury et al. (12 vols., 1923–1939; 3rd ed., 1970–).
The Cambridge Medieval History, ed. Henry M. Gwatkin et al. (8 vols., 1911–1936).
Encyclopedia of American History, ed. Richard B. Morris and Henry S. Commager (rev. ed., 1970).
An Encyclopedia of World History, ed. William L. Langer (5th rev. ed., 1972).
McGraw-Hill Encyclopedia of Russia and the Soviet Union, ed. Michael T. Florinsky (1961).
The New Cambridge Modern History, ed. George N. Clark et al. (14 vols., 1957–1970).

LITERATURE

The Cambridge History of English Literature, ed. A. W. Ward and A. R. Waller (15 vols., 1907–1916; 1933).
Cassell's Encyclopaedia of World Literature, ed. S. H. Steinberg (2 vols., 1953).
Princeton Encyclopedia of Poetry and Poetics, ed. Alex Preminger et al. (enl. ed., 1974).
A Literary History of England, ed. A. C. Baugh et al. (2nd ed., 1967).
Literary History of the United States, ed. Robert E. Spiller et al. (2 vols., 3rd ed., 1963).

The Oxford History of English Literature, ed. Frank P. Wilson and Bonamy Dobree (12 vols., 1945–1963).
The Reader's Encyclopedia, ed. William Rose Benét (2 vols., 2nd ed., 1965).

MUSIC

Grove's Dictionary of Music and Musicians, ed. Eric Blom (10 vols., 5th ed., 1955, 1961).
International Cyclopedia of Music and Musicians (10th ed., 1975).
The New Oxford History of Music (10 vols., 1954–1973, in progress).

PHILOSOPHY

Copleston, Frederick C. *A History of Philosophy* (8 vols., 1947–1966).
The Encyclopaedia of Philosophy, ed. Paul Edwards (8 vols., 1967).

RELIGION

Encyclopaedia of Religion and Ethics, ed. James Hastings (13 vols., 1908–1926).
Jewish Encyclopedia, ed. Isidore Singer et al. (12 vols., 1901–1906).
The New Catholic Encyclopedia (15 vols., 1967).
The New Jewish Encyclopedia, ed. David Bridger (1962).
The New Schaff-Herzog Encyclopedia of Religious Knowledge (13 vols., 1908–1912; 1950).
Universal Jewish Encyclopedia, ed. Isaac Landman et al. (11 vols., 1939–1944).

SCIENCE AND MATHEMATICS

The Encyclopedia of the Biological Sciences, ed. Peter Gray (1967).
International Encyclopedia of Chemical Sciences (1964).
International Encyclopedia of Physical Chemistry and Chemical Physics, ed. E. A. Guggenheim et al. (1960–).
McGraw-Hill Encyclopedia of Science and Technology (15 vols., 4th ed., 1977).
Universal Encyclopedia of Mathematics (1964).
Van Nostrand's Scientific Encyclopedia (5th ed., 1976).

SOCIAL SCIENCES AND EDUCATION

Complete Guide and Index to ERIC Reports thru December 1969.
A Cyclopedia of Education, ed. Paul Monroe (5 vols., 1911–1913).
Encyclopedia of Educational Research (4th ed., 1969).
Encyclopedia of the Social Sciences (15 vols., 1930–1935).
International Encyclopedia of the Social Sciences (17 vols., 1968).
International Yearbook of Education (1948–).
World Survey of Education, UNESCO (1955–).

Other standard reference works

ALMANACS AND YEARBOOKS

Information Please Almanac, 1947–.
   Complements *The World Almanac.*

The New York Times Encyclopedic Almanac, 1970–.
　All inclusive in scope.
The Statesman's Yearbook, 1864–.
　Historical on an international scale.
The World Almanac and Book of Facts, 1868–.
　Comprehensive in its coverage.
Yearbook of the United Nations, 1947–.
　Covers activities of the organization.
Yearbook of World Affairs, 1947–.
　Important in the social sciences.

ATLASES AND GAZETTEERS

Columbia Lippincott Gazetteer of the World (1962).
Encyclopaedia Britannica World Atlas (1977, frequently revised).
Goode's World Atlas (15th ed., 1978, frequently revised).
Historical Atlas, ed. William R. Shepherd (9th ed., 1964).
National Geographic Atlas of the World (3rd ed., 1970).
The Times Atlas of the World (5th ed., 1975).

BIOGRAPHY

Current Biography: Who's News and Why, 1940–.
　Features biographies of living newsworthy figures.
Dictionary of American Biography, 20 vols., 1928–1937.
　Main volumes include people who died before 1926. The five supplements update
　the work through 1955.
Dictionary of National Biography, 63 vols., 1885–1937.
　(Reprinted in 22 vols., 1938.) Covers notable British figures. The seven supplements
　update the work to include those who died through 1960.
International Who's Who, 1935–.
　Reissued annually. Includes people of current international reputation.
National Cyclopaedia of American Biography, 1892–.
　Includes lesser known figures, both living and dead.
Webster's Biographical Dictionary, 1962–.
　Frequently revised. Brief sketches of world figures, living and dead.
Who's Who, 1849–.
　Reissued annually. Brief sketches of prominent living figures, most of them British,
　but including also some Americans and others.
Who's Who in America, 1889–.
　Reissued every two years. Brief sketches of prominent living Americans.

BOOK REVIEW INDEXES

Book Review Digest, 1905–.
　Digests of book reviews, listed alphabetically by author.
Book Review Index, 1965–.
　Monthly guide to reviews of books in the humanities and social sciences.
Index to Book Reviews in the Humanities, 1960–.
　Issued annually. Includes social sciences.
　　Since 1974, book reviews have also been listed at the end of volumes of the

Humanities Index, Readers' Guide to Periodical Literature, Education Index, Business Periodicals Index, and *General Science Index.*

DICTIONARIES
See pp. 512–515.

INDEXES

The single most important index for the beginning researcher is *Readers' Guide to Periodical Literature.* It indexes approximately 165 of the most widely read popular magazines in contrast to the more specialized indexes that concern themselves with scholarly and less well-known periodicals.

Because *Readers' Guide* indexes articles by author and subject and lists literary works and movies by title, it makes available a vast amount of information from widely scattered sources.

The sample entries reproduced on p. 379 make clear exactly how works are indexed in *Readers' Guide.*

Other valuable indexes include:

Agricultural Index, 1916–.
Subject index.
Applied Science and Technology Index, 1958–.
Subject index.
Art Index.
Subject and author index.
Biography Index. 1946–.
Indexes books and articles on the living and dead.
Biological and Agricultural Index, 1964–.
Subject index.
Books in Print, 1948–.
Indexes books by author, title, and series; appears annually.

BIBLIOGRAPHIES OF BIBLIOGRAPHIES AND GUIDES TO LIBRARIES

The accumulation of special bibliographies, catalogs, records, and indexes has now made necessary another kind of publication: the bibliography of bibliographies. One of the best known is Theodore Besterman's *A World Bibliography of Bibliographies,* in five volumes, now updated to 1974 in two volumes compiled by Alice F. Toomey. *The Bibliographic Index,* which appears semiannually, includes bibliographies that are included in books and periodicals. But these are bibliographical aids beyond the needs of most beginning researchers. Of use, however, are several general guides:

Barzun, Jacques, and Henry F. Graff. *The Modern Researcher* (3rd ed., 1977).
Galin, Saul, and Peter Spielberg. *Reference Books: How to Select and Use Them* (1969).
Gates, Jean Key. *Guide to the Use of Books and Libraries* (3rd ed., 1974).
McCormick, Mona. *Who-What-When-Where-How-Why-Made Easy,* 1971 (paper ed.: *The New York Times Guide to Reference Materials* 1974).

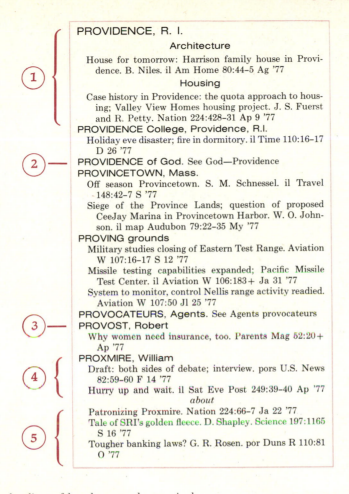

PROVIDENCE, R. I.

Architecture

House for tomorrow: Harrison family house in Providence. B. Niles. il Am Home 80:44-5 Ag '77

Housing

Case history in Providence: the quota approach to housing; Valley View Homes housing project. J. S. Fuerst and R. Petty. Nation 224:428-31 Ap 9 '77

PROVIDENCE College, Providence, R.I.

Holiday eve disaster; fire in dormitory. il Time 110:16-17 D 26 '77

PROVIDENCE of God. See God—Providence

PROVINCETOWN, Mass.

Off season Provincetown. S. M. Schnessel. il Travel 148:42-7 S '77

Siege of the Province Lands; question of proposed CeeJay Marina in Provincetown Harbor. W. O. Johnson. il map Audubon 79:22-35 My '77

PROVING grounds

Military studies closing of Eastern Test Range. Aviation W 107:16-17 S 12 '77

Missile testing capabilities expanded; Pacific Missile Test Center. il Aviation W 106:183+ Ja 31 '77

System to monitor, control Nellis range activity readied. Aviation W 107:50 Jl 25 '77

PROVOCATEURS, Agents. See Agents provocateurs

PROVOST, Robert

Why women need insurance, too. Parents Mag 52:20+ Ap '77

PROXMIRE, William

Draft: both sides of debate; interview. pors U.S. News 82:59-60 F 14 '77

Hurry up and wait. il Sat Eve Post 249:39-40 Ap '77

about

Patronizing Proxmire. Nation 224:66-7 Ja 22 '77

Tale of SRI's golden fleece. D. Shapley. Science 197:1165 S 16 '77

Tougher banking laws? G. R. Rosen. por Duns R 110:81 O '77

1 Subject headings of broad scope subcategorized.
2 Cross-indexing by subject. See also entry under Provocateurs.
3 Author entry. Under Robert Provost, the information means that an article entitled "Why Women Need Insurance, Too" appeared in *Parents' Magazine*, volume 52, page 20 and following pages, for August, 1977. Abbreviations of periodicals are explained at the beginning of each issue of *Readers' Guide*.
4 Articles or interviews by William Proxmire.
5 Articles about William Proxmire.

Sheehy, Eugene P. *Guide to Reference Books* (9th ed., 1976). Formerly listed under Constance M. Winchell.

Shove, Raymond, et al., *The Use of Books and Libraries* (10th ed., 1963).

Of particular value to the student of language and literature are two books, both available in paperback editions:

Altick, Richard D., and Andrew Wright. *A Selective Bibliography for the Study of English and American Literature* (6th ed., 1979).
Bond, Donald F. *A Reference Guide to English Studies* (2nd ed., 1971).

Bibliographies in English studies are numerous, but among the annual bibliographies four are of special importance:

Essay and General Literature Index, 1900–. Author and subject guide to essays and articles in collections.
MHRA (Modern Humanities Research Association). *Annual Bibliography of English Language and Literature*, 1921–.
MLA International Bibliography in Publications of the Modern Language Association of America, 1922–. The single most important index to literary and linguistic studies.
Year's Work in English Studies, 1919–.

QUOTATIONS

Familiar Quotations, eds. John Bartlett and E. M. Beck (14th ed., 1968).
The Home Book of American Quotations, ed. Bruce Bohle (1967).
The Home Book of Quotations, Classical and Modern, ed. Burton E. Stevenson (10th ed., 1967).
The Oxford Dictionary of English Proverbs, ed. William G. Smith and F. P. Wilson (3rd ed., 1970).
The Oxford Dictionary of Quotations (2nd ed., 1953).

Evaluating materials

Books and magazines are designed for different purposes and audiences; they are therefore not of equal value to the researcher. It may be difficult for beginners to know the reputation of writers on a particular topic or the trustworthiness of their opinions, but there are several general considerations that are important in choosing materials that you will use:

The audience

The nature of a publication comments generally on its audience. Encyclopedias, for example, address themselves to a broader and more varied audience than scholarly books. Popular magazines treating many topics are different from specialized periodicals addressed to experts. Textbooks for lower-division courses are different from those designed for graduate courses. The most specialized work is not necessarily the best for the beginning researcher (it may be too detailed), but you should recognize that your choice of sources will determine to a great extent the level and style of your own paper.

The length of a work does not alone determine the thoroughness of its coverage because a big book may treat a very broad topic. But given two works of approximately the same scope, it follows that the longer one will probably include more detail than the shorter one. The short one may in its outlines include as much support but not as much elaboration. An article in a scholarly periodical is often an extended, thoroughly documented treatment of a very limited topic and valuable for that very purpose. What the researcher needs to seek, therefore, is not long works as opposed to short ones but inclusion of works that are adequately detailed and documented as well as general ones.

The authoritativeness of a work will often depend on its sources of information. A primary source is an original record, statement, or document; a secondary source is something written about it. These two terms, however, are relative. If we consider a speech given by the President of the United States as a primary source, the newspaper commentary written about it is secondary. But if your topic is public opinion at the time of that speech, the newspaper commentary would then be considered primary. If a novel by a writer is the primary source, criticism of it is secondary. But if your topic is a writer's reputation at a particular period, the criticism would then become primary.

If a book derives its material only from what has already been written about primary sources and is wholly derivative, it may be valuable as a summary work but not as a source of new information. Returning to primary sources is a way of reinvestigating and reevaluating what already has been written. Works that ignore primary sources and depend entirely on secondary ones may be limited by the dependence they show on other people's findings.

The reputation of a publishing house, press, or periodical may often be taken as a general factor in evaluating books and periodicals. Over a period of time, you will learn which publishers are noted for carefully edited, definitive editions and which periodicals screen and check carefully the soundness of the material they publish. The name of a vanity press, which requires writers to pay the cost of their own publications, may suggest that these authors were unable to have their books published under other circumstances. Books published by vanity presses are frequently eyed with caution and seldom reviewed.

A famous name is not consistently a sure guide to the soundness of the author's work. Some writers are well known because they are controversial. In this respect, they are interesting and stimulating thinkers, but their opinions should be checked against well-documented scholarship. The titles of some writers may also be a clue to their qualifications. A full professorship at Harvard, for instance, is an impressive recommendation; long experience in the field or other publications may also be additional proofs. You should be alert to any special interest that enters as a factor in the writer's judgment. On particular topics, it may make a considerable difference whether the writer is a southerner or a northerner, a Mormon or a Catholic, a black or a WASP, a Democrat or a Republican. If a writer reveals strong prejudices of one kind or another, these must be considered as representing a special point of view.

Value

All of the factors that have been noted here—the degree of the author's objectivity, the length and documentation of the work, the use of primary and secondary sources, the audience, the date of the writing, and the publisher—will combine to create an effect that inspires either confidence in the work or a general wariness about it. Everything in print is not of equal value. You must learn to make discriminations.

Taking notes

Perhaps everyone has to go through the experience of writing a reference paper without using notes, with only books on hand, to know how difficult and frustrating it is. Notes are simple means of excerpting information from books so that the facts

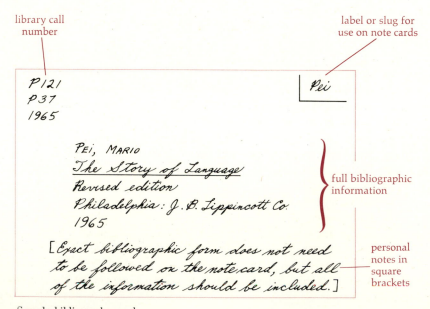

Sample bibliography card

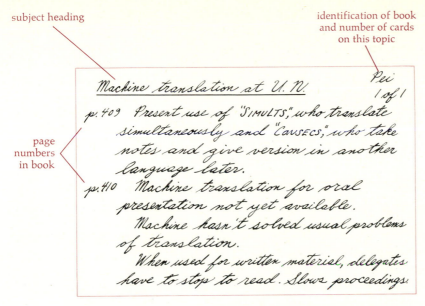

subject heading

identification of book
and number of cards
on this topic

page
numbers
in book

Machine translation at U. N.

Pei
1 of 1

p. 409 Present use of "Simults," who translate simultaneously and "Consecs," who take notes and give version in another language later.

p. 410 Machine translation for oral presentation not yet available.

Machine hasn't solved usual problems of translation.

When used for written material, delegates have to stop to read. Slows proceedings.

Sample note card

are easily available when you need them. A hundred cards drawing information from ten books can be sorted and shuffled; the pages of ten books cannot. In fact, it may not even be possible to have the ten books available. Notes therefore are a simple expedient.

Notes are also personal working cards; that is, there is no special reason why they have to follow a prescribed form. By the same token, there is no reason why every beginner should have to learn the pitfalls of note-taking the hard way. There are a few obvious facts that are often repeated for good reasons:

1. The first thing you should do is make up a bibliography card for each source used. Include *all* of the necessary data so that it is not necessary to return to the book. Choose some kind of label or slug, usually the author's last name, that can be used on note cards, since it is a waste of time to report all of the information on every note card (see sample bibliography card opposite).
2. Notes from a book or article should be taken according to subject headings so that they can be later sorted by topics. Cards 4 by 6 inches are a good size to use for notes.
3. Between the time of reading and the time of writing, note cards cool off—or the mind cools off. Notes therefore should not be too cryptic. It is also better to take too many notes than too few. Some can always be discarded.
4. The memory plays tricks. It forgets, but it sometimes remembers exactly. It is therefore advisable to put in quotation marks the phrases that seem worthy of quotation or that are likely to stick in your mind. It is embarrassing to come up with a fine phrase that actually belongs to someone else. In general, however,

notes should be a paraphrase of the original, avoiding as many of the author's own words as possible.

5. Any immediate reaction the reader has can be included in square brackets. Notes to oneself are often useful when the time to write arrives.

6. The page numbers must be included so that all of the information for writing a footnote is accessible. If a direct quotation occurs on two pages, it is advisable to use a slash to indicate where the wording on one page ends and the wording on another begins:

> pp. 295–296   "We are left with the impression of a painful sincerity and of a nobility that expresses itself only in definitions, not / in the activity of the imagination."[1]

7. If it takes three cards to jot down the notes on one topic, it is good to mark these as 1 of 3, 2 of 3, and 3 of 3 so that it is clear that one card has not been misplaced (see sample note card on p. 383).

The nature of the reference paper

In one sense, writing a reference paper is no different from writing any other expository theme. However, because the reference paper is ordinarily a more sustained piece of writing based on an extended project of several weeks or months, it sets its own requirements for the writer:

1. It requires more information, more facts, more variety of opinion than the ordinary essay.
2. It requires an ability to synthesize material into a larger frame of organization than a paper of lesser scope.
3. It requires more control on your part, more attention to orderliness and transition than you might ordinarily show in other kinds of writing.
4. It requires objectivity to differentiate clearly between your own opinions and the opinions of others, between matters of fact and matters of opinion. A reference paper need not be impersonal.
5. It requires support for its assertions and specific documentation.

These requirements focus attention on a series of steps that are important to writing a successful reference paper. The remaining sections of this chapter comment on each of these.

[1] Alfred Kazin, "A Condemned Man: Albert Camus," *Contemporaries* (Boston: Little, Brown, 1962).

Writing a paper: considerations

Limiting the subject

The subject must be adaptable to the length of the paper so that it can be treated in some depth. Three thousand words are not adequate for a paper on the position of women from Roman times to the present. In that space, by a judicious selection of material, you might possibly write about attitudes toward women in the Old Testament of the Bible, with a few added reflections on the influence of Hebraic concepts on later times.

Some topics are too broad and vague for anything except book length; others are too narrow and specialized because they require primary sources or original investigation beyond the beginning student. Even though extremes of broadness or narrowness are usually self-evident, you do not know precisely what the limits of a topic are until you have done considerable reading and see clearly the dimensions.

Selecting and organizing

It is wise to think of the organization of a long paper in terms of stages: first, a tentative outline of main topics which can be added to, developed, discarded, or regrouped. You should not try to settle on a plan too soon. The precise organization usually becomes more and more apparent as you complete your reading, sort your notes, re-examine them to find out where they are full and where they are sparse, where you have found your interest turning during the period of investigation, where the paper must place its emphasis to use the notes available, and what must be discarded. One big pitfall is to try to use everything you have collected. When the final plan becomes evident, some things have to go.

Paraphrasing, quoting, and plagiarizing

Plagiarism is the act of passing off someone else's ideas or words as your own. Some plagiarism represents deliberate dishonesty, that is, copying material word for word from a book and submitting it without the use of quotation marks or documentation as if it were your own. Perhaps a more common source of plagiarism, however, is carelessness—failure to take adequate notes that use quotation marks, failure to paraphrase in words sufficiently different from the original, or failure to get far enough away from the notes in writing the paper. These failures can be illustrated by considering specific examples.

If you were writing a reference paper on censorship, for instance, your reading would probably lead you to one of the classic statements on the subject, a speech by John Milton entitled *Areopagitica*, which appeared in 1644. For years excerpts of it appeared in many anthologies for Freshman courses. If you read that long and difficult work, you would eventually come across the following passage that would be tempting to copy on a notecard:

And yet, on the other hand, unless wariness be used, as good almost kill a man as kill a good book: who kills a man kills a reasonable creature, God's image; but he who destroys a good book, kills reason itself, kills the image of God, as it were, in the eye.[2]

What can best be illustrated here is that what is unfamiliar or new to you may be quite familiar to other readers. If you decided not to grapple with the complex reasoning of that passage and simply wrote "It is almost as bad to kill a man as to kill a good book" and then tried to pass it off as your own without reference to Milton or without any footnote whatsoever, many people would immediately recognize that you were not being honest with your source materials. This thought is Milton's; it is uniquely identified with him; it is a passage often quoted. It is not yours. Milton should get credit for it.

Let us consider a modern example, a passage from Alvin Toffler's *Future Shock:*

This is why the individual's sense of the future plays so critical a part in his ability to cope. The faster the pace of life, the more rapidly the present environment slips away from us, the more rapidly do future potentialities turn into present reality. As the environment churns faster, we are not only pressured to devote more mental resources to thinking about the future, but to extend our time horizon—to probe further and further ahead. The driver dawdling along an expressway at twenty miles per hour can successfully negotiate a turn into an exit lane, even if the sign indicating the cut-off is very close to the exit. The faster he drives, however, the further back the sign must be placed to give him the time needed to read and react. In quite the same way, the generalized acceleration of life compels us to lengthen our time horizon or risk being overtaken and overwhelmed by events. The faster the environment changes, the more the need for futureness.[3]

This passage has one particularly quotable sentence: "The faster the environment changes, the more the need for futureness." One way of using that sentence would be to quote it openly and honestly. In the context of other remarks of your own, you might say: "Alvin Toffler sees a relationship between the speed with which the times change and the amount of energy we have to give to thinking about future possibilities. He condenses that thought into a single sentence: 'The faster the environment changes, the more the need for futureness.'" This quotation would then be footnoted with a specific page reference to *Future Shock.*

Every direct quotation used should have justification. Direct quotations are justified.

- if the original phrasing is particularly striking and memorable;
- if the special feeling or style of the writer would be lost by paraphrasing it;
- if the original phrasing is so well known that a paraphrase would be a distortion;
- if the quotation itself is an example or proof of what is being discussed, for example, the print-out response of a computer grading a student theme;
- if the quotation is used to typify a writer or a character in a work of literature.

[2] John Milton, *Areopagitica* in *Masterworks of Prose*, ed. Thomas Parkinson (Indianapolis: Bobbs-Merrill, 1962), p. 56.

[3] (New York: Random House, 1970), p. 372

It should be emphasized that a reference paper does not automatically give you more license to quote. It is a paper, however, that ordinarily demands full support from various sources and may therefore lead you to use more quotation than you would in an essay expressing entirely your own opinions. Nevertheless, other people's words cannot be made a substitute for your own. A reference paper is not patchwork, a collection of other people's words in cut-and-paste style. It ought to be your own version of what you have learned from reading, with clear-cut references to the sources.

The difficulty with many direct quotations, like the one from Toffler, for instance, is that they fail to get at the heart of the reasoning. You will note that Toffler's sentence comes at the end of a paragraph. It is a kind of summary sentence, but its full meaning depends on all that has come before. A paraphrase would require more time and effort, but it might ultimately produce a better statement. For instance, instead of containing direct quotation, your note card might include this kind of paraphrase:

p. 372 The faster things in our environment change, the further we have to project our thinking and planning into the future to be ready. If we can't anticipate future events and plan for them, we can become victims of change. We need time to adapt. "The faster the environment changes, the more the need for futureness."

If you read this note two or three weeks after you made it, it would supply you enough of Toffler's thought to be able to produce statements like these:

```
Alvin Toffler thinks that human beings need lead-time to
prepare for future changes. The faster things change, the
longer the lead-time has to be.4
```

---

    [4] Ibid.

Or:

```
Alvin Toffler claims that one way to avoid future shock is
to have enough advance warning of what the future holds.
Human beings need time to adapt.5
```

---

    [5] Ibid.

These are both statements that depart considerably from the phrasing of the original, yet remain true to the writer's thoughts.

Rewording on note cards rather than putting down exact quotations guards against the telling phrases of a writer that may be far different from your own use of words. At the beginning of "Politics and the English Language," George Orwell writes, "It follows that any struggle against the abuse of language is a sentimental archaism, like preferring candles to electric light or hansom cabs to aeroplanes." (Note that Orwell writes "electric light" instead of the more familiar "electric lights." Accuracy is important in quoting.) If the phrase "sentimental archaism" crept into your own prose without quotation marks, it would be a dead giveaway. "Sentimental archaism" may be Orwellian or British, but it is not a phrase that many American students would write spontaneously. Paraphrase is insurance against plagiarism because it requires you to absorb a writer's thoughts and reproduce them in your own words. Paraphrase is an essential part of good reference paper writing. It does not, however, release you from the responsibility of acknowledging your source.

Revising and polishing

Because the reference paper holds you accountable for your sources as well as your own ideas, it may be a paper that can be less spontaneously written. You often have to consult your notes at the same time that you are writing. A series of drafts may actually be necessary to get a final paper that reads smoothly. Matters that often require particular attention in long papers include:

- using adequate transitional words and phrases between sections that may have been written at different times;
- varying the comments leading up to direct quotations so that they do not all read: "Bertrand Russell says";
- paring down the prose or expanding it, whichever may be necessary to get a clear, accurate statement;
- reordering material to get more coherent, effective discourse;
- supplying a detail or checking an item for accuracy.

Of course, the prose of reference papers is subject to the same care you would give to any essay. The principles set forth in Chapters 9–12 need to be applied strenuously for the simple reason that the more you write, the more opportunity you have to fall into error.

Supporting and documenting

Footnotes are the means commonly used to document specific statements within the main body of a reference work. These can be given at the bottom of the page on which they appear, separated from the main text by a rule across the page; grouped at the end of the paper in one continuous list; or, as some disciplines prefer, placed immediately after the citation in parentheses or immediately below the citation, separated by rules from the rest of the text in the manner illustrated here:[1]

```
    1Some footnotes are purely information notes as op-
posed to others which are references. Writers, however,
should avoid lengthy digressions in footnotes. If comments
are too long, they are best omitted.
```

Even though footnote forms often monopolize the attention of the beginning researcher, a far more substantive problem is to know when to footnote. A ten-page paper with a hundred footnotes is a parody of a reference paper, not necessarily a well-documented one. You must be able to discriminate between material that is considered common knowledge and material that is clearly identified with one particular writer or source. Facts and opinions that are recognized as general knowledge need not be footnoted. All others should be attributed to their source. The obvious example of material to be footnoted is the direct quotation, but the ideas of another person, even if they are freely paraphrased, are also to be footnoted.

What is and what is not general knowledge on any particular subject usually becomes apparent during the time of reading and notetaking. You will encounter the same basic information again and again. You may take notes on these facts one or two times and then come to the realization that information of this kind is common knowledge among those who write on this subject. You too can make the same assumption, even though you may consider yourself far less knowledgeable. General knowledge may be characterized as encyclopedic knowledge. On the other hand, special findings, opinions, and interpretations need to be accounted for.

The bibliography is a different kind of documentation; it is a list of books, periodicals, and any other source materials, either complete or selected, that you have used in preparing your paper. Ordinarily, if works like a dictionary or the Bible are referred to in the paper, these are not listed. But all other works referred to in the footnotes should be included.

Footnotes

Footnote forms are a conventional system, and they vary from discipline to discipline. If you submit a paper to your sociology professor or your engineering professor, therefore, you should consult a style manual in that discipline or refer to one of the established periodicals in that field. The forms given in this section are those ordinarily used in English studies and other related studies in the humanities.

The following practices are standard for typewritten papers:

1. A footnote is signaled by a number, slightly raised and placed after the material being cited.
2. Footnotes are most commonly numbered consecutively from 1 to — throughout the paper, whether they are put at the bottom of the page, in the text, or at the end.

3. Footnotes do not repeat any information given in the text. If the author's name is given in the comment leading up to a quotation, the note will supply only the title, place of publication, publisher, date, and page reference.

4. Although the name of the publisher may be omitted in the footnote, the latest style sheet of the Modern Language Association of America includes it. See footnote 7 for alternate form without publisher's name.

5. Footnotes are indented and typed single-spaced with a double space between them, separated from the text by a rule if they are placed at the bottom of the page.

6. All citations made on a particular page are included on the same page if the footnotes are placed at the bottom. If the last note is lengthy, it may be continued on the next page.

7. Footnotes should be as specific and limited as possible. A reference like "pp. 101–132" is not particularly helpful unless you are intentionally making a recommendation for additional reading.

8. In footnotes, the first name of the author comes first.

14A   *Sample footnote forms*

ARTICLES IN MAGAZINES OR PERIODICALS

[1]Archibald A. Hill, "The Tainted <u>Ain't</u> Once More," <u>College</u> <u>English</u>, 26 (1965), 301.

If the volume of a periodical is numbered consecutively throughout, it is not necessary to list the month. The month, however, may be given as a convenience to individuals who have unbound issues. When a volume number is not given, the page symbol (p.) is used, as in footnote 4.

[2]Archibald A. Hill, "Grammaticality," <u>Word</u>, 17 (Apr. 1961), 9.

[3]L. M. Myers, "Generation and Deviation," <u>CCC</u>, 18 (1967), 217.

CCC stands for *College Composition and Communication.* Long titles of periodicals are usually abbreviated in footnotes. The full titles are given in the bibliography.

ARTICLES IN PERIODICALS WITH NO VOLUME NUMBER

[4]"Rand McNally: More Than a Mapmaker," <u>Business</u> <u>Week</u>, Nov. 22, 1969, p. 66.

BIBLE

⁵John 1:1.

Books of the Bible are not italicized. The translation and edition are not given unless the differences in phrasing are a significant point in the paper.

BOOKS WITH A SINGLE AUTHOR

⁶James Sledd, <u>A</u> <u>Short</u> <u>Introduction</u> <u>to</u> <u>English</u> <u>Grammar</u> (Chicago: Scott, Foresman, 1959), p. 5.

If the publisher's name is not included in the footnote, the form changes slightly:

⁷James Sledd, <u>A</u> <u>Short</u> <u>Introduction</u> <u>to</u> <u>English</u> <u>Grammar</u> (Chicago, 1959), p. 5.

If the author is unknown, the note begins with the title of the book. If the date is not given, n.d. (no date) should be used. If the publisher's name is not listed, n.p. (no publisher) should be used.

BOOKS WITH TWO AUTHORS

⁸Anne Ruggles Gere and Eugene Smith, <u>Attitudes</u>, <u>Language</u>, <u>and</u> <u>Change</u> (Urbana, Illinois: National Council of Teachers of English, 1979), p. 29.

As many as three authors are usually listed by name.

BOOKS WITH MORE THAN THREE AUTHORS

⁹Alfred J. Ayer et al., <u>Studies</u> <u>in</u> <u>Communication</u> (London: Secker & Warburg, 1955), p. 34.

The words "and others" can be used instead of the Latin equivalent. See 14C.

BOOKS WITH AN EDITOR

¹⁰<u>Exploring</u> <u>Language</u>, ed. Gary Goshgarian, 2nd ed. (Boston: Little, Brown, 1980), p. 166.

This is a collection of essays by various authors. This footnote is a reference to a note by the editor on page 166.

BOOKS WITH A TRANSLATOR

[11]Karl Vossler, <u>The</u> <u>Spirit</u> <u>of</u> <u>Language</u> <u>in</u> <u>Civiliza-</u>
<u>tion</u>, tr. Oscar Oeser (London: Routledge & Kegan Paul,
1932), p. 15.

BOOKS IN LATER REVISED EDITIONS

[12]C. K. Ogden and I. A. Richards, <u>The</u> <u>Meaning</u> <u>of</u>
<u>Meaning</u>, 8th ed., Harvest Book (New York: Harcourt, Brace
and World, 1946), p. 140.

BOOKS PUBLISHED IN SEVERAL VOLUMES

[13]George P. Krapp, <u>The</u> <u>English</u> <u>Language</u> <u>in</u> <u>America</u>
(New York: Ungar, 1925), II, 147.

BOOKS PUBLISHED IN A SERIES

[14]James T. Hatfield et al., eds., <u>Curme</u> <u>Volume</u> <u>of</u>
<u>Linguistic</u> <u>Studies</u>, Language Monograph, No. 7, Linguistic
Society of America (Washington, D.C., 1930), p. 4.

DISSERTATIONS   See Unpublished material

DRAMAS

[15]<u>Macbeth</u> V.i.39.

If variant texts are available, the edition should be indicated in the first footnote and
listed in the bibliography. For example, the following would be included in footnote
15 in addition to the reference given:

All references to <u>Macbeth</u> are taken from <u>Shakespeare</u>:
<u>Twenty-Three</u> <u>Plays</u> <u>and</u> <u>the</u> <u>Sonnets</u>, ed. Thomas Marc Par-
rott, rev. ed. (New York: Scribner's, 1953).

ENCYCLOPEDIA ARTICLE

[16]"Language," <u>Encyclopaedia</u> <u>Britannica</u>, 14th ed.,
XIII, 700.

ESSAYS IN AN EDITED COLLECTION

[17]James D. McCawley, "The Role of Semantics in a
Grammar," in Emmon Bach and Robert T. Harms, eds., <u>Uni-</u>

versals in Linguistic Theory (New York: Holt, Rinehart and Winston, 1968), pp. 168–169.

GOVERNMENT DOCUMENTS

[18]U.S. Department of State, Language and Area Study Programs in American Universities, compiled by Larry Moses in cooperation with the Language Development Branch of Health, Education and Welfare Department (Washington, D.C.: External Research Staff, 1964), p. 105.

INTERVIEW

[19]Senator Henry M. Jackson, personal interview on student activism, Washington, D.C., May 7, 1980.

INTRODUCTORY MATERIALS WRITTEN BY ANOTHER AUTHOR

[20]Samuel R. Levin, Foreword to Otto Jespersen, Analytic Syntax, Transatlantic Series in Linguistics (New York: Holt, Rinehart and Winston, 1969), p. vii.

NEWSPAPER ARTICLES

[21]Seattle Times, June 3, 1979, Section C, p. 1.

If author and title are given, they can be indicated as in footnote 1.

QUOTATIONS FROM A SECONDARY SOURCE

[22]William of Nassyngton, Speculum Vitae as quoted in A. C. Baugh, A History of the English Language, 2nd ed. (New York: Appleton–Century–Crofts, 1957), p. 172.

This is a work dated 1325 and not easily available in any other source. In general, quotations from secondary sources should be avoided.

REVIEWS

[23]Noam Chomsky, rev. of Verbal Behavior by B. F. Skinner, Language, 35 (1959), 29.

UNPUBLISHED MATERIAL

[24]James E. Hoard, "On the Foundations of Phonological Theory," Diss. University of Washington, 1967, p. 120.

Second references to footnotes

Subsequent references to the same work differ from the first. Instead of the abbreviations of the Latin words *ibidem, opere citato,* and *loco citato,* commonly used in the past, current practice favors the use of the author's name or, if two works by the same author are used, the author's name and a short title. "Ibid." is still widely used, but not the other abbreviations. All readers, however, should understand their meanings:

ibid.—"in the same place." Ibid. is used to refer only to the citation immediately preceding it, although it may be used several times in succession. It is usually combined with a page number, for example, "Ibid., p. 20," but if it is used without a number, the reference means the same source and the same page. (The Latin abbreviation ibid. is no longer italicized. See 14C.)

op. cit.—"in the work cited." Op. cit. is used together with the author's name and the page reference, for example, "Vossler, op. cit., p. 18." Its use refers to a work previously cited but not immediately preceding.

loc. cit.—"in the place cited." Loc. cit. is used with the author's name but no page reference, for example, "Goodlad, loc. cit." It refers to an exact passage previously cited but not immediately preceding.

The following citations illustrate subsequent references to books and periodicals cited in the sample footnote forms above:

REFERENCE TO WORK IMMEDIATELY PRECEDING

[25]Hoard, p. 121.

REFERENCE TO SAME WORK IMMEDIATELY PRECEDING

[26]Hoard, p. 119.

REFERENCE TO n. 16.

[27]"Language," Britannica, XIII, 689.

REFERENCE TO n. 2, BUT TWO WORKS BY SAME AUTHOR

[28]Hill, "Grammaticality," pp. 7–8.

REFERENCE TO OTHER WORK BY HILL IN n. 1

[29]Hill, "Tainted Ain't," p. 301.

TITLE REPEATED TO AVOID CONFUSION WITH n. 28

[30]Hill, "Tainted Ain't," p. 302.

SAME WORK IN *n. 13*, DIFFERENT VOLUME

    [31] Krapp, I, 43.

SAME WORK, DIFFERENT VOLUME

    [32] Krapp, II, 149.

The same notes using ibid. would read:

    [25] Ibid., p. 121.
    [26] Ibid., p. 119.
    [27] "Language," <u>Britannica</u>, XIII, 689.
    [28] Hill, "Grammaticality," pp. 7–8.
    [29] Hill, "Tainted <u>Ain't</u>," p. 301.
    [30] Ibid., p. 302.

There is no confusion in n. 30 because ibid. refers to the citation immediately preceding.

    [31] Krapp, I, 43.
    [32] Ibid., II, 149.

Bibliography

The bibliography is usually the last portion of a reference paper, if it is used at all. If all of the footnotes contain full bibliographical information, the bibliography is superfluous except as a convenience to the reader. Articles in the humanities customarily do not use bibliographies.

    The following practices are standard for preparing bibliographies:

1. Books are listed alphabetically by the author's last name. If no author is given, the book or article is listed by its title.
2. The author's name is given last name first—a reversal of footnote form.
3. Full publishing information is given for books. If the name of a publishing house has been changed in recent years, the name given on the title page should be used.
4. The main parts of a bibliographical entry are punctuated differently from footnotes. See models in 14B.
5. Several works by the same author are listed in alphabetical order by their titles. A long dash substitutes for the author's name after the first reference.
6. Inclusive page numbers of articles and parts of books are listed. The page numbers of complete books are not given.
7. Items in a bibliography are not numbered.
8. Items are single-spaced, with the second line indented so that the author's name is prominent. Double spacing is used between items.
9. Books and periodicals may be grouped together or listed separately.

14B Sample bibliography forms

The items included in the footnotes above are listed here in bibliographical form. An actual bibliography is arranged alphabetically. See p. 431 for a model.

ARTICLES IN MAGAZINES OR PERIODICALS

Hill, Archibald A. "Grammaticality." Word, 17 (April 1961), 1–10.

————. "The Tainted Ain't Once More." College English, 26 (1965), 298–303.

Myers, L. M. "Generation and Deviation." College Composition and Communication, 18 (1967), 214–220.

ARTICLES IN PERIODICALS WITH NO VOLUME NUMBER

"Rand McNally: More Than a Mapmaker." Business Week, November 22, 1969, pp. 66–68.

BOOKS WITH A SINGLE AUTHOR

Sledd, James. A Short Introduction to English Grammar. Chicago: Scott, Foresman and Co., 1959.

BOOKS WITH TWO AUTHORS

Gere, Anne Ruggles, and Eugene Smith. Attitudes, Language, and Change. Urbana, Illinois: National Council of Teachers of English, 1979.

BOOKS WITH MORE THAN THREE AUTHORS

Ayer, Alfred J., et al. Studies in Communication. London: Secker & Warburg, 1955.

BOOKS WITH AN EDITOR

Goshgarian, Gary, ed. Exploring Language. 2nd ed. Boston: Little, Brown, 1980.

BOOKS WITH A TRANSLATOR

Vossler, Karl. The Spirit of Language in Civilization. Trans. Oscar Oeser. London: Routledge & Kegan Paul, Ltd., 1932.

BOOKS IN LATER REVISED EDITIONS

Ogden, C. K., and I. A. Richards. <u>The</u> <u>Meaning</u> <u>of</u> <u>Meaning</u>.
     8th ed. Harvest Book. New York: Harcourt, Brace &
     World, Inc., 1946.

BOOKS PUBLISHED IN SEVERAL VOLUMES

Krapp, George P. <u>The</u> <u>English</u> <u>Language</u> <u>in</u> <u>America</u>. Vol. II.
     New York: Frederick Ungar Publishing Co., 1925.

If both volumes were used, the entry would read "2 vols."

BOOKS PUBLISHED IN A SERIES

Hatfield, James T., et al., eds. <u>Curme</u> <u>Volume</u> <u>of</u> <u>Linguis-</u>
     <u>tic</u> <u>Studies</u>. Language Monograph, No. 7. Washington,
     D.C.: Linguistic Society of America, 1930.

DISSERTATIONS   See Unpublished material

DRAMA, COLLECTIONS OF

<u>Shakespeare</u>: <u>Twenty-Three</u> <u>Plays</u> <u>and</u> <u>the</u> <u>Sonnets</u>. Ed.
     Thomas Marc Parrott. Rev. ed. New York: Charles
     Scribner's Sons, 1953.

ENCYCLOPEDIA ARTICLE

"Language." <u>Encyclopaedia</u> <u>Britannica</u>, 14th ed., XIII,
     696-704.

ESSAYS IN AN EDITED COLLECTION

McCawley, James D. "The Role of Semantics in a Grammar,"
     in <u>Universals</u> <u>in</u> <u>Linguistic</u> <u>Theory</u>. Ed. Emmon Bach
     and Robert T. Harms. New York: Holt, Rinehart and
     Winston, Inc., 1968, pp. 124-169.

GOVERNMENT DOCUMENTS

 U.S. Department of State. <u>Language</u> <u>and</u> <u>Area</u> <u>Study</u> <u>Programs</u>
     <u>in</u> <u>American</u> <u>Universities</u>. Compiled by Larry Moses
     in cooperation with the Language Development Branch
     of Health, Education and Welfare Department. Wash-
     ington, D.C.: External Research Staff, 1964.

INTERVIEW

Jackson, Henry M., Senator. Personal interview on student
    activism. Washington, D.C., May 7, 1980.

INTRODUCTORY MATERIALS WRITTEN BY ANOTHER AUTHOR

Levin, Samuel R. Foreword to Otto Jespersen, <u>Analytic</u>
    <u>Syntax</u>. Transatlantic Series in Linguistics. New
    York: Holt, Rinehart and Winston, Inc., 1969.

NEWSPAPER ARTICLES

<u>Seattle</u> <u>Times</u>, June 3, 1979, Section C, p. 1.

REVIEWS

Chomsky, Noam. Review of B. F. Skinner, <u>Verbal</u> <u>Behavior</u>.
    <u>Language</u>, 35 (1959), 26–58.

UNPUBLISHED MATERIAL

Hoard, James E. "On the Foundations of Phonological The-
    ory." Ph.D. dissertation, University of Washington,
    1967.

14C Common abbreviations used in notes

The abbreviations for Latin words below were formerly always printed in
italics (underlined in manuscript). It is now increasingly common and accepted practice to print them in regular type (no underlining). "Sic,"
which is not an abbreviation, is usually used within a quotation to indicate that an obvious error appeared in the original; it is placed after the
error within brackets (see p. 231, third example under 10K).

c., ca. (*circa*)	about, approximately (ca. 1450)
cf. (*confer*), cp.	compare
ch., chs., chap., chaps.	chapter, chapters
cp.	compare
diss.	dissertation
ed., eds.	edited by, editor, editors
e.g. (*exempli gratia*)	for example
et al. (*et alii*)	and others
f., ff.	the following page(s) or line(s)
fl. (*floruit*)	flourished
ibid. (*ibidem*)	in the same place

i.e. (*id est*)	that is
il.	illustrated
l., ll.	line(s)
loc. cit. (*loco citato*)	in the place cited
ms., mss.	manuscript(s)
n.	note
n.d.	no date of publication
n.p.	no place of publication; no publisher; no page numbers
n.s.	new series
op. cit. (*opere citato*)	in the work cited
o.s.	old series
p., pp.	page(s)
pass. (*passim*)	throughout, here and there
q.v. (*quod vide*)	which see
rev.	revised
sic	thus
tr., trans.	translated by; translator
v. (*vide*)	see, consult
viz. (*videlicet*)	namely
vol., vols.	volume(s)

Sample reference paper **14D**

On the following pages, you will be able to read a complete reference paper with an outline and bibliography, together with a running commentary on the facing pages on features of the essay that deserve mention. Students were also asked to keep an informal research diary, giving the reason they chose their topic and then recording their progress and problems as they did the job. They were invited to put in whatever personal comments they wanted to make. The research diary of Kenneth Fellows, the author of the reference paper, follows the paper.

General typing instructions

A paper should be typed on $8\frac{1}{2} \times 11$ white bond paper (not lightweight tissue) with at least one carbon copy. Or you can dispense with the carbon copy and make a Xerox copy after you have finished typing. Type on only one side.

Spacing for the main body of the paper should be double or a space and one-half. Instructions for the footnotes and bibliography have already been given.

Pages should be numbered with arabic numerals at the top right corner of the page about five spaces below the edge of the paper. (On pages with major headings, you may place the number at the bottom of the page in the center.)

Make the typing look balanced on the page. Leave a margin of approximately one inch on both the left and the right sides of the paper.

Indent paragraphs five spaces. Leave two spaces after a period or other terminal punctuation mark (including a colon when it is followed by a complete sentence). Leave one space after any other kind of punctuation mark (including a colon when it is used within a sentence or other material).

TITLE PAGE   (see p. 402)

Many departments or individual instructors have their own requirements for the information to be included on the title page. Those instructions should be followed as prescribed.

When a title page is used, the title is not repeated on page 1 of the essay. A title page is not numbered, although it is counted as a page if other preliminary materials are included and numbered with small Roman numerals (ii, iii, iv).

The title page is sometimes followed by one blank page, which is also not a numbered page if used, although it is also counted if other preliminary materials follow. (See the front matter of published books.)

THE OUTLINE   (see p. 403)

If an outline is required by an instructor, it should be inserted following the title page or blank page. It is considered preliminary material. The pages of preliminary materials are usually unnumbered, or they may be numbered with small roman numerals, as prefatory pages in books usually are.

An outline is never submitted unless it is part of an academic assignment.

THEIR CANDLE KEEPS BURNING

The Tradition of the Yaqui Indians

Kenneth Fellows

English 172

Professor Irmscher

March 14, 1981

OUTLINE

Thesis: The Yaqui Indians of Arizona may represent a dying culture because of their separation from Mexican roots and the difficulty of maintaining their way of life in this country.

Introduction: Locating the Yaquis and asking three questions that their presence in Arizona raises

I. Who the Yaquis are

    A. Historical background

        1. Early period of resistance: 1519-1825

        2. Period of active rebellion: 1875-1910

        3. End of hostilities: 1927-present

    B. Division into _mansos_ and _broncos_

II. What the traditions are and how they came about

    A. Historical background: the Jesuits

    B. Description of a major religious ceremony

        1. The serious ritual

        2. The contrasting details

    C. Other fiestas and the importance of the ceremonial societies

III. What the effect of the traditions is upon Yaquis living in Arizona

    A. Work patterns

    B. _Limosna_ as an economic solution

    C. Sponsorship as a social and economic solution

Conclusion: Asking the open question whether the Yaqui culture can survive in the modern world

Page 1 is numbered because a title page is used. If the title is put on the first page, the number can be put at the bottom of the page or omitted altogether.

A quotation of this kind at the beginning of a work is called an epigraph. Its purpose here is to explain the metaphorical title of the paper, "Their Candle Keeps Burning." Fellows makes the image of the candle apply to the tribe as a whole. Note that no quotation marks are used because the direct quotation is set off by special indentation and single-spacing.

The opening paragraph is an introduction. It provides a general setting and overview. Nothing is footnoted because all of the material can be considered general knowledge. Fellows says in his research diary that he has seen the ceremonies. Some of the comments reflect his own opinions.

The last sentence of the paragraph is important because it sets up the organization of the paper as a whole. A look at the outline will show that the paper falls into three main sections answering these three basic questions.

Footnote 1: This is the first reference to a book. Fellows gives full bibliographical information for it. For other details about preparing footnotes, see pp. 389–390. Sample footnote forms are given on pp. 390–395.

> Each of us has a candle when he is born in
> the world. Any person who has a short candle
> has not long to live. Anyone with a tall
> candle will live a long time.[1]

1   During early spring, visitors to Tucson, Arizona,

can witness unusual ceremonies among the Yaqui Indians

of nearby Pascua village that undoubtedly differ from

anything they have ever seen before. The ceremonies are

in part the familiar observances of the Roman Catholic

church during the forty days preceding Easter, but they

are combined with ancient practices of the Yaquis that

predate their conversion to Christianity. The Pascua

fiesta is no Hollywood production done for the sake of

the tourist trade. It is a ceremony central to the

lives of the Yaquis, one that gives them a special

identity among Indian tribes. Three questions immediately

arise: Who are these Indians whom many people have

never heard of? How did the traditions that they

preserve come about? How do these traditions affect

the Yaqui way of life in the modern world?

---

[1]Rosalio Moisés, et al., The Tall Candle: A
Personal Chronicle of a Yaqui Indian (Lincoln: University of Nebraska Press, 1971), p. 88.

Paragraph 2 begins section I of the outline. It answers "who the Yaquis are."

The population figures are Spicer's estimate. That information is therefore footnoted. Someone else might give different figures.

Edward Spicer is identified as an authority on the Yaquis. Every author does not need to be identified, but Fellows' research diary tells us that Spicer is one of the leading authorities and the main source for this paper.

The three reasons for the special distinction of the Yaquis are also Spicer's. Footnote 3 gives him credit.

Note that the final sentence of paragraph 2 provides a transition from a discussion of the reputation of the Yaquis at the present time to a discussion of the historical background.

Paragraph 3 covers section I A 1 of the outline.

Footnotes 2 and 3: These are the first references to two other books. Fellows gives full bibliographical information for them. Spicer's full-length book on Potam (footnote 3) is part of a series, but the information given in the book did not permit Fellows to write a footnote that followed exactly the models given in either footnote 14 or footnote 20 on pp. 392–393. He asked what he should do. The answer, of course, was that he had to combine models, as you occasionally have to do when you encounter a book that will not fit a set form. Footnoting at times demands flexibility, although undue liberties should not be taken with the basic forms or punctuation.

2   The people of Pascua village and other parts of
Tucson represent about half of approximately 2,500
Yaquis who have lived in the United States since the
1880s, when they began to flee the persecutions of the
Mexican government in their native pueblos of Sonora,
Mexico.[2] Edward Spicer, who is an authority on the
Yaquis, says that they are distinctive for three main
reasons: (1) they are the last of the North American
Indians who were considered a serious military threat
by the white man; (2) they are the most widely scattered
of the North American Indians; (3) in spite of the fact
that they are separated in various parts of Mexico and
the United States, they keep their traditions as a mark
of their ethnic identity.[3] An understanding of the
Yaquis of Arizona therefore depends on knowing about
their Mexican background.

3   In 1939, Vicente Tava, a Yaqui living in Sonora,
dictated a letter to his daughter in Tucson. What he
said is an overview of the history of the Yaquis:

---

[2] Edward H. Spicer, _Pascua: A Yaqui Village in
Arizona_ (Chicago: University of Chicago Press, 1940),
pp. xiii-xiv.

[3] Edward H. Spicer, _Potam: A Yaqui Village in
Sonora,_ American Anthropological Association Memoirs
No. 77 (Aug. 1954), p. 1.

The quotation is the only extended one in the paper except for the epigraph. It is certainly a justifiable quotation. It is a direct statement from one who was a part of the history and who has strong feelings about the fate of the Yaquis. The short sentences joined by "and" are stylistically effective. If these thoughts were paraphrased, they would lose their impact.

Quotations set off by special indentation and single-spacing as this one is do not require quotation marks.

In a short paper of this kind, the entire history cannot be recounted. Fellows chooses to include what he calls "the main outlines." The remainder of this paragraph and the next two paragraphs narrate some of the important events that tell more about who the Yaquis are.

Footnotes 4–6 and 8–10 indicate that most of the historical material is taken from Kelley's long introduction to *The Tall Candle.*

Footnote 4: Full bibliographical information on the *The Tall Candle* was given in footnote 1. This is the first reference to Kelley's introduction. Since most of the references from this book are to the introduction, not to the book proper, the book is listed in the bibliography under Kelley's name.

Footnotes 5 and 6: Standard use of "ibid.," indicating that all of the information in these footnotes is the same as that in the preceding note except the page numbers, which are given.

> We have spilt much blood, and we have lost
> many lives, and we have lost much wealth,
> and we have suffered a thousand miseries,
> and we are despised. Both the soldiers and
> the civil population look upon the Yaquis with
> scorn. They call us Indians. They never say
> Yaqui.[4]

The history itself is confused since it has been handed
down mainly by word of mouth, but the main outlines are
clear. From the time of the Spanish invasion of Mexico
in 1519, the Yaquis resisted being absorbed or
exterminated. Although Captain Don Diego Martínez de
Hurdaide was successful in subjugating many of the
Mexican tribes, he was defeated three times by the
Yaquis during 1609 and 1610.[5] Yet for all of their
warlike resistance, the Yaquis often did not follow up
their advantage. Again in 1825, when the government
for the first time tried to collect taxes from the
Yaquis, under the leadership of Juan Banderas they
defeated the government soldiers but were later forced
to sue for peace when the Mexicans retrenched and
defeated them.[6]

---

[4] Jane H. Kelley, Introduction to Moisés, The Tall
Candle, p. xlviii.

[5] Ibid., p. xiii.

[6] Ibid., p. xiv.

Paragraph 4 is I A 2 of the outline.

Ordinarily, footnotes are held until the end of a sentence, but in this instance Fellows throws in an interesting phrase from Spicer, although the rest of the material is taken from Kelley. The matter is solved by putting extra footnote 7 immediately following the quoted phrase.

Notice that the history is told in broad terms, but there is enough detail, particularly in the use of names and dates, to add interest.

Paragraph 5 finishes the political and military portion of the history (I A 3) that explains how the Yaquis in Pascua, who are the subject of this paper, got to the United States.

There is the possibility that much more of the history is footnoted than needs to be. Some of the facts could be considered general knowledge, but Fellows chooses to play safe and indicate exactly where he is getting his material. The choice is wise: if in doubt, put a footnote in rather than leave it out.

Footnote 7: Because the paper uses two books by Spicer, the footnote must include a short title of the book, not the author's name alone.

Footnotes 9 and 10: If short titles were used exclusively throughout the paper instead of "Ibid.," these notes would read:

```
9Kelley, p. xviii.
10Kelley, p. xix.
```

In 1875, one of the major Yaqui leaders, José María Leyva, familiarly called Cajeme, one who "does not drink,"[7] succeeded in uniting the Yaquis and kept them in an active state of revolt until their disastrous defeat in 1886. Cajeme was executed in 1887.[8] The Yaquis were settled in eight major pueblos along the Rio Yaqui under strict Mexican control. But from this point on, the scattering began. Some Yaquis fled to the mountains to continue guerrilla resistance. Others worked as laborers on ranches and in mines. Others began to move to the United States. But the warring continued. The extermination policies of Rafael Izábal, Governor of Sonora from 1903 until the establishment of the Mexican Republic in 1910, intensified the hatred of the Yaquis for the Mexicans.[9]

Open hostility did not end until 1927, when the Mexican government placed garrisons in all the Yaqui pueblos.[10] Satisfactory settlement of affairs, however, did not come until President Lázaro Cárdenas recognized

---

[7] Spicer, _Pascua_, p. 19.

[8] Kelley, p. xvi.

[9] Ibid., p. xviii.

[10] Ibid., p. xix.

"Ceded in perpetuity" is, of course, an actual quotation from one of the official documents signed by Cárdenas, but it is also a familiar legal term used in land settlements. It is therefore not footnoted; it falls into the category of general knowledge about documents of this kind.

In paragraph 6, the refugees of Pascua are further identified as *broncos*. This paragraph covers section I B of the outline.

The final sentence of paragraph 6 provides a transition to the second major part of the paper about the religious traditions.

The opening sentence of paragraph 7 indicates that, even though we have moved to the next section of the paper, one additional part of the historical background about the early Jesuits needs to be filled in.

Fellows pays special attention to the accurate transcription of accents in Spanish names.

Footnote 11: First reference to an article in a scholarly journal. Full bibliographical information is given. Note that when a volume number is used in this footnote form, the abbreviation for pages (pp.) is dropped.

the autonomy of the Yaquis and "ceded in perpetuity" to them the lands they now occupy. Even though programs were initiated in 1960 to aid the Yaquis, basic differences between the political systems of the Mexicans and the Yaquis continue to cause friction.[11]

6   During the long struggle, the Yaquis were themselves divided between those who wanted to come to terms with the Mexican system and those who refused. The first were referred to as _mansos_ (tame) and the others as _broncos_ (wild). The refugees of Pascua in Tucson were originally _broncos_. In 1909, after a period of deliberately remaining obscure to protect themselves, they revived the ceremonies that identify them as Yaquis.[12]

7   The ceremonies, however, are another important part of the history. About 1620, the Yaquis of Sonora welcomed two Jesuit missionaries, Andrés Pérez de Ribas and Tomás Basilio, to their territory. Part of the teaching of the Jesuits was to dramatize the story of

---

[11]Gilbert D. Bartell, "The Yaqui and Mexican Government Conflict in the Perception of Power," _International Journal of Comparative Sociology_, IX (Sep. and Dec. 1968), 179-181.

[12]Muriel T. Painter, _A Yaqui Easter_ (Tucson: University of Arizona Press, 1971), p. 3.

Paragraph 8 gives a detailed description of one major ceremony. Fellows does not try to describe the entire fiesta, which goes on for many weeks. If he had done that, the paper would have been decidedly unbalanced.

Here, again, the use of native words lends both authenticity and interest to the writing.

Footnote 13: The "ibid." represents a conventional reference footnote. The remainder of the footnote gives additional information. Informational or explanatory footnotes are useful as long as they do not represent long digressions from the main thought of the paper. Unfortunately, some writers have a tendency to tuck into a footnote everything that they cannot legitimately get into the main body of the paper.

Jesus' crucifixion and death, but they did not force
the Yaquis to give up their native dances or rituals or
even their own myths.[13] Thus Yaqui Catholicism
developed separate from Mexican Catholicism. To this
day, the Roman Catholic diocese of Tucson maintains a
church close to Pascua village. The Yaquis maintain
and attend their own modest church structure.[14]

8   The ceremonies leading up to Easter are the most
important part of the Yaqui year. They are a drama-
tizing of a Passion play called La Fiesta de Gloria.
The entire fiesta continues for six Fridays, depicting
the slow pursuit of Jesus and his followers by Roman
soldiers and by Mary and her friends until Jesus is
finally arrested in Gethsemane and crucified. The most
spectacular part of the fiesta is the symbolic battle
between the forces of good and the forces of evil that
takes place on the Saturday before Easter. The
Chapayekas, who are the masked fariseos (Pharisees)
carrying wooden swords and daggers, first praise Judas.
The maestros, the lay priests of the village, sing the

---

[13]Ibid. Perhaps the largest collection of myths is
included in Ruth W. Giddings, Yaqui Myths and Legends
(Tucson: University of Arizona Press, 1959).

[14]Spicer, Pascua, p. 6.

Note how Fellows works into the description some of the myths and legends associated with certain religious practices. In this way, he carries out the theme of the second section: what the traditions are and how they came about.

Paragraph 9 continues the description of the ceremony, introducing other groups who participate. The topic listed as II B 1 in the outline requires two paragraphs.

The use of the Yaqui names gives both color and authenticity to the writing. The further importance of the ceremonial groups is discussed in paragraph 11. Here they are identified by their costumes and roles in the fiesta.

Footnote 15: Another example of an informational footnote. This material would not appropriately go into the main body, but it is useful information to have if one wanted to follow up the subject.

Gloria. Then the battle of flowers begins. The
fariseos are defeated by a rain of paper flowers and
confetti; they are symbolically defeated by the blood
of Jesus, because a Yaqui myth tells that the blood
falling from the side of Jesus on the cross caused
flowers to spring up.[15] Flowers are also closely
associated with Mary. A story tells that Mary always
had flowers with her; she remained a virgin because she
conceived by smelling a flower.[16] Flowers and symbols
of flowers are a part of the costumes and headdresses of
most participants.

The fariseos do not give up easily in the battle.
Small children representing angels beat them with
switches. Young unmarried girls wave flags. The
caballeros, the good soldiers who did not turn away from
Jesus, kneel and cross themselves. The costumed
matachinis, soldiers of the Virgin, wave feathered wands

---

[15]Muriel T. Painter, Faith, Flowers, and Fiestas
(Tucson: University of Arizona Press, 1962), p. 1.
Although the Yaquis ordinarily do not permit visitors to
take pictures, a few photographs appear in this book,
together with numerous paintings of the ceremonies done
by Yaqui schoolchildren. The well-known Arizona artist
Ted de Grazia has done a series of forty highly colorful
paintings covering the entire Lenten season. These are
published in De Grazia Paints the Yaqui Easter (Tucson:
University of Arizona Press, 1968).

[16] Spicer, Pascua, p. 254.

What is impressive here about the writing is the amount of information that is compressed into a small space. Notice the reference in footnote 17; what is described in Painter for three pages is here reduced to one paragraph.

Burlesque   Pascua
                                             191

263   Burlesque is part of
      the role of playing evil
      spirit.
           Important feature of
      ceremony.
           heap, shiver, scrape
      imaginary filth from legs
      when Mary's name mentioned.

Paragraph 10 covers II B 2 of the outline—the contrasting details. The six sentences beginning "All of the actions are not sacred and serious" are based on material from Painter and Spicer. The two note cards on this page will permit you to see how Fellows used the material on his cards; see footnote 20. (Students were asked to turn in all their cards with their final papers. Fellows turned in 198 cards.)

Pascolas   Pascua
                                             494

185   Crowd-pleasers. Keep spectators
      interested. Call people to fiesta.
      Keep them awake and active.

187   They clown. Imitate animal
      movements and cries.
      Horseplay with one another
      and crowd.
           Obscenities. Farce

and dance. The deer dancer, originally a part of the
ancient ritual of deer hunting among the Yaquis, joins
in also, shaking bells and rattles. Three times the
fariseos are driven back. Finally, in defeat, they
throw their swords and daggers and masks on a pyre to
which a straw figure of Judas has been tied, and all is
engulfed in flames. The victory is celebrated in an
all-night fiesta. The pascolas, the old men of the
fiesta, bare to the waist, dance dances of ancient
origin. At dawn, the matachinis perform a Maypole
dance. The way is prepared for the day of resurrection
and more ceremony.[17]

10   The intricate details of the long ceremonies during
the entire Lenten season are performed almost exactly
the same in all Yaqui villages, although there is no
written script.[18] All of the actions are not sacred
and serious. Because the fariseos represent evil, one
of their functions is to distract the maestros. The
fariseos play the role of clowns. They joke and perform
antics. They do things lefthanded and backward.[19] The

---

[17]Painter, A Yaqui Easter, pp. 36-38.

[18]Ibid., p. 6.

[19]Ibid., p. 12.

Paragraph 11 turns to topic II C of the outline. This paragraph tells more about the functions of the ceremonial societies and tells about the tradition of the *manda*. Notice from the footnote references in 21–24 that the material is drawn from four different sources. This would suggest that Fellows has absorbed his material and written his own version of it.

Footnotes 20 and 22: "pp. 187, 263" refers to two separate pages widely separated. Inclusive pages are indicated as in 177–179, but 182 is a separate page reference.

pascolas, who have names like badger, wolf, and turtle, imitate the actions of the animals and even make indecent gestures.[20]

11   Fiestas are not limited to the Easter season. Spicer estimates that at least 171 days of the year are devoted to some kind of public religious ceremony, and that figure does not include the private fiestas held at the time of baptisms, confirmations, marriages, and funerals.[21] Their ceremonial societies, five for men and two for women, serve basically as the social and civil structure of the Yaqui community. Each society has ceremonial obligations. What one group can do or when it can appear is well defined. The societies also carry on the administration of the village by a kind of diffuse, general, democratic decision-making. There is no chief.[22] Societies like the maestros, the matachinis, fariseos, and caballeros are dedicated either to Jesus or Mary. Groups like the pascolas and the deer dancer and his musicians do not take religious vows, but

---

[20]Spicer, Pascua, pp. 187, 263.

[21]Ibid., p. 204.

[22]Bartell, pp. 177-179, 182.

The discussion of the *manda* also relates to the mythic material previously mentioned. Many of the myths begin with a *manda* or promise.

Paragraph 12 moves to the third major section of the paper: what the effect of the traditions is upon the Yaquis living today in Arizona. The opening sentence is transitional. Two observations grow out of what has been discussed thus far. Commentary on the first point—that the ceremonies are time-consuming—is given in the remainder of this paragraph (III A).

Footnote 25: The source of this footnote, Spicer's *Pascua,* was published in 1940. One can assume that a great number of changes have occurred in the forty-year period since the time of Spicer's research. Fellows notes in his research diary that he tried unsuccessfully to get more recent data. The statement about cotton picking that Fellows makes, however, is couched in past tense; he does not make claims about more recent history that he has not been able to verify.

they cooperate in the ceremonies.[23] An individual usually becomes a member of a particular society as a result of a _manda_ or promise, often made during a time of illness. Sick people may dedicate themselves to serve if their health is restored, or a parent may dedicate a child to serve. A _manda_ is thought to be binding. Failure to carry it out will be punished by illness, accident, or death.[24]

12   Two things ought to be apparent about the ways of the Yaquis in the modern world: (1) the ceremonials and the preparation for them are time-consuming; (2) they are also financially demanding on a group of uneducated people who live on the lowest possible economic level. Everyone does not attend all ceremonies, yet a man if necessary will quit his job to meet a special ceremonial obligation. The work pattern of the people is strongly affected by the ceremonial pattern. Cotton picking was always popular because the season left the Yaquis free for the most important Easter fiesta of the year.[25]

---

[23]Kelley, pp. xxvi-xxvii.

[24]Painter, _A Yaqui Easter_, p. 9.

[25]Spicer, _Pascua_, pp. 48, 56-57.

Paragraph 13 moves to the economic solutions that the Yaquis make, relating to the second observation made in the previous paragraph that the ceremonies are financially demanding (III B of the outline). We are told what effect the *limosna* has on community spirit.

Paragraph 14 moves to a second solution (III C). The opening transitional phrase "Equally important" keeps the reader informed of the structure of the presentation.

Paragraph 15 continues the discussion of the topic given in III C of the outline.

Footnote 26: Notice that "ibid." can be used as the first footnote reference on a new page. It simply refers to the preceding footnote on p. 10 of the reference paper.

13 Within the village, people share with one another
through an institution called <u>limosna</u>, meaning "alms."
A fiesta means expenses for food and decorations. To
provide these for everyone, members of the dance
societies go from household to household to collect what
money or food is available. The village acts as a
common economic unit just as a household does, where
the members must share with their relatives.[26]

14 Equally important to the community spirit of the
Yaquis is the practice of sponsorship or ritual kinship.
Sponsors are provided for all of the ceremonial
occasions in an individual's life from baptism to death.
An ordinary person participating in all of the
ceremonials could accumulate as many as ten sponsors
during a lifetime. A member of the <u>fariseos</u>, who get a
new set of sponsors every three years, could accumulate
fourteen or fifteen. The average person has from five
to seven.[27]

15 Sponsors are more than friends or more than
godparents as we usually think of them in this country.
They have strong obligations. They serve an important

---

[26] Ibid., pp. 44-47.

[27] Ibid., pp. 100-101.

Paragraph 16 moves to the conclusion. Ralph Beals is mentioned for the first time in the paper; he is identified as "another leading authority" in addition to Spicer. The idea, of course, is to give strong weight to his opinion.

The outline lists the final paragraph as the conclusion. It is, but note that it is not a summary tagged on at the end. It grows out of the previous material and is a part of it; yet the conclusion has a point of its own. It is basically an expansion of the statement given as the thesis of the entire paper: can the Yaquis survive?

function in a society where blood kin are often separated from one another.[28] A child may live apart from his parents and be supported by another household. Few adults live alone. The household rather than the family is therefore the important unit of the Yaqui social structure. Members of several families may be living in one household.[29]

16   Despite the strong beliefs of the Yaquis, their way of life may be doomed. Ralph Beals, another leading authority on the Yaquis, contends that the culture of the Yaquis in the United States is dying, although he does not see the same thing happening among the Yaquis in Mexico.[30] The Yaquis in Pascua are no longer a strong homogeneous group. Some have moved away. Some do not believe in the ceremonies, although they still participate. The young show little interest in tradition. The modern way of life attracts them.[31]

---

[28]Ibid., p. 68.

[29]Kelley, pp. xlii–xliv.

[30]Ralph L. Beals, The Contemporary Culture of the Cáhita Indians, Smithsonian Institution Bureau of American Ethnology Bulletin 142 (Washington, D.C.: U. S. Govt. Printing Office, 1945), p. ix.

[31]Spicer, Pascua, pp. 264–266.

The entire final paragraph shows special attention to matters of style. The short sentences move the essay rapidly to a climax and to the final point.

The last sentence of the paper gives a unity to the paper as a whole. That sentence returns to the metaphorical implications of the title and the epigraph. It is Fellows' own commentary on the basis of what he has studied. He expresses a kind of cautious pessimism. Contrast this ending with other possible kinds of endings he might have written. It would not have seemed quite right to say "Surely modernism will not be able to crush their enduring spirit" or "Surely the Yaqui spirit will live on." These sentences express an optimism that the facts do not justify. Fellows' choice is realistic and imaginative without being unnecessarily fancy.

Footnote 32: If short titles were used throughout this paper, footnote 32 would read:

[32] Spicer, _Pascua_, pp. ix–x.

13

Yet the Yaqui identity continues strong. Those who
move away come back regularly. They continue to support
their kin. Those who stay allow the society to be
flexible enough to permit change. They have learned to
live with non-Indians because they are economically
dependent on them.[32] History shows that the Yaquis have
prevailed against extreme hardships in the past. Their
candle keeps burning, but it may now be burning low.

---

[32]Ibid., pp. ix-x.

Bibliography: The bibliography lists only the books and periodicals Fellows actually used in writing the paper and two books that he refers to in the footnotes. These he had obviously read and used for the value of the pictures.

Abbreviations used in footnotes are spelled out in the bibliography.

As previously mentioned, the book listed under the name of Jane H. Kelley is used in two ways. A good bit of the historical material is taken from the introduction; the epigraph of the reference paper is taken from the personal chronicle written by Moisés. Since the same book should not be listed in two different ways, a choice had to be made. Because the Kelley introduction was used for a substantial number of notes, Fellows chose in favor of that entry.

The long dash indicates that the book was written or edited by the person listed in the previous entry.

For other details about preparing a bibliography, see p. 395. Sample forms are given on pp. 396–398.

14

BIBLIOGRAPHY

Bartell, Gilbert D. "The Yaqui and Mexican Government Conflict in the Perception of Power." _International Journal of Comparative Sociology_, IX (September and December 1968), 177-187.

Beals, Ralph L. _The Contemporary Culture of the Cáhita Indians_. Smithsonian Institution Bureau of American Ethnology Bulletin 142. Washington, D.C.: United States Government Printing Office, 1945.

De Grazia, Ted E. _De Grazia Paints the Yaqui Easter_. Tucson: University of Arizona Press, 1968.

Giddings, Ruth W. _Yaqui Myths and Legends_. Tucson: University of Arizona Press, 1959.

Kelley, Jane H. Introduction to Rosalio Moisés et al., _The Tall Candle: The Personal Chronicle of a Yaqui Indian_. Lincoln: University of Nebraska Press, 1971.

Painter, Muriel T. _Faith, Flowers, and Fiestas_. Tucson: University of Arizona Press, 1962.

----------. _A Yaqui Easter_. Tucson: University of Arizona Press, 1971.

Spicer, Edward H. _Pascua: A Yaqui Village in Arizona_. Chicago: University of Chicago Press, 1940.

----------. _Potam: A Yaqui Village in Sonora_. American Anthropological Association Memoirs No. 77 (August 1954).

Research Diary of Kenneth Fellows

Reason I chose the topic: Before I came to the University of Washington, I lived in Tucson, Arizona. I saw the Yaqui ceremonies about four different times. They last for hours, sometimes in a kind of boring way, but they are also interesting because you constantly wonder what is going on and why they are doing certain things. I learned a little bit then, but I wanted to know more about the Yaquis. I also knew that Don Juan of Castaneda's books was a Yaqui, but I decided to leave him out of my paper completely because he's a big subject by himself and, anyway, I read that what he knew about drugs wasn't typically Yaqui. He learned from the Mexicans. I also heard the word "Yaqui" used recently on a Western TV show. That reminded me of them. The guy on the show said Yaqui to rhyme with "Jackie" to make it sound like they were no-gooders. Everybody in Tucson always said Yaqui to rhyme with "hockey." I knew that they were very poor people, but I also heard they were very proud and would not accept charity.

1. I started with encyclopedias. The first one handy was *Encyclopedia of the Social Sciences.* No entry. *Encyclopedia Americana* had a short article with reference to one book on Cahita Indians by Beals. No separate entry in *Collier's Encyclopedia.* Had to look in the Index to find Yaquis. Only mentioned by name. No details. Tried *Encyclopaedia Britannica.* Volume missing. I skipped it because I wasn't getting much good out of the encyclopedias anyway.

2. Went to the card catalog and looked up under Yaqui. Pleased to find 32 cards, some of them duplicates, however. Two books in Spanish. Made up 16 bibliography cards. Followed cross reference to Cahita Indians. Found the one book by Beals referred to in *Encyclopedia Americana.* Felt I had made good progress in a short time.

3. Checked *Readers' Guide* for a ten-year period to find recent stuff. No good. Found only a few things referring to Castaneda's books. Checked *International Index* for ten years. One was a very technical article on the Yaqui language. The other had possibilities. I wrote it down. I found one entry in the *Bibliographic Index.* I really thought I had enough to go on so I stopped searching.

4. I had the call numbers on the books. I had to look up one periodical. I ran into a dead end on the U.S. Bureau of Ethnology. The U.S. drawer said to see Ethnology. Ethnology said to see U.S. I had to get the librarian to bail me out. I sometimes think they do tricky stuff like that so we have to ask them questions. Otherwise, they can't feel important.

5. I began with the Bartell article. I realized almost immediately I was going to have to decide whether I wanted to write about the Mexican Yaquis or the Tucson Yaquis, but I wasn't ready to make the decision yet.

6. Since this was the first notetaking, I found myself hating to break things down into topics on separate cards. Then I remembered a paper I once wrote in high school when I took all my notes on big sheets of paper. I nearly wore out the sheets trying to find what I wanted and sometimes never did. No repeat of that, thank you.

7. Always a battle against the clock. I had more time to spend in the library, but the

announcement came through that the library was going to close at 5 (Friday afternoon). I managed to get three books checked out for the weekend.

8. I read the long 46-page introduction to *The Tall Candle*. Already I was finding out that Spicer and Beals are the big names on the Yaquis. Kelley, who wrote the introduction, refers to them. She ends up with a bibliography of 17 items. Suddenly I have more sources than I can possibly use.

9. I'm already thinking about choices. Do the religious/supernatural? The myths are really interesting. Do the historical? I'll have to do some of it whatever I write about. Do what I know a little bit about—the Tucson Yaquis? I'm fooled already because I thought I was choosing a little topic, and it's as big as Mexico.

10. I read the Painter book on *A Yaqui Easter* and decided the paper had to have something about the fiestas because they are probably the most important part of Yaqui life. I made up a very tentative outline, planning to start with the description of a fiesta, talk about the ceremonial societies, and then do a kind of flashback to give the background.

11. Second trip to the library. The saints of the Yaquis must be on my side. I looked for six books and found all of them in. That's the advantage of working on a topic that everybody in the University isn't studying at the same time. I checked out the books.

12. Spicer's work is specifically about the Yaqui Indians. Beals' work is broader about other groups closely related to the Yaquis. I see now that the few decisions I have already made about organization are helping me decide which notes to take and which ones to skip.

13. Third trip to the library. I wanted two more books. I goofed for the first time. I didn't look at a number right in the locator file and ended up walking to the Art library. There I found out that the book was in the main section where I was to start with. Oh well, I guess exercise is a part of researching. I got the other book too. Those are the last two I want. I therefore have clear sailing from here on.

14. When I found the statement by Spicer that the Yaquis are distinctive for three main reasons, I decided to change the organization of my paper. I am settling on two questions: Who are they? How did their traditions come about? That gives me some of the present and some of the past.

15. It didn't take me long to organize my note cards into stacks. I have a big stack on History, one on Ceremonies, one on the Supernatural, one on Civic/Social/Political/Economic. I think those are the main ones. Anyway, I know where to look when I want something.

16. I began writing. The outline is mainly in my head. I've been giving it a lot of thought. I actually got half of the paper written in one sitting. I'm making good progress because my notes are good. Two times I was hazy about some of the political history and had to go back to the books to get the facts straight. Good thing I still had the books.

17. I finished the paper in one more sitting. I wrote in long hand, putting in the footnotes at the bottom of the page by just listing the author and pages. I'll get those in correct form when I begin to think about the final draft.

18. The paper practically wrote itself, fortunately. When I finished and reread, I discovered something interesting. Instead of answering the two questions that I originally started out with, I ended up answering three questions. Only I didn't have three questions at the beginning. I went back and revised the end of paragraph one to read "three questions" instead of "two questions." I made up my final outline.

19. I ended up with two pretty big stacks of cards left over, although I used a few out of each of them. I think the paper might have been more interesting if I had been able to work in more of the myths, but it would have been twice as long. I'm really biting the bit over one story about the Devil blowing out the candle of a young man who tricked him. It's a good story and has a good quotable passage, but I can't force it in.

20. I see I ended up with only two extended quotations in the paper. You warned us so much about unnecessary quotations that maybe I went to the other extreme. But I don't think so. The only thing I really wanted to get in extra was the story about the Devil and the young Yaqui. Funny how something like that bugs you.

21. I typed up my longhand copy triple space so I could revise it easily. I found out there wasn't too much I had to do—a few sentences here and there for clarity and better style.

22. I wrote up the footnotes and bibliography. Everything is ready now for final typing.

23. From the first day I went to the library to the day I am adding the final entry to this diary, I've worked on the paper about three weeks. I could have done it faster, but I couldn't give it all of my time. Anyway, thinking about a subject helps even if you can't be writing on it.

Evaluating the reference paper

As a completed project, the reference paper is subject to the same criteria you use in judging the sources you chose for your paper. In brief, a reference paper is good

- if you have adequately canvassed the topic and carefully weighed the sources;
- if the material is up to date;
- if the material is authoritative and accurate;
- if the material is fully and accurately documented;
- if the paper is properly limited so that particular points can be handled with adequate detail;
- if the paper inspires in the reader a sense of confidence by its objectivity and the persuasiveness of its style.

Projects | *1.* Choose ten reference sources listed on pp. 374–380. Go to the library; locate each book and examine it. Test it by looking up something you think should be there. Provide the following information in less than fifty words for each book: (*a*) its call number; (*b*) its location in your school library as specifically as possible; (*c*) three or four details about the book's arrange-ment, ease or difficulty of using it, and comments about features that interest you.

2. Determine which library resources will meet these needs: (*a*) to introduce you to your topic with some suggestions for additional reading; (*b*) to find out what books are available on your campus on your topic; (*c*) to check the critical reputation of some books on your topic; (*d*) to find periodical mate-rial that will cover your subject; (*e*) to find the basic tools of library research in your subject area; (*f*) to find out the exact date of a national event.

3. Read the passage given below. Then do two things: (*a*) copy it accurately, word for word, as you see it; (*b*) compose in your own words an accurate paraphrase, paying attention to the overall meaning and emphasis. Let an-other member of the class check the accuracy of your first transcription. As a class, discuss the major implications of the passage as represented by the paraphrases.

> The facts of today's population crisis are appallingly simple. Mankind at first gradually, but recently with extreme rapidity, has intervened artificially to lower the death rate in the human population. Simultaneously we have not, repeat have not, intervened to lower the birth rate. Since people are unable to flee from our rather small planet, the inevitable result of the wide discrepancy between birth and death rates has been a rapid increase in the numbers of people crowded onto the Earth.
>
> The growth of the population is now so rapid that the multitude of humans is doubling every 35 years. Indeed in many undeveloped countries the doubling time is between 20 and 25 years. Think of what it means for the population of a country like Colombia to double in the next 22 years. Throughout its history the people of Colombia have managed to create a set of facilities for the mainte-nance of human beings: buildings, roads, farms, water systems, sewage systems, hospitals, schools, churches, and so forth. Remember that just to remain even, just to maintain today's level of misery, Colombia would have to duplicate all of those facilities in the next 22 years. It would have to double its human resources as well—train enough doctors, lawyers, teachers, judges, and all the rest so that in 22 years the number of all these professionals would be twice that of today. Such a task would be impossible for a powerful, industrialized country with agricultural surpluses, high literacy rate, fine schools, and communications, etc. The United States couldn't hope to accomplish it. For Colombia, with none of these things, with 30–40% of its population illiterate, with 47% of its popula-tion under 15 years of age, it is inconceivable.
>
> from Paul R. Ehrlich,
> "The Population Explosion: Facts and Fiction,"
> *The Sierra Club Bulletin* (Oct. 1968)

4. Arrange each of the following groups in some kind of order. Then offer an explanation for your arrangement or grouping:

A. 1776, 1201, 1066, 1492, 2001, 1914, 1984, 1941

B. let rise, eat, mix, knead, measure, bake, slice, cool

C. Isaac Asimov, Charles Ives, Andy Warhol, Ray Bradbury, Gian Carlo Menotti, Robert Heinlein, Samuel Barber, Jackson Pollock, Mary Cassatt

5. Write accurate footnotes based upon the miscellaneous information given below:

A. Reference to page 9 of an article entitled The Writer's Audience Is Always a Fiction, written by Walter J. Ong, S.J., and published in Volume 90 of the Publications of the Modern Language Association of America (usually referred to as PMLA), dated January 1975.

B. Reference to pages 44 through 46 of a book entitled The Rhetoric of Black Power, published by Harper & Row in New York in 1969. The authors were Robert L. Scott and Wayne Bockriede.

C. Reference to page 31 of an essay called On Defining Style written by Nils Enkvist and published in the second edition of a collection of essays entitled Modern Essays on Writing and Style, edited by Paul C. Wermuth and published in 1969 by Holt, Rinehart and Winston of New York.

D. Reference to p. 1380 of Aristotle's Rhetorica, translated by W. Rhys Roberts in Volume XI of The Works of Aristotle, edited by W. D. Ross and published by the Clarendon Press of Oxford in 1924.

E. Reference to p. 177 of Volume III of A History of Greek Philosophy published by Cambridge University Press in Cambridge, England in 1969. It was written by W. K. C. Guthrie.

6. Keep a research diary as you write your documented essay for the course. Use the one in this chapter as a model, although you will record your own experiences, decisions, and problems.

Suggestions for writing

1. List facts taken from a newspaper article about a news event; then write about the facts as if you personally had witnessed them.

2. Write a documented essay about what was going on in the world on the day you were born. Consult as many indexes and yearbooks as possible to determine the scene. Who was President? What was news? What was the focus of the people's attention? Who was big on the sports scene? In the movies? In literature? After you compile your facts, write a documented essay on your impressions of the times.

3. Below are facts and quotations taken from an article written by Saunders Redding, "Sojourner Truth," in *Notable American Women 1607–1950: A Biographical Dictionary*, ed. Edward T. James et al. (Cambridge: Belknap Press of Harvard University Press, 1971), III, 479–481. Using this material, rewrite the biographical sketch, based on an organization of your own. Read through all of the material first to determine how you can present the facts in an informative and effective way. You need not try to use all of the facts. Determine your emphasis; then eliminate what does not seem relevant.

[p. 479] Born: c. 1797. Died Nov. 26, 1883.

Given name: Isabella. Parents: James and Elizabeth, Slaves of Charles Harden-bergh, a Dutchman in New York. First language spoken: Dutch.

1810–27: Slave in the household of John J. Dumont, New Paltz, New York. Gave birth to five children by fellow slave named Thomas. Of four who survived infancy, two were sold by the master.

1827: Ran away to household of Isaac and Maria Van Wagener. Chose Isabella Van Wagener as her name.

1828: Mandatory emancipation of slaves in New York State. Quaker friends helped Isabella by legal proceedings to regain son Peter, who had been sold illegally.

c. 1829: Moved to New York with two youngest children. Worked as domestic. Religious activity as disciple of Elijah Pierson, "a wealthy fanatic who called himself 'The Tishbite.'" [p. 480] Her activities included preaching on the streets, "where Isabella's tall, gaunt, masculine figure and guttural Dutch-accented voice attracted welcome attention."

Between 1829–1831: Joined the household of Pierson and his wife Sarah, "Where they prayed together interminably and fasted for three days at a stretch." The Piersons and Isabella fell dupe to Robert Matthews by giving him their resources to establish "Zion Hill" in Sing Sing, New York. Venture of two years' duration resulted in death of Pierson and a scandal of immoral behavior involving Isabella. She won a libel suit that vindicated her.

Eight or nine-year period of living quietly in New York with her two children and earning her living as a domestic. Always subject to mystical experiences, seeing visions and hearing voices. In 1843, "the voices commanded her to take the name 'Sojourner Truth' and travel east to preach."

June, 1843: Alone, she began a walking, singing, preaching tour through Long Island and Connecticut. Knowledgeable about Bible, though illiterate all of her life.

Winter, 1843: Member of communal farm in Northampton, Mass., established by George W. Benson. Failure of experiment in 1846. Remained in Benson household as a servant and guest. During these years, encountered abolitionist movement for first time. Continued to travel and preach. Growing reputation.

c. 1850: Went west to Ohio, Indiana, Missouri, and Kansas. Became popular figure. Attracted large crowds.

Maintained herself by sales of *Narrative of Sojourner Truth* (1850), written for her by Olive Gilbert. Met Harriet Beecher Stowe, who called her "The Libyan Sibyl" in an article in *Atlantic Monthly* (April, 1863).

Accused of being a man. Bared her breasts at women's rights convention in Indiana to prove her sex. Continued for long years as supporter of women's suffrage movement.

Mid 1850s: Settled in Battle Creek, Michigan, with three daughters and their families. Solicited support for Negro volunteer regiments during Civil War.

1864: Received by President Lincoln at the White House. [p. 481] Until 1875, continued her travels in support of Negro rights, women's rights, temperance, and godliness.

Returned to Battle Creek, where she received visitors until her death in 1883. Funeral said to be the largest ever held in the town.

4. Visit your library. Observe its plan and the location of the card catalog, reference books, periodicals, etc. Collect as many useful facts as you can. Write a guide for a new student on "Getting Around Our Library."

5. Choose a topic you are interested in. Read about it first in one of the general encyclopedias, then in a specialized one. (For instance, you might read about Impressionism in *Encyclopaedia Britannica* and then in the *Larousse Encyclopedia of Modern Art.*) In as concise form as possible, list the facts found in each. Put an asterisk by those facts found in both. What similarities and differences are there between them? What features of either encyclopedia seem particularly useful? For what purpose would each best serve? Write a brief analysis (200–250 words) answering these questions and comparing the two encyclopedias on the basis of your analysis. Remember that your subject is the encyclopedias you are using, not the material you are looking up. However, use examples to illustrate whatever points you wish to make.

6. Plan a multimedia presentation on The City, using literature, paintings, photographs, music, film, or other media. Determine your purpose. Then research the topic. Write a program scenario explaining how you would arrange the material you have selected. Append a bibliography.

7. With the approval of your instructor, choose a topic that you can research as a major project for the course. Pay special attention to the bounds of the topic—whether it is too large or too limited; to the availability of materials on the topic—whether the library has crucial materials that may be necessary to treat the subject adequately; to the popularity of the subject—whether most of the books you need will be unavailable because they are currently being used by many students. In short, think in advance about some of the pitfalls you are likely to encounter.

Write a documented essay of a length specified by your instructor.

Everyone must write a business letter now and then—perhaps a letter of application, a letter of recommendation, a letter of inquiry, or a letter of complaint. Communications of this kind make a far better impression if they are typed on 8½-by-11-inch paper and follow a standard form. The two letters included (15A, 15B) show the two usual forms. The first is a letter of complaint, the second a letter of application followed by a resume (15C). General guidelines for business letters and a checklist for letters of application follow the resume.

Ordinarily, business letters should be kept brief and to the point. Yet if they deal with complex matters, their organization and development should be given the same reflection that an essay requires. Business letters represent a very special form of persuasion. They have a specific purpose; they are trying to make a point. The manner in which they are written is therefore of special importance. They must be clear and correct. Above all, they must maintain a tone appropriate to the purpose. Even a letter of complaint is more likely to receive careful attention if the case is reasonably stated. Threats, angry denunciations, and insults are more likely to antagonize than to persuade.

2638 Landor Avenue
Louisville, Kentucky   40205
April 11, 1981

Central State Insurance Company
347 Michigan Avenue
Peoria, Illinois   61614

To Whom It May Concern:

Re: Group Policy 2-A-5217

I have recently received my hospitalization policy from
your company, effective May 1, 1981. Included was a
statement asking for an advance payment of $65.50.

At the time I sent in my application for this policy, I
included my check in the amount of $65.50, and the
canceled check has been returned. Would you please see
that my account is credited with this payment?

Sincerely yours,

John F. Gerhardt

John F. Gerhardt

5251 Baker Street
Seattle, Washington 98107
May 10, 1981

Box 959
Yakima, Washington 98907

To Whom It May Concern:

Please consider my application for the position of Counselor-Manager of a group home for adults advertised in The Seattle Times, May 9, 1981. I am enclosing a resume.

You will notice that I have already had considerable experience working with senior citizens, as well as with younger people. In some positions, I have had supervisory responsibilities. Because I have had to work full time during my college career to support myself and a younger brother, I have required six years to complete my B.A. in Sociology. Although I have had to proceed more slowly than many students, I have gained invaluable experience working with people and have acquired an understanding of social problems that goes far beyond textbook learning. I have a complete dossier at the University Placement Service that includes a transcript of my record and letters of recommendation. If you wish, I will have a copy forwarded to you.

I am now free to relocate and would be able to assume responsibilities in residence at the home. If you wish to arrange a personal interview, I am willing to come to Yakima at a time most convenient to you.

Because I have become acquainted with halfway houses for adults through my work with the Department of Human Resources of the City of Seattle, I can assure you of my genuine interest in the kind of position you offer.

Sincerely yours,

Pamela Robinson

Pamela Robinson

Pamela Robinson
5251 Baker Street
Seattle, Washington 98107

Home telephone: (206) 486-7105

PERSONAL INFORMATION

Birth date: February 9, 1956
Marital status: single Dependents: none
Height: 5'3" Weight: 115 lbs.
Health: excellent
Physical handicaps: none

EDUCATIONAL BACKGROUND

B.A., University of Washington, March, 1981
                         (Accumulated grade point average:
                              3.3 on 4.0 scale)
    Major: Sociology (60 quarter credits)
    Related studies: Psychology (20 credits)
                       Social work and gerontology
                        (20 credits)
Special abilities: speak, read, and write Spanish;
                     play piano
Diploma: Queen Anne High School, Seattle, 1974

WORK EXPERIENCE

1980-present: full-time employment
    Department of Human Resources, Aging Division
       Mayor's Office, Seattle
    Duties: Resource person; research and consulta-
       tion; personal interviewing of senior citizens;
       planning of programs and solutions

1978-1980: full-time employment
    Neighborhood Youth Corps, Northwest Senior
       Center, Seattle
    Duties: General supervisor, responsible for
       operation and management of center; program
       planning

1974–1978: full-time employment
    The Ark, Seattle
    Duties: Graduated responsibilities from reception-
        ist to counselor of girls with problems of
        family and social adjustment

Summers, 1975, 1976: full-time employment
    Red Barn Ranch, Auburn, Washington
    Duties: Counselor and leader in day camp center

1974–1976: part-time employment, evenings
    Open Door Clinic (University district), Seattle
    Duties: Counseling, especially emergency situations

REFERENCES

Mr. W. Parkington Allen, Head
Department of Human Resources, Aging Division
City of Seattle
Seattle, Washington 98104

Professor Alvin Jacobs
Department of Sociology
University of Washington
Seattle, Washington 98195

Professor Henry Jenkins
Department of Sociology
University of Washington
Seattle, Washington 98195

Ms. Althea Foster, Coordinator, Neighborhood Youth Corps
Department of Human Resources
City of Seattle
Seattle, Washington 98104

Ms. Mary Sandmel (former supervisor of The Ark)
3465 Watts Boulevard
Seattle, Washington 98155

The resume

The resume (also called a data sheet or vita) consists of four parts: personal information, educational background, work experience, and references. The order of the first three parts can be varied according to specific circumstances, but references are always placed at the end. Work experience is usually listed beginning with the present or most recent employment and continuing in reverse chronological order. Although there is no prescribed form, it is advisable to arrange the data so that it is easily readable.

The resume on p. 442 can serve as a model; it can be varied to meet your own circumstances. If you have no special abilities you wish to mention, omit that category. If you have received special awards or prizes, add another heading. In short, adjust the resume to include all of your qualifications.

15D Guidelines for writing business letters

1. Even though the names of streets and states are usually spelled out, abbreviations may be used, depending on the formality of the letter. The Postal Service's two-letter state abbreviations are increasingly used and accepted in all kinds of correspondence. Note that both letters are capital letters and that no periods are used between or after them (NY, WV, PA, TX).
2. Some title should always be used before a person's name as a part of the inside address:

```
Ms. Julia P. Braker
16 Fifth Street
Cleveland, OH 44116
```

3. When a letter is not addressed to a known person, salutations like "Gentlemen:" or "Dear Sir:" were commonly used in the past. It is now considered more appropriate to substitute "To Whom It May Concern:" as a salutation to unknown groups of both sexes.
4. Complimentary closes vary in their formality:

Highly formal	Respectfully yours, Respectfully,
Formal:	Very truly yours, Yours truly,
Less formal:	Sincerely yours, Yours sincerely,
Personal:	Cordially, Sincerely,

5. Letters should always be signed, even though the name is typed for purposes of clarity.
6. The sender's address is not typed on stationery that already has a business or home address printed on it, but such a letter should otherwise follow one of the standard forms.

Checklist for letters of application *15E*

The immediate purpose of a letter of application is to get an interview; the ultimate purpose is to get a job. The letter you write, therefore, has to make a good impression for you. Further, you have to be careful not to send the wrong message by inadvertent carelessness or inattention to detail.

The following suggestions will serve as a checklist:

1. Be direct and concise. Provide all of the information asked for so that the addressee knows you can read accurately and follow directions.
2. Assume a confident but polite tone. The addressee undoubtedly wants a person who can do the job well but also one who can get along with others.
3. Be moderate. Indicate that you are proud of the things you have accomplished in the past, but use modest statements, not exaggerated boasts. It would be better to say "Upon two occasions during my college career I was given special awards for my skills in debate" rather than "My friends tell me I am the best debater at the University today."
4. Present your best side. Suppress the sob story or special pleading. Refer to your hardships only if the addressee is likely to interpret these as strong motives for your future success.
5. Follow conventional form. Use $8\frac{1}{2}$-by-11-inch white bond paper, type neatly, and fold the letter straight. Inattention to small things may be interpreted as a sign of sloppiness.
6. Proofread. See that the letter is completely correct in grammar and mechanics to indicate your concern for accuracy of detail. Make certain your addressee's name and address are correct if they are given.

The English language and its use   Part IV

The English language is our heritage, but we do not preserve it as a museum piece. We use it daily. We refurbish it. We discard parts of it that no longer seem suitable for our times. The language experiences a constant renewal through its speakers. We are not born with the capacity to speak a language; we grow up with it, we absorb it, we learn it, we practice it. By the time we go to school, we have mastered the fundamentals. From that point on, education attempts to develop our capacity with language and to familiarize us with the best of the heritage that has been preserved in the literature.

Language, therefore, is one form of human behavior. It is mainly social behavior, because it is our means of communication with one another, either spoken or written. Interaction between speakers keeps the language vital and flexible. Languages like Sanskrit and Gothic are known as dead languages because they no longer have an active history of living speakers. They are preserved only in a written literature. Nothing is altered, and nothing is added. Because the history of a language is largely an account of its changes, its history ends when change is no longer possible.

English is a relatively young language. Its history extends over a period of approximately 1500 years, although its origins may be traced back to a more distant past. But its development as a separate language coincides with the movement of tribes from the continent of Europe to the British Isles about the middle of the fifth century. The people already living in Britain were by no means without languages. Numerous dialects of Celtic were spoken, and surely Latin survived as a remnant from the earlier Roman occupation. But the native people of Britain could not resist the force of the invading tribes. English, the new language, predominated. The other languages died or managed to survive only because their speakers retired to isolated and remote parts of the island. In the years following, English underwent a natural course of development, but the facts of its origins and early development were lost. Not until the sixteenth century did the English show an interest in the study of Old English, and not until the nineteenth century did scholars throughout the world provide the evidence that established the concept of the Indo-European family of languages and the ties of English with that family (see table).

Indo-European Family of Languages

A. Hellenic (Mycenaean Greek, Attic, Ionic, Doric, Aeolic, Cyprian, Modern Greek)
B. Italic
  1. Oscan
  2. Umbrian
  3. Latin (Faliscan, Latin, Italian, Provençal, French, Spanish, Catalan, Portuguese, Rumanian)
C. Celtic (Gaulish, Welsh, Cornish, Breton, Irish, Manx, Gaelic)
D. Germanic
  1. East Germanic (Gothic)
  2. North Germanic
    a. East Norse (Swedish, Danish, Gutnish)
    b. West Norse (Norwegian, Faroese, Icelandic)
  3. West Germanic
    a. High German (Alemannic, Bavarian, Yiddish)
    b. Franconian (Dutch, Flemish)
    c. Low German, or Plattdeutsch
    d. Old Frisian, Modern Frisian
    e. English (Old English, Middle English, Modern English)
E. Indo-Iranian Branch
  1. Indic (Sanskrit, Pakrit, Pali, Hindi, Urdu, Hindustani, Bengali, Gujarati, Marathi, Panjabi, Singhalese, Romany)
  2. Iranian (Avestan, Old Persian, Pahlavi, Sogdian, Scythian, Balochi, Pashtu, Persian, Kurdesh, Ossetic)
F. Armenian Branch (Classical Armenian, Eastern and Western Armenian)
G. Albanian Branch (Thracian, Illyrian, Albanian)
H. Balto-Slavic
  1. Slavic (Old Bulgarian, Bulgarian, Serbo-Croatian, Slovenian, Czech, Slovak, Polish, Wendish, Great Russian, White Russian, Ukrainian)
  2. Baltic (Old Prussian, Lithuanian, Latvian)

Origins of English

The visit of Sir William Jones to India in the 1780s assumes special importance in tracing the origins of the English language because that visit brought him for the first time in touch with Sanskrit writings dating back to as early as 2000 B.C. Sir

William, a man learned in many languages, was impressed by the resemblances between ancient Sanskrit and the more familiar ancient languages of Latin and Greek. Sir William was not the first to notice these similarities, but he was the first to state with emphasis that the resemblances were surely not accidental and that languages of both the Western and Eastern worlds must have sprung from a common source.

Thus, the hypothesis of a parent for languages as widely separated in time and place as Sanskrit, Latin, and English was set down in 1786. The findings of men like Franz Bopp, Jacob Grimm, Rasmus Rask, and Karl Verner in the following century represent a remarkable feat of scholarship. What the first three of these men did was to tabulate corresponding words in widely scattered languages and to conclude that their differences could be explained in terms of regular and predictable sound changes. The work of the fourth, Karl Verner, conclusively established the principle of the orderly development of languages because he was able to explain changes that seemed to be exceptions to the principles of Grimm and the others. These principles of sound change are familiarly known today as Grimm's Law and Verner's Law.

Indo-European

The hypothesis of Indo-European as the original tongue may be stated briefly: enough evidence exists to conclude that Indo-European was a language spoken by a tribe, probably in north central Europe, in the late Stone Age. No written documents exist in the language because it was spoken before the invention of writing. About 2500 B.C., possibly earlier, the members of the tribe dispersed both to the west and to the east, moving eventually as far west as Cornwall and as far east as Chinese Turkestan, carrying with them a common language which was to undergo different kinds of change in scattered places of the world. Certain words, however, especially the numerals and terms for family relationships, did not completely lose signs of their origin. The study of these clues in the earliest written documents of many ancient languages has made possible the reconstruction of a lost language and its grammar.

Comparison of variant forms of many languages suggests that some languages have undergone more changes than others. Among modern languages, some scholars think Lithuanian is possibly closest to the parent language. Modern English represents a wide divergence. In the relatively brief period of its history, English has undergone vast changes, so that what we now recognize as English is quite different from the English of a thousand years ago.

The stages of development

The history of the English language is customarily divided into three periods: Old English, 450–1100, Middle English, 1100–1500, and Modern English, 1500 to the present. Some histories choose to distinguish between Early Modern from 1500 to 1800 and Modern, a later development from 1800 on. But these particular divisions are arbitrary. The dates vary slightly from history to history, but the breaks in this gradual and continuous evolution reflect events which had a strong impact on the development of the language. The earliest invasion of Germanic tribes that we know was A.D. 449; the Norman conquest of England occurred in 1066; William Caxton set up the first printing press in England in 1477; by 1800, England's political and social structure was remolded by the Industrial Revolution. These are only a selection of the external events that affected the conditions under which people lived and influenced the way they used the language.

Because a full account of the development of the English language would involve a detailed discussion of its grammar, vocabulary, and pronunciation in each of the periods, a handbook of this kind can give only an overview and some suggestion of the kinds of change that occurred.

Old English (450–1100)

The overall change that has occurred in English from its earliest period to the present may be summarized as a gradual shift from a basically synthetic language to a basically analytic language. A synthetic language is one that depends chiefly on a well-developed inflectional system for its operation; an analytic one depends mainly on word order. Indo-European itself was a synthetic language, and many of the branch languages, like Modern German and Russian, still utilize inflections extensively. The fact that Old English was a synthetic language causes it to resemble Modern German more closely than it does Modern English.

A quotation from an Old English translation of the Bible will quickly suggest some of the features of the language:

Ðās þing se Hǣlend sprǣc, and āhōf ūpp his ēagan tō   heofenum, and
Those things the Saviour spoke, and lifted up his eyes   to [the] heavens   and

cwǣð 'Fæder, tīd ys cumen; geswutela þinne Sunu, þæt þīn Sunu geswutelige
said: 'Father, time is come; glorify   thy Son,   that thy Son may glorify

þē; and swā þū him sealdest anweald ǣlces mannes, þæt he sylle   ēce   līf
thee; and as thou to him gavest power of each man, that he might give eternal life

eallum þām þe   þū   him sealdest. Ðis ys sōþlice ēce   līf, þæt hi oncnāwon
to all those whom thou him gavest. This is truly   eternal life, that they know

þæt þū   eart   ān sōþ God, and se þe   þū   sendest, Hǣlynde Crīst.'
that thou art the one true God, and he whom thou sendest, Saviour Christ.'

John 17:1–3

The strangeness of Old English is in part due to symbols we no longer use, like the þ (thorn) and ð (edh), used indifferently in Old English for either the *th*-sound in *thin* or the *th*-sound in *thine*. The symbol æ in the word *sprǣc*, the past tense of *sprecan* ("to speak"), stands for a sound like the *a* in *at*. These early forms of the verb "to speak" may be compared with Modern German *sprechen* and *sprach*.

The *-um* ending on *heofenum* indicates a dative plural, no longer used in Modern English. *Eagan* is an old plural form still recognizable in a word like *oxen*. The form of *Ðās* in *Ðās þing* shows that the noun is accusative plural, and the form of *þinne* in *þinne Sunu* shows that it is accusative singular. *Geswutela* is the imperative mood of *geswutelian,* a Class II weak verb; *geswutelige* is the same verb in the optative mood, expressing wish or desire. *Tīd* is an archaic word for *time* that we retain in words like "yuletide" and "eventide." *Ðū him sealdest* ("thou to him gavest") represents a word order we no longer follow, but the words can be understood in Old English because the inflected form of *him* indicates that it is dative after the verb *sealdest* and should be read "to him." These are only a few details that give a clue to the highly complex system of noun, pronoun, and adjective declensions, complicated verb classes and conjugations, and a spelling and sound system quite different from Modern English.

Middle English (1100–1500)

John 17:1–3 in John Wycliffe's translation in Middle English, about 1388, shows to what extent the language had evolved over a period of several centuries:

> These thingis Jesus spak, and whanne he hadde cast up hise iȝen into hevene, he seide: 'Fadir, the our cometh; clarifie thi sone, that thi sone clarifie thee; as thou has ȝovun to hym power on ech fleisch, that al thing that thou hast ȝovun to hym, he ȝyve to hem everlastynge liif. And this is everylastynge liif, that thei knowe thee very God aloone, and whom thou hast sent, Jesu Crist.'

Even though the spellings and forms of this passage continue to have a strange appearance, they have enough resemblance to Modern English that an interlinear translation is no longer necessary. The pronunciations of Middle English words differ from those of both Old English and Modern English. Vowel sounds in Middle English had basically the values of what are now referred to as continental vowels; that is, they were pronounced like vowels in Modern French, German, or Italian. Through the centuries, vowel sounds have shifted, so that a word like *stan* in Old English, which was pronounced with an *a* as in *father,* changed to Middle English *ston* or *stoon,* pronounced with an *o* as in *bought,* and finally reached its present fully rounded sound. Sound shifting is a complete history in itself.

The most significant change that took place in the Middle English period was a gradual erosion of the inflectional system. *Thingis* in the passage above has a plural ending that has been retained and become standard in Modern English (compare OE *Ðās þing* in the earlier passage); *iȝen* (eyes) is one of the irregular plurals that have been almost completely dropped except for *children* and *oxen,* although we retain a few other irregular forms. The most frequent ending in Middle English is the final *e,* but it serves only a limited grammatical function. The numerous inflections of Old English which distinguished case and number and gender of nouns and adjectives were gradually leveled to a single form *e.* No longer serving its former purpose, however, the ending was doomed to be dropped—first in pronunciation and later in spelling. Word order had already become fixed in Old English before the end of the Old English period so that the loss of inflections did not cause a loss of efficiency.

With the decay of the inflectional system, English had to depend on word order. By the end of the Middle English period, English had become essentially an analytic language.

The invasion of the Normans in 1066 exercised a major influence on the English language because French became an invading language, as Old English had at an earlier period. As the language of the aristocracy and of almost all official bodies, French might conceivably have replaced English. Or Latin, as the language of the church, might have undermined the importance of English in high places. But English always remained the speech of the common people and, in its struggle for survival, strengthened its resources by absorbing approximately 10,000 words from French and innumerable other words from Latin.

By the end of the thirteenth century, political and social conditions in England had dulled the prestige of French. The military struggle during the long Hundred Years' War in the fourteenth and fifteenth centuries brought about a growth of national feeling. By 1400, it was necessary for everyone in England—king, judge, professor, ecclesiastic, and common people alike—to know English. A flourishing literature at the end of the fourteenth century, particularly the work of Chaucer, seems to testify that English, as the language of its people, deserved survival.

Modern English (1500 to present)

By 1500, the English language had established the principles of operation we recognize as modern. Spelling, however, was to remain unstandardized for at least another two hundred years, and forms that we now recognize as obsolete were still in use. The pronunciations of the sixteenth century, vastly changed again from Middle English values, may have sounded more like Modern Irish than Modern English. Nevertheless, the language of 1500 was essentially the language of today. Tyndale's translation of John 17:1–3, given above in Old English and Middle English, will indicate exactly how the printed language appeared in 1534:

> **These wordes spake Jesus, and lifte uppe his eyes to heven, and sayde: 'Father, the houre is come; glorify thy Sonne, that thy Sonne maye glorify the; as thou hast geven hym power over all fleshe, that he shulde geve eternall life to as many as thou has geven him. This is life eternall, that they myght knowe the, that only very God, and whom thou has sent, Jesus Christ.'**

The forms *thou, thee,* and *thy,* commonly used in speech, fell into disuse during this period (today they are used only in poetry and certain types of formal address). *Ye,* as a distinguishing nominative plural of *you,* was dropped, although the King James version of the Bible (1611) continued to make the distinction: "For the Father himself loveth you, because ye have loved me . . ." (John 16:27).[1] Impersonal constructions like "it dislikes me that . . ." also disappeared. *Its* as the possessive of *it* made its appearance about 1600 instead of the former *his,* although Shakespeare does not use *its* in his plays. *Who* and *which* were added to *that* as relative pronouns.

[1]See also Glossary under *ye.*

Printing had its effect on the language, not only as a standardizing force but as a means of introducing new words. Words no longer had to be imported by mouth; books could serve the purpose. The sixteenth and seventeenth centuries were periods of extensive borrowing, particularly from Latin and Greek. At times, borrowings even displaced English words. The influx of strange words and their use in English sentences caused a reaction of distaste among writers of the seventeenth century. They denounced "inkhorn terms," their phrase for obscure and pedantic words like *accersited* for *bought* and *adjuvate* for *aid*, both derived from Latin. They expressed the view that the English language had to be kept pure—a theme that has been repeated at various times in various places throughout the ages and continues to have its advocates at the present.

The past four hundred years have produced unquestionable evidence of the force of analogy on language, both pronunciations and forms, but particularly on forms. Analogy works as a leveler, a force to make things the same. Thus, the irregular forms of nouns and verbs and adjectives that carried over from Middle English have been regularized. *Shoon* has becomes *shoes*, like most plurals; *holpen* has become *helped*, like most participles; *doth* has become *does*, like most third-person singulars. Of course, irregular forms remain in current English, but analogy continues to wear away at their nonconformity. *Indexes* is now a common substitute for *indices*, *syllabuses* for *syllabi*, and *hoofs* for *hooves*. Even the plural of *mongoose*, a much later addition than *goose*, reads *mongooses*, not *mongeese*.

Thus, time has changed English radically. Not much of Old English remains today in the active language. Eighty-five percent of Old English words have been lost, but those that have survived are among words that we use most frequently. Less than half of the Old English irregular strong verbs survive, and some of those, like *dive* and *thrive*, have been regularized. But, in the process of alteration, English has become a simpler language and a cosmopolitan one. Today, it is spoken by more than 300,000,000 people throughout the world. It is no longer exclusively the language of England and the United States. English has become an international language.

Projects

1. Examination of the Indo-European family of languages on p. 450 will indicate that many familiar languages like Chinese, Japanese, Tagalog, Algonquin, and Swahili are missing. These belong to other language families. Consult an encyclopedia or specialized book on language, and submit a table of at least one other family of languages that may interest you.

2. Many languages have interesting histories. Choose one as the subject for research, and prepare a ten-minute oral report for your class. Suggestions:

A. Basque

B. Berber

C. Coptic

D. Swahili

E. Celtic

F. The language of Jesus of Nazareth

G. Pidgin English

H. *Lingua franca*

I. Gullah

J. Louisiana Creole

K. Manchu

L. Middle English dialects

3. Choose approximately 100 words from an English prose passage written before 1700. "Translate" this passage into contemporary idiomatic English. Then list what kinds of changes you made in word choice, word order, combination of sentences, spelling, capitalization, and punctuation. Submit the original and the adaptation, together with your commentary on the changes.

4. Consult the *Oxford English Dictionary*. Be able to trace the changes in meaning of the following words: *honest, mansion, prevent, philosophy, wit, rhetoric, tenement, conceit, fancy* (n), *science.*

5. Trace the origins of the following names of flowers to see in what way their names are appropriate:

alyssum	delphinium
aster	gladiolus
carnation	iris
chrysanthemum	lilac
columbine	nasturtium
daisy	peony

Suggestions for writing

1. If you are a native speaker of English and have traveled in a foreign country, write about your experience with people who are native speakers of another language. Did you expect foreigners to speak English? Did you try to speak their language? What attitudes did you find yourself forming?

2. Consider the proposition that language makes a person rather than that a person makes language. How can language change a person? What are the practical implications? Does this statement apply particularly to foreign students and speakers of minority dialects? For instance, is it possible to go to college without being changed by its characteristic language? Write about the changes that you think language can make on anyone and has made on you.

3. In *Understanding Media*, Marshall McLuhan writes:

> Today computers hold out the promise of a means of instant translation of any code or language into any other code or language. The computer, in short, promises by technology a Pentecostal condition of universal understanding and unity. The next logical step would seem to be, not to translate, but to by-pass languages in favor of a general cosmic consciousness which might be very like the collective unconscious dreamt of by Bergson. The condition of "weightlessness," that biologists say promises a physical immortality, may be paralleled by the condition of speechlessness that could confer a perpetuity of collective harmony and peace.

Are McLuhan's speculations completely farfetched? Is speechlessness a condition of "collective harmony and peace"? Write an essay on thoughts that grow out of his comments.

4. Write an essay on your attitude toward the changing language. Is English deteriorating? Whether your answer is positive or negative, on what assumptions do you base your reply? What is a corrupted or uncorrupted language?

In popular usage, *linguistics* and *grammar* are overlapping terms. *Linguistics* is a collective term for historical and descriptive studies in the phonology, morphology, syntax, and semantics of the language. Grammar is a covering term for morphology and syntax, at times also for phonology, but it is most often used as a synonym for syntax alone. As a word, *linguistics* has connotations that relate it closely to science and theory. In the popular mind, *grammar* remains firmly associated with teaching and the practical matters of speaking and writing the language. Misunderstanding of the true nature of grammar often accounts for the unpleasant response that the word gets.

The meaning of grammar

Many people associate grammar so closely with rules about what should be said and should not be said that they fail to recognize what grammar actually is and how it operates. It may be well, first, to make a distinction between *grammar,* which can be called the working plan of our language, and *usage,* which is the way we put language to work for whatever personal, social, economic, or cultural reasons we might have. Grammar is therefore more concerned with meaningful communication than it is with socially approved communication.

Grammar is an inescapable fact of a language system, because it is the set of operating principles that permit orderly speaking and writing. A grunt may be expression, but it has little to do with grammar. The fact is that grammar would exist even if there were no books about grammar because it is essentially the unwritten agreement among speakers of the language about the ways they will express ideas most efficiently. Even children subscribe to the code of grammar before they ever learn about it in school, although at early ages they very frequently use a grammar characteristically their own. All native speakers are so accustomed to patterns of expression that grammar might be referred to as an imprint on their minds. Thus, grammar is the structure of speaking and writing that we accept—an internalized set of principles that enable us to use the language—whether or not we are students of grammar. Once we are students of grammar, we then concern ourselves with explicit descriptions of those operating principles.

If someone began to read words from the dictionary randomly, each word might convey some element of meaning, but the list as a whole would be essentially meaningless. We can illustrate briefly by considering just six words:

shoes   his   my   in   lay   corner

This series is obviously not without meaning because we recognize the six words. In fact, the associations among them are so close that we instinctively find ourselves trying to arrange them into a meaningful statement. We are first tempted by combinations that make sense: *my shoes* and *his corner*. From that point on, we have no great difficulty in combining *in his corner* and then arranging all six words into a complete pattern: *my shoes lay in his corner.* This arrangement, however, is only the most obvious one. The series might be combined to read: *his shoes lay in my corner.* In some particular context, the cluster beginning with *in* might be put in first position (*in my corner lay his shoes*), but this transposition would not alter the basic pattern or meaning. Note that *his corner lay in my shoes* makes no sense whatever, although it may be considered well formed.

Thus, combinations of words can be chaotic and senseless, but they can also be well formed and senseless. In these various examples, the six words do not change, but their relationship to one another does. The basic grammar of English reduces all of the possible combinations of these six words to a limited number of orderly and understandable ones. Thus grammar makes clear communication possible by placing limits on the combinations.

The operating principles of grammar

The devices grammar uses to limit meaning are its operating principles. The chief ones in the written language are (1) word order, (2) the addition of suffixes, including inflections, and (3) the use of function words. All are illustrated in the six-word sentences above.

1. The most important operating principle in the English language is word order. Our sense of grammar as native speakers leads us immediately to seek out words that combine with one another, like *my shoes, in his corner,* and *my shoes lay in his*

corner. The last arrangement breaks down into two parts—first, a subject (*my shoes*) and then a predicate (*lay in my corner*). Until the subject–predicate relationship is established, the pattern is neither complete nor fully meaningful. Until that arrangement is arrived at, transposing part of the sentence to another position for a different effect is impossible.

2. Four words in the series show grammatical features by inflection. *My* and *his,* as opposed to *I* and *he,* show possession. The form *lay* signals the simple past tense form of the verb *lie,* and the *s* of *shoes* shows that this word is plural.

3. Finally, the word *in,* a function word, signals a relationship between *lay* and *corner;* namely, the phrase *in my corner* tells where the shoes are lying.

In similar ways, all grammatical sentences in English depend on these three devices to express basic meanings and variations of meaning. Coherent meaning is not possible without grammar. A grammarless language would be only a discord of sounds.

The meaning of grammatical

In practice, grammar permits us to (1) analyze what has been expressed and (2) understand our own expressions. In either case, grammatical expression represents a norm. A writer or speaker either holds to the standard or deviates from it.

Deciding what is grammatical and what is not depends, of course, on a common definition of "grammatical." Grammarians themselves are by no means agreed on a definition, and native speakers of the language, when tested on whether particular sentences in their opinion are grammatical or ungrammatical, express doubts and often disagree widely. But the doubts and disagreements ordinarily concern sentences that seem to fall between examples that are unquestionably grammatical and ones that are obviously ungrammatical. Everyone will agree, for example, that *shoes his my in lay corner* is totally ungrammatical and that *my shoes lay in his corner* is fully grammatical. But there might be strong doubt about the opening of Lewis Carroll's famous poem:

> 'Twas brillig, and the slithy toves
> Did gyre and gimble in the wabe. . . .

This sentence shows conventional grammatical features and orderliness, but it does not make sense. The same doubts might be expressed about a grammarian's well-known test sentence:

> Colorless green ideas sleep furiously.

With such a sentence, we might compare lines from a poem by Andrew Marvell

> Annihilating all that's made
> To a green thought in a green shade.

The difficulty with the last two examples is that they violate our usual expectations of acceptable combinations in a literal sense: green is not colorless and not ordinarily an attribute of ideas or thought, although we might attempt to figure out a metaphoric association. Nor does *sleep* relate literally and sensibly with *ideas.* Yet in each of these examples, we react to the structure and try to impose meaning on the words. Carroll's poem and the grammarian's nonsense sentence are both well formed but uninformative. If we change *colorless green ideas sleep furiously* to *formless dull ideas die easily,* we see that the transition from one sentence to the other is not great, and some idea of what is fully grammatical begins to be apparent.

What we have to recognize is some intermediate degree between sentences that are fully grammatical, which are both well formed and informative, and sentences that are fully ungrammatical, which are both chaotic and meaningless. Such an intermediate degree might be called semigrammatical. Semigrammatical sentences, therefore, might be defined as well-formed sentences that are deviant in the way they combine words.

It is not surprising that two of the semigrammatical examples given above are excerpts from poems. Poets have traditionally been inventors of original expression. The imaginativeness of their work often springs from the departures they make from the ordinary. Yet their departures are structurally based. In one sense, poetic expression is an extension of the grammatical system. The grammar of our language is sufficiently flexible to allow deviations without falling into chaos. Thus, when Dylan Thomas writes *a grief ago,* we associate his phrase with time expressions like *a month ago* and *a while back* and proceed from that point on to interpret. Thomas' phrase is poetic, not conventionally factual. But only an analogy with a fully grammatical phrase makes an interpretation possible.

Grammar or grammars

The term *grammar,* as we have noted, is used in different senses, sometimes as the equivalent of what is called usage, sometimes as a broad term for the formal features and fundamental principles of a language, and sometimes in a more limited sense as a description of the structure and operation of a language. If grammar is considered a description of the structure and operation of a language, it then follows that descriptions may vary. A description of the grammar of German will differ from a description of the grammar of Chinese, and a description of Latin grammar will differ from a description of English grammar, although Latin and English grammar may have more features in common than German and Chinese grammar. It is also possible that descriptions of the same language will vary. Even though each language operates in its characteristic way, each description is a particular interpretation, a way of looking at it. Before the invention of the camera, painters depicted horses in full gallop with their fore limbs and hind limbs stretched out simultaneously before and behind the body of the horse. The invention of the camera, and particularly the evidence of still shots of movie sequences, revealed that horses gallop with their hoofs following one another in an orderly sequence. It is perfectly obvious that horses had not changed their way of running before and after the invention of the camera, but the camera altered people's way of seeing how they ran.

A similar situation has occurred in the history of grammar. In the last two hundred years, the operation of the language has not changed radically, but our views of how it operates have changed. As a result, we now have several descriptions, some based on verifiable evidence of a scientific nature. We no longer have *one* grammar, that is, one description, but several. The three main and most complete descriptions at the present time are those usually identified as traditional, structural, and transformational-generative. Their differences can be overestimated. One linguist has estimated that the three coincide in at least 95 percent of their facts. These three grammars merely represent different viewpoints and therefore emphasize different features of the language. They need not be thought of as competing with one another, although exponents of each have certainly competed for attention in the scholarly world. It is preferable to think of these three descriptions as phases of the development of grammar, and this book, therefore, emphasizes in what ways the three grammars supplement one another in order to give us a clearer notion of how the language operates.

Traditional grammar had its roots in the thinking and attitudes of eighteenth-century grammarians. It began with the assumption that Latin was superior to English and that English grammar should therefore use Latin as a model. Thus, the case of the pronoun *her* in a strongly Latinate construction like *I knew her to be an actress* (compare *I knew that she was an actress*) was explained in the same terms that Latin grammar would use to explain it—as the subject of an infinitive in the accusative case.

Eagerness for a fixed language, logical consistency, and uniform practice led early grammarians to be highly prescriptive about matters of usage. Their injunctions about double negatives and the use of *shall* and *will* still survive, because many individuals, including some teachers, think that these principles, having been set down once, remain inviolable. But all of the assumptions of traditional grammar need not be considered outmoded. In its coupling of form, function, and meaning and in its recognition of intuition as a strong factor in the functioning of a grammar, traditional grammar has by no means been displaced. In fact, it has evolved and continues to thrive. Many of its terms, definitions, and explanations of the grammatical process survive in current descriptions of the language.

Structural grammar, primarily a twentieth-century description, was an outgrowth of the historical and comparative studies of language in the second half of the nineteenth century. These studies reinforced the idea that language operates systematically and that the system can best be determined by describing exactly what occurs in the language, both in speaking and in writing. Structural grammar begins with the assumption that English is English and Latin is Latin. English is an analytic language; Latin is a synthetic language (see p. 452). English, therefore, has to be described in its own terms without reference to Latin grammar.

Structural grammar is basically a descriptive grammar. Historically, it served as a methodical inventory of English after a long period of failure to assess what the resources of our own language actually were. It established the priority of the spoken language over written language as a major influence on grammar. Books on structural grammar, by confining their description of the language to the observation of forms and patterns, divorced from meaning and logic and usage, necessarily limited themselves to the products of language—the written and spoken utterances—rather than to the process of language or the generation of language. Structural grammar, for instance, does not define a verb as a word showing action or being, but as a word that shows the difference between present and past tenses by various inflectional changes, like *know, knew, known,* or *act, acted, acted.* Parts of speech are identified by their characteristic forms and their typical positions in a sentence. For example, in *I knew her to be an actress,* the pronoun *her* can be explained as an object form because it is the object of the verb *knew,* not illogically as the subject of an infinitive. At the present time, structural grammar survives alongside traditional grammar, and its objective descriptions have contributed to our total knowledge of the language system.

The newest grammar, which is a product of the second half of this century, is transformational-generative, commonly referred to simply as transformational grammar. Taking advantage of the spadework performed by the structuralists, transformational grammarians have begun to build a structure they hope will ultimately account for all the well-formed sentences that can possibly be produced in the English language. Transformational grammar thus shifts its major emphasis from matters of form to matters of function. It is interested in the way native speakers are intuitively capable of producing complex structures that are seemingly combinations of many simple basic patterns of meaning. The breakdown of a sentence into layers or kernels reveals what is called its deep structure. Deep structure is a description of the sources of all constructions in a sentence in terms of the basic patterns from which they originated. The deep structure of the sentence *I knew her to be an actress* consists of two kernel sentences: *I knew her. She was an actress.* One of the kernels has undergone transformation. Thus, transformational grammar has added a new dimension to grammar—the deep structure of a sentence as well as its surface structure. Deep structure and the transformational process are theoretical concepts, but they help to explain how form and meaning are connected in the grammatical process. In emphasizing the role of intuition and meaning in grammar, transformationalists have returned to some of the concerns of the traditional grammarian. They are interested in describing not merely what has happened but what can happen. Within the bounds of its own rules for the formation of grammatical sentences, transformational grammar has assumed a highly prescriptive attitude, but that prescriptivism does not extend further to matters of usage. Usage seems to be a concern beyond the interest and consideration of the theoretical grammarian.

The possible limitation of transformational grammar is the scope of the task it has set for itself. In attempting to explain logically and completely everything that native speakers do naturally, transformational grammar has assumed a monumental task. Because most grammars never succeed in accounting for all of the irregularities of the English language, it is not uncommon to hear grammarians console themselves with the assertion that "all grammars leak."

In linguistic terms, the vowels and consonants of the language make up a group of sounds referred to as segmentals. Combined, they form words. Speech, however, permits an individual to vary the sound of segmentals by adjusting the stress with which they are spoken, altering the pitch of the voice and making pauses of different degrees between words or parts of words. These three devices—stress, pitch, and juncture—are called suprasegmentals.

The suprasegmentals are not the same in all languages. It is frequently difficult for a nonnative speaker to catch the intonation that is characteristic of another language. For example, pitch is a much more important feature in Chinese than it is in English, and what we sometimes refer to as a foreign accent may result from foreigners' attempts to use the suprasegmentals of their own language when they speak another one.

Because stress, pitch, and juncture occur simultaneously in speech, it is virtually impossible to speak of one without reference to the others. Linguists, however, generally recognize four degrees of stress, four levels of pitch, and four types of juncture in English. The degrees of stress are marked from heavy to weak as primary /ˊ/, secondary /ˆ/, tertiary /ˋ/, and weak /ˇ/. Pitch, of course, is relative to the speaker and what is ordinarily his normal speaking tone. The norm is identified as /2/. One level below is marked as /1/; the levels above are designated as /3/ and /4/. Level-four pitch is characteristically the kind of sound produced by a speaker during high excitement. Juncture is marked as:

- internal /+/
- level /|/ or /→/
- rising /‖/ or /↗/
- falling /#/ or /↘/

The only thing the writing system can do to indicate the suprasegmentals is to use punctuation and a few conventional mechanical devices like italics and ellipses. A phrase like "It is with . . ." would be spoken with one kind of pitch, stress, and juncture if it were part of the familiar phrase "It is with great pleasure. . . ." It would be spoken quite differently if it were a part of the following dialogue:

Can you read this word?
Yes, it is *with*.

In this reply, what appears to be a fragment in writing can be made a sentence in speech by giving the words the appropriate stress, pitch, and final juncture.

Furthermore, variations of the suprasegmentals determine the differences between statements, questions, and exclamations. These are grammatical differences. The writing system must use a question mark to indicate that "You really mean it?" is a question, not a statement or an exclamation. The rising intonation pattern of speech makes the distinction quite easily.

The stresses, pitches, and junctures of words are by no means constant. In a word like *primary*, the first syllable clearly gets the heaviest stress if the word is spoken by itself. When the form of the word is changed to *primarily*, the heavy stress shifts. When words are combined, other changes take place. In the phrase *primary goal*, *goal* gets the heaviest stress, and the stress on the first syllable of *primary* is reduced in relation to the heaviest.

Native speakers of the language ordinarily have no problem with suprasegmentals. They know how to make contrasts between *the White House* and *a white house*. If their pronunciation has not made clear whether they have said *a nice chest* or *an ice chest*, all that needs to be done is to exaggerate stress, pitch, and juncture to make the contrast. Therefore, the suprasegmentals are natural means of making ourselves understood, and they are the devices that give expressiveness to our speech. In fact, the whole rhythmic structure of the English language is based on them. The suprasegmentals are particularly important in teaching English to children and to foreigners. It is also highly likely that animals respond not so much to the words that we say as to the suprasegmentals we use in saying those words.

A microgrammar of English

Words, because of their great number and variety, have been traditionally classified into groups called *parts of speech*. The categories are determined mainly in terms of inflectional features, the positions words ordinarily take in a sentence, and the functions they perform. Because some words can assume various positions and do different things, the parts of speech do not represent inflexible categories. They do not represent absolute truths and are therefore subject to different definitions and interpretations. They are concepts that help us understand the working of the language.

The eight parts of speech are noun, pronoun, verb, adjective, adverb, preposition, conjunction, interjection. These terms, closely associated with traditional grammar, have been retained for the most part by modern grammarians, although they have tended to group them under two broad and meaningful headings. The first group includes the *form* words, those identified by the inflections they show and the positions they take (nouns, pronouns, verbs, adjectives, and adverbs). The second group includes the *function* words, those that are uninflected and therefore are mainly identified by their particular use and characteristic position (conjunctions and prepositions). Interjections are anomalous.

These two groups may be further contrasted by the exclusiveness they show. The form words are an *open* category; the function words are a relatively *closed* class. "Closed" means that all of the words may be catalogued, and users of the language show little tendency to add new ones to the list. On the other hand, "open" means that the category is undergoing constant change by the addition of new words and the shift of words from one part of speech to another. *Run*, for example, may be classified as a verb because it shows features of a verb and occupies typical verb positions, but it can also act like a noun if it assumes noun characteristics (*a run*, *running*) or occupies the position of a noun (*A run is invigorating*).

Modern grammarians have tried to define parts of speech exclusively in terms of form and function; nevertheless, usage tends to associate meaning with the words of particular categories—nouns with things, verbs with action, adjectives with qualities, adverbs with manner, and prepositions with direction, to mention only a few selected associations.

One of the most difficult tasks is to provide definitions for the working terms of the language because they often need to be explained in terms of one another. It is almost impossible to define the sentence usefully without reference to subject and predicate and to define these terms without reference to noun and verb. The following list of terms, therefore, is intended to provide only capsule definitions that depend mainly upon obvious examples to make their meaning clear, just as a mechanic might say "This is a box wrench," without trying to define it or explain its complications; or as a botanist might say "Examine a leaf," without bothering to explain a term familiar to everyone. The following definitions do not take into account numerous irregularities and exceptions.

Basic working terms

NOUN A noun is a word like *car* or *class* that indicates its plural and possessive forms by inflection: (*cars, classes; car's, class's; cars', classes'*) and serves as the model word for the subject of a sentence: (*The* ———— *began*).

NOMINAL A nominal is a noun or any other word, phrase, or clause that can assume the noun's position: the *cars* collided; *they* collided; *to push* is impolite; *what we thought* was trivial.

PRONOUN All pronouns are nominals: *I, you, he, we, they.* They substitute for nouns.

VERB A verb is a word like *collide* or *run* that shows differences between present and past time by inflection: *collide, collided; run, ran.*

VERBAL A verbal is a form of the verb that functions as another part of speech: The *driving* is strenuous (gerund as noun); *composed* a century ago, the song . . . (participle as adjective); *to enter* was impossible (infinitive as nominal).

ADJECTIVE An adjective is a word that may be compared by inflection (*big, bigger, biggest*) or any other word that can occupy a typical adjective position: *beautiful* day, time *immemorial,* he is *famous.*

ADVERB An adverb is a word that is often marked by the suffix *-ly* (*confidently*), often compared by using *more* and *most* (*more confidently, most confidently*), but, not showing these characteristics, it can be tested in one of several typical adverb positions. (We returned the books [promptly]. We returned the books [*to the library*]).

PREPOSITION   A preposition is a structure word or phrase like *to, from, at, across from, in front of.*

CONJUNCTION   A conjunction is a connective like *and, but, when, because,* and *either . . . or.*

INTERJECTION   An interjection is an independent word or construction which has no special features or special grammatical function: *ouch, oh goodness, hi.*

SUBJECT   A subject consists of a nominal and its modifiers placed in special relation to a verb, usually as its topic:

The two cars / collided.
A steady rain / fell.

PREDICATE   A predicate consists of a verb and its modifiers which act together as a commentary upon the subject:

The two cars / *collided at the intersection.*
A steady rain / *fell throughout the state.*

SENTENCE   A grammatical sentence is an independent clause that divides into a subject and a predicate with a finite verb:

The houses / showed signs of weathering.
I / didn't give the idea much thought.

CLAUSE   A clause is any combination of words that contains a subject and predicate. Some are independent, called sentences. Others are dependent, usually called subordinate clauses: *when he broke his glasses; if they were free.*

PHRASE   A phrase is a combination of words that acts as a single part of speech but does not contain both a subject and predicate as clauses do: *this envelope* (noun phrase), *on the floor* (prepositional phrase), *have been sleeping* (verb phrase).

MARKER   A marker is a word that helps to identify the words following it: *this* world (noun marker), *have been* helped (verb markers), *at* the circus (phrase marker), *if* he is in doubt (clause marker).

MODIFIER   A modifier is a general term for words like adjectives and adverbs that qualify in some way the meaning of other words: *a narrow* street; have been helped *significantly.* Or modifiers may take the form of phrases or clauses or other parts of speech that act like adjectives and adverbs (*adjectivals* and *adverbials*): ran *with determination;* a street *that was made of brick;* a *stone* fence.

HEADWORD   A headword is the word in any larger group that is modified: blue *sky*, exactly *two*, very *fiercely*, *drove* cautiously.

ANTECEDENT   An antecedent is an explanatory reference for another word:

The sophomores read *Gulliver's Travels*. They found it more relevant than many current works. [*Sophomores* is the antecedent of *they*; *Gulliver's Travels* is the antecedent of *it*.]

OBJECT   An object is a noun or other nominal that completes the actor-action relationship of the subject and verb (The crowd gave a *cheer*) or serves as the goal indicated by a preposition (in *town*, at a *minimum*).

COMPLEMENT   A complement is a collective term to include (1) the object of a verb: I told a *joke*; (2) a noun in the predicate after the verb *to be* or other linking verbs: he was an *officer*; and (3) an adjective in the predicate after the verb *to be* or other linking verbs: he was *brave*; he seemed *modest*.

APPOSITIVE   An appositive is a word or phrase that extends the meaning of another word of the same part of speech immediately preceding it and may act as its substitute:

The orchestra played his favorite song, "Tea for Two."

ABSOLUTE CONSTRUCTION   An absolute construction is a collective term for any sentence modifier that is attached to a sentence but has no grammatical ties to any particular word in the sentence:

The tributes having been given, the crowd dispersed.

Nouns *17A*

Inflected features of nouns *17AA*

1. Nouns show only the genitive case by inflection. It is commonly called the possessive case, but it shows other relations besides possession. These are sometimes referred to as inanimate genitives.

Possessive: my aunt's picture [one belonging to her]
my aunt's picture [a likeness of her]

Inanimate genitives: the committee's purpose
a month's duration
the film's perspective

2. Nouns regularly show plural by adding *-s* or *-es* to the base words: *brick, bricks; church, churches.* Other words have irregular plurals:

Irregular plurals of
Old English origin: mouse, mice; goose, geese

Irregular foreign plurals: hypothesis, hypotheses; alumnus, alumni

Singular and plural the same: Japanese, barracks, zebra, salmon

Even though words like *foot, inch, gallon,* and *pair* have plurals, the plural forms are frequently not used in idiomatic expressions with numbers: *a ten-foot ladder, a two-inch margin, a three-gallon bucket, four pair of socks,* but also the regular *four pairs of socks.*

17 AB *Functions of nouns*

1. **Subject of a sentence:** The *tornado* / struck violently.
2. **Direct object of a verb or preposition:**

   The tornado destroyed *homes* in its *course.*

   He led *them* a merry *chase.* [double object]

3. **Indirect object** after verbs like *give, make,* and *send.* The indirect object ordinarily precedes the direct object, with *to* or *for* implied after the verb: He sent [to] his *friend* a gift.
   When a sentence of this kind is transformed to passive voice, the object is retained: His friend was sent a *gift.*

4. **Subjective complement** (also called predicate noun or predicate nominative) following the verb *to be,* certain intransitive verbs like *become,* and the passive construction of transitive verbs:

   Mr. Wilson is the *headmaster.*

   Mr. Wilson became *headmaster.*

   Mr. Wilson was appointed *headmaster.*

5. **Objective complement,** a noun used to refer to the direct object as a way of completing the meaning of the predicate. The objective complement occurs only after certain verbs like *appoint, call, choose, elect, make, find, judge, keep, prove,* and *think:*

   We elected Cynthia *treasurer.*

   We considered her a fine *choice.*

6. **Appositive,** a noun used to complement the meaning of another noun immediately preceding it: Ms. Phipps, *the president,* called the meeting.

7. **Direct address:** *Ms. Phipps,* did you call a meeting?

1. **Common nouns** are words that identify general categories of things without reference to a particular one: *river, university, philosopher.*
Proper nouns identify a particular member of a group by a name given especially to it: *Mississippi River, University of Washington, Nietzsche.* Proper nouns are capitalized.

The distinction between the two categories determines how they are customarily used. Proper nouns are almost never used in the plural and may often be used in the singular without determiners.

2. **Mass nouns** are generally collective words like *fruit, water,* and *wheat,* not usually thought of in terms of numbered parts. In this sense, mass nouns are usually singular, although certain contexts may invite plural references: *All wools are not sheep wool.* Mass nouns do not require determiners; thus: *Pepper is expensive.*
Count nouns are nouns that are thought of as separate units and can therefore be numbered when they are plural: *a staple, staples, five hundred staples.* In the singular, count nouns require determiners, thus *a desk, the desk,* but in the plural the use is optional: *Desks are scarce. The maple desks are particularly scarce.*

The way we interpret a noun affects the way we use determiners with it. Some words can be used either as count nouns or mass nouns. The use of the determiner changes accordingly.

Mass noun: We are studying film. [art form]

Count noun: We saw a new film. [a separate item]

Mass noun: Cereal builds muscles. [collective sense as food]

Count noun: This cereal tastes good. [a particular one]

3. In terms of meaning, **abstract nouns** name qualities or ideas, like *interest, initiative,* or *justice,* which have no physical substance and therefore cannot be perceived by the senses.
Concrete nouns, in the same terms, name animate and inanimate objects, like *elephant, road,* and *flour,* which can be perceived by the senses.

Some words, like *man* and *animal,* can be used in either a generic sense (*Man is mortal*) or in a concrete sense (*That man is thin*). Many concrete nouns, like *treasure,* may also be used in a figurative, abstract sense: *His book is a treasure of odd facts.* Transformational grammarians note that abstract nouns usually act as mass nouns and therefore use the determiner differently. Concrete nouns usually act as count nouns.

4. **Collective nouns** are plural in meaning but singular in form, like *audience, flock,* and *committee.* The inflection of the verb in a sentence can suggest whether a group acts as a single unit or as individuals within a group:

The jury votes as one. [singular concept]

The jury were unable to agree. [as individuals among themselves]

Since groups can be thought of in a plural sense, some collective nouns have plural forms, like *fleets* and *orchestras.* Some, like *corps and grouse,* have the same form for the singular and plural. Words like *politics, data,* and *athletics* are plural in form but may be singular or plural in use.

5. **Nominals** are words and structures that fill noun slots but do no ordinarily show the characteristic features of individual nouns. Besides pronouns, treated in 17B, nominals include infinitives, gerunds, phrases, clauses, and other parts of speech shifting from their usual function. All of these noun substitutes are evidence of the flexibility of the grammatical categories to accommodate expression. A selection of examples will illustrate:

As subject:

The *best* didn't win. [adjective]

Running is good exercise. [gerund]

Spading the ground is hard work. [gerund phrase]

To run a mile is tiring. [infinitive phrase]

From New York to Los Angeles is a long drive. [prepositional phrase]

That we finish on time is crucial. [clause]

As direct object of verb:

They had their *ups* and *downs.* [prepositions or adverbs]

I will teach *whatever book is available.* [clause]

As object of preposition:

He went from *here* to *there.* [adverbs]

He did everything except *wreck the car.* [infinitive phrase without the *to* expressed]

He injured his shoulder by *swinging too hard.* [gerund phrase]

As indirect object:

Tell *whoever arrives late* that we have gone. [clause]

As retained object:

They were not told *what they should do.* [clause]

As subjective complement:

The decision of the hearing was *that he was negligent.* [clause]

As appositive:

The main point, *that he refused to come,* has been ignored. [clause]

Pronouns 17B

Inflected features of pronouns 17BA

1. Personal pronouns and the relative pronoun *who* show three cases by inflection: the subjective, objective, and possessive or genitive. The personal pronouns show two different forms of the possessive (see the paradigm below).
2. Most of the personal pronouns and the demonstratives (*this, these, that, those*) show singular and plural by change of form. Other pronouns do not, although they may be singular or plural by implication, like *everyone, anyone,* and *none.*
3. Personal pronouns vary their forms by person, a feature that nouns do not show. First person indicates whether someone is speaking (*I, we*); second person, whether someone is spoken to (*you*); and third person, whether someone is spoken about (*he, she, it, they*).
4. The three forms of the personal pronoun in the third-person singular distinguish between masculine, feminine, and neuter (*he, she, it*).

Paradigm of Personal Pronouns

	SUBJECTIVE	OBJECTIVE	POSSESSIVE, FIRST FORM	POSSESSIVE, SECOND FORM*
Singular				
1st person	I	me	my	mine
2nd person	you	you	your	yours
3rd person	he	him	his	his
	she	her	her	hers
	it	it	its	
Plural				
1st person	we	us	our	ours
2nd person	you	you	your	yours
3rd person	they	them	their	theirs

*The second possessive form of pronouns is used in typical noun positions:

　Hers is the one on top.

　The coat on top is *mine.*

　He is a friend of *theirs.*

The nonstandard forms *ourn, yourn, hisn, hern,* and *theirn* are formed by analogy with *mine.* The second possessive forms of these pronouns end in *s: ours, yours, hers, theirs. His* remains unchanged.

RELATIVE PRONOUN *WHO*

who   whom   whose

ARCHAIC FORMS OF PERSONAL PRONOUN

thou   thee   thy   thine

ye (singular and plural, both subjective and
objective)

17BB *Functions of pronouns*

The personal, indefinite, and demonstrative pronouns share with nouns most of their
uses as subject, direct object, indirect object, retained object, subjective complement, objective complement, appositive, and direct address:

Someone must act quickly. [subject]

Did the fire cause *that?* [direct object of verb]

Most of *them* responded. [object of preposition]

He owes *me* money. [indirect object]

Thanks were given *us*. [retained object]

I know *who* you are. [subjective complement]

We made him *one*. [objective complement]

Otello, the *one* by Rossini, is less well known. [appositive]

Hey, *you!* Come here. [direct address]

The reflexives, relatives, interrogatives, numerals, and reciprocal pronouns serve
only a limited number of these uses.

17BC *Kinds of pronouns*

1. Since pronouns have no independent meaning of their own, **personal pronouns** refer to beings and objects and assume the person and gender of the
antecedent. Personal pronouns are a stable category, that is, it is not likely that
new ones will be added, although a look at the history of the English language
shows that the pronoun system has undergone a number of changes.

2. **Reflexive pronouns** combine *-self* or *-selves* with the first possessive form of
first person and second person pronouns (*myself, yourself, yourselves*) and with
the objective form of third person pronouns (*himself, herself, itself, themselves*).
For this reason, forms like *hisself* and *theirselves*, which do not follow this
pattern, are considered nonstandard. Reflexives are used to express a reflex
action upon the subject:

He cut *himself*.

They blamed *themselves* for the accident.

The same forms are also used as **intensifiers:**

The topic *itself* is impossible.

I did it *myself.*

3. **Indefinite pronouns** are indistinguishable by gender. They are consistently used for third-person references: *all, another, any, anybody, anyone, anything, both, each, each one, either, everybody, everyone, everything, few, many, many a, much, neither, nobody, none, no one, one, other, several, some, somebody, someone, something.*

   Indefinite pronouns combined with *else* add *'s* to the end of the compound to form the possessive case: *anybody else's, everyone else's.*

4. **Reciprocal pronouns** combine various indefinite pronouns to suggest an interaction: *each other, one another.* Possessive forms: *each other's, one another's.*

5. **Demonstrative pronouns** have the special function of focusing on something or pointing out. They show number: singular forms: *this, that;* plural forms: *these, those.* Their possessive must be expressed by a phrase with *of: The point of that is clear.*

6. **Relative pronouns** introduce clauses that act as nouns or as modifiers. The simple relatives are *who, whom, whose, which, that,* and sometimes *what* (*He knows what works*). All of these forms except *that* combine with *ever* to form additional relatives: *whoever, whosever, whichever, whatever.* The forms *whosoever, whichsoever,* and *whatsoever* are archaic.

7. The **interrogative pronouns** *who, which,* and *what* and the combinations with *ever* are identical with relative pronouns in form, but different in function. Interrogatives phrase direct questions:

   What is his name?

   Whom did the newspapers mention?

   Whatever could he have meant?

8. **Numerals:** both the cardinals (*one, two, three*) and the ordinals (*first, second, third*) may be considered pronouns in certain uses:

   Two are enough for me.

   The *sixth* was the hardest.

Verbs and verbals **17C**

vb

Inflected features of verbs **17CA**

1. **Regular verbs** show four forms: *help, helps, helping,* and *helped.* **Irregular verbs** like *sing* show five: *sing, sings, singing, sang, sung.* Other verbs like *can,*

ought, spread, and *cut* may show fewer than four forms. The verb *be* shows eight. These forms differentiate the various uses of the verb.

2. With the exception of the verb *to be,* verbs show person and number by inflection in the third person singular of the present and present perfect tenses only (*sees, is seeing, has seen*).

3. Verbs have only two finite forms for showing **tense:** the simple present (*see*) and the simple past (*saw*). However, since the most characteristic way of thinking about time is in terms of present, past, and future, English expresses future time by means of phrases like *shall see* and *will see* or by the present or progressive forms of the verb: *I leave shortly; I am going tomorrow.*

17CB   *Other features of verbs*

1. **Aspect** is the property of verbs that extends their capacity to express many other time relations besides simple present, past, and future. These additional meanings include action occurring in the past and continuing (*has seen*), action completed at some past time (*had seen*), action to be completed by some future time (*will have seen*), action occurring in the present (*is seeing*), action repeatedly occurring (*keep singing*). All of these concepts are expressed by phrase structures. For convenience, *has seen, had seen,* and *will have seen* are called the perfect tenses (present perfect, past perfect, and future perfect). English, therefore, may be said to have six tenses. The *-ing* forms with a helping verb (*is seeing*) are called the **progressive** forms.

2. **Voice** is a property of verbs that permits the verb to show whether the subject is acting (*he hates*) or is acted upon (*he is hated*). These are called **active voice** and **passive voice.** Since Modern English has no specific forms for expressing voice as Latin does, it depends upon verb phrases.

3. **Mood or mode** is the capacity of verbs to indicate the manner of the speaker's expression. A verb may be **indicative** (expressing fact or inquiring about it), **subjunctive** (expressing condition, wish, or possibility), or **imperative** (expressing request or command). With the exception of the verb *to be,* subjunctive forms are identical with indicative forms except in the third person singular of the present tense of a verb (*if he see* instead of *if he sees*).

17CC   *Conjugation of the verb*

The changes of the verb by number, person, tense, aspect, voice, and mood may be set down in a complete arrangement called a **conjugation.** However, the same material can be indicated by a **synopsis,** that is, a conjugation in one or more persons. The accompanying synopsis of the verb *to see* in the third person singular and plural summarizes the verb system.

Synopsis of Verb **To See**

	ACTIVE VOICE, INDICATIVE MOOD	PASSIVE VOICE, INDICATIVE MOOD
Present	He sees	He is seen
Past	He saw	He was seen
Future	He will see	He will be seen
Present perfect	He has seen	He has been seen
Past perfect	He had seen	He had been seen
Future perfect	He will have seen	He will have been seen

PROGRESSIVE FORMS

Present	He is seeing	He is being seen
Past	He was seeing	He was being seen
Future	He will be seeing	*He will be being seen
Present perfect	He has been seeing	*He has been being seen
Past perfect	He had been seeing	*He had been being seen
Future perfect	He will have been seeing	*He will have been being seen

EMPHATIC FORMS

[Necessary for the formation of questions and negative constructions]

Present	He does see [*Does he see? He does not see.*]
Past	He did see [*Did he see? He did not see.*]

IMPERATIVE FORMS

See	Be seen
[*See what he is doing!*]	[*Be seen less often here.*]

SUBJUNCTIVE FORMS

[If] he see	[If] he be seen

*Although the paradigm invites these constructions, they would be extremely rare in use, if at all possible.

Function of the verb 17CD

A finite verb acts as a predicate to the subject; that is, it indicates the speaker's intention to write a fully grammatical sentence. As the focal word of the predicate, all the thought of the sentence turns on the verb. Without it, no comment could be made about the subject.

Kinds of verbs 17CE

1. **Finite verbs** are primary verb forms that show distinctions of person, number, tense, aspect, and mood. They therefore act as the focal word of the predicate. **Nonfinite verbs** include the gerund, participle, and infinitive, which show only some of the distinctions of finite verbs and cannot therefore stand alone as the verb of a predicate. (See verbals, pp. 480–482.)
2. **Linking verbs** are those that serve as a connection between a nominal in the subject and a nominal in the predicate (*He is a leader*) or between a nominal in the subject and an adjective in the predicate (*He is strong*). The verb *to be* is the most common linking verb, but a number of others can substitute for it: the sense

verbs, like *feel, look, smell, sound,* and *taste,* and others, like *appear, become, continue, grow, prove, remain, seem, stand,* and *turn.*

He *became* the leader.

The weather *continues* bad.

The future *looks* hopeful.

3. **Transitive verbs** are those that have direct objects (She *gave* a dollar). When verbs do not have an object, they are identified as **intransitive verbs** (*She cried*). Most verbs can be used either transitively or intransitively:

She *cried* tears of joy. [transitive use]

They *produced* automatic weapons. [transitive use]

The fields *produced* heavily. [intransitive use]

A few verbs like *arrive* and *lie* (to recline) are always intransitive. Transitive verbs are sometimes thought of as action verbs. The term is a technical one because some verbs in this category, like *possess, receive,* and *owe,* do not necessarily imply physical action. These verbs, however, like other transitive verbs, may take direct objects:

She *possesses* talent.

He *received* a medal.

We *owe* money.

4. **Auxiliaries** or **helping verbs** combine with other verbs to show tense, aspect, mood, voice, and various other degrees and manners of action. These include *be, can, could, dare, do, have, may, might, must, need, ought, shall, should, will,* and *would.*

Expressing possibility: I can go, may go, would go, could be going, might be going.

Expressing obligation: I must go, have to go, ought to go, have got to go, should have gone.

Expressing emphasis: I did go, dared to go, do need to go, will be going.

As these representative examples suggest, the auxiliaries and progressive forms permit the English verb to express a great number of highly refined and often subtle meanings beyond simple time relationships.

5. **Regular verbs** contrast the past tense and past participle from the base of the verb by adding *-ed* (*engage, engaged, engaged*). These three forms—the base, the past tense form, and the past participle—are called the ***principal parts of a verb.*** **Irregular verbs** are those that show variations, which have usually evolved from the earlier forms of these verbs in Old English. The irregular verbs fall into four main categories:

A. Verbs whose past tenses show a change from the base but whose past participles are the same as the past form:

BASE	PAST TENSE	PAST PARTICIPLE
bend	bent	bent
bind	bound	bound
bleed	bled	bled
breed	bred	bred
bring	brought	brought
build	built	built
buy	bought	bought
catch	caught	caught
cling	clung	clung
creep	crept	crept
deal	dealt	dealt
dig	dug	dug
feed	fed	fed
feel	felt	felt
fight	fought	fought
find	found	found
flee	fled	fled
fling	flung	flung
grind	ground	ground
hang [a painting]	hung	hung
have	had	had
hear	heard	heard
hold	held	held
keep	kept	kept
lay	laid	laid
lead	led	led
leave	left	left
lend	lent	lent
lose	lost	lost
make	made	made
mean	meant	meant
meet	met	met
read	read [vowel change]	read
rend	rent	rent
say	said	said
seek	sought	sought
sell	sold	sold
send	sent	sent
shoe	shod	shod
shoot	shot	shot
sit	sat	sat
sleep	slept	slept
slink	slunk	slunk
speed	sped	sped
spend	spent	spent

spin	spun	spun
stand	stood	stood
stick	stuck	stuck
sting	stung	stung
string	strung	strung
sweep	swept	swept
swing	swung	swung
teach	taught	taught
tell	told	told
think	thought	thought
weep	wept	wept
win	won	won
wind	wound	wound

B. Verbs whose past participles add *n* or *en* either to the base or to the past tense form, at times with a slight variation in spelling:

BASE	PAST TENSE	PAST PARTICIPLE
be	was	been
bear	bore	borne
bite	bit	bitten
blow	blew	blown
break	broke	broken
choose	chose	chosen
do	did	done
draw	drew	drawn
drive	drove	driven
eat	ate	eaten
fall	fell	fallen
forsake	forsook	forsaken
freeze	froze	frozen
give	gave	given
go	went	gone
grow	grew	grown
know	knew	known
ride	rode	ridden
rise	rose	risen
see	saw	seen
shake	shook	shaken
speak	spoke	spoken
slay	slew	slain
steal	stole	stolen
stride	strode	stridden
swear	swore	sworn
take	took	taken
tear	tore	torn
throw	threw	thrown
wear	wore	worn
weave	wove	woven
write	wrote	written

Two verbs show a unique pattern. Like other verbs in lists A and B, they are derived from Old English strong verbs, but have evolved differently.

come	came	come
run	ran	run

C. Verbs that show a change of vowel in both the past tense and past participle. The short list below includes verbs that at present have no alternate forms in standard usage. Additional verbs in this category that are undergoing change are listed under E:

begin	began	begun
fly	flew	flown
lie	lay	lain
ring	rang	rung
swim	swam	swum

D. Verbs that show no change in any of the principal parts. They are called **invariables:** *bet, bid* [at auction], *burst, cast, cost, cut, hit, hurt, let, put, set, shed, shut, split, spread,* and *thrust.*

E. Most important is the list of verbs that are currently undergoing change so that alternate forms are in use. An examination of the list will suggest the kinds of changes that typically occur. Naturally, a tendency exists to regularize any verb that is irregular. Therefore, *ed* forms appear for the invariables (*rid, sweat*) and for verbs that change vowels (*awake, thrive*). A second kind of change by analogy is to make a regular verb irregular (*dove* for *dived* to correspond to *drive-drove*) or to reduce the changes of vowel in the principal parts from two to one (*sink, spring*). A number of the participial forms listed appear to be antiquated. Although they may not be ordinarily used in forming the perfect tenses, they are used in passive-voice constructions (*was stricken, was shrunken*) and particularly as adjectives in such expressions as *thinly clad waif, rough-hewn board, badly swollen hand,* and *a sunken boat.* Other alternate forms like *spat* and *bade* seem clearly dated and little used. Up-to-date dictionaries attempt to record the changes that usage has established over a period of time.

BASE	PAST TENSE	PAST PARTICIPLE
abide	abode (abided)	abode (abided)
awake	awoke (awaked)	awoke (awaked, awoken)
beat	beat	beaten (beat)
bereave	bereaved (bereft)	bereaved (bereft)
beseech	beseeched (besought)	beseeched (besought)
bid [command]	bade (bid)	bidden (bid, bade)
bide	bode (bided)	bided
broadcast	broadcast (broadcasted)	broadcast (broadcasted)
chide	chid (chided)	chidden (chided, chid)
cleave [adhere]	cleaved (clove)	cleaved (clove)
cleave [split]	cleaved (cleft, clove)	cleaved (cleft, cloven)

clothe	clothed (clad)	clothed (clad)
crow	crowed (crew [Brit.])	crowed
dive	dived (dove)	dived
drink	drank	drunk (drank)
fit	fitted (fit)	fitted (fit)
forget	forgot	forgotten (forgot)
forecast	forecast (forecasted)	forecast (forecasted)
get	got	got (gotten)
heave	heaved (hove)	heaved (hove)
hew	hewed	hewed (hewn)
hide	hid	hidden (hid)
kneel	knelt (kneeled)	knelt (kneeled)
knit	knitted (knit)	knitted (knit)
light	lighted (lit)	lighted (lit)
mow	mowed	mowed (mown)
quit	quit (quitted)	quit (quitted)
prove	proved	proved (proven)
rid	rid (ridded)	rid (ridded)
saw	sawed	sawed (sawn)
seethe	seethed	seethed (sodden)
sew	sewed	sewed (sewn)
shave	shaved	shaved (shaven)
shear	sheared	sheared (shorn)
shine	shone (shined)	shone (shined)
show	showed	showed (shown)
shrink	shrank (shrunk)	shrunk (shrunken)
sing	sang (sung)	sung
smite	smote	smitten (smote)
sow	sowed	sowed (sown)
speed	sped (speeded)	sped (speeded)
spit	spit (spat)	spit (spat)
spring	sprang (sprung)	sprung
stink	stank (stunk)	stunk
strew	strewed	strewed (strewn)
strike	struck	struck (stricken)
strive	strove (strived)	striven (strived)
sweat	sweat (sweated)	sweat (sweated)
swell	swelled	swelled (swollen)
thrive	throve (thrived)	thriven (thrived)
tread	trod	trodden (trod)
wake	waked (woke)	waked (woke, woken)
wed	wedded (wed)	wedded (wed)
wet	wet (wetted)	wet (wetted)
work	worked	worked (wrought)

Other kinds of variants reflect the substitution of a *t* sound for the *ed* sound that we often make in speaking: *blent, blest, burnt, dreamt, gilt, girt, leapt, learnt, spilt, spoilt,* and *swelt.*

6. Verbals: gerunds, participles, and infinitives

   A. A **gerund** is an *-ing* form of the verb used mainly as a noun. It has both active and passive forms (*seeing, being seen*). It is identical with the present participle in form but different in function. Even though a gerund functions as a noun, it retains characteristics of a verb: it conveys the notion of a verb; it can take an object; and it can be modified by adverbs:

   gerund   obj.   adv.
Counting money daily is a tedious job.

          gerund   obj.   adv.
He liked *driving* cars fast.

B. **Participles** have a variety of forms in both active and passive voice:

ACTIVE VOICE		PASSIVE VOICE	
seeing	viewing	being seen	being viewed
seen	viewed		
having seen	having viewed	having been seen	having been viewed

Participles function mainly as adjectives, either as single words (a *broken* glass) or as phrases (*Having given a toast*, he broke his glass). Like gerunds, participles retain their characteristics as verbs: they also express the verb idea, take any kind of complement, and are modified by adverbs:

part.   obj.   adv. phrase
Having no money at the time, he was forced to hitchhike.

The participial phrase *having no money at the time* modifies *he*. Participles also function within absolute phrases as modifiers of the noun:

The argument *having ended suddenly*, we walked away.

I turned sharply, my face *confronting his*.

C. **Infinitives** have active and passive forms:

ACTIVE VOICE	PASSIVE VOICE
to see	to be seen
to be seeing	
to have seen	to have been seen
to have been seeing	

Infinitives retain verb characteristics by taking complements and adverbial modifiers. They often combine with other verbs to form verb phrases: *decided to go, was said to have been recommended*. Infinitives may function as nouns, adjectives, or adverbs:

To be known is *to be doubted*. [as noun, used as subject and subjective complement]

They tried all forms of appeal except *to go* in person. [as noun, object of a preposition]

They agreed upon a plan *to end the war.* [infinitive phrase as adjective]

She was too angry *to object.* [as adverb]

17CF *Nonstandard uses of the verb*

Many of the nonstandard forms of verbs may be accounted for by the tendency to regularize verb forms or to form them after the pattern of other verbs. Thus, the participle *swollen* gives rise to *swoll* as the past tense of *swell; snuck* as the past tense of *sneak* and *tuck* as the past tense of *take* are related to forms like *struck* and *stuck. Flang, swang,* and *wrang* as the past tenses of *fling, swing,* and *wring* imitate *sing-sang.* Irregular verbs treated as regular ones result in *knowed, blowed, runned, stinked, taked,* and *throwed,* common also in children's speech.

Other nonstandard forms of verbs, however, are less a matter of following a pattern than of following no pattern, giving rise to uses like *I sees, we was, he do, I taken it,* and *they boughten that.* Still other nonstandard uses result from the tendency to reduce the inflectional forms common to standard grammar. Thus, *s's, es's, ed's,* and other verb endings are omitted. Auxiliaries may be dropped from both statements and questions: *he goin' now* or *you do that?* In other instances, *been, done, done been,* and *ain't* are made to do general service for *has* and *have: done been finished, ain't been finished.* In like manner, *used to* substitutes for *formerly* in expressions like *used to couldn't* and *used to wasn't.* The use of auxiliaries as main verbs gives rise to *hadn't ought, might can,* and *might could.* Even though *might could, used to could,* and *ought to could* are generally considered nonstandard, they do appear commonly in the speech of educated southerners as dialect forms.

17D *Adjectives*

17DA *Inflected features of adjectives*

Some adjectives show three degrees of **comparison**—positive, comparative, and superlative—in either of three ways:

1. By adding *-er* and *-est* to the positive stem:

heavy, heavier, heaviest

short, shorter, shortest

2. By forming phrases with *more* and *most* or *less* and *least:*

meaningful, more meaningful, most meaningful

famous, more famous, most famous

promising, less promising, least promising

3. By using irregular forms:

bad	worse	worst
far	farther, further	farthest, furthest
good	better	best
little	littler, less, lesser	littlest, least
many, much	more	most
near	nearer	nearest, next
old	older, elder	oldest, eldest

Some adjectives may be compared in two ways: *true, truer,* (*more true*), *truest,* (*most true*). *Common, bitter, happy,* and *lovely* also have double forms. Other adjectives like *optimum, foremost, innermost, main,* and *chief* are ordinarily used in only one degree.

Functions of adjectives   **17DB**

1. **General modifier:** The primary function of adjectives and other words, phrases, and clauses acting like them is to describe or limit nouns and pronouns. Besides their most typical position preceding the noun, adjectives may also follow immediately after the noun:

Cherries jubilee is a treat *supreme.*

The crowd, *noisy* and *milling,* shoved forward.

The clerk *at the desk* apologized. [phrase modifying *clerk*]

The man *who could not stop coughing* finally left. [adjective clause, modifying *man*]

2. **Appositive:** One adjective may be used to interpret another adjective, for which it can also act as a substitute:

He assumed a paternal, that is, *authoritative* manner.

3. **Predicate adjective:** Adjectives in the predicate that modify nouns or pronouns in the subject occur with three types of verbs:
A. Verbs of being:

I am *honest.*

My check will be *good.*

The photographs were especially *clear.*

B. Other linking verbs:

She looks *healthy.*

The milk tastes *rancid.*

He remains *inflexible.*

C. Certain transitive verbs in passive voice:

The ceiling was painted *beige*.

The room was made *comfortable* by soft chairs.

The crew of the plane was found *dead*.

4. **Objective complement:** When sentences like those in 3 C above are converted to active voice, the adjective becomes an objective complement, modifying the direct object:

I painted the ceiling *beige*.

Soft chairs made the room *comfortable*.

The rescue party found the crew of the plane *dead*.

17 DC   *Kinds of adjectives*

The categories of adjectives are particularly important because some words function quite differently from others. The wide variety of words included under the general heading of adjective has prompted structural and transformational grammarians to discuss determiners as a separate part of speech, not as a subcategory of adjectives. When most people refer to the adjective, they commonly mean the descriptive adjectives.

1. **Descriptive adjectives** include all those words that represent the qualities of nominals: *ripe* peaches, *ingenious* writing, *comparative* literature.
2. **Proper adjectives** are derived from proper nouns and retain their capital letters: *Afro-American* movement, *Shakespearean* glossary.
3. **Adjectivals** are those words and structures that fill adjective positions but do not ordinarily show the characteristic features of individual adjectives. See also phrases, pp. 491–492, and clauses, pp. 492–493.

The room had a *brick* fireplace.

It was an *above-board* agreeement.

Theirs was a *going* affair.

We had to attend a *morning* meeting.

The dog was particularly *high-strung*.

The spirit of the group was *you-name-it-we'll-do-it*.

4. An interrogative pronoun in an adjective position functions as an adjective, referred to as an **interrogative adjective:**

Which question are you answering?

Whose belongings are these?

5. A relative pronoun in an adjective position functions as an adjective, referred to as a **relative adjective:**

He will do *whatever* job has to be done.

He witnessed for the man *whose* wallet had been stolen.

6. The **determiners** are modifiers that do not show regular adjective features and tend to limit nouns rather than describe them. They may be classified by the manner in which they combine with other determiners and adjectives:

A. Regular determiners, including

Articles: a, an, the

Demonstratives: this, these, that, those

Genitives: my, your, his, her, its, our, their, car's, John's

Indefinite adjectives: all, another, any, both, each, either, every, neither, no, some

Only one regular determiner may precede a noun.

B. Postdeterminers, including

Ordinals: first, second, next, last

Cardinals: one, two, three

Comparatives and superlatives: more, most, fewer, fewest, less, least

Indefinite adjectives: few, little, many, much, other, own, several

More than one postdeterminer may occur with a noun, but usually in a fixed order:

The *second most* admired athlete; *one last* man.

C. Predeterminers, including

Prearticles: all, only, both, just

all the people
both the keys
just a joke

Regular determiners and postdeterminers + of: all of, some of, most of, the first of, just the last of

Nouns of quantity + of: a slice of, a quart of, a piece of, a gallon of

Predeterminers precede both regular determiners and postdeterminers when there are a number of modifiers:

a gallon of that most delicious wine

all the hundred other possible versions

not one of her own three ancient Egyptian coins

17E *Adverbs*

Adverbs do not show identifiable features of inflection as do nouns, pronouns, verbs, and adjectives. They are identifiable mainly by their position in a sentence. The adverb is the most movable part of speech, even though there are constraints on its placement. An adverb may come before the subject, after the subject, after the verb, or occupy a number of other positions depending on the word it modifies:

Then I made an announcement.

I *then* made an announcement.

I made an announcement *then*.

I *also* made an *equally* important announcement.

I adjourned the meeting *very abruptly*.

A phrase, clause, or another part of speech that can fill an adverb position is referred to as an **adverbial.**

17EA *Comparison of adverbs*

Many adverbs, like adjectives, show three degrees of comparison, formed by the use of *more* and *most: promptly, more promptly, most promptly*. A few adverbs like *slow, fast, quick, loud, early, right*, and *deep* have two forms, one of them identical with the adjective form: *slowly, more slowly, most slowly* or *slow, slower, slowest*. *Soon* also compares in two ways (*sooner, soonest; less soon, least soon*), but it is always an adverb.

17EB *Functions of the adverbs and adverbials* 17EB

Adverbs function as:

1. **Modifiers of verbs, adjectives, and other adverbs:**

He read *thoughtfully*. [modifies the verb *read*]

He read *very* thoughtfully. [modifies the adverb *thoughtfully*]

His *particularly* thoughtful reading drew applause. [modifies the adjective *thoughtful*]

2. **Sentence modifiers:**

Yes, I know what is wrong.

Several hours ago, we would have welcomed the chance.

3. Sentence connectors:

You can cross the border; *however*, you have to be checked.

We had extra money; we *therefore* stayed longer.

4. Appositives:

They came home extremely late, *at 3:00 A.M.*

The job was done accurately—*with utmost precision*.

5. Interrogatives:

How did you get along?

Where is the game?

6. Clause markers (relative adverbs):

I didn't know *when* to get off.

This is *where* the battle was fought.

7. Correlatives:

The harder we tried, *the less* we accomplished.

The sooner we know, *the better*.

8. Idiomatic particles with verbs:

We looked *over* [scanned] the document.

He is going to try to hold *out* [endure].

Nearly all one-word prepositions like *in, to, up, down,* and *beneath* may also be used as adverbs. The forms are the same, but the function and often the meaning are different:

She / jumped at / the chance. [adverb, combining with *jump* to mean "accept eagerly"]

She / jumped / *at* the Olympics. [preposition, introducing phrase]

He / was driven *to* / madness. [adverb]

He / was driven / *to* the city. [preposition]

9. **Adverbials:** Nouns in adverb positions that express ideas of time, place, manner, or degree function as adverbs:

One *year* we had rain continuously for two days.

I went *home.*

We arrived *Sunday.*

17EC　*Kinds of adverbs*

Many adverbs may be grouped by meaning, although others are classified solely by their function in a sentence, as indicated in 17EB.

1. Adverbs of **time:** *immediately, today, ago, now, again, always, by and by, forever,* and other words and phrases answering "when."
2. Adverbs of **place** or **direction:** *here, there, everywhere, inside, forward, downward,* and other words and phrases answering "where" or "in what direction."
3. *Adverbs of* **manner:** *maybe, possibly, apart, happily, particularly, not, never, only,* and other words and phrases answering "how" or "to what degree." *Extremely, quite, rather, somewhat, too,* and *very* serve as special intensifiers of the words they modify.

17ED　*Confusion of adjectives and adverbs*

Ordinarily a word ending in *-ly* can be identified as an adjective instead of an adverb if it can be compared by inflection. Thus, *homely, homelier, homeliest* and *lowly, lowlier, lowliest* are adjectives, but *merely* and *badly,* which cannot be compared in this way, are adverbs. Confusion, however, occurs in actual usage. Adjectives and adverbs have separate uses in the following sentences:

1. Adverbs, not adjectives, modify verbs:

   I was driving along pretty *steady.* [colloquial use of adjective]
   I was driving along pretty *steadily.* [standard use of adverb]

2. Adverbs, not adjectives, modify adjectives and other adverbs:

   She seemed *terrible* upset. [colloquial use of adjective]
   She seemed *terribly* upset. [standard use of adverb]

   Most always we go on Mondays. [colloquial use of adjective]
   Almost always we go on Mondays. [standard use of adverb]

3. Complements referring to the subject after special linking verbs take adjectives, not adverbs:

I feel *badly.* [misuse of adverb after *feel*]
I feel *bad.* [correct use of adjective]

He looks *good.* [correct use of adjective after *looks*]
He looks *well.* [correct use. *Well* is both an adjective and an adverb; here it is used in its adjective sense of "in good health."]

Prepositions 17F

Prepositions show no identifiable features of form. They are uninflected. They have no characteristic suffixes. The simple prepositions may be listed, but some of these are identical with adverbs and conjunctions. Some grammarians have stressed the functional features of prepositions completely at the expense of their meaning. If prepositions had no meaning, any one of them might logically substitute for any other. Those that express spatial relations most clearly have meaning. *Above* means something quite different from *below* and *around;* and *in, on,* and *by* express relative positions. A failure to recognize the meaning of prepositions is a failure to recognize the subtle differences they are capable of expressing.

Functions of prepositions 17FA

1. The preposition is a structure word. It usually introduces a phrase that acts as a single part of speech, usually an adjective or adverb, and connects the phrase with another word in the sentence:

   He demonstrated the differences *between individual and group thinking.* [adjective use of phrase, modifying *differences*]

   The cities are full *of people.* [adverbial use, modifying *full*]

   The budget has been reduced *to its minimum.* [adverbial use, modifying *has been reduced*]

2. The prepositional phrase with *of* is an alternate way of expressing genitive relations: a third *of the group,* the top *of the building,* the collar *of my shirt.*
3. Prepositions are used idiomatically with nouns, adjectives, and verbs. The choice of idiomatic prepositions causes considerable difficulty even for native speakers, and the dictionary often provides no help in interpreting differences between *resemblance between, resemblance of,* and *resemblance to* or *agree to* and *agree with.* In most instances, a context will help; but, in stubborn cases, special dictionaries of prepositional and verbal idioms are available (see pp. 514–515).

Kinds of prepositions 17FB

1. **Simple forms:** The most commonly used prepositions are *of, on, to, at, by, for, from, in,* and *with.* Other familiar prepositions are *about, above, across, after, against, around, before, behind, below, beneath, beside, between, beyond,*

down, during, except, following, like, near, off, opposite, out, over, through, toward, under, until, and *without.* The total list numbers about sixty.

2. **Compound forms:** The simple forms combine with each other and with other words to form various other possibilities: *according to, because of, by means of, due to, except for, in addition to, in front of, in spite of, instead of, on account of, with regard to.*

17FC *Confusion of prepositions and conjunctions*

But, for, after, since, and *before* function as prepositions and also as conjunctions. Even though the forms are identical, the uses and positions make clear the differences. Conjunctions, for example, are seldom used at the end of a sentence unless the sentence is elliptical.

I was vaguely hopeful, *but* not optimistic. [conjunction connecting two adjectives]

I could do nothing *but* hope. [preposition in the sense of *except* with the infinitive [*to*] *hope* as object]

Here is a new collar *for* the dog. [preposition]

He protested, *for* it was the thing to do. [conjunction]

Even though *for* is very close in meaning to *because,* the part of the sentence beginning with *for* cannot be moved to first position as it could be if *because* were substituted.

Note: See also Glossary under **like, as.**

17G **Conjunctions**

Conjunctions, like prepositions, show no identifiable features of form. They are uninflected. They have no characteristic suffixes. A complete list of conjunctions would be a relatively short one, and the language shows little tendency to add new ones. Although the definition of a conjunction as a structure word duplicates that of the preposition, the two perform quite different structural functions.

17GA *Kinds of conjunctions and their uses*

As connectors and transitionals, conjunctions serve as one of the major devices for order and coherence in prose. The relations they signal provide a structure for clear communication. The way they are used, misused, or overused influences the whole matter of style. The various kinds of conjunctions have therefore been treated in previous sections of the book:

Coordinating conjunctions: p. 121
Subordinating conjunctions: pp. 122–123
Correlative conjunctions: p. 130
Conjunctive adverbs: pp. 223–224

As a group, interjections have no identifiable features of form. They are utterances used to attract attention or to express various degrees of feeling. They function as independent elements without grammatical connections with the rest of a sentence. They frequently stand alone as separate fragments or sentences. In speech, their effect depends more on the pitch and stress of the voice than on the meaning of the words.

Functions of interjections 17HA

1. Interjections are used as means of address: *Hi! Hey there! Come on! John, hurry up! O Lord, maker of us all!*
2. Interjections express feelings, either mild ones or strong ones.

Kinds of interjections 17HB

1. **Sound words:** Most interjections are expressive sounds. Some are relatively spontaneous and instinctive sounds without specific meaning, like *oh* and *ah* and *well;* others are conventional or cultivated sounds with implications established by usage, like *ouch* (pain), *eureka* (discovery), *shh* (be quiet), *psst* (pay attention). Included in this category also are a great number of swear words.
2. **Other parts of speech:** Any word, phrase, or short clause spoken with a stress or marked with an exclamation point can be made to serve as an interjection:

Mercy! [noun]

Oh me! [pronoun]

Outrageous! [adjective]

Watch out! [verb]

Not on your life! [phrase]

You don't say! [sentence]

Phrases 17I

The word *phrase* is often used loosely to mean any brief expression. Grammatically, it is a meaningful unit of more than one word which acts as a single part of speech. It differs from a clause in that it does not have both a subject and a finite verb, although it may have one or the other.

Kinds of phrases 17IA

1. **Noun phrase:** Prepositional, gerund, and infinitive phrases used as nouns are called noun phrases, but in transformational-generative grammar, a noun phrase consists of a noun and its modifiers: *the paper, a very indignant old gentleman, time immemorial.*

2. **Verb phrase:** A finite verb phrase consists of a verb and any other words that help it or complete its meaning: *have been going, have to study, put up with.*

3. **Gerund phrase:** A gerund phrase is a verbal phrase, nonfinite in nature, which acts as a noun:

We were interested in *gathering the facts.* [object of preposition]

Living the remainder of his life in isolation will be punishment enough. [subject of verb]

4. **Participial phrase:** A participial phrase is a verbal phrase, nonfinite in nature, which acts as an adjective:

The snow *piled high on the curb* was a barrier.

Acting with unusual intensity, the cast surpassed itself.

5. **Infinitive phrase:** An infinitive phrase is a verbal phrase, nonfinite in nature, which acts as a noun, adjective, or adverb:

To hear him is a treat. [as a noun]

It was a drink *to be sipped.* [as an adjective]

It would be appropriate *to send a card.* [as an adverb]

6. **Prepositional phrase:** A prepositional phrase consists of a preposition and its object. It acts as an adjective or adverb and occasionally as a noun:

We missed the sign *with a blinking light.* [as an adjective]

He did it *without thinking.* [as an adverb]

7. **Absolute phrase** or **nominative absolute:** A nominative absolute consists of a noun and some portion of a predicate, often a participle. It may be thought of as a transformed sentence. The absolute phrase acts independently; it modifies no particular word in the main clause:

She stood up, *her hands on her hips.*

The light of day just beginning to show, we started out.

He failed to respond, *his face impassive.*

17J *Subordinate clauses*

A subordinate clause is a sentence changed from independent status to dependent status by the addition of a signal word such as a subordinating conjunction or a relative pronoun. The signal word expresses the relationship between the subordinate clause and the main clause.

Two independent clauses: It is raining. We won't go.
One clause subordinated to express a new relation: *If* it is raining, we won't go.
We will go, *even though* it is raining.

Two independent clauses: The chair creaks. It is in his room.
One clause subordinated to express a new relation: The chair *that* creaks is in
his room.

Kinds of clauses *17JA*

1. A **noun clause** is one that occupies the position of a noun and serves its
functions:

Whoever is going should sign up. [subject of verb]

I don't know *what his name is.* [object of verb]

Give it to *whatever organization you choose.* [object of preposition]

The complaint was *that he was constantly late.* [subjective complement]

2. An **adjective clause** functions as an adjective by modifying nouns and pronouns. Typically, it follows the word it modifies:

The secretary, *who also had to double as treasurer,* was overworked. [modifying
the subject]

I see no reason *why we should be excluded.* [modifying the object of the verb]

This is a book *that I like.* [modifying a subjective complement]

Anybody *who denies this* is foolish. [modifying a pronoun as subject]

Adjective clauses that are introduced by a relative pronoun, relative adjective, or
relative adverb are called **relative clauses.** In these constructions, the relative
may substitute for the subject of the clause.

who confessed his involvement [the relative pronoun is the subject]

whom I was expecting [the relative pronoun is the object]

whose talents we know [relative adjective]

where I was heading [relative adverb]

3. **Adverb clause:** An adverbial clause functions as an adverb by modifying verbs,
adjectives, and other adverbs:

They made the attempt, *although the risk was great.* [modifying the verb *made*]

I am confident *that they'll succeed.* [modifying the adjective *confident*]

We accomplished considerably more *than we did yesterday.* [modifying the adverb
more]

Permanently

One day the Nouns were clustered in the street.
An Adjective walked by, with her dark beauty.
The Nouns were struck, moved, changed.
The next day a Verb drove up, and created the Sentence.

Each sentence says one thing—for example, "Although it was a dark rainy day
    when the Adjective walked by, I shall remember the pure and sweet
    expression on her face until the day I perish from the green, effective earth."
Or, "Will you please close the window, Andrew?"
Or, for example, "Thank you, the pink pot of flowers on the window sill has
    changed color recently to a light yellow, due to the heat from the boiler
    factory which exists nearby."

In the springtime the Sentences and the Nouns lay silently on the grass.
A lonely Conjunction here and there would call, "And! But!"
But the Adjective did not emerge.

As the adjective is lost in the sentence,
So I am lost in your eyes, ears, nose, and throat—
You have enchanted me with a single kiss
Which can never be undone
Until the destruction of language.

Kenneth Koch

Projects **1.** Choose three sentences from an essay. Analyze the sentences in terms of the three operating principles of the language described on p. 458; that is, what suffixes and inflections guide the meaning? What function words are present? Which parts are movable? Which parts must be kept together even if they are moved?

2. Observe the language of young children, particularly the uses that amuse us—*foots* for *feet* or *breaked* for *broke*, for instance. What deviations from the standard operating principles of the language do these uses represent? Are children's deviations systematic? How do they cope with the irregularities of the language?

3. Arrange at least ten of the following words and nonsense words into a sentence that seems grammatical. What inferences about the language can you draw from the way you proceeded?

would	lures	cotion
that	delisandro	would
delurts	more	hation
dimide	blot	blecked
than	energestly	
of	the	

4. Read a number of poems in an anthology to find at least five phrases that fall into the category of semigrammatical (see p. 460). What analogies with fully grammatical phrases help to interpret the meanings of these phrases? For example, "furnished souls" and "angry candy" appear in E. E. Cummings' poem "the Cambridge ladies who live in furnished souls." In addition, invent five semigrammatical phrases of your own.

5. See Section 17CC. Write a synopsis of a conjugation for the following sentences, as illustrated on p. 475:

it develops	he addresses the meeting
it tears	the earth shakes
she gives	we hate

Suggestions for writing

1. Why do many people seem to hate the study of grammar? Is grammar actually useless or only taught uselessly? Is the study of grammar simply intellectualizing about a process that works well without studying it, like explaining gravity, for instance? Write an essay advocating the study of grammar in the schools or advocating its elimination from the English curriculum.

2. Write an essay about your experience of learning another language. Did the study of a different grammar give you a perspective on the grammar of your own language? Is learning another language easy or difficult for you? Why?

3. Years of experimentation with chimpanzees have proved that these non-human beings are capable of two-way communication by means of sign language employing a grammar. The achievement opens up the possibility of a different world in which birds, fish, and animals might communicate with man if we found the proper means to establish communication with them. Let your imagination go. Write an essay envisioning this new world of communication.

4. Consider the effects of displacement if the human being is no longer unique in this world as a creature capable of generating language. Write an essay on the implications of the human being as equal to other beings on Earth, not dominant because of language skills.

Chapter 18   Usage

Usage is the active force of a living language on words and current structures, at times working contrary to established grammar and standard practices. Usage is the way people, both educated and uneducated, use the language, not necessarily how books say it should be used. Sometimes users of the language conform to prevailing practices; sometimes they deviate. In the use of language, there are individual, occupational, and regional differences, varying social patterns, degrees of formality and informality, and differences between speaking and writing. Every speaker and writer is faced with choices. Over a period of time, if the differences get obscured so that people no longer know that a choice exists, then the more popular form simply prevails. Thus we can assume that as long as a language is used, it will change.

Those who express a perennial longing for a pure and stable language look on change as erosion. But resistance to change does not alter the fact that human beings today show the same tendencies in their speech habits as they did a thousand years ago. The present dependence of English on word order as opposed to inflection grew out of the human being's sense of economy with sound. Inflections occurring in syllables of weak stress were lost because persons obscured them in speaking. Even today, sounds in similar positions are highly susceptible to change. Speakers of some dialects characteristically drop *ed*'s and *s*'s when the strong stress falls on a preceding syllable. Thus, *exercised* becomes *exercise; teacher* is reduced to *teach; going to* becomes *gonna.* The final syllable, which requires an extra effort to pronounce, tends to be weakened or is lost altogether. Even though dialects that operate on a reduced grammar are generally considered nonstandard, they illustrate the kind of changes that usage has forced on grammar in the past and that have now become standard. The written language still acts as a restraint on the changes that speech makes, but, in the past, oral usage has tended to prevail unless the literary tradition has been very strong. Today, editors of books and periodicals often act as a control over innovations that writers may want to include in their writing.

The now-established word order of the language acts constantly as a force for the change of traditional forms. A strict observance of grammatical principles would demand expressions like *It is I* and *Whom are you talking to?* In the first example, the pronoun *I* occupies a position normally reserved for the object of a verb; in the second example, the pronoun *whom* occupies a position ordinarily reserved for the subject of the sentence. Thus, usage has established the expressions *It's me* and *Who are you talking to?* Whether expressions such as these continue to function merely as idioms of the language or will in time affect the whole grammatical system of pronoun use cannot be predicted. Pronouns have been considerably altered in the past, and since they still remain one of the most complex parts of speech in the language, usage may well act in its characteristic way to simplify and regularize them.

The regularization typical of usage acts also on verbs and noun plurals. Irregular verb forms like *awoke, proven,* and *clad* now commonly appear with regular verb endings: *awaked, proved,* and *clothed.* Usage also provides regular plural forms for words borrowed from foreign languages. Thus *libretti* changes to *librettos, stadia* to *stadiums,* and *châteaux* to *châteaus.*

Usage has by no means acted as a chaotic influence on the language. In most instances, it has worked for greater efficiency and clarity. But recognition of change in language does not by any means condone permissiveness. Usage at any one period tends to be highly stable, although controversies always exist about particular usages and innovations. However, speakers of the language who are concerned about acceptable usage will usually find agreement among educated speakers on most matters of importance. Familiarizing yourself with the backgrounds of English to see what has happened in the past is one means of gaining confidence in the use of the language in the present.

Idiolect and dialect

The way an individual uses the language in choice of words, pronunciation, and grammar is that person's idiolect. One person's speech, however, does not ordinarily differ so greatly from another's that one of them cannot be understood at all. The common features of language that certain speakers share with one another represent their dialect. The elements that dialects share with one another establish a language.

Dialects in the United States differ from one another mainly in the pronunciation of certain sounds and in the selection of words for fairly common things. All of them share a common grammar and a large stock of words which everyone understands, even though the words may be pronounced with variations.

Language almost always operates within a community, either large or small. The community may be groups like the family, a circle of friends, a business organization, or a lodge. The language of these groups is shaped further by the locality—either the neighborhood, the city, or the region. Local characteristics are deeply rooted, so that persons moving from one part of the country to another usually carry with them the marks of their former communities. Because dialectal features are transferable in this way, dialectologists are particularly interested in population shifts. The speech traits of blacks in some ghettos of the North, for example, may be traced to patterns of speech in particular rural areas of the South. Big cities can usually be subdivided into local communities whose members share a common dialect.

Dialects thrive in isolation, but in an age in which transportation and communication have erased almost all natural geographical divisions, dialect differences tend to be diminished. Nevertheless, two opposite forces operate constantly on language. On the one hand, schools, the military, the press, radio, and television act as leveling influences, tending to iron out dialectal differences. On the other hand, local pride, racial consciousness, individualism, and the exclusiveness of tight groups with common interests tend to preserve these differences. Absolute uniformity in the use of language, even if it were possible, would scarcely be a virtue, because nonconformists in language have always acted as a stimulus to the growth of the language.

Dialects, therefore, may be studied in terms of regional differences, social patterns, or group functions such as an occupation, hobby, or sport.

Regional American dialects

Regional dialects are identified by attempting to determine boundaries, called isoglosses, where distinct pronunciations or the use of particular words and forms is divided. An expert linguist can locate a speaker's origin, sometimes within a radius of fifty miles, by using a series of test words and phrases like *merry, marry, Mary; wash, water, Washington; on, off, dog, oft, lot, log, sorry; about the house; greasy; park the car; first, bird; fur, four; horse, hoarse,* and others. These words provide a few of the clues to differences between speakers of the major dialect areas: northern, midland, and southern and, within those areas, regions like eastern Virginia, eastern New England, and New York City (see map, opposite).

In addition to pronunciation differences, the regions also represent certain other types of local characteristics that set off one dialect from others. A northerner, for example, may refer to a *pail* or *faucet* instead of a *bucket* or *spigot,* used predominantly by midlanders and southerners. *Polecat* for *skunk* is a southernism. A northerner characteristically uses *chipmunk* for *ground squirrel. Might can, might could,* and *used to could* are markedly southern expressions, even among educated speakers.

The massive task of mapping the linguistic geography of the United States has not yet been completed, but studies that have been published mark off boundaries on the basis of regional features, and they include maps showing the direction of migrations (see map, opposite). Dialects, of course, are no respecters of state lines. At one time,

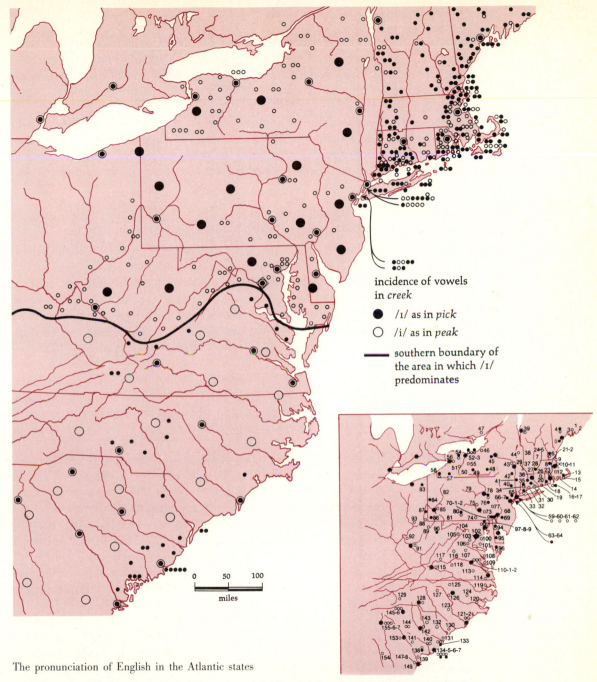

The pronunciation of English in the Atlantic states

The map indicates that the pronunciation of *creek* with an /ɪ/ as in *pick* predominates in the North except in southern New England and metropolitan New York. Pronunciation with an /i/ as in *peak* predominates in the South except for the coast of South Carolina. Since /i/ is used as a prestige pronunciation among educated speakers, the insert shows how their usage differs from that of the general populace.

mountains and rivers may have determined the major isoglosses, but today the existence or absence of a road may be the main factor that determines the degree of a region's isolation. Some dialects spoken today in isolated parts of the Appalachians and Ozarks preserve features of English that were common in seventeenth-century England.

The history of early settlement in a region is also an important part of the field work in dialect study, mainly because patterns of speech and usage in an area can often be traced to foreign influences. Thus, *stoop* for *front porch* or *steps* is used in northern areas where the Dutch settled; *smearcase*, common in midland areas, is a clear sign of German borrowing.

Social patterns: standard and nonstandard English

The social patterns of the United States are closely related to education and economics. Ours is not so much a class society as it is a status society, and it is a society divided to a great extent by the use of language. Uneducated people may make a fortune but find themselves excluded from the society of the educated rich because of their speech. On the other hand, educated individuals have sometimes found themselves accepted in social circles that they cannot well afford. Standard English, the speech of the majority of educated Americans, has become the prestige dialect of this country.

In a nation as diverse as this one, the existence of a standard dialect is inevitable. One dialect becomes the official language of the nation because it is used in official documents, in formal public gatherings, and in all serious deliberations. Knowledge of it is therefore helpful to anyone who intends to participate in the serious affairs of this nation.[1]

Standard English, however, is by no means one thing. It represents a wide range of formal and informal uses, particularly in the choice of words, although it should be stressed again that media, education, and transportation work much more strongly toward the uniformity of our language than toward its diversity. One of the usual characteristics of standard English is its adherence to the regular grammatical features of the language. An obvious sign of nonstandard English is a speaker's consistent and unaffected deviations. Uneducated speakers may say "I done it" because they are unaware of the standard models of the grammar, or they may impose a regular pattern on the grammar when irregularity exists so that they say, "She say she in trouble" instead of "She says she is in trouble."

Educated speakers also show lapses, particularly in matters of usage, but their choices, like the use of *ain't*, are sometimes quite deliberate, even affected. Often, our attitude toward the prevailing order of society influences the kind of language we use. Some speakers show a strong desire to conform. They may even know that there are guidelines for choices between *who–whom*, *I–me*, and *bad–badly*, though they lack confidence or experience to apply them correctly. Those who try too hard

---

[1] Standard English is now often referred to as Edited American English. This term reflects the fact that Standard English is English as it is often written, though the writer may or may not use it when speaking.

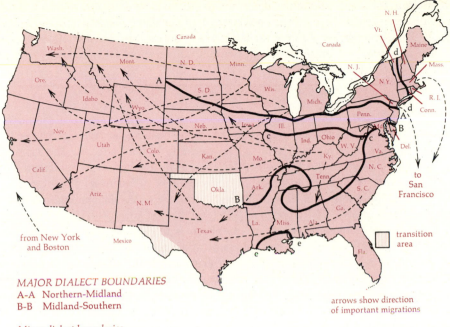

MAJOR DIALECT BOUNDARIES
A-A   Northern-Midland
B-B   Midland-Southern

Minor dialect boundaries
c-c   North Midland-South Midland
d-d   Coastal New England-Northern
e-e   New Orleans Focal Area-Southern

arrows show direction
of important migrations

Dialect boundaries mark off those areas where features of language and pronunciation clearly identify the speakers. The West is mainly a mixture of various groups.

fall into the unnaturalness and incorrectness of sentences like *Whom do you think you are? They gave the present to him and I,* or *I felt badly about the error.* Ungrammatical uses of this kind represent an "educated nonstandard" English. They result from a desire to be overly correct. They are quite unrelated to the typical unaffected characteristics of nonstandard speech.

The social revolution of the 1960s and 1970s in this country affected the attitudes of many individuals toward standards of English usage that had prevailed up to that time. Many language experts took the position that requiring students in the schools to use the prestige dialect was the equivalent of forcing everyone, regardless of ethnic background, to learn "white man's English"; students had a right to their own language. The protest movement raised serious questions about our attitudes toward language in this society and about the consequences of reshaping the identity of special groups, who as individuals characteristically find an identity by the use of their own language. Undoubtedly the movement worked toward breaking down rigid social barriers that language can erect and led to a new realization that bidialectalism and even multi-dialectalism are necessary if all individuals, not minority groups alone, are to function easily in various social situations, depending upon the place and occasion. The concept of a standard dialect, established in

England as early as the fourteenth century, has been tested and altered, but it prevails as a strong force in our society. People constantly seek authority for language use; they want to know what is right and acceptable. Further, the standard dialect serves the useful purpose of providing an accepted and common code for efficient communication.

Group dialects

Every occupation, hobby, and sport—in fact, every possible pursuit—gives rise to a certain number of terms that have special meaning in that activity. The language that identifies a trade or profession is referred to as its argot or jargon or shoptalk. It may even vary from place to place or from business to business. For example, a waitress changing jobs may have to learn a new set of terms for placing orders in a different restaurant.

If the purpose among speakers of any group is to exclude outsiders, that is, to carry on a kind of private or secret communication, then the language is referred to as cant. Slang is a common collective term that may include all of the occupational dialects but more commonly refers to rapidly changing words of popular speech that are deliberately invented to give language new vigor. Because slang is associated with every speaker's most casual and lighthearted way of talking, it is generally considered inappropriate for truly serious occasions. Also because most slang dies quickly, it is generally considered inappropriate for written work that may be read in the future. Using slang in writing may be a way of being in vogue, but it is also the fastest way of being out of vogue six months or six years later.

Despite these reservations, however, slang continues to create new words and phrases and to extend the meanings of old ones. Even though slang is sometimes invented by professional gagwriters and advertisers, it is more likely to spring up at any time or place in any situation without intention. Slang invites inventiveness. Without doubt, it is one of the most powerful influences on the living language.

Idiom

Idiom may be used in two senses. First, it may refer to a characteristic manner of English expression, as opposed to the way of saying something in another language. English idiom in this sense is almost synonymous with grammatical expression. In the second sense, however, idiom may be used to refer to any expression that does not quite fit the customary grammatical or logical expectations of English but has become established as a way of saying something in our own language. In this sense, idiom is a stereotyped expression. Thus, a sentence like *The team was riding high* is wholly idiomatic, although in a literal sense it is illogical (compare *The team was having great success*). Likewise, idiom establishes the differences in meaning between phrases like *make away with, make out, make over, make up,* and *make up to.* Because idioms are a vernacular feature of language, native speakers have little difficulty with them. Usage alone establishes an idiom.

Formal and informal usage

A newspaper account recently quoted the words of a judge who, in censuring an attorney appearing in his court, said, "It is the opinion of the court that you are under the influence of alcohol." It is difficult to think of any other situation in which this particular phrasing might be appropriately used. The sentence is impersonal, guarded in tone, and stiffly formal as compared with any of the following alternatives:

1. You appear to the judge of this court to be intoxicated.
2. You appear to me to be intoxicated. [his position as judge implied by the courtroom setting]
3. I think you're drunk.
4. You're smashed.

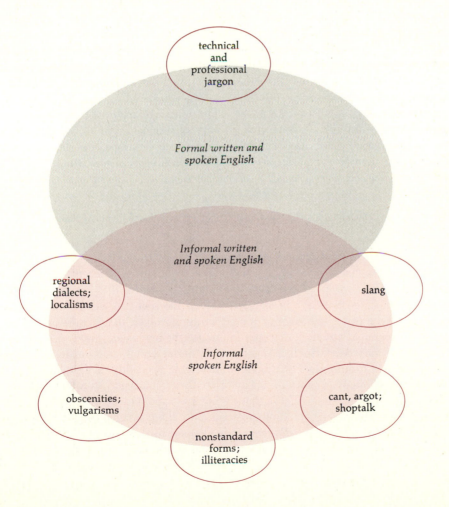

technical and professional jargon

Formal written and spoken English

Informal written and spoken English

regional dialects; localisms

slang

Informal spoken English

obscenities; vulgarisms

nonstandard forms; illiteracies

cant, argot; shoptalk

The test of any of these usages, including the judge's original statement, is not whether one is good English and another bad or whether one is correct and another incorrect but whether the statement is appropriate to the speaker and his relation to the listener at a particular time and place. A standard of appropriateness implies a concern for the opinions and reactions of others. In the courtroom, the judge might possibly have used alternatives 1 and 2 without jeopardizing the dignity of his position or the seriousness of his tone. Or, if he had been primarily interested in giving greater directness and emphasis to his remarks in that formal situation, he might also have chosen alternative 3 for purposes of contrast. In any formal situation, alternative 4 would be clearly out of place, although it is conceivable that the same judge might have said this to the attorney in private if the two of them were on close speaking terms.

The varieties of English account for confusion in the minds of many people about the actual use of the language. They want to know precisely what is correct and what is incorrect. They think of rules. They are perplexed by degrees of formality and intimacy, the differences between writing and speaking, and the various accommodations of language that a speaker can make for differing audiences and differing purposes. They are perplexed because they want choices to be clear-cut. Actually, there is considerable overlapping in the speech habits of any one individual. In terms of society as a whole, there is an intermingling and borrowing among the various dialects, as the diagram on page 503 suggests.

The discriminations we make in the use of language are therefore more relative and involved than any dictionary or glossary of usage can cover. At most, usage guides can suggest the formal or highly colloquial implications of certain words and phrases, but their prescriptions are almost always subject to exception. Good taste and judgment will help a speaker more than a stack of dictionaries.

Usage as etiquette

The regard for appropriateness in the use of language is often referred to as the etiquette of language—the adjustment of our speaking to different occasions and gatherings. The concept of language as etiquette is helpful if it clarifies the notion that individuals do not have to talk one way all the time any more than they dress one way all the time. The analogy is misleading, however, if it suggests that people are ill-mannered at any time that they fail to use the language in most precise terms. Almost any variety of English is acceptable under certain circumstances. Overly polite usage in an informal situation is as unsuitable as crudity on a somber occasion. The best manners in any form of behavior are those that a person follows intuitively in consideration of others. Those that do not arise spontaneously tend to be empty conventions. Some long-standing prescriptions about usage, like the distinction between *different from* and *different than*, belong to this category. *Different than* tends to be a more spontaneous form.

Writing is rather consistently a more highly conventionalized form of expression than speaking. Even dialogue set down in writing tends of be more abbreviated, controlled, and orderly than conversation is. Because writing is a slower process than speaking, writers can reflect on their own remarks, make decisions about phrasing, edit, and polish. Speaking in an informal situation does not allow the same degree of control.

Both speaking and writing may vary in their degree of formality, but the basic difference between the conditions under which the two are produced ordinarily affects usage. Speaking assumes that an audience is immediately present. The reading audience of written prose is removed in time and place. In fact, writers may create their own audience by the way they write, because a reading audience chooses what it will read or not read. Listeners, on the other hand, are captive, unless they intentionally leave or refuse to listen.

The immediacy of an audience gives a characteristic directness and simplicity to colloquial expression. Almost every technical term and learned phrase has a colloquial equivalent that permits speakers to talk about such things in an easy way. It is also true that colloquial expressions infiltrate written prose. If they do to a great extent, the writing merely takes on an increasingly informal quality. Twentieth-century writing has shown a marked preference for informality, so that hard and fast divisions between expressions appropriate to speaking or to writing are now being constantly obscured. The fact remains, nevertheless, that the nature and conditions of writing seem always to place greater restraints on writers, no matter how deliberately experimental they may try to be.

Projects

1. Indicate the characteristic terms you use in your family or home town for the categories indicated below. Compare your terms with those of other members of the class:

    A. Family word for *father*
    B. Family word for *mother*
    C. Word for *a member of the police force*
    D. Phrase for *skipping school*
    E. Phrase for *passing time idly*

2. Keep a slang notebook for one week, making notations about words and phrases you and others use. Indicate the context. Where were the words said? To whom? What particular words are used with consistency? Do their meanings vary?

3. In a nostalgic vein, assemble a list of at least ten popular terms from years past. You may have heard these from your parents or in films or read them in books. How were phrases like *cat's pajamas, trucking,* and *spit and polish* used?

4. Give at least two equivalent words or expressions in standard English for the following terms: lousy, elbow grease, flop, croak, blab, to snowball, spill your guts, stupe.

5. List ten words that mean one thing in a standard context and something quite different in a special jargon or cant. Define the special usage. In 1976, someone might have listed *pad, trip,* and *stoned.* Five years later, these words may be remembered only nostalgically, and a new set will have emerged. List current usages.

Suggestions for writing

1. Some people refer to standard English as "white man's English" and the teaching of it in schools as a device of the capitalistic society to maintain the oppression of minorities. Write an essay agreeing or disagreeing. Consider the question from the viewpoint of minorities as well as from the viewpoint of the dominant group.

2. Write an essay on the use of language by particular groups to exclude outsiders (special jargon or the lingo of subcultures) in addition to its function to communicate. Use specific examples.

3. Write an essay on styles of language as a reflection of styles of living. Are changes in language styles a strong factor in the gap between generations?

4. Write an essay on the discriminatory attitudes of the dominant society toward nonstandard usage. Try to define what the attitudes are (that users of nonstandard usage are not as intelligent as users of standard usage, for instance). In what way are the attitudes enforced (hiring practices, for instance)? How can these attitudes be changed? Should they?

5. Write your own version of one chapter of Haig Bosmajian's book *The Language of Oppression* (Washington, D.C.: Public Affairs Press, 1975): The Language of Anti-Semitism, The Language of White Racism, The Language of Indian Derision, The Language of Sexism, The Language of War.

Using a dictionary is an old and established custom, but the earliest word lists, called glosses, in no way resembled what we now think of as a dictionary. They were chiefly lists of difficult foreign words, with simple explanations, sometimes in the same language as the foreign words, sometimes in English. The first dictionaries of English words date from the beginning of the seventeenth century, but they remained lists of hard words and still concentrated upon foreign borrowings.

As the words of the language continued to increase, dictionaries became more and more a necessity, and their contents were expanded to include information about spelling, pronunciation, etymology, and usage. One of the most influential of early dictionaries was Samuel Johnson's *A Dictionary of the English Language* (1755), which continued to be used in various revisions until 1900. Johnson fully recognized the changing nature of the language, but he also thought it was the duty of the lexicographer to "retard what we cannot repel." Further, recognizing what he considered the "improprieties and absurdities" of the English language, he set out "to correct or proscribe."

No modern editors claim that a dictionary proscribes or prescribes. With consistency, they assert that a dictionary describes. It becomes an authority only insofar as it is a faithful and complete recorder of language as it is used. In this sense, the dictionary assumes only the role of adviser, what the editors of *Webster's New World Dictionary* call "a friendly guide, pointing out the safe, well-traveled roads."

The reliable dictionary

In what sense is a dictionary either good or unreliable?

First, no one dictionary is a definitive reference. Each is an interpretation of the language. Some modern editors assert that lexicography is now a linguistic science; others, like Philip B. Gove, the editor of *Webster's Third New International Dictionary*, say that it never will be a science because the interpretation of words requires "subjective analysis, arbitrary decisions, and intuitive reasoning." In whatever sense we think of dictionary making, the editors and staff are chiefly responsible for its reliability. The contributors and consultants must be specialists in language study. No modern dictionary is a one-man job. The staff may involve hundreds of scholars, and the total production may represent more than a million-dollar investment.

Whatever the degree of its authority is at any one time, a dictionary does not continue to be a reliable, current reference unless it is kept up to date. Desk or collegiate dictionaries, because of their relatively small size, are frequently supplemented or revised. Unabridged dictionaries may undergo major revisions only every twenty or thirty years. Many inexpensive dictionaries on the market today are only reprints of old editions, sold by a previous publisher to be retitled and distributed by another one.

The size of a dictionary is a clue to its coverage. The more information it contains, the more likely it will be able to serve the needs of its users. Since every dictionary must of necessity select certain words to be included and compress its definitions into the smallest possible space, the large dictionary naturally gains an advantage because of its size. *Webster's Third New International* lists more than 450,000 words. The popular collegiate dictionaries list from 100,000 to 150,000 words. These are ordinarily complete enough for the purposes of most college studies.

Every dictionary gives details about its coverage and arrangement in its prefatory materials. These sections, although usually printed in a forbiddingly small type, are the clearest guides to the reliability of the book.

Information included in a dictionary

Dictionaries, of course, vary in their emphasis. Besides basic definitions of words, some contain more encyclopedic information than others, some more etymological data, some more illustrations. But to varying degrees, all reliable dictionaries provide users with information of the following kinds:

Spelling and capitalization

Words that have variant spellings, like *catalog* or *catalogue*, are frequently given separate entries, although definitions are given only under one form. If a variant is not standard American, it is labeled. Thus, *defence* as a spelling for *defense* is labeled as a typical British spelling in most dictionaries. If no label is attached, all variants may be considered acceptable in American usage.

Capitalization of proper nouns is indicated.

Syllabication

Since the American system of dividing words by syllables in typed and printed copy involves numerous complicated principles, the simplest thing to do is to follow the divisions made in the dictionary for every entry of more than one syllable. Dictionaries vary, but each one follows its own system consistently.

Pronunciation

Each dictionary explains its own system for describing the sounds of words. Key symbols are given in the preface and at the bottom of pages for convenient reference.

In matters of pronunciation, the editors usually emphasize that they are not the arbiters of correct pronunciation. They merely record what pronunciations are used by educated native speakers. If one or more variants are accepted by a sufficiently large number of persons, these are listed. Each dictionary has its own way of indicating which pronunciation may be more common, if it is possible to make a judgment. In general, however, dictionaries do not label preferred pronunciations beyond suggesting how widespread a pronunciation may be. Any pronunciation that is entered may generally be considered standard unless it is given a special label.

What dictionaries cannot record, of course, is all of the changes in pronunciation tion that occur when words are used in context and subject to variations of pitch and stress. Therefore, what is listed as acceptable is at best only an approximation of the sounds we usually hear in conversation.

Parts of speech and inflected forms

The definitions of words are grouped in terms of the parts of speech. If a word is commonly used in several ways, the forms are given and labeled. A change in the part of speech sometimes requires additional definition. For example, *ideal* is defined separately as an adjective and as a noun.

Forms of the past tense and participles of verbs, the plurals of nouns, and the comparative and superlative forms of adjectives are given when these are irregular in form or spelling.

Etymology

A dictionary's own explanation of its symbols and abbreviations is the key to interpreting the etymological information, which is ordinarily placed either before or after the definitions. If the source of a word is obvious, like *mailbox,* no etymology is given. In addition, the sources of many words are uncertain. If an explanation is speculative or controversial, the word *probably* is often used as a qualifier.

The premium on space in a dictionary requires that all of the above information be condensed into a small space in the most abbreviated terms.

am·mo·nia \ə-'mō-nyə\ *n* [NL, fr. L *sal ammoniacus* sal ammoniac, lit., salt of Ammon, fr. Gk *ammōniakos* of Ammon, fr. *Ammōn* Ammon, Amen, an Egyptian god near one of whose temples it was prepared] **1** : a pungent colorless gaseous alkaline compound of nitrogen and hydrogen NH₃ that is very soluble in water and can easily be condensed to a liquid by cold and pressure **2** : AMMONIA WATER

Webster's New Collegiate Dictionary

Definition

The definitions of a dictionary attempt to cover as many meanings of a word as it commonly carries. The dictionary, however, cannot begin to explore all of the implications of a word or to concern itself with personal connotations. The extended and figurative meanings of words are not listed unless they have become established by frequent use. Dictionaries, therefore, seek as broad a coverage as possible in terms of most common usages. It is left to the users to select a particular meaning in terms of the context in which they find or use a word.

Each dictionary describes its own arrangement of definitions. Some begin with the etymology and earliest meaning and progress historically to current senses of the word. Others begin with the most frequently used definition and proceed in turn to more specialized and rare uses. Two citations will illustrate:

in·spire (in spīr′) *vt.* **-spired′, -spir′ing** [ME. *inspiren* < OFr. *inspirer* < L. *inspirare* < *in-*, in, on + *spirare*, to breathe] **1.** orig., *a)* to breathe or blow upon or into *b)* to infuse (life, etc. *into*) by breathing **2.** to draw (air) into the lungs; inhale **3.** to have an animating effect upon; influence or impel; esp., to stimulate or impel to some creative or effective effort **4.** to cause, guide, communicate, or motivate as by divine or supernatural influence **5.** to arouse or produce (a thought or feeling) *[kindness inspires love]* **6.** to affect with a specified feeling or thought *[to inspire someone with fear]* **7.** to occasion, cause, or produce **8.** to prompt, or cause to be written or said, by influence *[to inspire a rumor]* —*vi.* **1.** to inhale **2.** to give inspiration —**in·spir′a·ble** *adj.* —**in·spir′er** *n.*

Webster's New World Dictionary

in·spire (in spī°r′), *v.*, **-spired, -spir·ing.** —*v.t.* **1.** to infuse an animating, quickening, or exalting influence into. **2.** to produce or arouse (a feeling, thought, etc.): *to inspire confidence.* **3.** to influence or impel: *opposition inspired him to a greater effort.* **4.** to animate, as an influence, feeling, thought, or the like does. **5.** to communicate or suggest by a divine or supernatural influence. **6.** to guide or control by divine influence. **7.** to give rise to, bring about, cause, etc.: *to inspire revolution.* **8.** to take (air, gases, etc.) into the lungs; inhale. **9.** *Archaic.* to infuse (breath, life, etc.) by breathing. **10.** *Archaic.* to breathe into or upon. —*v.i.* **11.** to give inspiration. **12.** to inhale. [ME *inspire(n)* < L *inspīr(āre)* (to) breathe upon or into = *in-* IN-² + *spīrāre* to breathe] —**in·spir′a·ble,** *adj.* —**in·spir·a·tive** (in-spī°r′ə tiv, in′spə rā′tiv), *adj.* —**in·spir′er,** *n.* —**in·spir′ing·ly,** *adv.*

Random House Dictionary

The listings of synonyms and antonyms aid the user in finding a variety of similar or opposite terms. For many words, dictionaries sometimes add a short section in which they discriminate between the meanings of closely related words and illustrate by a quotation or citation.

> **beau·ti·ful** (bū′tə fəl), *adj.* having beauty; delighting the eye; admirable to the taste or the mind. —**beau′ti·ful·ly,** *adv.* —**beau′ti·ful·ness,** *n.*
> —**Syn.** BEAUTIFUL, HANDSOME, LOVELY, PRETTY refer to a pleasing appearance. That is BEAUTIFUL which has perfection of form, color, etc., or noble and spiritual qualities: *a beautiful landscape, girl* (not *man*). HANDSOME often implies stateliness or pleasing proportion and symmetry: *a handsome man.* That which is LOVELY is beautiful but in a warm and endearing way: *a lovely smile.* PRETTY implies a moderate but noticeable beauty, esp. in that which is small or of minor importance: *a pretty child.* —**Ant.** ugly.

American College Dictionary

In a similar way, the oftentimes special meanings of idiomatic phrases are added to a main entry. Thus, to the main entry of the verb *fall* are added phrases like *fall away* (withdraw support), *fall back* (retreat), *fall back on* (depend), *fall behind* (lag), *fall down* (disappoint), *fall for* (be deceived), and *fall in with* (meet by chance).

Labels

The special labels used in dictionaries help the user to understand what limitations particular words and meanings have. Some of these labels indicate usage in terms of region (*British, Southwest*), in terms of time (*archaic, obsolete*), in terms of subject (*philosophy, anatomy*), or in terms of style (*poetic, dialectal, nonstandard*). When the labels involve value judgments, as dialect or colloquial labels frequently do, they may vary from dictionary to dictionary. For controversial items of usage, *The American Heritage Dictionary* offers extended discussions, referring to the opinions of a special usage panel of more than a hundred prominent writers, educators, and public figures, selected by the editors:

> **ain't** (ānt). *Nonstandard.* Contraction of *am not.* Also extended in use to mean *are not, is not, has not,* and *have not.*
> **Usage:** *Ain't,* with few exceptions, is strongly condemned by the Usage Panel when it occurs in writing and speech that is not deliberately colloquial or that does not employ the contraction to provide humor, shock, or other special effect. The first person singular interrogative form *ain't I* (for *am I not* or *amn't I*), considered as a special case, has somewhat more acceptance than *ain't* employed with other pronouns or with nouns. (*Ain't I* has at least the virtue of agreement between *am* and *I.* With other pronouns, or nouns, *ain't* takes the place of *isn't* and *aren't* and sometimes of *hasn't* and *haven't.*) But *ain't I* is unacceptable in writing other than that which is deliberately colloquial, according to 99 per cent of the Panel, and unacceptable in speech to 84 per cent. The example *It ain't likely* is unacceptable to 99 per cent in both writing and speech. *Aren't I* (as a variant of the interrogative *ain't I*) is acceptable in writing to only 27 per cent of the Panel, but approved in speech by 60 per cent. Louis Kronenberger has this typical reaction: "A genteelism, and much worse than *ain't I.*"

The American Heritage Dictionary

Encyclopedic information and illustrations

Dictionaries vary widely in their encyclopedic information, that is, the extent to which they include miscellaneous biographical, historical, scientific, and literary information and foreign words and phrases, as well as pictures, diagrams, tables, and maps. Some dictionaries include information of this kind in the main alphabetical listing; others relegate some of this information to separate sections or exclude it altogether. Many dictionaries also provide basic handbook information on grammar and mechanics.

Types of dictionaries

Collegiate dictionaries

The following list represents a sampling of responsibly edited dictionaries that are kept current between major editions by minor revisions at the time of reprinting:

The American College Dictionary. New York: Random House (not fully revised since 1947).

The American Heritage Dictionary of the English Language. New College Edition. Boston: Houghton Mifflin Co.

Funk & Wagnalls Standard College Dictionary. New York: Harcourt Brace Jovanovich.

The Random House College Dictionary. New York: Random House.

Webster's New Collegiate Dictionary. Eighth Edition. Springfield, Mass.: G. & C. Merriam Co.

Webster's New World Dictionary of the American Language. Second College Edition. New York and Cleveland: Collins, William and World Publishing Co.

Unabridged dictionaries

Besides the greater number of entries in an unabridged dictionary, one of its significant advantanges is the fuller use of quotations or phrases to support particular meanings and usages. These dictionaries also vary in the amount of encyclopedic information they include.

One or more of the following unabridged dictionaries will be found in most public or college libraries:

Funk & Wagnalls New "Standard" Dictionary of the English Language
The Random House Dictionary of the English Language
Webster's New Twentieth Century Dictionary
Webster's Third New International Dictionary

The Century Dictionary: An Encyclopedic Lexicon of the English Language. 12 vols.

Since *The Century Dictionary* has not been revised in more than sixty-five years, many of its entries are out-of-date. It is not completely useless, however. For words of historical rather than current interest, the dictionary still provides a wealth of information.

Scholarly dictionaries

Scholarly dictionaries are primarily for students of the English language who are interested in the progressive history of meanings and in the various forms that English words have had in the past. One of the monumental projects of dictionary making in any language is *The Oxford English Dictionary* in twelve volumes and one supplement, originally published in ten volumes under the title *A New English Dictionary on Historical Principles.* Thus, it is familiarly referred to as the *OED* or the *NED*, and at times as *Murray's Dictionary*, because the name of Sir James Murray, the general editor, appeared prominently on the spine of the original volumes.

The project, which was first conceived as early as 1850, was in motion by 1879, when preparation in its present form began. The first volume appeared in 1884; the last, in 1928. The *Supplement and Bibliography* was issued in 1933, and work on a three-volume second supplement was in progress in the 1970s. The exhaustive entries in this dictionary are based on more than five million quotations, contributed by hundreds of teachers and scholars in Great Britain and America. In 1971, Oxford University Press issued *The Compact Edition of the Oxford English Dictionary*, in two volumes; the complete text of the thirteen volumes is included, reproduced micrographically. The *OED* is also available in three abridgments: a two-volume edition entitled *The Shorter Oxford English Dictionary*, a large one-volume edition called *The Oxford Universal Dictionary on Historical Principles*, and an essentially different one-volume, updated edition entitled *The Concise Oxford Dictionary of Current English.*

A comparable historical study of words as they have been used in the United States is *A Dictionary of American English on Historical Principles* in four volumes (1938-1944), edited by Sir William Craigie and J. R. Hulbert. Mitford Mathews' *A Dictionary of Americanisms* in two volumes (1951) adds further material to the total body of knowledge about English and American words. A one-volume edition appeared in 1956.

Besides these dictionaries for specialists, there are various other dictionaries that define words in Old English, Middle English, and Early Modern English. A number of dialect dictionaries also exist. A lengthy list of these by period is included in *A Bibliography of Writings on the English Language from the Beginning of Printing to the End of 1922* by Arthur G. Kennedy (1967). More recent additions may be found in the bibliography of *Readings in American Dialectology*, eds. Harold B. Allen and Gary Underwood (1971).

In addition to the standard dictionaries, innumerable other volumes have been compiled on almost any specialty that you can think of. Such dictionaries, of course, provide more thorough coverage than any general dictionary of the language is able to. A selection of those that are especially helpful to the reader and writer of English is listed below:

DICTIONARIES OF USAGE

Bryant, Margaret M. *Current American Usage* (1969).

Evans, Bergen, and Cornelia Evans. *A Dictionary of Contemporary American Usage* (1965).

Follett, Wilson. *Modern American Usage: A Guide* (1966).

Fowler, H. W. *A Dictionary of Modern English Usage* (2nd ed. rev., 1965).

Hornby, Albert S. *Guide to Patterns and Usage in English* (2nd ed., 1975).

Morris, William, and Mary Morris. *Harper Dictionary of Contemporary Usage* (1975).

Nicholson, Margaret. *A Dictionary of American-English Usage* (1957). Based on Fowler's *Modern English Usage.*

Usage dictionaries are not necessarily descriptive in the sense that other dictionaries are. A usage dictionary may reflect its author's bias, either conservative or liberal. Fowler's well-known work can hardly be considered of current use unless one deliberately wants to emulate Fowler's patrician views.

DICTIONARIES OF SYNONYMS, ANTONYMS, ACRONYMS, AND ABBREVIATIONS

Chapman, Robert L. *Roget's International Thesaurus* (4th ed., 1977).

Crowley, Ellen T. *New Acronyms, Initialisms, and Abbreviations: 1976 Supplement to Acronyms, Initialisms, and Abbreviations Dictionary* (5th ed.)

Hayakawa, S. I. *Modern Guide to Synonyms and Related Words* (1968).

Kay, Mairé Weir. *Webster's Collegiate Thesaurus* (1976).

Spillner, Paul. *World Guide to Abbreviations* (2nd ed., 1970–1973).

Webster's New Dictionary of Synonyms (1968).

DICTIONARIES OF ETYMOLOGIES

Klein, Ernest. *A Comprehensive Etymological Dictionary of the English Language.* 2 vols. (1966–1967).

Morris Dictionary of Word and Phrase Origins (1977).

Onions, C. T. *The Oxford Dictionary of English Etymology* (1966).

Partridge, Eric. *Origins: A Short Etymological Dictionary of Modern English* (1966).

Shipley, Joseph T. *Dictionary of Word Origins* (1945, repr. 1967).

DICTIONARIES OF SLANG, IDIOMS, AND CLICHÉS

Freeman, William. *A Concise Dictionary of English Idioms* (3rd ed., 1973).

Makkai, Adam. *A Dictionary of American Idioms* (rev. ed., 1975).

Phythian, Brian A. *A Concise Dictionary of English Slang and Colloquialisms* (2nd ed., 1976)

Wentworth, Harold, and Stuart B. Flexner. *Dictionary of American Slang* (2nd ed., 1975).

Wood, Frederick T. *English Prepositional Idioms* (1967).

——. *English Verbal Idioms* (1964).

DICTIONARIES OF FOREIGN AND DIFFICULT TERMS

Byrne, Josefa Heifetz. *Mrs. Byrne's Dictionary of Unusual, Obscure, and Preposterous Words* (1974).

Guinagh, Kevin. *Dictionary of Foreign Phrases and Abbreviations* (2nd ed., 1972).

Mawson, C. O. Sylvester, and Charles Berlitz. *Dictionary of Foreign Terms* (2nd ed., 1975).

Pei, Mario, and Salvatore Ramondino. *Dictionary of Foreign Terms* (1974).

Trench, Richard C. *Dictionary of Obsolete English* (1958).

Projects

1. Check a dictionary for variant spellings for the following words. Determine whether your dictionary indicates which is the preferred form: *appraise, blond, cater-cornered, catsup, choosy, doughnut, Eskimo, good-by, jujitsu, medieval, OK* (v), *T-shirt*.

2. Consult a dictionary to see what help you can get in pronouncing the following words: *Beaujolais, chiaroscuro, chic, Derby, eczema, foyer, Gloucester, Juan de Fuca, Luichow Peninsula, Magdalene College, phthisis, Poughkeepsie, quay, Septuagint, Vichy, Worcestershire sauce*.

3. Indicate what usage labels are given to the following words in your dictionary. If no label is given, mark the word "unqualified": *chutzpah, fain, roughneck, stoop* [porch], *tote, unto, wing* (n), *yore*.

4. From whose names have the following words been derived: *begonia, boycott, chauvinism, dahlia, dun* (v), *dunce, quixotic, sadism?*

5. Indicate the differences in meaning between the following pairs:

allude, elude	flaunt, flout
bloc, block	human, humane
canvas, canvass	ingenious, ingenuous
climactic, climatic	prescribe, proscribe
elicit, illicit	waive, wave

6. Indicate the difference in meaning between the capitalized forms of the following words and lower-case forms given here: *apocalypse, catholic, communist, democrat, dunker, epiphany, friend, genesis, jersey, passion, republican*.

7. Choose one or more antonyms for the following words: *delicate, devout, faithful, free, naive, romantic, solemn, urban*.

8. Choose two or more synonyms for the following words: *coarse, excessive, hate, loud, nasty, prevent, remiss, small*.

9. Find the derivations of the following terms: *Canary Islands, cocktail, crisscross, eureka, olympian, paddywhack, passion, riff-raff*.

10. Listed below are eight words given as meanings of the word *respond:*

to answer   to counter   to react   to reply
to chant   to match   to rejoin   to rise

Look up the definitions of each of these words and find additional synonyms and variants. Then look up the definitions of those synonyms, continuing the investigation until you come to a dead end or find words that clearly indicate that you have reached the full range of the word's meaning. For instance, *to rise* in the sense of *rebel* is a kind of responding and should be included, but *rise* in the sense of *ascend* indicates that this meaning belongs to another word cluster. The words you accumulate are called a *semantic cluster.*

A glossary of usage and linguistic terms

a, an, the The old school rule that says, "Use *a* before consonant sounds and *an* before vowel sounds" is still the surest guide to the use of *a* and *an*: *a sweater, a jacket, an onion, an African.* The distinction, however, is made on *sound*, not spelling. In certain contexts, the degree of stress or the degree of elision may alter the choice of *a* or *an*. Certain speakers say *a history course,* but *an historical event; a humiliating experience,* but *an humble man.* Words like *usury* and *eugenics* that are spelled with beginning vowels are actually pronounced with consonant sounds.

Both *a* and *an* come from an Old English word meaning *one* and are still used only with singular nouns. *The* was originally a form of the Old English demonstrative pronoun; it combines with both singular and plural words. In current usage, *the* still retains its demonstrative quality. Compare *the house,* for example, with *any house. A* and *an* are called indefinite articles; *the* is a definite article.

above, below *Above* is a standard way of referring to material that precedes a particular passage on a printed page. *Below* is the counterterm for something that follows: *The diagram above* [or *below*] *shows population growth in terms of individual countries.*

accept, except Verbs easily confused. *Accept* means "to receive." *Except,* derived from the preposition, means "to take or leave out."

He *accepted* the award.
Seniors were *excepted* from the regulation.

accusative case A term for the objective case, derived from Latin and used in the study of Old English and other Indo-European languages.

Words easily confused. *Affect* as a verb means "to influence": *His ideas affected future generations. Effect* as a verb means "to bring something about": *We will see if we can effect a workable plan.* The noun usage is almost always *ef-*

fect, meaning "result": *The effect of the storm was disastrous. Affect* is used as a noun by psychologists, but the usage has not become common.

affix   A covering term for any addition to the root of a word to form a new word. It includes prefixes (added before the base), suffixes (added after the base), infixes (added within the base), and reduplication (repeating part of the base form). Infixes and reduplication are not characteristic of Modern English words.

aggravate   *Aggravate* means "to intensify" or "to make worse": *The rigid attitude of the President only aggravated the political situation.* In an extended, informal sense, *aggravate* means "to annoy": *The people were aggravated by the President's manner.*

ain't   Still a highly controversial usage. Generally characteristic of nonstandard speech, but clearly used by educated speakers in an effort to be casual or funny, particularly in tag questions like *ain't I?* The word is inappropriate in expository prose unless dialogue is a part of the writing.

almost, most   *See* **most.**

alot, a lot   Although pronounced as one word, *a lot* is written as two words.

already, all ready   Forms sometimes confused. *Already* is an adverb meaning "prior to some designated time": *He has already gone. All ready* is an adjective phrase expressing preparedness: *We're all ready to start.*

alright, all right   *Alright* has not yet been fully established as an acceptable substitute for *all right.* Dictionaries reflect the divided usage. *Webster's New Collegiate* lists it without a usage label; *New World,* 2nd ed., identifies it as a disputed spelling; *Random House* labels it as nonstandard.

although, though   *See* **though.**

alumnus, alumna   The endings of these Latin borrowings show that *alumnus* pertains to a male graduate and *alumna* to a female graduate. *Alumnus* and its plural *alumni* are now commonly used to refer to anyone, either male or female, who attended or graduated from a school.

amidst, amongst   Acceptable variants of *amid* and *among,* but words that clearly sound like poetic diction now outmoded.

among, between   *See* **between.**

amount of, number of   Many writers make a careful distinction between the use of *amount of* with mass nouns expressing bulk and the use of *number of* with count nouns expressing a collection of particulars: *a small amount of pepper, a large number of boxes.* The use of *amount of* with count nouns, however, is increasingly common in speech: *The amount of people who came in was amazing.*

anyplace, anywhere   Standard usage no longer makes a distinction between the two, but *anyplace* has only recently established itself as an acceptable form. It is therefore subject to the usual lingering prejudice against new usages. *Anyplace* tends to be less formal than *anywhere,* and the equivalent term *someplace* tends to be less formal than *somewhere. See also* **everyplace, everywhere.**

anywheres, somewheres   Dialectal forms of *anywhere* and *somewhere.*

apt, liable, likely   *See* **liable.**

as   In speech, *as* has become a general utility word. When a word of this kind is made to serve many purposes, it loses its capacity to make fine distinctions of meaning. Writers therefore need to be aware of the extended and sometimes nonstandard uses of the word:

1. Because it expresses manner, time, and cause, *as* substitutes for *when, while, since,* and *because.* Those words might preferably be used to emphasize cause or time:

Lacking emphasis: As we are the only two who enrolled, the class has to be dropped.
More emphasis: Because we are the only two who enrolled, the class has to be dropped.

2. *As* acts as an obviously folksy substi-

tute for *who, that,* and *whether: Anybody as tries can succeed; I am not sure as I know; I don't know as I can go.*

Among the many other uses of *as,* several are particularly important:

As a preposition, meaning "in the function or part of": He was excellent as Romeo.
As a conjunction expressing simultaneous action: As I was leaving, visitors arrived.
As an adverb in comparisons, meaning "equally": as stately as a steeple.

as . . . as, so . . . as Traditionally, *as . . . as* makes a positive comparison; *so . . . as* is used with a negative comparison: *He is as skillful as John; he is not so skillful as Don.* In current usage, *as . . . as* is acceptable for both purposes.

as, like *See* **like.**

as well as, while Constructions with *as well as* invite ambiguity. *Lily sang the role as well as Joan* means either that the singing of one soprano is as good as that of the other or simply that they both sang a particular part. Rephrasing resolves the ambiguity:

Lily sang the role equally as well as Joan.
Lily and Joan sang the role equally well.
Lily sang the role; Joan did too.
Both Lily and Joan sang the role.

While may express concession or time. The ambiguity that results can be resolved by substituting other words:

Ambiguous: While the grass dies, the weeds flourish.
Concession expressed: Even though the grass dies, the weeds flourish.
Time expressed: At the same time that the grass dies, the weeds flourish.

awake, awaken *See* **wake.**

awful, awfully *Awful* is seldom used in the sense of "inspiring awe or reverence." It is now a colloquial synonym for "very bad" or "disagreeable": *an awful book, an awful person. Awfully* is used as an intensifier in expressions like *awfully good* or *awfully pretty.* Both usages are highly informal, common in speech but for the most part inappropriate in formal prose.

awhile, a while Two separate but acceptable usages. *Awhile* is an adverb: *we waited awhile,* which might also be phrased *we waited for a while.* In the second sentence, *while* is used as a noun.

bad, badly The grammar of the language calls for a predicate adjective after sense verbs. Thus, the choice between the adjective *bad* and the adverb *badly* after these special verbs is clear: *I feel bad, The corn tastes bad,* but *The saw cuts badly.* Speech, however, tends to follow the usual pattern of making adverbs modify verbs: *I feel badly, The corn tastes badly.* Even though usage is divided, a careful writer will observe the grammatical distinction. *Badly* in the sense of "very much" is colloquial: *I need a rest badly.*

barely *See* **hardly.**

because of *See* **due to.**

being as, being that Both nonstandard phrases for *since* or *because:*

Nonstandard: Being as I am here, I'll eat dinner.
Standard: Since I am here, I'll eat dinner.

below *See* **above.**

beside, besides Both *beside* and *besides* act as prepositions, but their meanings are different:

The runner-up stood beside the winner. [at the side of]
There was a runner-up trophy besides the winning trophy. [in addition to]

Besides in the same sense of "in addition to" is also used as an adverb: *Campaigning is fun besides.*

better *See* **had better.**

between, among *Between* is ordinarily used to express a relation between two things: *between you and me, between France and England. Among* is used to express a relation involving more than two: *among the nations, among the fish.* However, *between* is also used to express an interrelation between several things when they are considered individually rather than as a group:

We worked between Boston, New York, and Chicago.

There is an obvious difference between the three composers.

bi-, semi-   *Bi-* is a prefix that usually means "multiplied by two." *Semi-* is a prefix that means "divided by two." But *bi-* is not consistently used. *Bimonthly* means occurring every two months and *biennial* means every two years, but *biannual* means occurring twice a year. Confusion can be avoided by substituting *semiannual* for *biannual*.

bust, busted, burst   *Bust* was originally a dialectal variant of *burst*. Its principal parts are *bust, busted, busted. Burst,* the standard form, is invariable: *burst, burst, burst. Bust* has proved to be an adaptable word; it is used as a noun, adjective, or verb—all with different meanings:

The show was a bust. [failure]
I am busted. [without money]
I busted out. [escaped]
I busted chemistry. [failed]

These uses, of course, are either slang or strictly informal.

but that, but what   Both constructions are not considered standard, occurring usually in negative statements of doubt or concern:

I am not certain but that he is guilty.
I don't doubt but what he was disappointed.

In either sentence, a simple *that* serves just as well.

can, may   Formal usage observes a distinction between the two words—*can* expressing ability or power (*I can do it*) and *may* expressing permission or chance (*May I do it? I may do it*). Speakers tend to use *can* for both meanings, depending on tone of voice to convey the idea of request.

cannot, can not   Both forms are acceptable. If writing is published, the choice between them is usually the editor's. The one-word form is increasingly preferred.

can't help but   An acceptable American idiom: *I can't help but sympathize with him.* Many writers, however, still prefer the British usage: *I can't help sympathizing with him.*

censor, censure   Two verbs easily confused because they are often pronounced very much alike. *Censor* means "to examine in order to delete or suppress objectionable material." *Censure* means "to criticize or blame." *Censure* is a much more general term than *censor*.

center around, center about   A common idiom, even in writing, but one that easily offends some people who insist that the expression is illogical. Things ordinarily revolve around a center, not the opposite.

Informal: Our discussion was centered around the idea of civil disobedience.
Alternatives: Our discussion was centered on . . .

Our discussion focused upon . . .

cognates   Words in different languages that are related to one another because of their common ancestry, thus Modern English *sister*; German, *schwester*; Latin, *soror*; French, *soeur*; Italian, *suor*; Sanskrit, *svasar*; and Russian, *sestra*—all from Indo-European **swesor.* (A starred form is used to indicate a hypothetical form reconstructed on the basis of sound change or at times to identify an unacceptable or ungrammatical construction.)

common   *See* **mutual.**

compare, contrast   Although *contrast* means "to show differences," *compare* may mean "to consider in such a way as to show likenesses and differences." Joining the two terms, as professors often do on examinations, is a way of emphasizing that two things should be done: *Compare and contrast Pope's style and Wordsworth's style.*

compare to, compare with *Compare to* is used to emphasize the resemblance between two things: *He compared the surface of the pond to a mirror. Compare with* is used to show relative values, whether they are alike or different: *He compared the use of alcohol with the use of drugs.* The distinction is difficult to hold to, particularly since either *to* or *with* is used with the past participle: *Compared with [to] any other novel, this one is sensational.*

complected The awkwardness of the standard form *complexioned,* as in *dark-complexioned,* no doubt accounts for the currency of the colloquial form *dark complected.* The usage is probably better evaded than debated by saying *Her complexion was dark.*

consensus of opinion Now an idiomatic and acceptable phrase, even though it is redundant. *Consensus* means "a general harmony of opinion."

contact Widely used as a verb to mean "to get in touch with" without reference to a specific means of communication: *Mr. Smith should be contacted.* Many people object to the usage as a brand of commercial jargon. Without doubt, the word has already been disassociated from the world of salesmanship so that more and more it can be freely used without censure.

continual, continuous A useful distinction exists between the two words, although it is not always observed. *Continual* refers to happenings that recur with sufficient frequency to be considered a series: *There has been continual warfare for the last one hundred years. Continuous* refers to something that occurs without interruption: *My electric clock has a continuous hum.* Unfortunately, many established writers use the words synonymously.

contractions Contractions are abbreviated forms in writing that reflect speech habits: *I'm* for *I am; would've* for *would have; John's been sick* for *John has been sick.* Because contractions reflect the informality of speech, they are appropriate in writing when the situation and occasion are informal enough to justify them. Otherwise, they are out of place. Writers who are sensitive to the rhythm of their prose treat the use of contractions flexibly.

contrast *See* **compare.**

could of, would of *See* **of.**

couple In an exact sense, *couple* means "two." In speech, however, it is loosely used to mean "several": *a couple of minutes ago.* The difference in meaning may cause a writer to choose "two" if he needs to be absolutely precise.

credible, creditable, credulous Three words sufficiently similar in sound that they are confused in usage. *Credible* means "capable of being believed": *His story was credible. Creditable* means "worthy of recognition": *His writing is creditable. Credulous* means "gullible, too willing to believe without evidence": *Children are often credulous.*

dative A term borrowed from Latin to apply to one of the inflected cases in Old and Middle English and other Indo-European languages. The case of the indirect object in Modern English, formerly the dative case, is identical in form with the objective case (they gave *me* the money). The idea of the dative is now expressed by prepositional phrases: *to him, for her.*

declension A system of showing nouns, pronouns, and adjectives in all of their inflectional varieties. Since nouns and adjectives in Modern English have so few changes, declension is useful mainly in presenting the forms of the pronoun (see p. 471).

different from, different than *Different from* has traditionally been the preferred form in America; however, *different than,* the British usage, has become more and more common and acceptable in this country because it avoids the piling up of words that the use of *different from* sometimes requires. Two groups of sentences illustrate:

The spirit of Franz Hals's painting is considerably different from that of Rembrandt's.

The spirit of Franz Hals's painting is considerably different than Rembrandt's.

It's different from what you think.
It's different than you think.

digraph   A group of two letters representing a single speech sound (*ea* in *head*, *th* in *both*). The word is often confused with a ligature, which in printing is a character that combines two or more letters (Æēlfric), or with a diphthong, which is a combination of vowel sounds pronounced as one.

dinner, supper   Inasmuch as *dinner* is defined as the main meal of the day and *supper* as the evening meal, *dinner* may be substituted for *supper* or, of course, refer to the noon meal if that is the principal meal.

discreet, discrete   Words easily confused. *Discreet* means "prudent" or "careful": *She was discreet in what she said. Discrete* means "separate" or "discontinuous": *The naval research laboratory was a discrete unit of the campus.*

disinterested, uninterested   Two words that allow a useful discrimination of meaning, but now used interchangeably to mean "having no interest." *Disinterested,* however, is still often used to mean "impartial": *What the dispute needs is a disinterested mediator.* The person who knows the difference between *uninterested* and *disinterested* will understand such a sentence; the uninformed will remain confused.

due to, because of   Although both of these phrases are now used as prepositions in both speech and writing, it is useful to know the traditional distinction which many educated people still observe. They classify *due to* as an adjective and use it following the verb *to be: His success was due to years of hard work.* They reserve *because of* for prepositional phrases used as adverbs: *He was recognized because of his hard work.* Since the choice depends on some knowledge of grammar, it is easy to see why the distinction has been blurred.

effect   *See* **affect.**

e.g.   *See* **viz.**

enthuse, enthused   A back-formation from *enthusiasm,* giving rise also to the participial form *enthused.* Characteristically, back-formations tend to be scorned until their usage is so established that no one remembers why scorn was necessary. Our reactions to *peddle* and *reminisce,* also scorned at one time as back-formations, are now completely neutral. *Enthuse* and *enthused* are now widely used, but they are not yet so firmly established in standard English as to find complete acceptance.

-ese   A suffix used to refer to a language or literary style, used in words coined especially to designate special kinds of jargon: *officialese, commercialese, journalese.*

etc.   Abbreviation for the Latin phrase *et cetera,* meaning "and other things." To say "and *et cetera*" is to show ignorance of the Latin. Although *etc.* sometimes serves a useful purpose in technical writing to indicate an indefinite list of items, it is a lazy substitute in other kinds of prose for a fairly selective list. If the list is an unduly long one, the English words *and so forth* and *and so on* serve better than the Latin.

ever so often, every so often   Often pronounced alike, but their meanings are different. *Ever so often* means "very often": *We go to the theater ever so often. Every so often* means "now and then": *He writes a note every so often.*

everyplace, everywhere   Traditionally, *everywhere* has been the preferred form, but *everyplace* is now so commonly used that it must be recognized as standard English. *Everyplace* continues to be more informal than *everywhere. See also* **anyplace, anywhere.**

except   *See* **accept.**

expect   Colloquial usage in the sense of "suppose": *I expect he'll be coming soon.* In standard usage, *expect* means "to anticipate something": *I expect him soon.*

expletive   A general term in grammar meaning "filler." It is most commonly used to refer to *it* and *there* when they are used to fill in the subject position as a means of moving the subject ahead: *There was no reason to stay. It was his responsibility to call.* The term *expletive* also means an exclamatory word, especially a profane one.

farther, further   Originally, *farther* was a variant of the adverb *further;* the comparative form of the adjective *far* was *farrer.* In time, *farther* displaced *farrer* and became associated with distance: *Portland is farther from here than Vancouver. Further* expressed other ideas of advancement: *He went further in school than Al.* Current usage has blurred the former distinction. Perhaps the most accurate statement that can be made is that *further* is now a variant of *farther* and has become the predominant form. The difference between them is mainly a matter of regional variation.

faze   In most dictionaries, *faze* still carries some kind of usage label, either colloquial or informal. Since synonyms like *discomfit, disconcert, daunt, perturb,* and *abash* all seem to be much more formal in tone than *faze,* it is understandable why the word is being more and more used in both speaking and writing.

fewer, less   *Fewer* is used with count nouns expressing a collection of particulars, and *less* with abstract nouns and mass nouns expressing bulk: *fewer errors, less excitement, less salt.* However, *less* is popularly used with count nouns, so that it is not uncommon to hear expressions like *less voters* and *less words.* Careful writers tend to make a distinction between the two forms.

field   A standard and acceptable word in the language, but frequently overused, so that it ends up as deadwood in the sentence:

Deadwood: I have increased in the field of understanding.
Rephrased: I have increased in understanding.

flaunt, flout   Words easily confused.

Flaunt means "to make a showy display": *He flaunted his defiant attitude. Flout* means "to show scorn for": *He flouted conventional manners.*

folks   The formal plural of *folk* is *folk. Folks* is a popular plural, often used informally to refer to relatives.

former, latter   *The former* and *the latter* are relatively formal ways of referring to two things already mentioned. For a series of more than two, *first* and *last* are the appropriate terms for referring to the beginning and end.

freshman, freshmen   Although *freshmen* is the plural form of *freshman,* only *freshman* is used as the adjective form: *a Freshman theme, a Freshman meeting.*

further   See **farther.**

gender   Although gender is ordinarily associated with sex, grammatical gender has no necessary connection with it. In Old English, the word for *queen* was feminine, the word for *womanhood* masculine, and the word for *wife* neuter. Modern English nouns show no grammatical gender except for a few words referring to men that also have a corresponding feminine form in *-ess: host, hostess; actor, actress; prince, princess.*

Modern English may be said to follow natural gender in choosing pronouns to refer to nouns: *he* for *man* and *she* for *woman.* The exceptions are conventional: the tendency to refer to nature, boats, and countries as *she* or to refer to an animal or a baby as *it* when the sex is unknown.

get   One of the utility words of the language which has a variety of idiomatic uses, both standard and colloquial. *The Random House Dictionary*, College Edition, lists fifty-one subheadings under the word. Of particular interest is the use of *get* as an auxiliary verb: *I get to go soon,* signifying future; *I have got to finish,* emphatic use; *I got to thinking,* progressive implication; *I got caught,* passive sense. In questions, *got* serves as a filler: *What have you got to* *say?* The use of *got* by itself in sentences like *You got good sense* is colloquial. A writer would include *have: You've got good sense* or *You have good sense.*

go and   See **try and.**

good, well   Interchangeable words in certain constructions when they are both adjectives meaning "in a sound state of health." *I feel good* means the same as *I feel well.* But *She is well* is quite different from *She is good.* When *well* is an adverb (*She plays the flute well*), the substitution of *good* is nonstandard.

good and, good many   Colloquial uses to mean "exceedingly": *I was good and mad. I had a good many complaints.*

got, gotten   Past participles of *get. Gotten* is acceptable as an alternative to *got. Got* is normally used when the word means "have" or "possess." In other senses, the choice between *got* and *gotten* is largely a matter of rhythmic preference: The flowers *were gotten* this morning.

grapheme   A term sometimes used to differentiate the letters of the writing system from the phonemes of the language. One phoneme may be represented by several graphemes. Thus the phoneme /f/ appears as *f* in *fox,* as *ff* in *muffin,* as *gh* in *rough,* and as *ph* in *physics.*

had better, had best, you'd better   All acceptable idioms in standard English for *should* or *ought: You had [you'd] better report to the man in charge. I had best do it myself.* Any further shortening is strictly colloquial: *You better go.*

had of   A pronunciation spelling of *had've.* Either form is nonstandard.

Nonstandard: I wish I had of gone.
Standard: I wish I had gone.

had ought, hadn't ought   Nonstandard forms. *Ought* is an obsolete participle of the verb *owe.* Today it is used only as an invariable form, combined with infinitives: *I ought to speak up. He ought to be elected.*

half a, half an, a half, a half a   The first three are acceptable variants: *He worked half a day. We chatted for half an hour. I will take a half dozen. A half a* (*a half a piece*) is colloquial.

hanged, hung   When *hang* means "to execute," *hanged* is the preferred past form and past participle: *He was hanged at 10:00 A.M.* In other senses of "suspend," *hung* is used: *The decorator hung the picture.*

hardly, barely, scarcely   Since the meaning of all three adverbs is "not quite," the negative does not need to be re-expressed. Phrases such as *hardly didn't know* and *scarcely never went* are considered nonstandard.

have got   See **get.**

help but   See **can't help but.**

he/she, his/her   *He* and *his* have traditionally been used in a generic sense to refer to both males and females. The change of women's status during the 1970s focused attention on a usage that seems to deprive women of equal status by including them anonymously with the other sex. As a result, many writers and speakers now consciously try to avoid the generic *he.* The common way to solve the problem is to use *he or she.* This is unmistakable in meaning, but represents a clumsy construction that detracts from the total meaning by calling attention to itself. In some contexts it even produces unintended humor. Therefore, it is often better to reword a sentence:

Often unacceptable: If anybody expresses his opinion, he will be penalized.
Awkward: If anybody expresses his or her opinion, he or she will be penalized.
Rephrased: If any of us express an opinion, we will be penalized.
Rephrased: If any of you expresses an opinion, you will be penalized.
Rephrased: If any of them express an opinion, they will be penalized.
Rephrased: Anybody who expresses an opinion will be penalized.

Among the ways to avoid the generic *he* are first person plural, second person singular or plural, or third person plural—whichever is most appropriate to the sense and the context. A sentence can usually also be rephrased in a more impersonal way, as in the last rephrasing. *See also* **man, person.**

heteronym, homograph   Words of the same language that have identical written forms but different pronunciations and meaning: *dove* (the bird), *dove* (variant of *dived*); to shed a *tear,* to *tear* a page.

homonym   Words of the same language that have identical spelling and pronunciation but different meanings: *pool* of water, play *pool*; pole, Pole. *Homonym* is sometimes defined to include both homophones and homographs.

homophone   Words of the same language that sound alike but have different spellings and different meanings. They are a common source of puns and of spelling errors: *bear, bare; meat, meet; to, two, too; they're, their; threw, through. See* 12B.

hopefully   Now used frequently in the sense of "it is hoped that" (*Hopefully, we'll win*) rather than in the sense of "in a hopeful manner" (*I began hopefully*). Despite the strong objections the first usage generates among some individuals, most readers are now unaware that there is a "hopefully problem." English now seems to have adopted an adverbial usage, equivalent to the German *hoffentlich,* which is used as a sentence modifier.

human, humans   Now acceptably used as nouns, although *human beings, people,* and *persons* seem to predominate in formal writing as alternate ways of expression.

hung   *See* **hanged.**

i.e.   *See* **viz.**

if, whether   After verbs like *ask, doubt, know, remember, see,* and *wonder,* the two conjunctions are used interchangeably: *I'll see if [whether] I can go. I wonder if [whether] it'll rain.* If an alternative is expressed, *whether* is the preferred form in standard usage: *I don't know whether you can use the typewriter or not.*

imply, infer   The traditional distinction between the two words is worth preserving. *Imply* is concerned with sending out a suggestion; *infer,* with receiving it or drawing it out: *Your actions implied a sense of doubt. I inferred a sense of doubt from your actions.* Nevertheless, in practice, the distinction is fading. *Infer* is often used in the sense of *imply: I presume that anarchy was not inferred by your remarks.*

incredible, incredulous   Words easily confused. *Incredible* means "unbelievable": *It was an incredible feat of strength. Incredulous* means "skeptical": *He looked at me with an incredulous smile.*

ingenious, ingenuous   Two words easily confused. *Ingenious* means "clever" or "resourceful": *an ingenious composer. Ingenuous* means "frank" or "straightforward": *an ingenuous remark.*

in regards to, with regards to   Nonstandard forms for the standard phrases *in regard to* and *with regard to.*

inside of, outside of   When used as prepositional phrases, the *of* can be dispensed with: *We walked inside [of] the vault. We lived outside [of] the city.* When *inside* and *outside* are used as nouns, the *of* is necessary: *The inside of* [outside of] *the door is scratched.*

intent, intention   Both mean "determination to do something." *Intent* is the more formal and restricted term, often legal in its implications: *with intent to kill. Intention* is a more general, all-purpose word: *His intentions were good.*

in-, un-, il-, im-   All negative prefixes, but not often used interchangeably. Dictionaries indicate which words use *in-* (*incoherent, inartistic*), *un-* (*unlikely, unnecessary*), *il-* (*illiterate, illegitimate*), and *im-* (*immoral, impractical*). *In-* sometimes appears to mean "not" when it is actually an intensifier, for example, *invaluable* (very valuable) or *inflammable* (very flammable).

invite   As a shortened form of *invitation,* pronounced with the accent on the first syllable, *invite* is dialectal: *We got an invite to the party.*

irregardless A nonstandard variant of *regardless*. Since *-less* expresses the negative idea, the negative prefix *ir-* is unnecessary.

is when, is where *When* and *where* may sometimes introduce noun clauses after the verb *to be: The big decision is when we should start.* If the speaker is defining, however, a *when* clause or *where* clause usually supplies an example instead of a definition.

Awkward: A libation is when wine is spilled in honor of the deity.
Rephrased: A libation is an act of spilling wine in honor of the deity.
Awkward: The chancel of a church is where the clergy and the choir are.
Rephrased: The chancel of a church is that part reserved for the clergy and the choir.

its, it's Two forms frequently confused. *Its* is the possessive form of *it. It's* is a contraction of *it is.* The two are not interchangeable.

judgment, judgement *Judgement* is a British spelling; *judgment,* the common American form.

kind of, sort of Strictly colloquial when used as adverbs to mean "rather" or "somewhat":

Colloquial: He was kind of [kinda] peeved at what I said.
Standard: He was rather peeved at what I said.

laid, lain *See* **lie.**
latter *See* **former.**
lay *See* **lie.**
lead, led The verb *lead* (to conduct) and the noun *lead* (a metal) are spelled alike but pronounced differently (homographs). *Led,* the past tense and participle of the verb, rhymes with the metal. The confusion often leads to the misspelling of one of the forms.

leave, let Easily confused because their meanings overlap. When *leave* clearly means "depart" and *let* means "allow," no confusion occurs. But when both words mean "permit to remain," the choice between the two is difficult. Both *Leave me alone* and *Let me alone* are accepted as standard usage.

In many instances, *let* is followed by an infinitive: *Let the rope go. Let it stay.* In these constructions, *leave* cannot substitute.

lend, loan For a period of time, *lend* was a verb only and *loan* a noun only. *Loan,* however, has come to be used as a verb. Today, the two words are used interchangeably as verbs. *Loan* remains the only noun.

less *See* **fewer.**

lest A conjunction meaning "for fear that": *The government took unusual precautions lest the peace negotiations be endangered.* Because *lest* is very often followed by a verb in the subjunctive, it has become associated with formal expression, even a slightly archaic tone.

let's Since *let's* is a contraction of *let us,* it should not be used with *us:*

Colloquial: Let's us get together for lunch.
Standard: Let's get together for lunch.

liable, likely, apt *Likely* implies strong probability that something will happen: *It is likely to snow.* In speech, *liable* and *apt* might substitute in the same sentence. In its own right, *liable* implies susceptibility to something unpleasant (*The machine is liable to error*) or, in a legal sense, responsibility for damages (*He is liable for the damage*). *Apt,* in its own right, implies a natural tendency or inclination (*She is apt in sports*).

lie, lay Words easily confused because their principal parts overlap: *lie, lay, lain* (an intransitive verb meaning "to recline") and *lay, laid, laid* (a transitive verb meaning "to place"):

I lay down an hour ago.

If I lay the key on the table, will you pick
it up?
The hen laid an egg.

The past tense of *lie* is the source of most of
the trouble. Note that the principal parts of
lie, "to tell an untruth," are *lie, lied, lied.*

lighted, lit Both acceptable past tense
and participial forms of *light*. Because
lighted is a two-syllable word, it is usually
preferred in combinations like a *beautifully lighted tree* or *could have been
lighted earlier.*

like In informal speech, *like* has become a popular, all-purpose word, often
merely serving as a filler in almost any position. In many instances, it seems to be a
loose substitute for "for example":

Colloquial: Like our first lesson, most of us
didn't know the first thing about poetry.
Standard rephrasing: During our first lesson, for example, most of us didn't know
the first thing about poetry.

Colloquial: When you have your first introduction, they should like give meanings.
Standard rephrasing: When you have your
first introduction, they should give meanings, for example.

Colloquial: like lots of times; like when
they were kids.
Standard rephrasing: many times, for instance; when they were kids, for example.

like, as The traditional distinction between *like* as a preposition and *as* as a conjunction is being rapidly worn away. *Like*
is more and more commonly used as a conjunction, although that usage predominates
in speech rather than in writing:

Informal: Few tenors can sing top notes like
he does.
Formal: Few tenors can sing top notes as he
does.

Writers should be aware that the use of *like*
as a conjunction remains controversial; *as*
as a conjunction remains the safe choice.

likely *See* **liable.**
lit *See* **lighted.**
literally When *literally* means "in a

strictly accurate sense," it should be the
opposite of *figuratively*, which means "in
an imaginative or metaphorical sense." In
speech, however, *literally* is often used as
an intensifier in contexts that are clearly
figurative: *He literally split his sides
laughing* or *He literally sailed across the
room.* Since these are not literal statements, the use of *literally* seems not only
unnecessary but confusing.

loan *See* **lend.**

loose, lose, loosen *Loose* is either a
verb meaning "to unfasten" or an adjective
meaning "unrestrained." *Lose* is always a
verb, meaning "to be deprived of something." Confusion between the two is a
common cause of misspelling. *Loosen* is a
common substitute for *loose: Will you
loosen the knot for me?*

lots, lots of Colloquial substitutes for
much, many, a large number, or *a great
amount: a lot of courage* for *a great
amount of courage; lots of times* for *many
times; I resent that a lot* for *I resent that
very much.*

majority, plurality In elections, *majority* means "more than one half of the
total votes cast." *Plurality*, ordinarily used
when three or more candidates are involved, refers to "the excess of votes received by one candidate over those received by the next highest candidate."
Since *plurality* is not often used, majority
is sometimes extended to include its meaning.

man, person The use of *man* to refer
to "a human being of either sex" pervades
the English language. In fact, *woman* derives from the Old English word *wifman*,
meaning literally "a female human being."
The change of women's status during the
1970s has focused attention on words that
seem to mention only males in a preferred
way when both men and women are included. Thus, *chairperson* or simply *chair*
(a use of synecdoche) is now commonly
substituted for *chairman* to refer to either
sex. Other uses such as *salesperson, sports-*

person, maintenance person, or an expression like *to a person* instead of *to a man* are likely to find favor, although it is questionable whether words like *foreperson, freshperson,* and *woperson* ever will. The substitution of *person* for *man* in initial and medial positions seems especially unlikely when we consider examples like *personhole, personhour, personpower, sportspersonship, statespersonship,* and a verb like *personhandle.* Words of this variety introduce an element of absurdity. The changes that are occurring and being accepted, however, give us an opportunity to observe language in action. *See also* **he/she, his/her.**

may be, maybe *May be* is a verb phrase; *maybe* is an adverb meaning "perhaps": I *may be* late. *Maybe* I'll be late.

may *See* **can.**

may of, might of *See* **of.**

mighty Although *mighty* occurs in standard written English, it is highly informal when it is used as an intensifier meaning "very" or "extremely": *mighty useful, mighty good.*

morpheme The linguist's basic term for the smallest unit of language that conveys specific meaning. A morpheme may be free or bound; it may be a part of a word or a word itself. It is not to be confused with a syllable. *Incurable* is four syllables but three morphemes: (1) the root *cur[e]*, (2) *in-* meaning "not," and (3) *-able* meaning "capable of." *Kentucky* is three syllables but one morpheme. *Chairs* is one syllable but two morphemes: *chair* and the plural morpheme *s.*

most, almost *Most* is commonly used as an adverb to form the superlative degree of adjectives and adverbs: *most helpful, most strikingly.* Shortening *almost* to *most* is a common colloquialism:

Colloquial: A good night's sleep will help most anything.
Standard: A good night's sleep will help almost anything.

Ms. Now an accepted and inclusive term of address for women, regardless of their marital status. *Ms.,* therefore, equates with *Mr.,* which does not make a distinction between married and single status, as *Mrs.* and *Miss* do.

muchly *Much* is both an adjective and adverb form. The *-ly* is unnecessary.

mutual, common *Mutual* implies "having the same relation to one another": *a mutual agreement, a mutual exchange of gifts. Common* means "sharing something equally with each other or with others": *a common cause, common property. Common* is often substituted for *mutual:*

Misuse: They have a common admiration for one another.
Properly used: They have a mutual admiration for one another, a common respect for Faulkner.

need, needs Both third person singular forms of the auxiliary verb. *Need* is used in negative statements: *He needs to go. He need not go.*

nice The history of the word *nice* is long and varied. At different times among other definitions it has meant "foolish," "wanton," "strange," "tender," "coy," "thin," "appetizing," and "trivial." It now expresses only a very general and mild approval, little used by writers who are interested in precise words.

nominative A term for the subjective case, used in Latin and in the study of Indo-European languages, but also used at times by modern grammarians.

no place, nowhere, nowheres Of the three, *nowhere* is the most formal usage; *no place* tends to be colloquial; *nowheres* is nonstandard.

nowhere near Colloquial expression for "not nearly" or "not by a wide margin": *He was nowhere near right.*

nowheres *See* **no place.**

number of *See* **amount of.**

O, oh Two acceptable interjections varying in usage. *O* almost always combines with other words, usually in formal address or apostrophe: *O Lord our Lord. O moon of my delight!* It is capitalized and not followed by punctuation. *Oh* acts independently: *Oh, that isn't so. Oh! That's terrible!* It is not capitalized unless it begins a sentence; it is usually followed by a comma or exclamation point.

of   *Have* in unstressed syllables sounds very much like *of,* particularly when *have* is contracted in forms like *could've, would've, may've might've,* and *must've.* The tendency to transcribe the neutral sound as *of* instead of *have* accounts for such nonstandard forms as *could of, would of, may of, might of,* and *must of.*

off of   A colloquialism. The *of* can be dispensed with in writing: *A board fell off* [*of*] *the fence.*

O.K., OK, okay   Perhaps the most popular of all Americanisms, but clearly a colloquialism. All three transcriptions are acceptable in informal writing. The expression is made to serve as several parts of speech: *get an O.K.* (noun), *he OK'd it* (verb), *an OK guy* (adjective), *he ran O.K.* (adverb), *Okay!* (interjection).

olden   A Middle English inflected form of *old.* Clearly archaic and inappropriate in contemporary prose: *the olden days.*

only   As a modifier, *only* tends to move forward in a sentence. Thus, three versions of the same sentence may be quite acceptable:

You have to do *only* the first problem.
You have *only* to do the first problem.
You *only* have to do the first problem.

In other instances, however, the placement may directly affect the implication and tone:

A telescreen fell from a box to the audience below. Fortunately it injured *only* a standee. [not a regular subscriber]
Fortunately it *only* injured a standee [did not kill him]
Fortunately it injured *only* one standee. [not many]

ought   *See* **had ought.**

out loud   Colloquial for *aloud* or *very loudly.*

outside of   *See* **inside of.**

paradigm   A grammatical term for the arrangement of all of the forms of a word into an established pattern. It includes the declensions of nouns and pronouns and the conjugation of verbs (see pp. 471, 475).

particle   A rather loosely defined, inclusive term for uninflected parts of speech, including articles, prepositions, conjunctions, interjections, and adverbs used with verbs.

per   Standard in set Latin phrases like *per annum, per capita,* and *per diem.* When the Latin noun is translated and *per* is kept, the phrases become typical business jargon: *per year, per head, per day.* In these and other phrases like *per yard* and *per week,* the article can be substituted very naturally: *$12 a day, $7 a yard, 25 cents a head. Per* in the sense of "according to" (*per your instructions, per agreement*) is a carryover of business jargon into speech.

per cent, percent, percentage   *Percent* may be written as one word or two and does not require a period, even though *cent* is an abbreviation of Latin *centum.* The word is ordinarily used after numbers: *10 percent.* The symbol % is used only in technical and business contexts. In speech, *percent* and *percentage* have become synonymous, but some editors still insist on the distinction between *per cent* with numbers and *percentage* in other contexts: *a large percentage of the population.*

periphrastic construction   An alternate way of expressing the meaning of inflections by using particles and auxiliaries:

Periphrastic genitive: the beauty of Seattle *instead of* Seattle's beauty
Periphrastic comparison: more clean *instead of* cleaner
Periphrastic indirect object: gave to him *instead of* gave him
Periphrastic plural form: kinds of brilliance *instead of* brilliances

Periphrastic verb form: he does go *instead of* he goes

person   *See* **man.**

phase   Not to be confused with *faze.* *See* **faze.**

phoneme   A phoneme is a working term in linguistics to cover a range of sounds that we recognize as separate from any other range. A phoneme is the smallest unit of contrasting sound that makes meaning and understanding possible. If we could not hear the differences between /k/, /b/, and /m/, we would not be able to understand *cat, bat,* and *mat,* which differ only in the first phoneme.

The English language has approximately thirty-three distinct vowels and consonants, called segmental phonemes, and approximately twelve different degrees of pitch, stress, and juncture, called suprasegmentals. Linguists are not agreed on a uniform phonemic alphabet for English, and all speakers do not necessarily have all of the phonemes in their speech. Other languages have their own systems of phonemes, which may vary in number from thirteen to seventy-five.

playwrite, playwright   *Playwrite* is a logical but incorrect word for the writer of a play. The spelling *wright* is derived from an Old and Middle English word meaning "maker" or "creator." Compare *wheelwright.*

plenty   Its uses as an abverb meaning "very" or "fully" are colloquial: *plenty sore, plenty hot enough.*

plurality   *See* **majority.**

practical, practicable   Words easily confused but not interchangeable. *Practical* means "tested by experience," "concerned with applications," or "useful": *a practical method, a practical mind, a practical invention. Practicable* means "potentially useful" or "feasible" and does not apply to persons: *practicable material, the proposal is not practicable.*

prefix   A combining form attached to the beginning of a root or word base so as to change its meaning: *un*prepared (not prepared), *anti*social (averse to society).

presently   *Presently* is most frequently used to mean "in a little while, soon." It is also used informally to mean "at the present time, now." The context will usually decide which meaning the speaker intends, but most listeners expect the first meaning.

pretty   Overused as an adverb meaning "moderately," "somewhat," or "in good condition": *pretty bad, pretty clever, sitting pretty.* Even though *pretty* is well established in this sense, the usage remains basically colloquial.

principal, principle   Words commonly confused. As a noun, *principal* refers to the head of a school, a leading performer, or a sum of money (*principal and interest*). As an adjective, it means "main": *principal idea, principal stockholder, principal parts.* The noun *principle* means "theory, concept, or rule": *the principles that determine our conduct.*

proved, proven   Both acceptable past participles of *prove.* The choice between them is usually the writer's preference for a one- or two-syllable word in a particular context: *a proven proverb, a claim that has been proved again.*

provided, providing   Equally acceptable as subordinating conjunctions: *I will accept, providing [provided] the terms are favorable. Provided* is more commonly used in formal legal and business contexts.

qua   Adverb meaning "in the function of," "in the character of," or "as," used to designate in which of several roles a person acts: *He cannot act qua governor as he did qua private citizen.* Essentially a pretentious usage.

quite, quiet   Words easily confused in spelling. The adjective *quiet* means "calm." The adverb *quite* means "completely" or "positively": *They are quite mistaken.* Colloquially, the adverb is used to mean "rather" or "somewhat": *We live quite close to the center of town.*

quote, quotes   Used colloquially as a shortened form for "quotation" and "quotation marks." Even though the usage grows increasingly, it is still casual in tone.

raise, rear   *See* **rear** *and* **rise.**

rarely ever   Now an established idiom for *rarely if ever.* The *ever* is unnecessary and may be dropped in more formal writing: *I rarely* [ever] *pretend to be what I'm not.*

re   Strictly business or legal jargon for "in the matter of" or "regarding": *Re your letter of the 15th. . . .*

real, really   *Real* is the acceptable adjective form: *a real triumph, real trees. Really* is the acceptable adverb form: *a really enthusiastic crowd, things as they really are.* Colloquially, *real* is also used as an adverb: *a real nice conversation, a real good story.*

rear, raise   It is no longer true that one "raises cattle" but "rears children." *Raise* is now standard usage for "bringing up children."

reason is because, reason is that   Traditionally, a writer of formal prose used a noun clause introduced by *that* following the verb *to be: The reason he didn't vote is that he was out of town.* The common use of *because* constructions in speech, however, has influenced the accepted standard for written prose. *Reason is because* may be found in the prose of established persons writing for reputable journals.

regardless   *See* **irregardless.**

rise, raise   Verbs sometimes confused. The principal parts of *rise,* an intransitive verb, are *rise, rose, risen: The audience rose to applaud.* The principal parts of *raise,* a transitive verb, are *raise, raised, raised: The flag was raised. He raised his family well. See also* **rear.**

root   The base of a word without prefixes, suffixes, or inflections: *seg* (meaning "to cut") is the root of *suprasegmentals,* which includes the prefix *supra-,* the suffixes *-ment* and *-al,* and the plural inflection *s.*

said, same   The use of *said* and *same* to mean "the foregoing" or "above-mentioned" is strictly legal or business jargon and inappropriate to other kinds of prose: *The said motor is one of the best. I would like credit for same.*

scarcely   *See* **hardly.**

seldom ever   A colloquial expression for *hardly ever. Seldom,* of course, may be used alone: *I seldom go to the concerts.*

semi-   *See* **bi-.**

set   *See* **sit, set.**

shall, will   *Will* is rapidly replacing *shall* to express the future, although *shall* remains a mark of legal prose. In fact, the almost invariable use of *will* now gives *shall* a special formal tone. The old device of using *shall* in the second and third persons (*You shall go, He shall go*) and *will* in the first person (*I will go*) for special emphasis is a strategy that depends on the reader's knowing what the writer is doing. Linguistics has made clear that emphasis is not a matter of choosing one word or the other but of arranging words so that they fall into stressed positions: *They were told that they couldn't appeal. But they will.* The choice of *shall* in this sentence would not add to the emphasis that *will* naturally gets because of the rhythm of the sentence.

shan't   An acceptable contraction of *shall not* but even more formal in tone, possibly archaic, than the use of *shall* itself.

should of   *See* **of.**

sit, set   Words easily confused. *Sit* is almost always used intransitively; its principal parts are *sit, sat, sat.* The principal parts of *set* are *set, set, set. Set* is sometimes used transitively: *I set it down. I set the trap. Set* is also used intransitively: *Cement sets, chickens set,* and *the sun sets.*

smart   A highly adaptable word that tends to be overused. It has a variety of meanings in phrases like *a smart person, a smart pace, a smart blow, smart talk, smartly dressed.*

so, so that *So* has become an all-purpose word. It substitutes for other conjunctive adverbs like *accordingly, consequently, hence,* and *therefore;* it acts as a subordinating conjunction in place of *so that;* and it serves colloquially as an intensifier: *so lovely.* The problem is mainly one of overuse, particularly when subordination would be more effective:

Informal: This sketch is only a rough copy, so it lacks detail.
Rephrased: This sketch lacks details because it is only a rough copy.

some Lends itself to colloquial uses in such sentences as:

That was some game! [unusual]
You will have to go some to beat that. [to a great extent]
She is some better. [somewhat]

someplace, somewhere *See* **anyplace** and **everyplace.**
somewheres *See* **anywheres.**
sort of *See* **kind of.**
such, such that The use of *such* as an intensifier is informal: *He was such an effective speaker.* In written prose, *such* is ordinarily followed by a clause of result: *He was such an effective speaker that no one in the audience seemed to move at all.*
suffix A combining form added after the root or word base so as to change its meaning and often its grammatical classification. Suffixes are either derivational (consider*able,* improper*ly*) or inflectional (pillbox*es,* soft*er*).
supper *See* **dinner.**
sure and *See* **try and.**
sure, surely *Sure* is the adjective form; *surely,* the adverb. The use of *sure* as an adverb is common in speech mainly because *surely* manages to sound pompous in some contexts:

Colloquial: He sure can throw the ball far. [*compare* He surely can throw the ball far.]
Standard: We would surely discourage any kind of interference.

swell Colloquial in many of its uses: *a swell head* (short for *a swelled head,* a conceited person); *a swell show* (excellent); *a swell house* (fashionable).

than whom *Than whom* is ungrammatical but acceptable in such an idiomatic expression as *than whom none lived longer.* The phrase usually creates an awkward construction and is better avoided altogether.
that, which *See* **who, which, that.**
the *See* **a, an, the.**
therefor, therefore Used interchangeably by some persons. In a strict sense, *therefor* is an adverb, with the stress on the second syllable, meaning "for this" or "for it": *The company gave a new play; the setting therefor was Rome. Therefore* is also an adverb, with stress on the first syllable, and can be used as a conjunction to mean "as a result" or "consequently": *The setting was Rome; therefore, the stage director attempted to make it authentic.*
though, although Two acceptable subordinating conjunctions with no difference in meaning. Since one is a two-syllable word and the other a one-syllable word, the choice between them often depends on the rhythmic pattern of a clause. *Though* seems to be more frequently used, particularly in clauses following a verb: *He spoke hesitatingly, though he was not actually reluctant to tell his story. Though* is also used colloquially as a synonym of *however: They kept going to the meeting; I decided, though, that I wouldn't. Tho* and *tho'* are variant spellings but should be recognized as inappropriate to serious writing.
thusly *Thus* is an adverb. The *-ly* is unnecessary.
toward, towards *Toward* is the American form, *towards* the British. Usage in this country, however, is divided.
try and, come and, go and, be sure and All well-established usages in conversation: *Try and stop me, come and get me, go and see, be sure and do it.* All, however, are colloquial equivalents of the more ac-

cepted idioms for formal writing: *Try to, come to, go to,* and *be sure to,* which more clearly express an element of purpose.

type   Colloquial for *type of:*

Colloquial: He's not that type student.
Standard: He's not that type of student.

un-   *See* **in-.**

very, very much   Traditionally, glossaries of usage have held that *very* should be used to modify an adjective and *very much* to modify a verb or past participle: *very rich, very much inclined.* The main difficulty with such a usage is that it is not always possible to say with certainty what is a participle and what is an adjective: *I was very much [very] concerned about the matter.* General usage is rapidly wearing away the old distinction.

viz., i.e., e.g.   Latin abbreviations with separate meanings and uses. *Viz.,* now also acceptable without a period, is derived from *videlicet* and means "namely." It is the most formal of the three and is used to particularize: *The major sources of the novella, viz, 1._____, 2._____, 3._____. I.e.* is an abbreviation of *id est,* meaning "that is." It is commonly used to interpret: *He was Faulknerized; i.e., he was mesmerized by Faulkner's novels. E.g.* is an abbreviation for *exempli gratia,* meaning literally "for the sake of the example." It is used to introduce an illustration: *Shortened spelling forms exist for a number of words, e.g., "thru," "tho," and "til."* The Latin abbreviations now frequently appear without italics in print or without underlining in typed copy.

wake, awake, waken, awaken   The principal parts of these verbs cause uncertainty. Since all of them have overlapping meanings, they may often be used interchangeably:

| [a]wake | [a]woke *or* [a]waked | [a]woke *or* [a]waked |
| [a]waken | [a]wakened | [a]wakened |

want, want that, want for   The standard usage after *want* is an infinitive: *I want you to help me.* The other idioms are nonstandard: *I want that you should help me* or *I want for you to help me.*

well   *See* **good.**

what with   *What* combined with *with* is a very old but still acceptable expression, meaning "with the attending circumstances of": *What with the threat of a recession, we had better not sell our house.*

whereas   The use of *whereas* as a subordinating conjunction meaning "while on the contrary" often goes unrecognized: *Three of the five girls made a perfect score, whereas only one of the ten boys did. Whereas* is often treated only as a conjunctive adverb.

whether   *See* **if, whether.**

while   *See* **as well as, while.**

whilst   The British equivalent of *while.* Sometimes used in poetry for a special effect, usually to suggest antiquity.

who, which, that   *Who* is characteristically used to refer to people and some animals, *which* to things and animals, and *that* to both beings and things. *Which* to refer to people (*Joe which was here*) occurs in nonstandard dialects.

In some constructions, *which* and *that* can be used interchangeably, particularly if variety is needed: *Coordination is a relationship which [that] shows that two ideas are to be considered equal.* However, *that* is commonly preferred in restrictive clauses: *It is the kind of music that I like. Which* tends to be preferred in nonrestrictive clauses: *The text, which was first published in 1964, is now out of print.*

will   *See* **shall.**

win   In the sense of "defeat," *win* is colloquial: *I won him at tennis.*

-wise   A suffix for forming adverbs, found in certain established usages such as *lengthwise, otherwise, counterclockwise,* and *likewise.* In recent years, however, nonce words ending in *-wise* have flourished so that coinages of this kind have become associated with bad jargon: *exam-*

inationwise, weatherwise, timewise, distancewise. Undoubtedly, a number of useful words will survive out of this language fad; but, for the present, careful writers proceed with caution.

would of   *See* **of.**

Xmas   Commercial spelling of Christmas, but not a modern form. *X* is the first letter of the Greek spelling of *Christ.* The form was used in ancient times, and the *Oxford English Dictionary* records a usage in English as early as 1551.

X-ray, x ray   Variant forms. X was used by Roentgen, the discoverer of X-ray, to indicate the unknown nature of the ray.

ye   Old English for *the.* The form is a survival of early printing practices when a *y* was substituted for the Old English thorn. Thus þe was written as *ye* and still appears in deliberately contrived antique names like Ye Olde Coffee Shoppe. Not to be confused with *ye,* an archaic form of *you.*

you all   A familiar southern dialect form, often shortened to *y'all.* Most commonly used by southerners as a means of distinguishing *you* singular from *you* plural. Poor imitators of southerners use *you all* in the singular.

youth, youths   *Youth* may be used in a collective plural sense to mean young people in general: *Youth have always been restless. Youths* emphasizes individuals in a plural sense: *Six youths were injured in the bus accident.*

Sections most commonly needed for reference